Under the General Editorship of

Jesse W. Markham

Princeton University

Houghton Mifflin Adviser in Economics

THEORETICAL ISSUES
IN
INTERNATIONAL ECONOMICS

■

M. O. Clement
Dartmouth College

Richard L. Pfister
Indiana University

Kenneth J. Rothwell
University of New Hampshire

■

HOUGHTON MIFFLIN COMPANY • BOSTON
New York • Atlanta • Geneva, ILL. • Dallas • Palo Alto

EDITOR'S INTRODUCTION

Some of the most challenging problems in economics arise in the broad area of international relations. In the two decades that have followed World War II, these problems have multiplied and become more complex. The ever-proliferating new and underdeveloped nations seem to be handicapped by a chronic shortage of international exchange. Even industrially advanced nations such as France, the United Kingdom and the United States seem to be buffeted in the waves of trade surpluses and the troughs of trade deficits. From 1946 until the mid-1950's, the international finance problem was the dollar shortage; in the mid-1960's, at least from the United States point of view, the problem is the dollar glut.

New institutions have arisen in response to the newly defined problems in international trade. The World Bank facilitates the flow of funds into much-needed capital formation in underdeveloped nations. The International Monetary Fund softens the pressures on nations to revalue their currencies. Customs Unions, Common Markets, free trade areas and the General Agreements on Tariffs and Trade are created and exercised in hopes of furthering the gains from trade among nations.

The new and complex problems, and the responses to them in the form of the new international institutions, have severely taxed the capacity of traditional economic theory and, in consequence, have given rise to the creation of new tools of economic analysis. It is to the new problems and the adequacy of contemporary international trade theory to handle them that Professors Clement, Pfister and Rothwell have addressed this book. Because they have tried not to minimize the complexities of the problems and issues to which these problems give rise, they have not conveyed to the student the impression that any one of these problems has a single simple solution. Instead, they have applied to them all the relevant analytical tools with the objective of identifying clearly and unmistakably the effects of alternative policies.

The authors have purposely designed their book for students who have already had the introductory course in economics and, hopefully, have had training in the elements of international trade theory. However, the theoretical material presented in Part I will enable the perceptive and energetic student to understand the issues taken up in the rest of the book. The authors have tried to breathe life and meaning into these issues and thus effectively meet the students' customary criticism that economic theory is sterile and inoperative. Not only the students, but their professors as well, will welcome this refreshing approach to what should be among the most exciting areas of economic study.

Jesse W. Markham
Princeton University

PREFACE

Students of international economics are apt to be perplexed by the numerous policies proposed by experts in the field. How is it possible, they might wonder, that well-trained and prudent men can hold divergent, frequently diametric, views of the solutions to what appear to be rather simple problems? How is it possible, for example, for a dozen solutions to be offered to resolve the problem of international liquidity?

Perceptive students will have discovered that different normative standards are not solely responsible for the policy disagreements among economists; disagreements arise also from differences in analysis or explanation of the problems to be solved. But students may also have been led to believe that economic theory, properly employed, permits only a single result to emerge from a given set of phenomena. Students, therefore, may justifiably question whether economists' theoretical propositions are sufficiently developed to permit them effectively to employ these propositions.

Lack of training is, of course, only partly responsible for students' puzzlement. The mold of conventional textbook expositions is also contributory. All too often texts create a false impression that there is little professional disagreement over fundamental issues of international economic theory. Controversial aspects of recent theoretical exposition are frequently not discussed; differences in the explicit and implicit assumptions of theorists are overlooked. Indeed, at the introductory level it is difficult to do otherwise since pedagogy compels a certain amount of distillation and resolution of material. Ordinarily, texts must seem noncontroversial, if not non-partisan. It is apparent to any specialist, however, that on many topics there may be no simple, generally accepted, theoretical explanation. Rather, theoretical debate is still vigorous; basic constructs of international economic theory are still being formed and tempered; that part of the debate which will ultimately be acknowledged as accepted doctrine remains at issue. Those theoretical formulations that have achieved virtually unanimous adoption have done so only after an extensive period of development. Yet, conventional texts convey these impressions poorly, if at all.

Our experience in teaching international economics leads us to believe that many students find international economic theory arid partly because they do not appreciate the tentative, evolutionary nature of theory. It is thought, in addition, that standard texts do not place international economic theory in a perspective that highlights its values and limitations for the purposes of formulating policy. One result is the prevalent student attitude that theory, per se, is sterile and inoperative. We believe that knowing that economists may not have *the* answer to important economic problems, and realizing *why* they do not have the answer, will kindle and deepen student interest in the theory of international economics. It will as well contribute to a better understanding of theory's role in policy deliberations.

How are students to gain this awareness and how are they to acquire this perspective when conventional texts must encompass such a broad spectrum of knowledge and still must simplify? Certainly, treatises are available that capably expound and synthesize international economic theory. Monographic studies often provide the desired viewpoint. Unfortunately, many of these treatises and monographs, being pointed to the professional reader, are either too advanced for the ordinary student, are too recondite, or are largely outmoded. Much journal literature is inordinately difficult and frequently focused on narrow facets of the theoretical debate. In addition, the journal literature is relatively inaccessible for many students. Thus, in short, we have found no satisfactory analytical treatment of contemporary issues of international economic theory to which searching students with a moderate theoretical training can be directed.

The present book is our response to these impressions and dissatisfactions. We have selected for discussion subject areas in international economic theory which in particular have received widespread and intensive attention in the last two decades and in which signal contributions have been made. Others might have chosen different topics or given them different emphases. We believe, however, that the nine topics treated in this volume especially have whetted the interests of imaginative and critical intellects in the field of international economic theory. Furthermore, they represent areas of contemporary debate which have emerged from vital policy issues. We have tried, in what follows, to reflect these interests in a way that is faithful to the evolution of analytical thought on these topics and to convey a sense of the fascination of theoretical work and of the importance of theory to the solution of significant problems in international economics. Perhaps the most meaningful description of the book's content is that each of the chapters is a "survey article," as that term is commonly understood, developing the theoretical or analytical ideas that have been brought to bear on contemporary international economic issues. Not all issues have been analyzed with the same degree of elaborateness and rigor, of course. It is, therefore, inevitable that the level of difficulty of the several chapters will vary. Nevertheless, our hope is that the materials presented will be understandable to students who have competence in micro- and macro-economics, who have a conceptual grasp of elementary college-level mathematics, and who are either taking concurrently or have taken the "first course" in international economics. Moreover, our intention is that each chapter should stand on its own, independently of the rest, a possible exception being the first two chapters which are connected by some theoretical tools.

The book is, of course, a joint product, but the interests of the three of us naturally led to individual drafting efforts: Professor Clement had this responsibility for Chapters 1, 7, 8, and 9; Professor Pfister for Chapters 3, 4, and 6; and Professor Rothwell for Chapters 2 and 5. We have benefited greatly from the generous, painstaking, and most helpful comments of Professors Charles P. Kindleberger and Richard E. Caves, each of whom read approximately half the manuscript in its initial form. In addition, the wisdom of the various teachers of the authors, the challenging questions and frustrations of many classes of students, and the endless rounds of debates with colleagues are instilled in various ways in the pages of this book. The book is immeasurably better because of the advice received; however, the authors alone are responsible for its deficiencies.

M. O. Clement
Dartmouth College

Richard L. Pfister
Indiana University

Kenneth J. Rothwell
University of New
Hampshire

TABLE OF CONTENTS

NOTE ON CHAPTER BIBLIOGRAPHIES

The final section of each chapter is a bibliography of the works mentioned in the text of that chapter. Consequently, the list is not exhaustive, but it is thought to give a reasonably comprehensive coverage of the literature relevant to the subject of the chapter, especially for the postwar period. Each item in these bibliographies is identified by a number. The bracketed references in the text of the chapter refer to this identification number.

The following abbreviations of journal titles have been used in the citations. All other items are referred to by their full titles.

Abbreviated Title	Complete Title
AER	American Economic Review
BOUIS	Bulletin of the Oxford University Institute of Statistics
CJEPS	Canadian Journal of Economics and Political Science
Econa	Economica
Econia Internaz	Economia Internazionale
Ec Rec	Economic Record
EDCC	Economic Development and Cultural Change
EHR	Economic History Review
EJ	Economic Journal
Emet	Econometrica
JEH	Journal of Economic History
JFin	Journal of Finance
JPE	Journal of Political Economy
Kyk	Kyklos
Man Sch	Manchester School of Economic and Social Studies
Metroecon	Metroeconomica
OEP	Oxford Economic Papers
QJE	Quarterly Journal of Economics
REStat	Review of Economics and Statistics
REStud	Review of Economic Studies
SP	International Monetary Fund Staff Papers

PART I / Pure International Trade Theory

CHAPTER 1 / Trade and Relative Factor Prices

PREFATORY STATEMENT

Trade occurs in a world where the movement of goods and the mobility of productive factors are more or less imperfect. This is true within nations as well as between them but undoubtedly freedom of movement is in general relatively greater within a national economy than within the international economy. Furthermore, between countries the barriers to the flow of goods are usually insubstantial compared to the disinclination of productive factors to migrate across national borders. The assumptions of the pure theory of international trade reflect these differences; it is common to assume perfect mobility of factors nationally, completely free movement of goods within and across national boundaries, and complete immobility of factors internationally.

Under these conditions the theory of the pricing of commodities internationally differs little from the theory of the determination of goods' prices within national markets. The extension of factor pricing in the absence of international trade to the determination of factor returns when trade is occurring is not so readily apparent. A distinguishing characteristic of international trade theory is then in the explanation of factor price determination. The question arises: what will be the national prices of the various factors of production when goods are free to move easily between countries but factor movements are restricted solely to those within the confines of the nation? Alternatively, does the free international movement of goods substitute so effectively for perfect mobility of factors that the pattern of national relative factor prices in the absence of commodity exchange is also established when goods move internationally?

It is seen that, indeed, such a pattern will be determined. In a model of sufficiently simple and rigorous conditions, international trade causes the returns to all factors of production to be identical in each of the trading countries. But full international factor price equalization, as the pattern is called, can be upset by a number of rather realistic phenomena.

Moreover, in certain situations trade may not even tend to bring about convergence of relative factor returns internationally. With the relaxation of some of the assumptions of the simple model, the lack of empirical evidence of full factor price equalization, or of a tendency toward it, can be explained analytically. Thus, it can legitimately be said that the effect of the international exchange of goods on the relative and absolute factor returns of the various nations depends upon the economic features of the environment in which international trade is undertaken.

In a perfectly competitive world where goods move freely between nations, the minimum condition for the occurrence of international trade is that the relative domestic costs of production of different commodities should vary among nations. Demonstration of this principle of comparative advantage was based on a simple two-factor, two-commodity, two-country model in which productive factors were assumed to be completely immobile internationally and perfectly mobile domestically. In the Ricardian model comparative cost differences were due to the assumption that identical absolute combinations of the factors devoted to the production of a single commodity would produce different amounts of that commodity in different countries. In modern parlance, comparative cost differences in Ricardo's theory existed because the production function for a given commodity varied from one country to another and the extent of variation differed for the two commodities.

Chapter 2 discusses an alternative formulation for the basis of comparative cost differences attributable to Heckscher [13] and Ohlin [41]. In contrast to Ricardo, they posited that the production function for a given commodity was the same irrespective of the country of production. An identical absolute input of productive factors would result in the same output of a given good in any country. While production functions for any good were identical from country to country, they did, however, vary from commodity to commodity. One production function might require a relatively large supply of labor to combine with capital — and hence gave rise to a labor-intensive good — while the other production function might require relatively little labor — and therefore its associated good was capital-intensive. This factor-intensity difference in the production functions of the two commodities, in conjunction with observed differences in relative factor endowments of the countries, accounted for international differences in comparative costs of production.

This basis of comparative advantage was formulated in the famous Heckscher-Ohlin theorem: a country tends to export the commodity which uses intensively that factor with which the country is relatively

4

heavily endowed. In a two-commodity, two-factor model it is also true that a country tends to import that good which uses intensively that productive factor with which it is relatively poorly endowed. The theorem follows from the fact that in the formal Heckscher-Ohlin model, with its many simplifying assumptions, the relatively abundant factor commands a relatively low factor return and, therefore, the commodity whose production function happens to require relatively large amounts of the plentiful factor is produced more cheaply than the commodity requiring large amounts of the relatively scarce factor. Since countries possess different relative factor endowments they also have a comparative advantage in the production of different goods. Therefore, as long as each commodity has its own distinctive production function, internationally identical production functions and international disparities in relative factor endowments are sufficient to explain the profitability of trade.

In the absence of impediments to international trade, including costs of transporting goods, the price of each commodity traded internationally must be identical in all countries. In economies using money, for instance, the price of any good moving in international trade will be identical in all countries provided that the equilibrium exchange rate is taken into consideration. In a barter system, the standard framework for pure trade theory, the rate at which one commodity exchanges for another in one country will be duplicated in other countries. Real commodity prices, that is, will be identical in the trading countries. In a perfectly competitive situation and in the context of comparative cost differences, the opening of trade tends to eliminate comparative cost differences. Assuming increasing cost conditions in, say, country A, the domestic costs of the relatively cheap commodity, call it commodity X, increase as trade opens up while the domestic costs of the relatively dear commodity, commodity Y, fall; in country B the domestic costs of commodity Y rise relative to the domestic costs of commodity X. As long as both countries continue to produce both commodities, this cost adjustment proceeds until the relative costs of the two commodities are identical in the two countries. Free trade between the two countries will have made the pre-trade differences in comparative costs disappear.

Note, however, that trade itself does not cease when comparative cost differences are eliminated. Rather, the mechanism is that the volume of trade increases, causing changes in comparative costs, and this *increase* in trade stops at the point where comparative cost differences no longer obtain. Barring changes in certain underlying conditions — technology, factor supplies, commodity demands — the resulting volume of trade continues to take place and comparative cost differences are kept nonexistent. "At the margin," international commodity flows cease, yet international trade continues.

It is helpful at this point to review the conditions giving rise to the relative production cost changes depicted above. A framework of two commodities, two factors, and two countries in perfect competition gives simplicity to this review. Assume that country A is relatively well-endowed with labor compared to its capital stock in comparison with country B which is relatively capital rich compared to its labor endowment.[1] Assume further that the production functions of the two commodities are such that commodity X is labor-intensive and commodity Y is capital-intensive, regardless of the relative prices of the factors of production. Finally, suppose that the law of variable proportions holds and that returns to changes in the scale of output are constant. That is, if in the production of a given commodity the input of one factor, say, labor, is increased relative to the other factor, so that the proportion of labor to capital in the production of the commodity rises, output of the commodity rises but the marginal product of labor falls; but if the inputs of both factors are increased by equal percentage amounts, so that factor proportions do not change, output rises by that same percentage amount and the marginal product of either factor is not altered.

With these assumptions, as Meade explores [29, Chap. XIX], country A may produce commodity X but none of commodity Y and vice versa in country B; country A may become completely specialized in producing commodity X, producing none of good Y, while country B may continue to produce some of both commodities, or country B may completely specialize in commodity Y and country A may produce both; or specialization may be incomplete so that both goods continue to be produced in both countries. It is convenient to visualize a situation in which specialization is incomplete with both countries producing some of both goods, although a later section explores the consequences of complete specialization. With the conditions stated above, country A has a comparative advantage in the production of commodity X and exports it and imports commodity Y; country B has a comparative advantage in commodity Y, exports that good, and purchases some of commodity X from country A.

Look carefully at what happens in country A as international trade opens up. Since country A satisfies some of its demand for good Y by importing it, the output of good Y in country A falls, releasing factors of production in a certain proportion; the industry producing commodity X, the export industry, expands, absorbing factors. Since commodity Y is capital-intensive and commodity X is labor-intensive, a relatively larger amount of capital is released per unit of output reduction in industry Y than is taken up by a unit increase in the output of commodity X. Without a change in relative factor prices and unless the two goods can be produced with variable factor proportions, capital becomes unemployed unless there is some reduction in the return to

6

capital compared to that of labor. The assumption of perfect competition, in factor as well as goods markets, eliminates the possibility of unemployment because mobility and price flexibility are perfect. Output changes in the two goods-producing industries then result in a decline in the return to capital, the relatively dear factor in country A.

As capital becomes cheaper relative to labor, compared to the pre-trade situation, capital is substituted for labor in the production of both commodities. This reduces the proportion of labor to capital utilized in both industries in country A. Since, by assumption, the marginal product of the factors is dependent solely upon the factor proportions and is not influenced by the scale of output, this factor substitution results in an increase in the marginal product of labor, the relatively abundant and hence cheap factor in country A, and a decrease in the marginal product of capital, the relatively dear and scarce factor. Recalling that one of the equilibrium conditions in competitive markets is that productive factors receive returns equal to their marginal products, it is apparent that international trade, under the conditions assumed, results in a cheapening of the relatively expensive factor of production and an increase in the return to the relatively inexpensive factor. In country A the opening up of trade, at the very least, tends to reduce the disparity between the returns to the factors of production that existed in the pre-trade situation because labor was more abundant relatively than capital.

Analogously, in country B, industry Y expands its output to meet its domestic demand and the import demand of country A. Production of commodity X contracts as this commodity is imported from country A. This process releases relatively more labor than can be absorbed, at the going factor prices, in the capital-intensive industry Y. Relative factor prices change and, in country B, labor is substituted for capital in both industries. With the fall in the capital-labor ratio in country B, the marginal product of capital rises, as does the return to capital, the relatively cheap factor. Correspondingly, the return to labor, the relatively dear factor, falls. In country B, as in country A, factor returns, at the very least, tend to be equalized.

The opening up of international trade is, therefore, capable of effecting some sort of change in the pattern of relative returns to the factors of production. The analysis, deliberately, has not been as precise as possible. It has confirmed merely that "at the very least" the free movement of goods internationally "tends" to equalize "relative" factor returns in two countries. This is a weak conclusion, hedged as it is. The analysis has not, for example, eliminated the possibility that the returns to the factors of production in the two countries can be fully equalized, relatively and absolutely, by free trade. It has established only that, in the Heckscher-Ohlin model of international trade, forces are revealed which cause the development of a certain relationship among the returns to the

7

factors of production internationally. The task of this chapter is to ascertain as precisely as possible the sort of relationship among factor returns that is dictated by the existence of international trade. For example, does free trade cause a given factor to command the *same* return in every country — full or complete equalization of factor prices — or does it cause merely an incomplete tendency for factor prices to be equalized — partial equalization — or is the pattern of factor prices immune to the existence of international trade? More familiarly, the chapter examines the logic of the so-called "factor price equalization theorem."

It is important to acknowledge the limits this puts upon the scope of the discussion. The significant body of literature which treats the impact of trade on the way in which a country's productive factors share in the total domestic output or income is not discussed. Not that there is no relationship between factor returns and factor shares. Since factor shares are related to both the relative employment and the relative returns of the factors, the opposite is patently true. Moreover, a plausible case can be made that, in the instance of one of the independent statements of full factor price equalization, the analytical viewpoint had been supplied by previous work on the effects of trade protection upon relative factor shares.[2] But examining conditions of factor pricing is simpler and more instructive, and much that can be said about factor shares can be inferred from analysis of the factor price equalization process.

Additionally, the discussion centers on a purely static model. Total supplies of the factors of production are, with one exception discussed in the Appendix to this chapter, assumed to be fixed for each country, as are technology, income, and tastes. Again, the lack of dynamic qualities in the analysis limits the insight that can be given to several important issues. For example, Myrdal [40] leveled a grave, if misdirected and vaguely focused, charge against the logic of the pure theory of international trade. He argued that the operation of a free trade, international economy has stunted the economic growth of the underdeveloped areas with the result that the international inequality of income distribution has been aggravated. This would seem to be a refutation of the conclusion that trade leads to factor price equalization, for it is difficult to deny that the international distribution of income between the "have" and the "have-not" nations has been becoming relatively more unequal through time.

To accept Myrdal's premise, however, is not to accept his explanation. Meier [30; 31] pointedly and effectively demonstrated that Myrdal's criticism is not of the classical, static theory of international trade that has developed over the last century or so. Myrdal does not challenge the logic of static international trade theory; he does, however, question the applicability of a static international trade theory to some of today's problems.

The "dynamization" of trade theory is considered in the next chapter and this story will not be told here. Suffice it to say that continuing and even widening inequalities in per capita income do not constitute a challenge to the factor price equalization theorem *per se*. As Johnson points out in a comment 'on Linder's attempt to explain growing income inequalities on a basis alternative to that of Myrdal,[3] factor prices may tend to be equalized while international income per capita becomes more disparate if amounts of productive factors per capita are also diverging among nations. This is distinctly possible in view of the different saving habits, and therefore different rates of capital accumulation, of people in developed and underdeveloped countries [15, p. 89]. Interesting though they may be, these kinds of dynamic considerations are not brought into subsequent discussion.

In an examination of the development and elaboration of the factor price equalization theorem, the precise focus must be clearly understood. To this end, it must be mentioned that the term "factor price" clearly misrepresents the area of interest. Factor return, as generally employed, is a more appropriate expression. Using "factor price" suggests an intention to analyze the impact of international trade on the value which a unit of a productive factor commands in the market place. This is not the case, however. The analysis is not primarily concerned with the price of a piece of capital equipment or the price of a human laborer (a slave, for example). Rather, it focuses on the effects of trade on the market value of a unit of factor *service*. The wage for a man-hour of input, the price of an hour's running time for capital, the rental for a year's use of an acre of land exemplify these.

The price of a factor, as distinct from the price of the service of that factor, is determined by the discounting of a stream of future earnings. To the degree that the prices of the services of the various productive factors are equated between countries, the earnings of the various factors are also equalized; but this does not guarantee that the prices of the productive factors themselves are also equalized between countries. For that to be so, the rate at which the stream of earnings is discounted has to be identical for each country. Whether the national discount rates — the rates of interest — are also equalized by international trade is the subject of the most recent contribution to the debate about the relation between trade and factor returns. While this contribution is noted in the Appendix to this chapter, for the greater part it is convenient to ignore the difficult conceptual problems it raises. Thus, a concern with the conditions affecting the returns of the services of the various factors of production in the separate countries dominates the discussion. That the convention of using factor returns and factor prices interchangeably is continued should not divert attention from the market value of factor services.

9

From this introduction it would be possible, but peremptory, to move directly to a statement of the logic of the factor price equalization theorem, employing assumptions that would inevitably lead under free trade to a deduction of full international equality of the absolute price of any given factor. If this step were taken, discourse on the theorem would appear to have a precision and finality which it does not in fact have. Proof of the equalization theorem can be criticized because a number of commonly used terms and several assumptions are not completely free of ambiguity. Until concepts are carefully defined, the body of assumptions is susceptible to diverse interpretations which, in turn, reflect upon the logical deduction that factor prices are equalized by international trade. Therefore, before stating the assumptions upon which the theorem is built, a discussion of several conceptual problems will provide an antidote to the flavor of precision one is apt to get from much of the literature. Much has been written on these conceptual problems and the prospect for widespread agreement on definitions is not high. Many of the conceptual issues are not broached here, nor are the assumptions themselves challenged, except as the discussion of definitional problems does so. Questioning of assumptions is left for later sections and for the Appendix to this chapter. But enough of the more obvious and critical ambiguities are revealed to leave the impression that the debate over factor price equalization is not yet stilled.

In a model relying so heavily on relative endowments of the factors of production in order to explain different output patterns among countries, clear-cut notions of what is meant by a productive factor, by relative factor endowments, by a production function, and by a product are desirable. Yet mutual inconsistencies among these concepts make it impossible to adopt precise definitions. In order to assume realistically that a commodity's production function is identical in different countries, the concept of productive factor, or better its service, must be satisfactorily circumscribed. However, as Robinson describes [46, pp. 172–73], it is not always possible to distinguish between production functions and productive factors: countries having different climates may be considered as having different production functions, in the sense that the same combination of conventional factors, i.e., land, labor, and capital, can produce more wheat with a favorable climate than with an adverse climate; or countries may be considered as having different factors of production, by giving the production function an additional factor dimension.[4] In the former case, "productive factor" would be defined so as to exclude "climate," but insofar as climate influenced output and climate varied internationally, this influence would be reflected in different production functions. In the latter case, the production function could be made identical by incorporating a productive factor called "wheat-type climate" but then one country would be completely deficient in this factor.

Since it is vital to the derivation of complete equalization of the returns to factors that the production functions be identical internationally, it appears that the latter alternative must be adopted. A given productive factor must be assumed, and hence defined, to be identical from one country to another. Nevertheless, by using this device to keep production functions identical between countries, it is likely that the number of factors of internationally equal quality proliferate so greatly and are delineated so narrowly that, as suggested above, one of the countries has none of some particular factor. If, in a two-country model, a particular factor is found only in one country, the marginal products of the various factors common to the two countries will differ. Factor price equalization is not to be expected in the circumstances, a condition of which Ohlin was aware [41, pp. 105–06]. With an exception noted below, to derive the theorem satisfactorily the countries must have available the same bundle of identical types of factors and must be producing an identical bundle of types of goods.

There are other senses in which specification of a factor of production becomes troublesome. Balogh stresses that by assuming factors of production to be truly identical a most important cause of divergent production functions is ruled out. The effect of homogeneous factors can best be surmised by assuming them to be non-homogeneous. With non-homogeneous factors, different sized doses of the same factor applied to another factor would not be perfectly substitutable. Imperfect factor substitutability could be responsible for different patterns of increasing costs of production in two countries. Unless "the same pattern of imperfections in substitutability should be encountered in both regions," it is impossible with non-homogeneous factors to maintain "the assumption that identical production functions will exist in the two regions" [3, p. 194].

So far the definition of what constitutes a product has not been considered. In microeconomic theory the formal definition is that a commodity encompasses all those things for which the cross-elasticity of demand is infinite, the cross-elasticity of demand for all other things being zero. The difficulties this "convenient" definition causes for the theorist when he moves into an analysis of oligopolistic market structures and of the real world are familiar. No similar definition is proposed in the formal arguments on factor price equalization; indeed, a definition of "commodity" at this level of generality has not received any attention. It should not be inferred, however, that the definition of "commodity" is without significance. But again, as in the case of defining a factor of production, no satisfactory definition has been found; rather, the issue of arriving at a generic definition has not been squarely faced.

Nevertheless, specific uses of the term "commodity" have been suggested. The nub of the issue is that it is vital for the proof of factor price equalization, in a more general model containing many commodities and many factors, that the number of commodity types not be less than the number of types of factor. Harrod, observing no evidence of a tendency of factor prices to equalize, suggests the following definition of commodity: "any class of similar objects which require at least one specific kind of factor not also required by any other objects" [12, p. 246]. If this definition is adopted it would be impossible, according to later analysis, to get equality of factor returns for there are, by definition, as many factors as goods plus an additional number of factors which are non-specific in the sense that they are found producing more than one good.

Caves [7, p. 84] states that it would be difficult to defend the particulars of this suggestion. But he feels it contains a grain of truth in that it lumps together, if factors are properly defined, all commodities having identical production functions, since a minimal requirement of an identical production function is that it consists of the same combination of productive factors. If there are factors which are not generally employable for commodity production, then it is true that for each of these factors there should be a separate product. Here, however, Harrod's suggestion runs afoul of the difficulties of consistently defining factors and production functions. These are difficulties that have not been, and probably cannot be, satisfactorily resolved.

Travis, in a monograph which endeavors to explain the pattern of international trade by the existence of differential protection rather than differential factor endowment, is concerned that the number of factors may exceed the number of commodities, both presumably defined in some unspecified, conventional way. His redefinition, which unlike Harrod's is an effort to insure that the equalization of factor returns is not prevented in the multi-factor, multi-product situation, rests upon a vertical disintegration of the various production processes so that any number of intermediate goods may be created. To Travis the relevant focus of analysis is no longer a commodity as usually conceived; rather, it is an "activity" which must have the properties, such as given factor intensity, that have heretofore been attributed to goods. Each of these "activities" yields an intermediate good and the trading of these intermediate goods is sufficient to establish a tendency toward factor price equalization if other conditions prevail [56, pp. 9-11].

Travis' solution is attractive in that it recognizes, and takes advantage of, the fact that the vast bulk of international trade is in intermediate goods, not final goods. It has the additional benefit of increasing the likelihood that the one formal assumption of the factor price equalization model which has been most rigorously challenged — that a product is always made by using intensively the same factor irrespective of relative factor prices — holds. By judiciously breaking down the production process into sub-units (activities), it might be possible to insure somewhat against "factor-intensity reversal" — as this challenge has come to be called — and to enhance the meaningfulness of the necessary condition that production functions for a given product are identical throughout the world. But these suggestions are too new to have received the critical attention they deserve. Moreover, there are limits, as Travis realizes [56, pp. 10–11], to the effective vertical disintegration of the production process. And, in any case, if Harrod's specific and nonspecific factors are relevant to defining production functions, for activities as well as commodities, the old dilemma that the number of factors may exceed the number of commodities remains.

This discussion of specific definitions of commodities assumed that the relevant theoretical framework is one in which there are many productive factors and products. And indeed many of the formal properties of the factor price equalization theorem have been derived by exploring mathematical systems of simultaneous equations in just such a framework.[5] In contrast, the economic mechanism and adjustments in the price equalization process have been worked out in a simpler world of two commodities, as well as two factors and two countries. Some analysts would defend this simplification on the ground that some grouping is inevitable and always arbitrary in the sense that another classification is equally defensible. As long as grouping occurs, it is not possible to eliminate the so-called index number problem — weights must be assigned, shifts in the composition of the commodity group must be accommodated, and so forth. If it is thus impossible to obviate the difficulties attendant to indices of composites, why not ignore this range of problems and hence simplify in the extreme by lumping all commodities into just two (composite) goods?

Pearce raises this question rhetorically, only to issue a strong negative rejoinder. In the case of factor price equalization, he asserts the crux of the matter is precisely a facet of the index number problem. As will be seen, the derivation of equalization of factor returns depends upon there being a simple single-valued relationship between factor prices, on the one hand, and commodity prices on the other. Insofar as the commodity is a composite, says Pearce, this simple relationship is not inevitable, since any given composite commodity price can be consistent with a number of different factor prices, depending upon the ratio of factor inputs to product outputs. In Pearce's words [43, p. 726]:

> . . . The price of a composite commodity is precisely the weighted sum of the prices of the factors which produce it, the weights being the ratio of inputs to output. The factor-price equalisation theorem seeks to establish that the connection between factor prices and their weights is such that there is one,

and only one, way of building up any given commodity price, at the same time fulfilling all the economic conditions for equilibrium. If the world . . . contains many factors, whose relative prices vary independently, then we are simply assuming away the major part of our problem by trying to fit it into two dimensions. . . .

This is a telling point and, of course, the analysis of factor price equalization has come to grips with it. It is a particularly useful perspective when the concern is to show that, consistent with known facts, the equality of factor returns among nations is not an inescapable deduction. Broadening the scope of the analytical model not only increases the likelihood of the kinds of conditions that mitigate factor price equalization; the conditions themselves are qualitatively changed in a multifaceted model and the new conditions, inhibiting equalization of factor returns, presumably occur more commonly.

Generally speaking, these new conditions are not discernible in the economic mechanism of the factor price equalization model; rather they depend on relatively recondite properties of multiple equation mathematical systems.[6] But it is not necessary to incorporate more commodities and factors in the model in order to be justly skeptical of the applicability of the logic of full equalization of factor prices in the real world. To be sure, increasing the number of factor and commodity types does this. However, the simple model already contains enough unrealistic assumptions and, if these are relaxed in favor of realism, it is improbable that anyone should believe that free trade would actually bring about the equality of factor prices. Moreover, emphasis on the simple two-commodity, two-factor, two-country model facilitates the examination of the mechanism of factor price adjustment as international trade takes place. It is believed that, far from being self-deceiving and unfortunate as Pearce charges [43, p. 726], an understanding of this process leads to an increased awareness of the nature of Pearce's "index-number problem" that is glossed over in a two-commodity, two-factor world.

Specification of the relative endowments of the productive factors among the countries is an integral part of the analysis supporting factor price equalization. In the Heckscher-Ohlin formulation of international trade theory, with its identical production functions, perfect competition, and the like, relative factor endowments underlie the international pattern of comparative advantages and, thus, explain the structure of trade. On the face of it, the identification of relative factor endowments would seem to pose no difficult problem once an acceptable definition of a productive factor is found. This, however, is not so. It is essential to adopt a definition of factor endowment that does not foreordain any important aspect of the model and that promises to yield the most leverage in a manageable theoretical analysis. As Jones [16] and Bhagwati [4, pp. 737–38] suggest, a choice, along these lines, must be made among those definitions of relative factor endowment which are most frequently encountered.

The number of such definitions is not legion. It is immediately evident that an inventory of the physical amounts of factors available in each country is able to supply the kind of information needed to establish relative factor endowments. Indeed, this is the conception of factor endowment that best fulfills the criteria just set forth. Several other definitions have been suggested, however, and while it would be uninstructive to dwell on all of these they nevertheless should be mentioned.

Viner, for example [62, p. 276], opts for a definition of relative factor endowment based upon "relative efficiency prices" of the factors which reflect relative differences in product demand, factor supply, and factor marginal value product. As Viner suggests, there is much to commend this approach: even with imperfect competition, differences in factor qualities, and disparate technologies, relative efficiency prices unambiguously determine the structure of trade as long as factor intensity reversals are ruled out. Nevertheless, this concept of relative endowment has not been exploited in the literature, perhaps because at a manipulable level of theoretical simplification it does not differ from relative factor prices as a determinant of relative endowments.

While relative efficiency prices hold the prospect of opening up new avenues of theoretical effort on factor price equalization, an alternative formulation of factor endowment, attributable to Lancaster, closes off discussion of a major substantive issue. Lancaster implied that a country's scarce factor was ". . . that which is used more intensively in the good of which more is produced in isolation than in trade. . . ." [21, p. 208] — that is, presumably, the factor which is employed most intensively in producing the import good. As Bhagwati points out [4, p. 737], acceptance of this definition would amount to predetermining one of the aspects of the factor price equalization theorem whose determination should be integrated into the logic. It is, in other words, profitable to adopt a specification of relative factor endowments which at the outset is not directly dependent on the structure of trade, although it should be related to trade structure in some predictable fashion. Given this specification it is then of signal importance to ascertain the situations in which a country does indeed import the commodity which, when produced at home, utilizes the scarce factor relatively intensively.

A definition of relative factor endowment which, in the theoretical model, is independent of the existing trade structure is one based on physical amounts of the factors. Although a physical specification may be challenged on the practical grounds of immeasurability and incommensurability of factors, its simplicity and its failure to impose unnecessary rigidities on the analysis recommend it highly. In the simple two-factor, two-country model relative physical abundance of a factor is determined by adding all available units of service of each factor in each country, computing two ratios for those sums, and comparing these between the two countries. Thus, letting K_A and L_A stand for the physical amounts of capital and labor inputs, respectively, available in country A, and similarly for country B, country A is said to be relatively well endowed with labor if $(K/L)_A < (K/L)_B$, and in country B labor is correspondingly scarce with capital being relatively abundant.

This physical definition of factor endowments is not, apparently, the one originally used by Ohlin, who conceived of relative factor abundance primarily in terms of the ratios of the pre-trade prices of the factors. Following Jones' discussion [16, pp. 2–3] and indicating pre-trade[7] prices by P, country A is relatively labor rich if $(P_K/P_L)_A > (P_K/P_L)_B$, whereas country B is relatively capital rich and, hence, labor scarce. With this configuration of factor endowments, country A would find its comparative advantage in that commodity using labor relatively intensively and would inevitably export that commodity; country B would, in turn, export the capital intensive commodity. As long as the production function for each commodity is identical in the two countries, there can be no ambiguity on this unless a reversal of factor intensity is possible. Indeed, when non-reversal of factor intensities is assumed, as is usually the case in what follows, a relative factor price measure of factor endowments makes the logic of factor return equalization somewhat more cut-and-dried than it need be.

Moreover, if it is essential that there be no shift in pre-trade and post-trade factor endowments, it is hard to see how this conception stands up. If, after trade, the relative and absolute prices of the productive factors are identical in the two countries, this measure of factor endowments leads to the conclusion that the factor endowments of the two countries are also identical in the post-trade situation. Yet, in equilibrium, as noted above, trade is still taking place (merely disappearing at the margin) and the Heckscher-Ohlin theorem — that a country tends to export the commodity using intensively its relatively abundant factor — is no longer valid. In equilibrium the theorem becomes meaningless; the particular trade structure it predicts is only observable when the two countries are not in equilibrium.

This is not to deny that, in theory, factor price equalization will occur, for it will. The logic of the equalization theorem merely becomes less interesting under this definition of factor endowments. The reason is that by this conception the relatively scarce factor is, by definition, the high-priced factor and the abundant factor is low-priced. Since if relative endowments are specified by relative factor prices, a country always, with trade, produces more of and exports that commodity using a relatively large amount of the low-priced factor, the price of the scarce factor always rises and that of the abundant factor falls. If, in contrast, scarcity and abundance are defined without reference to factor prices, the opening of trade may cause the price of the "abundant" factor to fall while that of the "scarce" factor may be forced to rise. Factor price equalization then may occur in a manner seemingly perverse to the normal economic processes.

A physical definition of factor endowments admits this perverse process. As Rybczynski [47] and Jones [16, pp. 3–4] show, a capital rich country finds that it is biased toward producing the capital-intensive commodity. In Jones' terms ". . . if the output of the two commodities is in the same proportion in both countries, the relatively capital abundant country will be able to expand its production of the capital intensive commodity at a lower [real] opportunity cost than the other country" [16, p. 3, italics omitted]. A bias in favor of producing the capital-intensive commodity does not, however, necessarily lead to the export of that commodity. The capital-intensive commodity is exported provided that its price is relatively lower than that of the labor-intensive commodity, compared to the situation in the second country. Insofar as taste patterns in the two countries are similar, as empirical evidence suggests, this is likely.

Where taste patterns are disparate, however, the capital rich country (in physical terms) might find itself exporting the labor-intensive commodity and importing the capital-intensive commodity. But, if this were the case, physical abundance of capital is nevertheless associated with a high price for capital and physical scarcity of labor with a low wage. Trade still brings about the equalization of factor returns[8] provided that certain other conditions prevail, most notably that a good's production function is identical in both countries and that there are no reversals of factor intensities. Where these conditions hold, trade results in increasing the return to the physically scarce (but the relatively cheap) factor and reducing the return to the physically abundant factor.

Because, as Bhagwati puts it [5, p. 20], a physical specification leaves more scope for explanation, it is the conception of factor endowments used in this chapter. The factor price equalization theorem could be demonstrated more simply by recourse to the relative factor price definition of endowments. Pedagogically significant substantive issues would then be superficially treated. In particular, the role of commodity demand patterns would be neglected. In order to plumb the logic of factor price equalization to the fullest extent, it is important to consider the consequences of relaxing a number of the simplifying assumptions upon which the formal derivation of the theorem is based. Defining relative factor endowments in terms of the physical quantities of the factors expedites this.

The factor price equalization theorem states that under certain conditions international trade in commodities, like international movements of the productive factors, causes the absolute returns to each of the factors of production to be identical in each of the countries participating in the trading network.[9] If absolute factor returns are the same, so too are relative factor prices. The validity of this theorem is contingent upon the existence of a one-to-one relationship between relative commodity prices and relative factor prices so that if commodity prices are identical in the countries their factor prices must also be identical. The derivation of such a relationship and, hence, the proof of the "full equalization" theorem rests upon a number of exact, relatively unrealistic assumptions. Little wonder, in view of the unrealism of these assumptions, that the theorem has fallen short of validation in the real world. Nor should substantiation have been expected. Before the reasons for "failure" of price equalization can be examined, it is imperative to derive the theorem with some rigor. In this way the role of each of the assumptions becomes familiar.

The analysis proceeds, first, by stating explicitly the various assumptions that are necessary to derive complete equalization of absolute factor returns. Following itemization of the assumptions, a fairly full derivation of the theorem itself is sketched. A section is then devoted expressly to a relaxation of several of the more significant assumptions. Finally, the Appendix to this chapter brings out other ramifications of the factor price equalization analysis and discusses the consequences of relaxing other, less explored assumptions of the model. It will become clear, even in a strictly static model, that full factor price equalization is a most unlikely phenomenon. The highly restrictive nature of the assumptions needed for full equalization makes the theorem, as Harrod succinctly observes [12, p. 255], ". . . a *curiosum* in international trade theory. . . ." Yet the derivation and discussion of the factor price equalization theorem vividly display the "power and elegance" of *a priori* analysis; they illustrate as well the severe limitations of some kinds of pure theoretical work.

The Assumptions

1. Two countries (A and B), using two factors, capital (K) and labor (L), produce two commodities (X and Y) used solely for consumption purposes. Each factor and each commodity is of identical quality in the two countries. The two factors and the two commodities are relatively imperfect substitutes. Each country produces some of both commodities before and after trade takes place so that specialization in production is incomplete.

2. Perfect competition exists within each country in both factor markets and goods markets. Factors are perfectly mobile within each country. These assumptions, together with perfect factor and commodity price flexibility, mean that the factors of production are continuously fully employed.

3. The total effective supply of each of the factors is fixed in each of the countries. Thus, the productive factors, while perfectly mobile nationally, are completely immobile internationally. A further implication of this assumption is that the trade of the two countries is balanced so that international capital flows do not occur.

4. When international trade takes place, it is completely free and costless. Tariff protection, quotas, and the like are absent and transport costs are zero. Moreover, in the multi-commodity, multi-country case, each good may be exchanged for every other good and each country may trade with every other country.

5. The tastes of each consuming unit in both countries are identical and unchanging. Moreover, the taste pattern is accurately presented by isoquants which reflect linear homogeneous demands.[10] This assumes away any problems which might be created by the international redistribution of income as factor prices move toward equalization. It also means that in essentials the demand patterns of the two countries are identical — in this instance, at any given commodity price ratio, each country demands the two commodities in the same proportion.[11]

6. The factor endowments of the two countries, measured by their respective ratios of physical quantities of the two factors, differ. Country A is relatively labor abundant while country B is relatively capital rich, i.e., $(K/L)_A < (K/L)_B$.

7. The relationship between the inputs of the two factors and the output of each of the commodities is the same for both countries. In other words, the production function for each commodity is identical in both countries. However, each commodity has a different production function. These relationships between factor inputs and outputs of goods exhibit the following characteristics.

a. Returns to changes in the scale of production are constant. Therefore, if the input of each of the factors is doubled, the output of the commodity being produced is exactly doubled.

b. For any given ratio in which the factors are combined in the production of each commodity, the relative prices of the factors are identical. Thus, the relative prices of the factors depend only upon the proportion in which factors are combined in the productive processes.

c. In order to maintain a given output of the commodity, as more of one factor relative to the other factor is used in the production process, increasingly larger doses of the first factor are needed to offset a unit reduction in the input of the second factor.

Taken together, these conditions determine that each of the production functions is linear homogeneous[12] and that the marginal rate of substitution of the factors in the production process is diminishing. The "law of variable proportions" is assumed to hold so that, if the input of one of the factors is increased, the input of the second factor remaining constant, the marginal product of the first factor will have fallen.[13] These conditions mean also that Euler's theorem — that paying each of the factors a return equal to marginal product will completely use up the total output in factor payments — is applicable. It is worth noting, moreover, that where a production function is linear homogeneous any single isoquant from that production function provides an accurate picture of all the significant properties of the production function. This feature of linear homogeneity permits convenient simplification of the graphical presentation of the factor price equalization theorem.

8. Each commodity can be classified by its factor intensity according to whether its production uses relatively much or relatively little of one of the factors when compared to the manner of production of the other commodity. It is assumed that commodity X is relatively labor-intensive and therefore that commodity Y is relatively capital-intensive. Since this is also a property of the production function, the factor intensity of each of the commodities is invariant between the countries. It is also stipulated that the factor intensity of a given product is not subject to "reversal" as the relative prices of the productive factors change. Thus, at any relative factor price $(K/L)_X < (K/L)_Y$ and this holds for both countries.[14] It should be noted that the ratio of capital to labor in the production, say, of commodity A is not identical in the two countries in the pre-trade situation. Different relative factor endowments insure this. This assumption means that the capital-labor ratio in the production of commodity X, while different in each country, is less than the capital-labor ratio employed in making commodity Y, which is also different in each country before trade. Indeed, the gist of the demonstration of factor price equalization, early recognized by Samuelson [50, p. 182], is that trade brings about an alteration in the factor ratios used in the production of each commodity — ratios which are initially different in each country — so that the factor ratios employed become identical in both countries for each commodity.

The Demonstration of Factor Price Equalization

On the basis of these extreme simplifying assumptions, the factor price equalization theorem can be demonstrated using the analytical tools commonly employed in modern microeconomic theory. These tools are the familiar indifference curves, commodity isoquants, production possibilities curves, and the less well-known Edgeworth-Bowley box diagram. The demonstration in this framework can be complete, in the sense that all of the logical steps in the argument are made readily apparent. Moreover, it is the underlying basis for a second approach to the issue of relative factor prices — that attributable in rudimentary form to Samuelson [50], but refined by Harrod [12] and fully elaborated by Johnson [14]. The Harrod-Johnson graphical formulation relies, as does Jones' suggestive treatment [16, pp. 8–9], upon the existence of a known relationship between factor price ratios and commodity price ratios, a relationship which can only be established by recourse to the more traditional approach. The specific effort of the traditional approach is to determine, with the above assumptions, that only a single factor price ratio is consistent with a given commodity price ratio and that these two price ratios are identical for the two countries. Where this can be shown, equalization by trade of relative and absolute factor prices is also demonstrable. But this one-to-one relationship between relative commodity prices and relative factor prices need not exist. It is easiest to explore this latter possibility using the Harrod-Johnson approach.

Thus, the first step is to employ the traditional tools of microeconomic theory to prove that international trade does lead to full equalization of factor prices under sufficiently rigorous assumptions. The more interesting of these assumptions are then relaxed, seriatim, to determine the consequences of more realistic conditions for the factor price equalization theorem. At this point it becomes convenient to utilize the Harrod-Johnson diagrammatic analysis. But from time to time it is also helpful to revert to the traditional approach, using it to emphasize differences between the simplified model, described by the above assumptions, and a more realistic structure of underlying conditions.

The traditional formulation / To prove the ultimate equalization by free trade of the price of each productive factor in both countries it is first necessary to establish that the prices of the two commodities will be identical in both countries after trade occurs. This is conventionally undertaken by constructing production possibilities curves for each country, showing the possible combination of outputs of commodities, given the factor endowments of the two countries and given also that the above assumptions imply that goods and factor prices are perfectly flexible and that productive factors are always fully employed. When the production possibilities curves are superimposed on an indifference map — reflecting the taste preferences as between the two commodities — relative prices for the two commodities in each country can be determined. It can be shown that these relative commodity prices are identical after trade occurs, although they are different in the pre-trade situation. The first step in the demonstration is, then, the derivation of the production possibilities curve for each of the countries.[15]

The shape of the production possibilities curve is related both to relative factor endowments and to the commodities' production functions. In assumption 8 above, it is stipulated that commodity X is labor-intensive compared to commodity Y for any relative price of the productive factors. The nature of this assumption is clarified by referring to Figure 1-1. In Figure 1-1A the quantity of labor input is measured on the abscissa; the quantity of capital input is measured on the ordinate. The two solid curves represent isoquants for each of the commodities, X and Y. For example, the isoquant designated by YY shows that a given, unspecified amount of commodity Y can be produced by various combinations of capital and labor, one of which might be OK_Y of capital and OL_Y of labor. Similarly, XX gives those factor combinations that can produce a given, unspecified amount of commodity X. Which factor combination will be used in the production of these quantities of commodities depends, of course, on the relative factor price.

First assume some relative factor price given by the slope of the price-line P_1P_1. Ignoring algebraic signs, the greater is the slope of the price-line the higher is the price of labor relative to that of capital; moreover, a price-line of any given steepness implies a constant relative factor price. Recall also that a price-line represents an isocost line. That is to say, any point along P_1P_1 connotes a constant level of expenditure on capital and labor combined, given their relative price. In this context, a rational entrepreneur faced with the isocost line P_1P_1 and the isoquant YY will so combine his factors that OK_Y of capital and OL_Y of labor are put into the production of commodity Y. In this way he maximizes his output of Y for the given expenditure on capital and labor at their given relative factor price. Similarly, if the entrepreneur were interested in producing only commodity X, and were faced by the same isocost line P_1P_1, he would combine OK_X of capital with OL_X of labor.

At the factor price ratio depicted by the slope of P_1P_1, commodity X is relatively labor intensive and commodity Y is relatively capital intensive. It will be remembered that this property was given by $(K/L)_X <$ $(K/L)_Y$. Thus, it is only necessary to compare the factor combinations in each commodity as shown in Figure 1-1A. The comparative factor intensities are OK_X/OL_X and OK_Y/OL_Y. By inspection, it is apparent that $(OK_X/OL_X) < (OK_Y/OL_Y)$; therefore, commodity X is relatively labor-intensive — at the factor price ratio given by the slope of P_1P_1.

This is also shown in Figure 1-1B, initially used by Samuelson [51], pp. 172–73], where the factor price ratio (P_L/P_K) is plotted against the factor input ratio (K/L). Thus, for the designated factor price ratio, P_1 in Figure 1-1B, the factor input ratio is lower for commodity X, $(K/L)_{X_1}$, than for commodity Y, $(K/L)_{Y_1}$. Commodity Y is seen to be capital-intensive compared to commodity X, which is therefore labor intensive.

A similar demonstration can be made using a higher relative price of labor, say the slopes of $P_2'P_2'$ or P_2P_2 (Figure 1-1A) which are identical. This factor price ratio is equal to P_2 in Figure 1-1B. The relative factor

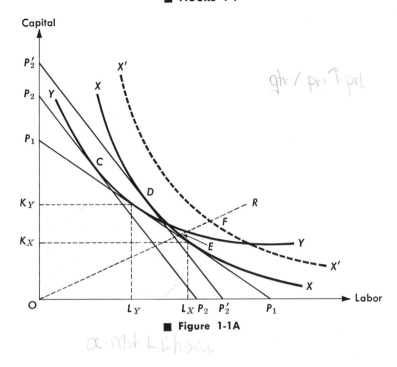

■ **Figure 1-1A**

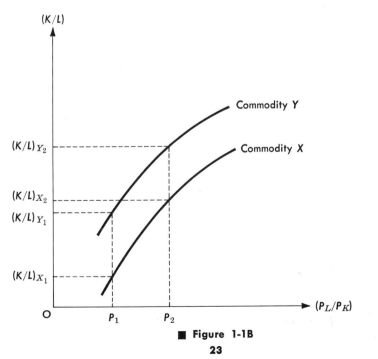

■ **Figure 1-1B**

inputs are not shown in Figure 1-1A although they are derivable by noting the input requirements of C and D on the isoquants. These factor input ratios are equal to $(K/L)_{Y_2}$ and $(K/L)_{X_2}$ in Figure 1-1B. At the new factor price ratio, commodity Y remains relatively capital-intensive and, therefore, commodity X remains relatively labor-intensive. Moreover, the isoquants XX and YY are drawn so that this is true at any positive relative factor price. Figure 1-1 diagrams, therefore, a situation in which factor intensity reversals are not possible and the "strong" Samuelsonian factor intensity assumption is applicable.[16] Had there been reversal the curves of Figure 1-1B, plotting the factor input ratio against the factor price ratio, would have crossed (at least once) and the isoquants XX and YY would have been tangent at some point or would have intersected (at least twice).

The meaning, for our purposes, of the assumption that the two production functions are linear homogeneous can conveniently be clarified at this point. The homogeneity assumption is particularly salient in later parts of the factor price equalization demonstration, it being imperative that relative and absolute returns to the factors depend solely upon the ratios in which the factors are employed. Homogeneity can be shown by referring, in Figure 1-1A, to the two isoquants, XX and $X'X'$, which are presumed to be derived from a linear homogeneous production function. For any given combination of factor inputs, such as that represented along the ray OR, the slope of the isoquants is constant. Conventionally the slope of the isoquant at any point equals the marginal rate of substitution of labor for capital at that point. The homogeneity assumption then means that at the points where the ray OR intersects the two isoquants the marginal rates of substitution are identical. Moreover, in equilibrium the marginal rate of substitution is equal to the ratio of the price of labor to the price of capital. Consequently, along any given ray — that is, for any given factor proportion — the factor price ratio is constant; relative factor prices therefore depend upon relative factor input proportions. Since this is true for all isoquants derived from a given linear homogeneous production function, any single isoquant, such as XX, precisely represents all others in this family of isoquants and also precisely represents the production function itself.

The meaning of the linearity assumption is more difficult to depict as Figure 1-1A is constructed. Because it is usually assumed that the axes mark-off factor inputs in equal units an exercise of mental gymnastics is required to show linearity. As already noted, the assumption of linearity in the production function means that output of the commodity, say X, is subject to constant returns to scale. With isoquants this is shown in the following way. Imagine that the units by which factor inputs are designated in Figure 1-1A are so selected that producing at F requires one-quarter more of both the inputs of capital and of labor than does producing at E. When this is the case, the linearity assumption compels the quantity of output of commodity X associated with isoquant $X'X'$ to be one-quarter larger than the output designated by isoquant XX. Since the marginal rates of substitution are identical at E and F, there is, in equilibrium, no change in relative factor prices. In consequence, total costs of production rise by one-quarter (reflected in a movement to a parallel isocost curve) but costs per unit of output remain constant — as is true of scale increases under constant returns to scale.

In the Appendix to this chapter the linearity or constant returns assumption is relaxed and the effects of relaxation on factor price equalization are discussed. For the moment, however, the importance of this assumption should be readily apparent: with constant average costs in a competitive model, the price a commodity commands in the market is equal to the average and marginal costs of producing the number of units of the commodity sold. How this feature of linear homogeneous production functions contributes to the demonstration of complete equalization of factor returns becomes clear in the paragraphs to follow.

The next step in the derivation of the production possibilities curves brings factor endowments into the picture. This is most conveniently accomplished by means of the box diagram. It saves some space and also adds to facility in using box diagrams if the production possibilities curve between commodities X and Y is simultaneously derived for both countries. This procedure makes more convincing the underlying characteristic of the comparative advantage doctrine: a country typically has a comparative advantage in the commodity which uses relatively intensively the factor which the country possesses in relatively abundant amounts.

Recall from assumption 6 that country A is relatively labor abundant, country B being relatively capital rich. Moreover, the meaning of the assumption that commodity X is relatively labor intensive and commodity Y relatively capital intensive has been noted. The effect of assumption 6 is shown in Figure 1-2A by the dimensions of the two boxes. The units in which the inputs of each factor are measured, in using the box diagram, are to be considered as equal. In Figure 1-2A the dimensions of the box for country A are such that it has available $O_X L_A$ units of labor input and $O_X K_A$ units of capital input. The factor endowment for country B, however, is $O'_Y L_B$ units of labor input and $O'_Y K_B$ units of capital input. That is to say, the dimensions of the boxes, which indicate factor endowments, are such that with labor inputs measured horizontally and capital inputs vertically the box for country A rests on its side while that for country B stands on its end. Therefore, country A has more labor relative to capital when compared to the factor endowment of country B: $(O_X K_A / O_X L_A) < (O'_Y K_B / O'_Y L_B)$. Country A is relatively labor rich. The positioning of the two boxes — so that one corner of each box coincides at O_X — is done solely for the convenience of the next step in the graphical derivation of the production possibilities curves.

That step consists of transplanting the linear homogeneous production functions depicted in Figure 1-1A into the two boxes. In doing this, due care must be given to the fact that with respect to commodity Y the axes are rotated 180°. In the box diagram the output of commodity X is measured conventionally, with the origin of the isoquants at O_X; commodity Y's isoquants, however, have their origin for country A at O_Y and for country B at O_Y'. Recalling that the production function for each commodity is identical in both countries one set of isoquants is sufficient (for both countries) in the case of commodity X; whereas, because of the impossibility (due to disparate factor endowments) of "coinciding" O_Y and O_Y', two sets of isoquants are needed for commodity Y. Yet it must be stressed that these two sets of isoquants for commodity Y depict the same production function. In Figure 1-2A these isoquants are denoted respectively by XX and YY.

The two sets of isoquant maps — one set for each country — permit the derivation of two maximum efficiency locus curves, or contract curves, for the two countries.[17] The maximum efficiency locus for country A is the heavy curve O_XO_Y and that for country B is the curve O_XO_Y'. These contract curves are drawn through the various points of tangency in the two isoquant maps and represent the loci of possible equilibrium combinations of the productive factors in the production of the two commodities, given the assumptions listed above. Although proof will not be given here, the points on a single contract curve represent factor combinations (at specific outputs given by the isoquants) where the marginal rates of substitution of the factors in the production of both commodities are equal, as are the ratios of the marginal products of the factors. Also, in a perfectly competitive factor market the ratio of the factor prices is identical in each of the two industries producing commodities X and Y. Referring, for example, to the potential equilibrium at E on the maximum efficiency locus of country A (Figure 1-2A), O_XL_E units of labor and O_XK_E units of capital are employed in the production of, say, 80 units of commodity X; country A also uses O_YL_F $(= L_EL_A)$ units of labor and O_YK_F $(= K_EK_A)$ units of capital to produce, say, 50 units of commodity Y. By simple addition of these quantities of factor inputs, it is seen that E represents full employment, as does every point on the contract curve. Indeed, factor prices adjust — the factor price ratio changes — so that full employment is insured and, also, so that the factor price ratio is identical in each industry for factor combinations on the contract curve. (The means of deriving the factor price ratio at E are not included in Figure 1-2A; they are seen, however, in Figure 1-4.)

With the maximum efficiency locus determined, it is an easy step to the production possibilities or transformation curve showing the real

26

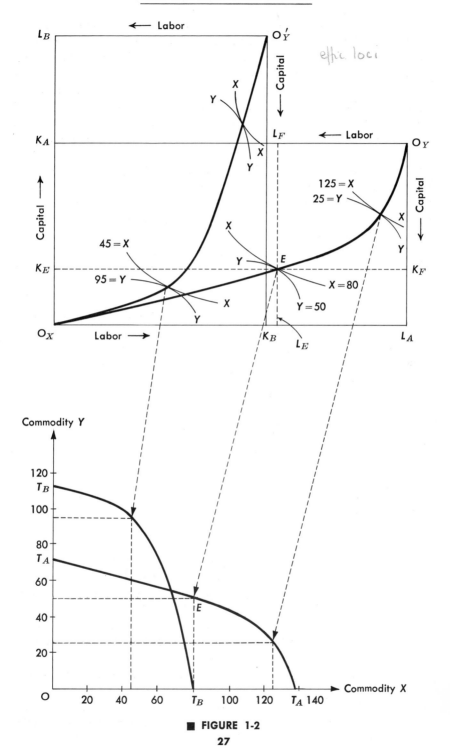

■ **FIGURE 1-2**

27

opportunity costs in terms of one commodity of producing a second commodity. One such transformation curve is shown in Figure 1-2B for each country. These transformation curves, $T_A T_A$ and $T_B T_B$, are "mapped" from their respective contract curves, $O_X O_Y$ and $O_X O'_Y$, in a manner indicated by the dashed arrows joining the two portions of the figure. Since the entire box diagram surface is filled with isoquants and since the maximum efficiency loci represent tangency points of isoquants, each point on the contract curves provides not only a factor input combination but also a commodity output combination. As Figure 1-2 is drawn, for example, the combination of labor and capital given by E on the maximum efficiency locus $O_X O_Y$ produces 80 units of commodity X and 50 units of commodity Y. These output quantities give a single point, also designated by E, in the two-commodity coordinate system which is also a point on the transformation curve $T_A T_A$. Other points on the transformation curves are similarly derived: for each point on a contract curve there corresponds a single point on a production possibilities curve.

Remembering the assumptions of the model, especially that production functions in the two countries are identical, the different shapes of the transformation functions, $T_A T_A$ and $T_B T_B$, are attributable solely to differences in factor endowments.[18] The relative slopes of $T_A T_A$ and $T_B T_B$ imply that country A has a comparative advantage in the production of commodity X; whereas country B has a relative advantage in the production of commodity Y. In this instance, comparative advantage must be interpreted in a particular way suggested by Jones [16, p. 3]: for any given output proportion in the two countries (i.e., for any given ray through the origin of Figure 1-2B) in order to produce one more unit of commodity X, country B has to give up production of a substantially greater amount of commodity Y than has country A. Contrastingly, for a unit increase in the output of commodity Y, country B is forced to forego the production of fewer units of commodity X than is country A. In technical language, the marginal rate of transformation of commodity X for commodity Y at any output proportion in the two countries is lower for country A than for country B, as reflected in the lesser slope of $T_A T_A$ than of $T_B T_B$ at, say, their point of intersection.

So much for the derivation of the transformation curves. These curves (of Figure 1-2B) are reproduced in Figure 1-3, along with a set of indifference curves showing taste patterns for commodities X and Y. Consistent with assumption 5 above, a single indifference map is common to both countries. The equilibrium condition for a system of production and consumption, it will be recalled, is that consumers in each country allocate their expenditures between the two commodities so that the marginal rate of substitution (in consumption) of commodity X for commodity Y equals the ratio of the price of commodity X to commodity

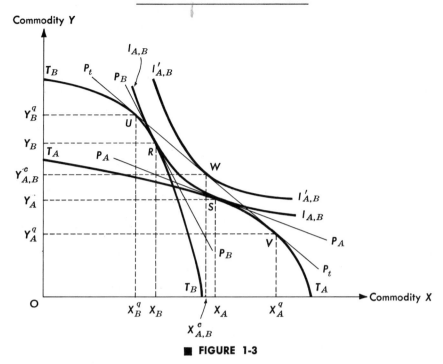

■ FIGURE 1-3

Y's price; in each country producers likewise contribute an output combination in which the marginal rate of transformation (in production) of
commodity X for commodity Y is equal to the same price ratio. Thus,
the equilibrium condition in each country is:

$$MRS = P_X/P_Y = MRT, \qquad (1\text{-}1)$$

where MRS stands for marginal rate of substitution, MRT for marginal
rate of transformation, and the P's for the prices of the respective commodities. When the countries are isolated, so that trade cannot occur,
this equilibrium condition is typically satisfied at a different commodity
price ratio in each country. Where factor endowments differ and production functions and taste patterns are identical, as here, this is always the
case. These equilibria are depicted in Figure 1-3 by the points (S and R)
of common tangency of $T_A T_A$, the indifference curve, $I_{A,B}$, and the price
line, $P_A P_A$, and of $T_B T_B$, $I_{A,B}$ and $P_B P_B$. Therefore, this pre-trade
equilibrium production *and* consumption are, in country A, OX_A of
commodity X and OY_A of commodity Y; in country B the output and
consumption are respectively OX_B and OY_B. By inspection it can also be
observed that $(P_X/P_Y)_A < (P_X/P_Y)_B$, these ratios being given by the slopes
of the price lines. In other words, commodity X is relatively cheap compared to commodity Y in country A, while in country B commodity Y is
the relatively cheap good. A basis for international trade exists.

29

If these countries now begin trading with each other, country A will become more specialized in the production of commodity X, whereas country B specializes further in the production of commodity Y. (Specialization does not become complete, however.) In the absence of trade barriers and transport costs, the commodities will exchange at identical prices in both countries. This common post-trade price ratio is shown by the slope of $P_t P_t$. Again, by inspection it is apparent that $(P_X/P_Y)_A <$ $(P_X/P_Y)_t < (P_X/P_Y)_B$; trade raises the commodity price ratio in country A and diminishes the commodity price ratio in country B. The effect of this relative commodity price movement is to lower country A's consumption of commodity X and raise its consumption of commodity Y; the contrary occurs in country B. Indeed, after trade the consumption patterns of the two countries are the same. In both countries, trade permits a higher level of satisfaction as indicated by the fact that the price line, $P_t P_t$, is tangent (at W) to a higher indifference curve $I'_{A,B}$ than was either of the pre-trade price lines. Thus, when equilibrium is established with international trade taking place, the following condition exists:

$$(MRT)_B = (MRS)'_B = (P_X/P_Y)_B = (P_X/P_Y)_t$$
$$= (P_X/P_Y)_A = (MRS)'_A = (MRT)_A \qquad (1\text{-}2)$$

the prime referring to the higher indifference curve. These equalities are simultaneously satisfied when country A is producing at V on its transformation function, country B is at U on its transformation function, and both countries are consuming at W on their common indifference curve, $I'_{A,B}$. The marginal rates of transformation and of substitution between the commodities and the relative commodity prices are identical in both countries. This post-trade equilibrium establishes the following situation (taken from Figure 1-3):

Equilibrium Situation After Trade

	Country A	Country B
Production:		
of X:	OX^q_A	OX^q_B
of Y:	OY^q_B	OY^q_B
Consumption:		
of X:	$OX^c_{A,B}$	$OX^c_{A,B}$
of Y:	$OY^c_{A,B}$	$OY^c_{A,B}$

The difference between each country's production pattern and consumption pattern is made up by international trade. In a two-commodity, two-country model, country A's exports are identical to country B's imports and country B's exports are identical to country A's imports. These respectively are given by $X^c_{A,B} X^q_A (= X^q_B X^c_{A,B})$ of commodity X

and $Y^c_{A,B}Y^q_B(= Y^q_A Y^c_{A,B})$ of commodity Y. Moreover, valued at the price ratio $(P_X/P_Y)_t$, the slope of P_tP_t, the value of the trade balance of each country is zero. In consequence, the post-trade commodity price ratio, $(P_X/P_Y)_t$, is an equilibrium ratio and, hence, there is no reason for these various magnitudes to change. Figure 1-3 depicts a situation of comparative statics: both pre-trade and post-trade equilibrium relationships are denoted; with free, unfettered trade, and other assumptions mentioned, a single commodity price ratio rules in both countries.

The final, most complicated step in the proof of full factor price equalization is to translate these commodity-trade equilibrium conditions back into the box diagram. While Figure 1-3 can show relative commodity prices, it cannot show factor prices. Conversely, the box diagram can directly show factor price ratios but it cannot show commodity price ratios. But as already established, for any point on the maximum efficiency locus there corresponds a single point on the production possibilities curve. The reverse is also true.[19] This unique relationship between points on the two types of curves is the key to the demonstration. Figure 1-4, which duplicates the essentials of Figure 1-2A, is drawn to illustrate the significance for factor prices of the movement from the pre-trade to the post-trade equilibrium depicted in Figure 1-3.[20]

Pre-trade production in country A has been determined in Figure 1-3 to be OX_A and OY_A units of commodities X and Y respectively. This output proportion corresponds to the isoquants for commodity X and commodity Y that are tangent to each other at S in Figure 1-4. While these isoquants are not sketched in Figure 1-4, it is the case that country A uses $O_X L^X_A$ of labor and $O_X K^X_A$ of capital to produce OX_A of commodity X; in order to produce OY_A of commodity Y, the remaining labor, $L^X_A L_A$, and capital, $K^X_A K_A$, are employed in its production. Similarly, in country B, where the pre-trade equilibrium is indicated by R, $O'_Y L^Y_B$ of labor and $O'_Y K^Y_B$ of capital are devoted to the production of OY_B units of commodity Y, while $L^Y_B L_B$ of labor and $K^Y_B K_B$ of capital go into making OX_B of commodity X. At these factor combinations, the relative factor price in country A (the slope of $K^P_A L^P_A$) is such that capital commands a relatively high return compared to the factor price ratio in country B (the slope of $L^P_B K^P_B$), where labor is relatively dear compared to capital. Clearly, in the pre-trade situation, while the relative return to both factors in the production of commodity X is identical to that received in the production of commodity Y in each country, relative factor prices in the two countries are not equal. Nor are absolute factor returns.

This condition is subject to change once free trade opens up. Trade permits greater specialization in each country so that the proportions in which the countries produce the two commodities are altered. With the assumptions of relative factor endowment and relative factor intensity specified above, as Lancaster proves [20, pp. 24–28], country A produces

31

relatively more of commodity X while country B increases relatively its output of commodity Y. (See also Mookerjee [38, p. 4].) In Figure 1-4 this is shown by a movement along contract curve $O_X O_Y$ from S to V and on contract curve $O_X O'_Y$ from R to U. This movement, it should be emphasized, reflects a similar movement along the transformation functions of Figure 1-3 from S to V and R to U respectively. In Figure 1-3 at U and V identical commodity prices obtain in the two countries; there is no incentive for a further expansion of trade and, hence, no inducement for a further change in the proportions in which the commodities are produced. So too in Figure 1-4: U and V reflect post-trade equilibrium output proportions and, therefore, equilibrium factor combinations.

The adjustment of output as trade occurs is mirrored in an adjustment in factor input combinations. In country A, on the one hand, $O_X L_A^{X'}$ of labor and $O_X K_A^{X'}$ of capital go into commodity X's production, so that inputs of both factors into the production of commodity Y are reduced. The resulting changes in factor combinations in country A are that, at V, both commodities are produced with a higher capital-labor ratio than at S. This being so, the marginal product of capital falls and that of labor rises in accordance with the "law of variable proportions." In country B, on the other hand, more of each factor is placed in producing commodity Y; specifically, $O'_Y L_B^{Y'}$ of labor and $O'_Y K_B^{Y'}$ of capital are involved in the production of commodity Y after trade occurs. In country B, the capital-labor ratio in producing both commodities falls and, hence, capital's marginal product rises relative to that of labor. Since in the model the factors, in equilibrium, earn a return equal to their marginal products it is seen that the opening up of trade *tends*, at the very least, to equalize the *relative* return of the factors.

This is shown more directly in Figure 1-4 by the fact that $K_A^{P'} L_A^{P'}$ is steeper than $K_A^P L_A^P$ and that $L_B^{P'} K_B^{P'}$ is less steeply sloped than $L_B^P K_B^P$.[21] The alteration of factor combinations attendant to the opening of trade increases the price of labor relative to the return to capital in country A, whereas factor prices move in the opposite direction in country B. Since before trade, capital was relatively dear in country A and labor was relatively dear in country B, this changing slope of the factor-price lines again shows a tendency for trade to equalize relative factor returns.

But, with the given assumptions, trade is capable of more than this. It can be shown that the slopes of $K_A^{P'} L_A^{P'}$ and $L_B^{P'} K_B^{P'}$ are identical. Therefore, trade *completely* equalizes the factor price ratios of the two countries, and not only tends to equalize them. Observe in Figure 1-4 that the ray $O_X G$ goes through both U on country B's contract curve and V on the maximum efficiency locus of country A, signifying that the same factor combination is used in the production of commodity X in both countries. Since linear homogeneous production functions are assumed,

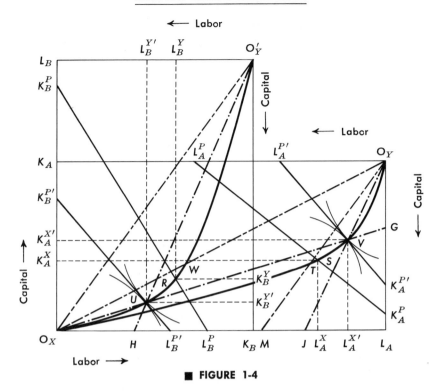

■ FIGURE 1-4

the relative marginal products of the factors must be identical at these two points, it being a property of linear homogeneity that marginal product ratios depend solely upon the proportions in which the factors are used. At U for country B and at V for country A:

$$(MRS)_B = (MRS)_A = MP_L/MP_K. \tag{1-3}$$

Here the marginal products (MP's) may be measured either in terms of commodity X or commodity Y. On the maximum efficiency locus, the slopes of the isoquants for commodity X and for commodity Y are equal so that the ratio of the factor marginal products in the production of either commodity is identical.

Alternatively, it can be shown that the two rays, $O'_Y H$ and $O_Y J$, indicating factor proportions in the production of commodity Y in country B and country A respectively, are parallel. This being so, by an argument analogous to that just above, the marginal rates of substitution must be equal to the ratio of the factors' marginal products measured in terms of commodity Y. Consequently, at U and V the following condition prevails: $(MP_L/MP_K)_A = (MP_L/MP_K)_B$. And since in perfect competition a factor's return is equal to its marginal product it is apparent that relative factor prices in the two countries are fully equalized, i.e., $(P_L/P_K)_A = (P_L/P_K)_B$.

To this point it has not been necessary to bring Euler's theorem into the analysis. To prove that absolute factor prices are equalized by international trade Euler's theorem — for any good in equilibrium the sum of the products of factor inputs and their associated marginal products equals the total amount of output — can no longer be ignored. Also it is necessary to invoke the linearity property of the production functions: where returns to scale are constant, the ratio of the output of a commodity to the attendant input of either factor is also constant. In other words, linearity entails a fixed average output to each of the factors. These two features of the model can be used to demonstrate absolute factor price equalization, as in Lancaster's formulation [20, pp. 23–24].

Deriving quantities from the equilibrium point V in Figure 1-4, Euler's theorem holds that:

$$(OX_A^q) = (O_X L_A^{X'}) \cdot MP_L + (O_X K_A^{X'}) \cdot MP_K, \qquad (1\text{-}4)$$

the first terms of the two elements of the right side of the equation referring to the appropriate factor inputs and OX_A^q referring to the total output of commodity X (given by the abscissa of V in Figure 1-3). Manipulating the equation to determine the average output of capital at V yields:

$$\frac{(OX_A^q)}{(O_X K_A^{X'})} = \frac{(O_X L_A^{X'})}{(O_X K_A^{X'})} \cdot MP_L + MP_K. \qquad (1\text{-}5)$$

Finally, rearranging the right side of the equation gives:

$$\frac{(OX_A^q)}{(O_X K_A^{X'})} = MP_K \left[1 + \frac{(O_X L_A^{X'})}{(O_X K_A^{X'})} \cdot \frac{MP_L}{MP_K} \right]. \qquad (1\text{-}6)$$

The preceding analysis shows that MP_L/MP_K is constant at any given factor proportion so that MP_L/MP_K is the same at any point on the ray $O_X G$ in Figure 1-4. Moreover, constant returns to scale means that for any given factor proportion (such as any point on ray $O_X G$) $(OX_A^q)/(O_X K_A^{X'})$, the average product of capital, is constant. Further, by definition the factor proportion, at V given by $(O_X L_A^{X'})/(O_X K_A^{X'})$, is constant along ray $O_X G$. Consequently, what is true of the magnitudes at V on ray $O_X G$ must also be true at any other point on the ray such as U. Thus at V the bracketed component and the left side of equation 1-6 are identical to their values at U; hence, the only remaining element of equation 1-6, MP_K, must also be identical at V and U. That is to say, since V refers to country A and U refers to country B, $(MP_K)_A = (MP_K)_B$. A similar sequence shows that $(MP_L)_A = (MP_L)_B$. And lastly, because of the assumption of perfectly competitive markets, $P_K = MP_K$ and $P_L = MP_L$. Therefore, $(P_K)_A = (P_K)_B$ and $(P_L)_A = (P_L)_B$. Given the assumptions of the present model, international trade brings about the full equalization of the *absolute* returns to each of the factors in the two trading countries.

The Harrod-Johnson formulation / The alternative graphical presentation supporting equalization by trade of relative factor prices in the two countries seems much simpler than the one just given. The simplicity is a mirage, however. It is gained through explicitly relying upon a fact established only by the above analysis: there exists, under the listed assumptions, a one-to-one relationship between the ratio of commodity prices and the factor price ratio. One, and only one, factor price ratio is consistent with any single commodity price ratio. Without a pre-existing proof of this relationship, the Harrod-Johnson diagrammatic formulation of equalization of relative factor prices in the two countries is groundless. Thus, the formulation about to be presented is a summarizing capstone for the previous argument — and not at all an alternative proof of relative factor price equalization.

Moreover, in that it relies upon the traditional formulation which provides a proof of absolute factor price equalization, the Harrod-Johnson alternative method also results in equalization of absolute factor prices insofar as it establishes relative factor price equalization. All hinges, therefore, on the proof already presented. Yet the advantage of the Harrod-Johnson technique is that, in glossing over this absolutely fundamental demonstration of a unique commodity price-factor price relationship, it paves the way for a facile examination of the theorem under assumptions alternative to those enumerated above.

Figure 1-5, the basis of the Harrod-Johnson demonstration of relative factor price equalization, shows the relationship between the factor price ratio, the commodity price ratio, and the optimum capital-labor ratio. The upper part of the diagram is derived from the underlying production functions and hence is similar to Figure 1-1B. It shows that for each relative factor price, (P_L/P_K), when factors are allocated in the production of the commodities so that the marginal products are equated to factor prices, the optimum capital-labor ratio in commodity Y is higher than that in commodity X; the "factor-ratio curve" for commodity Y, as Michaely calls this relationship [33, p. 536], is higher than the factor-ratio curve for commodity X. Moreover, in accordance with the initial assumption of non-reversal of factor intensity, the factor-ratio curves do not intersect so that commodity Y, for the range of the factor-ratio curves drawn, is always capital-intensive and commodity X is always labor-intensive. The factor-ratio curves are by assumption identical for each country. Each country is differentiated, however, by different relative endowments of the two factors. Reflecting the assumptions, country B is relatively capital abundant and its over-all factor endowment ratio is given by E_B. The relatively labor rich country A has an over-all endowment ratio equal to E_A.

These endowment ratios, in conjunction with the factor ratio curves, determine the limits of the range of relative factor prices in the two countries. If, for example, country A devoted all of its resources to production of good Y, its factor price ratio would be F_A^Y. In contradistinction, if it produced only commodity X its factor price ratio would be F_A^X. The greater relative price of labor in the production of good X reflects the fact that at a given factor input proportion, E_A, and hence different outputs of the two commodities, the marginal product of labor is higher in the labor intensive commodity than it is in the capital intensive commodity and vice versa for the marginal product of capital.

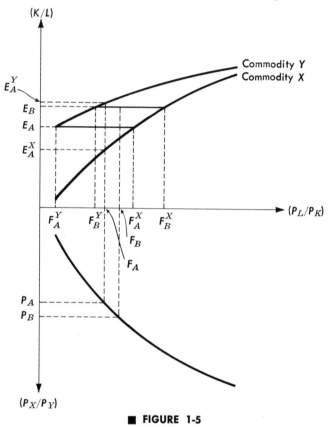

■ FIGURE 1-5

The factor ratio curves show that as the relative price of labor rises in country A from F_A^Y toward F_A^X the capital-labor ratio in the production of both commodities rises as capital is substituted for labor. This might appear odd in view of the fixity of the over-all factor endowment ratio, E_A. But this over-all ratio is distributed, as it were, between two industries, producing X and Y, in disparate proportions. The increase in the capital-labor ratio in both industries is reconciled with the fixed over-all factor endowment ratio by virtue of the fact that the movement of the factor price ratio also induces resources to shift out of the production of commodity Y, which being the capital intensive good releases the capital needed for increases in the capital-labor ratio in both industries.[22] Thus, assuming that the ruling factor price ratio in country A is F_A, the capital-labor ratio in industry X is E_A^X and in industry Y it is E_A^Y; but so much more of commodity X is produced relative to commodity Y that, when the factor input ratios are weighted by their respective outputs, the weighted average factor input ratio equals E_A. A similar relationship exists for any other relative factor price.

Correspondingly, for country B, whose endowment of capital is relatively abundant, a factor price ratio range can also be demonstrated. Consistent with the assumption of internationally identical production functions and E_B being higher than E_A, the minimum relative price of labor, F_B^Y, would be higher in country B than in country A. Country B would also have the higher maximum relative price of labor, F_B^X. As the factor-ratio curves are drawn, the possible range for the factor price ratio in the capital rich country is narrower than that of the labor abundant country. This latter aspect of the diagram reflects an implicit assumption of higher substitutability of capital for labor in commodity X than in commodity Y so that, because commodity X is labor intensive, the difference in the factor intensity of the two goods narrows as the price of labor rises relatively.

The lower portion of Figure 1-5 plots relative factor prices against relative commodity prices and hence differs slightly from Johnson's formulation [14] where commodity costs are used. As the price of labor rises relative to that of capital, the price of the labor-intensive commodity must also rise relative to that of the capital-intensive commodity. This is true whether or not factor intensity reversal is possible. As the axes are denominated and since commodity X is, for the range of the factor price ratio depicted, labor-intensive compared to commodity Y, the price ratio curve, as the relationship between the two price ratios is called, must be positively sloped: the higher the relative price of labor the higher the relative price of commodity X. Reflecting the different substitutability of capital for labor in the two production functions at higher relative labor prices, the price of commodity X rises relatively less rapidly compared to the change in the price of commodity Y, so that the relationship between the two price ratios tends to flatten out for higher factor price ratios. Intuitively, it can be seen that this phenomenon is attributable to the convergence of the factor intensity ratios in the two commodities. If both commodities were to exhibit the same factor intensity ratio — if the factor ratio curves touched — a change in the relative factor price ratio would cause no adjustment in the commodity price ratio.[23]

There is, as the diagram indicates, a definite relationship between the two portions of Figure 1-5. For any given factor price ratio there is an optimum combination of factors in the production of each commodity and also a relative commodity price which reflects the factor input combinations for the two commodities at the given relative factor price. As Johnson states [14, p. 22]: given the taste patterns of consumers, for a particular ratio of labor to capital prices there is a corresponding specific pattern of output, a corresponding distribution of income, and a corresponding relative price of the commodities at which the quantity of each commodity purchased is just equal to the amount of the commodity produced. As an example, for the relative price of labor designated by F_A, the relative price of commodity X is given by P_A. Correspondingly, if F_B were the relative labor price ruling in country B, the commodity price ratio there would be given by P_B. The values of the equilibrium factor price and commodity price ratios in any country are those which equate the relative commodity production costs with the commodity price ratio at which the quantities produced of the two commodities will just be taken off the market.

It is being assumed here, since $P_A \neq P_B$, that the countries are not engaged in international trade and, moreover, it should be recalled that their taste patterns are identical (assumption 5 above). Because of this latter assumption, it is clear that the same price ratio curve exists in each country. It is evident, and vital to the demonstration of factor price equalization using this technique, that in the situation depicted by Figure 1-5 (and for the assumptions enumerated in a previous section — specifically, the absence of factor intensity reversal) there is a unique relationship between the factor price ratio and the commodity price ratio: for each relative factor price there is only one relative commodity price; and vice versa, for each commodity price ratio there is only one factor price ratio. These are the same for both countries. Hence, since the opening up of costless international trade brings about the same commodity price ratio in both countries, provided specialization is incomplete, it must also be the case that relative factor prices are identical in the two countries. With the assumption of identical production functions internationally, this means that absolute factor prices are likewise equated in the two countries.

Equalization of relative factor prices may be described in the following way. Assume in Figure 1-5 that in the pre-trade situation the equilibrium price ratios are F_A and P_A in country A and F_B and P_B in country B. This reflects the conventional presumption that in the relatively labor rich country labor is comparatively poorly paid whereas in the capital abundant country labor is relatively well paid. Correspondingly, the labor rich country A has a comparative advantage in the production of commodity X, the labor-intensive commodity, and country B possesses a relative advantage in the production of the capital-intensive good, i.e., $P_A < P_B$, which is to say that $(P_X/P_Y)_A < (P_X/P_Y)_B$.

This need not have been the case, of course. As Johnson carefully analyzes [14, pp. 25–26], this pre-trade equilibrium situation could have been reversed, with the capital abundant country B, measured in physical terms, having a comparative advantage in the labor-intensive commodity X and the opposite for country A. This would be illustrated in Figure 1-5 if the positions of F_A and F_B (and consequently P_A and P_B) were reversed, so that country B had a relatively low price for labor.

But keeping to the situation diagrammed in Figure 1-5, when international trade takes place, country A exports commodity X. It transfers resources from industry Y to industry X, the relative price of labor rises, and therefore the relative price of the labor intensive commodity X also increases. In country A, then, F_A moves toward F_B and P_A moves toward P_B as trade occurs. Similarly, country B, having a comparative advantage in the capital intensive commodity Y, exports that commodity. It transfers resources from industry X to industry Y, the price of capital is driven up relative to the price of labor, and the price of the capital-intensive commodity Y rises relative to that of good X. Thus, in country B the opening up of trade between the two countries forces F_B to move toward F_A and P_B toward P_A. When trade is absolutely free of impediments and transportation is costless, as is assumed, the opening up of international trade would result in $P_A = P_B$. Then the unique and identical relationship between the commodity price ratio and the factor price ratio in each country would establish also that $F_A = F_B$. It should perhaps be mentioned that these processes would have occurred even though the pre-trade comparative advantage situations of the two countries were reversed in the manner stated in the preceding paragraph. Indeed, Johnson's description of the process takes up this reverse case.

It must be reiterated that Figure 1-5 precludes analysis of the effects of factor intensity reversals and complete specialization upon the factor price equalization theorem. Admission of these and other realistic conditions to the analytical model forces a different assessment of the likelihood of the equalization of relative factor prices. While the above analyses demonstrate the inevitability of factor price equalization (or, alternatively, of complete specialization), these are theoretical demonstrations and, like all of their kind, they are no more reasonable than the assumptions upon which they are based. A discussion of the consequences that other, more realistic assumptions have for the effects of international trade upon relative factor prices is undertaken in the next section and in the Appendix to this chapter. It will be shown that the analysis so far, while essential to a full comprehension of the effects of trade upon relative factor prices, proves too much. Under alternative assumptions factor price equalization is by no means an inevitable result of free international trade.

☐ ANALYTICAL CLARIFICATIONS AND EXTENSIONS

Even in its initial formulations, it was recognized that the factor price equalization theorem held only under rather unusual circumstances. The fact, for example, that international trade involves transportation costs and also restrictions of various sorts means that trade does not normally bring about the equality of commodity price ratios among countries; hence, relative factor prices are not equalized. If the introduction of transportation costs and trade impediments precludes full factor price equalization, it does not eliminate a tendency for trade to move factor prices toward equality. If goods move at all across national boundaries — if transportation costs are not prohibitively high — some equalization of factor price ratios occurs.[24] Moreover, the existence of non-identical production functions among countries prevents equalization of factor returns. Although commodity price ratios in the separate countries become the same through trade, disparate production functions typically result in the marginal products, and consequently the returns, of the various factors being different internationally.[25] Further, demand conditions can be stipulated which, in conjunction with the income redistribution that inevitably accompanies factor reallocation, can weaken the factor price equalizing qualities of free international trade.[26]

Generally speaking, these phenomena have not been carefully analyzed as yet — either because the consequences for relative factor prices are so obvious as to be uninteresting or because the ideas are too novel. In any event, it can be seen that relaxation of some of the rigorous assumptions required to demonstrate full factor price equalization quite naturally has an impact on the pertinence of the theorem itself. In some cases, the impact is to make the complete equalization through trade of relative factor prices impossible but the tendency toward equalization is merely mitigated and not obliterated; in other cases, the tendency for trade to equalize relative factor prices itself is destroyed and instead trade can widen international discrepancies in relative factor prices. This distinction should be borne in mind in the discussion that follows.

Factor Intensity Reversal

In the traditional demonstration of full factor price equalization it was assumed that one commodity could be designated as relatively labor-intensive — and the other commodity as relatively capital-intensive — irrespective of the relative price of the two factors. This is called the strong Samuelsonian factor intensity assumption, arising, it might be said, from an implicit assumption that the production functions for the two commodities, while different from each other, nevertheless both possess the property of having unitary elasticity of substitution between the factors. It was thought by Samuelson [48, pp. 121–22] that reversal of factor intensities could occur, to be sure, but that this was not apt to happen within the range of the factor-price ratio that might in practice be observed internationally. Nevertheless, it was subsequently found by Arrow, Chenery, Solow, and Minhas [1] and by Minhas [34; 35] that Samuelson's casual empiricism was not quite justified and, indeed, that when production functions permitting factor intensity reversal — the so-called constant elasticity of substitution (CES) functions — are fitted empirically, reversal is found to be a rather common phenomenon.[27] Thus, because factor intensity reversal may be of practical relevance and, more pointedly, because it makes a profound difference to the influence of trade on relative factor prices, the effects of reversal will be considered with some care. For this discussion it is assumed that neither of the countries becomes completely specialized in the production of either commodity subsequent to the opening up of trade.

Assume, unlike Figure 1-1A, that the isoquants for commodities X and Y are as depicted in Figure 1-6A. The production functions remain linear homogeneous, the sole difference being that in the production of commodity X the factors are more highly substitutable than in the production of commodity Y. In order to demonstrate factor intensity reversal, consider the factor price ratios designated by the slopes of the several price lines drawn in. If it is assumed that the ruling relative factor price is that given by P_1P_1 (and $P_1'P_1'$) it is apparent that commodity X is capital-intensive compared to commodity Y. The capital-labor ratio at F is greater than at G. Correspondingly, these ratios are designated by P_1 and $(K/L)_{X_1}$ and $(K/L)_{Y_1}$ in Figure 1-6B. Alternatively, if the factor price ratio is given by the slope of P_2P_2 (and $P_2'P_2'$), commodity X is the labor-intensive commodity relative to good Y. The capital-labor ratio at J is greater than the factor proportion at K. Again, these ratios are designated by P_2 and $(K/L)_{Y_2}$ and $(K/L)_{X_2}$ in Figure 1-6B. Still again, assume that the ruling factor price ratio is that determined by the slope of P_3P_3. In this event, the factor proportions at H, in the production of both commodities, are identical, $(K/L)_{X_3} = (K/L)_{Y_3}$. The relative factor price determined by the slope of P_3P_3, or what is the same thing the factor input proportions at H, in Figure 1-6A are, therefore, critical in that they represent the situation at which factor intensity reversal occurs. Hence at P_3 the factor-ratio curves intersect. There is then for the production functions indicated by the representative isoquants XX and YY a reversal of factor intensity. At a relative price of labor less than P_3, commodity X is relatively labor-intensive and commodity Y capital-intensive; at a relative price of labor in excess of P_3 commodity X is comparatively capital-intensive and commodity Y

41

labor-intensive. It should be noted, moreover, although it is not shown in the diagram, that isoquants which give more than a single reversal of factor intensity may be drawn — a condition which Lerner [25] was the first to analyze.

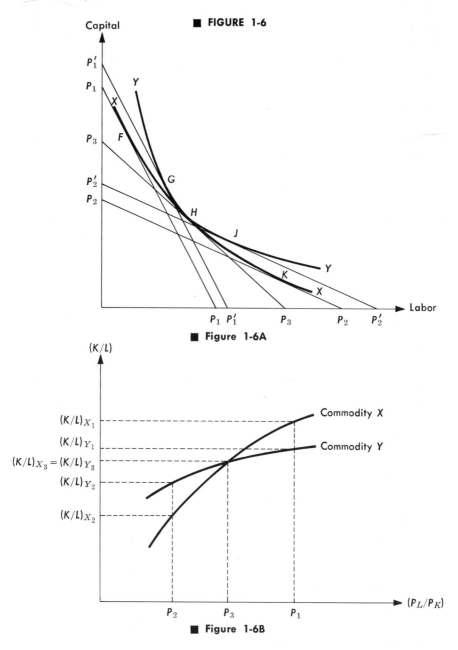

■ FIGURE 1-6

■ Figure 1-6A

■ Figure 1-6B

The impact of factor intensity reversal on relative factor prices is easily demonstrated in the Harrod-Johnson framework. Recall that the factor-ratio curves of Figure 1-6B are the upper portion of the Harrod-Johnson diagram. Corresponding to the point of intersection of the factor ratio curves is a maximum point on the price ratio curve which plots commodity price ratios against factor price ratios. Since any rise in the relative price of labor raises the price of the labor intensive good relative to the price of the capital intensive commodity, for increases in the factor price ratio at ratios lower than P_3 the price of commodity X rises relative to commodity Y; for increases in the relative labor price where the factor price ratio is greater than P_3 commodity Y's price rises relative to that of good X; and at P_3, since factor proportions are identical in the two commodities, any marginal change in the relative factor price has no effect upon the commodity price ratio. This relationship between relative labor prices and relative commodity prices, where there are single-reversing factor ratio curves, is illustrated in Figure 1-7.

The most arresting feature of the lower portion of Figure 1-7 is that, unlike Figure 1-5, the one-to-one relationship between relative commodity prices and relative factor prices has been lost. To be sure, for each factor price ratio there is only one commodity price ratio. But the reverse is not true and this is due solely to factor intensity reversal. With only a single reversal there are for each relevant commodity price ratio two relative labor prices which are consistent with the conventional equilibrium conditions. Thus, it is by no means certain that the equalization of commodity price ratios through international trade brings about the full equalization of factor prices.

The existence of a single reversal of factor intensity has no impact on the validity of the factor price equalization theorem if the point of reversal is itself merely potential rather than actual. That is, if the over-all factor endowments of the countries are not too dissimilar, so that the endowment ratios in both countries lie on one side or the other of the intersection of the factor-ratio curves, free trade causes full equalization of relative (and absolute) factor prices. This is nothing more than the case already described by Figure 1-5.

But suppose that over-all factor endowments in the two countries are so dissimilar, relative to the technologies of the two commodities, that their respective endowment ratios are separated by the ratio at which reversal takes place. Suppose, that is, that country A remains labor abundant compared to country B and that the endowment ratios are given by E_A and E_B respectively in Figure 1-7. In this case the factor reversal is no longer merely potential but is of material analytical significance.

Assume, for instance, that demand conditions in the two countries establish pre-trade factor price and commodity price ratios at F_A and

P_A in country A and F_B and P_B in country B. Accordingly, country A, the labor abundant country, has a comparative advantage in, and will export, commodity X which is, at the relevant factor price ratio, labor-intensive. Country B finds its comparative advantage in the production of commodity Y which at its relevant factor price ratio, F_B, is also labor-intensive. At the pre-trade equilibrium both countries produce relatively cheaply commodities which, while different, are both produced by using relatively high proportions of labor.

When trade opens up, the relative price of good X rises in country A and falls in country B, continuing until the post-trade commodity price ratio is identical in the two countries, somewhere between P_A and

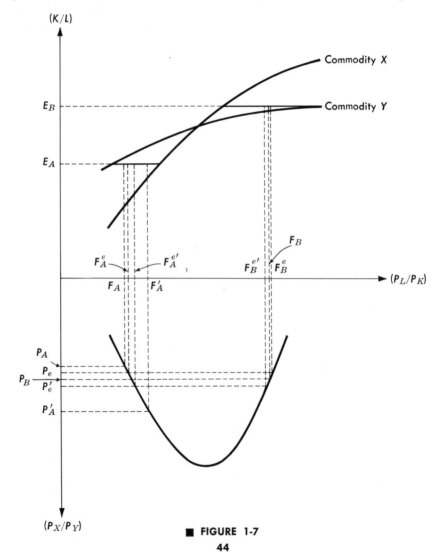

■ **FIGURE 1-7**

P_B. Assume that this post-trade equilibrium commodity price ratio is P_e. Under the implied conditions of demand and consistent with the Stolper-Samuelson theorem [54], the relative price of labor rises in both countries, from F_A to F_A^e in country A and from F_B to F_B^e in country B. There can be no full equalization of relative factor prices so long as factor intensity reversal is interposed between the endowment ratios. Moreover, it is not certain that the factor price ratios tend to converge as a consequence of trade taking place. Since the factor price ratio rises in both countries, convergence or divergence depends upon relative increases in the two countries. This in turn is related to the nature of the demand patterns in the countries as relative commodity prices adjust upward and downward from the pre-trade equilibria ratios to the post-trade equilibrium.

In addition, factor price ratios in the two countries can also decrease as trade occurs. To take another example from Figure 1-7, assume that the demand conditions in each country are such as to establish that pre-trade price ratios in the two countries are F_A' and P_A' in country A and F_B and P_B, the same as previously, in country B. Country A then has a comparative advantage in good Y, its relatively capital intensive commodity, while country B finds a relatively low price for good X, its relatively capital intensive commodity. Again, free trade eliminates discrepancies in the international commodity price ratios. When the countries undertake to trade the post-trade equilibrium commodity price ratio becomes, say, P_e'. The factor price ratios in each country fall, in one country from F_A' to $F_A^{e'}$ and in the other from F_B to $F_B^{e'}$. Again relative factor prices cannot be made equal by international trade. Again the factor price ratios may or may not tend to become more equal. As Figure 1-7 is drawn, divergence of relative factor prices due to trade is depicted because $F_A' - F_A^{e'} > F_B - F_B^{e'}$ and F_A' initially is lower than F_B. But without distorting the economics underlying Figure 1-7, it would be equally plausible to illustrate a situation in which the relative price of labor tended toward equality (without actually reaching it) even though the factor price ratio changed in the same direction in both countries.[28]

Since the box diagram is the foundation for the Harrod-Johnson presentation of the effects of trade on international factor price ratios, it is reasonable to expect that the consequences of reversal can also be explained within the traditional framework. In the case of a single factor intensity reversal, however, the maximum efficiency loci or contract curves of the two boxes are no longer as shown in Figure 1-4, where the two curves are on the same side of the diagonals of the boxes. With a single factor reversal the respective comparative advantage commodities are produced in each country with either labor-intensive or capital-intensive methods but not with both, as in the case of non-reversal. Therefore, the maximum efficiency loci lie on opposite sides of the diagonals. If it is assumed, for example, that good X is relatively labor-intensive in country A, good Y being capital-intensive, and good Y is labor-intensive in country B, commodity X being capital-intensive, the box diagram would be as in Figure 1-8.[29]

Suppose the pre-trade commodity price ratios in the two countries, determined by the tangency of the indifference curves and production possibilities curves (which are not diagrammed), are such that, in a closed economy, production of the two commodities in country A is given by the isoquants (not shown) tangent to each other at S in Figure 1-8 and in country B by the isoquants tangent at R. In the pre-trade situation, then, the factor price ratio in country A is designated by the slope of $L_A^P K_A^P$ and in country B by the slope of $L_B^P K_B^P$: labor in country A is relatively cheap compared to the relative price of labor in country B. Also at S, and at any other point on the contract curve, production of commodity X in country A is labor-intensive compared to its production of commodity Y, whereas commodity Y is relatively labor-intensive and, hence, commodity X capital-intensive in country B. Assume now that the pre-trade commodity price ratios (not shown) give country A a comparative advantage in the production of good X and country B a comparative advantage in good Y. As trade opens up, country A expands its output of good X and country B expands its output of good Y. That is, the two countries move along their contract curves, country A moving from S toward V and country B from R toward U. Concomitantly, factor proportions change in the two countries. In country A the ratio of capital to labor utilized in the production of either commodity rises; consequently the relative price of labor rises. In country B, unlike the movement from R to U depicted in Figure 1-4 where the capital-labor ratio fell, the proportion of capital to labor in the two productive processes rises; hence the relative price of labor rises in country B, as well as in country A, with the opening of trade. As Lancaster [20, pp. 37–38] shows, V and U represent post-trade equilibria in the two countries, i.e., at outputs associated with these points the commodity price ratios in the two countries are identical. For factor price ratios consistent with these points the relative price of labor has in country A risen to the factor price ratio given by the slope of $L_A^{P'} K_A^{P'}$ and in country B it has increased to the slope of $L_B^{P'} K_B^{P'}$. The relative price of labor remains higher in country B than in country A; there is no full equalization of factor price ratios. Whether trade causes a tendency toward equality or toward greater inequality depends, since the relative labor price in both countries rises, upon the relative slopes of $L_A^P K_A^P$ and $L_B^P K_B^P$ compared to the relative slopes of $L_A^{P'} K_A^{P'}$ and $L_B^{P'} K_B^{P'}$.

The alternative factor price adjustment process with a single factor intensity reversal is also demonstrated in Figure 1-8. As in the discussion of the Harrod-Johnson diagrammatic technique, the pre-trade output

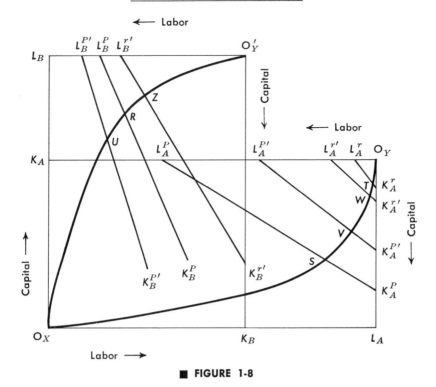

■ FIGURE 1-8

composition, commodity price ratio, and factor price ratio in country B are not changed. This again is represented by R and the slope of $L_B^P K_B^P$. In country A, however, it is here assumed that demand conditions have altered so that the pre-trade output composition is given by T (rather than S as previously) and that the relative price of labor is given by the slope of $L_A^r K_A^r$. Thus, country A has a higher relative labor price than formerly but this higher factor price ratio remains lower than that ruling in country B. Suppose, furthermore, that the change in the output proportion in country A is reflected in a much higher relative price for commodity X — so much higher that country A now finds its comparative advantage in commodity Y while country B has a relative advantage in commodity X. When trade takes place, therefore, country A produces more of good Y and country B expands its output of good X. Country A moves from T toward W on its maximum efficiency locus; country B moves from R toward Z. Once more W and Z represent post-trade equilibrium situations. The relative price of labor has fallen in both countries. Still, country A pays, compared to the return to capital, relatively less for its labor than does country B. No complete equalization of relative factor prices is possible. And again, there may or may not have been a tendency for factor prices to become equal because of the opening of trade.[30]

47

An even more obvious instance of the failure of trade to equalize relative factor prices — or even to tend to equalize them — can arise where there are two relevant factor intensity reversals. Such a condition cannot exist when production functions are restricted to those of the general CES type. But where the elasticity of substitution is itself variable at different factor input combinations the possibility of more than one reversal is present. The elementary case is to assume, in the Harrod-Johnson framework, rather disparate over-all factor endowment ratios in the two countries with two intervening factor intensity reversals. This situation is diagrammed in Figure 1-9.

The case constructed in Figure 1-9, as in Johnson [14, pp. 27–28], is one in which relative factor prices diverge in the two countries because the factor price ratio in country B, with the higher relative price of labor, rises while the ratio in country A falls. It is also plausible, how-

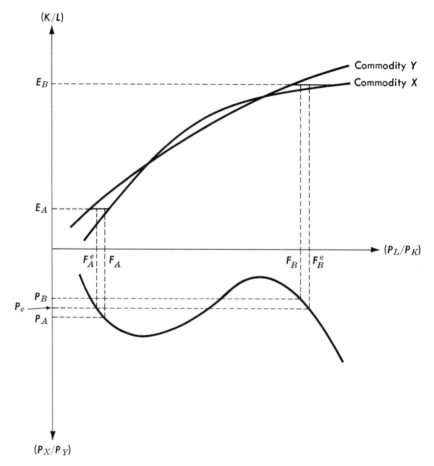

■ **FIGURE 1-9**

ever, that the factor price ratios in the two countries would tend to converge; in the double reversal case the factor price ratios must move in opposite directions. While convergence of relative factor prices is not unlikely, double factor reversal nevertheless precludes full factor price equalization. The case of convergence is not depicted in the diagram, its construction being reasonably obvious.

As before, assume that internal demand conditions in the two countries establish pre-trade price ratios at F_A and P_A for country A and F_B and P_B for country B. Since $P_A > P_B$, country A has a comparative advantage in its capital intensive commodity Y, whereas country B has a comparative advantage in its labor intensive commodity X. (It should be noted that the structure of production is here assumed to differ from that predicted by the Heckscher-Ohlin theorem, since country A is richly endowed with labor compared to country B.) The existence of disparate pre-trade commodity price ratios makes trade profitable. With the opening of trade, the relative price of commodity X falls in country A and rises in country B, becoming equal in the two countries at P_e. To accomplish this, factors in country A respond by moving from commodity X into commodity Y which reduces the capital-labor ratio employed in producing both commodities. In contrast, in country B the reallocation of factors increases the capital-labor input combination. Since relative factor prices, according to the assumption, are determined by the proportions in which the factors are employed, it is clear that the relative price of labor falls (relative capital price rises) in country A and vice versa in country B. This is illustrated in Figure 1-9 by a movement of the factor price ratio in country A from F_A to F_A^e and in country B from F_B to F_B^e with the achieving of post-trade equilibrium conditions. The relative prices of labor diverge in the two countries. In the example pictured, there is certainly no tendency for trade to equalize relative factor returns.

Reflection on these examples of factor intensity reversals poised between the over-all endowment ratios of the two countries should suggest the generalization that the existence of one or more reversals effectively prevents trade from establishing equal relative and absolute factor prices internationally. Nevertheless, there is no easy generalization with respect to the impact of reversal on the tendency for trade to bring about convergence of factor price ratios. Either divergence or convergence (but not equality) of relative factor prices is possible, depending upon the existing conditions of demand. Without regard to demand conditions, however, the following assertion is valid: when there are an odd number of factor intensity reversals between the over-all factor endowment ratios, relative factor prices must move in the same direction in both countries when trade takes place; when there are an even number of relevant reversals, the opening of trade forces relative factor prices to move in opposite directions in the two countries. The assertion was shown to be true for both single and double factor reversals; it holds true irrespective of the number of relevant factor reversals.

Interestingly, when more than two countries are admitted to the analysis the existence of factor reversals does not normally mean a complete absence of full equalization of factor prices. If reversals are spaced relatively far apart, in terms of the endowment ratios at which intersections of the factor-ratio curves occur, the several countries may be grouped into regions where reversal for countries included in the region is not possible. For example, in Figure 1-9 several countries may have over-all endowment ratios clustered closely around E_A, several other countries may be similarly clustered around E_B, and perhaps the factor endowment ratios of a third group of countries fall between the two endowment ratios at which reversal takes place. In this event, provided that all of the other assumptions still hold, trade would bring about full factor price equalization within each regional grouping. In short, there would not be as many factor price ratios as there are countries; rather the number of distinct factor price ratios is equal to the number of segments of the factor-ratio curves. The number of factor price patterns would be one greater than the number of meaningful factor intensity reversals. This so-called "local" version of the factor price equalization theorem has been suggested by, among others, Samuelson [50, pp. 192], Minhas [34, pp. 152–53], and Balassa [2, p. 120] and highlights the point that factor intensity reversal does not entirely eliminate all vestiges of full factor price equalization in the more comprehensive multi-country model.

Complete Specialization in Production

Reverting to a model where factor intensity reversals are not permissible, it is possible to explore the impact of complete specialization in production on the factor price equalization theorem. It is arguable, of course, whether complete specialization is a sufficiently probable condition to warrant being considered. After all, at least in the developed economies of the world, almost the entire range of manufactured products produced in any one country is produced also in the rest. But this is not true of agricultural commodities and of raw materials; also it is not the case that underdeveloped economies produce a wide range of manufactured goods. Moreover, as Travis takes pains to point out [56, p. 9], the fact that specialization in manufactured goods is incomplete in the developed areas has little bearing on the issue. The incomplete specialization observed can be attributed to the existence of trade restrictions and transportation costs, while the relevant consideration is whether specialization would remain incomplete with perfectly free trade. The little extant empirical research indicates that the incomplete specialization condition implied by the full factor price equalization theorem —

one version of the theorem being that, under the assumptions sketched previously, either trade will equate absolute factor prices internationally or will cause complete specialization in production — is not a promising prospect. The possibility of complete specialization is apt to be a matter of appreciable moment.

It can be shown that the greater the difference in over-all factor endowment ratios in two countries, for any given difference in the factor intensity of the two commodities, the more likely does complete specialization become. Conversely, when the production functions of the two commodities require the combination of factors in very similar proportions, complete specialization is more likely for any set discrepancy in the factor endowment ratios. This becomes obvious in the course of demonstrating the fact that, with one highly unlikely situation excepted, complete specialization, like factor intensity reversal, is sufficient to prevent full equalization of relative (and hence absolute) factor returns between nations. In no case, however, does the advent of complete specialization because of trade negate the tendency for relative factor prices to equalize.

To show the consequences of complete specialization for the effect of international trade on factor prices, we must refer back to the Harrod-Johnson diagram where factor intensity reversal is ruled out. The factor ratio curves and the price ratio curve of Figure 1-5 are here reproduced in Figure 1-10. Note, however, that, in order to accommodate complete specialization by both countries, the relative factor endowment ratios of the two countries are presumed to be rather different from the endowment ratios illustrated in Figure 1-5. E_A, the capital-labor ratio in country A, remains as before. For illustrative purposes, country B is assumed to have three possible capital-labor ratios, given by E_B, $\bar{E}_B$ and $\hat{E}_B$. It may be thought, that is, that country B is a proxy for three different countries but, since the model is still one of two countries, only one of these countries is at any particular instant in a position to trade with country A.

Johnson enunciates the principle upon which the type of specialization rests [14, p. 23]: given that the post-trade commodity price ratio must lie between the pre-trade commodity price ratios in both countries, a country will continue to produce both commodities as long as the identical international commodity price ratio falls within its range of permissible relative commodity prices. Recalling that this range is determined by the (horizontal) gap between the factor ratio curves at the country's given endowment ratio, it is seen in Figure 1-10 that country A will not specialize if the post-trade commodity price ratio is within the range given by $P_A P_A'$. By way of contrast, if country B has the high capital-labor ratio $\bar{E}_B$, it will not specialize as long as the post-trade commodity price ratio falls within $\bar{P}_B \bar{P}_B'$. Since these two ranges, $P_A P_A'$ and

$\bar{P}_B \bar{P}'_B$, do not overlap, if trade were to open up between country A and a country with the endowment ratio of $\bar{E}_B$, specialization in at least one of the countries would be complete. Moreover, with endowment ratios of E_A and $\bar{E}_B$ it is possible, although not certain, that both countries would specialize. Specialization by both countries would occur if the post-trade commodity price ratio fell in the range bounded by P'_A and $\bar{P}_B$. If country A were to specialize completely, in either the one-country or two-country specialization case, it would perforce produce only commodity X; if country B were to specialize in either of the cases, its "specialty" would necessarily be commodity Y. It should be apparent, however, that this ability to certify specialization in the commodity using intensively the factor with which the country is relatively well endowed is limited to the non-reversal model in which overlapping ranges for the commodity price ratio are ruled out. Where any number of reversals is a meaningful phenomenon, the "specialty" good does not necessarily conform to the dictates of the Heckscher-Ohlin theorem, although which commodity would become the "specialty" good would still be demonstrable.

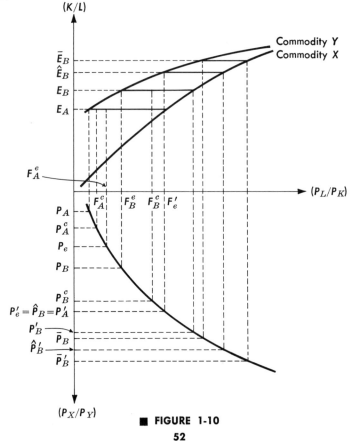

■ FIGURE 1-10

The more interesting case is illustrated by countries with factor endowment ratios E_A and E_B. This is the case developed above when the demonstration of full factor price equalization was laid out. There, however, care was used in selecting the ruling post-trade factor price and commodity price ratios in the two countries so that complete specialization would not occur; for in light of the above principle about specialization, it can now be seen that if the commodity price ratio had come to rest in the post-trade situation in either of the two ranges $P_A P_B$ or $P'_A P'_B$, one or the other country would have become specialized in production. Had the post-trade commodity price ratio been in the $P_A P_B$ range, for example, country B would have specialized in producing good Y with country A very probably continuing to produce both commodities. Country A would have become specialized in commodity X if the post-trade commodity price ratio fell in the range $P'_A P'_B$, with country B not specializing. Contrastingly, however, neither country would find specialization profitable if the post-trade commodity price ratio were to come to rest within the range bounded by P_B and P'_A and this was the case analyzed with the help of Figure 1-5.

The effect of complete specialization in one country on relative factor prices can now be observed. Assume that countries A and B are exemplified by capital-labor ratios of E_A and E_B and that the closed economy commodity price ratios in the two countries are P^c_A and P^c_B respectively. The relative price of labor in country A is F^c_A, low compared to F^c_B in country B. Country A has a comparative advantage in commodity X and country B in good Y. Now suppose the total demand by the two countries for commodity Y is so intense compared to that for commodity X that when trade opens up, the post-trade equilibrium commodity price ratio is P_e.[31] The relative price of labor in country A is driven up, coming to rest at F^e_A; both commodities are still being produced in country A. In country B, however, the factor price ratio cannot fall below F^e_B. As trade takes place, the commodity price ratio moves from P^c_B to P_e and the relative labor price decreases from its original level at F^c_B as country B expands its output of commodity Y and cuts back its production of good X. When the factor price ratio hits F_B, there can be no further reduction in the relative labor price in country B. Since only commodity Y is being produced — since specialization is complete — factor proportions become and remain equal to the over-all factor endowment ratio E_B. There can be no further change in the ratios of the marginal products of the factors.

There is a further adjustment in the commodity price ratio in country B as it falls below P_B. Since factor returns reflect the value of marginal output, it might be concluded that relative factor returns continue to adjust away from F^e_B as well. This is not the case however. Since the ratio of the marginal products of the two factors is fixed at the over-all

53

endowment ratio by complete specialization and since the changing commodity price ratio applies equally to both the marginal product of labor and of capital, the effect of the continuing commodity price adjustment is to leave relative factor prices in country B unchanged. While trade, even with complete specialization in one country, tends to reduce the international inequality in relative factor prices, the existence of complete specialization prevents full equality of the factor price ratios.

If the two countries had factor endowment ratios of E_A and $\bar{E}_B$, this generalization still would be accurate. Whether one or both countries specialize completely, trade cannot bring about equality of the factor price ratios in the two nations although it does bring the ratios closer together. This example is not illustrated in Figure 1-10. To do so, it would only be necessary to apply the discussion of the preceding two paragraphs on the assumptions, say, that the pre-trade commodity price ratio in country A is P_A^c, in country B somewhere between $\bar{P}_B$ and $\bar{P}_B'$, and that the post-trade commodity price ratio, to get both countries specializing completely, falls in the range $P_A'\bar{P}_B$.

An interesting but obviously extremely unlikely case in which complete specialization in both countries does not rule out full equality of factor price ratios is that in which country B has the endowment ratio $\hat{E}_B$ while country A still remains at E_A, the factor ratio curves of course remaining fixed. With these relative endowments, the pre-trade commodity price ratio in country B could well be given by $\bar{P}_B$ and P_A^c could be the equivalent price ratio in country A. When trade opens up between these countries, the commodity price ratio might, although it need not necessarily, come into equilibrium at $P_e' = \hat{P}_B = P_A'$. Notice that this is precisely at the outer and inner boundary of the ranges in which the countries will not completely specialize. Should this international price ratio rule, country A has all of its resources producing commodity X whereas country B specializes completely in the production of commodity Y. The factor price ratios in the two countries are exactly equated at F_e'.

This possibility is very remote, depending as it does on a particular configuration of relative factor endowment ratios in the two countries, of relative factor intensities in producing the two commodities at these endowment ratios, and of international demand conditions for the two goods. Slightly less unlikely would be the case of single-country complete specialization and full relative factor price equality. This would be depicted by a post-trade commodity price ratio of P_B. In this event the relative labor price would be F_B^e in both countries and country B, now having an endowment ratio of E_B, would be completely specialized in commodity Y. These types of equilibria are very rare and need not be discussed further.

The above considerations can, with greater complexity and more elegant proof, be demonstrated by recourse to the box diagram construction. For the sake of brevity this can only be sketched here, although an adequate discussion is available in Lancaster [20, pp. 28–30] and an exhaustive, very complex treatment is in Travis [56, Chaps. I and II].

Consider Figure 1-4 again, which is the case exemplified by E_A and E_B in Figure 1-10 just above. It was noted in Figure 1-4 that V on the contract curve of country A and U on the contract curve of country B, called "corresponding points" in the literature, have the property of equating relative commodity prices and relative and absolute factor prices in two countries with incomplete specialization. Suppose, however, that the post-trade relative price of commodity X were lower than that relevant to U and V. In this event, the "corresponding points" U and V would move along their respective contract curves toward O_X. This would be reflected in a counter-clockwise rotation, anchored at their respective origins, of the straightline segments $O_Y VJ$ in country A and $O'_Y UH$ in country B. The slopes of the segments give the capital-labor input ratios in the production of commodity Y. The capital-labor proportions in the production of commodity Y in both countries would fall. When, however, V coincides with T on the contract curve in country A, where the slope of $O_Y TM$ equals the slope of $O'_Y O_X$, the "corresponding point" in country B becomes O_X. That is to say, if the post-trade equilibrium conditions are to be met when country A is producing commodities X and Y at T and hence employing a capital-labor input proportion in the production of commodity Y equal to $O_Y L_A/L_A M$, country B must be using the same capital-labor ratio in its production of commodity Y and this is equal to $O'_Y K_B/K_B O_X = O'_Y K_B/O'_Y L_B$. Given the contract curve (constrained by the production functions and demand conditions) in country B, this can only be achieved by applying all of the factors in country B to the production of good Y. Country B, then, becomes completely specialized at the post-trade commodity price ratio compatible with T on the maximum efficiency locus of country A; for points between O_X and T on the contract curve of country A there are no "corresponding points" in country B and hence there is no equality of relative factor prices in the two countries. The equilibrium commodity price ratio consistent with T in Figure 1-4 has the properties of those compatible with P_B in Figure 1-10.

By corresponding reasoning, it can be shown that at a relative price of commodity X similar to that given by P'_A in Figure 1-10, country B would be producing at W on its contract curve (Figure 1-4). In country B, the capital-labor ratio in producing commodity X would be given by $O_Y L_A/O_X L_A$. Country A would then have to be completely specialized in the production of commodity X, having to use all of its resources for that purpose in order to match the capital-labor input proportion country Y is employing in producing commodity X. Consequently, for points on the contract curve of country B between W and O'_Y there exist no "corresponding points" on the contract curve of country A. Country B could be producing both commodities at factor proportions and factor price ratios that country A cannot match. Although the proof is not given here, there can be no equality of relative factor prices in the two countries; it is demonstrable that the factor price ratios are more disparate before than after international trade takes place.

Proliferation of Countries, Products, and Factors

Up to this point the discussion of this chapter has been in terms of the relatively simple, and graphically convenient, world of two countries, two commodities, and two productive factors. The world is not at all like this and a number of scholars have analyzed the impact of international trade on factor prices in a world of many countries, many products, and many factors. Meade's extension of the analysis to three factors [28] and then to three commodities and factors [29, pp. 378–83] is one of the earliest departures from the simple two-dimensional world and, due to the very limited proliferation of factors and products, he was able to state his argument without recourse to mathematics. The discussion of Land [22] is similarly instructive in its simplicity. But when the world becomes multi-dimensional, the number of factors and commodities exceeding three, the analysis of the model becomes completely unmanageable verbally and diagrammatically. Inevitably, the analytical "factor price" properties of trade in the multi-dimensional world are exposited in terms of systems of simultaneous equations. Conceptually, the mathematical formulation of the model is not difficult, although the notation may be awesome. In contrast, the solutions of the equation systems, and more particularly the properties of these solutions, entail relatively unfamiliar mathematical principles. These will be treated cavalierly here, although the flavor of the analytical problem in the multi-dimensional world should become apparent.

When the world is divided into many countries, each with the same two factors and producing the same two commodities, the results of the factor price equalization theorem are in no way invalidated. In terms of Figure 1-5, it is merely necessary to add more factor endowment ratios to the diagram and as long as specialization is incomplete and there is no factor intensity reversal, full factor price equalization is brought about by free trade.[32] Given that the assumptions of the factor price equalization theorem hold in every country, each country exhibits identical factor ratio curves and an identical price ratio curve and the logic of the Harrod-Johnson demonstration continues to apply. There exists the same unique relationship between factor price ratios and commodity price ratios in all countries and the equating by trade of the commodity price ratios among all countries inevitably makes factor prices equal.

It was noted above that the existence of factor intensity reversals in a multi-country world prevents the establishment of a single factor price pattern for the world; but nevertheless a number (unrelated to the number of countries but dependent upon the number of meaningful reversals) of distinct patterns is brought about by trade. "Localization" of factor price equalization may be the result also of a type of complete specialization in a multi-country world. Tinbergen [55, p. 44] and Laursen [23, pp. 554–55] state that complete specialization is more likely in a many-country model; but Caves [7, pp. 82–83] suggests that if a group of countries can be found producing and freely trading enough of the same types of commodities, there is going to exist factor price equalization within this group of countries. The number of localized factor price patterns in this case depends upon the number of such completely specializing groups, rather than on the number of relevant factor intensity reversals.

A warning is necessary, however. Meade points out that the ways in which countries (localized regions) can be linked together, and hence have equal factor prices, is not limited to free trade among all countries in the same commodities. A factor price equalizing trade network can be rather intricate. In a three-country, two-factor, two-product world, for example, country C need only "produce something of both of two commodities (either or both of which may be, but need not be, one of the commodities which link [countries A and B]), that something of each of these two commodities should be produced in at least one of the other countries, that there should be free and costless trade in each of these commodities between [country C] and at least one of the other countries in which that commodity is also produced, and that all the products which serve as links between the three countries should stand in an unchanging order of labour-intensiveness in production" [29, pp. 345–46]. In any realistic situation the trade links between countries (and localizing regions) may be quite devious and the nature of the complete specialization pattern that prevents global factor price equalization is correspondingly complex.

The more interesting aspects of the multi-dimensional world appear when the number of commodities (n) and number of factors (r) exceed two. If it can be shown that there remains a unique relationship between commodity prices and factor prices under these conditions, the factor price equalization theorem is then applicable generally. The relationship, as already suggested, is no longer as easily interpretable as the price ratio curve of the two-dimensional Harrod-Johnson framework; but the relationship may exist in many dimensions and if it is determinate and unique conditions for factor price equalization exist.

Adopting Samuelson's multi-dimensional formulation [52] and simplifying along the lines suggested by Caves [7, pp. 83–84], unit isoquants for the commodities, and hence linear homogeneous production functions, are spelled out as:

$$1 = f_i \left(\frac{\theta_{i1}}{Q_i}, \ldots, \frac{\theta_{ij}}{Q_i}, \ldots, \frac{\theta_{ir}}{Q_i} \right) \text{ for } (i = 1, 2, \ldots, n), \qquad (1\text{-}7)$$

where f_i indicates the functional relationship, θ_{ij} stands for the input of factor j of r factors in industry i of n industries, and Q_i is the output of commodity i. Equations 1-7 — n of them — specify, then, the input coefficients for the unit isoquants of the various commodities. In a perfectly competitive equilibrium each factor is paid the value of its marginal product so that:

$$P_j = \frac{\phi_i \partial f_i(\theta_{i1}/Q_i, \ldots, \theta_{ij}/Q_i, \ldots, \theta_{ir}/Q_i)}{\partial \theta_{ij}}$$

$$\text{for } (i = 1, 2, \ldots, n) \text{ and } (j = 1, 2, \ldots, r), \qquad (1\text{-}8)$$

where P_j is the price of factor j, ϕ_i is the price of commodity i, and the partial derivative gives the marginal product of factor j in producing commodity i. Equations 1-8 are nr in number. As things stand, the system of equations cannot be solved to derive the general equilibrium solution: the number of unknowns greatly exceeds the $n + nr$ independent equations 1-7 and 1-8. But also as things stand the equation system is incomplete.

The crux of Samuelson's presentation is to complete the system by prescribing that commodity prices — the ϕ's — are arbitrary constants or possibly determined in international markets. If it is then found that for these ϕ's the equation system gives a unique set of P's, factor price equalization is verified in the multi-dimensional case, since each country can be represented, under the assumptions, by an identical set of equations. When the ϕ's are the same in every country, so too are the P's. But when the ϕ's are so prescribed, the only unknowns in the equation system are the P's — r in number — and the (θ/Q)'s, numbering nr. Therefore, a system of $n + nr$ independent equations is available to provide the solution to $r + nr$ unknowns.

Whether this system has a solution depends upon the number of commodities — the size of n — and the number of factors — the size of r. A soluble system must contain as many independent equations as unknowns. Nevertheless, though the equation system is soluble, the solution need not be unique. This, as Samuelson expresses it, depends upon the "quality" of the equations [50, pp. 192–93; 51, pp. 5, 9–10]. Recall that, in the two commodity-two factor case, uniqueness of the values of the price ratio curve depended on non-reversal of factor intensity. Similarly in the multi-dimensional model a kind of factor intensity condition must be specified for uniqueness but the condition seems no longer to be expressible in words.[33] Provided this condition is met by the equations and provided they equal in number the unknowns to be found, the model system specified by equations 1-7 and 1-8 has a unique solution giving, under free trade, full equality of factor prices among any number of countries.

Clearly, when the number of factors and the number of commodities are equal — when $n = r$ — factor price equalization pertains, for then the $n + nr$ equations equal the $r + nr$ unknowns. Adding any number of countries to the analysis does not upset this. As noted by Tinbergen [55, p. 44] and Samuelson [52, pp. 12–13], the inclusion of more countries merely contributes an equal number of independent equations and unknowns so that the system is still capable of a unique solution. What, however, is the effect of trade upon international factor prices when $n \neq r$? This is a more interesting case as it would be mere happenstance that the number of factors and of commodities was identical. When $n \neq r$ two alternative cases, each having its own peculiar properties, must be considered.

Suppose the number of commodities exceeds the number of factors, i.e., $n > r$; the number of equations therefore exceeds the number of unknowns by $n - r$. Tinbergen [55, pp. 45–47] thought that this system would be partly overdetermined and partly underdetermined and, therefore, generally incapable of an equilibrium solution. He contended, as did Pearce [42, p. 117], that complete specialization was the likely outcome of this situation and that consequently factor prices would not be equalized by trade. This early position of Tinbergen was, however, criticized by Meade [28; 29, Chap. XX], Laursen [23, pp. 442–53], and Samuelson [52], the gist of their objections being that not all n goods need be included in the equation system for the purpose of solution. They suggest that if there is a subset of n' goods which satisfy the uniqueness conditions, such that $n' \geq r$, a unique solution exists and equality of commodity prices means equality of factor prices.[34] To be sure, a form of indeterminacy still exists: in Meade it is the absolute domestic outputs of the commodities that cannot be established; in Samuelson the number of commodities produced in excess of the number of factors is not determinable, nor is the international pattern of productive activity [52, pp. 6–7]. But importantly, for the case where $n > r$, the factor prices, P's, and the input coefficients, (θ/Q)'s, are determinate, which, together with uniqueness, is the essential condition for full factor price equalization.

Moreover, contrary to Tinbergen's original presumption of complete specialization, Laursen [23, p. 553] and Samuelson [50, p. 192] agree that the case where $n > r$ would not be as likely to result in complete specialization as where $n = r$, so that, mathematical properties aside, factor price equalization is more probable in the more commodities than factors case. Apparently the correctness of viewpoint on this issue is contingent on the type of good being added, as it were, to the model. To Laursen and Samuelson the commodities added to the model are apt to have quite different factor intensities, thereby reducing the likelihood of complete specialization. Land [22, pp. 140–42], however, shows that where the added commodities are similar in factor intensity, so that there is a "denser . . . spectrum of commodities in terms of their factor intensities," factor price equalization is less likely to occur, as Samuelson [50, p. 192] recognizes too.

Turning to the case where the number of factors exceeds the number of commodities, where $n < r$, it is universally conceded that factor price equalization via free trade is virtually impossible — except, that is, under "strong and bizarre assumptions," in Bhagwati's phrase [5, p. 32]. These assumptions apparently relate to the absolute factor endowments of the countries, as briefly discussed by Samuelson [52, pp. 7–8] and Kemp [17, pp. 52–53]. Indeed, where $n < r$ the "equilibrium" determined by solving equations 1-7 and 1-8 is a multiple one, there being an infinite number of possible equilibrium factor prices consistent with the model. In short, there are $r - n$ fewer equations than unknowns.

Samuelson overcomes this underdeterminacy by stipulating a new set of equations requiring that the fixed factor endowments of the countries must be fully employed. These equations are given by:

$$\Sigma\theta_{ij} = \left(\frac{\theta_{1j}}{Q_1}\right) Q_1 + \left(\frac{\theta_{2j}}{Q_2}\right) Q_2 + \cdots + \left(\frac{\theta_{nj}}{Q_n}\right) Q_n = \theta_j$$

$$\text{for } (j = 1, 2, \ldots, r) \quad (1\text{-}9)$$

Thus, n unknowns, the Q's, are thereby added to the problem of determining equilibrium; at the same time r new equations are also supplied. With the inclusion of this full employment constraint, the system given by equations 1-7, 1-8, and 1-9 contains $r + nr + n$ unknowns which can be determined using the $n + nr + r$ independent relations. While this procedure provides a unique solution to the equation system it must be emphasized that the equilibrium values of the factor prices (P's) are dependent upon the factor endowments (θ's). Generally, since different countries must be considered as having different factor endowments, the equilibrium factor prices are different in different countries, even though these countries face identical commodity prices. The assumptions of the factor price equalization theorem, where the number of factors is greater than the number of commodities, do not necessarily imply either full factor price equalization or a tendency for factor prices to become equal with the opening of trade.[35]

CONCLUDING REMARKS

In providing a formal demonstration that international trade, under certain specifiable conditions, causes complete equalization of the prices of equivalent productive factors in the separate countries, the haunting suspicion lingers that too much has been proved. The kinds of conditions that lead to exceptions to the equalization of factor returns are altogether too apparent. The tremendous diversity of factor combinations in particular industries throughout the world strongly suggests the realism of factor intensity reversal, if indeed it does not imply non-uniformity of production functions. Complete specialization when trade is free and without impediment is a serious possibility, although the observable evidence, resulting as it does from a trading system where transportation costs and trade restrictions are substantial, might lead to the contrary inference. The taxonomic jungle that must be cleared in a meaningful specification of "product" and "factor" is a cause for consternation. Eyebrows should be raised at the assumptions of perfect competition, of constant returns, of fixed factor endowments, and others. Surely, the omnipresence of conditions disruptive to equalization of factor returns through trade should long ago have cast doubts on the practical relevance of the factor price equalization theorem.

But this also is hinting at too much. The original propounders of full factor price equalization harbored no illusions about its practicality. Their service in stating the theorem in its strictest terms was to provide a machinery to facilitate subsequent qualifications and emendations. These, rather than the formulation of the theorem itself, have been the major interests of theorists over the years just past. Their motivation has undoubtedly been, to a substantial degree, that some nuance of the formulation of the theorem — or some path opened up by it — remained to be explored. Equally, also, their motivation was discontent with a conclusion so palpably denied by empirical observations. Yet the tools of theory and the limitations of the mind are such that realism can be approached only slowly and step-by-step. These are the explanations of the unfolding analysis of the impact of trade on relative and absolute factor returns. These also warrant the expectation of further theoretical elaboration of the factor price equalization theorem in its fullest scope. That the development of this body of doctrine requires theoretical models of increasing complexity is the price exacted by an approach to the explanation of phenomena of the real world.

FOOTNOTES

1. For purposes of this chapter, the *absolute* amount of the factors in any country is immaterial. A relative discrepancy in the size of the two countries, in the sense that one country possesses much more of both factors than the

other country, does not alter the conclusions of the analysis, provided that the assumptions listed below continue to hold in both countries. Specifically, it must be cautioned that size disparity should not lead to complete specialization in production in either of the countries. Barring this, only the *relative* amount of the factors in each country is relevant.

2. Samuelson's statement of the full factor price equalization theorem [51; 50] follows quite clearly ideas developed some years earlier in a pioneering joint article (with Stolper) on trade and factor shares [54]. A major conclusion of the earlier article is that international trade results in an increase in the share of domestic output of that factor which is used most intensively in the export industry. That this conclusion needed restatement was noted especially by Metzler [32] and Lancaster [21]. The original factor shares theorem and its modification and elaboration are discussed in Caves [7, pp. 68–76]. A marked similarity between Caves' statement and the discussion which appears above will be noticed.

The other independent statement (besides Samuelson's) of full factor price equalization is that of Lerner [25], enunciated initially at a very early date, 1933, but not generally accessible until 1952.

3. Linder's explanation is based upon his assumption that trade accelerates growth in relatively developed areas, where the ability to reallocate resources is quite high, but does not increase growth where reallocative ability is negligible. Presumably, income per capita in the reallocating economies expands whereas in the non-adaptive economies it stagnates [26, pp. 135–36]. Johnson inveighs against validating an empirical phenomenon by the questionable assumption that underdeveloped areas lack the capacity to reallocate resources [15, p. 89].

4. Samuelson [51, p. 181] raises this point and, like Robinson, is unable to resolve it satisfactorily. A similar idea is found in Brown [6, pp. 67–68, 72–73]. Brown suggests that the differential impact of the excluded "factor" on the production functions of different manufactures is so significant that it, rather than a combination of factor proportions and relative factor returns, is primarily responsible for the pattern of comparative advantage. See also [51, pp. 182–83], Viner [61, pp. 122–23], and Mrs. Robinson [45, pp. 202–03] — where further complications in the relationship between definitions of productive factor and production functions are raised.

5. The best examples of these are Tinbergen [55], Samuelson [52], Pearce and James [42], Meade [28], McKenzie [27], Uzawa [57], Reiter [44], and Kemp [17, pp. 50–53].

6. These properties, not discussed here, are elegantly and rigorously formulated in McKenzie [27], Reiter [44], and Uzawa [57]. Pearce [43] attempts to give a visual image of the nature of these properties.

7. It must be assumed for a straight-forward demonstration of the equalization of relative factor returns through international trade that the relative factor endowments of the country, however defined, do not change as a consequence of trade. Where relative endowments are specified by efficiency prices or just plain factor prices this may be a potentially significant stricture. To be secure, therefore, it ought to be assumed that expressing relative factor endowments in terms of pre-trade or post-trade prices will not alter the relative factor scarcities in the two countries. If endowments are defined in physical terms, trade is not so likely to cause a shift in endowment patterns, although even in this instance given sufficient time international trade might so alter the relevant propensities (to work or to form capital) that an endowment pattern shift is

not out of the question. The brief comment on this by Viner [62, p. 276] is of some interest.

8. That the factor price equalization theorem — as distinct from the Heckscher-Ohlin theorem of trade structure — is not negated by the existence of disparate demand conditions is demonstrated by Samuelson's general proof of the theorem [52], in which taste patterns are left unspecified.

9. It is perhaps necessary to mention that if the analysis were to be conducted in monetary terms, the factor prices would become identical only when properly adjusted by the equilibrium exchange rate. The theorem, however, is derived in real terms and, therefore, it is in real terms that the price of a given factor becomes equal internationally. The meaning of this will become clear as the analysis progresses.

10. The meaning of "linear homogeneous" is explained below in the discussion of the production function. That discussion is easily translated into the income differences and relative commodity prices which are meaningful for demand analysis. Such a translation is left to the reader.

11. Robinson [46, Part IV, esp. pp. 185–86] notes that identical taste patterns may be incompatible with identical demands except where linear homogeneity prevails. This is a point of some theoretical interest but need not be summarized here. When the time comes to relax the simplifying assumption of identical demand conditions, it is stipulated merely that the commodity-purchase combination for the two countries is different for identical commodity-price ratios. Taste patterns, *per se,* need not be considered.

12. Assuming linear homogeneous production functions denies the existence of the conventional U-shaped long-run cost curves. Hence, the number of firms producing any given commodity is indeterminate. This does not significantly affect the derivation of factor return equalization, however. See Laursen [23, p. 542].

Also, Travis [56, pp. 8–9] notes that linear homogeneity is an unnecessarily restrictive assumption. It need only be assumed that the scale of an industry is large relative to the capacity at which constant costs of production begin. He also suggests that industries with increasing returns to scale need not be excluded. These suggestions, however, have not been fully exploited in the Heckscher-Ohlin framework.

13. Samuelson [52, p. 2] further clarifies the special nature of the "variable proportions" law that is required for the full validity of the price equalization argument. Non-increasing marginal returns to incremental factor input must set in from the very beginning — a more restrictive condition than is conventionally associated with the law of variable proportions. It is to be noted that this does not exclude a constant marginal product; only increasing marginal products are ruled out.

14. In a more general multi-commodity framework it would have to be stated that, regardless of the factor price ratio, the optimal combination of capital and labor always gives a capital-labor ratio for any given commodity which is greater than or less than that for any other commodity. This is often called the "strong" Samuelsonian intensity assumption. It means that commodities can be uniquely ranked according to their relative factor intensities and the ranking is unaltered by changes in relative factor prices. As Jones demonstrates [16, pp. 5–6], this ranking is in accordance with comparative advantage and when demand conditions are brought into the analysis the division between exports and imports can be determined.

Even in a two-commodity model there are difficulties attending an assumption of non-reversal of factor intensity. It complicates the problem of finding an acceptable definition of a productive factor. See Mrs. Robinson's comment [45, pp. 202–03].

15. Savosnick [53] and Travis [56, pp. 19–28] provide a more complete and elegant demonstration of this derivation. A comparison of these works with the following presentation will reveal a drastic and inaccurate shortcut in the graphical technique used here. Specifically, the quantity of output given by the isoquants must be transferred into the production possibilities curve not directly from the contract curve but from an additional construction line whose slope is determined by over-all factor endowment of the country concerned. See especially [53, pp. 186–89]. While Travis' presentation is diagrammatically more elegant than that of Savosnick, the latter's technique underlies the discussion of the following pages.

16. It can be noted that the factor input ratio curves of Figure 1-1B are described by an elasticity of factor substitution in the production of each commodity. Elasticity of substitution in this context can be defined as

$$\frac{d(K/L)}{(K/L)} \bigg/ \frac{d(P_K/P_L)}{(P_K/P_L)}.$$

More accurately, the denominator should consist of factor marginal products rather than factor prices but in perfect competition these are identical. With equal and constant elasticities of substitution the two factor input ratio curves cannot intersect. A given percentage increase in the price of labor relative to that of capital will result in an equal percentage increase in the capital-labor ratio in each commodity as the relatively less expensive input (capital) is substituted for the relatively dearer input (labor). This equal and iso-elasticity property of the factor input ratio curves is mirrored in the isoquants by identical degrees of curvature. Were commodity Y to have a lower elasticity of substitution than commodity X, isoquant YY would bend more sharply than isoquant XX.

17. These curves are derived on the assumption that the factors are imperfect substitutes in the production of each of the goods. This imperfect substitutability is assumed to be continuous, however. Eckaus [9, pp. 544–53] develops the maximum efficiency locus and its associated production possibilities curve on the basis of more restricted substitutability — for any given productive "process," the proportion in which factors can be combined is fixed and the number of such processes is limited. Under his assumptions the generality of the factor price equalization logic breaks down.

18. It should be noted that there are various explanations, summarized by Caves [7, pp. 31–35], of the "bowing outward" of the transformation functions. The explanations are rather technical and are not sufficiently integral to the issue of factor price equalization to warrant attention here.

19. Vanek [58; 59, pp. 208–10] gives a short alternative proof of the factor price equalization theorem which relies upon the uniqueness, in both directions, of the relationship between the contract curve and the production possibilities curve. He also provides an intuitive geometric proof of the failure of trade to bring about factor price equalization in the three-factor, two-commodity case.

20. A very thorough exposition of the conditions derivable from Figure 1-4 is that of Lancaster [20]. His statement of the "theorem of corresponding points" and the "theorem of inverse points" is somewhat more comprehensive

than is required for factor price equalization but the derivation of these theorems constitutes a formal derivation of factor price equalization. In this chapter all elements of the proof will not be fully supported but the reader can refer to Lancaster for a more complete and painstaking exposition. Travis [56, Chap. I] covers the same ground — and more besides. It should not be read until Lancaster's concepts are mastered.

Ford's proof of the factor price equalization theorem [10, pp. 407–18] is less formal than Lancaster's and skips over some of the material presented in this section.

21. That the relative slopes of these various price lines must be of the nature indicated is demonstrated by Mishan [36]. The price lines are tangent to the isoquants, which themselves are tangent, at every point on the contract curve. Mishan shows that for contract curves bowing downward to the right, as drawn in Figure 1-4, a movement rightward and upward along the contract curve is accompanied by an increasing slope for this tangent. That is to say, as output of the capital intensive commodity is reduced and output of the labor intensive commodity expands, the price of capital falls relative to that of labor or, what is the same thing, a unit of capital can substitute for more units of labor [36, p. 358]. The converse is, of course, also true.

22. Johnson asserts that there is a definite pattern between the factor price ratio and the employment of the factors in the two industries. Thus, "the proportions of the total labour supply employed in one of the industries is equal to the ratio of the difference between the other industry's capital:labour ratio and the overall ratio, to the difference between the capital:labour ratios in the two industries. . . ." [14, p. 21] In terms of Figure 1-5, at relative factor price F_A commodity X uses a proportion of the labor force given by

$$(E_A^Y - E_A)/(E_A^Y - E_A^X).$$

23. From this discussion it is seen that the potential range of the factor price ratio, and of the commodity price ratio, that is possible in any country depends upon the difference between the optimum capital-labor ratios in producing the two commodities and the degree of substitutability of capital for labor in the two industries. See Johnson [14, p. 21].

24. A good discussion of the effects of transportation costs is that of Meade [29, Chap. XXII]. Travis [56, pp. 6–8] suggests that the relative significance of transportation costs as a block to factor price equalization depends upon whether factor endowment differences are substantial. If they are insubstantial and there is an appreciable trade in goods that are inexpensive to transport, the tendency to equalization of factor prices should be nearly complete — provided, of course, that the other conditions of the theorem hold.

25. See, for example, Laursen [23, pp. 556–57] and Ford [10, pp. 426–28]. Travis [56, p. 8] also offers an interesting, but unresearched, suggestion about the relationship between the existence of international trade and a tendency for production functions to become identical. Uzawa [57] uses a mathematical model containing the possibility of different production functions internationally (as well as different taste preferences) and finds that factor price equalization would occur only if the initial factor endowments of the countries are those which would be achieved in equilibrium under free trade and international factor mobility. He specifies that relatively small comparative advantages in the commodities and a relatively small trade volume are conditions for this equilibrium. Reiter's model [44] considers non-identical production functions

and also is one of the few to relax the assumption of linearity of production functions. With regard to the linear homogeneity assumption, see also Danière [8].

26. Viner [62, p. 283], for example, reflects that "the influence of the opening of trade on relative prices of factors, therefore, operates via changes in relative domestic demands for products which result directly from changes in the occupational allocation of resources . . . and as well as from changes in the regional patterns of distribution of income associated with the changes in relative factor-prices. . . . It is hard to see whether these particular added interdependencies would work to strengthen or to weaken any factor-price-equalization tendencies otherwise inherent in . . . trade." Consider, also, the arguments of Robinson [46, pp. 179–88].

27. In the CES production functions the elasticity of substitution, while constant for each commodity, need not be unitary. The so-called Cobb-Douglas production functions, however, are of unitary substitution elasticity and yield non-reversal of factor intensity. Likewise, fixed coefficient production functions, such as used by Leontief in his input-output analysis, have zero elasticity of substitution and also lead to non-reversal.

Two reviewers of Minhas' [35], Mrs. Robinson [45] and Leontief [24], are not convinced by his findings. Mrs. Robinson takes an "agnostic" position, believing that Minhas' exercise is largely irrelevant since CES production functions are not likely to be found in practice. Leontief, however, adopts Minhas' data and shows that reversal is not likely for countries with such supposedly diverse factor price ratios as India and the U.S.

28. Mookerjee [38, pp. 10–16; 37, pp. 67–69] provides an ingenious variation on the Harrod-Johnson technique. By relating relative commodity prices directly to capital-labor ratios, rather than to relative factor prices as in the Harrod-Johnson diagram, he shows that for each capital-labor ratio there are two commodity price ratio curves, one for each factor ratio curve. He then demonstrates that complete factor price equalization is not possible when the factor endowment ratios of the two countries give rise to a meaningful reversal of factor intensity. The particular advantage of the Mookerjee variant is that the demonstration of the effects of reversal and of complete specialization are virtually identical.

29. Proof of this proposition is too long to be given here and, after demonstrating the properties of the box diagram for non-reversal of factor intensity, it would serve little purpose. A complete explanation can be found in Lancaster [20, pp. 32–37] and Travis [56, Chap. I]. See also the comments of Robinson [46, p. 178].

30. Lancaster [20] calls points on the contract curves having the properties of U and V or of W and Z "inverse points." They are equilibrium points in every sense. In particular, when two countries are producing at either of these sets of points, the marginal product of labor in the production of both commodities in country A equals the marginal product of capital in the production of both commodities in country B. The inverse also holds. Thus, at U and V or at W and Z, $(P_L/P_K)_A = (P_K/P_L)_B$. It is for this reason that the points are called inverse points. See also the discussion of Ford [10, pp. 422–23] and Travis [56, Chap. I].

31. Meade [29, pp. 383–85] describes the effects of what might be called demand skewness, and of very disparate industry and country sizes, upon the movement of relative factor prices. The picture given in Figure 1-10 of a

relatively small change in country A compared to the change in country B is consistent with the demand assumption here.

32. Meade [29, p. 346] notes that with two factors — and many commodities — trade need only be free in two of the commodities. The remainder of the goods may be heavily protected and bear substantial transportation costs and factor price equalization would still occur.

33. There are several possible formulations of the condition of uniqueness. In addition to Samuelson's, see that of Kuhn in the mathematical appendix to Land [22] and that of McKenzie [27]. Pearce's contribution [42; 43] has already been mentioned in the section on definitional problems. There is continuing interest in this uniqueness issue; Bhagwati [5, pp. 30–32] refers to several unpublished works on the subject.

34. The process by which the n-n' goods are eliminated depends upon the assumption made regarding the determination of the commodity prices. When the ϕ's are arbitrarily set, specialization will occur because a sufficient number of high priced industries will be competed out of existence. Alternatively, if the ϕ's are set in international markets, it is implicit that the prices of n-r goods would have already accommodated themselves to the prices of any r goods. In both instances, the number of excess equations would be expelled from the system and a determinate solution is possible. See Samuelson [52, pp. 6–7].

35. Meade [29, pp. 378–83] states the case for non-equalization of factor returns in a simple two-country, two-commodity, three-factor model. The conclusion hinges, of course, upon a difference in the post-trade situation in the marginal physical products of the factors in the two countries. His account makes profitable reading.

Short summaries of the multi-dimensional model elaborated here are in Caves [7, pp. 82–86], Kemp [17, pp. 50–53], and Bhagwati [5, pp. 31–32]. These all adopt the basic framework of Samuelson [52], rather than the frameworks of Tinbergen [55] or Laursen [23].

APPENDIX

Reversal, specialization, and "multi-dimensionalizing" of the factor price equalization theorem have, of the extensions and emendations of the basic model, received the lion's share of scholarly attention. Research has by no means been completely restricted to these areas, however. Several other analytically significant issues bearing upon the effects of trade on international factor prices have been explored. These issues have been much less systematically assayed in the literature — and the work already done has been scrutinized less intently — than those extensions of the simple model so far considered. Salient points applicable to the analysis of the consequences of trade for factor prices have been raised, however, and these merit notice. The object of this Appendix is to discuss these amplifications.

Non-constant returns to scale / Incorporating increasing and decreasing returns to scale results in a tremendously complicated model. Do increasing or decreasing returns exist in one or both industries? Are marginally increasing returns to scale greater at small than at large industry outputs? Both of these are conditions whose consequences were spelled out by Meade [29, pp. 351-56]. Where production functions are more complex than implied by these questions, is one country likely to have increasing returns and the second country decreasing (or constant) returns in the same industry? An affirmative reply to this question is not inconsistent with the assumption of identical production functions in the two countries. Are the sources of increasing returns internal or external to the firm? The answer determines whether the assumption of perfect competition is aborted. If returns to scale are increasing, what is their relative strength compared to the strength of the decreasing returns to factor proportions? As Kemp observes [17, pp. 119-20], the relative adjustments in the marginal product of each factor in each industry hinge upon the response to this question. These and other issues concerning non-constant returns to scale have been considered and it is necessary to resolve them before even a start can be made in analyzing the full impact of trade on factor prices. Depending upon their resolution — or rather the combination of resolutions — the opening up of trade may have quite different results.

Apart from the analytical complications attendant to non-constant returns, one safe generalization emerges. Once increasing or decreasing returns enter the model, the possibility of full absolute factor price equalization must typically be ruled out. As Kemp suggests [17, pp. 118, 122], assuming that perfect competition continues to be the relevant market structure in the analysis and that the economies are external to the firm (while internal to the industry), the factors are still paid a return equal to their value of marginal product; the firm's production function, but not that of the industry, remains linear homogeneous. Since in the post-trade situation the commodity prices are identical in the two countries, the equating of absolute factor prices entails equal proportions in combining the factors to produce each good *and* the same scale of production in each industry as well. These two conditions mean that absolute factor prices can only be equated by trade when the countries have identical absolute factor endowments — an improbable situation in practice and a sterile case theoretically. Thus, the analysis of the factor price equalization theorem with non-constant returns to scale is concerned solely with the question of relative factor prices between countries — with whether trade equalizes or tends to equalize relative factor prices.

The answer to this question is not intuitively obvious. Recall that the Harrod-Johnson demonstration of the impact of trade on factor prices is contingent upon the existence of an identical price ratio curve in both countries. In a provocative article, Laing [19] shows that, under non-constant returns to scale, the "position" of the price ratio curve depends upon the scale of output. Where the scales of production in the two industries differ between the two countries, it is no longer the case that the relationship between relative factor prices and relative commodity prices is the same in both countries. Indeed, in Kemp's skeletal summary of Laing's analysis [17, pp. 118–27], wherein the number of examples is expanded beyond Laing's formal efforts, the price ratio curves can be shown to take on very peculiar shapes under non-constant returns. Besides the "position" of these curves being dependent on scale, the slopes of the price ratio curves are dependent not only upon the relative factor intensity of the two industries (as in the case of constant returns to scale) but also upon the concavity or convexity of the production possibilities curve.

Generalizations about relative factor price equalization through trade under these types of conditions are truly difficult. Clearly, for relative factor price equalization to be even possible, the price ratio curves in the two countries must intersect. A careful examination of Kemp's analysis and a glance at his diagrams reveal that the price ratio curves either intersect twice or they do not intersect at all; international equalization of factor price ratios (but not of factor prices) may occur at one or the other of two different relative commodity prices or it may not occur at all. Moreover, except in the case where the production possibilities curve is S-shaped, the intersections of the price ratio curves, and hence the possibility of relative factor price equalization, are found at commodity price ratios where one or the other of the two countries specializes completely. Since there is no particular reason why the post-trade commodity price ratio, which is determined by international demands for the commodities, should fall at one of the two relative factor price equalizing points, it must be concluded that the presence of non-constant returns to scale generally invalidates the factor price equalization theorem — even when relative factor prices are the point of focus.

Similarly, with respect to the tendency for free trade to cause convergence of factor price ratios, production functions with non-constant returns to scale can lead to very strange outcomes. The possibilities for relative factor price movements shown in Kemp range through the spectrum that was found relevant in the case of factor intensity reversal, i.e., unambiguous convergence, unambiguous divergence, and divergence or convergence (or no change) with the factor price ratio moving in the same direction in both countries. With increasing returns to scale, however, another stratum of possibilities emerges. Under certain rather realistic assumptions, the movement of pre-trade commodity price ratios toward the post-trade equilibrium may result in factor price ratios first converging and then diverging and, hence, during the adjustment passing through, or overshooting, a condition of relative factor price equality. To state this another way, there may exist in each country different pre-trade commodity price ratios at which relative factor prices are equal but when trade opens up inequality of the factor price ratios in the two countries sets in. Clearly, the opening of trade does not inevitably lead to a convergence of relative factor prices between nations.

Neither Laing, who is responsible for the development of the argument underlying this discussion, nor Kemp fully explores all of these various possible situations. The presence of non-constant returns to scale opens up such a host of combinatory assumptions about the production functions that an exhaustive treatment would test the mettle and patience of the most assiduous scholar. The outlines of the effects of trade on factor prices under non-constant returns have been sketched, however; they indicate that the validity of the factor price equalization theorem — in any of its guises — is generally questionable insofar as non-constant returns are the ruling technological condition.

Categories of commodities / The discussion of factor price equalization usually proceeds on the basis of implicit assumptions that no commodity is used as an input in the production of some other good and that all products enter into trade once trade becomes possible. In other words, the absence of intermediate goods and of purely domestic goods is typically postulated. It is, however, well known that for any complex commodity a substantial fraction of the input is in the form of semi-finished or crude materials; intermediate products therefore are prevalent. Moreover, some "commodities" may not be capable of entering international trade at all — some services come to mind — and yet their production has an influence upon the returns paid to the factors. The question arises whether the inclusion in the formal model of intermediate products and of purely domestic goods has a significant bearing upon the relationship between trade and relative factor prices between nations.

The little research done on the impact of either of these commodity categories fails to demonstrate the need to augment the analysis already developed. Samuelson [52, p. 1 and Mathematical Appendix], for example, claims this for a multi-dimensional productive system in which "each good requires in its production every *other good* as an input," where goods serve "as intermediate as well as final goods." Vanek [60], using Samuelson's mathematical treatment as a backdrop, demonstrates geometrically the same point using a two-factor, two-commodity model in which each commodity is a fixed coefficient input for the other commodity and is also a final traded output. The factors are substitutable so that variable factor proportions pertain.

Vanek's demonstration is in two steps. First, he derives from the conventional no-intermediate-product production possibilities curve (like those of Figure 1-3) a production possibilities curve reflecting the use of the two products as inputs and hence reflecting the unavailability of some output of the two products for final purchasers. He derives, as it were, a transformation function between the *net* outputs of the two goods from the transformation curve for the total output of the two goods. The translation from one transformation function to the other depends solely upon the size of the fixed coefficients representing the input of, say, commodity X per unit of commodity Y and, vice versa, the input of Y per unit of X. The second step is to show that the equilibrium product price ratios determined from the "net output" transformation function stand in a one-to-one relationship with the factor price ratios given by the maximum efficiency locus of the box diagram, the maximum efficiency locus of course relating factor input combinations and total (not net) output combinations. Using the technique he developed earlier [58; 59, pp. 208–10], where factor price equalization is shown using a modified box diagram presentation, Vanek gives a clever proof that, under the typical assumptions of the factor price equalization theorem with the additional condition that intermediate, traded products are present, "given factor prices will always correspond to given product prices, whatever the factor endowments of an economy" [60, p. 137]. Consequently, in a model admitting interindustry product flows the factor price equalization theorem is shown to hold.

While the existence of traded intermediate goods has no unsettling results for the customary effect of trade on factor prices, such is not true of the existence of purely domestic — or non-traded — goods. This has been exhibited in a four-commodity, two-factor analysis undertaken by Morgan and Rees [39]. Their conclusions are somewhat less firm regarding relative factor prices and also more realistic because it is assumed that transportation costs on all of the goods are substantial enough to countermand pre-trade comparative cost differences in two of them. Transportation costs give rise to two non-traded commodities and also, of course, prevent full factor price equalization. Nevertheless, given that their assumption precludes internationally equal factor prices, Morgan and Rees show that the difference between factor price ratios remaining after trade opens is greater when some purely domestic goods are produced than when all goods are traded internationally.

The basis of this finding is in one sense simple and obvious. As trade takes place, the factors released by the contracting import-competing industry, which is possibly most intensive of the four goods in terms of utilization of one of the factors, are taken up not only by the expanding export industry but also possibly by the expanding domestic goods industries. This phenomenon suggests that complete specialization (in the meaningful sense of one of the countries failing to produce one of the traded commodities) becomes more likely when non-traded goods are considered.[A-1]

But the situation just depicted need not be the case at all. Transportation costs may block out of international markets the commodities which use most intensively of the four goods the relatively scarce factor

71

in each country. Then if the outputs of these commodities expand as trade occurs the demand for the scarce factor tends to remain high and the tendency for the price of that scarce factor to fall relatively is diluted and possibly even reversed. This can be happening in both economies with readily apparent consequences for the adjustment of relative and absolute factor prices.

From these two examples, superficially discussed, it is seen that trade impediments may prevent exchange of two goods at the extremes of factor intensities, of two goods adjacent in factor intensities, or of two goods whose factor intensities are separated by that of a third good. Which of these is the case affects the way non-traded goods can impede the tendency of trade to equate factor prices. Moreover, the output of one or both of the purely domestic goods may contract as trade opens up, contrary to the assumption of the above examples. Whether this is the case is a function of the substitutability (or complementarity) relationships among the four commodities in consumers' taste patterns. The possibility of decreasing production of purely domestic goods also alters the effect of non-traded commodities on the factor price equalization theorem.

As with non-constant returns to scale, the inclusion of non-traded goods within the model opens up numerous analytical paths. Perhaps one generalization is possible with a non-traded goods assumption: the greater the post-trade expansion of output of the domestic good using the scarce factor most intensively, and the more intensively (relatively) the scarce factor is employed in making that commodity, the stronger will be the offset of the existence of non-traded goods to the factor price equalizing qualities of international trade. And this leads to a further observation. Full factor price equalization is in any event frustrated by transportation costs. Nevertheless trade brings about closer factor prices between the countries the smaller is the purely domestic sector relative to the export and import-competing sectors and the greater is the volume of international exchange.

Capital and the interest rate / Using capital as one of the homogeneous productive factors in the analysis gives rise to a complexity which may have come to the reader's mind but has so far been ignored. In reciting the proof of the factor price equalization theorem and in discussing the analytical extensions of the theorem, it was noted that the "price" of the factor should more accurately have been called a return or a "rental" for the services of the factor. The meaning of this in the case of labor — or land for that matter — leads to no ambiguity, for the rental return to labor is strictly speaking its wage rate. With respect to capital, however, the interest rate, which is commonly thought to correspond to the wage rate, is not capital's rental return. This is made evident by recalling that the formula for computing the present value (price) of an asset involves capitalizing a stream of earnings by use of the interest rate. Thus, it may be said that the present value, V, of a piece of capital equipment is given by the formula:

$$V = P_k \left(\frac{1}{(1 + i)} + \frac{1}{(1 + i)^2} + \cdots + \frac{1}{(1 + i)^m} \right), \qquad (1A\text{-}1)$$

where i is the interest rate, m is the number of periods over which the capital good will last, and P_k is the stream of earnings or rental return of capital, which, in this case, is assumed to be constant through time. The factor price equalization analysis for capital and labor in fixed supply shows merely that the P_k's in all countries are equalized by trade (under certain assumptions). The interest rate, i, may or may not be equalized among nations by the existence of trade and, as Kemp observes [17, pp. 48–49], only if the i's are equalized, along with the P_k's, is the price, V, of an identical capital asset the same in every country. This is also apparent from equation 1A-1.

There is a second kind of ambiguity arising from the use of capital. Labor (and land) does not deteriorate with use; capital does. This distinction between the productive factors in the factor price equalization model has also been overlooked until very recently. In a way, it has been implied that capital is just like labor in respect to depreciation and it was not required to distinguish whether the return to the factors was a "gross" rental, making no allowance for deterioration in use, or a "net" rental, which allows for the fact that the factor may indeed wear out. Therefore, the point which Samuelson [49] makes is important: the rental return that trade, under certain conditions, equalizes between nations is the "net" return. Indeed, under plausible assumptions, the "gross" return to capital is not even uniform between industries within a given country, wherein both commodities and factors are completely mobile, whereas the "net" rental to capital is. This interindustry equalization is, of course, a pre-condition to international equalization of returns through trade. Thus, a "net" rental to capital appears as P_k in equation 1A-1. Since depreciation has no relevance to the labor factor, as labor is typically defined, the distinction between "gross" and "net" wage has no meaning.

But it is to the question of interest rate — not "net" capital rental — equalization through trade that Samuelson addresses his analysis [49]. Samuelson makes the case that under certain assumptions the interest rate also becomes equal among trading countries. His crucial assumptions, in addition to those conventional for full factor price equalization, are: (1) capital is a homogeneous, produced factor, using a combination of labor and capital; (2) capital is an intermediate, non-traded good used, along with labor, in producing two traded commodities; (3) gross capital formation, although not necessarily net capital formation, is positive; and (4) the interest rate is positive.[A-2] Given these conditions, Samuelson proves the international equality of the interest rate by the now modish technique of establishing that in equilibrium each possible price ratio between the two traded goods permits only a single factor price (net rental) ratio and for each possible factor price ratio there is only one consistent interest rate. Since these functional relationships are identical in every country, when the same commodity price ratio rules in each country, as it does in post-trade equilibrium, the same interest rate must rule in every country. The conclusion depends intimately upon the assumptions listed above; other assumptions about the nature of capital may nullify interest rate equalization through free trade.

Kemp [17, p. 49] offers a simple, intuitive explanation of this conclusion, probably based upon Samuelson's formulation. With full equality of factor prices in every country it follows from the assumptions of factor price equalization that the cost of producing the homogeneous capital good is the same in every country. In perfect competition the price of capital must equal its cost and must, therefore, be the same in every country. Looking at equation 1A-1, the V's are identical for every trading country as are the P_k's. It then follows from the general applicability of the capitalization formula that the i's are also the same in each country. Although this glosses over a host of complications mentioned in Samuelson's paper, Kemp's discussion puts Samuelon's argument in elementary and understandable terms.

Variable factor supply / The entire preceding analysis has involved the assumption that the over-all factor endowment ratio of each of the countries is unchanging. The dimensions of the boxes in the box diagram, or alternatively the factor endowment ratios of the Harrod-Johnson formulation, were given and fixed. Possibly, this assumption can be justified in the context of the conventional foreign trade model, where complete international factor immobility is postulated. But even with this postulate the assumption of fixed capital-labor ratios is an extreme oversimplification. Specifically, some elasticity in the supply of factors over time and in response to changes in relative factor returns — and to real income as well — is observable. Even if one factor were to remain in fixed supply (as with land, for example), the variation of the second factor would be sufficient to affect the over-all endowment ratio.

This has not escaped the attention of theorists and several avenues of pursuing the consequences of variable factor supplies have been opened in the literature. One approach, typified by Guha's recent article [11], proceeds by changing the dimensions of the box diagram and analyzing the consequent impact upon the maximum efficiency locus and the production possibilities curve. This technique of accommodating variable factor supplies is discussed in Chapter 2 and will not be summarized here.

A second approach, that of Walsh [63], ignores explicit use of the box diagram and treats instead the direct effects on the production possibilities curve of changes in the amount of labor supplied — or more accurately leisure taken. Taking up these approaches in order to examine the impact of variable factor supplies on relative factor prices would lead to analytical complexities greater than those already presented. Caves [7, Chap. IV, especially pp. 114–19] provides an effective resumé of this literature, pointing out that admitting variable factor supplies to the model modifies the equalization of factor prices only in that it enhances the likelihood of complete specialization.

This result can be shown more facilely by adapting the Harrod-Johnson diagram in the manner indicated by Kemp and Jones [18] mathematically and by Kemp [17, Chap. 7] geometrically, both presaged by a brief aside of Johnson [14, pp. 21–22]. Specifically, an increase in the relative price of labor normally would cause an expansion in the labor supply relative to the capital stock; the over-all capital-labor endowment ratio of a country is therefore inversely related to the relative labor price. Curve RR in Figure 1A-1 reflects this relationship. For illustration, assume as before that country A has a fixed endowment ratio, E_A, but that country B has a variable endowment ratio according to RR. With this assumption, provided the post-trade price comes to rest in the range $P'_B P_A$, specialization is incomplete and factor price equalization is established. But this "equalizing" commodity price range, $P'_B P_A$, in which specialization can be incomplete and factor price equality can rule, is appreciably narrower than would have been the "equalizing" range, i.e., $P_B P_A$, had the over-all endowment ratios of the two countries been fixed at E_A and E_B. Yet RR is constructed so that, it might be said, the "average" over-all endowment ratio in country B approximates E_B.[A-3] With flexible endowment ratios, the chances of factor price equalization through trade are reduced commensurately with the responsiveness of the endowment ratio. Johnson notes, as an extreme case, that if the supply of labor in country B is perfectly elastic with respect to the factor price ratio — RR would become a vertical straight line — factor price equality is possible at only a single commodity price ratio [14, p. 22]. Moreover, equality would be ruled out unless the vertical RR took on the value of E_A somewhere between the factor price ratios in country A that would force that country to specialize completely.[A-4] Thus, once the factor endowment ratio becomes related to changes in relative factor prices, the likelihood of factor price equalization through free trade varies directly with the relative factor price responsiveness of relative factor supplies.

Kemp [17, pp. 98–99] poses an interesting question which this line of thought raises. He asks whether, with factor endowment ratios responding to relative factor price movements, trade would always cause factor price equalization if country A and country B had identical RR curves. The answer is yes, as can be established from Figure 1A-1, but only as long as the solid RR curve is the relevant one. Suppose, however, that the labor supply responds to other variables than factor price ratios, as already implied. Kemp suggests that these other variables might be the prices of the two commodities and the value of leisure — what might be called "real income" in an expanded meaning of income. Under these conditions the factor endowment ratio may, at low factor price ratios, fall as the relative price of labor increases and then, as the factor price ratio rises sufficiently, the capital-labor ratio might rise with further increases in (P_L/P_K). This is consistent with the hypothesis of a "backward-bending" supply curve of labor and is illustrated in Figure 1A-1 by RR'.

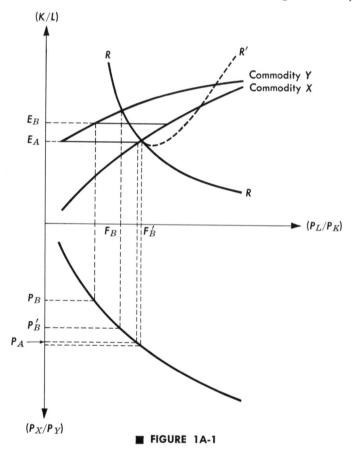

■ FIGURE 1A-1

If RR', rather than RR, were to pertain in both countries, factor price equalization is no longer inevitable with trade. Relative commodity prices would of course be equal in the two countries but specialization might occur in at least one of the countries before factor prices could be equalized. This would be the case if one country were operating, between the factor ratio curves, on a portion of its RR' curve that is positively sloped while the second country is operating on the negatively sloped segment of its (identical) RR' curve. Full factor price equalization is not ruled out by identical RR' curves if the pre-trade factor price ratios are sufficiently similar; if dissimilarity is relatively great inequality of factor prices persists even after trade is opened up.

As Figure 1A-1 is drawn, a tendency toward convergence of factor price ratios is dictated by the factor endowment response illustrated by RR' with disparate capital-labor ratios in the two countries; trade tends to equate factor prices in this case. With an intervening factor intensity reversal — with the factor ratio curves intersecting between the two portions of RR' relevant to this example — other possibilities can be imagined. Divergence of the factor price ratios in the two countries is certainly possible when variable factor endowment ratios and factor intensity reversals are permissible. Movements of factor price ratios in the same direction, with either divergence or convergence, are also conceivable outcomes.

Footnotes to Appendix

A-1. The further conclusion, valid in the discussion of preceding sections, that with complete specialization further tendency to factor price equalization is impossible, must not be made.

As Morgan and Rees clearly see, one of the more fascinating analytical possibilities with non-traded goods is the following: with non-traded goods being produced, the coming on of complete specialization need not halt the movement of factor prices. The domestic goods industries may release productive factors to the completely specialized industry with the prospect of further changes in the factor proportions and factor rewards. For factor prices to converge further, once complete specialization has taken place, it is only necessary that factor intensities vary among the traded and non-traded goods in a particular pattern and that the volume of trade itself continues to increase. See Morgan and Rees [39, pp. 337–38].

A-2. Where gross capital formation is zero (by definition, gross capital formation cannot be negative), the factor rentals may still be equalized between countries while their interest rates are not, the interest rate difference resulting from differences in time preference in the countries.

A positive interest rate is required, as Samuelson's model is set up, to insure that the present value of the homogeneous capital is greater than zero.

A-3. The average over-all endowment ratio in country B, with the variable endowment ratio depicted by RR, would approximate E_B in the sense that a random fluctuation in the factor price ratio in country B between its extremes of specialization (from F_B to F'_B would result in E_B being the average endowment ratio over the period of the fluctuation in (P_L/P_K).

A-4. That is, if the factor endowment ratio of country B were perfectly flexible and the endowment ratio of country A were fixed at E_A, factor price equalization would be possible only if the vertical RR curve intersected the solid horizontal line which has been drawn in at the endowment ratio E_A — and it would be possible at one, and only one, relative commodity price.

BIBLIOGRAPHY

[1] K. J. Arrow, H. B. Chenery, B. S. Minhas, and R. M. Solow, "Capital-Labor Substitution and Economic Efficiency," *REStat* (August 1961).

[2] B. Balassa, "The Factor-Price Equalization Controversy," *Weltwirtschaftliches Archiv*, No. 1 (1961).

[3] T. Balogh, "Static Models and Current Problems," *OEP* (June 1949). Reprinted in Balogh, *Unequal Partners*, vol. I, chap. 15 (1963).

[4] J. Bhagwati, "Protection, Real Wages and Real Incomes," *EJ* (December 1959).

[5] ————, "The Pure Theory of International Trade," *EJ* (March 1964).

[6] A. J. Brown, "Professor Leontief and the Pattern of World Trade," *Yorkshire Bulletin of Economic and Social Research* (November 1957).

[7] R. E. Caves, *Trade and Economic Structure: Models and Methods* (1960).

[8] A. Danière, "American Trade Structure and Comparative Cost Theory," *Econia Internaz* (August 1956).

[9] R. S. Eckaus, "The Factor Proportions Problem in Underdeveloped Areas," *AER* (September 1955).

[10] J. L. Ford, "The Effects of Commodity Trade on Factor Prices," *Econia Internaz* (August 1963).

[11] A. Guha, "Factor and Commodity Prices in an Expanding Economy," *QJE* (February 1963).

[12] R. F. Harrod, "Factor-Price Relations Under Free Trade," *EJ* (June 1958).

[13] E. Heckscher, "The Effect of Foreign Trade on the Distribution of Income," *Ekonomisk Tidskrift* (1919), as reprinted in American Economic Association, *Readings in the Theory of International Trade* (1949).

[14] H. G. Johnson, "Factor Endowments, International Trade and Factor Prices," *Man Sch* (September 1957), as reprinted in Johnson, *International Trade and Economic Growth* (1958).

[15] ————, "Review of S. B. Linder, *An Essay on Trade and Transformation*," *Econa* (February 1964).

[16] R. W. Jones, "Factor Proportions and the Heckscher-Ohlin Theorem," *REStud* (1956–1957).

[17] M. C. Kemp, *The Pure Theory of International Trade* (1964).

[18] ———— and R. W. Jones, "Variable Labor Supply and the Theory of International Trade," *JPE* (February 1962).

[19] N. F. Laing, "Factor Price Equalization in International Trade and Returns to Scale," *Ec Rec* (September 1961).

[20] K. Lancaster, "The Heckscher-Ohlin Trade Model: A Geometric Treatment," *Econa* (February 1957).

[21] ————, "Protection and Real Wages: A Restatement," *EJ* (June 1957).

[22] G. H. Land, "Factor Endowments and Factor Prices," *Econa* (May 1959).

[23] S. Laursen, "Production Functions and the Theory of International Trade," *AER* (September 1952).

[24] W. Leontief, "International Factor Costs and Factor Use," *AER* (June 1964).

[25] A. P. Lerner, "Factor Prices and International Trade," *Econa* (February 1952). Reprinted in his *Essays in Economic Analysis* (1953). Originally given at a seminar at the London School of Economics in December 1933.

[26] S. B. Linder, *An Essay on Trade and Transformation* (1961).

[27] L. W. McKenzie, "Equality of Factor Prices in World Trade," *Emet* (July 1955).

[28] J. E. Meade, "The Equalisation of Factor Prices: the Two-Country Two-Factor Three-Product Case," *Metroecon* (December 1950).

[29] _____, *Trade and Welfare* (1955).

[30] G. M. Meier, *International Trade and Development* (1963).

[31] _____, "International Trade and International Inequality," *OEP* (October 1958).

[32] L. A. Metzler, "Tariffs, the Terms of Trade, and the Distribution of National Income," *JPE* (February 1949).

[33] M. Michaely, "Factor Proportions in International Trade: Current State of the Theory," *Kyk*, Fasc. 4 (1964).

[34] B. S. Minhas, "The Homohypallagic Production Function, Factor-Intensity Reversals, and the Heckscher-Ohlin Theorem," *JPE* (April 1962).

[35] _____, *An International Comparison of Factor Cost and Factor Use* (1963).

[36] E. J. Mishan, "Factor Endowment and Relative Commodity Prices. A Comment," *Econa* (November 1956).

[37] S. Mookerjee, *Factor Endowments and International Trade: A Study and Appraisal of the Heckscher-Ohlin Theory* (1958).

[38] _____, "Factor Proportions, Comparative Advantage and Factor Prices, *Arthaniti* (May 1958).

[39] E. V. Morgan and G. L. Rees, "Non-Traded Goods and International Factor Price Equalisation," *Econa* (November 1954).

[40] G. Myrdal, *An International Economy* (1956).

[41] B. Ohlin, *Interregional and International Trade* (1933).

[42] I. F. Pearce and S. F. James, "The Factor Price Equalisation Myth," *REStud,* No. 2 (1951–52).

[43] I. F. Pearce, "A Further Note on Factor-Commodity Price Relationships," *EJ* (December 1959).

[44] S. Reiter, "Efficient International Trade and Equalization of Factor Prices," *International Economic Review* (January 1961).

[45] J. Robinson, "Factor Prices not Equalized," *QJE* (May 1964).

[46] R. Robinson, "Factor Proportions and Comparative Advantage," *QJE* (May, August 1956).

[47] T. N. Rybczynski, "Factor Endowment and Relative Commodity Prices," *Econa* (November 1955).

[48] P. A. Samuelson, "A Comment on Factor Price Equalisation," *REStud,* No. 2 (1951–52).

[49] —————, "Equalization by Trade of the Interest Rate along with the Real Wage," in R. E. Caves, H. G. Johnson, and P. B. Kenen (eds.), *Trade, Growth, and the Balance of Payments: Essays in Honor of Gottfried Haberler* (1965).

[50] —————, "International Factor-Price Equalisation Once Again," *EJ* (June 1949).

[51] —————, "International Trade and the Equalisation of Factor Prices," *EJ* (June 1948).

[52] —————, "Prices of Factors and Goods in General Equilibrium," *REStud,* No. 1 (1953–54).

[53] K. M. Savosnick, "The Box Diagram and the Production Possibility Curve," *Ekonomisk Tidskrift* (September 1958).

[54] W. F. Stolper and P. A. Samuelson, "Protection and Real Wages," *REStud* (November 1941). Reprinted in American Economic Association, *Readings in the Theory of International Trade* (1949).

[55] J. Tinbergen, "The Equalisation of Factor Prices Between Free-Trade Areas," *Metroecon* (April 1949). Reprinted in *Selected Papers,* L. H. Klaassen, *et al.* (eds.) (1959).

[56] W. P. Travis, *The Theory of Trade and Protection* (1964).

[57] H. Uzawa, "Prices of the Factors of Production in International Trade," *Emet* (July 1959).

[58] J. Vanek, "An Alternative Proof of the Factor Price Equalization Theorem," *QJE* (November 1960).

[59] —————, *International Trade: Theory and Economic Policy* (1962).

[60] —————, "Variable Factor Proportions and Inter-Industry Flows in the Theory of International Trade," *QJE* (February 1963).

[61] J. Viner, *International Trade and Economic Development* (1952).

[62] —————, "Relative Abundance of the Factors and International Trade," *Indian Economic Journal* (January 1962).

[63] V. C. Walsh, "Leisure and International Trade," *Econa* (August 1956).

CHAPTER 2

Trade and Relative Factor Supplies

PREFATORY STATEMENT

This chapter focuses on a small, though significant, part of the corpus of pure trade theory. It deals with the current debates involving the supply side of international trade — the supply of factors which influence the supply of commodities. The problem of the factor-composition of commodities exchanged in international trade has not been examined in depth until comparatively recently. We will begin then with a review of this basic approach to trade theory — frequently referred to as the Heckscher-Ohlin approach — and compare it with the classical approach.

Theoretical and empirical studies have shaken the basis of many notions concerning the operation and structure of international trade. The emergence of contrary propositions generated by the Leontief "Paradox," in which empirical facts seem to refute widely accepted theory, has set in motion a series of searching examinations into the theoretical basis of trade under static and dynamic conditions. The studies suggest that relatively capital-rich economies may not always export relatively capital-intensive commodities. Other studies have shown how trade tends to equalize the price of factors. Our concern in the chapter is with the disputes over how the factors of production are geared physically to international trade rather than with matters which deal with trade effects on factor prices.

When assumptions regarding the fixity of factor endowments are relaxed, the production frontier itself is no longer fixed and some crucial considerations of economic growth are introduced. It is shown that with relatively changing proportions of factors used in production, the production effects and resulting trade patterns are not as easily determined as they were by the earlier Hechscher-Ohlin approaches. Furthermore, the role of natural resources and intermediate products in trade, as well as the role of technology, affect patterns of trade not easily appreciated in two-factor, two-country models of comparative statics which begin with given factor proportions. The effect of economic growth on trade has considerable contemporary significance and gives us insights into problems of developed countries, as well as of developing countries.

"Trade and Relative Factor Supplies" is concerned with how the direction and pattern of trade change when there are alterations in the supplies of factors of production. It deals with the causes of change in trade created by production changes which influence relative commodity prices but it attempts to avoid further examination of effects on factor prices. Inevitably, some of the foundational material already made familiar must be re-examined but, wherever possible, repetitious formulations are avoided. The concentration on relative factor endowments is warranted because of the relevance of factor proportions theory and changing factor supplies to contemporary problems of economic growth and economic development.

The fundamental approach to supply aspects of the pure theory of international trade has been through the comparative cost doctrine. Although many details of the doctrine have been greatly changed, in essence it has withstood most attacks. The classical formulations of the theory have absorbed numerous modifications proposed by advances in general economic theory and by the demands of public policy. In turn, re-examination of the formulations has aided the progress of general economic theory and policy development.

Stated in simplest terms, the comparative cost doctrine claims that, under conditions of free trade, each country exports that commodity the production of which is relatively cheaper than other commodities when compared to the relative production costs of the same commodities abroad and imports that commodity in which other countries have a comparative cost advantage. This traditional explanation of international trade has tended to remain an analysis of static equilibrium assumed to apply to all countries, rich and poor, although it is modelled on short-run domestic market conditions in advanced countries.[1] General economic theory, in contrast, has recently begun to reach more and more into the area of long-period dynamic equilibrium analysis [Meier, 44, p. 1]. Viner points out that international trade theory based on classical approaches has tended to possess serious shortcomings as a guide to national and international policies in the contemporary world [65, p. 1]. Long ago Williams pointed out that traditional trade theory with its assumptions of fixed productive factors fully employed is hardly applicable to the real world; attention should be given to the relationships between international trade and the emergence of new resources and productive forces [67, p. 196].

82

Contemporary theory centers upon the role of resources and production in trade and shows how the relationships are useful in understanding policy problems. The theory, formally associated with the names of Heckscher [25] and Ohlin [50], is based on the proposition that a country exports those commodities produced with relatively large quantities of the country's relatively abundant factor. This theorem is not in contradiction of, or in competition with, the comparative cost doctrine. In its full development the theorem lends powerful support to traditional doctrine. It provides an explanation of why production costs might differ from one country to another and it shows the possible causes of relative commodity cheapness. Nevertheless, since about 1950, the major propositions of both theories have been subjected to closer scrutiny. Theoretical and empirical studies have raised doubts about the validity of some of the propositions and the main assumptions have been closely reappraised.

Before examining the relevance and implications of the Heckscher-Ohlin theorem for our particular purpose, a brief review of its theoretical antecedents and its place in the economic literature is in order.[2] The theory of comparative costs, said to originate with Ricardo and Torrens,[3] was supported by two ideas which are now discounted and were not really necessary for the fundamental validity of the doctrine. These ideas were the labor theory of value and the assumption of the international immobility of factors; essentially, only the factor of labor was significant. Since it was assumed that the production function of a given commodity differed internationally, relative commodity prices then referred to relative labor costs which Ricardo showed through his value theory to be linked to money costs and money prices. In short, comparative commodity prices were based on comparative labor productivity.

Ricardo's comparative cost approach neglected the role of demand and showed only the range of possible barter terms of trade. Mill introduced demand into the picture when he developed a theory of international values and determinate prices which utilized the concept of demand elasticity. Marshall, and others, extended this demand analysis still further, particularly through the analytical device of reciprocal demand and supply curves. This approach made possible a general equilibrium solution to international trade — a solution in which prices and quantities in production and consumption were accounted for. This is in contrast to the earlier partial equilibrium solution which dealt only with supply conditions. The improved approach used Marshall-Edgeworth offer curves, representing the loci of possible points of trade equilibrium under the assumption that domestic adjustment has been made for each trading position given on the offer curve.

83

One major deficiency on the supply side of the classical theory of trade was the labor theory of value assumption. It was originally assumed that labor was the only factor of production with complete domestic mobility and complete international immobility. Early attempts to deal with this deficiency replaced the notion of labor cost with the notion of real cost which is based on subjective cost or disutility. Cairnes, for example, spoke of comparative cost in terms of human cost, meaning labor and abstinence [see Viner, 64, p. 456]. A more acceptable replacement was the notion of opportunity cost.[4]

In the opportunity cost model of trade and production equilibrium, the supply of factors is assumed constant and inelastic with respect to price. The approach recognizes the existence of many different factors of production including a whole range of different kinds of labor, land, natural resources, and capital. It does not depend on basic cost conditions for each separate item. For determining equilibrium commodity prices, the marginal cost of producing one commodity is related to the marginal cost of producing another, assuming factors of production are held constant and are in full employment.

It is possible to achieve a fully developed theory of general equilibrium from the opportunity cost approach, assuming no trade restrictions and transport costs and using the concept of community indifference curves. This approach more adequately copes with situations involving increasing costs than the earlier theories which almost invariably had to assume constant costs.

An alternative approach to general equilibrium theory of international trade, with differences largely on the supply side, is seen in the Heckscher-Ohlin approach. Heckscher's main contribution lay in explaining foreign trade flows in terms of relative scarcity or abundance of the various factors of production. The classical approach, based on comparative costs, made little attempt to locate the root of comparative cost differences. Heckscher went further by using marginal productivity theory and by showing that the comparative advantage of output arose from the relatively large supply of the factors of production which one country possessed and which were most important in the production of the output.

One of Heckscher's purposes was to show the effect of foreign trade on the distribution of income under free trade conditions. Certainly, the new approach opened the way to a more thorough treatment of the concept of income distribution and factor shares. Heckscher explained how foreign trade evens out the scarcity of the factors of production if their supplies are inelastic [25, p. 285] and how it has a tendency to equalize the relative returns to the factors throughout the world. Heckscher concluded that free trade, in redistributing income, is better than any other commercial policy because unlike other policies it creates the possibility of maximum satisfaction of human wants.

Ohlin modified and refined the Heckscher treatment in several studies.[5] He used a two-region, many-commodity, many-factor model for his analysis and assumed a given rate of exchange. Unlike Heckscher, Ohlin disassociated his theory from the classical theory mainly by a complete rejection of the labor theory of value. The comparative cost doctrine nevertheless was enhanced by a clearer analysis of why costs differ in different regions. Following Heckscher, Ohlin found the reason to lie in different factor endowments, although he allowed that different demand conditions could also lead to price differences. Differential endowments embrace both qualitative and quantitative characteristics of the factors and also the influence of social institutions.

In general, the classical hypothesis presupposed the existence of inter-country differences in production functions, while the Heckscher-Ohlin hypothesis presupposed identical inter-country production functions, and factors of production which were identical in a qualitative sense [Balassa, 2, p. 231]. The opportunity cost approach is an alternative approach to the classical system relying on real costs. But both the method of opportunity cost and comparative costs based on relative productivities can be used for exploring the underlying cost conditions represented by factor proportions and factor supplies.

In the classical comparative cost approach, in which labor was the only factor, relative factor supplies had little meaning. Because of the assumption of inter-country differences in production functions, however, export commodities would tend to have smaller labor inputs in terms of labor time than non-export commodities. Money costs were regarded as proportional to these real costs and variations in domestic production conditions which made possible differences in labor productivity were taken for granted rather than being incorporated in technical production functions. There were few attempts to develop supply functions for labor in connection with trade theory. Furthermore, with the assumption of international factor immobility, factor supplies were not variable on account of migration.

In the opportunity cost model developed by Haberler, the quantity of each factor is taken as given and output varies depending on how the available supply of factors can be utilized in the alternative optimal productions. There are no restrictions on the number of factors employable or on how they are employed but one set of factors lies behind each transformation curve. Costs are in the form of foregone alternative production and are conditioned by the degree to which the factors can be substituted for one another. Factors which are not highly substitutable create sharply increasing opportunity costs when production of one commodity is increased. Factors can be combined in variable proportions but any increase in absolute supply leads to an extension of the production frontier. International trade leads to an increased output of the commodity produced at lower comparative opportunity cost and an increase in the relative employment of those factors contributing most to the output.

In the Heckscher-Ohlin model the relationship between absolute amounts of factor supplies determines the pattern of production and trade. The relatively plentiful factor is used most commonly in production, making possible the emergence of comparative advantages and hence international trade. The comparative advantages emerge because of differences in basic factor endowments and because of differences in factor intensities in producing commodities. If relative factor endowments were the same for the countries involved and factor intensities were the same in all commodities produced, no comparative cost differences would be created. The pre-trade conditions which create comparative cost differences depend upon absolute factor endowments, relative factor intensities, and multiple factors — all identical qualitatively in the two countries.

The Heckscher-Ohlin model, however, does not provide all the answers to the dynamic problems of international trade. With trade, for example, relative factor supplies are likely to change; the relatively scarce factor becomes less scarce and the relatively plentiful factor becomes less plentiful until there is equalization of factor supplies. Relative factor supplies then could be influenced by the presence of trade itself, particularly if it is recognized that capital goods flow in international trade. Increases in factor supplies at disproportionate rates can create a reversal in the initial factor endowment, while changes in relative factor supplies due to an alteration in the composition of output can reverse initial comparative advantages.

The influences of relative factor supplies and their variation are the subject of the analysis which follows. The three separate approaches to the study of international trade are frequently merged to provide a basis for a better understanding of the role of factors in international trade. Most attention is given to the nature of relative factor endowments, the relevance of production conditions to the Heckscher-Ohlin theorem, the effects of changes in factor supplies, and the attempts to verify empirically the basis of trade.

☐ THE HECKSCHER-OHLIN METHOD

The Assumptions Affecting Factor Supplies

That trade depends on relative factor endowments is widely accepted in modern international trade theory. Nevertheless, the immediate cause of trade in the modern approach is the same as in the classical: inequalities of relative commodity price ratios. The difference is that in the classical approach any probing for causes ceases with the acceptance of comparative cost differences, while in the modern approach an attempt is made to explain how cost ratios come to differ in the first place.

Most of the assumptions of the Heckscher-Ohlin approach are crucial for examining the role of factor supplies. The complete list of assumptions, however, makes for an unwieldy model — a model sometimes regarded as unrealistic and too restrictive. Several of the assumptions have recently come under critical attack and some of the conclusions are in doubt. The major assumptions of the simplified two-country, two-commodity, two-factor version of the Heckscher-Ohlin theorem, relevant to a study of factor supplies, are briefly stated here: [6]

1. perfect competition exists in factor and goods markets in both countries;
2. complete mobility of factors applies internally and complete immobility externally;
3. production possibility curves are concave to the origin, meaning that we are dealing with increasing cost industries and factors with partial substitutability;
4. techniques of producing identical goods are the same in both countries, meaning that a given bundle of tangible factors yields the same quantity of a given output in both countries;
5. the different production functions for the two commodities are linear and homogeneous, meaning constant returns to scale of inputs used;
6. factor intensity in the production of a commodity distinguishes production functions and goods can be uniformly classified by their factor intensity;[7]
7. factors are of identical quality in the two countries;
8. factor supplies are given, are fixed and are fully employed — though each country is differently endowed.

While the model is two-factor, two-commodity, and two-country the possibility of a multi-factor model, as Ohlin recognizes, is not antithetical to the major conclusions of the theory. The model implies, as Ford notes [21, p. 460], that the physical quantities of the factors can be measured and that hence the relative factor endowments can be compared. The greater relative abundance of one factor over another further implies that its price will be relatively lower. All comparisons in the Heckscher-Ohlin model are relative measures: we compare relative factor endowments of the two countries, relative factor proportions of the two commodities, and relative commodity prices in the two countries.

In two countries, A and B, the two factors, in units, are capital, K, and labor, L, and the two commodities, in units, X and Y. Country A is relatively more endowed with labor than country B.[8] Commodity X is relatively more labor-intensive than commodity Y; therefore Y is relatively more capital-intensive.

The absolute factor endowments, E, are:

in country A, $E_A = K^X + K^Y + L^X + L^Y$
in country B, $E_B = K^X + K^Y + L^X + L^Y$,

where superscripts are used to denote the commodity which draws on the factor inputs and where subscripts refer to the countries. All supplies of factors are fully employed. With no labor theory of value and no common physical measure of the two factors, there is no determinate real measure of E.

The relative factor endowments are indicated by:

$$\left(\frac{L}{K}\right)_A > \left(\frac{L}{K}\right)_B \quad \text{or} \quad \frac{L_A}{L_B} > \frac{K_A}{K_B},$$

where $K = K^X + K^Y$ and $L = L^X + L^Y$ in the respective countries. This simply indicates that A is relatively more abundant in labor than B. It follows from this statement that A is relatively less endowed with capital, and that B is relatively less endowed with labor and relatively more endowed with capital. Given any one of these statements, the other three are automatically determined.

The production functions for X and Y in both A and B are:

$$Q^X = F(K^X, L^X)$$
$$Q^Y = G(K^Y, L^Y).$$

The two outputs draw upon and hence compete for the two factors under the stipulated full employment conditions. The two outputs are produced in the two countries in precisely the same way; F and G have no nationality. The two sets of factors are not distinguished by productive capabilities peculiar to a location. There is the implication that technology has free international mobility, although capital and labor do not.

A commodity can be regarded as relatively labor-intensive when, at the same relative prices for the factors in both industries, it requires more units of L than K in each unit of output as compared with the other commodity. Given X is labor-intensive relative to Y:

$$\frac{L^X}{K^X} > \frac{L^Y}{K^Y} \quad \text{or} \quad \frac{L^X}{L^Y} > \frac{K^X}{K^Y}.$$

When either of the two commodities is stated as using one of the factors in greater proportions, the three other relative factor-intensity conditions follow automatically.

With production functions for each commodity the same in A and B, a series of isoquants showing various levels of output of the commodity X and another series for Y would be identical in the two countries. If no factor substitutability were admitted, only one productive process would exist and this would dictate the applicable factor intensity. With constant returns to scale and a single productive process, the maximum output would be limited by some multiple of the available supply of the relatively scarce factor. In this case, the transformation curve for outputs would exhibit constant opportunity costs over the whole range only if factor intensities were the same in both industries, meaning they used identical production processes. With a different process for each industry, the transformation curve would show two segments of constant opportunity costs and only one point — at which the opportunity costs changed — as a situation of full employment of the two factors.

The case of constant opportunity costs which can be derived from the classical assumptions of given factor endowments (although all factors are based on labor and production functions are the same for both industries), can be used to illustrate the simple effects of factor expansion on trade and specialization. In Figure 2-1, country A's constant cost production possibilities are represented by combinations of commodities X and Y along VU. Country B's constant cost production possibilities, HU, are added to A's to give a world transformation curve BWA. The figure VBW represents B's production possibilities with the origin at V rather than at O. The slope of BW (= slope of HU) indicates the marginal rate of transformation (MRT_B) of ˙one commodity for another in country B and the slope of WA (= slope of VU) indicates the MRT_A in country A. The curve BWA for the two countries is similiar to the transformation curve of a single country when factors are non-substitutable and single but different productive processes apply in each industry.

Obviously A has a comparative cost advantage in the production of commodity Y and normally will specialize in producing Y while country B will specialize in X. But if country B's output and hence factor inputs are very small, its available exportables will not meet country A's possible demands and MRT_A will dominate. On the other hand, if B is very large, country A's exportables will not be sufficient to meet B's demands and MRT_B will dominate. To show this we introduce world demand and indicate several sizes for country B relative to A. World production possibility curve BWA, is tangential at Z to a world consumer indifference curve assumed to be based on identical preference maps for the two countries. World prices then will be

89

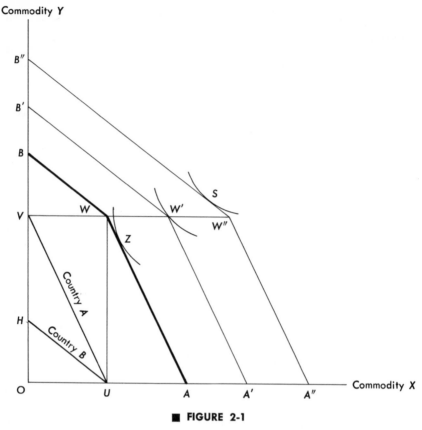

Commodity Y

Commodity X

■ FIGURE 2-1

equivalent to MRT_A or opportunity costs in A. Country B will specialize completely, but A will not since world demands for X are greater
than B's capacity to supply this commodity — given as OU. With a
growth in the factors and hence outputs of B so that the world production possibility curve becomes $B'W'A'$, the indifference curve through
W' is not tangential to the MRT of either country and both countries
will specialize. With a still greater expansion in B the world production
possibility becomes $B''W''A''$ and S becomes a point of tangency with
a higher world indifference curve. World prices then are dominated
by MRT_B and country A will specialize but B will not.

Absolute factor endowments of each country are significant in determining the relative trading prices, the pattern of trade, and the
extent of specialization — provided it is possible to sum the different
factors or give a definite statement that $(L/K)_A > (L/K)_B$. With the assumptions used, it can be said that small countries are more likely to
specialize than larger countries and economic growth is likely to ne-
cessitate diversification.

With some factor substitution, the production possibility curve does not exhibit constant costs, more than one production process is available, and more than one degree of factor intensity is possible. With the assumption of perfect competition among factors and full internal factor mobility, full employment of factors exists at all points on the transformation curve. As was shown in the earlier chapter, the transformation curves for the two countries are derived from their maximum efficiency loci in the box diagram.

Another version of the factor endowment model which focuses on world factor supplies is given in Figure 2-2. The factor endowments, K_A and L_A, of country A are represented by the box $XDOE$ and the factor endowments of B, K_B, and L_B are represented by the box $YJOH$ under the assumption that $(L/K)_A > (L/K)_B$. World labor supply, L_W, is given by XG and world capital supply, K_W, by YG. The curve XUO is the familiar maximum efficiency locus of country A in producing commodity X, measured from point X, and in producing commodity Y, measured from point O. Similarly, the curve OVY is the maximum efficiency locus of country B. At U and V, the ratio of marginal physical products of L and K are equal to relative factor prices and represent

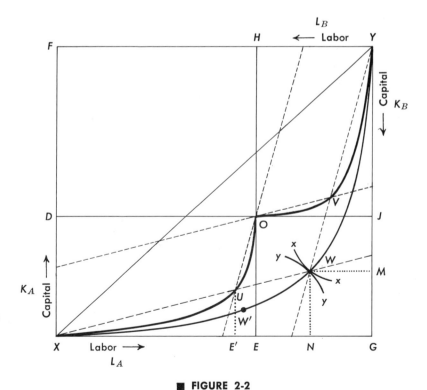

■ FIGURE 2-2

after-trade equilibrium points for the respective countries. The rays XU and OV indicate that the production of X is relatively labor intensive to the same degree in both countries and the rays OU and YV indicate that the production of Y is relatively capital intensive to the same degree in both countries.

The assumption carried over from the classical model — the assumption that factors do not move internationally — means that factor price equalization will be brought about by most cases of commodity price movements and trade. Both countries use more fully their relatively abundant factor. With the possibility of factor movement, however, factor price equalization will still occur and factor movement will act as a substitute for commodity movement [Ohlin 51, p. 169].

In Figure 2-2, the curve XWY represents the maximum efficiency locus of producing X and Y, using the given production functions and allowing factor movement between countries as well as between industries. World outputs of X and Y are represented by the isoquants xx and yy, respectively, which are tangential at W. The same factor intensities are used at these higher levels of output as at the lower because with constant returns to scale and the same relative commodity prices, relative factor prices will be the same and relative marginal productivities of the two factors in the two industries will be the same as before. The marginal product of labor is the same at U as at W and the marginal product of capital is the same at V as at W. Therefore the same proportion of factors will apply at W.

In order to achieve a higher output of X in country A, an immigration of labor from B equal to EN will have to occur. For country B the higher level of Y necessitates a flow of capital from A equivalent to JM. Both countries employ more of their relatively scarce factor as well as more of their relatively abundant factor in the expanded production of the commodity in which they have a comparative advantage. Factor movement between countries makes the XWY curve similar to the maximum efficiency locus of a single country where factors are free to move between industries. With factor movement possible, specialization in production is complete in both countries at the position given for W, as it would be for two industries. The result is the same as in the case of constant costs considered earlier where the size of each country is sufficient to ensure meeting possible exchanges of the other country. In the present case, small size means that factor movements will be proportionately greater for the small country just as small size means that commodity movements will be proportionately greater. With factor movement, trade is still undertaken if the original consumption preferences, which are assumed not to correspond with world production patterns, are preserved. Factor movement then is not a complete substitute for commodity movement.

Point W on the curve XWY is only one of the possibilities given by varying demand conditions. If production took place at W', country A would send to B some of both of its factors. Were production to take place in B's factor box, some of both factors would move from country B to A.

The relative size of countries can be indicated by varying the position of the DJ and HE lines in the box diagram of world factor supplies. The only condition necessary to pursue the Heckscher-Ohlin analysis is that $\dfrac{XD}{XF} \neq \dfrac{XE}{XG}$ or that $\left(\dfrac{L}{K}\right)_A \neq \left(\dfrac{L}{K}\right)_B$. Assume again no international factor mobility. If country A has only L_A equal to or less than XE' instead of XE and only K_A equal to or less than UE' instead of EO — so that O in effect is shifted to U — country A will produce only commodity X at the given world commodity price ratio. With O shifted to U, V will coincide with W and country B will produce some of both commodities. Specialization for country A would also occur if it had L_A greater than XN and more K_A than NW but less than would be given by any point along the line WY.[9]

The production from factors mobile only within countries compared with production from factors with complete international mobility is shown in Figure 2-3. The transformation curve for country B, BG, is added to the transformation curve for country A, HA, to produce a world transformation curve $B'WA'$. The pre-trade MRT_A is given by the slope at S and pre-trade MRT_B is given by the slope at R. At U and V, the $MRT_A = MRT_B$ and marginal productivities of the factors are equalized. The commodity price line, UCV, is tangential to the common indifference curve at C. On $B'WA'$, $U'C'$ is parallel to UCV, C' being the point of tangency to the world indifference curve which is double the consumption pattern at C so that $OC = CC'$.

If factor mobility is possible, another world transformation curve would be produced — given as $DC'F$. Despite the condition of constant returns to scale, there is no reason to expect that the employment of both factors of production in both countries in the production of commodity X would yield a higher level of output than the employment of the world's factors in producing X in a single country. One reason for this is that, if producing only X, the differently endowed countries use production processes different from those used by the world as a whole. The marginal productivities of the factors therefore will be different at the concentration points. Maximum production of commodity X, with factors separated by countries, will lie at A' and world maximum production of X will be at F. If one country is very small relative to the other in terms of factor endowments, there will be a greater divergence than that shown between the combined transformation curve $B'WA'$ and the world transformation curve $DC'F$.

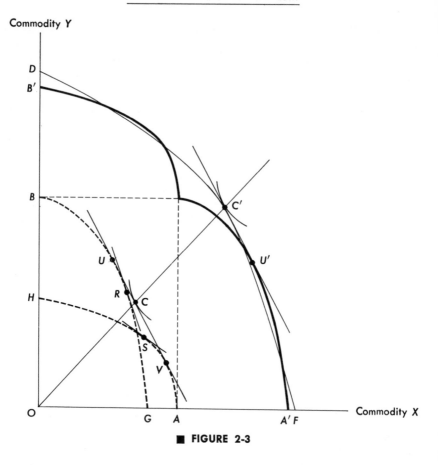

■ FIGURE 2-3

Further Implications of Factor Endowments and Factor Proportions

An extension of Heckscher-Ohlin trade theory has been provided by employing the input-output ideas of interindustry flows. Adopting the opportunity cost curve with the conventional assumption of fixed supplies of primary productive factors and given technologies, Vanek adds the assumption of possible substitutability between primary factors and of possible absorption of output from one industry as input of another; he is thus able to speak of an "input-output opportunity cost curve" [62, p. 135]. This ties together the transformation curve of productive capacities based on substitutable fixed factors and input-output analysis based on output substitutability and fixed production coefficients. In input-output analysis no factor substitution is usually admitted whereas in production possibilities, with changing opportunity costs, factor substitution is essential.

From a given production possibility curve of two outputs and two primary factors limited in supply and assuming fixed coefficients of one output used as input of the other output, Vanek derives an input-output opportunity cost curve shown as a concave curve, flatter than normally, lying inside the concave production possibilities curve. [62, p. 133]. All points on the curve correspond to given fixed relative factor endowments. With an increase in absolute endowments of a factor, the output of the product for which this factor is most intensive will also expand. This requires that output of the other commodity must be withdrawn from final consumption in order to provide inputs for the expanding industry. With demand conditions geared to comparable proportions of final consumption of the two commodities, relative factor endowments will still determine the commodity exported. This approach sustains the factor proportions theory of international trade by showing that it holds for both direct and indirect factors of production.

There are several definitional problems encountered in the notions of relative factor endowments, supplies, and proportions. If country B is relatively capital-rich, it has, physically, a higher proportion of capital to labor than country A — both types of endowments being fixed in supply. But relative factor abundance can be based on relative factor prices. For Ohlin, for example, the *pre-trade* ratio of factor prices in the two countries indicated relative factor abundance. In the capital-rich country then the price of capital before trade is relatively lower than the other factor. The pre-trade factor price ratios are related to pre-trade commodity prices. A third level of defining relative abundance is that based on relative factor intensity of exports [Lancaster, 36]. Only when factor endowments are defined in a physical sense, however, are commodity prices not necessarily related to factor proportions, since dissimilar demands can interpose to influence the relationship. The physical endowment differences as usually presented in the Heckscher-Ohlin model impart a bias on the supply side which does not ensure general validity of the proposition. Jones [32] shows that this bias is best seen in the relationships between the transformation schedules of the two countries. The transformation curves differ in shape because of different relative factor endowments. If relative endowments were in the same proportion, although not identical absolutely, the transformation schedule of one country would have a direct scale relationship to the other. With different endowments, however, different shapes in transformation curves are produced.

A relatively capital-rich country, B, has a production pattern favoring the capital-intensive commodity; it is able to expand output of this commodity at a lower opportunity cost than country A. However, country B may have a ratio of capital-intensive commodity prices to labor-intensive commodity prices higher, because of demand preferences, than the ratio in country A. By expanding output of its lower-priced commodity, country B will export it in exchange for capital-intensive commodities for which there is a greater relative demand. Thus, the Heck-scher-Ohlin theorem may not always be applicable in practice because of the demand conditions imposed.

The view has been expressed that, in evaluating the comparative cost doctrine of trade theory, the nature of trade rather than the gains from trade should receive prime consideration [Robinson 53, p. 169]. Robinson felt that a successful theory should be able adequately to account for the pattern of trade. He thought that, since both capital goods and raw materials are involved in trade, the notion of given relative factor supplies has little significance. He strongly attacked the basis of factor proportion theory, finding the assumptions too demanding and the argument tautological. By subsuming all supply phenomenon under uniform production functions and fixed factor endowments, nothing is left on the supply side to explain differing commodity prices.

Ford [21] maintained that two theories of trade emerge from Ohlin's idea.[10] He labeled these the "basic" and the "subsidiary" theories. The basic theory is derived from explicit and implicit assumptions, not completely realistic, although not damaging, to the theory in superficial testing. The subsidiary theory aimed at being more realistic. Ohlin clung to the conclusions of the basic theory as being the fundamental explanation of trade. The *cause* of trade for Ohlin was no different from the classical theory of comparative advantage: trade is caused by differences in relative commodity price ratios. The *basis* of trade, however, is given by the elements which cause differences in relative commodity price ratios. The only possible basis of trade then for Ohlin is an unequal endowment of productive factors in different countries. Ohlin's factor proportions theory was not a good \theory, according to Ford, because its premises were unrealistic and thus it failed the sternest test of a theory [21, p. 470]. The assumptions of perfect competition, equal factor qualities, no product differentiation, absence of increasing returns to scale, and identical production functions are not general in the real world. Furthermore, the Ohlin theory omits any socio-economic factors. Despite numerous criticisms, however, most writers agree that the basic theory of Ohlin was sound in being logically consistent and of value in being superior to the formulation based on labor-cost-theory which it sought to replace.

☐ EMPIRICAL STUDIES OF FACTOR PROPORTION THEORY

The factor proportions theory of trade has widespread acceptance, largely because of its simple explanatory variables and its apparent relevance to the practical world. It seems highly apt for trade in raw materials where differences in factor and resource endowment are easily discernible. Nevertheless, attempts to show convincingly the practical operation of the theory have been largely unsuccessful and its applicability to trade in manufactures remains largely illusory.

In order to test the factor endowment theory, verification of comparative differences in commodity prices and costs would have to be based on comparative differences in factor endowments. This seemingly easy task has not been satisfactorily accomplished. While many tests of comparative costs have been made to support the basic classical proposition, investigations into the apparatus behind comparative costs have turned up results which tend to disprove the factor endowment doctrine or at least to show exceptions to it. This in turn has accelerated intensive examinations of factor endowment theory.

Comparative Cost Analysis

One fairly recent test of the classical comparative cost doctrine was made by MacDougall [42]. He compared productivity in the United Kingdom with productivity in the United States — in light of the general rule that each country will export that commodity for which its output per worker, relative to the other country's output per worker, exceeds its money wage rate, relative to the other country's money wage rate. MacDougall [42, p. 697–98] pointed out that, before World War II, U.S. weekly wages in manufacturing were about twice those of the U.K. In industries where U.S. output per worker was more than double that of the U.K., the U.S. predominated in the export market; in industries where U.S. output per worker was less than double that of the U.K., the U.K. predominated in the export market. Although these countries were not trading with each other in all goods which possessed comparative advantage, this was due to the fact that tariff barriers, monopolistic competition, and transport costs in each country offset comparative advantage. It was concluded, therefore, that the analysis tended to support the comparative cost theory.[11]

Some critics of MacDougall's methods point out that many other variables were not considered — variables which might have been relevant to the study. For example, import preference differences and import-content of exports could influence the results. Likewise, the theory of non-competing groups showing industry differences in wage levels could affect export ratios in the two countries — an objection raised in several studies and summarized by Caves [12, p. 269–71].

An extension of the MacDougall study has been undertaken by Stern [55] who sought to verify comparative cost doctrine using ratios of output per worker, per unit labor costs, per unit net costs, and export prices of selected U.K. and U.S. manufactures. He aimed at explaining the relative export performance of the U.S. and the U.K. to third countries by comparing data for 1937, 1950, and 1959. Stern found that comparative costs, as indicated by the measures employed, accounted for comparative export performance in 1950 and 1959. The range of comparative costs narrowed between 1937 and 1959, since the U.K. increased productivity and exports in industries which normally are highly productive in the U.S. and the U.S. improved productivity in its low productivity industries. Technological communication and different patterns of technological development and factor substitution accounted for productivity and export changes.

MacDougall and others [43] have made a study which is in line with Stern's investigations but independent of them. It largely substantiates earlier findings, although it uses different samples and methods. This later study notes that tariffs, which by 1950 were no longer higher in the U.S. than in the U.K., were rarely an important offset to comparative advantage in 1950 as contrasted to 1937.

Kravis [35] likewise assessed the relative, short-run importance of various factors which influence the commodity composition of U.S. trade. He considered that differences in relative wages were not the controlling factor; differences in relative output per worker were probably more significant as explanations, particularly for third markets. His conclusions stressed the notion of "availability" as being of the greatest importance. When commodities are unavailable at home due to lack of natural resources in relation to demand, the comparative advantage doctrine is irrelevant.

Another and more recent test of comparative costs has been made by Balassa [2]. He examined recent U.K. and U.S. productivity figures for 28 selected industries producing roughly 42 per cent of manufacturing output in each country. Relative productivity differences were compared with export performance to third countries. Balassa found a high correlation between productivity ratios and export shares. No definite relationship between wage ratios and export shares could be established, however [2, p. 236]. Thus productivity advantages in a particular industry were not offset by higher wages.[12] Similarly, differences in capital cost per unit of output did not appear to influence exports. The classical position which, narrowly interpreted, assumed capital requirements did not vary significantly from commodity to commodity was therefore supported by Balassa's test. Differences in wage and capital costs seem far less successful than productivity differences in explaining international trade.

The Leontief "Paradox"

By extending the comparative cost test referred to above, MacDougall [42] conducted one of the earliest tests of the factor endowment theory. He endeavored to find out whether U.S. exports were relatively more capital-intensive than U.K. exports. This would have been shown if the U.K. had had a relatively smaller share of the world market — and the U.S. a relatively larger share — in relatively capital-intensive commodities. MacDougall measured capital intensiveness of comparable industries by reference to horsepower used at prevailing factor prices. His somewhat negative conclusion was that the U.K. did not tend to export to the U.S. commodities with low capital intensity relative to labor. Likewise the U.S. did not appear to be an exporter to the U.K. of relatively capital-intensive commodities. This test, however, cannot be regarded as adequate refutation of the factor endowment theory: the enquiries were not exhaustive, the samples were small, and neither horsepower nor net assets per dollar of receipts can be regarded as satisfactory measures of capital employed.

In one of the most widely discussed tests of the factor proportions theory, Leontief [38; 39] attempted to reveal the relative factor-proportions structure of U.S. participation in international trade. It was considered that a country's exports should contain relatively intensive inputs of relatively abundant domestic factors; imports should consist of commodities requiring relatively more of the relatively scarce domestic factors. Leontief's first study was based on computations from input-output tables constructed for the year 1947. He computed for various industries the direct and indirect capital and labor required to produce a given dollar value of output. He then calculated the effects on capital and labor use of a given reduction in both U.S. imports and exports so that the relative commodity composition of exports and imports remained the same. The conclusion was that the given value of U.S. exports embodied less capital and more labor than would be required to expand domestic output to provide an equivalent amount of competitive imports [38, p. 343]. Expressed inversely, U.S. import replacement industries required more capital relative to labor than did U.S. export industries.

The Leontief conclusion that, in the international division of labor, the U.S. specialized in labor-intensive rather than capital-intensive goods contradicted the widely accepted view derived from the Heckscher-Ohlin proposition. Since it was not doubted that the U.S. was relatively capital-abundant and relatively labor-deficient, it would seem that, following the theory, exports should be capital-intensive and imports labor-intensive. At first there was no dispute over the Heckscher-Ohlin proposition; rather there was a dispute over the particular empirical contradiction presented by Leontief. Leontief himself explained the contradiction by reference to measures of labor supply. A concept more relevant than treating labor as a homogeneous item internationally and measuring it in man-years would be treating it as "efficiency units" — of which the U.S., because it has more productive labor, has relatively more efficiency units than it has units of capital. Even working with the same amount of capital, the U.S. worker is more efficient than his foreign counterpart.[13]

Implications of the Leontief findings are that a marginal reduction of U.S. trade would release from the export industries relatively more labor than capital, compared with what would be required by import-replacing industries. Thus tariff protection would seem to harm United States labor and capital accumulation would tend to reduce the comparative advantage enjoyed by United States industry in international trade [Leontief, 38; Diab, 17, p. 56].

It has been maintained that Leontief's computations of capital-labor ratios in U.S. export and import replacement industries neglected the role of natural resources [Buchanan, 11; Vanek, 63]. Some evidence has also been produced to show that the factor structure of American exports and competitive imports mirrors relative resource scarcity rather than capital scarcity [Diab, 17, ch. 5; Vanek, 63]. The factor requirements ratios of exports and competitive imports have been calculated by Vanek:

	Exports/Competitive Import Replacement
Labor	1.07
Capital	.83
Natural Resources	.54

From these relationships it could be presumed that the U.S. is relatively well endowed with labor and relatively undersupplied with natural resources. If it is assumed that natural resources could substitute as well for labor as for capital, there are grounds for presuming that the U.S. is relatively well endowed with labor compared with capital. Capital and natural resources, however, appear to be strongly complementary. Vanek is thus able to offer the conclusion that although capital may actually be a relatively abundant factor in the United States, it appears to be in inputs relatively less abundant because scarce natural resources enter efficient production only in conjunction with large amounts of capital [63, p. 135].

Another attempt to verify empirically the factor proportions conclusion of the Heckscher-Ohlin theory of trade has been made by Bharadwaj [7]. This attempt, employing data compatible with that used by Leontief, endeavors to support widely held notions that Indian exports to the U.S. are labor-intensive compared to competitive imports which are relatively capital-intensive. The results depicted a situation for India, as Leontief showed for the United States, in direct contrast to what is usually expected in trade theory based on factor proportions. On the basis of the figures examined, Indian exports in 1951 were capital-intensive and not labor-intensive as usually understood.[14] Several conditions are offered as explanations of these particular violations of factor proportion theory: climatic conditions in the particular year examined, the existence of a higher degree of disguised unemployment in Indian primary industries than in Indian manufacturing industries, and extreme ranges of divergent production technologies.

Evidence accumulated so far does little to dispel the Leontief paradox. Factor endowment theory has not been validated by the empirical studies mentioned. On the other hand, the theory has not been replaced; it could be that the theory has not been really tested.

Explanations of Divergence between Theory and Fact

Many critics of Leontief's first study [38] concentrated on statistical and methodological matters. Most of their suggestions were accepted and tested by Leontief in his broader second study [39] which confirmed his earlier findings. Swerling [56], for example, questioned the statistical results of the first study and the validity of the capital-labor ratios used in the analysis. He argued that with low capital-labor ratios certain industries excessively influenced the results and that the results were biased by the way in which transport, commercial services, and wholesale trade were incorporated into the analysis. He also argued that capital-output ratios for agriculture and fisheries were excessively high. Another argument against capital-labor ratios employed was given by Buchanan [11] who maintained that Leontief's capital coefficients were essentially investment requirements coefficients unless the durability of capital was the same in all industries. This is so, Buchanan argued, because the coefficients show the amount of investment in capital goods for unit values of output used on the average in the various industries.

That the Heckscher-Ohlin theory cannot be put into reverse has been pointed out by Jones [32, p. 8]. He asserted that the theory cannot be used to infer factor endowments from trade patterns. Thus Leontief, in arriving at the conclusion that the U.S. is labor abundant if efficiency is taken into account, was not basing his analysis on relative factor endowments in different countries. He made no direct comparison of factor endowments in the U.S. with those abroad. It could be possible that *both* U.S. exports and import-competing products are produced in the U.S. with more capital-intensive methods than abroad.

Valavanis-Vail asserted that the method used by Leontief was inappropriate [58; 59]. The input-output approach, based on fixed input coefficients, Valavanis-Vail claimed, was logically incompatible with international trade analysis which usually assumes varying production processes to achieve full employment equilibrium. Caves takes issue with this explanation, pointing out that a fixed-coefficient production model usually implies less than full employment in one or more factors, although, operationally, coefficients vary less than other variables [12, p. 279].

Other lines of attack on the Leontief "paradox" tend to be directed not at statistical, methodological, or factual matters but at theoretical points which aim to reconcile the empirical findings with traditional theory. The non-statistical explanations of the Leontief paradox have been summarized as follows [Clemhout, 14]:

(1) that foreign labor yields less in efficiency units than U.S. labor (the explanation given by Leontief);
(2) that in the U.S. production functions differ from those of foreign countries;
(3) that the relationship of factor intensities between U.S. exports and imports is not clearly distinguished;
(4) that demand conditions in the U.S. absorb more of the commodities in which the U.S. enjoys a comparative advantage than it is able to supply.

The Leontief paradox cannot be explained by reference to some notion of superior entrepreneurship since what is required is some element raising the measure of labor productivity rather than that of capital [Mookerjee, 47, p. 76 fn]. Leontief's own explanation that U.S. labor is relatively more efficient than foreign labor, even when using the same amount of capital, could mean that entrepreneurship and managerial requirements are less per unit of output in the U.S. than abroad. This, however, suggests a lack of uniformity in the production functions. Furthermore, the existence of factors other than those explicitly included implies that the capital-labor production functions are not homogeneous and with multi-factor approaches the notion of factor intensity, essential for the Heckscher-Ohlin approach, becomes increasingly ambiguous. The existence of other factors destroys the symmetry of the theoretical two-factor model. Because the U.S. exports labor-intensive commodities, it is not necessary that it import capital-intensive commodities.

Clemhout [14] offers an explanation of the paradox in terms of differences in production functions. He aims at expanding the scope of the Heckscher-Ohlin theory so as to embrace a conclusion revealed by the Leontief study. It is possible that scarce factors other than labor and capital influence foreign trade structures, a possibility which was recognized but never systematically explored by Leontief. It is obvious that in actual situations relative prices are influenced by more than factor proportions. Relative efficiency among countries and industries is possibly one of these influences. While studies of relative efficiency are scarce, studies of production function differences are even more scarce.

Parameters which are of importance to differences in production functions are those measuring efficiency and returns to scale. Thus a country may have comparative advantages arising from relative efficiency or returns to scale quite apart from comparative advantages arising from relative factor proportions and natural endowments [14, p. 108]. There is no reason why these different types of comparative advantage must correspond for each industry. Exports, therefore, might occur for reasons other than factor proportions. It is possible that the Leontief structure of trade could be explained by these other influences. As an example of a special type of influence, Clemhout introduces tariff protection as the cause of different production functions [cf. Travis, 57]. In effect, Clemhout has tried to alleviate the conflict between the Heckscher-Ohlin theorem and the Leontief investigation by relaxing some of the assumptions on which the theorem is based.

In a systematic analysis, Travis [57] argues that the Heckscher-Ohlin theory is the only complete and general explanation of international trade. Using empirical data he shows that trade patterns fail to reflect relative factor endowments because of distorting tariff effects. Evidence was produced to show that Leontief's study essentially measured U.S. and foreign tariff effects on relative factor prices. He emphasises the need to incorporate relative degrees of protection in any positive trade theory.

If a country's demand conditions are sufficiently biased towards output using intensively its relatively abundant factor, exports may not agree with factor endowments. This has been emphasized by Robinson [53] and Valavanis-Vail [58]. If U.S. exports are unrelated to factor endowments because of demand biases, the U.S. would consume relatively more of its capital-intensive commodities. It seems, however, according to Brown [9], that the U.S. consumes relatively more of its labor-intensive goods such as services.

Ford [21, 22] doubts that Leontief's study refutes the basic Heckscher-Ohlin theorem. He points to several deficiencies in the study which debar it as an adequate test of the theory. Basing his attack on the methodological approach employed, Ford believes that the correct approach would have been to compare input coefficients for actual exports and actual imports rather than to compare input coefficients for export industries and competitive import-replacements as Leontief did. In order to use this method, it would be necessary to examine the production functions for outputs in the U.S. and in all other countries with which the U.S. traded [21, p. 466–67]. Import replacements are considered in the Leontief study in terms of productive practices in the U.S. and therefore are likely to be biased in favor of capital intensive practices. Ford felt that, with the favorable endowment of capital in the U.S. its general productive processes would tend to substitute capital for labor more readily than most other countries. Furthermore, import replacement could require materials not readily available in the U.S. but nevertheless capital-intensive in their production. In the U.S., Ford claims it can be expected that import replacement industries are capital-intensive compared to export industries.[15] He is thus able both to accept the

Leontief conclusions without rejecting the Heckscher-Ohlin theorem and to claim that the Leontief studies are no test of the theory.

The paradox then has not been resolved. On the one side, there is a closely knit theory of trade based on relative factor proportions. On the other side, weighty empirical studies have been made which show that the facts of the real world seem unlike the theoretical propositions. Clearly the theory requires more detailed scrutiny and the facts derived from empirical observations need refinement in order to adequately test the situation described by the theory or some modification of it.

□ CHANGES IN FACTOR SUPPLIES AND INTERNATIONAL TRADE

The matter of trade effects following a change in factor supplies is of increasing significance, particularly in connection with problems of economic development. It involves, from the world viewpoint, more efficient use of available factors of production or — what amounts to the same thing analytically — an overall improvement in the quality of the factors. Our concern in this section is with an autonomous change in factor supplies as occurs with economic growth and the effect of this on international trade. Factor supply changes through migration have already been considered. In a later section we will consider the effect of trade on factor supply.

In classical writings, there was an assumption of a given quanta of productive factors already in existence and in employment. The importance of the development of new resources and productive forces referred to in these earlier writings is only now being more fully realized. The interaction between trade and increase in factor supplies and the reverse was not overlooked by Ohlin[16] but he emphasized simple one-way causation and abstracted from the dynamic conditions of production and trade. Among more recent writers, Robinson [53], for example, recognized the overriding significance of international trade in providing the stimulus for creating *new* productive factors. He considers that the gains from the new factors exceed the gains derived from raising the marginal productivity of existing factors.

Basically, the Heckscher-Ohlin model assumed fixed factor supplies in the pre-trade situation. In the post-trade situation, relative factor supply changed in response to changing factor prices; it was the influence of trade on factor prices and hence on factor supplies that was the subject of much of the detailed analysis in Ohlin's work. Furthermore, much of the literature following the original formulation has been concerned with factor price equalization. The fixity of factor supplies makes the determination of relative factor endowments rather simple, since relative proportions are a constant and the factor relatively abundant can be easily identified. With changing relative proportions, however, relative factor abundance and relative factor scarcity are not easily determined.[17] Depending upon rates of change, one factor would not necessarily always be the relatively abundant factor. Thus, with factor change, particularly in a physical rather than a price sense, the basis of trade is severely affected.

Increase in a Single Factor — Rybczynski's Theorem

In investigating the effect of an increase in factor supply on production, consumption, and the terms of trade, Rybczynski [54], showed that — in the case of the two-country, two-commodity, two-factor model — when one factor increases autonomously, there is an absolute expansion in production of the commodity using a considerable quantity of the increasing factor and a reduction in the production of the commodity using relatively little of that factor. This analysis is based on an assumption of linear, homogeneous production functions and unchanged marginal rates of substitution in production with the same terms of trade. Rybczynski also showed that an increase in one factor would always lead to a worsening of the terms of trade or a decline in the relative price of the commodity using relatively more of the increasing factor. If the commodity is also the export commodity, external terms of trade would worsen; if it is an import commodity, external terms of trade would improve [54, pp. 340, 341].

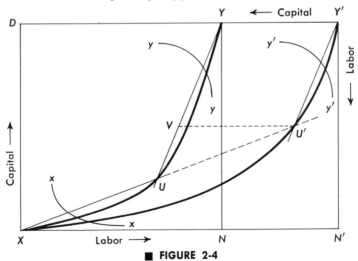

■ FIGURE 2-4

The Rybczynski theorem can be demonstrated by use of a box diagram for a single country as in Figure 2-4. Commodity X is relatively labor-intensive and Y is relatively capital-intensive. Output is in equilibrium at U on the maximum efficiency locus XUY. Labor (L) is now increased from XN to XN', capital endowment (K) remaining unchanged absolutely, at XD.

Point Y' is now the new origin of the series of isoquants showing production of the capital-intensive commodity; the origin of the xx isoquants remains at X. Through the origin Y', $Y'U'$ is drawn parallel to YU; XU is extended to XU'. Point U' is the intersection of these two lines and can be shown, as in Lancaster [36], to lie on the new maximum efficiency locus. The series of xx isoquants convex to X are intersected by XU and its extended version XU' at the same marginal rate of substitution of factors because the production function is linear and homogeneous. Likewise, $Y'U'$ intersects all yy isoquants, which are the same as those originally convex to Y, at the same marginal rate of factor substitution. At U' the marginal rates of factor substitution involved in producing X are the same as those involved in producing Y and U' lies on the new maximum efficiency locus.

Relative commodity output can be measured under linear conditions by the ratio of one radial from the origin X to another radial from Y' [Rybczynski, 54, p. 337]. Because $Y'U'/XU' < YU/XU$ and $Y'U' < YU$, the output of commodity Y must be less at U' than at U and the output of commodity X more.

The extent of the relative change in production can be shown geometrically by constructing VU' parallel to YY' so that $Y'U' = YV$. Then commodity X has increased in the proportion UU'/XU' and commodity Y has decreased in the proportion UV/UY.

Subsequent writers dealing with the Rybczynski theorem have tended to use an alternative diagrammatic presentation which has several advantages in dealing with economic growth [Mundell 48; Vanek 60]. One of these advantages is that it can show the effect of changing commodity prices and production. Figure 2-5 shows a production possibilities curve, PP, of commodity X, which is relatively labor-intensive, and commodity Y, which is relatively capital-intensive. As before, production functions are linear and homogeneous, diminishing returns apply, neither commodity is an inferior good, and it is assumed that the terms of trade remain unaltered. For this country, point N is the production point, point C is the consumption point, and the slope of CN indicates the given terms of trade.

With an expansion in L alone, more labor is available for the production of X and Y and the production possibilities curve moves outward from PNP to QMQ. On PNP, where N is the original production equilibrium at the given terms of trade, the relative exchange ratio between quantities of X and Y, the MRT, it given by the slope of CN. The tangent at N' has the same slope as the tangent at N and must lie on QMQ below NS, since the increase in L is used more intensively in the production of commodity X which expands more than proportionally

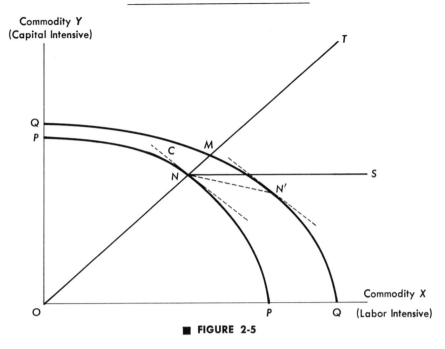

Commodity Y
(Capital Intensive)

Commodity X
(Labor Intensive)

■ FIGURE 2-5

compared with Y. This is the result which is given in the Rybczynski theorem. Since the supply of L has expanded, the relative factor price of L will fall and the price of commodity X will fall relatively to that of commodity Y. The curve QMQ then must be flatter than the curve PNP at point M which is on the production expansion path, OT, with relative marginal productivities remaining the same. With the slope of the tangent at N' equal to that at N, the original price ratio between commodities X and Y is preserved. Because neither of the commodities is an inferior good, the increase in output and income implies an increase in the consumption of both commodities absolutely. Irrespective of the demand conditions, however, the price of commodity X must have fallen relative to that of commodity Y and the ratio of the output of commodity X to the output of commodity Y will have increased.

If the terms of trade are allowed to move, production equilibrium for this country will not be at N' but at a point higher up on QMQ where the terms of trade are less favorable than those indicated at N and N'. The MRT then will not be equal to the slope of CN and its parallel through N'. More of the export commodity X will be offered in exchange for a given amount of the import commodity Y.

Increase in Two Factors

The Rybczynski analysis just discussed showed that an increase in one factor, say, labor, lowers prices of labor-intensive outputs relative to capital-intensive outputs. Rybczynski maintained that the analysis could be extended to show variations in quantities of two factors, although he did not develop this investigation. Other attempts have been made to show effects of increases in supplies of more than one factor.[18]

Corden [15] has examined the effects of economic expansion in one country, the other country remaining unchanged. It can be shown that if in a closed economy production expands along an expansion path with constant returns to scale, either due to an increase in labor productivity or capital stock, and demand also expands on a constant scale, the proportionate increase in output and demand must be the same at a given price ratio. Corden's concern was with the effects of possible output expansion in an open economy. He noted that the nature of the output depended on many items, including the relative rate of productivity increase, relative factor intensities, relative factor expansion, and relative economies or diseconomies of scale [15, p. 225]. Necessarily with expansion and unchanged prices, the output of import-competing goods became a smaller fraction of total output relative to the amount of imports in consumption; import demand expanded faster than domestic output of import-replacements; and domestic demand for exportables expanded at a slower rate than output. In general, the result is a worsening of the terms of trade for the expanding country. Using the Rybczynski theorem, Corden extended his conclusions to show that the trading conditions could be derived without considering demand conditions. If an output expansion was in the export industry only and there was a greater relative increase in the commodity using the factor more intensively (the exportable), there was a deterioration of the terms of trade. If, in contrast, the output expansion was in the import-replacement industry only, the terms of trade must improve [15, p. 227].

Extending single factor growth to multiple factor growth involves comparing relative rates of growth. If both L and K expanded at the same rate in one country, so that relative endowments were unchanged, then, under the usual assumptions of factor proportions theory and the assumption of fixed terms of trade, there would be a uniform increase in outputs of X and Y and the MRT would be unaffected. If, however, the rates of factor change are not equal, distortions in relative output would take place, depending upon relative factor ratios in production processes.

The Rybczynski theorem has been expanded and put into more general form by Amano [1], although a similar examination by Guha [23] is more complete. Consider a proportionate rate of increase in one factor, say, L, greater than in another, K. In terms of Figure 2-6 this means that from the initial endowment, labor expands NN'/XN while capital expands DD'/XD and $NN'/XN > DD'/XD$. Amano shows that an absolute output expansion in commodity X, which uses relatively more of L, and an absolute curtailment in the output of commodity Y occurs only if the ratio of the absolute increase in labor to the absolute increase in capital is less than the ratio of L and K used in commodity X [1, p. 413]. That is, if ΔL is the absolute increase in labor ($=NN'$) and ΔK the absolute increase in capital ($=DD'$), while L^x and K^x are the factor inputs used in producing X, the condition for the above proposition to hold is: $\Delta L/\Delta K > L^x/K^x$.

If in Figure 2-6, point U is the pre-expansion equilibrium output of commodities X and Y, then the increase in the two factors will shift output to a new point at U', the intersection of XU extended, and $Y'U'$ which is parallel to YU. Both commodities are still produced by relative factor proportions identical with the pre-expansion proportion, but the relative outputs will have changed. Let us construct UP parallel to YY', the slope of which indicates the given relative expansion of labor to capital. Now the original output of commodity Y, YU, is indicated by $Y'P$. In order to show when the output of commodity X expands more than the output of Y, it is necessary to show when $UU'/XU > PU'/Y'U'$ under differing relative increases in the factors. In the example given, commodity X expands greater proportionately than commodity Y, since UU'/XU is greater than $PU'/Y'U'$.

Likewise for any increase in labor relative to an increase in capital greater than that indicated by the slope of YG, which is the relative factor proportions in the initial endowment, the labor-intensive commodity X

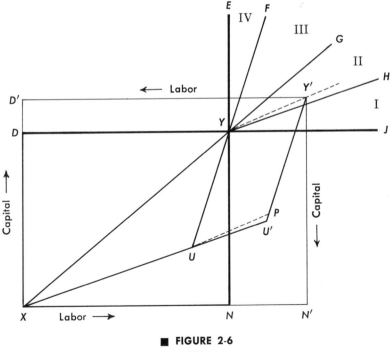

■ **FIGURE 2-6**
109

will increase proportionately more than the capital-intensive commodity Y. If, however, the relative increase in factors is that indicated by the slope of YF, which corresponds to the factor intensity of producing commodity Y and shows that the relative increase in K is greater than the relative increase in L, then point U' will coincide with U. The output of commodity X will remain unchanged while commodity Y will expand. Thus the crucial relationship for the relative change in outputs and hence their relative prices is the relationship of the incremental labor-capital ratio to relative factor intensities of productive processes [Guha 23]. The labor-intensive commodity will increase in output relative to the output of the other commodity only if the incremental labor-capital ratio is greater than the labor-capital ratio used in the productive process.

The results can be summarized by considering four possible zones of expansion as indicated in Figure 2-6. Zone I, for example, is given by the zone JYH where YH is parallel to XU, the factor proportions of the labor-intensive commodity X. In this zone, the increment of labor to capital is greater than the input of labor relative to capital in the production of X. The table below summarizes relative output results:

Zone	Change in Factor Supply	Factor Intensity	Change in Relative Output
I.	$\dfrac{\Delta L}{\Delta K}$ $>$	$\dfrac{L^X}{K^X}$	$\uparrow X, \downarrow Y$
II.	$\dfrac{\Delta L}{\Delta K}$ $<$	$\dfrac{L^X}{K^X}$	$\Delta X > \Delta Y$
III.	$\dfrac{\Delta K}{\Delta L}$ $<$	$\dfrac{K^Y}{L^Y}$	$\Delta X < \Delta Y$
IV.	$\dfrac{\Delta K}{\Delta L}$ $>$	$\dfrac{K^Y}{L^Y}$	$\downarrow X, \downarrow Y$

Zone I is obviously equivalent to the Rybczynski case, where output of commodity X increases and that of Y decreases. If expansion is along YH, the output of commodity Y is unchanged; if expansion is along YG, the output of both commodities increase in the same proportions; and if expansion is along YF, the output of commodity X remains unchanged. Expansion along YJ and YE are single factor expansion paths where the Rybczynski theorem holds.

In the above analysis, relative commodity prices were held constant — a possible type of growth in a small country facing price patterns determined in the international economy. In the normal case of an open economy, however, the terms of trade would turn against the country if the output using more of the strongly growing factor were exported.

If the assumption of fixed factor supplies of the traditional model is relaxed, the elasticity of labor supply with respect to changing wage rates becomes greater or less than zero. In a study by Kemp and Jones [33], the authors take the view that a removal of the assumption makes possible a reduction in the output of a commodity in association with an increase in its price. A backward-bending offer curve is also possible, so that a larger quantity of imports is demanded at a higher price associated with a deterioration in the terms of trade. In order to produce this result, the labor supply must decline with rising wages at a faster rate than the decline in output of importables associated with increasing prices. This is necessary because — to take the reverse case — when labor supply increases, the rising income induces more importables demanded at the same time as the output of importables increases. The perverse results which the authors develop use an elasticity of labor supply of less than zero and depend on income inducements to importables being greater than output effects on importables.

The possibility of factor-intensity reversal destroys the tightness of the Heckscher-Ohlin theorem concerning factor proportions and trade patterns. Nevertheless, another dimension is added. Countries with abundant labor and low wages, for example, might obtain a comparative advantage in capital-intensive industries where there is a low elasticity of substitution between capital and labor. This development may be possible because, technologically, a given capital intensity determines the feasible minimum size of plants independently of relative factor prices. At larger sizes, factor proportions can be varied depending upon factor substitutability. The phenomenon of factor-intensity reversal destroys the predictive powers of the factor-proportions theory with respect to the direction of trade [cf. Robinson, 53, p. 174 and Minhas, 45, p. 154].

Influence of Technological Progress on Factor Supplies and Trade

The assumption of similar and unchanged production conditions in the trading countries facilitates many of the conclusions of factor proportions theory concerning trade patterns. It is quite possible, however, for differences in technology to be the basis for trade in the absence of differences in factor endowment.[19] In the Heckscher-Ohlin model, of course, the level of technique was assumed to be constant and identical for the countries involved. In the classical approach, technology as an influence in trade was traced largely through effects on the terms of trade. In recent years, the role of technological change has assumed considerable importance in international trade theory as well as in certain branches of general economic theory. Both the long-run dollar imbalance and economic development of backward countries, for example, have been viewed as problems of international trade involving differentials in technological advance.

The nature of technological change has not been uniformly dealt with. The most common view of technological progress is of a change

111

in the production function.[20] Technological change may involve higher output with unchanged combinations of factor inputs or increased efficiency of one input relative to another. It may also involve the increase in effective factor supply. Innovations, for example, have been classified by reference to their effect on factor supply. Johnson [29], in examining effects of technological change, treats a labor-saving innovation as equivalent to an increase in the marginal productivity of capital and in the "effective" supply of labor. A neutral technological improvement has been regarded as one in which factor proportions remain constant for the same level of output with unchanged factor prices. The same absolute combination of factors, however, produce at higher levels of output [Vanek, 60, p. 26].

In technological progress, where the restrictive assumption of neutral innovations is employed, factors of production are combined in the same proportions before and after trade. Johnson [29] claimed that if there was neutral technical progress in one industry, no change in the technology of the other industry, and if total factor endowments remained unchanged, then output of the other industry would fall, provided relative commodity prices remained constant.[21] It was not necessary that exports occur in that commodity using most intensively the factor with which a country was most heavily endowed.

Technical progress need not occur in all industries at the same rate. Similarly, it may affect factors of production differently. Findlay and Grubert [20] have reconsidered and restated the various cases of technical progress. In speaking of neutral technical progress, meaning a reduction in the quantities required to produce a given quantity of output, in the same proportion, Findlay and Grubert show that such progress has the immediate effect of raising output in the industry in which it occurs and of reducing costs of initial factor prices. If factor prices are to be retained at the same level, it must be assumed that factors shift from other industries to the improved industry.

By influencing factor supply, either relatively or absolutely, technological change has impacts on relative outputs as between industries, as well as between countries. Under technological progress, the shape of the production possibilities curve will alter, thus affecting both the relative commodity prices and the quantities of goods exchanged internationally.

Role of Natural Resources in Development and Trade

Although the Heckscher-Ohlin theory and comparative cost approach recognized the role of natural resources in affecting comparative commodity prices, almost all of the analyses developed concentrate on labor and capital. Empirical studies made from time to time usually provide measures in terms of labor and capital. The reason for such concentration is that the study of resource structure in foreign trade presents unusual difficulties mainly in the matter of measurability. There are very few meaningful ways of measuring natural resource availability and employment. Kindleberger points out that natural resources must be described in relation to a given technology; changes in technology change the characteristics, the availability, and the value attached to natural resources [34, pp. 28, 29]. Frequently, the natural resource factor is inseparably combined with other factors, particularly capital. Nevertheless, size of land area, its fertility, the distribution of minerals and fossil fuels, and other aspects of natural resources, combined with the availability of labor, capital, and technology, make for the differences in endowment which is basic to the development of foreign trade.

The way in which resource elements enter into a country's foreign trade and the way in which the relationship may be affected by changes in factor endowments, technology, and demand conditions have been examined by Vanek in both theoretical and empirical terms [60; 63]. He grapples with the measurement problem as one of the first tasks. Vanek rejects the notion of economic rent as a measure of natural resources employed and instead employs the notion of "value of resource products." Resource products are all commodities using natural resources in their productive processes [63, p. 10]. The resource content of resource products, Vanek observes, is on the average much greater than the resource content in highly fabricated products. It is assumed that any change in resource products included in exports and imports can be taken to reflect changes in resource content of foreign trade generally [63, p. 11]. Capital and labor can be viewed as a joint factor so that the model continues to be essentially a two-factor one.

Long-run development means an outward extension of the transformation curve and a consumption path leading to higher levels of national economic welfare — as indicated in Figure 2-7. The long-range relationship between production and consumption will be influenced by the prospects of foreign trade. Vanek's hypothesis is that natural resources in foreign trade will reflect the relative abundance of this factor in the economy; the natural resource content of foreign trade will change with changes in relative abundance of natural resource [63, p. 14]. An economy with a relatively abundant supply of one factor will tend to expand so as to exploit this factor. Output of the commodity using this factor more extensively will be increased relatively more than the other commodity and will become the exportable item. Thus for the American economy in 1870–1880, land was the relatively abundant factor supply and land-intensive commodities were the major exports. Natural resources tended to become relatively more scarce as capital and population increased. Capital-labor-intensive commodities offered increasing potential in foreign trade so that the United States turned from acting as a

Natural Resource-
Intensive Commodities

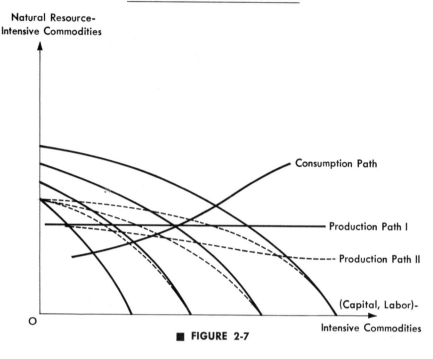

Consumption Path

Production Path I

Production Path II

(Capital, Labor)-

O

Intensive Commodities

■ **FIGURE 2-7**

net exporter of resource products and a net importer of capital-labor intensive products, to acting as a net importer of resource products and a net exporter of the capital-labor intensive products.

The results which arise from disproportional growth in the various factors are similar to those arising from technological improvement. Unchanged factor endowments, combined with a faster rate of technological improvement in one industry than in another, produce outcomes very much the same as uneven increases in factors with no technological improvement. In Figure 2-7, the series of unbroken transformation curves are produced by technological improvements in capital-labor-intensive industries at faster rates than in other industries which produce commodities intensive in natural resource inputs.

One important difference is dealt with by Vanek [63, pp. 29–30]. If technology were stationary in the resource sector and advancing in the capital-labor-intensive industry so as to provide incomes equal to those produced by a growth of factor supplies, there would be a greater effect on trade than that produced by factor growth alone. Technological improvements in a single industry expand output of that industry, leaving the other industry unaffected; but factor increases, by being substitutable as between industries, add something to both outputs under most conditions. Thus there would be a greater change in relative commodity prices with biased technological growth than with factor growth and greater comparative cost differences in international trade. This is shown in Figure 2-7 where the series of broken transformation curves represent one-sided technological change. The consumption path remains unchanged in the two situations but production path II tends to be more negatively sloped in the case of one-sided technological change than in the other case represented by production path I. Thus international trade, which is the difference between the consumption and production paths, would be relatively greater.

In the empirical analysis, Vanek established within reasonable limits the expected impact of technology and natural resource scarcity on the relative resource requirements of U.S. trade [63, p. 107]. In the case of mineral resources, demand conditions or other factors were probably responsible for changes in the mineral resource content of foreign trade. Mining and manufacturing seem to have increased in efficiency faster in the U.S. than abroad, while agriculture showed no divergent trend. The Malthusian dilemma of population growth relative to natural resources is put aside by Vanek who points to the fact established by his own studies and by others that the apparent scarcity of the world's natural resources has changed relatively little in the past century [63, p. 137]. For the U.S., however, in contrast to the rest of the world, natural resources, especially non-renewable resources, have become scarce relative to other factors. This would have occurred even in the absence of foreign trade which fostered greater use of natural resources.

The economic development of the less developed countries will, because of these trends, cause a relative decline in the economic superiority of the countries already well developed [63, p. 137]. The underdeveloped countries are largely net exporters of natural resource-intensive commodities and the developed countries are net importers. With greater population growth in underdeveloped than in developed countries, the relative abundance of natural resources to labor declines more rapidly for the underdeveloped than for the developed, with the consequence that patterns of international trade are certain to alter with respect to resource content. Natural resources in the future will become comparatively less abundant in the developing countries than they are at present and so they will tend to figure less in the exports of these countries [63]. A more rapid rate of technological innovation and capital formation or a reduction in uneven population growth in the developing countries would offset these trends.

Economic Development and International Trade

Many of the matters considered in earlier portions of this section have dealt with elements of growth and their impact on foreign trade. The nature of the growth and a country's stage of growth naturally influence the trade structure in different ways.[22] Most theories of economic development give considerable attention to the international aspects of development. In this connection there is a two-way influence — that of development on trade and that of trade on development. In this section attention is directed primarily at the influence of development on trade, abstracting from the possibility of factor movement between countries.

Factor proportions are significant in helping to explain the relationships between economic development and trade. Differential rates of growth of factors, of factor efficiency, and of technology — all culminating in differential rates of economic development — alter basic comparative advantages and induce trade changes. Undoubtedly, economic development involves an increase in the capital/labor ratio and makes possible capital deepening. Given that underdeveloped countries are relatively deficient in capital, imports initially might comprise capital-intensive commodities and exports might comprise labor-resource intensive commodities, although much of the capital for social overhead cannot be imported directly and domestic capital can be increased if imports free productive factors. After an initial expansion in foreign trade under the stimulus of economic development, foreign trade seems to decline proportionately to total economic activity. This tendency of a declining share of the international sector has been partially confirmed by empirical studies, although there are many uncertainties and exceptions not explained [Kindleberger, 34, p. 179].

In economic growth, foreign trade can be enlarged because of increased income and its influence on imports. For equilibrium to be maintained in the growing country, a rate of growth of exports has to be established which will permit a balance between growing effective demand and productive capacity. Johnson [29] has maintained that a growth rate of exports permitting equilibrium growth at a constant rate can only apply when the country's initial equilibrium rate of output growth is equal to the initial rate of growth of return on capital.

There is the vital question of whether imports increase more than proportionately to the increase in national output, or in the same proportion, or less than proportionately to the increase in output. Growth then can be viewed as making the country relatively less self-sufficient, relatively more self-sufficient, or leaving it with the same degree of self-sufficiency. This raises, in turn, the question of whether exports of the foreign country or the rest of the world increase at rates faster or slower than to its growth in output or equal to it.

Three types of growth have been considered [Johnson, 29; 30; 31]:

(1) pro-trade biased growth which increases the country's demand for imports or supply of exports more than in proportion to the expansion of output;

(2) neutral or unbiased growth which increases the country's demand for imports or supply of exports in proportion to the expansion of output;

(3) anti-trade biased growth which increases the country's demand for imports or supply of exports less than proportionately to the expansion of output.

In addition to these three cases, two extreme cases are considered: in ultra-pro-trade bias, expansion reduces the supply of importables; in ultra-anti-trade bias, the expansion reduces the supply of exportables. The effect of growth on import demand results from the effect of growth on consumption and domestic supply. Consumption and production shifts could be biased in the same direction or they could be biased in opposite directions. The major types of economic growth have different effects on the trade patterns involved. Johnson distinguishes growth due to technical progress, growth due to population increase, and growth due to capital accumulation. In technical progress, the production functions of the economy are altered, whereas with population increases and capital accumulation, there is an addition to the quantity of productive factors but no alteration of production functions. The various effects of the three major types of economic expansion through consumption effects and production effects on trade are summarized in a general proposition: expansion will lead to an increase in the developing country's demand for imports.[23] Expansion in either country or in both will turn the terms of trade against the faster developing country.

An analysis by Black [8] shows how trade balances and the terms of trade change between two countries when supplies of exports and demands for imports in each country change with economic development. It is assumed that each country deals in four commodities — exportables, importables, a commodity which is produced but not exported, and another which is consumed but not produced. This approach makes it possible to separate long-run demand and supply influences at work in a partial equilibrium model. It is further assumed that the proportion in which the fixed total of productive effort is divided between the production of non-trade goods and exports in each country is determined by relative prices of goods. Export supply curves are based on the assumption that price levels of home non-traded goods are held constant.

Shifts in demand and supply curves depend on the form of development which may be export- or import-biased because of consumption influences or production changes. In examining instances of ultra-bias on both export and import sides, Black found, on the one hand, that the home country's trade balances tend to improve with a faster rate of growth of the foreign country and with more export biased development of foreign demand [8, p. 211]. On the other hand, export bias in the development of foreign supply worsens domestic trade balances in the circumstance that domestic demand price elasticity exceeds unity.

The attention given to effects of economic development on international trade has given concern in some quarters to the possibility of harm to the growing country. This has been termed "immiserizing growth" by Bhagwati [5]. If the economic expansion is confined to one country, for example, and it increases output sufficiently, the terms of trade may deteriorate to such an extent that the economic gains to the country become negative. To Bhagwati, the crucial conditions for immiserizing growth are an inelastic offer curve by the rest of the world and a reduction of domestic production of importables at constant relative commodity prices. This reduction in output of importables caused by economic growth agrees with the Rybczynski theorem and can be produced with relatively simple assumptions.

It has been claimed that differences in factor proportions between developed and underdeveloped countries have led to restrictions on the pace of development in underdeveloped countries [Eckaus, 18]. The particular problem is seen as one of dualism in which the underdeveloped country is split into two sectors. One sector is directly involved in foreign trade; the other is remote from this type of activity. Production for the country is export biased and the export sector is the developing area surrounded by a low productivity region. In the advanced sector, methods of production are capital-intensive. Technical coefficients are relatively fixed and average income is relatively higher. In the backward sector, production is labor-intensive and the factors of production are usually combined in variable proportions. As a consequence, inflows of foreign capital to the advanced sector reduce employment opportunities for labor in the area dominated by capital-intensive activities. Increased population growth in the advanced sector is forced back into the underdeveloped region where variable input coefficient operations apply. Disguised unemployment, therefore, becomes apparent in this region. Technological progress takes place in the capital-intensive, fixed-coefficient sector and labor-saving innovations reduce still further the capacity of the advanced sector to create employment opportunities. At the base of this development is the growth of exports which promoted the advanced sector and retarded the backward sector.

International Trade and Economic Development

One of the new areas of controversy in international trade theory involves the role of trade in economic development. On the one side, there is the view that trade is the important engine of growth for facilitating development in advanced and unindustrialized countries. On the other side, there is the view that international trade inhibits the development of the poorer countries.[24]

The problem can be stated as a conflict between the gains from trade and the gains from growth [Meier, 44, p. 153; Chenery, 13, p. 15]. Meier emphasizes that if production increases are according to comparative advantage and trading occurs at the international exchange ratio, there is a gain or increase of real income because of more efficient resource allocation. This is equivalent to an outward shift in the country's production frontier, even in the case of fixed resources and unchanged techniques of production. Most of traditional trade theory accepts the view that gains from trade are equivalent to gains from growth; one follows the other.

The early formulations of trade theory, such as those of Adam Smith, pointed to the allocative efficiency of production as an important consequence of international trade. After that time, however, effects of trade are most frequently expressed in terms of gains from trade. Trade has different impacts on different countries depending upon "reallocative ability" [25] and most contemporary approaches deal with trade effects for separate categories of countries — developed and underdeveloped.

Classical economists saw the major effect of trade on domestic factor supply as an increase in the capital stock [Meier, 44, p. 158]. As real income increases, the capacity to save rises and international trade facilitates more efficient resource allocation for this purpose. The broadening of the market through overseas trade stimulates investment, particularly under conditions of increasing returns. Extended markets also permit economies of large-scale production and the adaptation of the most advanced techniques of production. In short, trade makes possible a greater and more economical use of domestic factor supplies. Static gains from better utilization of resources were supplemented by a greater access to technology, skills, and managerial talent, to capital equipment, and to raw materials as well as by the extension of competition. From these generalizations the classical economists concluded that international trade was the great stimulant to economic development.

Along with the classicists, many proponents of factor endowment theory saw economic development following trade, although there is a growing view to the contrary [Chenery, 13]. The factor-proportions model of Heckscher-Ohlin suggested that factor price changes, which were brought about by trade, were instrumental in altering the use of factors of production.[26] Factor reallocation, however, did not necessarily result in a reallocation of gains from trade. As is accepted in traditional trade theory, a country under conditions of free trade is able to move to a higher level of consumption than prevailed before trade. However, frequently it may be prevented from doing so by inflexible factor prices. Welfare, nevertheless, can still be increased and the gains from international trade realized by a reallocation of consumption. Gains are realized by a reallocation of consumption rather than by a reallocation of production.

Much depends upon reallocative ability, a condition which tends to distinguish the developed from the underdeveloped country. In the developing country with factor price inflexibility, output of the import-competing commodity with greatest use of the factor subject to inflexible returns will decrease [Linder, 41]. Unemployment of the factor will result. Losses in economic welfare may be greater than the gains obtained from consumption reallocation. Such conditions are likely to prevail in underdeveloped countries where the reallocative ability is very low. Factor price flexibility which entails factor reallocation, therefore, will ensure the realization of some gains from trade. For these countries, where there is a lack of reallocative ability or an absence of factor flexibility, the opening-up of trade may be to their long-run disadvantage.

Empirical evidence has been used in many instances to show that economic development does not follow from foreign trade. In contrast to the traditional theory, there is a belief that considerable growth in foreign trade does not always produce sustained domestic development. Nevertheless, many countries can point to successful development which has followed foreign trade. Exports of both industrial products and raw materials have made contributions to these successful cases of economic development. One of the marks of an underdeveloped country today is the high proportion of total activity in foreign trade. It is to be noted too that much of the policy advocated in national economic councils is to make the proportion higher. National economic policy has to begin with, and operates most immediately upon, natural resources and factor endowments — and their value is usually higher in world use than regional use.

FOOTNOTES

1. The theorems of international trade have been neatly arranged into theorems in statics, theorems in comparative statics and theorems in dynamics by Bhagwati [6].

2. Caves has stressed the contrast between the classical comparative cost model and the "separate group of model builders, claiming the Scandinavian ancestry of Wicksell and Cassel" [12, pp. 5, 93]. He notes that Heckscher-Ohlin give considerable emphasis to production processes, whereas the classical writers avoided detailed discussions of this area after assuming production processes were the same in all industries of a country, although different as between countries. See Wijnholds [66].

3. The origin of the doctrine is seen as a development of the criticism of mercantilist policy. Viner has dealt with origins in great detail [64, Ch. VIII].

4. Haberler first propounded the opportunity cost theory of value in 1936 never claiming that any difference existed between the opportunity cost approach and the "outright income approach" which is derived from an extension of real cost considerations [24, pp. 12, 13]. Vanek, however, shows that the "opportunity cost and real cost theories of value, if properly stated, are perfectly compatible" [60].

5. The original refinement by Ohlin is given in [50] which was subsequently incorporated and improved in his best known work, completed in 1931 [51].

The originality of the Heckscher-Ohlin approach — as distinct from the theory — has been questioned by Viner; he points to commonplace expressions of the theory in the 16th century. See J. Viner's contribution in *Ekonomi, Politik, Samhalle* (Stockholm 1959) cited in Linder [41, p. 15]; also Viner [64, pp. 500–16]. Ohlin himself expresses awareness of earlier statements of the basic idea of his theory [51, pp. 30–34].

6. These are derived from Ohlin [51, Ch. I and 5 and Appendix 1] and are given varying emphasis in Bharadwaj [7, pp. 106, 107]; Caves [12, pp. 38–44]; Ford [21, pp. 460–63]; Mookerjee [47, Ch. II, III].

7. Thus a commodity which is capital-intensive in one country is automatically capital-intensive in the other. The second commodity in both countries is consequently labor-intensive. A commodity classified as intensive in one of the factors remains so, irrespective of relative factor prices. A commodity is intensive in one of the factors if relatively more of that factor is used in one output than in another.

8. A country can be regarded as relatively well endowed with capital if it possesses more units of capital per unit of labor than does another country [Ford, 23, p. 274]. This will mean that the second country is relatively well endowed with labor.

9. Some proof of this is given in the discussion of corresponding points given later. See also [Lancaster, 36; and Travis, 57, p. 18].

10. Other writers have detected two separate theories of comparative advantage in Ohlin's work; one is more fully analyzed than the other but the two are not compatible. Note Laursen [37]. Ford would like to replace the Heckscher-Ohlin theory by what he calls a "development stage theory" of trade which would employ the concept of relative factor endowments but modified by less restrictive assumptions [21, p. 476].

11. Although the data do not support factor proportions theory, it has been pointed out that the figures of horse-power used are inadequate measures of capital [42, pp. 707–8]. Note Hoffmeyer [26].

12. High productivity and high wages do not necessarily go together; this is in opposition to the common contention that they do. Likewise, the low correlation found by Balassa between export shares and wage ratios refutes the common arguments that low wages determine export patterns [2, p. 238]. See Beckmann [4].

13. Leontief subsequently produced another computation involving more industries and weighting labor in each sector by its average wage [39]. These results arrived at similar paradoxical conclusions.

14. A similar, paradoxical picture emerges from an empirical study of Canadian-U.S. trade and Canadian-U.K. trade. See Bhagwati [6, p. 25] and Travis [57, pp. 194–96]. French-U.S. trade and factor structures yields a similar conclusion [Travis, 57]. Note Balogh [3].

15. To replace imports by its own production would require relatively more of the scarce factor in the United States [cf. Ford, 21, p. 467; Ellsworth, 19, p. 280; Kravis, 35].

16. He states for example: "The supply of productive factors is not given once for all, nor is it variable only under the influence of circumstances which have nothing to do with trade and pricing. . . . The supply of industrial agents may sometimes more adequately be described as the *result* of trade than as its

cause." [51, p. 67]. In developing his basic model, Ohlin assumes the supply of factors to be constant and given [51, pp. 18, 553]. But, in examining trade effects he tends to treat the supply of a factor as a function of factor price [51, pp. 19, 129].

17. Caves points out that the situation is determinate in a general equilibrium model if the factor supply is a unique function of its own real wage [12, p. 102]. He observes that changing factor supplies is more a matter of economic theory in general than of international trade theory in particular.

18. Mishan has suggested, however, that it would be difficult to make unambiguous generalizations about multi-factor changes [46].

19. Linder, for example, has attempted to discount the factor endowment theory of trade by endeavoring to show the relationship between high incomes and trade in manufactures where technological change is more relevant than factor endowments [41]. Posner examines the conditions under which trade may take place through differences in technical change apart from differences in factor endowments [52].

20. Vanek uses "technological change" and "change of total productivity" as synonymous. He finds that they agree in general usage with "efficiency," meaning a change of the production function in contrast to movements on a single production surface [60, p. 26].

21. The proposition which requires that diminishing returns apply as a sufficient condition can be extended to a case of more than two goods and factors [Bhagwati, 5, p. 205; Findlay and Grubert, 20, p. 112]. In general, a country undergoes economic growth by first engaging in export-biased innovations in developments which, although increasing the volume of trade, worsen the terms of trade. The pattern of comparative advantage changes in the process [Johnson 29].

22. The different impacts of economic development on foreign trade have been compactly tabulated by Kindleberger [34, p. 178].

23. The possible exceptions are technological progress at only slightly higher rates in the developed than in the underdeveloped country and population growth with only slowly diminishing marginal productivity in the underdeveloped country [29, p. 83]. A bibliography dealing with matters of relevance to economic development and trade is given in [31, pp. 99–103].

24. The controversy about the role of the theory of comparative advantage in development policy has been reviewed by Chenery [13]. Note also Myint [49] and Lewis [40]. Kindleberger refers to three models: export-led growth; trade as a balancing sector; and trade-lagging growth [34, Chap. 12].

25. Linder, for example, [41, pp. 12, 13] refers to the concept as the ability to reallocate resources as distinct from the ability to consume resources. Underdeveloped countries or countries lacking positive economic growth do not possess this reallocative ability, developed countries or growing countries do. Note also Brown [10].

26. As already mentioned, Ohlin considered that the supply of factors may sometimes be the result of trade rather than the cause [51, p. 67]. The Heckscher-Ohlin model of comparative advantage is most useful for development policies, since its measures of comparative advantage do not depend on perfect competition and initial equilibrium [Chenery, 13, p. 19].

BIBLIOGRAPHY

[1] A. Amano, "Factor Endowment and Relative Prices: A Generalization of Rybczynski's Theorem," *Econa* (November 1963).

[2] B. Balassa, "An Empirical Demonstration of Classical Comparative Cost Theory," *REStat* (August 1963).

[3] T. Balogh, "Factor Intensities of American Foreign Trade and Technical Progress," *REStat* (November 1955).

[4] M. J. Beckmann, "International and Interpersonal Division of Labor," *Weltwirtschaftliches Archiv*, Heft 1 (1957).

[5] J. Bhagwati, "Immiserizing Growth: A Geometrical Note," *REStud* (June 1958).

[6] _____, "The Pure Theory of International Trade," *EJ* (March 1964).

[7] R. Bharadwaj, "Factor Proportions and the Structure of Indo–U.S. Trade," *Indian Economic Journal* (October 1962).

[8] J. Black, "Economic Expansion and International Trade: A Marshallian Approach," *REStud*, No. 3 (1956).

[9] A. J. Brown, "Professor Leontief and the Pattern of World Trade," *Yorkshire Bulletin of Economic and Social Research* (November 1957).

[10] _____, "Factor-supplies and Comparative Costs in Underdeveloped Countries," *Pakistan Economic Journal* (March 1959).

[11] N. S. Buchanan, "Lines on the Leontief Paradox," *Econia Internaz* (November 1955).

[12] R. E. Caves, *Trade and Economic Structure* (1960).

[13] H. B. Chenery, "Comparative Advantage and Development Policy," *AER* (March 1961).

[14] S. Clemhout, "Production Function Analysis Applied to the Leontief Scarce-Factor Paradox of International Trade," *Man Sch* (May 1963).

[15] W. M. Corden, "Economic Expansion and International Trade: A Geometric Approach," *OEP* (June 1956).

[16] A. Danière, "American Trade Structure and Comparative Cost Theory," *Econia Internaz* (August 1956).

[17] M. A. Diab, *The United States Capital Position and the Structure of its Foreign Trade* (1956).

[18] R. S. Eckaus, "The Factor Proportions Problem in Underdeveloped Areas," *AER* (September 1955).

[19] P. T. Ellsworth, "The Structure of American Foreign Trade: A New View Examined," *REStat* (August 1954).

[20] R. Findlay and H. Grubert, "Factor Intensities, Technological Progress, and the Terms of Trade," *OEP* (February 1959).

[21] J. L. Ford, "The Ohlin-Heckscher Theory of the Basis of Commodity Trade," *EJ* (September 1963).

[22] _____, "Measures of Factor Endowments and of Factor Intensities," *OEP* (November 1963).

[23] A. Guha, "Factor and Commodity Prices in an Expanding Economy," *QJE* (February 1963).

[24] G. Haberler, "Some Problems in the Pure Theory of International Trade," *EJ* (June 1950).

[25] E. Heckscher, "The Effect of Foreign Trade on the Distribution of Income," *Ekonomisk Tidskrift* (1919). Reprinted in translation in *Readings in the Theory of International Trade* (1949).

[26] E. Hoffmeyer, "The Leontief Paradox Critically Examined," *Man Sch* (May 1958).

[27] W. Isard, and M. J. Peck, "Location Theory and International and Interregional Trade Theory," *QJE* (February 1954).

[28] H. G. Johnson, "Factor Endowments, International Trade and Factor Prices," *Man Sch* (September 1957).

[29] —————, "Economic Expansion and International Trade," *Man Sch* (May 1955).

[30] —————, "Equilibrium Growth in an International Economy," *CJEPS* (November 1953).

[31] —————, "Economic Development and International Trade," *National Ekonomisk Tidskrift* (Bund 5). Reprinted as Chap. IV, in *Money Trade and Economic Growth* (1962).

[32] R. W. Jones, "Factor Proportions and the Heckscher-Ohlin Theorem," *REStud*, No. 1 (1956).

[33] M. C. Kemp, and R. W. Jones, "Variable Labor Supply and the Theory of International Trade," *JPE* (February 1962).

[34] C. P. Kindleberger, *Foreign Trade and the National Economy* (1962).

[35] I. B. Kravis, "Availability and Other Influences on the Commodity Composition of Trade," *JPE* (April 1956).

[36] K. J. Lancaster, "The Heckscher-Ohlin Trade Model: A Geometric Treatment," *Econa* (February 1957).

[37] S. Laursen, "Production Functions and the Theory of International Trade," *AER* (September 1952).

[38] W. W. Leontief, "Domestic Production and Foreign Trade; the American Capital Position Reexamined," *Proceedings of the American Philosophical Society* (September 1953), as reprinted in *Econia Internaz* (February 1954).

[39] —————, "Factor Proportions and the Structure of American Trade: Further Theoretical and Empirical Analysis," *REStat* (November 1956).

[40] W. A. Lewis, "Economic Development with Unlimited Supplies of Labor," *Man Sch* (May 1954).

[41] S. B. Linder, *An Essay on Trade and Transformation* (1961).

[42] G. D. A. MacDougall, "British and American Exports: a Study Suggested by the Theory of Comparative Costs," *EJ* (Part I: December 1951, Part II: September 1952).

[43] —————, P. F. Dowley and S. Pugh, "British and American Productivity, Prices and Exports: An Addendum," *OEP* (October 1962).

[44] G. M. Meier, *International Trade and Development* (1963).

[45] B. S. Minhas, "The Homohypallagic Production Function, Factor-Intensity Reversals, and the Heckscher-Ohlin Theorem," *JPE* (April 1962).

[46] E. J. Mishan, "Factor Endowment and Relative Commodity Prices: A Comment," *Econa* (November 1956).

[47] S. Mookerjee, *Factor Endowments and International Trade: A Statement and Appraisal of the Heckscher-Ohlin Theory* (1958).

[48] R. A. Mundell, "International Trade and Factor Mobility," *AER* (June 1957).

[49] H. Myint, "The Classical Theory of International Trade and the Underdeveloped Countries," *EJ* (June 1958).

[50] B. Ohlin, *Handelns Teori* (1924).

[51] _____, *Interregional and International Trade* (1935).

[52] M. V. Posner, "International Trade and Technical Change," *OEP* (October 1961).

[53] R. Robinson, "Factor Proportions and Comparative Advantage," *QJE* (Part I: May 1956, Part II, August 1956).

[54] T. N. Rybczynski, "Factor Endowment and Relative Commodity Prices," *Econa* (November 1955).

[55] R. M. Stern, "British and American Productivity and Comparative Costs in International Trade," *OEP* (October 1962).

[56] B. C. Swerling, "Capital Shortage and Labor Surplus in the United States," *REStat* (August 1954).

[57] W. P. Travis, *The Theory of Trade and Protection* (1964).

[58] S. Valavanis-Vail, "Leontief's Scarce Factor Paradox," *JPE* (December 1954).

[59] _____, "Factor Proportions and the Structure of American Trade: Comment," (followed by W. W. Leontief's reply); *REStat* (February 1958).

[60] J. Vanek, "The Natural Resource Content of Foreign Trade, 1870–1955, and the Relative Abundance of Natural Resources in the United States," *REStat* (May 1959).

[61] _____, "An Afterthought on the 'Real Cost–Opportunity Cost' Dispute and Some Aspects of General Equilibrium under Conditions of Variable Factor Supplies," *REStud* (June 1959).

[62] _____, "Variable Factor Proportions and Inter-Industry Flows in the Theory of International Trade," *QJE* (February 1963).

[63] _____, *The Natural Resource Content of United States Foreign Trade, 1870–1955* (1963).

[64] J. Viner, *Studies in the Theory of International Trade* (1937).

[65] _____, *International Trade and Economic Development* (1953).

[66] H. W. J. Wijnholds, "The Theory of International Trade: A New Approach," *South African Journal of Economics* (September 1953).

[67] J. H. Williams, "The Theory of International Trade Reconsidered," as reprinted in American Economic Association, *Readings in the Theory of International Trade* (1949).

CHAPTER 3 / The Terms of Trade

PREFATORY STATEMENT

The classical economists were primarily concerned with three questions about foreign trade: (1) what goods would a country buy and sell in trade with other countries; (2) what would be the terms of exchange between the goods bought and sold; and (3) what happens to reestablished equilibrium when a disturbance occurs to trading relationships. The first two chapters of this book are concerned primarily with the first question, that is, what goods would a country buy and sell in trade with other countries and the effects of trade. This chapter deals with the second question, the terms of exchange between the goods bought and sold or, as it is more commonly called, the terms of trade.

Since World War II there has been great interest in the terms of trade, especially on the part of countries whose foreign trade is large relative to income and output. For such countries changes in the terms of trade may have a major impact upon the level of income. Another reason for the widespread interest is the possible role the terms of trade may play in explaining changes in income differentials among countries. Changes in the terms of trade may affect the international distribution of income and there is particular interest in whether or not unfavorable terms of trade may provide some explanation for the low levels of income in many countries. Furthermore, some economic historians consider the terms of trade to be an important variable in explaining the course of economic history. The behavior of the terms of trade plays an important role in many problems of economic policy today.

In the simple models of the classical economists there was no ambiguity concerning the meaning of the terms of trade. In the real world, with many commodities, non-constant costs, capital movement, payments imbalances, etc., there is no simple meaning to the terms of trade. Among the several different measures of the terms of trade, the most commonly used by far is the net barter terms of trade, which is an index of export prices divided by an index of import prices. A complication arises in interpretation because the various measures of the terms of trade may not all move in the same direction over a given period of time.

The theory underlying the terms of trade is concerned primarily with the causes of changes in the indexes or with the effects on the indexes of changes in the various determinants. Basically changes in supply and demand for internationally-traded goods cause changes in relative prices of exports and imports for a given country. Affecting the supply and demand, and thus the terms of trade, are tariffs, changes in exchange rates, international transfer payments, and economic growth (including technological change). These are the topics discussed in this chapter.

Despite the shortcomings and uncertainties concerning their computation and their interpretation, the terms of trade are of considerable importance in international economics.[1] They are particularly important to those countries whose foreign trade is large relative to national income because changes in the terms of trade may have a great impact upon the balance of payments and national income. The terms of trade are also a convenient indicator of the net effect of many forces acting upon international economic relations and they may be important in determining changes in welfare for the countries engaged in trade [Rostow, 60, pp. 167–169; and Kindleberger, 42, pp. 1–5].

There are several different measures of the terms of trade, each representing a different concept [Viner, 71, pp. 558–63; Haberler, 27, pp. 24–29; and Meier, 48, pp. 40–45]. The different measures are the net barter, gross barter, income, single factoral, and double factoral terms of trade.[2] The most widely used is the net barter terms of trade, also called the commodity or merchandise terms of trade. It is simply an index of export prices divided by an index of import prices with the quotient expressed as a percentage $[(P_x/P_m) \times 100]$. A rise in the net barter index over time means that a given volume of exports will exchange for a larger volume of imports than formerly. But the index does not indicate what has happened to the physical volume of commodities traded. Only if the values of exports and imports were equal in the base year and in the year under study would an improvement in the net barter terms of trade mean that a country actually obtained more imports with a given volume of exports.

Changes in the physical volume of exports and imports are apt to accompany changes in the ratio of export prices to import prices. Two of the other concepts embody volume changes. The gross barter terms of trade is the index of the quantity of exports divided by the index of quantity of imports $[(Q_x/Q_m) \times 100]$. The resulting index represents the rate of exchange between the aggregate physical exports and imports of a country. The meaning of changes in this measure are ambiguous whenever the value of exports and the value of imports are not equal. For instance, a fall in the index suggests an improved position because a given quantity of exports exchanges for a larger quantity of imports. But the change may be due entirely to a transfer receipt or a capital inflow; the favorableness or unfavorableness depends upon the type of transaction that changes the index. This index has not been very useful in analytical work because analysts generally have preferred to work directly with the causes of changes in the quantities rather than indirectly through the gross barter terms of trade [Meier, 48, p. 42].

The other concept that uses a quantity index is the income terms of trade [Dorrance, 21]. It consists of the index of the value of exports (a quantity index times a price index) divided by the index of import prices. The index is actually the net barter terms of trade times the index of the quantity of exports $[(P_x/P_m) \times Q_x]$. A rise in the index means that a country can obtain a larger quantity of imports from its sale of exports in a given year relative to the base year. Although frequently called a measure of the capacity to import, the index does not reflect the total capacity to import because that capacity depends upon net capital inflows and net receipts from invisibles in the current account as well as from commodity exports. Note that the income terms of trade and the net barter terms of trade may move in opposite directions. If, for instance, import prices remain constant but export prices fall by 5 per cent, the net barter terms of trade deteriorate from 100 to 95. But suppose the quantity of exports increases by 10 per cent. The value of exports increases and the income terms of trade rise from 100 to 104.5 $[(95/100) \times 110 = 104.5]$.

The three concepts discussed so far relate to the exchange between import and export commodities. Two other concepts — the single and double factoral terms of trade — relate to the exchange of productive factors embodied in traded goods. The single factoral terms of trade consist of the net barter index adjusted for productivity changes in the production of exports. The double factoral terms of trade entails the adjustment for productivity changes in both exports and imports. The adjustment for productivity changes actually involves the calculation of the prices of factors embodied in the traded goods. For instance, if the export price index falls 10 per cent while the productivity index for exports rises 20 per cent (both relative to 100 for the base year), the price of factors embodied in exports has actually risen to 108 $[(90 \times 120) / 100]$. If, further, the index of import prices remains at 100, the single factor terms of trade are 108, an improvement despite the decline in the net barter terms of trade from 100 to 90. The rise in the single factoral index means that the country receives more imported goods per unit of productive factors incorporated in exports as compared with the base year. If the productivity index for imports had risen to 110 in the example and if the import price index still remained constant, the double factoral terms of trade would have declined from 100 to 98.2 [$\{(90 \times 120)/(100 \times 110)\} \times 100 = (108/110) \times 100 = 98.2$]. This index shows the change in the rate of exchange between a unit of domestic productive factors used in producing exports and a unit of foreign productive factors used in producing imports. The factoral terms of trade are not operational because of the impossibility of defining and measuring a unit of inputs and hence of calculating a meaningful productivity index. A simple index of labor productivity is not a satisfactory measure of productivity changes for all inputs [Devons, 20].

The temptation is strong to equate changes in a country's terms of trade with changes in its welfare or in its gains from trade. But the deduction of the welfare effects of changes in the terms of trade is not simple and direct. It depends upon the particular circumstances — upon the underlying forces that cause any given change in the terms of trade. An adverse change in a country's net barter terms of trade suggests that the country is worse off than in the base year because it has to export more goods to pay for a given quantity of imports. The country will indeed be worse off if the adverse change results from a decline in the foreign demand for its exports, all other things remaining unchanged. If, by contrast, the decline in export prices results from technological change that lowers production costs, and if the decline in costs is more than proportionate to the decline in the terms of trade, the country will be better off because it obtains more imports per unit of productive factors employed in producing exports than it did in the base year. In this case, the net barter terms of trade deteriorate while the single factoral terms of trade improve; but the single factoral index correctly indicates an improvement in welfare. If the double factoral terms deteriorate, welfare in the foreign country or countries increases also and it might increase more, assuming some way of comparing welfare gains among countries.

The income terms of trade do not reliably indicate welfare changes. Assume that import prices and quantities remain unchanged and that exports and imports are equal in value in both the base year and current year. If export prices rise, the country is better off in welfare terms because it obtains its given volume of imports with a smaller volume of exports as compared with the base year, i.e., its real national income is larger. The income terms of trade are unchanged, however, so they do not reflect the welfare gain. As previously mentioned, a country's income terms of trade might improve at the same time that its net barter terms of trade deteriorate. The quantity of exports could increase sufficiently to cause a rise in the index for income terms of trade despite a relative decline in export prices. For a developing country, the capacity to import can be very important to its development program and its welfare might improve over time despite an adverse movement of the net barter terms provided the capacity to import increases.

Because the net barter terms of trade depend only upon merchandise trade, they do not necessarily indicate a country's position for the entire current account. For instance, a country might experience a decline in its net barter terms of trade but still be better off because of realizing more favorable terms of trade for the invisible items in the current account. The country may be able to borrow on better terms, to get a greater share of the profits earned by foreign enterprises, and so on. A later section of this chapter will point out specific situations in which a country has improved terms of trade for the entire current account despite a deterioration for merchandise alone.

Only the net barter terms of trade receive much attention; they are computed currently for most countries and are available for longer periods for a few countries.[3] The theoretical issues in the remainder of this chapter relate almost entirely to the net barter concept, so the terms of trade will refer to the net barter concept unless clearly stated otherwise. In the short run, changes in the terms of trade may result from numerous causes — among which are demand shifts, changes in commercial policy, depreciation, and transfers. In the long run, changes in the terms of trade result from structural shifts in demand and supply associated with economic development and growth. The following sections of this chapter will take up each of these factors.

□ THE EFFECTS OF DEMAND SHIFTS [4]

One cause of changes in terms of trade is a shift in demand for the exports or imports of a country. The theoretical analysis of this topic consists of determining the effect of special demand shifts as reflected in a movement of an offer curve. The model is the usual one with two countries (A and B) and two commodities (X and Y). Both countries have competitive economies and both maintain full employment at all times.

Elasticity of the Foreign Offer Curve

In Figure 3-1, OA and OB are the original offer curves of the two countries.[5] A's demand for B's export good increases and causes a shift in the offer curve to OA'. The new offer curve, OA', has the same elasticity as OA at each quantity of B's good (Y).[6] For each quantity of good Y, OA' lies to the right of OA by the same percentage. For instance, T' is approximately 20 per cent farther to the right of OY than the point on OA corresponding to the same quantity of Y; similarly, all

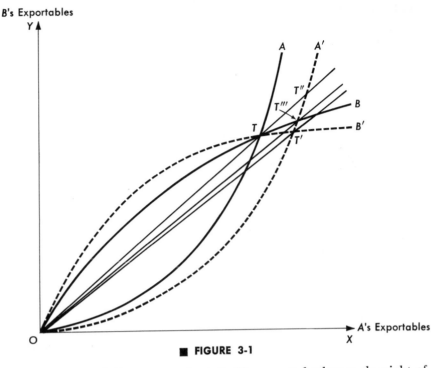

B's Exportables

■ FIGURE 3-1

other points on OA' are approximately 20 per cent farther to the right of OY than the corresponding points on OA. An increase in demand for B's good that shifts A's offer curve to OA' will cause A's terms of trade to deteriorate from the slope of OT to the slope of OT'''. Had B's offer curve been more inelastic, say OB', A's terms of trade would have worsened more (the slope of OT' is less than the slope of OT'''). By contrast, if B's offer curve had been more elastic than OB, A's terms of trade would have deteriorated less. In the extreme case of an infinitely elastic B offer curve, the terms of trade would not change because B's offer curve would be the ray OT''. The shift in A's demand would then have moved the equilibrium from T to T'', indicating a greater volume of trade but unchanged terms of trade. The geometry of Figure 3-1 thus demonstrates that the increase in A's demand with constant elasticity (at given quantities of Y) causes its terms of trade to deteriorate and that the deterioration is less the more elastic is B's offer curve [Dasgupta, 19].

Elasticity of the Home Offer Curve

The next question is how the elasticity of A's offer curve affects the terms of trade when A's demand for B's good increases, the elasticity of B's offer curve being given. In Figure 3-2, OA' again has the same elasticity as OA at given quantities of Y. The point t is directly to the right of T, and t will always be below OB as long as OB has elasticity

131

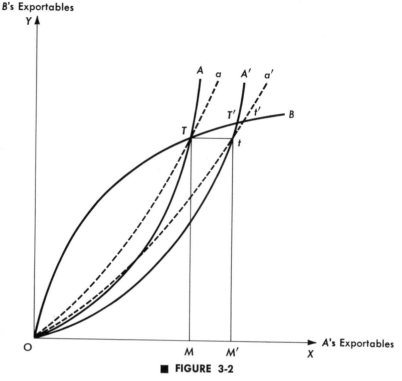

B's Exportables

■ FIGURE 3-2

greater than one. Any number of A's offer curves could pass through T, each having different shape and elasticity. But the shifted offer curves corresponding to each curve passing through T will necessarily pass through t provided each shifted curve represents the same percentage shift to the right as does OA' in relation to OA. In Figure 3-2, Oa' represents the same percentage shift to the right from Oa as does OA' relative to OA. Oa and Oa' are, however, more elastic than OA and OA'.

The offer curves of the two countries intersected originally at T; OA' intersects B's offer curve at T' while Oa' intersects at t'. A's terms of trade are less favorable when the intersection is at t' instead of T', and the intersection at t' is for the more elastic of A's two offer curves. Figure 3-2 therefore illustrates that the more elastic is A's offer curve, the more unfavorable A's terms of trade become when A's demand for B's good increases (no change in the elasticity of A's offer curve), provided the elasticity of B's offer curve is given.

Alternative Demand Shifts

In a comprehensive article on demand shifts, Kemp [36, p. 41] points out that an increase of demand with no change in elasticity is subject to three different interpretations. The first is the one used above, namely, a uniform percentage increase in the amount of A's good offered for any given amount of B's good. The second is a uniform percentage increase in the amount of $\hat{A}$'s good offered for B's good at all terms of trade. To illustrate this type of shift, draw a series of rays from the origin (representing various terms of trade) intersecting both OA and OA', the original and the shifted offer curves. For each ray, the intersection with OA' would be the same percentage farther out on the ray from the corresponding intersection with OA. The third is a uniform percentage decrease in the amount of B's good demanded for a specified amount of A's good, or a uniform downward (rather than horizontal) shift in A's offer curve.

The preceding discussion of demand shifts involved those of Type 1 in Kemp's classification. The analysis of the other two types is straightforward and can employ the same geometric technique as used for the Type 1 shift. The relationship between elasticities and changes in the terms of trade varies, depending upon the type of demand shift. All three types of increases in A's demand for B's good will, however, worsen A's terms of trade provided A's offer curve has an elasticity greater than one. In actual practice, there will generally be no way of predicting which type of shift is apt to occur or whether the shift will be one of the pure types or some combination of them.

□ THE EFFECTS OF TARIFFS

The effect of imposing a tariff on imports is to shift the offer curve of a country as that offer curve appears to foreigners, so the analysis of the effect on the terms of trade is similar in many ways to that in the preceding section. Elasticities are again important in determining the outcome but new elements in the analysis are the method of payment of the duty and the government's disposition of the tariff proceeds. Introductory textbooks in international economics commonly illustrate the effects of tariffs by using partial-equilibrium diagrams. Although such diagrams are useful for some purposes, they are not well-suited for showing the effect of a tariff on the terms of trade because they assume that the change in the foreign price of imports alone indicates the change in the terms of trade. If a tariff affects a substantial share of trade between two countries, it will almost certainly affect export prices as well as import prices. An advantage of offer-curve analysis is that it includes both exports and imports.

Tariff Paid with the Import Good

In Figure 3-3, OA and OB are again the free-trade offer curves of the two countries. They intersect at T, so the slope of the ray OT (not drawn) is the terms of trade with no tariffs. Now assume that the government in country A imposes a tariff of 100 per cent on imports, payable in kind with the import good. OA continues to be A's domestic offer

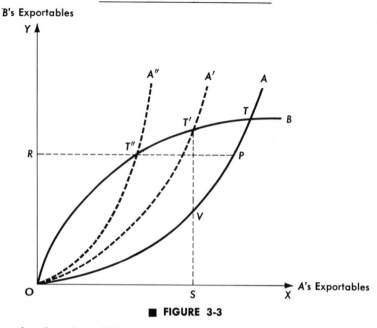

■ FIGURE 3-3

curve, showing the willingness of private traders to exchange X for Y. But to pay the duty, private traders will now have to transfer to the government a quantity of the import good equal to that which they keep for themselves. As a result, private traders in A will now demand twice as much Y as formerly from sellers in country B in exchange for any given quantity of X. Before the tariff, they offered OS of X in exchange for SV of Y in Figure 3-3 at the terms of trade given by the slope of the ray OV (not drawn). With the 100 per cent duty payable with the import good, they now demand ST' (two times SV) of Y in exchange for OS of X. A's offer curve as it appears to foreigners shifts to OA', constructed so that any point on it is twice as far above OX as the corresponding point directly below on OA. T' is the new equilibrium position; private traders exchange OS of X for ST' of Y but turn over VT' to the government as the duty. The international terms of trade (the slope of OT') improve for A because any given quantity of X now exchanges in the international market for a larger quantity of Y than under free trade. The duty causes the terms-of-trade line to become steeper, the shift being from the slope of OT to the slope of OT'. The slope of the ray OV gives the domestic price ratio including the duty on imports; the tariff thus causes the domestic price of the imported good to rise relative to the price of the exported good.

Tariff Paid with the Export Good

The shift in the terms of trade is different if the government collects the 100 per cent duty in the form of the export good. Private traders in

A will now have to transfer to the government as much X as they exchange for a given quantity of Y in dealing with foreign suppliers of Y. As before, OA continues to be A's domestic offer curve, showing the different quantities of X that private traders are willing to exchange for various quantities of Y. But half the quantity of X given in exchange for a particular quantity of Y must now go to the government as payment of the duty. Prior to the tariff, private traders in A offered RP of X to traders in B for OR of Y when the price ratio was the slope of OP (not drawn). After the tariff, traders in A will offer only RT'' of X to traders in B for OR of Y and will transfer $T''P$ of X to the government as payment of the 100 per cent duty.

The duty shifts A's international offer curve (the one seen by foreigners) from OA to OA''. The new offer curve bisects all horizontal lines between OA and OY and intersects B's offer curve at T'', the new equilibrium position. Country A exports RT'' of X and imports OR of Y. The terms of trade shift in favor of country A by a greater amount than when the duty was payable in the import good as manifest by the steeper slope of OT'' compared to OT'. The slope of OP gives the domestic price ratio in A, which, of course, includes the duty. The increase in the domestic price of the imported good (Y) relative to that of the exported good (X) is less than when the duty was payable in the import good $(OP$ is steeper than $OV)$.

The Foreign Offer Curve

If the foreign offer curve (OB) were infinitely elastic — a straight line from O, a tariff would not, of course, change A's terms of trade. It would only increase the domestic price of imports by the amount of the tariff and would reduce the volume of trade. Even when B's offer curve is less than infinitely elastic, a tariff might not improve A's terms of trade if B retaliates. A retaliatory tariff by B would shift its international offer curve downward toward the X axis so that the terms of trade could finally shift either way or be the same as before tariffs were imposed. The prices of imports would rise in both countries and the volume of trade would decline. The conclusions derived from Figure 3-3 depend, therefore, upon the absence of retaliation and upon the existence of a foreign offer curve with elasticity less than infinity.

A tariff by country A would cause a decline in the domestic price of the imported good if the foreign offer curve is highly inelastic at the initial intersection as it is in Figure 3-4. The foreign offer curve (OB) is inelastic beyond the point where it bends down toward the horizontal axis. Assume that A imposes a 100 per cent tax on imports payable with the export good. The tariff causes A's international offer curve to shift to OA' with A importing OR of Y in exchange for RT' of X. The slope of OP gives the domestic price ratio; it is greater than the slope of the

B's Exportables

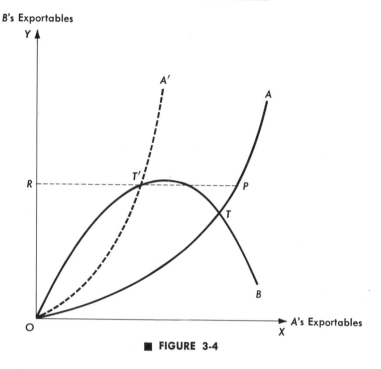

■ FIGURE 3-4

free-trade price line (OT), indicating that the tariff caused a relative decline in the domestic price of the imported good.[7]

The Government's Disposition of Tariff Revenues

The preceding analysis assumes that the imposition of the tariff does not affect private demand for the commodities [Baldwin, 4, p. 67]. The offer curve indicates the willingness of private traders to exchange X for Y — whether the slope of a ray from the origin to any point on the offer curve represents the free-trade or the post-tariff price ratio within the country. As Baldwin pointed out, this assumption implies either that the government destroys its tariff receipts or that the public consumption of the receipts does not affect the private offer curve. An alternative and perhaps more plausible assumption is that the government redistributes the proceeds of the tariff either by a reduction of taxes or by a distribution of the tariff receipts.

The distribution of the benefits associated with the government's allocation of the tariff receipts will generally affect the offer curve of private traders and will thus alter the eventual effect of a tariff on the terms of trade. On the one hand, the net effect of a tariff will be to shift the post-tariff international offer curve of country A in toward the Y-axis if the absolute value of the free-trade elasticity of demand for imports exceeds the marginal propensity to import. On the other hand, the post-tariff curve will shift outward from the Y-axis if the absolute value of the free-trade elasticity of demand for imports is less than the marginal propensity to import. Therefore, the terms of trade will improve for the tariff-imposing country if the absolute value of the elasticity of demand for imports exceeds the marginal propensity to import and will worsen if the elasticity is smaller.[8] The proof of this proposition [Baldwin, 4, pp. 74–75] is quite involved but the common-sense meaning is simply that the tariff increases the domestic price of the imported good, thus reducing imports by an amount that depends upon the price elasticity of demand. The redistribution of the tariff revenue increases the demand for imports (*ceteris paribus*) by an amount that depends upon the marginal propensity to spend on the imported good. If the absolute value of the price elasticity is greater than the import propensity, the demand for imports declines on balance and the foreign price will fall, yielding improved terms of trade.

The preceding discussion of tariffs assumes an initial position of free trade. In a real world situation, the question is apt to be one of the probable effect of raising or lowering an existing tariff.[9] The techniques used above will, however, apply to the alteration of an existing tariff, except that the initial equilibrium will be one with a tariff already in existence.

☐ THE EFFECTS OF DEPRECIATION

The relationship between depreciation and the terms of trade arises in discussions of the effects of devaluation upon national income. The question of interest to economists is whether devaluation increases import prices relative to export prices and thereby reduces a country's real income through an adverse movement of the terms of trade. An interesting outcome of the literature on this topic is that adverse changes in the terms of trade do not necessarily cause real income to fall [Machlup, 44]. But the primary topic of this section is the relationship between depreciation and the terms of trade.

When a country devalues, the foreign price of its exports typically falls. By contrast, the domestic price of imports normally rises. Many people conclude, therefore, that devaluation worsens the terms of trade because it reduces export prices and increases import prices. This seemingly straightforward interpretation rests upon an incorrect definition of the terms of trade because it uses the foreign price of exports and the domestic price of imports. The correct procedure is to compare export and import prices in the same currency, either domestic or foreign.

Devaluation normally causes both export prices and import prices to rise in domestic currency and to fall in foreign currency. More information is necessary to determine whether export prices fall relative to import prices, with both expressed in the same currency.

Role of Elasticities

Suppose, for instance, that the elasticities of supply were infinite for both imports and exports. Devaluation would then cause no change in the domestic price of exports but would cause a proportionate rise in the domestic price of imports. A 5 per cent devaluation would cause a 5 per cent deterioration in the terms of trade. If, by contrast, the elasticity of demand for imports were infinite for both the home and the foreign country, devaluation would cause the domestic price of exports to rise in proportion but would leave the domestic price of imports unchanged. A 5 per cent devaluation would now cause a 5 per cent improvement in the terms of trade. If the devaluing country were small and had no effect on world prices (foreign supply of imports and foreign demand for exports both are infinitely elastic), devaluation would not affect the terms of trade because the domestic prices of imports and exports would both rise in proportion to the devaluation. Although these illustrations are the limiting cases, they demonstrate clearly that the effect of devaluation depends upon demand and supply elasticities for exports and imports.

Joan Robinson demonstrated the mathematical relationships between the four elasticities and the terms of trade [59, p. 219]. She expressed the four elasticities in terms of prices in the home country's currency and then demonstrated that devaluation would worsen the terms of trade if the product of the two supply elasticities exceeded the product of the two demand elasticities. Algebraically the condition is that $s_m s_x > d_x d_m$, where s_m is the foreign elasticity of supply for imports, s_x is the domestic elasticity of supply for exports, d_x is the foreign elasticity of demand for exports, and d_m is the domestic elasticity of demand for imports.[10]

Probable Outcome

The question that arises next is whether there is a presumption that actual conditions would cause a worsening of the terms of trade for a devaluing country. Mrs. Robinson concluded that the terms of trade would probably deteriorate because countries tended to be more specialized in exports than in imports [59, pp. 219–220]. Therefore a country will be more dominant in the world supply of the goods it exports than it is in the world demand for the goods it imports, thus tending to make d_x less than s_m. In addition, the elasticity of demand for imports would tend to be low because countries generally import many goods that they cannot produce domestically. Finally, the elasticity of supply for exports would be high if the exporting country had some unemployment. The combined effect of these factors would tend to make $s_m s_x$ exceed $d_x d_m$ and thus devaluation would tend to worsen the terms of trade.

The subsequent literature on devaluation and the terms of trade discussed extensively the probable relationship in the real world. Some writers agreed with Mrs. Robinson, some disagreed, and others discussed the probable outcome under a variety of conditions [Machlup 44, pp. 417–20, traces chronologically the views of various writers]. Empirical testing has not been entirely successful [Kindleberger, 42, Ch. 5] and has thus not resolved the disagreement. One empirical study showed that exports were more concentrated in a few commodity classes than imports for a majority of countries [Michaely, 53]. But for most of the large industrial countries, commodity concentration was stronger or only slightly weaker in imports than in exports [53, p. 50]. Therefore, no generalization appears to be warranted — the outcome simply depends upon the conditions facing each country.

Shortcomings of Partial Elasticities

Mrs. Robinson used demand and supply elasticities to determine the effect of devaluation upon the terms of trade. The elasticities involve partial-equilibrium analysis: they show the ratio between relative quantity changes and relative price changes for one good, assuming incomes, other prices, and all other determinants of demand and supply remain constant. Such partial-equilibrium analysis will give a good first approximation, even though all variables adjust to the change in one price, *provided* expenditure on the one good is an insignificant part of total expenditures and that cross elasticities with other goods are small [Sohmen, 64, p. 2]. Neither of these provisos is apt to exist in the actual devaluation of a currency. If, as seems probable, devaluation changes the relationship between the prices of many traded and nontraded goods, some of the cross elasticities will probably be large and will significantly affect the demand for imports. Extensive changes in relative prices of many goods may significantly affect real income which will, in turn, influence the final demand for imports. Partial elasticities may, therefore, be far different from the total or general-equilibrium elasticities that allow all variables to adjust in moving to a new equilibrium. The total elasticities are the relevant ones in discussions of devaluation.

Kennedy [39] has developed a model that allows for some internal repercussions of devaluation. His model is thus more general or comprehensive than the strictly partial-equilibrium analysis of Mrs. Robinson. The resulting condition under which devaluation would worsen the terms of trade is very complex but Mrs. Robinson's condition remains valid provided that demand is independent of income (any changes in income must change saving, not expenditure) and that the trading countries can expand the production of home (nontraded) goods without affecting the production of export goods. If the home country has full employment (no expansion in home goods is possible without a reduction in exports), but the foreign country has some unemployment, the terms of trade will not change. With full employment in both countries, Kennedy's model gives no determinate solution. He concludes, however, that Mrs. Robinson's formula understates the probability of adverse movements of terms of trade when both supply and demand elasticities are high and may overstate the probability when only the supply elasticities are high.

Another shortcoming of the simple elasticity condition is that the analysis on which it is based ignores money and monetary policy. The effect of devaluation on the home and foreign price levels depends upon wage, monetary, and fiscal policies [Haberler, 26, pp. 150–51]. Kemp [35] broadened the analysis of depreciation and the terms of trade by formally introducing money and monetary policy. In his model, demand and supply depend upon the real value of the stock of money and upon prices as well. He assumes that the authorities keep the stock of money constant but he emphasizes that other assumptions are equally plausible and would, of course, alter the outcome. He treats money simply as another commodity and assumes that all goods (including money) are substitutes for each other. By this he means that a rise in the price of one good causes an increase in the demand for the others. A fall in prices of goods represents an increase in the price of money and will cause an increase in the demand for goods.

In this model, devaluation by the home country necessarily causes its money prices to rise — but less than in proportion to devaluation; foreign prices fall — but again less than in proportion to devaluation. These price changes cause the real value of the constant stock of money to fall at home and to rise abroad, thereby increasing the foreign demand for commodities and decreasing the home demand. The effect on the terms of trade depends upon the ratio of marginal propensities of the two countries, precisely as it does with transfer payments (see the following section on transfers). Specifically, the terms of trade will improve for the devaluing country (A) if the ratio of its marginal propensity to buy import goods to its marginal propensity to buy export goods exceeds the corresponding ratio of the foreign country (B) for the same goods. The expression is

$$\frac{M_{AY}}{M_{AX}} > \frac{M_{BY}}{M_{BX}},$$

where the M's are marginal propensities, Y is country A's import good (B's export good) and X is country A's export good (B's import good). It is reasonable that the same condition should apply to both devaluation and transfer payments because the change in real value of money assets imposes a loss and a windfall corresponding to the changes in purchasing power accompanying a transfer [Kemp, 35, p. 321].

Economists have long discussed the effects on the terms of trade of transfer payments from one country to another [Samuelson, 61, pp. 278–280]. Despite its long history, the discussion has continued since World War II, an indication of the difficulty economists have encountered in reaching agreement on the proper analysis. The problem is simply what happens to the net barter terms of trade when country A makes a transfer payment to country B. The exact nature of the payment is not important; analysts generally assume it to be a unilateral or unrequited payment, such as war reparations. But the same problems arise with respect to the terms of trade regardless of whether the transfer is a loan, a repayment of a loan, an interest payment, or a grant [Kemp, 34, p. 79]. And it may take place between governments, between individuals, or between a government and individuals.

The two basic approaches are to consider the transfer as a *real* problem and as a *monetary* problem [Johnson, 33]. The approach in real terms requires a model based on the classical assumption that economies maintain full employment of resources at all times. All transactions occur as barter arrangements; money does not affect the actual operation of the economy — only physical quantities are significant. By contrast, the monetary aspects dominate the analysis of transfers in models based on the Keynesian assumption of unemployed resources. Supply curves are perfectly elastic and aggregate demand determines the level of output and income.

Two problems arise in both classical and Keynesian models. The first concerns whether the financing and disposing of the transfer payment will create the trade surplus and deficit necessary to effect the transfer fully, without causing a disequilibrium in the balance of payments. The paying country effects the transfer by exporting more goods and services, by importing less, or by a combination of both so as to develop an export surplus equal to the amount of the transfer; the receiving country will have a corresponding import surplus. On the one hand, the financing of the transfer payment will generally reduce disposable income and the demand for imports in the paying country. On the other hand, the transfer will generally increase disposable income and the demand for imports in the receiving country. The balance of payments will remain in equilibrium only if the change in the trade balance between the two countries is equal to the transfer payment; when this situation prevails, the transfer is fully effected without other changes. The transfer is under-effected or over-effected according to whether the change in the trade balance falls short of, or exceeds, the transfer. And the paying country has a deficit or a surplus in its balance of payments as the transfer is under- or over-effected.

The second problem concerns the operation of the adjustment process, provided the transfer is not exactly effected. The analysis presented here assumes that changes in the terms of trade eliminate any disequilibrium that may arise. It assumes further that the sum of the elasticities of demand for imports is greater than one so that a deterioration of the deficit country's terms of trade (or depreciation of its currency) will restore equilibrium. Conversely, a favorable movement in the terms of trade will tend to eliminate a surplus.

The paying country incurs a primary burden — perhaps more accurately called a budgetary burden — in raising the funds for the transfer payment. The primary burden will, therefore, generally cause a decline in disposable income and a decline in spending. Interest in the terms of trade originated in the question of whether the paying country bears a secondary burden or reduction of real income because import prices rise relative to export prices, that is, because the terms of trade deteriorate. The orthodox view consists of a strong presumption that the terms of trade will turn against the country making the transfer payment. Recent theoretical discussions have questioned the orthodox view and have shown that the terms of trade can, under certain circumstances, move in either direction. The following discussion examines the problem in a classical model and in a Keynesian model with pegged and with flexible exchange rates. The models all assume two countries, A and B, both of which produce two goods, X and Y. Country A exports good X, and country B exports good Y. Country A makes the transfer payment to country B.

The Classical Model

In the classical model, both countries automatically maintain full employment and constant prices (initially).[11] These assumptions require that when country A makes a transfer payment, it must reduce its aggregate expenditure by the amount of the transfer and country B must increase its expenditure by the same amount. An examination of the expenditure equations for the two countries will demonstrate this statement. Domestic expenditures in A (E_A) equal the value of production for the two goods $(X_A + Y_A)$ minus the net capital outflow (represented by T, the transfer). In B, domestic expenditures equal the value of production plus the transfer. Thus, the two expenditure equations, both in terms of the same currency, are

(1) $E_A = X_A + Y_A - T$, and
(2) $E_B = X_B + Y_B + T$.

T is actually A's trade in balance, that is, the algebraic value of exports minus imports.

Assume that T is zero before A begins the transfer payments, so

142

that domestic expenditure equals national income (money value of production). To make the transfer, A must reduce its domestic expenditure so that its savings exceed its investment by the transfer. In B, national income cannot rise with receipt of the transfer because of the initial full employment; the transfer simply increases domestic expenditures so that investment exceeds savings by the amount of transfer. There are no multiplier effects in this model because of the assumption that both countries maintain full employment constantly. The assumption that prices initially remain constant means that each country will produce constant amounts of X and Y; the transfer simply causes a reallocation between the countries of their fixed output of the commodities.[12] The changes in expenditures in each country resulting from the transfer will induce changes in aggregate demand for the two commodities.

The reduction of expenditures in A will reduce its demand for imports while the increase of expenditures in B will increase its demand for imports. Both effects will improve A's trade balance: the exact improvement expressed as a percentage of the transfer is the sum of the percentage of the transfer spent on imports in B and the percentage of the transfer by which imports fall in A. If the sum is exactly 100, the transfer is fully effected because A's export surplus is equal to the transfer; there is no disequilibrium in the balance of payments. If the sum exceeds 100, the transfer is over-effected so that A has an export surplus greater than the transfer. Finally, if the sum of the percentages is less than 100, the transfer is under-effected because A's export surplus is smaller than the transfer. If, as is commonly assumed, the paying country finances the transfer with an income tax and the receiving country distributes it as a general income subsidy, the sum of the marginal propensities to spend on imports in the two countries indicates the extent to which the transfer is effected. If this sum is less than one, the transfer is undereffected, and so forth.

If the transfer is over- or under-effected, the terms of trade must change to make A's export surplus match the transfer, i.e., to restore the balance of payments to equilibrium. The terms of trade will move against the paying country (A) if the transfer is under-effected (assuming the sum of the price elasticities of demand for imports is greater than one). The greater the sum of the elasticities, the more effective are relative price changes and the smaller is the required change in the terms of trade to make the export surplus equal the transfer. If the transfer is over-effected, the terms of trade will improve for country A. Finally, if the transfer is fully effected, there will be no change in the terms of trade.

The preceding analysis suggests that the orthodox conclusion with respect to the change of the terms of trade rests upon the assumption that the sum of the proportions of the transfer spent on imports in the two countries is less than one. In other words, the reduction in expenditures on imports in A plus the increase in expenditures on imports in B is less than the transfer. It follows, therefore, that A's terms of trade must deteriorate.

But Samuelson argued convincingly that if transport costs are and always have been zero (as assumed in classical trade models) and if no other impediments to trade exist, the orthodox presumption is without justification [61, pp. 289–304]. For the sum of the marginal import propensities to be less than one, the two countries together would have to show a greater combined marginal propensity for home goods than for imports (assuming that for each country the sum of the two marginal propensities equals one). With no impediments to trade, Samuelson sees no reason to believe that consumers in a country would prefer home goods to foreign goods. There is no reason to assume a priori that the marginal import propensities in each country will be greater or less than one half. Consequently, the terms of trade in the classical model may move either against or in favor of the paying country, depending upon the actual import propensities existing in each situation.

The existence of tariffs or transports costs or both may, however, add support to the orthodox view that the terms of trade will turn against the transferring country [Samuelson, 62, p. 289]. Transport costs and tariffs cause a divergence between expenditures by residents of each country on imports and the receipts of the foreign exporters. Part of this difference between expenditures and receipts will probably be spent upon the domestic goods of each country. Therefore, the critical value for the sum of the marginal physical propensities to import will be greater than one. If the sum is less than this critical value, the transfer is incomplete and the terms of trade will turn against the transferring country. A critical value greater than unity increases the probability that the sum of the import propensities will be too small to make the transfer complete without a worsening of the terms of trade. The orthodox position is not a strong one, however, because the terms of trade could still move in either direction — the outcome would depend on the actual propensities in each specific situation.

The Keynesian Model

The central assumption in the classical model is that the countries maintain full employment at all times. By contrast, the central assumption in the Keynesian model is that the countries have unemployed resources, thus making supply curves perfectly elastic at fixed domestic price levels. In such a model, aggregate demand determines the level of output, income, and employment. The following discussion considers the transfer process with both pegged exchange rates and flexible exchange rates. Chapter 6 will discuss the operation of these two exchange systems in greater detail.

There are two major differences between the transfer problem in classical and Keynesian systems. First, the financing and disposal of the transfer under Keynesian assumptions will not necessarily cause aggregate expenditures in the two countries to change by the amount of the transfer — as occurred under classical assumptions. The paying country could finance the transfer wholly or partly by drawing down savings while the receiving country could dispose of the funds wholly or in part by adding to savings. Second, any change in expenditures caused by the transfer will have multiplier effects upon income and the balance of payments. Therefore, the analysis of the extent to which the real transfer is effected depends upon whether, after allowing for multiplier effects, the paying country's balance of trade improves by the amount of the transfer, by more, or by less.

Fixed exchange rates / Initially assume that the countries establish a pegged exchange rate and fixed interest rates, although they may adjust both if a payments disequilibrium persists. Assume further that levels of national income do not influence international capital movements but that national monetary authorities engage in financial transactions to finance payments imbalances temporarily. Johnson developed the most complete model of a transfer between two underemployed economies with a fixed rate of exchange between their currencies [33, pp. 217–221].[13] He followed the usual practice of setting up an income equation for each country and an equation for the first country's balance of payments. For each country the change in income is the result of changes in spending on domestic goods and on imports. Spending on each type of good consists of an autonomous and an induced component. The change in autonomous spending on domestic goods in *B* (the country receiving the transfer payment) is the amount of the transfer spent on domestic goods. Similarly, the change in autonomous spending on imports in *B* is the amount of the transfer spent on imports. The changes in autonomous spending cause changes in income that, in turn, induce further changes in spending on domestic goods and on imports. The parameters are the marginal propensities to import for each country, the marginal propensities to consume domestic goods, the proportion of the transfer spent on domestic goods and on imports in each country.

If the transfer causes a deficit in *A*'s balance of payments, the resulting changes in spending have failed fully to effect the transfer. To eliminate the deficit, *A* must deflate relatively or devalue. Either step will worsen *A*'s terms of trade because supply is infinitely elastic in the model. If the transfer causes a surplus in *A*'s balance of payments, the transfer is over-effected and the corrective measures will cause

A's terms of trade to improve. Whether the transfer is under-effected, fully effected, or over-effected depends upon the parameters in the model; any outcome is possible and there is no reason a priori to expect one outcome rather than another. If a transfer has the same effect on spending for domestic goods and imports as any other change in income, then the transfer would necessarily be under-effected provided that all marginal propensities were positive [Metzler, 51]. The proof of these propositions is quite complicated and so it is not given here; the curious reader can go to the works cited but must expect some tedious going in working through the proofs.

Flexible exchange rates / Now consider the transfer in a Keynesian model with flexible rather than fixed exchange rates [Kemp, 38]. Assume that the fiscal measures associated with financing and disposing of the transfer have no effect on the amount and pattern of spending out of any given level of disposable income. Let the paying country use three different methods of raising the funds for the transfer payment: an income tax, borrowing from the central bank, and a tax on imports or exports. A flexible exchange rate maintains payments equilibrium at all times and there are no loans between national monetary authorities to offset the transfer payment. Because the home-currency price of exports remains constant, exchange rate changes represent changes in the terms of trade. If a currency depreciates by 10 per cent, the terms of trade deteriorate by 10 per cent because imports rise in price (in the home currency) by that amount with no change in the price of exports. Assume further that total spending out of any given money income remains the same, even though changes occur in the price ratio between imported and home-produced goods. Finally, assume that transport costs are zero.

First, let country A levy an additional income tax yielding an amount equal to the transfer payment and let country B distribute the full amount of the transfer to its residents. Assume that A's balance of payments moves to a new equilibrium such that A has an export surplus equal to the transfer. As a result of these assumptions, disposable incomes in the two countries do not change. Disposable income in A (D_A) equals total spending by A's residents on domestic and imported goods (E_A) plus the trade balance ($x_A - y_A$, with x_A being value of exports and y_A being value of imports) less the transfer (T): $D_A = E_A + (x_A - y_A) - T$. The preceding assumptions mean that the trade balance ($x_A - y_A$) increases by the amount of the transfer (T), leaving A's disposable income unchanged. The deflationary effect of the income tax matches exactly the inflationary effect of the improved trade balance so that the net multiplier effect on income is nil. The opposite result occurs in B where the positive transfer offsets the adverse change in the trade balance, leaving disposable income unchanged. Therefore, no income changes occur to induce a change in the balance of payments: the entire burden of adjustment falls on the exchange rate or the terms of trade. Assuming the sum of the import elasticities exceeds one, A's currency must depreciate (its terms of trade must deteriorate) to maintain equilibrium. The extent of depreciation will vary directly with the size of the transfer payment and indirectly with the initial volume of trade and the sum of the import elasticities [Kemp, 38, p. 111].

If the government in B does not distribute any of the transfer, B's disposable income will fall at least by the amount of the transfer because there will be no offset to the resulting import surplus. Provided the multiplier in B is greater than one, there will be a secondary decline of income induced by the initial decline. The fall of B's income will tend to cause imports to fall, thus requiring an additional depreciation of A's currency to make the balance of payments accommodate the transfer. The required depreciation will be greater, the greater is B's marginal propensity to import and the smaller is B's marginal propensity to save. And the larger the proportion of the transfer that B's government distributes, the less will be the required depreciation of A's currency.

If country A finances the transfer by borrowing from the central bank, disposable income will rise initially by the increase of A's export surplus. This initial rise will induce a further rise provided the multiplier is greater than one. The increase of disposable income in A tends to increase imports and to make more difficult the generation of an export surplus equivalent to the transfer. The depreciation of A's currency (or deterioration of its terms of trade) will be greater the smaller A's marginal propensity to save and the larger A's marginal propensity to import. For any given distribution of the transfer by B's government, A's currency will depreciate more when the transfer is financed by central bank credit than when it is financed by an income tax [Kemp, 38, pp. 113–114].

If A raises the funds for the transfer payment by imposing a uniform import tax, there is a possibility that A's currency will appreciate. The import tax will raise the prise and reduce the quantity of imports from B. If the price elasticity of demand for imports in A is unity, total spending on imports will be constant provided disposable income does not change. Therefore the expenditure on imports net of the tax will fall by the amount of the tax proceeds. Because the tax proceeds equal the transfer, the resulting export surplus for A is equal to the transfer. The terms of trade and the exchange rate do not change. In B, the effect on disposable income of the decline in exports is just equal to the effect of distributing the transfer, so B's imports do not change. If the elasticity of A's demand for imports is greater than unity, A's currency will appreciate and the terms of trade will improve, provided again that B's government distributes all the transfer. If the elasticity is less than one, A's terms of trade will worsen. If B does not distribute all of the transfer, the elasticity of A's demand for imports must be greater than one for the transfer to be fully effected without a change in the terms of trade.

Several conclusions stand out in the discussion of the transfer in a Keynesian model with flexible exchange rates. First, the paying country would prefer the various methods of financing the transfer in the following order, assuming it considers only its own welfare: an import tax, an income tax, and central bank credit.[14] With an import tax, the terms of trade might improve; with an income tax, the terms of trade must deteriorate; and with central bank credit, they will deteriorate more than with an income tax. The general conclusion with a classical, fully employed economy was that the terms of trade may move either in favor of or against the paying country, depending upon the preferences for imports versus home goods in the two countries. But with an underemployed economy, the terms of trade must deteriorate for the paying country if it finances the transfer with central bank credit or an income tax.

Probable Effects

The preceding discussion of transfers suggests that the terms of trade may go either way, depending upon the actual circumstances of each transfer payment. But is there any way of generalizing about the actual conditions and hence about the probable outcome? In the real world, of course, there are transport costs, more than two goods, and more than two countries. The existence of transport costs may, as Samuelson suggested, create a presumption that the terms of trade will move against the paying country but the presumption is still a weak one. Graham argued that in a world of many commodities and many countries, the terms of trade between any pair of countries are virtually useless for analytical purposes and are probably not measurable in any event [25, pp. 284–85]. Empirical testing of the effects of capital transfers (lending or reparations payments) has been inconclusive [Kindleberger, 42, ch. 6]. Verification of theoretical conclusions based on the highly abstract models is generally not possible because the assumptions of the models are not approximated in the real world. Furthermore, longer-run forces are apt to swamp the short-run effects of the transfer with respect to the terms of trade.

Suppose the transfer payment is a loan or grant from a capital-rich country with low interest rates to a capital-poor country with high interest rates. Such a transfer is apt to cause a relatively large rise in the receiving country's income but is not apt to cause much change (if any) in the money income of the lending or paying country. Kindleberger believes that the income multiplier and import propensity of the receiving country under these circumstances will probably be high enough to cause the transfer to be fully effected initially [40, p. 371]. The subsequent movement of the terms of trade will depend upon the kind of spending to which the transfer leads in the receiving country and upon relative supply elasticities. Investment projects may require large amounts of imported capital goods because the capital-poor countries lack a large capital goods industry; other projects may use primarily local resources as in the case of some construction. The change in spending on the goods of the lending and receiving countries will vary from one investment project to another and will vary with the stage of economic development [42, pp. 126–127].

If the transfer causes a change in the total spending on the goods of one or both countries, the supply elasticities will, of course, have an effect upon the resulting change in the terms of trade. When there is an equal increase in spending for the goods of both the paying and receiving country, the terms of trade will move favorably for the country with the less elastic supply because the increased spending will drive its prices up more. The models discussed above tend to understate the role of supply elasticities because they assume supply curves to be completely elastic or completely inelastic. The supply elasticities have no effect upon the outcome only if the transfer causes equal but opposite income changes in the two countries and if the sum of the marginal import propensities equals unity. Under these conditions, no change occurs in total spending for the goods of each country.

A consideration of supply elasticities and relative demand changes suggests that the terms of trade are likely to shift in favor of the capital-poor country receiving the transfer but that the shift will be small. Any increase in spending on goods of the lending country is not apt to affect prices for two reasons. First, the lending country will probably be large relative to the borrowing country so that the change in demand for the lender's goods will be small in relative terms. Second, supply elasticities for exports of the lending country (probably an industrially advanced country) are apt to be relatively high so that a small increase in demand will not affect prices significantly. By contrast, the borrowing country may be highly specialized in exports and its supply curves will tend to be inelastic in the short run. But the country may consume small and inelastic amounts of its exports so that its increased income will not greatly affect export prices. The difference in assumed supply elasticities suggests, therefore, that any movement that may occur in the terms of trade will probably favor the capital-importing country.

Thus for transfer of capital from industrial countries to less developed countries, theoretical considerations suggest minor changes in the terms of trade, with any change likely to favor the borrowing country.

149

But for lending, reparations, or other unilateral transfers among industrial countries, there is no basis for assuming *a priori* that the terms of trade will move one way or the other. The outcome will depend upon income changes, propensities, and supply elasticities. Only an empirical study of these determinants will indicate the probable effect of the specific transfer on the terms of trade.

☐ THE EFFECTS OF ECONOMIC GROWTH

After World War II, discussions of the dollar shortage and the problems of underdeveloped countries created a great interest in the effects of economic growth and technological change on international trade. This section summarizes the aspects of the literature on this topic that relate to the effects of growth on the terms of trade. Chapter II contained a brief discussion of these effects. Economic growth means simply increased output — whether caused by technical progress, capital accumulation, or increase of the labor supply.

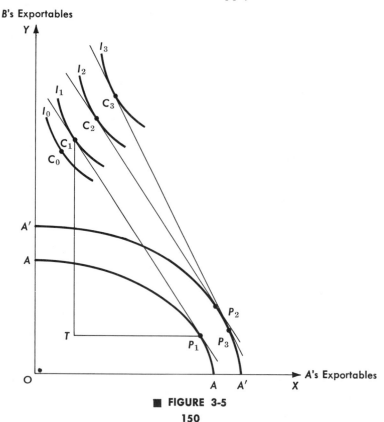

■ FIGURE 3-5
150

The analysis relies upon the usual model with two countries, two factors, and two commodities. Both countries maintain continuous full employment and factors cannot move from one country to the other. No money exists in the model, so the analysis is in real terms. Additional assumptions are that the production blocks (production possibilities curves or production frontiers) are convex from above and that the community indifference curves are convex from below. Initially, growth occurs in one country only.

The first step is to show the possible outcomes resulting from growth, assuming that the increase in productive capacity occurs without changing tastes, i.e., without changing the community indifference map. In actual practice, changes in tastes will undoubtedly accompany growth. The assumption of constant tastes simplifies the analysis, however, and does not invalidate the analytical technique. The second step is to consider what determines the direction of the change in the terms of trade. The simple model used in this discussion shows only the *direction* of change; more elaborate models are necessary to indicate the *extent* of the change. The concluding section discusses the implications of the theoretical analysis for probable changes in the terms of trade in the real world.

□ GROWTH IN ONLY ONE COUNTRY [15]

Figure 3-5 shows the production blocks and community indifference curves of the growing country. Pre-growth production is at P_1 on the production block AA, and the pre-growth consumption at C_1 on indifference curve I_1. The country exports TP_1 of X and imports TC_1 of Y; the slope of P_1C_1 gives the equilibrium terms of trade. As a result of growth, the production frontier shifts outward from AA to $A'A'$. If a new equilibrium occurs with no change in the terms of trade, production will be at P_2 and consumption at C_2 (the slopes of P_2C_2 and P_1C_1 are the same). The growth of real income is thus proportionate to the growth of output. If the terms of trade improve, consumption could perhaps move to C_3 on indifference curve I_3, making the growth of real income exceed the growth of output. If the terms of trade deteriorate, the gain from increased output could exceed the loss from worse terms of trade, in which case consumption would be on an indifference curve between I_1 and I_2. A highly adverse shift in the terms of trade could move consumption to an indifference curve below I_1, say at C_0 on I_0. At C_0 the growing country would have lower real income because the loss from the deterioration of the terms of trade exceeded the gain from increased output.[16]

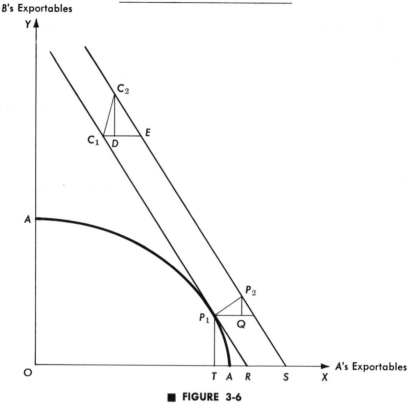

■ **FIGURE 3-6**

Determining factors / The next step is to investigate the factors that determine the direction of shift in the terms of trade. In Figure 3-6, AA is again the pre-growth production curve with pre-growth production and consumption at P_1 and C_1. After growth takes place, production would be at P_2 and consumption at C_2 if there were no change in the terms of trade (the slopes of P_1C_1 and P_2C_2 are the same). The indifference curves and the outward-shifted production block were not drawn in order to keep the diagram simple. C_1 and C_2 represent tangencies between the lines RC_1 and SC_2 and two separate indifference curves; P_1 and P_2 represent tangencies between RC_1 and SC_2 and the two production frontiers. The direction of shift in the terms of trade will depend upon whether consumption or production of the imported commodity would increase more at constant terms of trade as the country expands its output. At constant terms of trade, growth would cause the country to increase consumption of the imported commodity by DC_2 and to increase production of the same commodity by QP_2. If DC_2 exceeds QP_2, as it does in Figure 3-6, the net demand for imports increases and causes the import price to rise. The new equilibrium will thus cause the terms of trade to shift against the growing country. Thus, the shift in the terms of trade depends upon how growth affects both the demand for, and the supply of, the imported commodity.

Output elasticities / The literature employs the concepts of output-elasticity of supply (E_{SY}) and output-elasticity of demand (E_{DY}) in analyzing the effects of growth on the terms of trade [Bhagwati, 8]. Output-elasticity of supply is the percentage change in production of importables divided by the percentage change in total productive capacity, assuming unchanged relative commodity prices.[17] Output-elasticity of demand is the percentage change in consumption of importables (at constant relative commodity prices) divided by the percentage change in total productive capacity. Both elasticities indicate the real income effects of growth; they measure, in effect, the real income elasticity of production and consumption of imports at unchanged relative commodity prices.

The demand effects of growth are considered neutral if $E_{DY} = 1$, anti-trade biased if $E_{DY} < 1$, and pro-trade biased if $E_{DY} > 1$. An output elasticity of demand greater than one means that growth has caused the percentage increase in demand for importables to exceed the percentage increase in productive capacity. If the output elasticity of demand should be negative, i.e., if growth causes the amount of importables demanded to fall, the demand effect of growth is ultra-anti-trade biased. Similarly, the demand effect would be ultra-pro-trade biased if growth caused an absolute decline in the amount of exportables demanded. Both of these ultra-demand effects require the existence of inferior goods. Because exports and imports of any country are not apt to be inferior goods in the aggregate, there is no serious loss in simply ruling out this possibility [Meier, 48, p.33]. The production effects of expansion are neutral if $E_{SY} = 1$, pro-trade biased if $E_{SY} < 1$, and anti-trade biased if $E_{SY} > 1$. An elasticity greater than one for production means that growth has increased the supply of importables by a greater percentage than it has increased total productive capacity, thus tending to reduce the demand for importables. If growth reduces the domestic supply of importables, it is ultra-pro-trade biased; if it reduces the supply of exportables, it is ultra-anti-trade biased. The ultra-supply effects of growth, in contrast to the ultra-demand effects, receive a good deal of attention in most discussions of growth and the terms of trade.

A word of warning is in order at this point. A neutral demand effect occurs when expansion causes the demand for importables to grow at the same rate as productive capacity, assuming no change in the terms of trade. Similarly, a neutral supply effect is a unit elasticity reflecting equal percentage increases in domestic output of the importable good and in aggregate productivity capacity, again at constant terms of trade. The definitions of neutrality and bias are arbitrary ones and they do not refer to the direct effect upon the terms of trade. For instance, a neutral demand effect accompanied by a neutral supply effect is not neutral in impact upon the terms of trade. It is unfortunate in a chapter on the terms of trade that neutraltiy and bias do not refer directly to the effect upon the terms of trade. Nevertheless, this discussion follows the definitions prevailing in the literature — because to introduce new definitions more appropriate to the immediate purpose might hopelessly confuse a student who refers to the professional literature.

Figure 3-7 provides a geometric illustration of these elasticity concepts. C_1 and P_1 are the consumption and production points before growth. The C's and P's on the line parallel to C_1P_1 represent possible consumption and production points after growth with constant terms of trade. If consumption shifts to C_2, the percentage increase in consumption of both goods is C_1C_2/OC_1. The percentage increase in productive capacity, measured in good X, is RS/OR, which is the same as the ratio C_1C_2/OC_1. Consequently, the demand effect of growth will be neutral $(E_{DY} = 1)$ when consumption shifts to C_2. The effect will be pro-trade biased $(E_{DY} > 1)$ if consumption shifts to a point between C_2 and C_3; ultra-pro-trade biased above C_3; anti-trade biased between C_2

B's Exportables

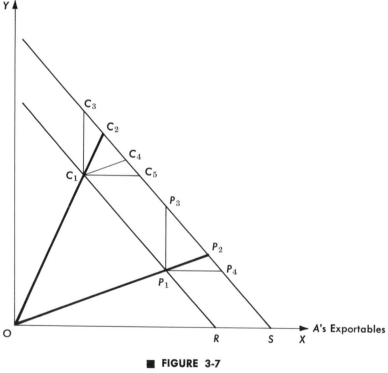

■ FIGURE 3-7

and C_5 ($E_{DY} < 1$); and finally, ultra-anti-trade biased ($E_{DY} < 0$) if consumption is below C_5 on the line SC_3. The production effect will be neutral ($E_{SY} = 1$) if production shifts to P_2; anti-trade biased ($E_{SY} > 1$) if between P_2 and P_3; ultra-anti-trade biased if above P_3; pro-trade biased ($E_{SY} < 1$) if between P_2 and P_4; and finally, ultra-pro-trade biased ($E_{SY} < 0$) if below P_4 on SC_3.

Total effect / The total effect of expansion is the result of combining the production and the consumption effects. In Figure 3-7, the length of P_1C_1 indicates the desired amount of trade (at the going terms of trade) because it is the hypotenuse of the trade triangle before growth. With neutral production and consumption effects, the desired trade after growth (at constant terms of trade) is P_2C_2. If the after-growth trade line is longer than P_2C_2 but shorter than P_4C_3, the total effect of expansion is pro-trade biased. If the trade line is longer than P_4C_3, the overall effect is ultra-pro-trade biased. By contrast, the total effect is anti-trade biased if the trade line is shorter than P_2C_2 but longer than P_2C_4 ($P_2C_4 = P_1C_1$ because C_1C_4 is parallel to P_1P_2). Ultra-anti-trade bias exists if the trade line is shorter than P_2C_4.

Whenever the new trade line (at constant terms of trade) is longer than the pre-growth trade line P_1P_1 in Figure 3-7), the demand for imports has increased and the terms of trade will worsen for the growing country. When both demand and supply effects of expansion are neutral, the total effect is also neutral with respect to consumption and production. But it causes an adverse shift in the terms of trade because the demand for imports increases (P_2C_2 is longer than P_1C_1). Only if the new trade line were equal in length to P_1C_1 would the terms of trade remain constant. In Figure 3-7, P_2C_4 is equal to P_1C_1; hence, the terms of trade may remain constant with a neutral production effect combined with an anti-trade biased consumption effect. In fact, the terms of trade will improve for the growing country only if the total effect is ultra-anti-trade biased, i.e., if the new trade line is shorter than P_1C_1.[18]

More Elaborate Models

There are numerous other and more elaborate models to show the effects of growth on the terms of trade but they are generally quite complicated and would require lengthy explanations if presented here. A few comments will, however, indicate the general features of some of these models. A logical extension of the preceding model is to postulate growth in both countries rather than in just one. The movement of the terms of trade will then depend on the relation between the net change in demand for imports in country A as it grows and the net change in supply of these imports by country B as it also grows [Bhagwati, 8, p. 402]. If the net demand for imports in A increases by more than the net supply in B, the terms of trade will turn against country A.[19]

The preceding models indicate only the direction in which the terms of trade must move. Bhagwati [10] developed a single formula that includes the determinants of the extent of change in the terms of trade necessary to restore equilibrium. These determinants are (1) the elasticity of substitution between exportables and importables in consumption; (2) the elasticity of transformation in production between exportables and importables; (3) the effect on consumption caused by the change in real income resulting from the altered terms of trade; and (4) the elasticity of the foreign offer curve facing the expanding country.

Johnson [31, pp. 78–83] analyzed separately the effects of expansion caused by technical progress, by capital accumulation, and by population growth (increase of labor supply). His model is necessarily elaborate because he assumes (1) different factor intensities in the production of each good; (2) different output elasticities of demand for the two goods; (3) neutral technical progress, i.e., neither capital saving nor labor saving; and (4) more rapid technical progress in one industry than the other. Findlay and Grubert [23] have extended the analysis to include non-neutral technical progress, i.e., labor saving and capital saving innovations. Bardham [6] suggested that shifts in the distribution of income caused by technical change may be important and could reverse some conclusions of models that assume no change in the distribution of income. Kemp [37] analyzed the effects of technological change on the terms of trade in an underemployed world with flexible exchange rates.

Probable Effects

What are the implications of this theoretical discussion for probable shifts of the terms of trade in the real world? A number of economists have suggested at least tentative implications of various models. Bruton [14], for instance, concluded that the terms of trade were not apt to deteriorate for a less developed country vis-a-vis an advanced country that was growing through technological advances if the technical change uniformly reduced the inputs required for producing given outputs in all industries of the advanced country. In reaching his conclusions, he adopted (1) alternative assumptions concerning the behavior of U.S. prices and money income and (2) what he believed were rough but reasonable values for the elasticities, based on previous statistical studies.

Triantis [66] analyzed the possible effects of changes in per capita incomes of poor countries on their terms of trade vis-a-vis the advanced countries. A rise in per capita incomes of the poor countries would tend to turn the terms of trade against them if the income elasticity of demand were higher, as it probably would be, for imports from the advanced countries than for their own exports. If the expansion in poor countries originated in a rapid population growth so that per capita incomes fell, the terms of trade might move in favor of the poor countries because of a greater reduction in demand for imports from industrial countries than for their own export goods. But the influence coming from changes in per capita incomes of the poor countries would probably be overwhelmed by changes in the advanced countries, so that a more realistic assumption would be that growth is more rapid in the advanced countries.

Black and Streeten [13] suggested two reasons why the growth of demand in industrial countries is apt to be anti-trade biased or perhaps even ultra-anti-trade biased. The first is the tendency of technical progress to reduce the inputs of raw materials per unit of output. On the assumption that raw materials are obtained primarily from the less developed countries, such technical progress would tend to turn the terms of trade against these countries. The second factor is the tendency for consumers to spend more of their incomes on services as incomes rise. The import content of services, with the exception of foreign tourism, is low, so the demand effect accompanying increased income in advanced countries tends to be biased against trade. But these demand effects could be wholly or partially offset by the production effects of expansion, so the two demand considerations suggested by Black and Streeten do not lead to a definite conclusion with respect to the terms of trade. Also, as indicated above, the terms of trade could shift in favor of the less developed countries even if the total effect of the expansion in advanced countries is anti-trade biased.

Black and Streeten correctly pointed out that much technical change results in new or improved products. They went on to suggest [13, p. 141] that an improvement in the quality of a country's export good would tend to divert spending by foreigners from their own domestic goods to the improved import good. Therefore, quality improvement in export goods makes foreign demand more trade biased and it tends to shift the terms of trade in favor of the innovating country. The improved product might also divert domestic spending in the innovating country toward its exportables, producing a tendency to anti-trade bias and strengthening the favorable shift in the terms of trade. But price indexes used in computing the terms of trade cannot satisfactorily reflect the effects of new products or improved products. If the new or improved product is better but costs more, the buyer may be better off than if he bought the old product at a lower price. So it is not valid to say that the terms of trade deteriorate for the importing country when it pays a higher price for the improved product because price indexes cannot satisfactorily handle new or improved products.

Johnson [31, pp. 92–93] warned that two-country models have limitations in providing guidance for probable effects in the real world. The use of two countries rather than many exaggerates the relative effect of growth on the terms of trade. In addition, a two-country model generally posits sharply different factor proportions and thus stresses complementarity rather than competitiveness among nations in international trade. An analysis of two broad categories of countries, such as industrial countries and primary producing countries, does not indicate the effects of output expansion in any one country of either group. The countries in each group are imperfect competitors, so that growth in any one would affect the terms of trade of the others in the group. The magnitude of the effect would depend upon the share of the growing country in world trade, the world demand for the exportables of the group to which it belongs, and the extent of substitutability in world consumption between its exports and imports and those of other countries. Consequently, the shift in the terms of trade of any one country may depend more upon its rate of growth compared to that of its rivals than upon the aggregate rates of growth for the two groups of countries.

☐ THE TREND FOR PRIMARY PRODUCTS VS. MANUFACTURES

Although the long-term trend in the terms of trade between manufactures and primary products may seem to belong to the preceding section on growth and the terms of trade, it generally has a separate position in the literature and it will occupy a separate section here. Many writers consider the terms of trade between developed and underdeveloped countries as equivalent to the terms of trade between industrial and primary products. The reason for this assumption is, of course, that underdeveloped countries export mainly agricultural products and raw materials while the developed countries export most of the manufactured goods. But as will be pointed out later, the terms of trade for developed versus underdeveloped countries is not identical to those for manufactures versus primary products.

The underdeveloped countries are much concerned over shifts in their terms of trade for a number of reasons. The volume of international trade for them is generally large in relation to their national incomes. Trade is vital because it provides them with technical knowledge, skill, capital, machinery, and equipment — all of which are essential for economic development. These countries will naturally be intensely concerned with all aspects of their trading relationships, including their terms of trade. Any worsening of their terms of trade, other things being equal (particularly no changes in productivity in producing their exports and no change in export volume), will reduce their capacity to import and shift income away from them, thus hampering their efforts to promote economic development.

Two Views

The classical economists believed that the terms of trade would shift in the long run in favor of primary products and against manufactures because primary products are subject to diminishing returns whereas manufactures are subject to increasing returns. With increased factor supplies but unchanged technology, this meant that production frontiers were moving out more rapidly along the axis for manufactures than along the axis for primary products. On the supply side the growth of inputs would have an anti-trade bias in the less developed countries and a pro-trade bias in the developed countries. The net effect of the production change would be, therefore, a reduction in the prices of manufactures and an increase in the prices of primary products.[20] The classical view ignored the demand effects of growth.

Today, however, a group of prominent economists argue that the terms of trade have actually deteriorated for the poor countries rather than improved [Prebisch, 67; Singer, 63; and Myrdal, 57]. The original basis for this view (hereafter called the secular-deterioration hypothesis) was the trend in the terms of trade for the United Kingdom from the latter part of the nineteenth century to the late 1930's. At the end of this period, a given quantity of primary products exported to Great Britain would have purchased 40 per cent less of manufactured goods than at the beginning [United Nations, 68]. Later refinements in the price indexes show less of a shift against primary products [Kindleberger, 42] but the new data have not shaken the belief of this group of economists that the long-term trend is against the poor countries.[21]

Theoretical Basis for the Secular-Deterioration Hypothesis

The early proponents of the secular-deterioration hypothesis suggested three causes for the shift in the terms of trade. The first is that the developed countries keep most of the gains from increased productivity in manufactures by increasing wages and profits and not reducing prices. By contrast, productivity growth in primary products results in lower product prices so that the gains accrue primarily to buyers of these products rather than to the factors of production. If all prices fell in proportion to the increasing productivity, the reductions would be less for primary than for manufactured products because technical progress has been greater in manufacturing.[22] Therefore, as the gap between productivity trends for primary and manufactured products widens, the terms of trade should shift in favor of the poor countries. But, according to this argument, the opposite happened because improvements in productivity did not lead to lower prices for manufactures.

The second reason for the shift against the poor countries is the contrasting cyclical behavior of prices for manufactures and primary products. The argument is that primary product prices rise sharply during prosperous periods but fall just as sharply during the cyclical downswing, losing all the increase of the upswing. The prices of manufactures, by contrast, do not rise as much during prosperous periods and they do not fall as far during the downswing as they rise in prosperity. The prices of manufactures are less flexible in the downward direction because of monopolistic factor and product markets. As a consequence of this contrasting cyclical behavior of prices, there is a widening of the gap between the prices of primary and manufactured products over successive cycles.[23]

A third reason is that there has been a relative increase in demand for manufactures and a relative decrease in demand for primary products. The explanation is partly because of Engel's Law which states that as income rises, a smaller share is spent on food. The income elasticity of demand is thus presumably lower for agricultural products than for manufactures. The other part of the explanation is that technical progress in manufacturing has reduced the amount of raw materials used in producing any given amount of finished products. In terms of the models in the preceding section, the demand effects of income growth are anti-trade biased in the industrial countries and pro-trade biased in the poor countries, causing a shift in prices against the poor countries. Technical change in the industrial countries is also anti-trade biased in that it reduces the demand for raw material imports. In the poor countries, technical change reduces the domestic demand for the export goods (raw materials) and is thus pro-trade biased. Technical change and Engel's Law work together in causing a deterioration of the terms of trade for the poor countries.

Kindleberger [43, pp. 342–347] subsequently proposed a somewhat different explanation of the trend in the terms of trade. He sought to determine whether the trend is attributable mainly to conditions of demand or of supply. If manufactures and primary products have the same productivity growth, Engel's Law and the tendency for manufactures to incorporate less and less raw material per unit of product would cause demand for manufactures to rise relative to demand for primary products and thus cause a worsening of the terms of trade for primary products. And given these demand conditions, the developed countries have a further advantage on the supply side in that their resources are more easily shifted. They can reallocate resources toward the production of those products for which demand is rising and away from those products for which demand is falling. By contrast, according to Kindleberger, the poor countries are less able to shift resources out of primary products subject to declining demand; therefore, the prices of primary products fall drastically when demand declines. The supply response is asymmetrical, however, because supply increases in response to higher prices, even though it does not decrease in response to lower prices. Kindleberger's conclusion is that in industrial countries entry and exit are easy for both manufacturers and primary producers; in underdeveloped countries entry is easy for primary producers but exit is difficult and entry is difficult for manufacturers of relatively complex products. Thus, in the less developed countries the supply of primary products does not fall when prices fall but it does rise when prices rise. By contrast, a price increase for imported manufactures does not generally cause an increase in the domestic supply of such goods. The lack of trained workers, the shortage of capital, the lack of technical knowledge, and the lack of managerial skills all combine to prevent the shifting of resources that would enable the underdeveloped countries to avoid the unfavorable effects of declining relative prices for their exports.[24]

Kindleberger [43, p. 343] also suggests that the exports of underdeveloped countries face more inelastic foreign demands than the exports of developed countries because the less developed countries are more specialized in production. Their exports are not widely consumed at home nor widely produced abroad, so that the elasticity of supply of these products tends to be low, as does the foreign demand for them. If the importing country has domestic production that competes with the imports, the domestic supply may be highly elastic for price rises, thus minimizing the rise. By contrast, the supply may not fall in the face of price weakness because import restrictions protect producers. The increase in domestic production prevents large price increases, but there is nothing to set a floor for the price of exports of less developed countries.

Criticisms of the Data

Other economists have criticized both the statistical and analytical arguments advanced in support of the secular-deterioration hypothesis [Haberler, 28; Viner, 70, pp. 141–146; Meier, 48, pp. 55–63; Morgan, 54 and 55]. This hypothesis was originally based on the "inverse" of Great Britain's terms of trade because the appropriate data were not available to show the terms of trade of individual underdeveloped countries over a long period. This inverse had serious weaknesses that made it unacceptable as support for the hypothesis. First, British import prices were c.i.f. while export prices were f.o.b., so import prices included transportation costs but export prices did not. During the period from 1870 to 1938 ocean transport costs declined a great deal. Consequently, the British c.i.f. price could have fallen yet the price received by the exporting country for primary products could have risen. Similarly, the prices paid by the poor countries for British goods could have fallen, even though the British f.o.b. prices rose.

Most computations of the net barter terms of trade have included prices for only the merchandise items in the current account.[25] There is, however, no logical reason for omitting the service or invisible items in the current account from the computations. Changes in the price of services entering international accounts affect the welfare of the trading countries just as do changes in the prices of commodities. The underdeveloped countries have been, on balance, heavy importers of services from the advanced countries. The trend in the terms of trade for services has clearly favored the less developed countries [Kindleberger, 43, p. 342]. The cost of transport and long-term interest rates for foreign loans have fallen over time. Probably even more important is the change in the division of profits between direct investors in industrial countries and the governments of the less developed countries. The share accruing to the host governments has increased sharply during recent years.[26] For these reasons, any computation of terms of trade that omits service items would be biased against the underdeveloped countries.

A second defect of the terms-of-trade index is that the U.K. import and export price indexes for the period 1870 to 1938 both include such broad categories of products that they conceal widely divergent price movements for individual products. No single underdeveloped country exported all of the products in the U.K. import price index and no individual industrial country exported the same products as Britain. Kindleberger's study demonstrated that the terms of trade for other industrial countries behaved somewhat differently than Great Britain's [42, pp. 53–57, p. 233]. Undoubtedly the terms of trade of individual poor countries would also have shown considerable divergences. Furthermore, the terms of trade between manufactures and primary products were not the same thing as those between developed and underdeveloped countries because some developed countries exported primary products (coal, wheat, cotton, lumber, woodpulp, and so forth) and some underdeveloped countries exported manufactures (cotton textiles, burlap, and other relatively simple manufactures).

Bhagwati [11] has shown that the arguments by proponents of the secular-deterioration hypothesis actually comprise as many as five distinct hypotheses. And data that support one of the hypotheses frequently do not support the others. By examining each hypothesis separately, Bhagwati is skeptical that the historical evidence has cumulated to support a general hypothesis that the terms of trade have turned against the underdeveloped areas. In fact, he says the supposed cumulation of evidence in support of the hypothesis is only a myth.

Finally, there are some general problems associated with the construction of price indexes that lead to skepticism concerning the real meaning of any terms of trade index. The methods of constructing price indexes cannot adequately allow for the introduction of new commodities or for improvements in the quality of old products. The failure adequately to cover new products gives an upward bias to the price indexes because the prices of new products typically decline during the early years of their production. Similarly, the failure to allow for quality improvements imparts an upward bias to the price indexes. Because the introduction of new products and the improvement of old ones is much more common among manufactured than among primary products, the price index for traded manufactures contains a strong upward bias relative to the index for primary products. Consequently, empirical evidence showing an adverse shift in the terms of trade for primary products may be misleading.

In his major study of the terms of trade, Kindleberger constructed detailed price indexes for manufactures and primary products [42, ch. 11]. His conclusion was that the indexes did not show a tendency in the long run to shift against primary products and in favor of manufactures. On the contrary, he suggested that if it were possible to define units of equal quality for both groups of products, the terms of trade might have worsened for manufactures. But paradoxically the terms of trade have turned against the underdeveloped countries — at least when no adjustment is made for quality changes. Kindleberger believes this generalization will hold even after allowing for changes in the price of services. By contrast, Morgan [55] examined data from numerous sources and concluded that they did not support generalizations but rather emphasized the variety of price experience. He feels that the fluctuations in the terms of trade are better explained by the particular circumstances for a particular product, country, and time than by the generalizations advanced by Prebisch and others.

Unless someone produces better price indexes than are now available, the empirical evidence will never completely resolve the issue of whether the terms of trade have moved unfavorably for primary products. Skeptics will point to the failure of the indexes to include new products, quality changes, and changes in prices for services, and they will probably conclude, as Haberler did [28, p. 283], that the empirical evidence does not show a long-term trend against primary products.

Criticisms of the Theory

The analytical basis for the secular-deterioration hypothesis also has numerous weaknesses [Haberler, 28]. One argument advanced in support of the hypothesis is that the underdeveloped countries have strong competition among both factor suppliers and primary producers, so that any technical improvement in production causes prices to fall but does not change money wages or profits. By contrast, factor suppliers (particularly workers) and manufacturers have monopoly power in the developed countries so that they are able to capture the benefits of technical change through higher money wages and profits with no decline in prices. There is no question but that technical progress in industrial countries has led to higher money wages with stable or rising prices rather than to constant money income with falling prices. But this behavior does not automatically mean that the terms of trade for the industrial countries will improve. It is important to note that monopoly at the factor level cannot affect the terms of trade unless there is also monopoly at the product level *in the world market* [Kindleberger, 42, p. 247]. National price-wage policies cannot affect the terms of trade if the foreign supply and demand in international trade are highly elastic. Even if domestic monopolies raise the price level in industrial countries, they will not affect relative world prices of primary and manufactured products unless exporters have monopoly power in the world markets. Even when this power exists, its effects on the terms of trade are not certain because monopolists sometimes hold down prices when competition would force them up. If exporters lack this monopoly power, they could not raise export prices without pricing themselves out of world markets — unless the exchange rate rose. As Kindleberger pointed out [42, p. 247], differences among countries in wage-price policies will affect their balance of payments and perhaps their exchange rates but not their terms of trade, unless individual countries have monopoly power in the world markets for their exports. As an illustration he mentioned that although domestic prices increased 50 times in Italy and increased only 4 times in Belgium between 1938 and 1952, Belgium's terms of trade improved while Italy's declined. Also, the rapid increase in price levels in many South American countries in recent years has not improved their terms of trade because world demand and supply for their exports were such that the countries had to devalue their currencies as domestic prices rose.

When monetary factors alone cause industrial prices to rise, the less developed countries can protect themselves from any real burden by appreciating their currencies or by allowing an equal degree of domestic inflation. These countries would be hurt only if there were an unfavorable shift in their *real* (as distinguished from their monetary) terms of trade. Such a real shift could occur, according to the secular-deterioration hypothesis, if these countries were to sell competitively-priced primary products and buy monopolistically-priced manufactures. But the mere existence of monopoly in the exporting of manufactured goods will not give rise to a *trend* in the terms of trade against primary products; it could cause the index to be less favorable both at the beginning and at the ending of a period than it otherwise would be. Monopoly power would influence the trend in the terms of trade only if the degree of that power were to change during the period under study.

Furthermore, there is considerable evidence to suggest that competition in world markets for manufactures is greater now than in the past [Haberler, 28, p. 284; Kindleberger, 43, pp. 345–46].[27] More individual firms and particularly more countries now export capital goods, machinery, and industrial technology than formerly. The recent formation of the European Economic Community indicates a greater reliance on competition, especially among manufacturing firms. Many countries are much concerned about their balances of payments and whether their exporters are pricing themselves out of world markets. Even if a country has only a single producer of a particular product, that producer may face strong competition from foreign producers in both domestic and foreign markets. In minerals production, there may, in fact, be more monopoly than in manufacturing. World production of minerals is typically dominated by a few large firms that attempt to maintain prices. Agriculture is, however, generally competitive, at least until governments step in to protect or assist it. But the monopoly-power explanation still does not provide much support for the secular-deterioration hypothesis.

The other major analytical basis for the hypothesis is that the demand for primary products has declined relative to the demand for manufactures because of Engel's Law and because of the tendency for technical progress to reduce the amount of raw materials consumed per unit of manufactured products. Therefore, a rise of incomes causes a relative decline in the demand for food and raw materials and a relative increase for other goods and services, including manufactures.[28] But demand effects alone do not determine the terms of trade — supply also plays a role. Shifts in the supply curves in the industrial countries could offset the effect of the different income elasticities of demand, so that prices need not turn against primary products. In theory, the terms of trade could still move either way, despite Engel's Law and despite reduced raw material requirements per unit of manufactures.

The preceding discussion concerns only the net barter terms of trade. Even though a country suffers a deterioration in its net barter terms of trade, it could still realize a welfare gain, provided its single factoral terms of trade were to improve by more than the decline in the net barter index. Also, as mentioned in the introduction, the income terms of trade can improve even though the net barter terms decline. Changes in the net barter terms of trade therefore do not necessarily indicate the effect on a country's welfare. But proponents of the secular-deterioration hypothesis generally say they are primarily interested in the division of the gains from trade rather than in these other measures. And they argue that over time more and more of the gains accrue to the developed countries.

To summarize, the proponents of the secular-deterioration hypothesis feel that empirical evidence indicates a downward trend in the terms of trade for underdeveloped countries. They have proposed several theoretical explanations for this trend. The opponents of the hypothesis argue that the evidence is faulty and that it does not establish a trend against the underdeveloped countries. Furthermore, the opponents reject most of the analytical arguments advanced in support of the secular-deterioration hypothesis. Unless there are some major advances in the statistical and theoretical issues pertaining to this discussion, proponents and opponents of the hypothesis will probably find enough support for their respective positions to keep the debate alive for a long time.

FOOTNOTES

1. For a skeptical view of the value of the terms of trade, see Benham [7], McLeod [46], and Staehle [65].

2. Viner [71, pp. 558–561] also distinguishes a real cost terms of trade and a utility terms of trade. These indexes would show directly the welfare effects of trade, provided it were possible to calculate the needed utility measures. The gain from trade would be the excess of the total utility attributable to imports over the disutility associated with producing and foregoing consumption of the exported goods. No way exists to calculate the desired utility measures, however, so the welfare effects must be obtained indirectly through use of other terms of trade indexes.

3. Major studies of the terms of trade for long periods are Devons [20], Imlah [30], Kindleberger [42], Martin and Thackeray [45], and Rostow [60].

4. The analysis was begun by Alfred Marshall whose conclusions were criticized by Viner and Graham. For a summary of this controversy, see Allen [1], Caves [15], Dasgupta [19], and Kemp [36]. Kemp's article [36] appears to have settled the controversy by pointing out the various possible interpretations of an increased demand curve that has the same elasticity as the original one.

5. For those not acquainted with offer curves, this footnote provides a brief explanation. In Figure 3-1, OA is the offer curve of country A. It shows the amount of X that commercial traders in A will export in exchange for specific amounts of Y, the import good. OB shows the amounts of Y that traders in B are willing to export in exchange for specific amounts of X. The slope of a ray from the origin to a point on an offer curve gives the ratio of exchange between the commodities at that point. The line from the origin is generally called the price line or the terms of trade line because it reflects the relative prices of the two goods. The offer curves tell us the quantities of the two goods each country would want to exchange at various terms of trade or rates of exchange between the goods. The intersection of the two offer curves determines the equilibrium price ratio between the goods. In Figure 3-1, the initial intersection is at T, and the slope of OT gives the equilibrium price ratio. For a more complete explanation, see Kindleberger [40, pp. 107–111].

6. The elasticity of A's demand for B's good at point c in the accompanying figure is $\dfrac{-Oa}{Ob}$ where Cb is tangent to OA at c and Ca is perpendicular to OX. [For a proof, see Vanek, 69, pp. 236–239]. Because the ratio $\left|\dfrac{Oa}{Ob}\right|$ is greater than one, the demand is elastic at c. At the point d on Oa where the tangent is perpendicular to OX, the elasticity of OA is unity (minus one). Beyond d on OA (when OA bends back toward the Y axis), the elasticity is less

than one, and demand is therefore inelastic. A straight line offer curve starting at the origin would be infinitely elastic because the segment Ob becomes zero. A similar geometric technique will indicate the elasticity of B's demand for A's good along B's offer curve.

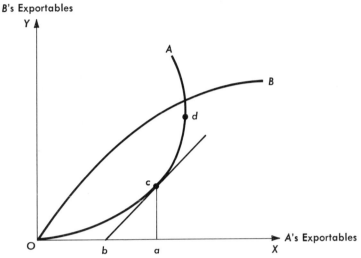

B's Exportables

A's Exportables

7. Metzler [50] has shown that if a tariff causes a decline in the domestic price of the imported good, it will shift income away from the scarce factor, assuming the protected good requires relatively intensive use of the scarce factor. He has thus found an exception to the general conclusion that a tariff alters the distribution of income to favor the scarce factor as compared to the distribution with free trade.

8. This conclusion actually rests upon restrictive assumptions. These assumptions and effects of relaxing them are discussed in Bhagwati and Johnson [12].

9. Gorman [24], for instance, concludes that the removal of existing tariffs would greatly expand the volume of trade but would have a relatively small effect on the terms of trade.

10. The derivation of this condition requires a good deal of algebraic manipulation and so will not be presented here. Briefly the procedure is to express the change in the foreign price of exports and imports as a function of the change in the exchange rate, to substitute these expressions into the formulas for the four elasticities so as to get all elasticities in terms of domestic prices, and then to substitute from the reduced elasticity formulas into the inequality showing a greater percentage change in import prices than in export prices (both in domestic currency). Haberler [26] employed a geometric technique to reach the same condition for a worsening of the terms of trade. He further demonstrated that if devaluation caused a deficit in the trade balance, it must worsen the terms of trade. But the trade balance could improve, even though the terms of trade deteriorated.

11. If the transfer causes a disequilibrium in the balance of payments, prices will have to change to restore equilibrium.

12. To allow for variable production would not alter the direction in which the terms of trade must move but might affect the extent of movement [Samuelson, 62].

13. Metzler's paper [51] is the classic one in the discussion of transfers between underemployed economies. His main interest, however, is in determining the amount of the transfer that will be effected by income changes, given various spending propensities and unchanged prices, interest rates, and exchange rates. He concludes that under the most reasonable assumptions, income changes will not fully effect the transfer. He is not directly concerned with what happens to the terms of trade.

14. It can be shown that A's terms of trade are less apt to improve if A finances the transfer with a sales tax on all home-produced goods than if it employs an import tax. Because a sales tax restricted to home-produced goods is so highly improbable as an actual policy measure, the analysis of such a tax is omitted, even though Kemp [38] discussed it.

15. This presentation follows closely the analysis of Bhagwati [8].

16. Bhagwati [9] has studied the possibility that growth might cause real income to decline because of a highly adverse shift in the terms of trade, a situation that he calls "immiserizing growth." Although Bhagwati considers this possibility more than just an intellectual curiosity, Meier [48] considers it unlikely to occur in the real world. Provided a country has some flexibility to alter its pattern of production in response to changing conditions, the elasticities of demand and supply are not apt to be such to cause immiserizing growth. Even if this flexibility is lacking, a country could still gain some of the benefits of expanded production by imposing appropriate taxes on traded goods.

17. Total productive capacity is measured in terms of just one of the goods. Production of the other good is converted to the first good at the pre-growth terms of trade for measuring capacity both before and after growth.

18. Meier [48] gives a complete summary of the overall biases that may result from various combinations of production and consumption biases.

19. Algebraically the net change in country A's demand for imports is

$$\text{(I)} \quad \frac{dQ_A}{Q_A} (Y_B \cdot E'_{SY} - C_{BY} \cdot E'_{DY})$$

where $\frac{dQ_A}{Q_A}$ is the percentage change in A's productive capacity, C_{AY} is A's consumption of importables (commodity Y), Y_A is the domestic production of importables, and the E's are the output elasticities as previously described. The net change in country B's supply of its exportables (commodity Y) is

$$\text{(II)} \quad \frac{dQ_B}{Q_B} (C_{AY} \cdot E_{DY} - Y_A \cdot E_{SY})$$

where $\frac{dQ_B}{Q_B}$ is the percentage change in B's productive capacity, Y_B is B's production of its exportable good (Y), the prime on the E's indicates B's output elasticities, and C_{BY} is B's consumption of its exportable good. The terms of trade for A will deteriorate if expression (I) exceeds expression (II), that is if A's net demand for imports increases more than B's net supply of imports to A [Bhagwati, 8, p. 402].

Meier [48] elaborates on the effect of various total biases when both countries are growing. The terms of trade may move either way, of course, depending upon the type and degree of bias and the rate of growth for each country.

20. Projections by Aubrey [3] and Clark [16 and 17] called for the future terms of trade to shift in favor of primary products and against manufactures as the classical view suggested.

21. Atallah [2] using an econometric model, predicted a 30 per cent worsening of the terms of trade for primary products in the decade after 1952–54. His prediction contrasts sharply with the predictions of Aubrey and Clark.

22. Viner [70] states that there are no grounds for contending that productivity growth has been more rapid in manufacturing than in primary production.

23. The cyclical behavior of prices of primary products and manufactured products suggests that the terms of trade of underdeveloped countries (exporting mainly primary products and importing mainly manufactures) deteriorate during cyclical downswings and improve during upswings. The opposite would presumably hold for the developed countries. By and large, this expected behavior is borne out by the data, although there are a number of exceptions [Kindleberger, 42, Ch. 7]. Before 1914, the British terms of trade generally improved in booms and deteriorated in depressions. The reason apparently was that coal, iron, and steel were important British exports and the prices of these basic commodities fell sharply during depressions. Transportation costs showed large cyclical variations that frequently lessened the impact on primary producers of depressions in advanced countries. Nevertheless the cyclical fluctuations of primary product prices cause serious problems for the less developed countries, aside from considerations of the long-run trend in the terms of trade, and these countries have urged commodity agreements to stabilize their export earnings — at least when primary prices were unfavorable.

24. Meyer [52] has developed an explanation of the trend in the terms of trade between manufactures and primary products that also relies on relative changes in supply and demand. He employs a model with highly aggregated measures of demand and supply changes for manufactures and for primary products. He relates changes in the terms of trade to the rate of growth of: (1) world trade in manufactures; (2) total world trade; (3) world production of manufactures; and (4) world production of primary products. His primary interest is in the statistical relationship; his explanation of how the system works is not as elaborate as Kindleberger's.

25. See Kindleberger [42] for an attempt to estimate the terms of trade on current account for industrial Europe. The inclusion of services reduces long-term fluctuations in the merchandise terms of trade. Price data are, of course, much more readily available for merchandise than for services.

26. Kindleberger [43] cites an example from an unpublished doctoral dissertation (Clark W. Reynolds, "Development Problems of an Export Economy: The Historical and Developmental Relationships of the Copper Industry to the Economy of Chile," University of California, Berkeley, 1961). Between 1925 and 1955 Chile's merchandise terms of trade declined from 100 to 65 but its terms of trade for the value of copper exports retained in Chile through domestic expenses and taxes rose from 100 to 300. Myint [56] stresses that the terms of trade for commodities may, in some manner, reflect the gains from trade for a country only if the residents receive all of the export earnings.

27. In the early years following World War II, there was not, of course, much competition in world trade in manufactures because of wartime destruction and depreciation of productivity capacity. This was a temporary situation and does not constitute an exception to the general trend in competition.

28. Where incomes are very low, as they are in underdeveloped countries, the income elasticity of demand for food may be rather high. But Engel's Law certainly holds for the industrial countries where the major increases of income have occurred.

BIBLIOGRAPHY

[1] W. R. Allen, "The Effects on Trade of Shifting Reciprocal Demand Schedules," *AER* (March 1952).

[2] M. K. Atallah, *The Terms of Trade between Agricultural and Industrial Products* (1958).

[3] H. G. Aubrey, "The Long-Term Future of the United States Imports and Its Implications for Primary-Producing Countries," *AER* (May 1955).

[4] R. E. Baldwin, "The Effect of Tariffs on International and Domestic Prices," *QJE* (February 1960).

[5] ——————, "Secular Movements in the Terms of Trade," *AER* (May 1955).

[6] P. K. Bardhan, "A Short Note on Technical Progress and Terms of Trade," *OEP* (March 1963).

[7] F. C. Benham, "The Terms of Trade," *Econa* (November 1940).

[8] J. Bhagwati, "Growth, Terms of Trade and Comparative Advantage," *Econia Internaz* (August 1959).

[9] ——————, "Immiserizing Growth: A Geometrical Note," *REStud* (June 1958).

[10] ——————, "International Trade and Economic Expansion," *AER* (December 1958).

[11] ——————, "A Skeptical Note on the Adverse Secular Trend in the Terms of Trade of Underdeveloped Countries," *Pakistan Economic Journal* (December 1960).

[12] ——————, and H. G. Johnson, "A Generalized Theory of the Effects of Tariffs on the Terms of Trade," *OEP* (October 1961).

[13] J. Black and P. Streeten, "The Balance and the Terms of Trade and Economic Growth," an appendix in P. Streeten, *Economic Integration* (1961).

[14] H. J. Bruton, "Productivity, the Trade Balance and the Terms of Trade," *Econia Internaz* (August 1955).

[15] R. E. Caves, *Trade and Economic Structure, Models and Methods* (1960).

[16] C. Clark, *The Economics of 1960* (1942).

[17] ——————, "The Future of the Terms of Trade," *International Social Science Bulletin* (Spring, 1951).

[18] W. M. Corden, "Economic Expansion and International Trade: A Geometric Approach," *OEP* (1956).

[19] A. K. Dasgupta, "The Elasticity of Reciprocal Demand and the Terms of International Trade," *The Indian Journal of Economics* (October 1941).

[20] E. Devons, "Statistics of United Kingdom Terms of Trade," *Man Sch* (September 1954).

[21] G. S. Dorrance, "The Income Terms of Trade," *REStud* (1948–49).

[22] P. T. Ellsworth, "The Terms of Trade between Primary Producing and Industrial Countries," *Inter-American Economic Affairs* (Summer, 1956).

[23] R. Findlay and H. Grubert, "Factor Intensity, Technological Progress, and the Terms of Trade," *OEP* (February 1959).

[24] W. M. Gorman, "The Effect of Tariffs on the Level and Terms of Trade," *JPE* (June 1959).

170

[25] F. D. Graham, *The Theory of International Values* (1948).

[26] G. Haberler, "Currency Depreciation and the Terms of Trade," in *Wirtschaftliche Entwicklung und sociale Ordnung,* edited by Ernst Lagler and Johannes Messner (1952).

[27] —————, *A Survey of International Trade Theory,* Revised and Enlarged, Princeton University, International Finance Section, Special Papers in International Economics, No. 1 (1961).

[28] —————, "Terms of Trade and Economic Development," in *Economic Development for Latin America,* edited by Howard S. Ellis (1961).

[29] J. R. Hicks, "An Inaugural Lecture," *OEP* (June 1953).

[30] A. H. Imlah, "The Terms of Trade of the United Kingdom, 1798–1913," *JEH* (November 1950).

[31] H. G. Johnson, *International Trade and Economic Growth,* 1958. Chapter III is a revision of "Economic Expansion and International Trade," *Man Sch* (May 1955).

[32] —————, "The Transfer Problem: A Note on Criteria for Changes in the Terms of Trade," *Econa* (May 1955).

[33] —————, "The Transfer Problem and Exchange Stability," *JPE* (June 1956).

[34] M. C. Kemp, *The Pure Theory of International Trade* (1964).

[35] —————, "The Rate of Exchange, the Terms of Trade and the Balance of Payments in Fully Employed Economies," *International Economic Review* (September 1962).

[36] —————, "The Relation between Changes in International Demand and the Terms of Trade," *Emet* (January 1956).

[37] —————, "Technological Change, the Terms of Trade and Welfare," *EJ* (September 1955).

[38] —————, "Unilateral Transfers and Terms of Trade," *AER* (March 1956).

[39] C. Kennedy, "Devaluation and the Terms of Trade," *REStud* (1950–51).

[40] C. P. Kindleberger, *International Economics,* Third Edition (1963).

[41] —————, "The Terms of Trade and Economic Development," *REStat* (February Supplement, 1958).

[42] —————, *The Terms of Trade, a European Case Study* (1956).

[43] —————, "Terms of Trade for Primary Products," in *Natural Resources and International Development,* edited by Marion Clawson (1964).

[44] F. Machlup, "The Terms-of-Trade Effects of Devaluation upon Real Income and the Balance of Trade," *Kyk* (1956).

[45] K. Martin and F. G. Thackeray, "The Terms of Trade of Selected Countries, 1870–1938," *BOUIS* (November 1948).

[46] A. N. McLeod, "Trade and Investment in Underdeveloped Areas: A Comment," *AER* (June 1951).

[47] F. Mehta, "The Effects of Adverse Income Terms of Trade on the Secular Growth of Underdeveloped Countries," *The Indian Economic Journal* (July 1956).

[48] G. M. Meier, *International Trade and Development* (1963).

[49] —————, "Long-Period Determinants of Britain's Terms of Trade, 1880–1913," *REStud* (1952–53).

[50] L. A. Metzler, "Tariffs, the Terms of Trade, and the Distribution of National Income," *JPE* (February 1949).

[51] —————, "The Transfer Problem Reconsidered," *JPE* (June 1942). Reprinted in American Economic Association, *Selected Readings in the Theory of International Trade* (1949).

[52] F. V. Meyer, *The Terms of Trade* (1962).

[53] M. Michaely, *Concentration in International Trade* (1962).

[54] T. Morgan, "The Long-Run Terms of Trade between Agriculture and Manufacturing," *EDCC* (October 1959).

[55] —————, "Trends in Terms of Trade, and Their Repercussions on Primary Producers," in *International Trade Theory in a Developing World*, edited by Roy Harrod (1963).

[56] H. Myint, "The Gains from International Trade and the Backward Countries," *REStud* (1954–55).

[57] G. Myrdal, *The International Economy: Problems and Prospects* (1956).

[58] D. H. Robertson, "The Terms of Trade," *International Social Science Bulletin* (Spring 1951). Reprinted in *Utility and All That and Other Essays* (1952).

[59] J. Robinson, *Essays in the Theory of Employment* (1937).

[60] W. W. Rostow, *The Process of Economic Growth,* New York, 1952. [Chapter 8 is "The Terms of Trade in Theory and Practice," *EHR* (1950); Chapter 9 is "The Historical Analysis of the Terms of Trade," *EHR* (1951)].

[61] P. A. Samuelson, "The Transfer Problem and Transport Costs: The Terms of Trade when Impediments Are Absent," *EJ* (June 1952).

[62] —————, "The Transfer Problems and Transport Costs, II: Analysis of Effects of Trade Impediments," *EJ* (June 1954).

[63] H. W. Singer, "The Distribution of Gains between Investing and Borrowing Countries," *AER* (May 1950).

[64] E. Sohmen, *Flexible Exchange Rates: Theory and Controversy* (1961).

[65] H. Staehle, "Some Notes on the Terms of Trade," *International Social Science Bulletin* (Spring 1951).

[66] S. G. Triantis, "Economic Progress, Occupational Redistribution and International Terms of Trade," *EJ* (September 1953).

[67] United Nations, Department of Economic Affairs, *The Economic Development of Latin America and Its Principal Problems* (1950). (Raul Prebisch wrote the report.)

[68] —————, *Relative Prices of Exports and Imports of Underdeveloped Countries* (1949).

[69] J. Vanek, *International Trade: Theory and Economic Policy* (1962).

[70] J. Viner, *International Trade and Economic Development* (1952).

[71] —————, *Studies in the Theory of International Trade* (1937).

CHAPTER 4

The Theory
of Customs Unions

The pure theory of international trade considers the effects of impediments to free trade as well as the effects of free trade. One impediment is, of course, the tariff. Tariff theory has generally been concerned with nondiscriminatory tariffs, that is, tariffs that are the same for all imports of a given commodity irrespective of the country of origin. Discriminatory tariff changes arise, however, in the formation of regional trade blocs such as customs unions, free trade areas, and common markets.

The members of regional trade blocs agree to reduce or eliminate tariffs on each others' goods but not to reduce them as much on goods imported from non-member countries. The result is, of course, to give preferential tariff treatment to goods imported from member countries and thus to discriminate against goods imported from non-member countries. These discriminatory changes in tariffs disturb existing economic relationships; they may cause changes in (1) production patterns, (2) consumption patterns, (3) the terms of trade, (4) the balance of payments, and (5) perhaps the rate of growth. The theory of customs unions is concerned with these various changes that may result from the discriminatory alteration of tariffs.

The milestone in the theory of customs unions was Jacob Viner's book *The Customs Union Issue,* published in 1950. This book was the first rigorous study of some effects of customs unions. Prior discussion of their effects had been largely oral and had led to the conclusion that a customs union would increase world welfare because it was a step toward free trade. Viner's major contribution was to demonstrate that the effects of the formation of customs unions are both beneficial and detrimental effects. The net effect then depends on which of two opposing effects is greater. The subsequent work has resulted in a clarification and elaboration of Viner's original contribution, has expanded the theory to take account of numerous effects not considered by Viner, and has built up a general and refined theory of economic integration.

173

Interest in customs union theory is not restricted to scholars. The apparent success of the European Economic Community has greatly stimulated awareness of both the theoretical and practical aspects of customs unions. Political leaders and government officials throughout much of the world are familiar with the key concepts of the theory. Moreover, the theory is useful in analyzing any discriminatory trading system that yields a less-than-optimal solution. For instance, economists have found it valuable in analyzing the economic effects of existing federations or common markets that are the result of past political and economic unification.

The theory of customs unions is concerned with an explanation of the economic effects of integration. The position of this theory in the field of international economic theory can be viewed in two different ways. On the one hand, the theory of customs unions is a special type of international trade theory that is broader or more general than traditional trade theory [Vanek, 34, p. 345]. Most international trade models include just two countries, while customs unions models must normally include three or more countries — the two or more countries forming the union and a nonmember country representing the rest of the world.[1] On the other hand, the theory of customs unions is a special branch of tariff theory. A customs union gives rise to a tariff system that discriminates among countries because identical imports are subject to different duties depending upon the country of origin. The theory of customs unions is therefore a special branch of tariff theory that deals with the effects of geographically discriminatory changes in trade restrictions [Lipsey, 20, p. 496]. By contrast, the usual discussion of tariffs concerns nondiscriminatory tariffs, that is, those that apply to all imports of a product, irrespective of the country of origin.

The theoretical analysis of customs unions has contributed importantly to the development of the theory of the second best. The best static solution, assuming a competitive world economy, is universal free trade because that will satisfy the Pareto optimum conditions. A customs union represents a step toward universal free trade since it expands the area of free trade. But it does not necessarily increase aggregate welfare by bringing the world closer to the best solution. This was Viner's major contribution to customs union theory and he thereby demonstrated one of the paradoxes in the theory of the second best [Lipsey and Lancaster, 21]. As long as all conditions for an optimium solution are not fulfilled, a change that increases the number of conditions fulfilled does not necessarily increase welfare.

In addition, the study of customs unions brings out clearly several differences between international and interregional trade. Even though no tariff exists on trade among members of a customs union, goods and factors will not move as freely as in interregional trade. Differences among members — in language, customs and traditions, tastes, institutions, and tax systems — are normally greater than among regions of one nation and thus create greater obstacles to the movement of goods and factors. The adjustment to payments disturbances is also apt to differ because regions within a nation are subject to common policies imposed by central authorities whereas members of a customs union are apt to act independently in adopting different and perhaps conflicting policies.

In the years immediately following World War II there was discussion of some form of general economic integration for Western Europe. The earliest formal step toward integration after the war was the organization of the Benelux Customs Union, followed by the European Coal and Steel Community. Subsequent negotiations led to the signing of the Treaty of Rome in 1957, a document that provided the framework for the European Economic Community (generally called the EEC or Common Market). Although there had been numerous actual and proposed customs unions in the past [see 35 and 36], it was the postwar movement toward integration that aroused the interest of the economics profession sufficiently to spur numerous studies of customs unions and economic integration. Moreover, the impressive performance of the EEC countries and the formation and proposed formation of other unions strengthened this interest in customs unions.

Although the theory of international trade has a long history, the theory of customs unions has a short one. Prior to Jacob Viner's major breakthrough in 1950 in the theoretical study of customs unions [35], no one had studied rigorously the effects of integration and no one had questioned seriously the prevailing opinion that a customs union was a movement toward free trade and would therefore bring about an increase in world welfare [Lipsey, 20, pp. 496–7]. Viner's major contribution — to show that the prevailing view was not necessarily correct because customs unions could, under certain circumstances, reduce world welfare — as mentioned above, helped develop the theory of the second best.

Most theoretical studies of customs unions focus on the welfare effects resulting from shifts in production and consumption. The effects on price behavior, balance of payments, and level of employment have received less attention. There have been several attempts to make quantitative estimates of the effects of integration in Europe [2, 4, 12, 14, 15, 16, 17, 29, 30, and 33]. There has also been considerable interest in the potential use of customs unions by groups of less developed countries [1, 3, 5, and 26].

There are various interpretations or meanings for the term *customs union*. A union may assume different forms, the most limited being a mutual reduction or elimination by a few countries of protective devices on just one product. The most complete union involves the removal of all restrictions on the movement of goods and factors and the adoption of common monetary and fiscal policies, including a common currency. A complete union necessarily requires political as well as economic integration. A common characteristic in all forms of customs unions, however, is that the member countries mutually liberalize trade among themselves while continuing to restrict imports from nonmembers.

In the literature on customs unions, various terms refer to the different degrees of economic integration, although there is frequently some overlap between one type and the next [3, p. 2]. A *free-trade area* abolishes tariffs and other trade restrictions among members but each country retains its own tariffs on imports from nonmembers, i.e., members do not adopt common tariffs on imports from outside the union. A *customs union* goes one step further in that all members maintain common tariffs on trade with nonmembers. In a *common market* members remove restrictions on both trade and factor movements among themselves in addition to imposing common trade restrictions on nonmembers. An *economic union* is a common market plus some coordination of national economic policies. *Total economic integration* involves the establishment of a supra-national agency with authority to determine common monetary, fiscal, and social policies for the member countries.

The following discussion assumes, as a minimum requirement in all cases, that integration involves elimination of tariffs and trade restrictions among member countries and adoption of a common tariff on imports from the outside. Certain sections will discuss problems or effects where the integration is more complete but such discussions will make clear the degree of integration assumed. In general, the terms customs union and integration will be used interchangeably, with the integration being partial rather than total.

☐ THE PROBLEM OF ASSESSING WELFARE EFFECTS

The desirability of a customs union depends upon its effect on welfare. The primary interest may be in the welfare of just one country (member or nonmember), of all member countries, of all nonmember countries, or of the world as a whole; most often the primary interest is in world welfare. The general practice of economists is, of course, to exclude the noneconomic aspects of welfare. Even so, the net effect upon economic welfare is difficult, if not impossible, to determine because modern welfare theory generally does not permit inter-personal comparisons of utility. This means that the net effect on aggregate welfare is unknown if a change makes one or more persons better off but also makes one or more worse off. An increase in the welfare of one or more persons leads to an increase of aggregate welfare *only if* no other person experiences a decline in welfare or if compensation is given to those who are hurt. Thus, rigid adherence to the rules of modern welfare theory precludes any conclusion as to the net welfare effects of shifts in income distribution among nations or among individuals within nations.[2]

Among other things, the formation of a customs union will change the amount and pattern of production, consumption, and trade. It will also alter the distribution of income among nations and among individuals within each nation. If a union leads to a more efficient use of resources so that given inputs lead to greater output, it is customary to gloss over the distributional effects and to conclude that welfare is increased.[3] Generally the formation of a union will cause some shifts to less efficient and other shifts to more efficient production. A comparison of the efficiency gains and losses is necessary to determine the net effect.

The discriminatory reduction in tariffs affects consumption by making goods from member countries cheaper relative to domestic goods and to imports from countries outside the union. As a result, a member country will tend to substitute imports from other union members for both domestic goods and imports from nonmembers. Some of the shifts in consumption will increase welfare by increasing the efficiency of exchange (consumption) while others will reduce it, so the net effect again depends upon a comparison of the increases and decreases.[4] A later section describes the various aspects of efficiency in consumption.

It is common to distinguish between static and dynamic effects of customs unions. A change in efficiency of production and exchange at a given moment of time is a static effect while a change in the rate of growth or progressiveness is a dynamic effect [see Belassa, 3; and Thorbecke, 33]. Static effects include the allocation effect on production (trade creation and trade diversion), consumption effects, and changes in the terms of trade. Dynamic effects include the potential effects of larger markets on the rate of growth through affecting the rate of technological change and investment, through increasing the effectiveness of competition, and through the possible existence of internal and external economies. Static and dynamic effects need not, of course, change welfare in the same direction; the formation of a union could reduce static welfare (efficiency) but enhance dynamic welfare (increase the rate of growth) or vice versa.

The discussion in this chapter makes no attempt to resolve the complicated issues involved in assessing the impact of integration upon welfare. It makes the usual assumption that welfare increases if integration leads to a static improvement in efficiency of production and exchange. The primary concern is with world welfare, although the discussion occasionally concerns only one country or the member countries versus the outside world. The major division in the discussion of static effects is between partial-equilibrium and general-equilibrium analysis. Then comes a discussion of dynamic effects, followed in turn by discussions of the terms of trade, the balance of payments, and the maintenance of equilibrium.

□ PARTIAL EQUILIBRIUM ANALYSIS

Production Effects

The formation of a customs union may affect the efficiency of production in several ways. It may increase efficiency because of a better allocation of production, that is, a better division of labor among countries in accordance with static comparative advantage. It may increase efficiency because of internal and external economies of scale, intensified competition, and lessened uncertainty: these ways are the topic of a later section. This section takes up only the static effect on production, generally called the allocation effect.

Viner [35, pp. 41–52] analyzed the welfare aspects of customs unions in terms of trade creation and trade diversion. A union will ordinarily shift the national locus of production of some commodities. If it shifts production from a higher-cost source to a lower-cost source, it creates trade and moves toward the free trade position. If the shift is from a lower- to a higher-cost source, it diverts trade and moves away from the free trade position. Such shifts in production constitute the allocation effect of a customs union — they affect the static efficiency of resource use.

A simple example will illustrate these concepts. Assume the money costs of producing a particular commodity in three countries are those shown in Table 4-1 (all costs converted to dollars at fixed exchange rates). The assumption underlying these figures is that costs are constant, i.e., that supply curves are infinitely elastic. If country A has a tariff of $15 per unit, the domestic product will be less expensive than the imported product. Country A will therefore produce the good domestically. Now

TABLE 4-1
Production Costs Per Unit for a Particular
Commodity in Three Countries

Country		
A	B	C
$25	$20	$15

let A and B form a customs union with no tariff on each other's good but a common external tariff of $15 per unit. Country A buys the product from *B* at a cost of $20 per unit, which is lower than either the domestic production cost of $25 or the price of $30 for imports from *C*, including the $15 tariff. If the union were between *A* and *C*, *A* would import the product from *C* for $15 per unit. Either case provides an example of trade creation. Country *A* ceases to produce the good and buys it from another country, thus shifting the locus of production to a lower cost source.[5] Because of the assumed constant costs, *A* obtains all of the product from just one country, depending upon which can sell at the lower price in *A*'s domestic market.

If, by contrast, the tariff initially had been just $7, country *A* would have been importing the product from country *C* before formation of the union. Then if *A* and *B* form a union with a common $7 external tariff, *A* buys the good from *B* at $20, which is lower than *C*'s price plus the $7 tariff. This is an example of trade diversion or a movement away from the free trade solution because production shifts from a lower-cost source to a higher-cost source. Trade diversion thus results in a less efficient allocation of world resources while trade creation results in a more efficient allocation.

The formation of a customs union will probably cause both trade creation and trade diversion; it might do so for a single commodity but it is virtually certain to do so when many commodities are involved. Assuming measurement of these effects is possible, the efficiency of resource use improves if the positive effects of trade creation exceed the negative effects of trade diversion. An increase in efficiency means simply that more can be produced with given resources or that the same amount can be produced with fewer resources. It does not necessarily mean that welfare has risen — because the locational changes in production will probably benefit some individuals and some countries but injure others. An increase in efficiency does mean, however, an increase in total production so that some individuals or countries could be better off, without making others worse off, by providing compensation to any individual or country that would otherwise be injured. To say that an increase in efficiency is also an improvement in welfare ignores the distributional problem unless compensatory transfers are assumed to take place. As mentioned above, many persons ignore this distributional question and assume any increase in efficiency leads to a more desirable situation.

Valid comparisons of the gains and losses arising from trade creation and diversion are not easy to make. Under the assumed conditions of constant costs, an estimate of the gain from trade creation can be obtained by multiplying the difference in unit costs between the old and new source by the physical volume of trade created [Meade, 25, pp. 35–36]. Similarly, the losses from trade diversion can be estimated by multiplying the difference in costs by the volume of trade diverted. A comparison of these two measures will then show whether the net effect is to increase or reduce efficiency in production. But to be valid, this method requires both constant costs and fixed consumption of the good in question. Without these two conditions, the assessment of gains and losses becomes very complicated if not impossible.

With increasing costs in production, the difficulties of measuring gains and losses are much greater. Assume that all three countries produce good X under conditions of increasing costs and that country A obtains its total quantity of X through buying some from domestic producers, some from producers in country B, and some from producers in country C. (This discussion no longer refers to Table 4-1.) If A now forms a union with B, A's import duty will no longer apply to imports from B but will continue to apply to imports from C. Because of increasing costs in all countries, A will import more of X from B while reducing both imports from C and domestic production. Trade creation occurs because part of the increased imports from B displaces the higher cost domestic production. But the remainder of the increased imports from B constitutes trade diversion because it displaces lower cost production in C.[6] There is no simple way of comparing the gains and losses because costs rise with the increase of output in B but fall with the decline of output in A and C.

Despite the lack of a satisfactory method of quantifying the gains and losses, two qualitative conclusions follow from the increasing-cost example. The first is that the favorable effects of trade creation will be larger the greater is the elasticity of supply in country A. This means that trade creation will be greater because the high-cost domestic producers will cut back sharply when they lose the tariff protection against lower-cost producers in other member countries. The second is that the higher the elasticity of domestic supply in country C the greater will be trade diversion and unfavorable effects on productive efficiency. When C's producers lose sales in A, the price in C will fall and the greater is the elasticity of supply the more production will decrease. This will, in turn, mean greater trade diversion as union producers displace C's producers in the union market.[7] The example assumes consumption is constant; otherwise the elasticity of demand in A would affect the diversion and creation of trade.

In the constant-cost case, the gains from trade creation accrue only to the union members.[8] In this simple model, with constant consumption, imports from and exports to nonmembers do not change, unless there is trade diversion. Trade diversion reduces efficiency of production within the union and probably in third countries. Within the union, it causes resources to shift into industries that have a comparative disadvantage vis-a-vis industries in the rest of the world. The reduced exports of third countries, while not affecting unit costs of the commodity, will presumably cause a shift of resources to the production of goods in which third countries have a lesser comparative advantage.

If increasing costs prevail, trade creation will, of course, still benefit the member countries. With trade creation but no trade diversion, neither the trade nor the welfare of third countries is affected. But trade diversion will clearly have detrimental production effects on both members and nonmembers. With decreasing costs in the affected industries, trade creation among union members will bring about even greater gains than when costs are constant or rising. If, however, those industries affected by trade diversion operate under decreasing costs, the losses may be greater [Meade, 25, p. 94].

Consumption Effects

Viner's path-breaking analysis concerned only production effects; it ignored changes in consumption. Subsequent analysis showed that the discriminatory tariff change acompanying a customs union will alter relative prices and lead to changes in consumption patterns. In the example based on Table 4-1, A's domestic price of the product fell from \$25 to \$20 when the union was between A and B; it fell to \$15 when the union was between A and C. In all cases the buyer in A pays a lower price for the product; and unless the demand for the product has zero elasticity, consumption will increase. Even when there is trade diversion, A's domestic consumption and imports increase. The increase of imports in excess of the amount of diverted trade is called trade expansion by Meade [25, pp. 40–41]. There is some economic gain from the increase of imports, provided the cost of production in the union partner is below that in the importing country.

In formalizing Viner's model, Lipsey showed that it implicitly assumed goods were consumed in some fixed proportion irrespective of relative prices [20, pp. 499–500]. This assumption means that the elasticity of demand for any one product is zero. But as long as demand is not completely inelastic, the formation of a union will change consumption and will thereby affect welfare. Efficiency in consumption (or exchange) is just as relevant for welfare as efficiency in production. The formation of a union will probably have positive and negative consumption effects similar to positive and negative production effects.[9]

Meade [25, pp. 44–52] analyzed consumption effects in a model that reversed the assumptions made by Viner. He assumed a fixed pattern of production but allowed the pattern of consumption to change with the formation of the union. To fix the production pattern, he assumed that each of three countries could produce a fixed amount of one and only one product, thereby making the supply elasticities zero. The formation of a customs union then changes relative prices, consumption patterns within each country, and trade among the countries. Meade evaluated the effects of changes in exports and imports of individual countries by comparing the ratios of the marginal utility of products within the individual countries as indicated by their domestic price ratios.

To summarize Meade's example, let country A produce good X, country B produce good Y, and country C good Z. Country A has a duty of 10 per cent on imports, country B has a duty of 20 per cent, and country C a duty of 30 per cent. Assume that A and B form a customs union. Before the elimination of internal tariffs, the ratio of the price of good Y to the price of good X, and so the ratio of their marginal utilities, was greater in A than in B. Good Y is made scarce in A by the 10 per cent duty and good X is made scarce in B by the 20 per cent duty. The ratio of the marginal utility of Y to the marginal utility of X is 30 per cent higher in A than in B. Meade suggests that this figure gives some indication of the potential gain in living standards in the two countries that would result from an *initial* increase in unit value of trade between them induced by tariff reductions. The gain from additional increases in trade steadily declines thereafter because the growth of trade reduces the difference between the ratio of marginal utilities in the two countries.

When A removes its tariff on good Y, it will increase its consumption (imports) of Y and probably will reduce its consumption of both X and Z. A similar development occurs in country B: its imports of X rise, imports of good Z from C fall, and exports of good Y rise. In C, imports of Y and X decline, as do exports of Z. The contraction of trade between C and the union members will tend to reduce living standards in all three and is thus an offset to the gain from increased trade between A and B. After formation of the union, C will have less X .but more Z while the union members will have more X but less Z in spite of the fact that X is relatively more valuable in C and Z relatively more valuable in the union.[10]

Meade concluded that the net effect on living standards (welfare) depends upon the initial structure of tariffs and the demand elasticities [25, pp. 50–52]. The higher the original tariff of union members relative to tariffs of outside countries the greater will be the amount of trade created and the greater will be the gains in consumption per unit of increased trade. Even so, the early stages of tariff reduction on trade between union members will bring larger gains than the late stages. The union is more likely to raise than to lower welfare the higher is the tariff of A and B and the lower the tariff of C — because these conditions increase the gain on intra-union trade with elimination of tariffs and reduce the loss on the contraction of trade between C and the union countries. Also the net gains will be larger the greater the degree of substitutability among products of member countries and the lesser the degree of substitutability between products of member countries and those of nonmembers. These substitutability conditions mean high elasticities of demand by union members for each other's goods and low elasticities of demand by union members for outside goods, conditions that tend to cause a large increase in trade among members (substantial trade creation) and a small reduction of trade between union and non-union members (little trade diversion).

The Total Effect

The previous sections demonstrate that customs unions affect welfare through influencing both production and consumption. Although the discussion treated production and consumption effects separately, they are not in fact independent. Shifts in production will affect the pattern of consumption and changes in consumption will similarly affect production. Lipsey feels that a better distinction of the effects of customs unions is between *inter-country substitution* and *inter-commodity substitution* [20, p. 504]. Intercountry substitution consists of Viner's trade creation and trade diversion, whereby the locus of production shifts. Inter-commodity substitution consists of the substitution of one commodity for another because of a shift in relative prices. Either substitution normally will lead to changes in patterns of both production and consumption.

A partial equilibrium diagram will illustrate both production and consumption changes for one commodity [Humphrey and Ferguson, 7]. Figure 4-1 depicts these changes for one commodity; it shows the changes in production and consumption for one country and the shift in both quantity and origin of imports caused by the formation of a customs union. The demand and supply curves are all linear; the home country, country A, has increasing costs while the two foreign supply curves are infinitely elastic. Such elasticities make the analysis less complicated and they could represent an actual situation where the home country was very small relative to the two foreign countries. The supply curves of the large countries could reasonably appear completely elastic in relation to the internal market of the small country. As is usual in partial equilibrium analysis, each demand and supply curve in Figure 4-1 rests upon the assumption that all other things remain unchanged. The assumption of a fixed exchange rate permits the conversion of prices in foreign currency to the currency of country A.

The home demand for the product is DD', the home supply is SS', the supply curve of country C is CC', and the supply curve of country B is BB'. With a tariff of CT, country A imports $Q_2 Q_3$ from country C and nothing from B. The domestic price in A is OT, domestic production is OQ_2, and total consumption is OQ_3. Domestic welfare in A is (by definition) the sum of consumers' surplus (the area under the demand curve but above TT'), producers' surplus (the area above the domestic supply curve but below TT'), and the tariff revenue (CT times $Q_2 Q_3$).

Now suppose country A forms a customs union with country B. The tariff of CT no longer applies to imports from the partner but it still applies to imports from country C. The problem now is to compare the new situation with that existing when the tariff applied uniformly to all imports. The price in the home country falls from OT to OB, domestic production declines from OQ_2 to OQ_1, and consumption increases from OQ_3 to OQ_4. The volume of imports increases from Q_2Q_3 to Q_1Q_4 but all imports now come from B instead of from C. The increase in imports, which is trade expansion, is equal to the contraction of domestic production (Q_1Q_2) plus the expansion of domestic consumption (Q_3Q_4). The extent of trade diversion is represented by Q_2Q_3, the amount of imports previously supplied by country C but now supplied by country B.

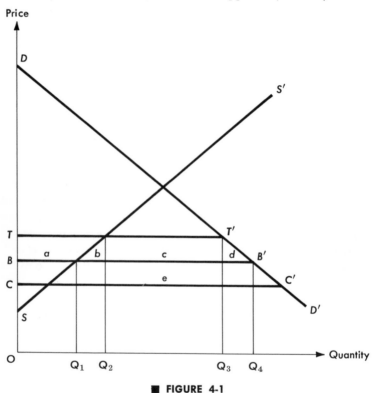

Price

Quantity

■ FIGURE 4-1

What is the welfare effect of the trade diversion and trade creation upon the home country? Consumers' surplus increases by $BTT'B'$, the total tariff revenue (area c + area e) is lost, and producers' surplus declines by area a. Part of the lost tariff revenue (area c) accrues to consumers because of the lower price for the product while the remainder (area e) is the net loss from diverting imports to a higher-cost source. The increase of consumers' surplus in A exceeds the loss of producers' surplus and the transferred tariff revenue (c) by the triangle b plus the triangle d; these two areas represent the net gain in welfare resulting from trade creation. Area b is the positive production effect and area d is the positive consumption effect. Area e, the net loss from diverting imports to a higher cost source, represents a payment to the higher-cost producers in B. The net welfare effect depends upon whether the gains from trade creation ($b + d$) are greater or less than the loss from trade diversion (e).

Because of the assumed horizontal supply curves in countries B and C, the trade diversion and creation causes no change of price in either country. Consequently, producers' and consumers' surplus will not change in either. The approach employed in Figure 4-1 can also be used when the supply curves of A and B slope upward but the diagram and explanation both become extremely complex [Humphrey and Ferguson, 7]. With upward sloping supply curves, producers' and consumers' surplus will change in all countries, thus adding to the complexity of the geometry and the explanation.

A glance at Figure 4-1 shows that the gain from trade creation will be greater (relative to the loss from trade diversion) the higher the initial tariff, the less the cost differential between the partner and the third country, and the less the absolute values of the slopes of the domestic supply and demand curves. For the most part, these conclusions are the same as those stated previously in the sections dealing separately with production and consumption effects, except here the condition refers to the slopes of the demand and supply curves instead of to their elasticities. The use of producers' and consumers' surplus to assess gains and losses is subject to a serious defect, however, because to add the surpluses of individual producers and consumers requires that utility be measurable.[11] Furthermore, the partial equilibrium approach in Figure 4-1 has serious limitations in analyzing the effects of customs unions because there are apt to be large changes in tariffs, thus violating the *ceteris paribus* assumptions underlying the supply and demand curves for an individual product. Such large and numerous changes as will occur in forming a customs union would undoubtedly cause shifts in these curves. Nevertheless, partial equilibrium has appeal because it neatly illustrates many effects of the formation of customs unions.

Determinants of the Effects: A General View

Although the preceding sections on production and consumption indicated some of the conditions that determine the magnitude of the effects, they did not present a general discussion of the determining conditions. Such a general discussion is the object of this section. It precedes the general equilibrium analysis because the conditions are easier to derive from, and apply to, the partial equilibrium analysis. A major part of this section consists of a discussion of the probable effects of customs unions in various situations in the world today.

Several of the conditions mentioned in the separate sections on production and consumption can now be briefly summarized. The higher the elasticities of demand and supply in union countries for goods traded with each other before forming the union, or for goods that will be traded with each other following the elimination of tariffs on intra-union trade, the greater will be the trade creation. The lower the elasticities of supply in the outside world for goods exported to the union and the lower the elasticity of demand in the union for these same goods the less will be the trade diversion. The greater the proportion of pre-union foreign trade of each member-to-be that is with other members-to-be (i.e., the lower the proportion of pre-union trade with countries not included in the union) the greater is the probability that the union will raise welfare.

A common generalization not previously mentioned is that the larger the economic size of the union the greater will be the gains through re-allocation of production [Viner, 35, p. 51, and Meade, 25, p. 109]. The larger the union the greater is the potentiality for internal division of labor because of the probable greater variety of resources available and the larger markets.[12] In addition, the larger the union the less is the possibility of trade diversion. In the limiting case, a union including all countries of the world could not cause any trade diversion but only trade creation.

The height of tariffs will also affect the gains ensuing from the formation of a customs union [Viner, 35, pp. 51–52; Meade, 25, pp. 108–109; and Balassa, 3, p. 44]. As Figure 4-1 illustrated, beneficial effects will be greater the higher the level of tariffs on trade between the countries forming a union because the amount of trade creation will be greater following the removal of the tariffs. And the amount of trade diversion will be less the lower the level of the common union tariff on outside goods. The lower this common tariff the less is the probability that the formation of the union will cause a union producer to displace an outside producer in supplying the union market. A final but controversial generalization is that the gains will be greater the lower is the tariff of countries outside the union [Balassa, 3, p. 44]. The lower the tariff of outside countries on imports from countries forming the union the less will be the diversion of trade from outside countries to union members when the union is formed. And the lower such tariffs the smaller is the loss when trade diversion occurs with respect to exports of union members to the outside countries. The argument against this position is that the higher is the tariff level on exports of union countries to outside countries the less trade there is to be diverted [Viner, 35, pp. 51–52].

Actually, there is no way of settling this issue without studying individual situations because the outcome depends upon demand and supply elasticities as well as the tariff.

The conditions existing in the countries forming any particular customs union will undoubtedly result in some beneficial and some detrimental shifts in production and consumption. The question that naturally arises is what types of countries are apt to realize net beneficial effects in forming a customs union and what types are apt to realize net detrimental effects. There has been extensive discussion concerning whether greater benefits will result from a union among complementary economies or from one among rival economies. The discussion pertains primarily to trade creation and trade diversion, with little or no explicit reference to consumption effects. The omission of consumption effects probably results from the greater difficulty of determining the potential effects of a union upon the efficiency of consumption. Some analysts believe that consumption effects are much less important than production effects because consumption patterns adjust slowly to changes in price ratios (i.e., demand elasticities are low).

Prior to Viner's 1950 book, the common view had been that a customs union among complementary economies would be more beneficial than one among rival economies. Complementary economies were loosely defined to be those with different patterns of production so that each tended to specialize in different products. By contrast, rival economies had similar patterns of production — there was much overlapping in the types of goods produced. The argument was that differences in costs of producing individual commodities were greater among complementary economies than among rival economies. A union of complementary countries would, therefore, be apt to yield greater savings in costs. Viner contradicted this view by arguing that customs unions among rival economies are more apt to be beneficial because they will cause greater trade creation [35, p. 51]. To illustrate the argument, assume that there are two groups of products subject to tariffs by all the countries coming together in a customs union [see Lipsey, 20, pp. 498–99]. The first group consists of commodities produced in all countries forming the union; the second consists of commodities produced in only one of the countries. Following the removal of tariffs on intra-union trade, the most efficient producing country for each product in the first group will probably capture the bulk of the union market. This shift in production is trade creation and it improves the efficiency of resource use. Similarly, the one country producing each product in the second group will undoubtedly capture most of the union market but in so doing it will displace imports by the other members from lower-cost producers in outside countries. Such displacement is trade diversion and it reduces the efficiency of resource use. Because rival economies will have relatively more products in the first group, a union among them is apt to cause a greater trade creation.

Subsequent discussion of Viner's analysis revealed ambiguities in his definition of rivalry and complementarity [Balassa, 3, pp. 29–33]. The terms now commonly refer to differences in comparative costs. Rival (or competitive) economies are those with similar cost ratios between pairs of products and complementary economies are those with dissimilar cost ratios. But Makower and Morton pointed out the technical difficulties of defining rival and complementary economies [22]. They showed that there is no single measure of the degree of similarity or dissimilarity in cost ratios because of the multi-dimensional nature of costs. An international comparison of costs must necessarily fall back upon the foregone alternatives (opportunity cost) to get the analysis into real rather than money terms and, furthermore, the cost ratios among countries will vary depending upon which good is the numeraire. Makower and Morton concluded that if a union creates trade, the gains will be larger the more dissimilar the cost ratios of the goods involved in the trade creation. Or, alternatively stated, *given that trade creation will occur,* the gains will be greater for a union of complementary rather than rival economies.

The Makower-Morton conclusion does not, in fact, contradict Viner's [Lipsey, 20, p. 499]. If two economies are complementary in the sense that there is little overlap in the types of commodities produced, a union between them will probably lead to more trade diversion than creation. By contrast, if the two economies are competitive in the sense of producing many of the same goods and if these goods are subject to tariffs, a union will permit the more efficient country to capture a greater share of the union market, thereby creating trade and increasing efficiency. Viner's conclusion was simply that trade creation was more likely to be dominant if the economies were competitive.[13] Makower and Morton showed that if trade creation does occur, the gains will be greater the greater the difference in production costs in the two countries for the goods involved in the trade creation, a conclusion with which Viner specifically agrees [35, p. 51].[14]

The countries in the European Common Market appear to satisfy several of the conditions necessary for the outweighing of the detrimental effects by the beneficial effects. A high proportion of the pre-union trade of the member countries was with each other. The industrial production and foreign trade of the member countries show much overlap in commodities and suggest a high degree of rivalry [Balassa, 3, pp. 33–34]. The EEC should, therefore, cause substantial trade creation. The rapid growth of intra-EEC trade in the years following the signing of the Rome treaty appears to verify this expectation.[15] Scitovsky argues that differences in production costs are small among the member countries for industrial goods, so the gains from trade creation will not be great [30, pp. 32–34]. But others argue that the differences are substantial and that trade creation will be highly beneficial in increasing efficiency. Attempts at statistical estimation of the production effects have not been conclusive [Balassa, 3, pp. 49–53]. There will be some trade diversion in manufactures because producers in outside countries sell many such products in the EEC market in competition with producers of member countries.[16] Trade diversion in raw materials will be small because EEC countries produce little of the raw materials they consume.

By contrast, complementarity exists in agriculture between the EEC countries and the former overseas dependencies. Therefore, the formation of the common market will cause substantial trade diversion in tropical agricultural products. In particular, members formerly importing tropical products from Latin America will eventually prefer to buy many such products from the former French dependencies in Africa that are associate members receiving preferential tariff treatment. The U.S. is the low-cost producer of numerous temperate-zone agricultural products and there will be some trade diversion of these [Salant, 29, pp. 106–111]. In general, however, customs unions among industrial countries with reasonably similar patterns of production, such as the EEC countries, appear to promise a substantial net gain in efficiency of resource use even though they will cause some trade diversion.

In comparison with the EEC members, the seven countries in the European Free Trade Association (EFTA) are considerably more complementary and less competitive. Britain is the major manufacturing country of the group; Austria and Switzerland export some manufactures; but the other countries are important exporters of food and raw materials. The proportion of total foreign trade carried on with members was much lower for the EFTA countries than for the EEC countries [Balassa, 3, p. 53]. This situation suggests that trade diversion will be substantial with the elimination of intra-union tariffs in EFTA and that it will occur in all three categories of goods — manufactures, food, and raw materials.

The underdeveloped countries included in the various proposals for customs unions generally do not trade much with each other. Although foreign trade is large relative to national income, a high proportion of the trade is with advanced countries. This situation suggests the strong likelihood of detrimental production and consumption effects. Because these countries export mainly food and raw materials, they are not generally complementary, although they differ with respect to the commodity composition of exports. But there is not much scope for trade creation among the primary products these countries produce. When the countries have in common protected manufacturing industries, there is a possibility for some trade creation if the countries will permit it.[17]

The major effect of a union may be the substitution of protected domestic manufacturers for imports from the outside and this is trade diversion. Thus, customs unions among underdeveloped countries are more apt to reduce than to increase static efficiency of resource use.[18]

An interesting question that has received some attention is the potential effects of a union among countries in different stages of development. Suppose Greece, a relatively underdeveloped country, immediately became a full member of the EEC. What would be the likely effect on the welfare of Greece, of the EEC, and of the world? The application of the preceding generalizations will provide a beginning to the answer for this question but a complete analysis would require a lengthy discussion of long-term dynamic factors that is beyond the scope of this chapter.

□ GENERAL EQUILIBRIUM

Most of the discussion thus far has consisted of partial equilibrium analysis. This section will describe some of the efforts to analyze the effects of customs union through use of general equilibrium. The first two subsections illustrate effects on one union member when the pattern of consumption is fixed and then when production is fixed. Next the discussion turns to more general models, using offer curves and permitting both production and consumption to vary. These models show effects on three countries — two union countries combined and a third country representing the outside world. Needless to say, general equilibrium models are more complicated than partial equilibrium ones.

Trade Diversion, Consumption Pattern Fixed

As mentioned above, Viner's model implies that a country consumes goods in some fixed proportion. Figure 4-2 is a model that Lipsey [20] used to demonstrate that trade diversion lowers welfare, given the assumption that two goods are consumed in a fixed proportion. Country B produces OA units of commodity Y, the only commodity it produces. Country B exchanges Y for commodity X which is obtained from country C, the low-cost producer. The slope of the line AC gives the terms of trade or the rate at which C will exchange X for Y. Assume further that with free trade country B maximizes welfare at point e by consuming Od of Y and de of X. Country B thus exports dA of Y in exchange for de of X.

The equilibrium point will not change when country B imposes a tariff, provided that it is not high enough to permit B's high-cost domestic producers to produce X in competition with imports from C. The tariff will, of course, change relative prices to consumers in B. The equilibrium will remain at e, however, provided (1) consumers in B insist

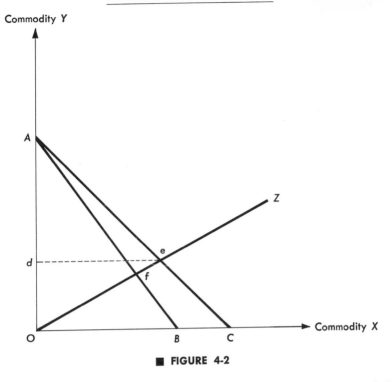

■ FIGURE 4-2

on consuming the two goods in the proportion given by the slope of OZ, (2) country C continues to exchange X for Y at the terms given by the slope of AC, and (3) the government redistributes the tariff revenue to consumers or spends it on the same goods consumers would have in the absence of the tariff.

Suppose now that B forms a customs union with country A and that A's costs of producing X are higher than C's but lower than B's. The exchange rate between Y and X is now given by the slope of AB which is greater in absolute terms than the slope of AC, reflecting a rise in the cost of X. Although A is a less efficient producer of X than C, imports from A are cheaper in B because they enter duty-free while imports from C (not a member of the customs union) are subject to a duty. The line AB now represents the possible combinations of Y and X that country B can obtain through trade with A. Assuming that B will continue to consume Y and X in the proportion given by the slope OZ regardless of the price ratio, the new equilibrium will be at point f. Country B will be consuming less of both goods so its welfare will clearly fall; an indifference curve passing through f (not necessarily tangent to AB) will be below one passing through e. In this special case, trade diversion reduces consumption in B and necessarily lowers its real income. By contrast, trade creation would shift the equilibrium outward on OZ and increase real income.

Trade Diversion, Consumption Pattern Variable

Trade diversion does not necessarily reduce welfare, however, when consumers may alter the pattern of consumption in response to a change in the price ratio. Figure 4-3, adapted from Lipsey [20], provides a geometric portrayal of this situation. Let OA again represent country B's production of Y, the only good it produces. The line AC again indicates the rate at which country C, the lowest cost producer of X, will trade X for Y. With free trade, equilibrium will be at e, the point of tangency between AC and indifference curve I_2. A tariff, even though it does not shift the source of X away from C, will now change the pattern of consumption in B. Suppose that the tariff causes the domestic price ratio in B to be that given by the slope of $A'C'$; the external or world price ratio continues to be the slope of AC. The equilibrium point will still be along the line AC because that line represents the world terms of trade and hence shows the possible combinations of X and Y that B can obtain through trade with C. Consumers in B will adjust their purchases of X and Y to the domestic price ratio (the slope of $A'C'$) that includes the tariff on X. Equilibrium will thus occur at a point along AC where the slope of $A'C'$ is equal to the slope of an indifference curve. Because the slope of $A'C'$ is greater than the slope of AC, the appropriate indifference curve will cross AC somewhere between e and A. The reason is that indifference curves intersecting the segment eA have slopes greater in

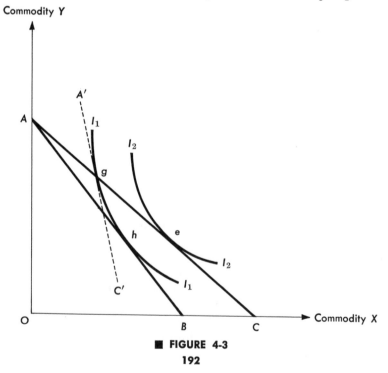

Commodity Y

■ FIGURE 4-3

absolute value than the slope of AC. Point g lies on AC and is also the point of tangency between $A'C'$ and indifference curve I_1, so g is the equilibrium point with the tariff. As would be expected, the tariff caused a decrease in consumption of the imported good and an increase in consumption of the domestic good. Welfare declined because country B is on a lower indifference curve than it was with free trade.[19]

Country B can now form a trade-diverting customs union and still improve its welfare position, that is, B's real income can increase despite trade diversion.[20] To demonstrate this, draw the line AB originating at A and tangent to I_1. Country B can form a customs union with country A, have terms of trade given by the slope of AB, and be no worse off than before when equilibrium was at g because h is on the same indifference curve as g. If the terms of trade with country A were worse than that given by the slope of AC but better than AB, then country B could be on a higher indifference curve than I_1, even though the union causes trade diversion. The movement to an indifference curve higher than I_1 is possible because consumers in B get X at a lower relative price after forming the union than they did before in paying a tariff on imports from C. The change in B's internal price ratio permits it to move to an indifference curve to the northeast of I_1. The favorable consumption effect thus more than compensates for the unfavorable effect of trade diversion that is manifest in the worsened external terms of trade. Trade diversion would reduce B's welfare only if its terms of trade with A were worse than that given by the slope of AB.

The favorable consumption effect occurs because consumers in B are able to adjust their consumption to the same price ratio as that at which the country can exchange commodity Y for commodity X by trade with country A. Previously, consumers in B adjusted consumption to an internal price ratio that included the tariff and thus represented a higher price for X than the rate at which Y could be transformed into X by trade with country C. To satisfy one of the Pareto conditions for maximizing welfare, consumers in country B must adjust consumption to a price ratio equal to the actual rate of transforming the one good into another by domestic production or trade — whichever is more advantageous. This condition was not satisfied prior to the formation of the union with A. After formation of the union, B had to export more Y for a given quantity of X because of the less favorable external terms of trade but it was then able to satisfy the optimum consumption condition. Provided the terms of trade line is between AB and AC in Figure 4-3, the beneficial consumption effects outweigh the detrimental production effects.

With just two commodities, complete specialization, and constant costs — as in the model portrayed by Figure 4-3, there is only one condition necessary for optimum consumption: the domestic price ratio facing consumers must equal the price ratio in international trade, i.e., there must be no tariff to drive a wedge between internal and external price ratios. But the conclusion drawn from a two-commodity model may not apply for situations where there are more than two commodities.[21] A model with at least three commodities provides more reliable conclusions concerning the welfare effects of changes in consumption. Let X be country A's good, Y be country B's good, and Z be country C's good. As before, let B, the home country, form a customs union with A. Assume that B imports X and Z both before and after the formation of the customs union.

Table 4-2 shows the domestic and international price ratios in three

TABLE 4-2
Domestic and International Price Ratios Between Pairs of Commodities Under Free Trade, a Uniform Tariff, and a Customs Union

Free trade	Uniform ad valorem tariff on all imports	Customs union between A & B
$\dfrac{P_{Yd}}{P_{Yd}} = \dfrac{P_{Xi}}{P_{Yi}}$	$\dfrac{P_{Xd}}{P_{Yd}} > \dfrac{P_{Xi}}{P_{Yi}}$	$\dfrac{P_{Xd}}{P_{Yd}} = \dfrac{P_{Xi}}{P_{Yi}}$
$\dfrac{P_{Xd}}{P_{Zd}} = \dfrac{P_{Xi}}{P_{Zi}}$	$\dfrac{P_{Xd}}{P_{Zd}} = \dfrac{P_{Xi}}{P_{Zi}}$	$\dfrac{P_{Xd}}{P_{Zd}} < \dfrac{P_{Xi}}{P_{Zi}}$
$\dfrac{P_{Yd}}{P_{Zd}} = \dfrac{P_{Yi}}{P_{Zi}}$	$\dfrac{P_{Yd}}{P_{Zd}} < \dfrac{P_{Yi}}{P_{Zi}}$	$\dfrac{P_{Yd}}{P_{Zd}} < \dfrac{P_{Yi}}{P_{Zi}}$

* P refers to price; X, Y, and Z are the products of countries A, B, and C respectively; d is the domestic price in country B (including tariff); and i refers to the price in the international market. (See text for a more complete explanation.)
Adapted from Lipsey [20].

possible situations. The P's are the prices of the commodities indicated by the first subscript. The subscript d refers to the domestic prices in country B and subscript i refers to prices in the international market outside country B. The price ratios in the international market represent the rate at which B can transform one good into another through international trade. The optimum conditions require that domestic price ratios for the three pairs of goods equal the international price ratios. Free trade results in the satisfaction of all conditions as illustrated in the first column of Table 4-2. If country B imposes a uniform ad valorem tariff on imports from A and C, the prices of the goods X and Z will be higher in the domestic market of B than in the international market. The inequalities in the second column of the table will then exist. The domestic price ratio for X and Z is the same as the international ratio because both goods are subject to the same ad valorem tariff.

Now suppose countries B and A form a customs union. Commodity X will no longer be subject to a tariff, so the first condition will be satisfied, as indicated in the third column of the table. However, the second and third conditions are not satisfied because commodity Z is subject to the tariff while X and Y are not. The formation of the customs union fulfills one condition that was not previously satisfied but it disturbs one condition that was previously satisfied. Country B's consumption is non-optimal both before and after the formation of the customs union and it is not possible *a priori* to say whether the union increases or decreases B's welfare. A gain results from satisfying the first condition but a loss occurs when the second condition is no longer fulfilled. The net effect on welfare of these gains and losses resulting from changes in consumption depends upon the actual circumstances in the countries involved.

If foreign trade is small relative to domestic production and consumption, the favorable consumption effects are more likely to outweigh the unfavorable. In this situation there are many goods in the Y category (domestic goods) in Table 4-2 but few goods in the X and Z categories. The formation of the union results in satisfaction of condition (1) involving the many Y goods but in disturbance of condition (2) involving relatively few X and Z goods. For any given amount of foreign trade, the larger the proportion that is with the union member the greater the likelihood that the beneficial consumption effects will outweigh the detrimental ones. If most of B's pre-union foreign trade is with A, there will be more goods in the X category than in the Z category. Consequently, the loss from disturbing condition (2) in Table 4-2 will tend to be balanced by the gain from satisfying condition (1). If the Z goods were many relative to the X goods, the loss from disturbing condition (2) would be more likely to outweigh the gain from satisfying (1).

Production and Consumption Variable

Vanek [34, pp. 346–359] has developed the most comprehensive general equilibrium analysis of customs unions: the discussion that follows is a summary of his work. His technique consists of using offer curves to represent an equilibrium between three countries for two goods. The model requires the usual assumptions associated with offer curves: the maintenance of full employment, competitive markets, and no external economies or diseconomies. Two countries, A and B, form a customs union while a third country, C, represents the outside world. Commodity X represents A's exportables, and commodity Y represents B's exportables. Assuming there is trade between A and B before forming the union, their offer curves could be OA and OB as shown in Figure 4-4.

The key step in Vanek's analysis is to construct an excess offer curve for the two countries forming the union. It shows the net offer curve of A and B acting jointly in trade with the third country. If the terms of trade in Figure 4-4 are the slope of OE, the trade of A and B is in balance with no excess supply or demand for either product. The excess

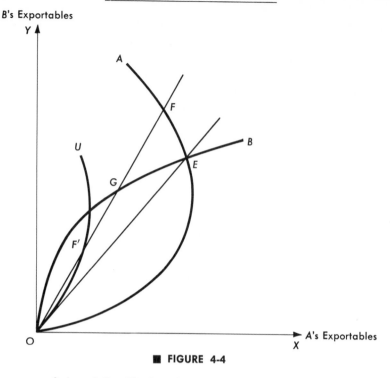

B's Exportables

■ FIGURE 4-4

offer curve of A and B will, therefore, pass through the origin when the price ratio is the slope of OE. With price line having the slope OF, A's demand for Y exceeds B's offer of Y or, alternatively, A's offer of X exceeds B's demand for it. The line GF represents this excess offer of X for Y; F' is the distance GF measured from the origin on OF. It is one point on the excess offer curve of A and B acting jointly. The same technique will determine other points along OU which is the excess offer of X for Y by A and B in their trade with country C. For terms of trade lines having a smaller slope than OE, the excess offer curve would be concave to the OX axis, indicating that the union would offer the outside world Y in exchange for X. Figure 4-5 brings together the excess offer curves of A and B and the regular offer curve of country C. The intersection of these two offer curves gives the price ratio (the slope of OE) that clears the markets for both goods in all three countries.

To demonstrate more fully the effects of forming a customs union, assume that both A and B previously imposed tariffs on imports from the other. Figure 4-6 shows the offer curves of the two countries with and without the tariffs. The subscript f identifies the free-trade offer curves, and the subscript t indicates the curves as modified by tariffs. The formation of the customs union means, of course, that A and B will no longer apply tariffs on each other's goods but they will apply a common tariff on imports from C. To show the effect of forming a union, it is

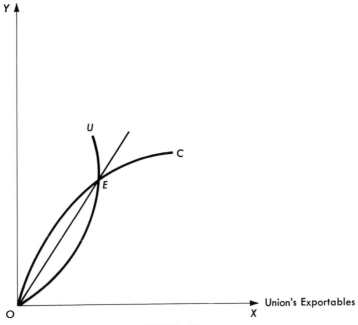

■ **FIGURE 4-5**

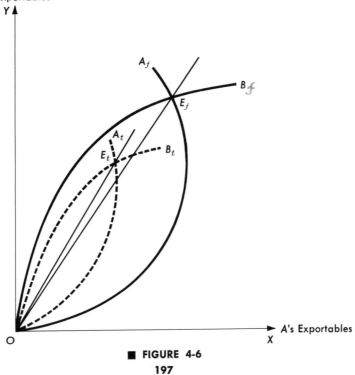

■ **FIGURE 4-6**

therefore necessary to construct the excess offer curve of A and B for the situation in which they have tariffs and the situation in which they do not have them on each other's goods. In Figure 4-7, OU_f is the excess offer curve with free trade within the union. OU_p is the pre-union excess offer curve when A and B still had their original tariffs. E_p is therefore the equilibrium for trade among the three countries prior to formation of the union. The excess offer curve after formation of the union will be OU_t; it reflects the common tariff on imports from country C. It is simply the shift of the free-trade excess offer curve (OU_f) caused by the common tariff on the union's imports from country C representing the rest of the world. Eu is the equilibrium for the three countries after A and B form a customs union.[22]

Figure 4-7 conveniently demonstrates some effects of the union between A and B. The terms of trade worsen for country C as they shift from the slope of OE_p (pre-union terms) to the slope of OE_u.[23] The terms of trade within the union countries are the slope of OE_f which differs from the slope of OE_u by the common tariff of the union on imports from nonmembers. The shift in the intra-union terms of trade benefits B (the exporter of Y) at the expense of A. Country B realizes improved terms

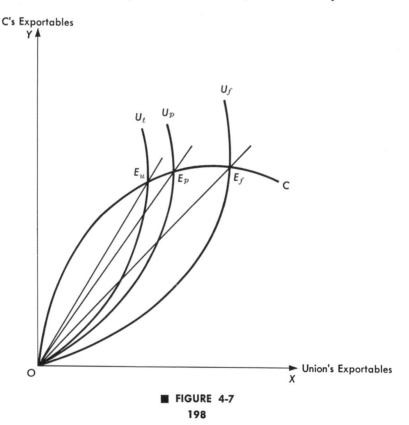

■ FIGURE 4-7

of trade because the pre-union price ratio was the slope of OE_p and afterwards it is the slope of OE_f. The shift of the equilibrium from E_p to E_u reflects the discrimination against country C and the reduced trade of union countries with C. The greater is the common tariff on nonmember goods, the greater will be the discrimination and trade diversion. Although country A's terms of trade worsen, it benefits from trade expansion — it will export more of X to country B.

The model is asymmetrical, however, in that it describes only one set of the possible trade relationships. It illustrates the case when the rest of the world imports country A's export good, that is, when the union partners have an excess supply of commodity X at the relevant terms of trade. If the model had used commodity Y as the one in excess supply by the union members, the same analysis would apply, except that it would reverse the role of the two union countries. Actually, there should be four groups of commodities to make the analysis complete: (1) A's exportables that are imported by C (the above model); (2) A's exportables that are exported by C; (3) B's exportables that are imported by C; and (4) B's exportables that are exported by C. In a real situation, all four groups would probably be traded simultaneously. Consequently, the analysis presented above for just one group would not correctly indicate the effects, particularly for the union members.

☐ **DYNAMIC PRODUCTION EFFECTS**

The previous discussion of the gains from improved allocation of production concerned static efficiency. The gains from "large-scale economies" — defined to include increased efficiency resulting from internal and external economies, from intensified competition, from possible acceleration of technological change, and perhaps from lessened uncertainty — concern the dynamic efficiency of production. There is disagreement concerning the probable significance of the large-scale economies emerging from the formation of customs unions. Balassa is a strong proponent of the view that the enlarged markets of a union will cause substantial economies in production, in addition to their static allocation effects [3, pp. 101–188]. But much of the evidence is consistent with other hypotheses. Theory is not much help in assessing the importance of large-scale economies and the conclusions of some of the empirical studies are in conflict or are subject to differing interpretations. Therefore, the actual significance of the dynamic production effects is open to dispute and will certainly vary from one situation to another.

Balassa believes that integration in Western Europe will give rise to important internal and external economies [3, pp. 131–138 and 159–162]. But Johnson [9], for instance, argues that Britain could expect only minor gains from economies of scale by joining with other European countries in some form of integration. He writes ". . . it is not at all obvious that an agglomeration of national markets, each with its own language, customs, and distribution methods, would offer the same opportunity for mass distribution as a homogeneous national market of the same size. Again, observation of the American market suggests that the mass consumer is a special consuming type, qualitatively different from a mass of consumers" [9, p. 34]. To paraphrase Johnson, free trade among union members offers not an escape from the straitjacket of the domestic market of a country but freer access than previously to a part of the world market. Kindleberger suggests that there is little evidence to indicate that European firms in general are too small to be efficient [13, p. 212]. He also suggests that some firms in the U.S. may be too large for optimum efficiency. Furthermore, firms in any one country are not limited solely to the domestic market because they can sell in export markets. Firms in small countries do this, an indication that they do not suffer inefficiencies in comparison with firms in larger countries [see Robinson, 28, Chapters 3–7]. If integration projects among underdeveloped countries do not become protectionist schemes, external economies may be an important benefit. But the evidence concerning both internal and external economies of scale for industrial countries is inconclusive and it does not provide convincing support for generalizations about the effect of hypothetical customs unions. Careful study of each proposed integration project is necessary to determine probable dynamic effects.

The formation of a customs union may affect the efficiency of production by changing market structures and thus either increasing or decreasing competition. Again there is a range of views. Some suggest that a customs union will serve as a catalyst for the formation of cartels and the growth of monopolies. It is argued that monopolists within a single country may extend their monopoly power to other union members after the removal of tariffs. Also, where cartel agreements are common within nations, they may grow to cover all producers of certain products throughout a union. If internal economies are important, the formation of a union will reduce the number of firms producing a particular commodity for the total union market and thereby increase concentration. Under *ceteris paribus* assumptions, an increase in concentration will reduce the effectiveness of competition.

Many persons feel, however, that a customs union will undermine monopolies and that the greatest gain from integration will stem from more effective competition [Balassa, 3, pp. 164–65; and Scitovsky, 30, pp. 19–48]. In countries where only one or a very few firms produce a given product, the removal of tariffs will increase the number of potential competitors and reduce the market power of the domestic producers, even if the union as a whole has fewer firms because of scale economies. Scitovsky

[30, pp. 22–30] argues that competition in Europe has been lethargic. Close personal relations among businessmen, the desire for a quiet life and stable income, and ignorance of demand elasticities have prevented the development of effective competition. By enlarging the market and increasing the number of competitors, a customs union will tend to break down these obstacles to vigorous competition. With a greater number of firms competing in each national market, competition is less personal, the fear of retaliation is less, and the reluctance to encroach upon the markets of rivals is less. Imports of slightly different but similar products should intensify competition — as should the spread of information regarding products, prices, services, and market outlets throughout the union. Free trade among members should also discourage government subsidies to small inefficient firms. The union should, however, adopt and enforce measures to outlaw various restrictive practices in order to prevent a return of the old relationships that could reduce the vigor of competition [Balassa, 3, p. 167].

In effect, Scitovsky argues that some countries in Western Europe are not on their production possibility curves because of inefficient resource use. More vigorous competition would increase efficiency and put the economy out on its production possibility curve. An alternative explanation would be that production possibility curves could be pushed out by more effective competition. In Scitovsky's view, the major gains in productive efficiency would stem from the reorganization of production within countries rather than among countries. In other words, he does not believe the major benefits will result from trade creation.

Another potential dynamic effect of the formation of a customs union is to speed up the rate of economic growth. A common view is that a union such as the EEC will accelerate economic growth because of important large-scale economies and because the enlargement of the market will cause more rapid technological change [Belassa, 3, pp. 101–116]. According to this view, the enlargement of the market will cause the size of firms to grow and, because large firms spend proportionally more on research and development than small firms, technological advance will be more rapid. Furthermore, it is suggested that there are important large-scale economies in research that will contribute to more rapid technological advance. The arguments for this view are, however, not entirely convincing. Clearly the largest firms in the U.S. spend proportionally more on research than the smallest firms. But studies of innovation have failed to show a superior performance by the largest firms in comparison with medium-sized firms. Therefore, even if integration brings about an increase in the size of firms and in spending on research, technological progress will not necessarily be more rapid.

Even if integration does increase productivity because of large-scale economies, this does not necessarily lead to a sustained increase in the

rate of growth. At the time of the productivity advance, growth accelerates but, after this initial surge in output, the rate of growth will not
necessarily be more rapid than before. The coalescence of national markets quite possibly could cause a once-for-all increase in productivity after
which the rate of growth would return to its former level. Those who
argue that a union will speed up growth do not have a satisfactory explanation of how the formation of the union will favorably affect the
determinants of growth (Streeten, 32, p. 284).

The formation of a customs union should contribute to the growth
of trade among members by reducing if not eliminating a major risk in international trade. An exporter frequently incurs the risk that foreign
markets will disappear because of changes in tariffs, subsidies, quotas, exchange rates, or exchange restrictions. These risks may inhibit certain investments that would improve the efficiency of resource use. A customs
union will do much to insure the stability of markets in member countries by the more or less permanent commitments in regard to abolition
of tariffs and other trade restrictions. There will still be some uncertainty as long as there are escape clauses and as long as monetary, fiscal,
and social policies are not highly coordinated. Nevertheless, such risks
will clearly be less in a customs union.

The effect of integration on the level of real income and its rate of
growth has important implications for the outside countries. A customs
union is virtually certain to cause some trade diversion and thus to harm
third countries. But if real income in the union rises, and especially if
growth accelerates, imports from the outside world will also rise. The increased income within the union could, in the long run, partially and perhaps wholly, offset the initial adverse effect of trade diversion on the outside world. The extent of the offset will depend upon the additional
growth of income generated by the union in the member countries and
upon the marginal propensities to import of the member countries.

☐ **THE TERMS OF TRADE**

Figure 4-7 provides an illustration of the effect of a customs union
upon the terms of trade in the special case where country A's export good
was imported by the outside world. Even though the model represented
a special case, it demonstrates how a union can alter the terms of trade
of union countries and the outside world.[24] This section contains a discussion of factors influencing the terms of trade under conditions less
restrictive than those necessary for easy portrayal with offer curves.

If a union leads to trade diversion, the value of imports from and
exports to nonmembers will decrease. Diversion thus implies a reduction in demand for outside goods and a reduction in supply of union goods

for the outside world. Under normal circumstances, the union's import prices will fall and its export prices will rise, thus causing a favorable movement of its terms of trade. The subsequent effect on the balance of payments will bring about additional changes in the terms of trade. The shifts in exports and imports will normally cause a surplus in the balance of payments of the union and a deficit for the rest of the world. In the long run, it is reasonable to assume that restoration of balance-of-payments equilibrium will require either secondary price increases in the union relative to the rest of the world, or an appreciation of the currencies of union members vis-a-vis currencies of the rest of the world, or both. In any event, the secondary effects will normally bring about additional changes in the terms of trade favorable to union countries.

The economic size (in terms of income) of the union will have an influence on the terms of trade. For a very small union, the offer curve of the rest of the world may be infinitely elastic so that the union cannot affect the terms of trade. The larger the union the more elastic will be its offer curve vis-a-vis the outside world; and the smaller the outside world the less elastic will be its offer curve relative to the union. The less elastic the outside offer curve the more the union can improve its terms of trade by discriminatory tariff reductions. The formation of a union will also strengthen the bargaining power of members with the rest of the world in trade negotiations and thus perhaps contribute still more toward improved terms of trade.

The effect of integration on the terms of trade is greatly complicated by considering income and price effects of productivity changes. The static allocation effect may improve efficiency of resource use within the union and thus increase income and the demand for imports. The increased demand for imports would, *ceteris paribus*, tend to worsen the terms of trade for the union. If integration speeds up technological advance, productivity and incomes will rise even more. The net effect on the terms of trade will depend heavily upon what specific industries experience the major productivity gains [Scitovsky, 30, pp. 70–74].

If the productivity increase occurs only in domestic industries that neither export nor compete with imports, the terms of trade will probably turn against the union because of increased real income and increased demand for imports. If productivity increases only in industries exporting to nonmember countries, the terms of trade could move either way, depending upon such factors as the effect of the productivity change on export prices, the elasticity of outside demand for the union's exports, and the effect of the income change on the union's demand for imports from the outside. If the productivity increase occurs only in industries that compete with imports from outside countries, the union will almost certainly reduce its imports from the outside and experience an improvement in its terms of trade.

If the union's productivity improvement takes place in purely domestic industries, most of the gain will accrue to members but some may accrue to outside countries. Nonmembers may gain because the cost reduction may stimulate output of goods requiring imported inputs and because the rise of real incomes will increase the demand for imported goods. If the cost reduction occurs primarily in export industries, both member and nonmember countries will gain. On the assumption that prices of exports fall, the nonmembers will gain, as will consumers of these goods within the union. There will probably be additional effects on the terms of trade and balance of payments. The decline in the price of exports will cause foreign buyers to spend more or less on these goods, depending upon the elasticities of demand. Cost reduction will generally lead to an increased demand for imports to produce more exports. Thus the balance of payments and terms of trade could be moved in either direction, as could the distribution of gains from cost reduction. A still different situation arises when the cost reduction occurs primarily in industries that compete with imports from nonmember countries. This reduces the union demand for outside goods so that the rest of the world loses because of the subsequent effects on the terms of trade and balance of payments.

There is a general presumption that the formation of a customs union will improve the terms of trade with the rest of the world. The preceding discussion suggests that, because of the many possibilities associated with productivity changes, this expected result might not always occur. Still the early part of this section seems to provide substantial reason for going along with the general presumption.

☐ MAINTAINING EQUILIBRIUM

As indicated previously, the formation of a customs union will undoubtedly affect the balance of payments of members vis-a-vis each other and vis-a-vis the outside world. Those members having the highest duties before integration will probably experience an adverse shift in their balance of payments with those union members having the lowest duties. And the union as a whole will probably realize an improved balance-of-payments position with the rest of the world.

As long as the major currencies of the world are convertible, each member needs only to maintain an overall payments equilibrium with the rest of the world, including both member and nonmember countries. Surpluses with nonmember countries can finance deficits with member countries or vice versa. If the formation of the union disturbs a previous equilibrium, an appropriate revision of the exchange rates or realignment of wage and price levels can restore the equilibrium. It will probably be easier to correct the initial disequilibrium by exchange rate adjustments and then to maintain equilibrium primarily through use of monetary and fiscal policies. The adjustment problem is frequently troublesome because countries are unwilling to permit the balance of payments to dictate domestic policies. And so long as there is unemployment or payments surpluses and deficits, genuine equilibrium does not exist in the economic relations among countries.

The precise effect of a customs union on the adjustment process depends upon the degree of integration. In most customs unions, the members can no longer resort to import or exchange controls with respect to intra-union trade. The union as a whole may still use direct controls to affect their balance of payments with the outside world, but such action requires close cooperation. If financial policies of the members are closely coordinated, union authorities can adopt domestic financial policies to maintain internal stability (stable prices and full employment) within the union as a whole and can, if necessary, restort to a joint program of control over trade and payments with the outside world to keep the balance of payments of the union as a whole in equilibrium. There might, however, have to be different rates of inflation or else exchange rate changes among countries within the union to maintain full employment and overall balance-of-payments equilibrium for each country.

If full employment is to be maintained without direct controls or restrictions on trade, countries must cooperate in coordinating financial policies and must be willing to employ various policy weapons. Surplus countries must prevent deflation and perhaps appreciate their currencies in case of severe disequilibrium. Deficit countries must avoid inflation and perhaps be willing to depreciate. The division of the adjustment burden among deficit and surplus countries will depend upon the internal conditions of each country. A deficit country, for instance, should not deflate if it already has unemployment. Similarly, a surplus country should not inflate if inflationary pressures are already strong. Exchange rate variations will work effectively only if accompanied by appropriate domestic policies aimed at preventing disruptive speculative transfers of funds.

The closer the coordination of national policies within the union, or the more complete the integration, the more nearly the adjustment process among union members will resemble that among regions within a country. Interregional adjustments within countries seem to take place smoothly because regional balance-of-payments difficulties are generally not a serious problem. The relative ease of interregional adjustments as compared with international adjustments is generally attributed to greater mobility of factors (labor and capital) among regions and to the role of government transfers.

Meade argues that the smooth adjustments of interregional disequilibria result from a common currency and a supra-national monetary authority [23]. Others feel that less formal cooperation will suffice to bring the needed mobility of capital that allows for easy adjustments by members of a customs union [Balassa, 3, p. 261; Ingram, 8]. If capital movements are to contribute to a smooth adjustment, a large volume of short-term securities held by financial institutions must be acceptable as a means for settling balance-of-payments deficits among member countries. This condition, in effect, increases intra-union reserves because such short-term securities perform the function of reserves in settling intra-union claims. Thus, highly mobile capital may finance temporary deficits so that there will not be a large immediate contraction of the money supply in the deficit country. This will, of course, help make adjustments easier by permitting them to take place more slowly.

Short-term capital movements cannot, however, take care of a persistent disequilibrium. When a disequilibrium persists, the automatic price and income changes are not sufficient to restore equilibrium. The problem could be less acute if the deficit countries could attract an inflow of long-term capital. But long-term capital movements can be disequilibrating as well as equilibrating. Long-term capital will probably not move to a depressed country or region; it is more likely to move out. Therefore, the restoration of payments equilibrium for a depressed area probably requires a relative downward movement of incomes and prices, outward migration of labor, and perhaps governmental transfers.

FOOTNOTES

1. Some international trade models include n countries but the vast majority incorporate just two countries. An analysis of customs unions needs to have at least three countries.

2. Some economists make welfare judgments in cases of income redistribution but in doing so they inject value judgments into the analysis. Economists who make such judgments usually say that welfare rises if the redistribution of income is in accordance with generally accepted ideals of equity.

3. Greater efficiency in production means that more goods will be available from a fixed amount of productive resources. Consequently, it would be possible to divide the greater output so as to prevent injury to anyone while making some persons better off. See the later discussion of this in the text.

4. Just as it may be possible to reallocate a given quantity of resources to increase efficiency in production, so also it may be possible to reallocate the consumption of a given quantity of goods to increase welfare by increasing efficiency in consumption or, perhaps better, efficiency in exchange.

5. The example ignores what happens to the factors of production in country A that formerly produced the good in question. It could be assumed that the displaced factors are absorbed in the production of other goods.

6. Assume at this point that A's consumption of X is constant.

7. A slightly different type of trade diversion occurs if, prior to the union, country B exported the commodity to D, a fourth country. The union then causes a diversion of B's exports from D to A, a union member. Then the gain from trade creation between A and B is larger the greater is the elasticity of supply of X in B; but the loss through diversion is larger the greater is the elasticity of supply in D.

8. This ignores the possible beneficial effects on nonmembers of higher real income in the union and thus greater imports from nonmembers.

9. The section on general equilibrium provides a more complete explanation of the effect of forming a customs union on the efficiency of production and the efficiency of exchange.

10. Greater generality can be achieved if more commodities are included in the model, as it is then possible to discuss secondary effects resulting from complementarity and rivalry in the consumption of the various products. Meade provides an elaborate discussion of secondary effects [25, pp. 67–82] but the application of the principles involved are straightforward and there is little to gain by repeating his exercise here. Secondary effects generally appear in the more elaborate general equilibrium models.

11. Meade [25, pp. 56–66] proposed a method of evaluating the gains and losses caused by a customs union. For changes in the quantity of a good produced and consumed, he compares the marginal utility of the good to the producer and to the consumer. Suppose, for instance, the cost of producing an additional unit of a product in one country is $2 and that a consumer in a second country would buy another unit of the product at a price slightly below its present price of $3 which includes a $1 tariff. If a slight reduction of the tariff causes this consumer to buy an additional unit, the excess of the utility gain to the consumer over the utility loss to the producer, measured in dollars, is just under $1. This is the net gain in economic welfare from the transaction. To compute the net welfare effect of forming a customs union, multiply the change in quantity of goods traded in all markets by the excess of the price paid by the buyer over the price received by the seller and add the results. The formation of a union will decrease trade in some goods and increase it in others. If the utility gain from increased consumption of some goods exceeds the utility loss from reduced consumption of others, the union increases economic welfare. This method is subject to a serious conceptual defect because it assumes that all buyers and sellers in all countries have the same marginal utility of money income. This condition is not apt to prevail, so any conclusions reached by applying the above method are of doubtful value.

12. Small domestic or intra-union markets need not prevent the formation of large efficient producers of any given product provided the producers can sell in the world market. Nevertheless, the existence of a large domestic market is undoubtedly more conducive to the development of large efficient firms than the existence of domestic markets too small by themselves to support such large producers [28, pp. 265–90].

13. See Spraos [31] for a further refinement in the conditions necessary to insure net beneficial effects when the countries have overlapping production.

14. More recently Streeten [32, p. 286] argued against using the terms rivalry and complementarity because they are ambiguous and may be misleading. He says that discussions should be in terms of comparative cost ratios and the level of tariffs.

15. For a skeptical view of the role of the common market in this growth of trade, see Lamfalussy [18].

16. For an estimate of the amount of trade diversion of U.S. manufactured goods, see Salant [29, pp. 97–104].

17. Allen [1] and Mikesell [26] do not believe that the underdeveloped countries will permit competition within a proposed customs union to eliminate existing manufactures in one country even if they are less efficient than those of another member. See also Kindleberger [13, p. 211] for an expression of doubt concerning the success of customs unions among less developed countries.

18. Balassa [3] tends to believe, however, that the dynamic effects over a long period might be beneficial and overcome the immediate detrimental effects.

19. Assume that the government of B consumes the tariff revenue and does not redistribute it, so the imposition of the tariff does not alter the demand schedules of the private sector in B.

20. This example implicitly assumes, as do all examples in this chapter, that the members of the customs union previously imposed tariffs on each other's goods.

21. Gehrels [6], using a two-commodity model, concluded that the consumption effect of a customs union would nearly always be favorable. With a three-commodity model, however, there is no a priori reason to believe that the consumption effects will be favorable, as the text explains.

22. Vanek [34, pp. 356–357] goes on to show the equilibrium for all three countries in a diagram containing the production blocks of A and B. The diagram is complex and therefore is not as convenient as the offer curves as in Figures 4-4 through 4-7.

23. Although this result will be the usual one, it is not a necessary one. If country B has a sufficiently inelastic offer curve at certain price ratios, the excess offer curve OU_t can be to the right of OU_p so that C's terms of trade improve [see Vanek, 34, pp. 354–355].

24. See Mundell [27] for a rigorous analysis of the effects of a customs union on the terms of trade of union members and the outside world.

BIBLIOGRAPHY

[1] R. L. Allen, "Integration in Less Developed Areas," Kyk, Vol. XIV (1961)

[2] B. Balassa, "The Future of Common Market Imports," Weltwirtschaftliches Archiv, Band 90, Heft 2 (1963).

[3] —————, The Theory of Economic Integration (1961).

[4] B. L. Bentick, "Estimating Trade Creation and Trade Diversion," EJ (June 1963).

[5] R. S. Bhambri, "Customs Unions and Underdeveloped Countries," Econia Internaz (1962).

[6] F. Gehrels, "Customs Unions from a Single Country Viewpoint," REStud (1956–57).

[7] D. D. Humphrey and C. E. Ferguson, "The Domestic and World Benefits of a Customs Union," Econia Internaz (1960).

[8] J. C. Ingram, "State and Regional Payments Mechanisms," *QJE* (November 1959).

[9] H. G. Johnson, "The Criteria of Economic Advantage," *BOUIS* (February 1957).

[10] _____, "Discriminatory Tariff Reduction: A Marshallian Analysis," *The Indian Journal of Economics* (July 1958, Part I).

[11] _____, "The European Common Market — Risks or Opportunity," *Weltwirtschaftliches Archiv* (1957).

[12] _____, "The Gains from Free Trade with Europe: An Estimate," *Man Sch* (September 1958).

[13] C. P. Kindleberger, "The United States and European Regional Economic Integration," *Social Science* (October 1959).

[14] L. B. Krause, "European Integration and the United States," *AER* (May 1963).

[15] _____, "The European Economic Community and American Agriculture," *Factors Affecting the United States Balance of Payments*, Compilation of Studies prepared for the Subcommittee on International Exchange and Payments of the Joint Economic Committee, U.S. Congress, 87th Congress, 2d Session (1962).

[16] I. B. Kravis, "The U.S. Trade Position and the Common Market," *Factors Affecting the United States Balance of Payments*, Compilation of Studies prepared for the Subcommittee on International Exchange and Payments of the Joint Economic Committee, U.S. Congress, 87th Congress 2d Session (1962).

[17] M. E. Kreinin, "European Integration and American Trade," *AER* (September 1959).

[18] A. Lamfalussy, "Europe's Progress: Due to Common Market?" *Lloyds Bank Review* October 1961).

[19] R. G. Lipsey, "Mr. Gehrels on Customs Unions," *REStud* (1956–57).

[20] R. G. Lipsey, "The Theory of Customs Unions: A General Survey," *EJ* (September 1960).

[21] R. G. Lipsey and K. Lancaster, "The General Theory of the Second Best," *REStud* (1956–57).

[22] H. Makower and G. Morton, "A Contribution Towards a Theory of Customs Unions," *EJ* (March 1953).

[23] J. E. Meade, "The Balance-of-Payments Problems of a European Free-Trade Area," *EJ* (September 1956).

[24] _____, *Problems of Economic Union* (1953).

[25] _____, *The Theory of Customs Unions* (1955).

[26] R. F. Mikesell, "The Theory of Common Markets as Applied to Regional Arrangements among Developing Countries," *International Trade Theory in a Developing World*, edited by Roy Harrod (1963).

[27] R. A. Mundell, "Tariff Preferences and the Terms of Trade," *Man Sch* (January 1964).

[28] E. A. G. Robinson, editor, *Economic Consequences of the Size of Nations* (1960).

[29] W. A. Salant and others, *The United States Balance of Payments in 1968* (1963).

[30] T. Scitovsky, *Economic Theory and Western European Integration* (1958).

[31] J. Spraos, "The Condition for a Trade-Creating Customs Union," *EJ* (March 1964).

[32] P. Streeten, "Common Fallacies about the Common Market," *Weltwirtschaftliches Archiv*, Band 90, Heft 2 (1963).

[33] E. Thorbecke, "European Economic Integration and the Pattern of World Trade," *AER* (May 1963).

[34] J. Vanek, *International Trade: Theory and Economic Policy* (1962).

[35] J. Viner, *The Customs Union Issue* (1950).

[36] United Nations, Department of Economic Affairs, *Customs Unions, A League of Nations Contribution to the Study of Customs Unions Problems* (1947).

PART II / International Monetary Theory

CHAPTER 5 / The Adjustment Mechanism
in International Payments

PREFATORY STATEMENT

Unlike pure trade theory, the monetary theory of international trade takes account of differences in national currencies and attempts to explain the differences in the offerings of one currency in exchange for another. This chapter on the adjustment mechanism deals with the problem of how differences in exchange volumes arise and how they are resolved.

Correct notions of balance of payments equilibrium and disequilibrium are basic to an adequate monetary analysis of international trade. Contemporary goals of economic policy influence the notion of payments equilibrium, since items that might be the criteria for equilibrium in the internal economy may not be the same as those for external equilibrium. An examination of concepts of equilibrium, therefore, becomes one of the prime aims of the chapter.

Conflicts in analysis of the adjustment mechanism are due primarily to differences between the so-called classical approach focusing on the influence of price changes and the so-called modern approach focusing on the influence of income adjustments. Other conflicts have been caused by different evaluations of the contemporary international economy. On the one side, the view prevails that equilibrium is basic to the international economy and traditional remedies can always be applied, while on the other, many maintain that the present national economic policies which deny traditional remedies perpetuate a disequilibrium system. Much of the theoretical analysis of the adjustment mechanism draws upon the experience of a few isolated countries, chiefly the United States and the United Kingdom and is closely linked with the problem of international liquidity. Precise economic theory, however, taking account of causes of imbalances originating in the capital account as well as in the current account, must also deal generally with causes originating internally and those originating abroad and abstract from the special conditions of reserve currency countries. The chapter emphasizes some of the analysis relevant to general policy remedies. In practice, however, many difficulties are found because non-traditional policies are needed for adjusting the imbalances which have been created by other measures aimed at different goals.

□ SCOPE OF CONTROVERSY

Analyses of the process of adjustment to the payments balance of the international accounts differ extensively. Nevertheless, concerted efforts have been made in recent years to bring together and reconcile the major streams of analysis. These divergent streams reflect the fact that, in the past quarter century, there has been a considerable shift of theoretical emphasis and consequently of policy solution. To a large degree, these shifts are associated with the Keynesian revitalization of economic theory and with the new responsibilities assumed in governmental policy.

Major areas of controversy arise from conflicts between classical formulations of mechanical adjustment, relying on the price system, and the more recent formulations of involuntary adjustment, relying on the level of income. In the classical system, adjustments emerge primarily through changes in the relative price structure and secondarily through monetary effects of changing gold holdings or changing foreign exchange reserves. In the more recent systems greater emphasis is given to adjustments through income effects. The more recent theories are sometimes geared to the notion of disequilibrium as contrasted to the classical systems where equilibrium is always possible in the long-run. Notions of certainty in automatic adjustment mechanisms tend to be replaced by notions of uncertainty. Despite numerous analytical gaps, progress has been made recently in the attempts to integrate price and income effects of the adjustment mechanism.

The matter of balance in international payments arises as a pressing policy problem but policy for balance of payments adjustment involves a wide area of conflict. Some of the more vigorous of these controversies are extracted in subsequent chapters. Thus the policy problem of fixed versus flexible exchange rates is treated in Chapter 6 and the elasticity and absorption approaches to devaluation are treated in Chapter 7.

Fundamentally, the adjustment process is concerned with how a nation reacts to imbalance in the balance of payments and how the balance of payments returns to equilibrium. This problem can be expressed as how differences between the demand for and the supply of a given foreign exchange at a given price are reconciled [Kindleberger 33, p. 63]. It can be insisted, however, that the effects cannot be studied independently of the causes. Under this approach, a particular item operating on the balance of payments has to be singled out and identified as the cause; its impacts on the national economy must then be traced through time. The validity of much of this type of analysis depends on how the balance of payments is defined and what constitutes an equilibrium or balance in the accounts.[1]

Many theoretical analyses of the adjustment process have used autonomous capital transfers as the initiator of payments imbalance. This has led to a thorough study of what has come to be known as the transfer problem which, although reaching a climax with the Keynes-Ohlin debate in the 1920s, is still under examination. In turn, consideration of the adjustment problem under differing causal factors has led to a clearer interpretation of income effects and the gradual weakening of the emphasis on price effects. A number of other causes, such as harvest conditions, inflation, business cycles, technological change, and innovation, have been used traditionally in examining adjustment effects. It is clear, however, that a particular cause need not be associated with a particular effect. One of the great problems of adjustment analysis is to show the general effects that arise from any disturbance to equilibrium in the balance of payments.

Scope of Variables and Policy Measures

The model of imbalance in international accounts must be carefully described; it can embrace many variables. Many controversies concern the suitability of variables and their special place in the model. Indeed, many seeming controversies arise simply because models and variables for two rival explanations are not exactly comparable.

Vanek [75, p. 48] has listed certain variables deemed most important in balance of payments adjustments: domestic and foreign price levels; the exchange rate; the interest rate; real and money wages; income; employment; income distribution; productivity; institutional factors such as monetary, fiscal, and commercial policy; and time. Obviously, few models have been constructed which can deal successfully with all of these variables. Variables which show one set of relationships before international payments equilibrium was disturbed are not likely, in fact, to show the same set of relationships after international equilibrium is restored. Stipulation of initial equilibrium conditions in theory usually establishes the essential conditions for ultimate equilibrium after the effects of adjustment are played out.

The selection of a special item as a cause of payments imbalance invariably presupposes a set of relevant factors which are more immediately connected with the cause than some other set of variables. For example, it could be said that disturbances originated on the monetary side in the form of different rates of inflation or that they originated in real terms in the form of different rates of productivity [39, p. 13]. Such approaches usually point to a certain type of policy as the most relevant. The isolation of causes may predetermine the factors affected and thus predetermine the policy to correct a payments imbalance. These are matters of methodology which we cannot pretend to solve here.

In the period since World War II, policy-oriented models for dealing with balance of payments adjustment have been widely used. Foremost among these model builders are Meade [45] and Tinbergen [69; 70]. Meade attempted to construct models which reconcile policies of full employment with policies of equilibrium in the balance of payments. He gave much attention to the notion of internal and external balance.[2] Tinbergen's method is a more general approach in which models are constructed to reconcile various policy objectives with the tools available. Different policies require different tools which have varying effects on all variables in the model. The significant feature of both approaches, which will be examined in more detail later, is that each policy objective requires an independent instrument.

Policy for solving balance of payments problems is obviously not limited to exchange rate manipulations; the numerous items comprising monetary policy, fiscal policy, or commercial policy have important impacts too. As a contemporary issue, the specialized balance of payments problem — created by the use of selected currencies as international exchange reserves — involves refinements of policy for which only limited experience and strongly competing theoretical solutions are currently available.

It has been stated that balance of payments problems are basically monetary problems [28, pp. 18–19]. This means only that the monetary claims of a country created over a stipulated period do not match the monetary obligations incurred. By varying the time period, the problem can become more or less severe and by segregating the different international claims and obligations, the problem can be treated as more or less intense. The cause of the problem may be monetary mismanagement but the solution to the problem, apart from improving management, may not necessarily involve monetary policy. The fact that the problem is one of international monetary imbalance does not preclude its solution by non-monetary policies.

Classical Views of the Adjustment Mechanism

The classical explanation of the adjustment process has had a longer period of acceptance than any other. Prior to the publication of Keynes' *General Theory* in 1936, the generally accepted view was that the monetary and price system reacted in such a way as to preserve equilibrium in the balance of international payments automatically.[3] If a deficit occurred, the balance would be made up in gold transfers. Gold transfers affected the countries' price structures so as to restore the balance of payments to equilibrium. This was the basis of the familiar price-specie-flow mechanism developed by Hume, Smith, Ricardo, Mill, and others.

The price-specie-flow mechanism relied on explicit acceptance of the "quantity theory of money," as well as on other assumptions of the classical system. These assumptions implied that output and employment remained unaffected by international monetary disturbances. A payments deficit inducing a gold outflow caused a reduction in the quantity of money which in turn lowered prices through a smaller aggregate money demand for goods and services. Because factors were assumed to be mobile domestically and prices were assumed to be flexible upward and downward, prices and costs were affected but not output and employment. Lowered domestic prices made domestic goods more attractive internationally and foreign goods relatively more expensive. Because demand was presumed to be elastic, the value of exports would rise and imports fall. The reverse effects would take place in the country experiencing an initial surplus in its balance of trade. Eventually the trade balance would improve for the deficit country and equilibrium would be restored.

This simplified statement of the price-specie-flow adjustment mechanism was subsequently improved and expanded to take account of newer institutional developments. The influence of interest rates on capital movements was recognized, suggesting that gold flows were not essential. Similarly, recognition was given to similarities between gold movements and changes in foreign balances. Fractional reserve banking was also introduced without destroying the basic features of the classical explanation.

Early tests of the validity of the classical explanation were undertaken by Taussig, Williams, Viner, and H. D. White.[4] These empirical studies seemed to support the classical theory in concluding that the balancing process had taken place in accord with theory but they led to doubts because of the seeming rapidity of adjustment. Later examinations of practices under the gold standard suggested that central bank policies, by stimulating capital flows, helped produce what was regarded as "automatic" adjustment [7; 49].

Other areas of doubt concerning the reliability of the classical system of adjustment arose from factual observations of price elasticities. Attempts during the 1920s and 1930s to measure the responsiveness of demand to price changes showed that demand elasticities were considerably less than unity.[5] These empirical findings made it difficult to accept the classical explanation of adjustment which depended so heavily on high degrees of responsiveness to price changes.

Subsequent to the factual doubts, erosion of the rigid assumptions of the classical approach took place, largely through a rejection of the doctrines linked to the "quantity theory of money" and Say's law of markets. With these doctrines discredited, it was possible to explore the effect of international imbalances on output and employment and to concentrate on saving and aggregate demand as affecting the circular flow of income. Keynesian economics provided a new framework which made possible a clear rejection of the classical assumptions.

Thus, a new theory of balance of payments adjustment emerged. The works of Joan Robinson, Harrod, Paish, Haberler, Salant, Kindleberger, Metzler and Machlup were important in shaping the Keynesian approach.[6] Basically, the approach asserted that an imbalance in international payments would involve an adjustment in income, employment, and output no matter what happened to prices and no matter how the deficit was financed. If, for example, one country encountered a deficit in its balance of payments, income in surplus countries would rise and increase their imports relative to exports. This meant increased exports in the deficit country, reversing in part or completely the initial deficit. The adjustment to the payments imbalance through income and employment changes relied little upon traditional monetary policy. Income and employment were related more to changes in aggregate demand than to changes in interest rates or bank reserves *per se*, a condition which is reinforced if domestic investment is viewed as nonresponsive to changes in interest rates.

The theory of adjustment which stresses income changes is both a theory of disequilibrium and of equilibrium. In contrast, the classical theory can be regarded as an application of static equilibrium theory where adjustment is always complete. Adjustment is automatic in the income approach but it might be only partially complete in initiating adjustment. The imbalance in international payments must affect the domestic income stream. Thus, in the income theory, as contrasted to the classical price theory of adjustment, different degrees of adjustment may arise due to different income responses to the disturbance. The newer theory heightens the contrast between domestic stability and international equilibrium and makes clear that, under static productivity conditions, lower national income is one result of a payments deficit. With optimum rates of economic growth the focal point of national economic policy, the need for a balance of payments policy becomes obvious. Moreover, the desire to avoid reductions in income levels because of payments imbalances throws much of the burden of adjustment on price changes which, in their turn, may conflict with the national objective of price stability.

In the classical framework, international payments imbalances were assumed to adjust automatically. Mechanistic balancing was possible under either the pure gold standard or inconvertible paper currency. Balance of payments equilibrium was restored through reactions in the national economy.

Briefly, under the pure gold standard, free gold flows caused interest rates to rise in one country and to fall in the other. Demand and price levels were reduced in the first country and increased in the second. With inconvertible paper currency, adjustment took place through free exchange rate adjustments which equated demands and supplies of foreign currency, implying perpetual equilibrium in international payments. In both systems certain economic policy reactions were implied by the automatic mechanisms of adjustment. To a large extent, policy was dependent upon international forces and was assumed to take shape in predetermined ways. This is in sharp contrast to the more modern analysis where policy reaction rather than being molded by the forces of international payments imbalance is more closely coordinated with national economic aims.

The gold standard was a case of fixed exchange rates. The international value of a domestic currency is maintained by a fixed relationship to gold, supported by a willingness on the part of the monetary authorities to buy and sell gold at a price set in domestic currency. In practice, of course, the export and import of gold was determined by interest differentials and by costs of shipping, handling, and insuring. The freedom of the exchange market, nevertheless, was limited.

The classical approach assumed that a natural distribution of the precious metals prevailed. This distribution depended upon relative economic strengths and could not be altered through monetary policy. The distribution ensured that price ratios were appropriate to general equilibrium. Thus a loss of gold occasioned by a fall in exports and a payments deficit would reduce the volume of money in circulation — causing prices to fall.

Similar results are obtained under a system of variable exchange rates based on inconvertible paper currencies. This system assumed complete freedom in all markets. Price changes were, as before, the means by which international adjustment took place. Potential deficits were corrected immediately by a depreciation in the exchange rate. In the long term adjustment, the structure of domestic production would alter to reflect changing relative prices.

Neither of the special cases — gold system or variable exchange rates — has extensive application in the contemporary world. Neither system of analysis provided for domestic stability, since wages and prices were treated as perfectly flexible. Both systems allowed the price mechanism to bear the burden of adjustment and both systems stressed automaticity of adjustment. The systems assumed full employment and quick and considerable reactions of all supply and demand to price changes. Both systems invited reactions by monetary authorities to deal with price changes, leaving income and employment free to fluctuate under international pressures.

The classical view of automatic adjustment to international payments imbalance did not disappear completely with the advent of Keynesian doctrine. Nevertheless, by virtue of the fact that the classical model operated with variable prices and fixed incomes and the newer models operated with variable incomes and fixed prices, there was a definite break in the development of adjustment theory.[7] The classical theory yielded ground to the newer theory, tending to become a supplement to the income approach [36, Ch. 3]. The two approaches have not yet been merged satisfactorily, although strenuous attempts have been made in this direction. The adjustment process clearly operates through both the price mechanism and income forces, although there are many who accept the supremacy of the income approach and treat price adjustments as decidedly subsidiary [55, p. 269].

The income approach to the adjustment process had forerunners prior to the Keynesian revolution but this approach suffered from the lack of an analytical model of employment and income determination.[8] The new approach contributed to a more thorough understanding of international monetary relations and international transmissions of the business cycle.

Because the classical system is geared to static equilibrium, while the income approach illuminates both equilibrium and disequilibrium positions, a redefinition of international equilibrium has been required. One test of equilibrium is given by the equality of total receipts for current transactions, plus long-term capital imports and total current payments, plus long-term capital exports at full employment, and without trade restrictions [Scammell 61, p. 49; Lary 34]. Seemingly, international equilibrium may occur at less than full employment domestic equilibrium. If, however, domestic equilibrium requires full employment, international equilibrium may be disturbed. Thus relationships between income or output and the balance of payments are significant forces in a world seeking full employment through national economic policy.

Neither analysis of the adjustment process takes account of all factors; the classical approach lacks realism by overlooking employment levels and the newer approach discounts the actual cases in which prices change. There is still need to clarify the role of price effects on the balance of payments adjustment, especially as governments consider the possibility of altering exchange rates without relinquishing the goals of full employment and domestic price stability.

Theory of the Foreign Trade Multiplier

It is now widely accepted that, on the one hand, incomes may change to facilitate equilibrium and that, on the other hand, changing incomes may produce disequilibrium in the balance of payments. An autonomous increase in exports gives rise to an increased demand for materials and capital and growing demands for the factors of production. Initial income increases in export industries spread to other industries. Thus aggregate money incomes and employment rise if the economy is not initially at full employment. Aggregate demand for goods and services, including those provided from abroad, expand. The increase in imports reduces the initial export surplus in the balance of payments.

In the money markets, the initial expansion in exports increases claims on foreigners and supplies of foreign currency. The conversion of these holdings of foreign currency into domestic currency by the banking system tends to increase the domestic money supply, bank reserves, and bank loans. Increased lending tends to increase money incomes and employment. An increase in imports follows from these developments, reducing the export surplus as before.

Imports are not increased because of rising domestic prices but because of rising incomes. Domestic prices, of course, would rise as the money supply increased and full employment in the economy was reached. They would also rise as a result of the reduction in domestic supplies caused by withdrawals for export. In these circumstances imports would increase as a result of both rising money incomes and relative price changes. Fundamental to the basic multiplier analysis, however, is the assumption of unchanged prices.

The multiplier principle demonstrates the extent of income increases following an autonomous increase in spending on current output. National income increases as a multiple of the additional expenditure because of respending by recipients of new money income. Employment and output rather than prices increase as a result of the new expenditure if unemployment exists. New expenditures on current goods and service fuels the multiplier process no matter what their source or purpose.

The simplest demonstrations of the multiplier in an open economy show that it depends on the marginal propensities to import and save. These are leakages from the expenditure stream limiting the extent to which the new expenditure can generate new incomes. Another important factor, however, should be introduced: as imports into one country increase, the incomes of the supplying country increase which, in turn, leads to the demand for more foreign goods. The second country's increased demand leads to increased imports from the first country, thereby stimulating income in the first country. This foreign repercussion affects the size of the multiplier in each country [Kindleberger 32; 33, Appendix E; 26].

Taxes constitute a leakage in the system, just as do imports. The marginal propensity to collect taxes is given by the ratio of additional

221

taxes collected to an increase in incomes. The multiplier (k) incorporating all these leakages is the reciprocal of the sum of the marginal propensities to import, (m), to save, (s), to collect taxes, (t), and a term (r) to reflect foreign repercussions: $k = \dfrac{1}{m + s + t + r}$.

If new expenditure or exports is the initiating factor, the initial surplus in the international accounts will be reduced more by the existence of a relatively large m, other propensities remaining unaltered, than by the existence of a relatively small m. Even where the total leakages of new expenditure are 100 per cent — assuming $0 < (s + t + r) < 1$ — there is still a positive trade balance and, although adjustment is complete, payments disequilibrium is still in effect. Equilibrium in the balance of payments under static conditions will come about only if the sole leakage is through imports.

If the amount of the change in expenditure is to be equal to the change in the balance of payments exactly, the sum of the marginal propensities to import in the two countries must be equal to one. These are the conditions under which a transfer or a switch in expenditure from one country to another is fully effected through the balance of payments and income changes [33, pp. 197–98].

Greater realism to the foreign trade multiplier and to its application to adjustment mechanisms is given if account is taken of the role of intermediate goods. It has been pointed out by Miyazawa that in the usual formulation of the foreign trade multiplier income changes relate to final goods produced alone, whereas imports include intermediate goods as well [48, p. 53]. In the usual Keynesian system no distinction is made between the leakage in the expenditure process and leakages in the production process represented by imported intermediate goods used in the production of consumption and investment goods. Combining the separate circular flow of intermediate products with the circular flow of final products reduces the numerical value of the foreign trade multiplier. If all the output of intermediate goods is absorbed domestically and there are no imports of foreign intermediate goods, this modified multiplier reduces to a Keynesian sort of foreign trade multiplier in which only induced imports of finished goods are considered [48, p. 56]. Adjustment processes will vary, depending upon the role played by foreign raw materials in domestic production and the degree of intermediate production in the total value added. The greater the volume of intermediate products produced relative to total output the smaller the multiplier and the weaker any given increase in exports.

Many of the adjustment effects demonstrated through multiplier analysis depend upon which factor initiates the change and which factor responds to the change. Most models of the multiplier, including several of Machlup's earlier formulations [40], rely on autonomous changes in exports. This usually implies autonomous increased foreign demand for domestic goods at the expense of foreign goods.[9] As a consequence, the initial rise in domestic incomes corresponds to an initial fall in foreign incomes. When foreign repercussions are taken into account, the higher domestic level of equilibrium income is related to a balance of payments surplus which matches in amount the balance of payments deficit at a lower foreign level of equilibrium income. If saving, rather than consumption, is reduced as a result of an autonomous increase in imports, income in both countries could rise [26; 32] but the import-export balance for both countries would be larger. Again, if autonomous investment were the cause of higher incomes in one country leading to expanded imports, both countries would experience higher income levels. When other induced factors are introduced, the adjustment mechanism may be used to show over- or under-compensation to changes in either exports or imports [5, pp. 263–67; 33].

Not all contemporary economists have placed great faith in multiplier analysis. Balassa, for example, seriously questions the value to be attached to theories based on money-income multipliers [6, p. 602]. The foreign trade multiplier presupposes, he claims, an availability of increased resources which may be unrealistic. He doubts also that a meaningful interpretation can be given to the marginal propensity to import expressed in money terms; instead, he advocates giving separate consideration to income and substitution effects. The multiplier is a Keynesian less-than-full employment notion; with full employment it loses meaning and significance.

Equilibrium and Disequilibrium Systems

The idea of equilibrium in the balance of payments or, more abstractly, in international trade, is a methodological device or a tool for analysis rather than an observable phenomenon [43, p. 11]. Adjustment theory uses the tool to show how variables in a model react to disturbances which may initiate disequilibrium or how the variables of a system already in disequilibrium change to produce ultimate equilibrium. Adjustment to disequilibrium involves changes induced by defined stimuli or impulses. These responses may force the variables in the system toward or away from a new equilibrium or new disequilibrium position. The theory must pursue the changes until these forces are expended. At that point a reassessment can be made to test either for equilibrium or disequilibrium.

Various writers have had different understandings of basic starting and concluding points in the analysis. To Joan Robinson the notion of *the* equilibrium rate of exchange which implied equilibrium in the balance of payments was a chimera [60, p. 208]. It was a relative concept which could change with the rate of interest, the level of effective demand, and the level of money wages. Each reacted upon the other. To Nurkse, concerned with constructing practical monetary policies, the equilibrium rate of exchange existed when no net change took place in a country's "reserve of international means of payments" over a period of five to ten years [54]. He was careful to point out that "true equilibrium" prevailed only if no additional restrictions on trade were introduced and if there were no domestic depression or unemployment. Machlup has described this view of equilibrium as one of "built-in politics and simulated stability" and doubts the analytical value of such a concept [43, pp. 15–16]. The analytical value of the concept is reduced because it attempts to make average *ex post* statistics equivalent to *ex ante* norms or data. Nevertheless, Nurkse's idea of equilibrium in international transactions has been widely accepted and used.

Equilibrium in the balance of payments in more modern formulations assumes government policy operating to ensure full employment. The existence of unemployment itself is a sign of disequilibrium. Political repercussions are a feature of the model. Thus writers such as Bernstein are able to discuss the implications of a "proper balance of payments" or other normative or "desirable" aspects [8, p. 123].

In dealing with balance of payments disequilibrium, Meade focuses on the "potential" deficit or surplus in the balance arising from autonomous transactions rather than the "actual" imbalance [45, pp. 13–15]. The actual imbalance is given by the amount of accommodating finance used in any period. He suggests that this potential imbalance may be permanent or temporary. Theoretically, therefore, a persistent disequilibrium could emerge. As Machlup points out, however, this is an inconsistent use of the concept of equilibrium. He charges that Meade employs three distinct approaches to equilibrium; as a value judgment; as a relation between factors; and as a tool of analysis [43, p. 20]. The inconsistency is partially resolved by Meade's use of two equilibria — "internal balance" and "external balance." Internal balance consists of full employment and price stability; external balance is maintained through use of trade controls and exchange rate adjustments. Meade's discussions of the conflicts between internal and external balances produce the basis for much of the contemporary analysis of economic policy as an integral part of adjustment theory.

Another viewpoint of balance of payments equilibrium concepts, as given by Streeten, is that they are "persuasive definitions" because they have built-in politics and "conceal within the definition criteria based on value judgments not widely shared" [67, p. 87]. Streeten argues against the convention of assuming stable exchange rates, full employment, stable prices, and unrestricted trade within the definition of equilibrium because of the policy aims implied. If, for example, import restrictions are associated with disequilibrium, the correct policy measure is seen as the removal of the restrictions. Streeten finds that definitions incorporating such criteria reduce their analytical usefulness to the economist although he recognizes the need to accept some normative goals to make economic analysis meaningful.

While classical theory uses a long-run static approach and assumes that disequilibrium is a transitory phenomenon, the modern system with a long experience of payment imbalances is sometimes treated as a disequilibrium system [50; 51, pp. 153–54, 28, pp. 15–16]. In the disequilibrium system, domestic political factors prevent surplus countries from deflating and deficit countries from inflating. The international disequilibrium system arises because, in order to achieve full employment without inflation, the monetary authorities prevent externally induced gold flows from affecting the internal supply of money [Mundell, 51, p. 170]. This newly practiced policy which works against the automatic price-specie-flow mechanism of Hume and the income-specie-flow mechanism of Keynes substitutes management for automaticity.[10] It has frequently been inferred, although wrongly, that the disequilibrium system arises because the Keynesian foreign trade multiplier generally shows that a given increase in exports initiates a smaller rise in imports so that the initial imbalance cannot be corrected.

The international system in recent times has become a disequilibrium system because a "policy vacuum" has been created; present policy weapons are directed primarily towards attaining domestic objectives while few new weapons have been created to cope specifically with imbalance in international payments.[11]

To Mundell, general equilibrium in an open economy means that balance exists in all markets. This requires that the current supply of goods equal their current demand, that the existing stock of money is demanded, and that there is no imbalance in international payments [51, p. 155]. Mundell assumes that these balances in the goods, money, and exchange markets depend upon the level of money income, the rate of interest, and the quantity of money. It is further assumed that the rate of interest, in responding to changes in money supply, influences the level of effective demand and the balance of payments [51, pp. 155–57; 14]. An imbalance in the foreign exchange market implies an imbalance in the other markets taken together. In practice, countries have remained unbalanced in external markets over long periods of time using foreign reserves and hoping for a change in external conditions to correct the disequilibrium. The conventional adjustment process therefore is prevented from applying corrective remedies unless foreign reserves are exhausted and hopes for a countervailing disturbance are evaporated [37].

The equilibrium conditions in foreign exchange markets have been the subject of a long endured controversy. The argument centers on the demand elasticity for exportables and thus on whether an alteration in the exchange rate or removal of exchange controls will help eliminate a payments disequilibrium. Assuming initial payments equilibrium and infinite supply elasticities, the sum of elasticities of demand for imports in two countries must exceed unity in order for a depreciation of the currency of either country to improve its trade balance; this is commonly called the Marshall-Lerner condition.[12] Pessimistic views on the possibility of these conditions being realized in practice has led to recommendations against devaluation and flexible exchange rates in order to adjust payments imbalances. There is strong feeling by the pessimists that demand elasticities would not be high enough to ensure improvement in the balance of payments and that a stable equilibrium exchange rate at any point is improbable. Under this point of view, fixed exchange rates are advocated, supported if necessary by monetary policies or direct controls. Optimists, on the other hand, see possibilities of the sum of elasticities being greater than unity in practice. Hence, they are able to present arguments for flexible exchange rates and support policies of devaluation to cure deficits [Friedman, 16]. This viewpoint rejects the notion of static instability in the foreign exchange market.

This argument is quite apart from the conflict between the elasticities and absorption approaches in explaining effects of devaluation.[13] It is concerned essentially with the theoretical and empirical validity of the Marshall-Lerner condition. Subsequent chapters deal with fixed verus flexible exchange rates, as well as with the elasticities versus the absorption approaches.

Contemporary discussion of the basic tenets of the elasticities approach has been highlighted by the exchanges between Sohmen [62; 63; 64; 65] and Johnson and Bhagwati [10; 11]. Sohmen supports the theoretical validity of Marshall's contention concerning the necessity of stable equilibria by claiming that an unstable equilibrium *has* to be bounded by two stable equilibria. Johnson and Bhagwati for their part contend that stable equilibria need not occur at finite rates of exchange. They claim that the proposition of unstable equilibrium being bounded by stable equilibria is derived from offer curves whose shapes are based on the assumption that wants are both insatiable and terminable [11, p. 427]. If insatiability in fact applies, demand for any commodity could increase indefinitely as its relative price falls. The shape of the demand curve, then, helps determine whether or not a given price of foreign exchange can constitute a stable equilibrium.

Due to the fact that reactions to exchange rate movements occur slowly, it has frequently been argued that demand elasticities in foreign trade are higher in the long- than in the short-run. Exchange rate instability therefore may arise because low elasticities of the short-run tend to dominate. Under these circumstances it may be impossible for a system of flexible exchanges to work. If, however, short-run speculative capital movements are stabilizing and if the long-run elasticities are high enough for stable equilibrium in the exchange markets, short-run instability could be overcome.

The issue of elasticity has been relevant to many policy considerations. Effects of tariffs, import restrictions, and exchange rate adjustments upon the balance of payments, and hence the advocacy of these measures, depend upon the elasticities. Empirical investigation has not resolved the theoretical impasse. Actual estimates of demand elasticities have invariably, on first examination, given support to the pessimistic side. The strength of the support nevertheless has been reduced by critical statistical evaluations of the empirical results. Some economists believe that the relevant demand elasticities have declined in recent decades because of increases of monopolistic competition in foreign trade. Sohmen refutes this position and claims that the relevant elasticities of demand are more likely to exceed unity the greater the extent of market imperfections [62, p. 15]. Thus, in both the theoretical efforts and the empirical studies, some doubt still prevails on the questions of how measures which alter relative prices impinge upon the balance of payments and whether or not equilibrium is possible. These uncertainties help contribute support to policies which treat devaluation and flexible exchanges as inefficient adjustment devices.

Treatment of International Investment
in the Adjustment Process

Great interest has been shown for a considerable time in adjustment problems created by the transfer of donated or loaned funds from one country to another. The so-called transfer problem is really produced when the amount of the transfer is not reflected completely by equal but opposite alterations in the balance of payments and hence in the underlying activities in the two economies involved. It is possible for under-transfer or over-transfer to take place, either under the classical assumptions or under Keynesian approaches [Vanek, 75, pp. 111–23]. In this section, attention will be directed toward the more recent treatment of international transfers, particularly the types associated with international investment.

Attitudes toward international investment changed greatly during the 1930s. Earlier, international capital movements had been treated as part of the system of adjustment; in general, they were unrestricted and outside the scope of national economic policy. International investment in the 1930s, however, became subject to direct and indirect control, especially in its relation to other economic aggregates such as employment, investment, and savings. At first, there was a tendency to treat international investment simply as equivalent to the net change in the balance of payments or the difference between exports and imports in a given period [Robinson 60, pp. 186–87; Buchanan 13, p. 312]. International investment had previously been examined with emphasis on motivations or purpose and effects on monetary markets, interest rates, and prices. In its new role, international investment became less of a free functional factor and more of a residual adjustable factor. This had important consequences for how domestic investment, employment, and income might change in the adjustment process.

Domestic full employment policies which use fiscal, exchange, or trade controls to maintain external balance have been favored over policies of free capital movement. In other respects, private capital movements have been supplemented by public capital movements. The argument was accepted that just as public investment at home might aid domestic employment and income so might public investment abroad. The argument became more significant when, on the one side, underdeveloped countries were seen as outlets which facilitated some adjustments to world imbalances and when, on the other side, underdeveloped countries saw foreign investment as a means of reducing income differences. Thus the notion of a "foreign investment policy" and policies for underdeveloped countries are almost wholly postwar occurrences. Largely concerned at first with the avoidance of double taxation of incomes derived from foreign investment, foreign investment policy later embraced a long list of devices to foster, or to liberalize, or, at the other extreme, to deemphasize international capital flows. The interest equalization tax in the United States, for example, is a recently conceived device designed to modify flows of international capital for balance of payments purposes.

There have been important changes in the theory of adjustment for international capital flows as well as in the policy approach to adjustment. Income theory has been used to elaborate and to modify the traditional theory of international investment [40; 47]. Metzler examined the effects of capital transfers in a two-country model where marginal propensities to consume, to import, and to invest differed and where less than full employment existed. His assumptions of unemployment along with rigid monetary wage structures, competitive industries, and constant returns were sufficient to ensure that changes in monetary demand affected levels of output rather than prices. With a fixed-exchange rate, measurements of all changes could be made in the currency of the lending country. Whether or not induced changes in income and the trade balance would bring about the capital transfer depended upon conditions in each of the two countries in isolation. If for each country the sum of the marginal propensities to consume, to import, and to invest was less than unity, a stable equilibrium was possible. In contrast, if one of the countries was unstable in isolation, as it might be if the sum of the propensities was greater than 1, the capital transfer would take place through induced changes — provided the unstable country permitted the transfer to affect its income directly [47, p. 411]. Metzler felt that in actual circumstances, however, few countries would have marginal propensities to consume, import, and invest large enough to place them in the unstable category.

The notion that foreign investment had favorable effects on domestic employment was questioned by Hinshaw [23]. He observed that the foreign contribution to domestic employment soon evaporated, unless lending abroad rose rapidly to offset the increasing return flows of interest and amortization. He considered that domestic employment could be promoted best through loans at very low rates of interest (although incomes for both lender and borrower were enhanced by foreign investment in much the same way as domestic investment). The basic problem was how the transfer was effected.

Later, Domar formulated relationships between return flows from foreign investment and the rate of new lending [15]. He concluded that the return flow need never be greater than the gross outflow if the rate of growth of new lending exceeded the rate of interest applied to the lending. Domar's examination implied that private investment alone could not be sufficient to cause the rate of new investment to exceed the yield. This followed because either the yield rate must be extremely low or the rate of new investment must be extremely high. Domar himself considered the best approach to be a combination of public lending with low rates of interest and private lending so that the average rate of interest charged in foreign borrowing was equivalent to the rate of growth of new loans.

Only since World War II has attention been given to balance of payments adjustments inflicted upon underdeveloped countries and countries needing reconstruction through international capital flow. Polak, for example, examined relationships between capital imports, domestic expansion, and commodity imports for countries severely deficient in capital [58]. An inflexible wage rate and the lack of capital implied extensive unemployment, low incomes, little savings, stagnant levels of productivity, and of course an imbalance in international payments. Foreign credits become essential to finance imports. Polak's main concern was the degree of danger to the balance of payments during the period of capital import. Although his methods precluded general quantitative conclusions, Polak reached several qualitative conclusions. Lending countries could not be assured of early correctives to the payments imbalances of borrowing countries; indeed, the imbalances might deteriorate rapidly if the domestic rate of investment in the borrowing country

229

was too high. He also thought that the initial rate of capital inflow tended to set the rate of total investment, given the marginal propensities to consume and to import.

Kindleberger [33, pp. 398–402] has taken exception to the arguments of Hinshaw, Domar, and Polak; he considers it a fallacy to think that foreign lending and borrowing must be continued cumulatively. Lenders do not necessarily lend all their interest returns and borrowers do not always borrow for unproductive purposes. Interest received by the lender is partly consumed and partly saved. Only a portion then is available for relending.[14] Similarly, capital borrowed, if productive, will yield income greater than the amount of interest payable and cause a shift of resources among sectors. Thus the adverse implications for the balance of payments will in practice be offset by more favorable developments.

Kahn has made critical observations on the general rule that countries engaged in reconstruction or development should invest an amount sufficient to yield additional export goods or services [31]. The rule, advanced by Polak and others, was to provide insurance against balance of payments difficulties after the period of capital formation. Kahn did not consider that investments whose products were not exportable involved any inherent threat to the balance of payments — because real and money incomes could be increased without increasing imports. Kahn contended that the rule's erroneous conclusions followed from an assumption of a marginal propensity to import always greater than zero. Even if the new investment leads to inflation there is still no presumption that imports will be higher eventually, provided there is no change in savings. He thought that a net marginal propensity to import of zero is possible, especially if prudent monetary policies are pursued [31, p. 47].

Transfer analysis has had a wider application than is usually realized. Streeten, for example, made use of the approach in 1954 in discussing "the transfer problem of the dollar shortage" [67, p. 110]. Johnson found it useful in analyzing the nature of exchange stability and in studying the effects of trade intervention [27]. He emphasized that the transfer problem can be posed as a real problem or as a monetary problem, that is, as an issue either in the classical full employment system or in the Keynesian system where aggregate effective demand determines output, incomes, and employment. One effect in the classical system is that the terms of trade are presumed to turn against the transferring country. Since this effect depends upon relative marginal propensities to spend, which have not been measured, Johnson is inclined to reject any lingering presumptions still attached to the claim. In the Keynesian approach the transfer problem is concerned with whether the transferor's balance of payments worsens or improves by the amount of the transfer after all multiplier effects involved in the financing and disposal of the transfer have been accounted for.

Historically there have been two competing theories of adjustment. The classical approach, as we have seen, stressed price or price-exchange rate adjustments; price elasticities played a crucial role. The Keynesian theory on the other hand stressed income effects; the foreign trade multiplier was the critical instrument. Several recent attempts have been made to combine the two approaches into one single theory and, in some cases, to include the rate of interest as well as money market conditions [18; 36; 45; 59; 68; 74].

Polak in one study [59] and Neisser and Modigliani in another [53] have provided important empirical evidence showing the extent to which national incomes adjusted to trade imbalances during the 1930s. Harberger, however, criticized this work as giving too little attention to the role of prices in the adjustment process [19]. He pointed to the lack of statistical significance in the estimated price elasticities of import demand used in the two studies and the numerical smallness of import and export elasticities. The small elasticities resulted, Harberger maintained, because income fluctuations overshadowed price movements in the period examined, because the short period analysis did not reflect the long-run effectiveness of price changes, and because of the statistical methods used. Orcutt [57] has also criticized empirical estimates of elasticities as leaving a downward bias.

An examination of numerous studies investigating prewar as well as postwar data enabled Harberger to conclude that "the price mechanism works powerfully and pervasively in international trade" [19, p. 521]. He advanced the rule that elasticities for the typical country were:

short-run import demand ——— $-.5$ to -1.0

short-run export demand ——— around -2

These bold claims and the ingenious methods used to derive them have in turn been challenged [Gehrels, 17]. The approach using price elasticities as the chief explanation of balance of payments adjustments has come into sharp conflict with the absorption approach. Chapter 7 examines this conflict in detail. Because of the empirical and theoretical conflicts, it is desirable to have tools of analysis that clearly show the forces of price and income in an international system.

Vanek has made a noteworthy attempt at theoretical synthesis [74, 75]. Noting that the classical system had a production function, which under Say's Law was associated with constant full employment output and a fixed rate of exchange, Vanek observes that the balance of payments was the only true variable in the system. Any imbalance in international payments would correct itself automatically through the price-specie-flow mechanism. The elasticity of demand for imports, exchange rate alterations, and the rate of interest were largely ignored. When interest rates were incorporated into the analysis they were treated as an element in the monetary adjustment rather than as a function of real adjustment.

Using the notion of interdependence between the rate of exchange and the balance of payments on current account, Vanek shows that equilibrium in the foreign exchange market under classical assumptions corresponds to equilibrium in the balance of payments. A correspondence exists between the elasticity of supply of foreign exchange and the elasticity of demand for exports if an infinite elasticity of supply for exports is assumed. Similarly, the elasticity of demand for foreign exchange can be related to the elasticity of demand for imports, assuming infinite elasticity of supply of imports. In order for the balance of payments to improve through a change in the exchange rate, the sum of the demand elasticities must be greater than 1 provided the balance was initially in equilibrium. The elasticity approach is imperfect, as Vanek points out, because it is unrealistic to assume an infinite elasticity of supply of exports and imports, especially since changes in output of these goods affect employment and output.

Building onto the simple Keynesian multiplier analysis, Vanek develops a more realistic theory of the adjustment mechanism where both income and relative prices are used as adjustment variables. The usual foreign trade multiplier depends on marginal propensities to save and to import and the simple Keynesian equilibrium system for an open economy relates the level of savings and imports to the level of investment and exports. This balance, however, depends on the fact that savings and imports (as well as induced investment) depend upon the interest rate, in addition to the level of real income. With these two dependent variables affecting the outcome, an infinite number of solutions are possible — as is expressed graphically, with contour AA in Figure 5-1 [74, p. 15; 75, p. 134]. Thus AA traces out the equilibrium path for the goods markets (S-I) and the foreign balance (X-M) when related to interest rates and *real* income. Important assumptions underlying this construction are that imports of, and prices in, foreign countries are constant. If domestic prices increase, for example, the terms of trade improve but there is reduced expenditure on domestic goods in favor of foreign goods. Thus the effective demand for domestic goods is reduced and there is a decline in real incomes. This means a movement of AA to the left, a movement such as to $A'A'$. The same movement could reflect an appreciation of the domestic currency.

The LL curve corresponds to the liquidity preference and the demand for money under conditions of a given price level, a fixed supply of money and the familiar liquidity trap. A reduction in the supply of money or in the price level shifts the portions of the LL curve, which are less than infinitely inelastic, upwards and to the left. Since a limit exists to real income, Y_o represents the full employment level. Point E is the

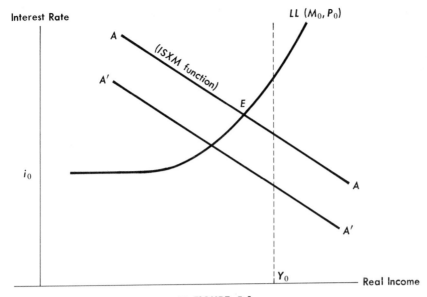

■ FIGURE 5-1

initial equilibrium situation where, with given prices and supply of money, domestic and foreign trade are compatible with liquidity preference and savings propensities. It indicates a deflationary gap, since it is below full employment income.

Devaluation, which causes E to decline in the terms of trade of the country in this model, will cause income and employment to increase if the equilibrium situation is stable and the marginal propensity to import of the foreign country is less than its marginal propensity to absorb its own products. Vanek finds that under these conditions and when incomes are taken into account, it is necessary for the sum of demand elasticities for imports to be much greater than 1 for devaluation to improve incomes [74, p. 36]. He thinks that import demand elasticities are fairly high in actuality but income effects offset expected results of exchange rate alterations. Both the partial equilibrium or elasticities approach to payments imbalances and the absorption approach are considered only as special cases to the more general theory of adjustment in Vanek's model.

□ ADJUSTMENT AS A POLICY PROBLEM

The Balance of Payments as a Distinct Problem

In its earliest stages the modern approach to the adjustment mechanism tended to discount automatic price adjustment and recognize only automatic income adjustment. Later, it took a new path whereby the policy variables were regarded as more flexible and separable from the process of adjustment itself. Equilibrium in the balance of payments was then regarded as only one part of stable national and international full employment equilibrium. Balance in the external sector could not be achieved without regard to the balance in the internal sector; instruments of control were needed for both external and internal sectors.

Economic policy thus took on new significance; it became important for bringing about adjustments to economic imbalance.[15] Unlike the older system, which tended to incorporate into the analysis firm sets of rules rather than independent policy measures, the newer approach regarded policy as quite distinct and independent from the adjustment system. Policy measures were exogenous variables which could make a difference as to whether or not international accounts were in balance.

Typically, a persistent deficit has been dealt with as a serious economic policy matter. In theory, any payments deficit implies a reduction in the availability of money; receipts by residents are less than payments by residents, excluding the operations of monetary authorities. The deficit means that residents are running down their cash balances while the velocity of circulation of money is increasing or that monetary authorities are expanding the monetary supply internally to offset the external drains [28, p. 18; 73]. If only residents ran down cash balances and the forces created were free to operate, the balance of payments would automatically correct itself in the long-run, since the rate of interest would rise attracting foreign capital. This alternative, however, has had little application since the 1930s because few countries have had sufficient foreign reserves to finance the deficits until adjustment is complete and monetary authorities have been concerned with the short-run stabilization of the rate of interest or the level of incomes.

The absorption approach makes clear that deficits in payments are linked with an excess of expenditure over output or income. The policy solution then is obviously to reduce expenditure or increase output. Johnson has categorized these policy approaches as "policies of expenditure reduction" and "policies of expenditure switching" [28, p. 19; 29, pp. 162–167]. The first type of policy means a reduction of aggregate demand that affects both expenditure and domestic output directly and through multiplier effects indirectly; it involves use of such instruments as higher taxes or interest rates. Policies of expenditure switching involve the diverting of spending on foreign-produced goods to home-produced goods. Among policies of this type are devaluation and import restriction. We shall return to these particular policy measures later.

An actual deficit need not always be the basis for a balance of payments problem. Bernstein, for example, says that "a country whose balance of payments is not a proper one has a payments problem" [8, p. 133]. He describes a "proper" balance of payments as an equality between payments and receipts for current transactions and "ordinary" capital movements — which means that the country is not compelled to keep economic activity below a "desirable" level or to restrict imports solely for balance of payments purposes and that the country is adding to its monetary reserves proportionately to the increase in world monetary stocks. Given that different countries "desire" different things, it would be possible under this definition for all countries in the world to have payments problems simultaneously. Also international payments could be in balance while a "problem" persisted; but the balance would be artificial or forced. In his own discussions, however, Bernstein deals with the payments problem as evidenced by large and persistent deficits. Remedial correctives are directed at these types of deficits, although usually with a time lag.

Different rates of inflation in different countries usually produce balance of payments disequilibria because exportables of the country with the greater inflation become over-priced in world markets and the list of potential importables grows as domestic prices surge upwards [Lutz, 38, 39]. International differences in the rates of economic growth also have important, as well as complex, consequences for balance of payments equilibria. A country with a faster rate of growth than another may incur a deficit, since imports into the country may rise more rapidly than imports by the rest of the world. Much depends on the contribution of expanding exports to economic growth.

Balance of payments problems can be created through capital account transactions quite apart from those in the current account. All unilateral and capital transfers involve a switch of purchasing power from one country to another. Income effects are produced which in turn influence the trade balance. Reactions in the trade balance, however, may not be sufficient to remove the imbalance initiated by the transfer. As explained earlier, there is widespread doubt and pessimism as to whether elasticities of demand and supply are such that they could permit the real transfer to take place.

In any actual situation, several causes of imbalance will be at work and in no two cases will the same degrees of contribution arise from the different factors. For example, excessive credit expansion in a large country, with a low average and marginal propensity to import, would contribute proportionately less to a balance of payments deficit than in a small country with high propensities to import and to substitute foreign for domestic goods. In any balance of payments problem, many separate items contribute some measure to the imbalance and it is difficult to determine precisely what causes are mainly responsible for what part of the imbalance. In spite of these difficulties in determining elements and causes, detailed information on the new forces at work is needed for policy formulation.[16]

It is generally acknowledged that there are four major national policy instruments to deal with a persistent deficit in the balance of payments. These are: deflation, devaluation, import controls, and flexible exchanges. The instruments do not all have the same effects; they do not induce the same changes in the variables; and they do not produce the same speed of adjustment.

These policy measures operate at the national level. Internationally other instruments are available: policies of internationl credit expansion or contraction and policies of coordination among monetary authorities of the world [Tinbergen, 71]. International credit expansion is a means of expanding international liquidity and international monetary coordination entails, essentially, the equalizing of interest rate changes.

Deflation affects expenditure and production by reducing the money supply, forcing money incomes and possibly prices down, and making new expenditure, particularly on investment, less attractive. Expenditure on foreign goods is reduced along with expenditure on domestic goods. In other words there is a decrease in absorption. A fall in domestic income is accompanied by a reduction of some domestic prices relative to foreign prices. Income and price changes both operate to lower imports and increase exports, although changes in the cost-price structure may be slow in appearing. The extent of the change, however, depends upon the complex mixtures of price elasticities and spending propensities at home and abroad.

Devaluation is usually a single-stroke act premeditated in secret and announced suddenly. It deals most effectively with price-cost disparities if they are the sole cause of payments imbalance. It may bring about redistribution in incomes for a limited time, promoting savings and investment but compressing consumption, particularly if real wages are not subsequently restored to former levels. Because price-cost disparities are themselves caused by excessive aggregate demand, in most actual situations a joint policy of price stabilization and devaluation is usually desirable. Normally, devaluation can only be introduced after a deficit occurs or a series of deficits takes place and a fall in reserves has been accentuated. In practice, devaluation must err on the side of too much rather than too little; but unfortunately, the extent of devaluation can only be guided by the most arbitrary measures.

A policy of flexible exchange rates as a complete solution to payments imbalances has been advocated by many [16, 62]. Much support is given to this policy because it is maintained that continuing automatic adjustment to payments problems is given by flexible exchange rates and it reduces the urgent needs for increased international liquidity. To many, this policy represents the chief alternative to balance of payments controls. This controversy is dealt with in Chapter 6.

An adjustment policy based on trade controls will have many instruments to choose from.[17] Meade has grouped direct controls over trade into two groups — financial and commercial [45, Ch. 20 and 21]. These controls aim at influencing particular elements in the balance of payments directly, in contrast to monetary policy and exchange rate policy which, by influencing the general mechanism of money prices and money incomes, affect the balance of payments indirectly. Among financial controls, Meade includes exchange controls, multiple exchange rates, and fiscal controls to cover taxes and subsidies. Among commercial controls, he includes quantitative restrictions, tariffs, quotas, and state trading monopolies.

Direct controls affect the balance of payments, the level of national income and its distribution within and between countries. They have some effects similar to the methods of adjustment operating through price mechanisms but they are necessarily discriminatory. Moreover, they do not correct for relatively over-priced goods; the currency is usually left over-valued. The size of demand elasticities in the countries involved influences considerably the choice between measures of balance of payments adjustment using price mechanisms or direct controls [Meade, 45, p. 323]. With large demand elasticities, the price mechanism will provide significant adjustment without too much manipulation of the items of trade. But if demand elasticities are small, the price mechanism by itself may be insufficient to remove the full force of the disequilibrium. Meade presumes elasticities will be reasonably large if trade barriers are not numerous and if sufficient time is allowed for the price adjustments to work themselves out [45, pp. 323–24].

Direct controls may be of great significance if other measures to influence the balance of payments fail. Because they are selective, they can, for example, lessen the adverse price effects created by exchange depreciation. Direct controls may, however, impair efficient resource utilization and create artificial balances in the international payments that may involve perpetual and even increasingly extensive controls.

Monetary Policy as an Adjustment Device

As is well known, in the early 1950s, after an interval of over twenty years, the monetary authorities of most countries reintroduced monetary policy as an active instrument for controlling economic imbalances. In the 1930s, monetary policy, which up to that time had been relied upon heavily, tended to be discarded in favor of fiscal and commercial policy. The main tool of monetary policy — interest rates — had generally been found wanting as an efficient regulator of investment. National economic goals were linked with low levels of interest and substantial treasury operations. The partial rehabilitation of monetary policy took place when it was conceded that low interest rates had much to do with inflationary forces that had emerged in the 1940s and 1950s. Nevertheless, it was recognized that high interest rates impeded attainment of new goals of rapid economic growth and, in general, that monetary policy was not as keenly edged a tool as formerly presupposed.

To be fully effective in a modern economy, monetary policy must aid in regulating aggregate spending so that full employment is maintained and price instability avoided. When the monetary authorities also have to encounter influences originating abroad, it becomes more apparent why doubts are cast on the full efficacy of national monetary policy. Unless they are able to alter the exchange rate, monetary authorities find it difficult in the long-run to prevent inflation from being imported [Lutz, 38, p. 37]. A payments surplus expands foreign reserves and increases national liquidity, which becomes the basis for a primary deposit expansion. Even an increase in reserve requirements and the sale of securities by the central bank may not be sufficient in the long-run to remove excess liquidity and dampen secondary deposit expansion. The limit here is set by legal reserve requirements and the central bank's portfolio of securities. Loss of control over the money supply entails loss of control over aggregate spending, unless recognition is given to international market forces by adjusting exchange rates.

In Mundell's view, monetary authorities have two alternatives in attempting to achieve society's goals of full employment and balance of payments equilibrium [50; 51]. They may stabilize the exchange rate by using monetary policy to maintain external equilibrium, leaving the price mechanism to maintain internal equilibrium; or they may stabilize the price level by using monetary policy to maintain internal equilibrium, leaving exchange rates free to maintain external balance.[18] Where avoidance of exchange rate alteration and trade control imposition are desired, it is suggested that monetary policy should deal with external objectives and fiscal policy with internal objectives [52]. Thus a deficit country experiencing unemployment should tighten interest rates and move towards a government budget deficit.

Mundell finds that if capital is highly mobile, the fixed exchange rate system will operate effectively since equilibrium is attained more speedily and more directly. If capital is immobile, however, the flexible exchange rate system appears more appropriate. Efficiency of adjustment is enhanced by high capital mobility under fixed exchanges because the interest rate has a direct affect on the balance of payments. If interest rates do not induce this responsiveness in the balance of payments directly, they must do it through the price level and reactions in goods markets.

Selective credit policy and manipulations of the pattern of interest rates are more refined monetary instruments; they have been used very rarely. It is possible to create situations which favor or discourage importers or exporters or international investors as the situation warrants.

By and large, however, the discriminatory features of such policies have been avoided by most monetary authorities. The efficacy of the "twist" — an attempt in the United States to segregate the short-term capital market from the long-term capital market by raising interest rates in the short-term market so that foreign funds are attracted and lowering interest rates in the long-term market so that higher investment contributes to faster economic growth — has not yet been tested empirically. More experimentation seems needed in the realm of monetary policy under a regime of fixed exchange rates. Certainly, the finer tools of monetary policy yet to be tested will require special controls and safeguards because such policy measures, being more selective, produce greater possibilities of evasion and mishandling.

Devaluation as a Policy of Adjustment

Considerable attention has been given in the literature to the effect of devaluation on the trade balance.[19] Devaluation has the immediate effect of altering critical price relationships. It usually provides a unique opportunity to assess the responsiveness of demand to price changes and thus has considerable appeal to the theoretician and statistician as a matter for investigation.

Two basically different approaches to the problem of adjustment under devaluation have been used, as Chapter 7 explains in detail. The Marshallian partial equilibrium approach stresses the effects of devaluation in terms of the demand and supply elasticities of exports and imports. A more general approach is through income theory linked to the balance of payments. This examines the way in which devaluation, by changing the terms of trade and altering demands for different goods, changes the level of expenditure made possible by a given level of income.

A major comparison of the two approaches is seen in the basic conditions necessary for the production of favorable effects from a devaluation. Briefly, in the partial equilibrium approach, the balance of trade is improved — which means that the algebraic sum of export changes and import changes is positive — when the sum of demand elasticities for imports at home and abroad is greater than one. More strictly, a necessary condition for no worsening in the trade balance in the Marshallian approach is that the sum of elasticities be not less than 1. The approach, however, ignores cross relations between supply and demand of exports and importables [Johnson, 28, p. 20].

The more general approach takes account of income determination, the cross relations between demands for different goods, and the possible direct effects of changes in the terms of trade on the level of expenditure from a given income. Using these factors, the requirements for making devaluation effective are sums of elasticities greater than 1 and higher than the Marshallian elasticities [28, p. 23; 29, p. 179].

The price relationships which are changed by devaluation introduce strong international forces of change. But devaluation also introduces significant impacts on domestic income, output, and employment through multiplier effects. Such income effects can be arrived at independently of the price effects, although price changes cannot be ignored in the complete analysis and it is widely felt that income effects modify the severity of the price effects. If devaluation creates an excess of domestic currency demand over domestic currency supplied, there is an injection into the domestic money stream that produces expansionary effects. In the foreign country, reverse forces operate [Allen, 4]. Thus an initial increase in exports, sponsored by the relative price changes in the devaluating country, may be partially offset by a decrease as foreign income and demand fall off. Similarly, an initial decline in imports caused by changes in relative prices may be offset by an increase in imports induced by income changes. It is theoretically unsatisfactory to superimpose separate unrelated multiplier or income effects on price effects; a comprehensive system of analysis is required to consider both effects simultaneously [Tsiang, 72, pp. 912–13].

One of the difficulties in assessing the results of devaluation on the balance of payments results from the uncertainty of effect on the terms of trade. Writers disagree as to the probable effect; a majority appear to believe that devaluation will worsen the terms of trade. The matter is complicated by the recognition of several types of terms of trade which could serve as indicators of improvement or deterioration and by the inconclusiveness of empirical studies.

If it were known in what direction and by how much the terms of trade would move as a result of devaluation, it still would not be clear to what extent national income would alter as a consequence and further how this would affect the balance of trade. Machlup feels that determinate effects on real income could be established only if productivity and the allocation of resources remained unchanged [42, p. 420]. Nevertheless, there is a strong presumption that devaluation would bring about a more efficient allocation of resources.

The belief is widespread that, if a currency is overvalued and payments disequilibrium is apparent, any policy of devaluation to correct the situation must be accompanied by deflationary monetary and fiscal policies since there will be an inevitable rise in domestic prices as a result of the devaluation. Such beliefs have been used as strong arguments against devaluation. Devaluation implies a domestic price rise for import goods if there is no change in foreign currency prices. At the same time the use of domestic resources for increased exports induced by the devaluation adds to the inflationary pressures at home.

Sohmen has argued against this view [64; 65]. The view, he thinks, could be supported if commodity movements were perfectly free and accommodating transfers bridged the gap in the balance of payments. In equilibrium, domestic prices would then always be equal to their foreign price times the exchange rate. Rarely, however, are these conditions found. Countries cannot ignore large deficits for any long period. Trade controls are frequently used to check the potential deficit, so that external and domestic prices diverge considerably based on the legal exchange rate [64, p. 275]. Sohmen feels that any balance of payments disequilibrium can only be corrected if all overvaluation of the currency and all trade controls are eliminated. Devaluation need not be inflationary, he thinks. On the contrary, falls in domestic price levels are possible, since any removal of import controls made possible by devaluation must lower import prices.

Controls Over Trade and Investment

For some time immediately following World War II, it was held that the imposition of direct controls on imports was preferable on welfare grounds to adjustments of price variables. Restrictions on imports as the sole means of securing an improvement in the balance of payments, however, have been somewhat discredited in recent years — due largely to the force of the absorption approach to the adjustment mechanism [Alexander, 1]. The elasticities approach, on the other hand, suggests that import restrictions inevitably improve a payments balance [Nurkse 56, p. 138; cf. 21, p. 483]; moreover, there are numerous practical problems in attempting to do away with trade restrictions [Bhagwati, 9; cf. 29, Ch. 6].

For an improvement in the balance of payments to take place within the scope of the absorption approach, savings must increase, investment decrease, or both. Import restrictions unaccompanied by measures which remove the excess absorption are not capable of providing, with any certainty, a net savings increase. In conditions of full employment and inflexible prices, import restrictions may, by distorting expenditure, bring about a fall in net savings and only a weak improvement in the payments position. Import restrictions usually have favorable effects on the import side of the balance of payments but they can also have unfavorable effects on the export side and on employment if exports are typically labor-intensive. In contrast, deflation, no matter what its role in foreign trade, usually has adverse effects on employment but favorable effects on both sides of the balance of payments.

It has been argued that supplementary policy is required for import restrictions, largely because the effect of import restrictions is felt through an improvement in the terms of trade, whereas alternative measures such as deflation exert downward pressures on all prices. Import restrictions improve the terms of trade by reducing the buying price of imports and by raising the domestic selling price of imports which in turn can increase export prices [Hemming and Corden, 21, pp. 508, 509]. Deflation, in contrast, tends to force prices of home-market goods down, bringing about a shift of domestic demand from imports and exportables to domestic goods. Deflation has an import-replacing influence as well as an export-promoting influence but it is limited by a downward inflexibility of domestic prices relative to prices of other goods. It is possible, of course, using an econometric system advanced by Tinbergen, to derive an ideal combination of policies of deflation and import restriction given the margins of adjustment necessary [69, pp. 114–148; 70, Ch. II].

If, because of violent and unexpected external disturbances, prices do not bring adjustment smoothly and quickly, direct controls may be necessary. When international markets for exports and imports are subject to sizable disruptions, the price mechanism by itself is usually too slow to produce the necessary adjustment. As a consequence, the loss of foreign reserves and gold will be more than can be sustained. If the catastrophic events then cannot be avoided or accommodated by international collaboration, direct control — rather than price adjustment through depreciation — seems preferable. The relative wealth and income positions of deficit and surplus countries also must be considered in order for world economic welfare to be maximized.

Policies controlling capital transfers have been retained or reinstituted long after policies controlling trade items have vanished. The present situation is one in which new uses are being found for controls on, as well as incentives for, capital movements [39, p. 51]. Rather than permit price levels to rise, countries with balance of payments surpluses on current account sometimes find it easier to encourage the export of capital. The surplus, which may also attract short-term funds, is offset and the growth of foreign exchange or gold reserves is reduced. Countries with deficits, by reducing unilateral payments abroad and increasing short-term liabilities to other countries, attempt to stem the loss of gold and reserves. The main assumption behind such policies is that the existing relative price level is the one to be preserved and that unilateral transfers should be in such an amount and in such a direction as to induce commodity flows which contribute to the preservation of that price level. In the new approaches, relative profitability and interest rate differentials are regarded as less vital than in the traditional approach of capital transfers. Whether or not capital export eventually reduces persistent surpluses depends upon repercussion effects. It is possible that increased unilateral transfers may boomerang through new export demands and make the surplus worse. If this always happened, a deficit country might worsen its position by reducing its unilateral and capital transfers, since the trade balance would deteriorate still further as exports fell off.

The effectiveness of policy concerning capital transfers can be gauged by whether there are changes in total world real investment or merely a change in the composition of foreign assets held. If, as a result of the policy, the surplus country accumulates long-term claims rather than short-term claims, while the deficit country reduces its short-term foreign liabilities as well as its rate of foreign long-term lending, there is no necessary feed-back through current account changes. In fact, under some definitions of payments balance, the surplus and the deficit are removed. In contrast, if the policy in the surplus country enables capital exports to make a net addition to total world investment, export feed-back mechanisms will operate and the export surplus will not be eliminated. It thus seems that specialized conditions or exchange controls are needed if international equilibrium is to emerge from uncoordinated full employment policies [Stolper, 66, p. 566; Machlup, 44].

In most of this analysis of the adjustment process, we have treated changes in trade as though all trade were alike. The truth of the matter is, however, that international trade has both qualitative and quantitative implications. We have not considered, for example, the problems that can arise when the pattern of trade alters so that one group of countries might be affected in a way different from another group. Adjustment policy and the choice of instruments, therefore, will be influenced by the composition of trade as well as by changes in overall magnitudes.

It has become apparent in the contemporary world that adjustment to payments imbalances is not automatic, either through domestic or international institutions; clearly the problem is not a matter solely for national policy. Small countries are perhaps more conscious of the adjustment problem than large countries, since adjustment to a given change in the value of world trade will have a greater effect — proportionately — on their economies than on larger economies. In recognizing this, most of the larger countries need to adopt adjustment policies that, while helping to solve their own payments problems, do not transfer an intensified problem to smaller countries.

FOOTNOTES

1. Adjustment analysis usually means the study of the transition from one equilibrium to another after the initial equilibrium has been disturbed. See Machlup [43] and Meade [45, pp. 52–58]. But what may be initial equilibrium for one purpose may not be equilibrium for another. Any adjustment analysis therefore should make clear the precise framework in which change is to be examined. The balance of payments for example can be arranged to show the trade balance as the test of equilibrium or can combine current account items with certain capital account items. Machlup [41] has emphasized the problem of differentiating between the "accounting balance," the "market balance," and the "program balance." Lary [34, pp. 137–162] also examines various ways of presenting the balance of payments.

2. An application of the internal and external balancing technique, where import restrictions is a possible instrument of control, is given in Corden [14].

3. Not all writers in the classical period supported the idea of the automatic price mechanisms of adjustment. Wheatley, Longfield, and Bastable in particular stood apart from the traditional positions. See Viner [76, Ch. VI and VII]. It was not until 1926, with the writings of Ohlin, that compelling attention was paid to an alternative formulation of the adjustment mechanism.

4. The relevance of these tests to the development of international trade theory is summarized in Metzler's outstanding review [46, pp. 212–215]. Many subsequent tests were made of the classical explanation but few gave it support. Noteworthy among these is the exhaustive treatment of Morgenstern [49].

5. The elasticity of demand for imports in the United States was estimated to be about .5 in one attempt and in the United Kingdom about .6 in another [Hinshaw and Chang quoted in 46, p. 215].

6. Relevant works of these authors are cited in Metzler [46, p. 213].

7. Joan Robinson presented one of the earliest attempts to relate Keynesian variables to a classical mechanism of adjustment [60, pp. 183–209].

8. Treatment of income effects in a general equilibrium analysis has been traced back to 1720 and to Isaac Gervaise who analyzed the adjustment mechanism both for relatively stable and for fluctuating rates. See Letiche [36, pp. 26, 27].

9. In order to show the effect of a change in imports as income changes, it is necessary to show that expenditures on current domestic output are altered. One way of doing this is to assume a substitution between foreign goods and domestic goods or a reduction in consumption of domestic goods as imports increase. See [Allen, 4, p. 376]. A more advanced treatment using financing and disposal effects is given by Johnson [27] and is considered briefly in the next section.

10. In effect, it represents a replacement of the "bullionist principle" by the "banking principle." For a discussion of the historic role of this controversy see Harris [20]. The banking principle was a recognition of the need to adjust the domestic economy to the needs of domestic trade: the bullionist principle sought to adjust it to the forces of foreign trade by altering the domestic supply of money with the inflow and outflow of gold.

11. Exchange controls, exchange rate manipulations, and trade restrictions are regarded as *ad hoc* policies dealing inconsistently with special circumstances [Mundell, 51]. Linder and Cohen point out that countervailing disturbances initiated by government are new adjustment mechanisms being increasingly used. The disturbances include pressures on surplus countries, changes in foreign tastes, economic growth, and customs unions [37].

12. Were imports to exceed exports before depreciation, an improvement in the balance of payments would be possible even though demand elasticities were low. It has also been argued that low supply elasticities can offset unfavorable effects of low demand elasticities [Streeten, 67, pp. 85–86]. For a summary of the postulate known as the Marshall-Lerner condition, see [Kindleberger, 33, pp. 175 and 656–58].

13. Streeten, for example, suggests that if attention is turned from price elasticities to income elasticity of demand, a more important element in balance of payments mechanisms is used and the way is open for a less pessimistic view [67, pp. 110–112].

14. The proportion of change in saving which is devoted to the purchase of foreign assets has been described by Johnson as the "marginal foreign investment ratio" [29, pp. 182–83]. This ratio will determine the extent to which the transfer will be over-effected or under-effected.

15. The adjustment mechanism has become "institutionalized" at the international level. For example, the purpose of the IMF is "to shorten the duration and lessen the degree of disequilibrium" in balance of payments. Article (1) cited in Allen [3, p. 149].

16. There are those who propose that "the remedies for payments difficulties should be selected in the light of their causes" [8, p. 135].

17. Advocates of trade controls as a superior instrument of adjustment are perhaps not as numerous as the advocates of flexible exchange rates. They are usually counted among the "elasticity pessimists." Note, for example, Henderson [22, p. 7] and Alexander [2].

18. It is assumed that money prices are flexible unless stabilized by the monetary authorities; that equilibrium conditions of two markets dominate — the domestic market for goods and services and the market for foreign exchange; that both markets are subject to the influences of the rate of interest and the terms of trade; that interest rates are determined by the monetary authorities; and that all foreign prices, incomes, and interest rates are constant [50, pp. 228–30].

19. The analysis is sometimes known as the problem of exchange stability which covers the problem of flexible exchanges as well as the question of devaluation. It is impossible here to cite the most relevant theoretical or empirical works on the devaluation topic; the following selection represents a modest sample of recent writings — [1; 12; 18; 24; 25; 30; 72].

BIBLIOGRAPHY

[1] S. S. Alexander, "Effects of a Devaluation: A Simplified Synthesis of Elasticities and Absorption Approaches," *AER* (March 1959).

[2] _____, "Devaluation versus Import Restriction as an Instrument for Improving Foreign Trade Balance," *SP* (April 1951).

[3] W. R. Allen, "The IMF and Balance of Payments Adjustments," *OEP* (June 1961).

[4] _____, "A Note on the Money Income Effects of Devaluation," *Kyk* (Fasc. 3, 1956).

[5] W. R. Allen and C. L. Allen, *Foreign Trade and Finance* (1959).

[6] B. Balassa, "Notes on K. K. Kurihara's Cost Disinflation and Export Expansion," *Kyk* (Fasc. 4, 1961).

[7] W. E. Beach, *British International Gold Movements and Banking Policy 1881–1913* (1935).

[8] E. M. Bernstein, "Strategic Factors in Balance of Payments Adjustment," *REStat* (February 1958).

[9] J. Bhagwati, "Indian Balance of Payments Policy and Exchange Auctions," *OEP* (February 1962).

[10] J. Bhagwati and H. G. Johnson, "Notes on Some Controversies in the Theory of International Trade," *EJ* (March 1960).

[11] _____, "Notes on Some Controversies in the Theory of International Trade: A Rejoinder," *EJ* (June 1961).

[12] J. Black, "A Savings and Investment Approach to Devaluation," *EJ* (June 1959).

[13] N. S. Buchannan, "International Investment," in B. F. Haley (Ed.) *A Survey of Contemporary Economics*, Vol. II (1952).

[14] W. M. Corden, "The Geometric Representation of Policies to Attain Internal and External Balance," *REStud* (October 1960).

[15] E. D. Domar, "The Effect of Foreign Investment on the Balance of Payments," *AER* (December 1950).

[16] Milton Friedman, *Essays in Positive Economics* (1953).

[17] Franz Gehrels, "The Effect of Price on Europe's Exports to the United States," *Kyk* (Fasc. 1, 1961).

[18] A. C. Harberger, "Currency Depreciation, Income and the Balance of Trade," *JPE* (February 1950).

[19] _____, "Some Evidence of the International Price Mechanism," *JPE* (December 1957).

[20] S. E. Harris, *International and Interregional Economics* (1957).

[21] M. F. W. Hemming and W. M. Corden, "Import Restriction as an Instrument of Balance of Payments Policy," *EJ* (September 1958).

[22] Hubert Henderson, "The Function of Exchange Rates," *OEP* (January 1949).

[23] Randall Hinshaw, "International Investment and American Employment," *AER* (May 1946).

[24] _____, "Currency Appreciation as an Anti-Inflationary Device," *QJE* (November 1951 and February 1952).

[25] A. O. Hirschman, "Devaluation and the Trade Balance: A Note," *REStat* (February 1949).

[26] F. D. Holzman and Arnold Zellner, "The Foreign Trade and Balanced Budget Multipliers," *AER* (March 1958).

[27] H. G. Johnson, "The Transfer Problem and Exchange Stability," *JPE* (June 1956).

[28] _____, "The Balance of Payments," *Pakistan Economic Journal* (June 1958), as reprinted *Money, Trade and Economic Growth* (1962).

[29] _____, *International Trade and Economic Growth* (1958).

[30] R. E. Jones, "Depreciation and the Dampening Effects of Income Changes," *REStat* (February 1960).

[31] A. E. Kahn, "Investment Criteria in Development Programs," *QJE* (February 1951).

[32] C. P. Kindleberger, "The Foreign Trade Multiplier, The Propensity to Import and Balance of Payments Equilibrium," *AER* (March and September 1949).

[33] _____, *International Economics* (1963).

[34] H. B. Lary, *Problems of the United States as World Trader and Banker* (1963).

[35] Sven Laursen and L. A. Metzler, "Flexible Exchange Rates and the Theory of Employment," *REStat* (November 1950).

[36] J. M. Letiche, *Balance of Payments and Economic Growth* (1959).

[37] S. B. Linder and B. J. Cohen, "Balance of Payments Adjustment in a Disequilibrium System," *Kyk* (Fasc. 1, 1964).

[38] F. A. Lutz, *International Payments and Monetary Policy in the World Today* (1961).

[39] _____, *The Problem of International Economic Equilibrium* (1962).

[40] Fritz Machlup, *International Trade and the National Income Multiplier* (1943).

[41] _____, "Three Concepts of the Balance of Payments and the So-Called Dollar Shortage," *EJ* (March 1950).

[42] _____, "The Terms of Trade Effects of Devaluation Upon Real Income and the Balance of Trade," *Kyk* (Fasc. 4, 1956).

[43] _____, "Equilibrium and Disequilibrium: Misplaced Concreteness and Disguised Politics," *EJ* (March 1958).

[44] _____, *Plans for Reform of the International Monetary System*, Special Papers in International Economics, No. 3, Princeton University, 1962.

[45] J. E. Meade, *The Theory of International Economic Policy*, Vol. I, The Balance of Payments (1951).

[46] L. A. Metzler, "The Theory of International Trade," in H. S. Ellis (Ed.), *A Survey of Contemporary Economics*, Vol. I (1948).

[47] _____, "The Transfer Problem Reconsidered," *Journal of Political Economy* (June 1942), as reprinted in H. S. Ellis and L. A. Metzler (Eds.), *Readings in the Theory of International Trade* (1949).

[48] Kenichi Miyazawa, "Foreign Trade Multiplier, Input-Output Analysis and the Consumption Function," *QJE* (February 1960).

[49] Oskar Morgenstern, *International Financial Transactions and Business Cycles* (1959).

[50] R. A. Mundell, "The Monetary Dynamics of International Adjustment under Fixed and Flexible Exchange Rates," *QJE* (May 1960).

[51] _____, "The International Disequilibrium System," *Kyk* (Fasc. 2, 1961).

[52] _____, "The Appropriate Use of Monetary and Fiscal Policy for Internal and External Stability," *SP* (March 1962).

[53] Hans Neisser and Franco Modigliani, *National Incomes and International Trade* (1953).

[54] Ragnar Nurkse, "Conditions of International Monetary Equilibrium," *Essays in International Finance*, No. 4, Princeton, 1945.

[55] _____, "Domestic and International Equilibrium," in S. E. Harris (Ed.), *The New Economics: Keynes' Influence on Theory and Public Policy* (1948).

[56] _____, "The Relation between Home Investment and External Balance in the Light of British Experience, 1945–1955," *REStat* (May 1956).

[57] G. H. Orcutt, "Measurement of Price Elasticities in International Trade," *REStat* (May 1950).

[58] J. J. Polak, "Balance of Payments Problems of Countries Reconstructing with the Help of Foreign Loans," *QJE* (February 1943).

[59] _____, *An International Economic System* (1954).

[60] Joan Robinson, *Essays in the Theory of Employment* (1937).

[61] W. M. Scammell, *International Monetary Policy*, 2nd Ed. (1961).

[62] Egon Sohmen, *Flexible Exchange Rates: Theory and Controversy* (1961).

[63] _____, "Notes on Some Controversies in the Theory of International Trade: A Comment," *EJ* (June 1961).

[64] _____, "The Effect of Devaluation on the Price Level," *QJE* (May 1958).

[65] _____, "Reply to Vanek and Hinshaw," *QJE* (November 1958).

[66] W. F. Stolper, "The Multiplier, Flexible Exchanges and International Equilibrium," *QJE* (November 1950).

[67] Paul Streeten, "Elasticity Optimism and Pessimism in International Trade," *Econia Internaz* (February 1954).

[68] Gerhard Stuvel, *The Exchange Stability Problem* (1950).

[69] Jan Tinbergen, *Economic Policy: Principles and Design* (1956).

[70] _____, *On the Theory of Economic Policy* (1952).

[71] _____, "International Co-ordination of Stabilization and Development Policies," *Kyk* (Fasc. 3, 1959).

[72] S. C. Tsiang, "The Role of Money in Trade-Balance Stability: A Synthesis of the Elasticity and Absorption Approaches," *AER* (December 1961).

[73] U.S. Congress, Joint Economic Committee, *Factors Affecting the United States Balance of Payments*. Compilation of Studies prepared for Subcommittee on International Exchange and Payments (1962).

[74] Jaroslav Vanek, *The Balance of Payments, Level of Economic Activity and the Value of Currency* (1962).

[75] _____, *International Trade: Theory and Economic Policy* (1962).

[76] Jacob Viner, *Studies in the Theory of International Trade* (1937).

CHAPTER 6

Exchange Rates:
Fixed or Flexible?

PREFATORY STATEMENT

The preceding chapter referred to the controversy between advocates of flexible exchange rates and advocates of fixed or pegged exchange rates. The purpose of this chapter is to explore this controversy in considerable detail. The only serious discussion of flexible exchange rates takes place among academic economists — public officials and policy makers simply avoid (understandably in most cases) discussion of such a major change in our international monetary system. Even among academic economists there appears to be a predominance of support for the system of pegged exchange rates. Nevertheless, there has been an increase in the discussion of flexible exchange rates in recent years, probably because of dissatisfaction with the functioning of the present international monetary system.

Critics of the present international monetary system see a potentially serious conflict between the domestic goals of full employment and satisfactory growth rates and the foreign goal of maintaining reasonably free movement of goods and capital among nations. They seek an international monetary system that is sufficiently flexible to reconcile the objectives of freer trade, continued or expanded foreign aid, and high rates of domestic expansion. They also want sufficient flexibility in the system so that it can cope with major disturbances that require extensive readjustments. These critics feel that the present system of pegged exchange rates does not provide this flexibility and that eventually countries will be forced to choose between a system of free international trade and satisfactory performance of their domestic economies.

The opponents of flexible exchange rates feel that the present system has actually worked quite well, even though it obviously has some defects. Furthermore, they feel that, with relatively minor modifications, the present system can be greatly improved. Most of the modifications involve greater cooperation among the major trading nations in the economic policies they adopt. These persons feel that a system of flexible exchange rates would have even greater flaws because of the tendency for the rates to be unstable and disruptive of international economic relations.

The preceding chapter briefly described the adjustment process under both fixed and flexible exchange rates. This chapter describes the operation of the two systems in greater detail and presents arguments for and against both systems. The term fixed exchange rates will refer to the adjustable peg existing today under the articles of the International Monetary Fund (IMF). In the strict sense, fixed exchange rates refer to the international gold standard that existed prior to 1914 under which countries defined their currencies in gold at a ratio assumed to be fixed indefinitely. A presumed but unstipulated rule of that system was that countries must follow whatever policies were necessary to maintain the gold value of their currencies. This rule meant that the condition of the balance of payments determined national financial policies. Although today a few people advocate a return to the pre-1914 gold standard, most do not seriously consider this possibility in discussing exchange systems.[1] Those currently advocating fixed rates are actually defending the system of the adjustable peg under which countries commit themselves to maintain a specified exchange rate but may, under certain circumstances, infrequently alter the rate. In discussing fixed exchange rates, this chapter is concerned with the adjustable peg of the IMF rather than with the old international gold standard.

Although the overwhelming majority of businessmen, government officials, and economists prefer fixed exchange rates, in recent years there has been increasing discussion of flexible exchange rates. The reason for this increased interest in flexible rates is that the present system of pegged rates has turned out to have some serious and unexpected defects. An analysis of these defects and of ways to overcome them has led some economists to advocate flexible exchange rates. A later section of this chapter indicates that different kinds of disequilibria require different remedies and that neither exchange system provides the better remedy in every situation.

The following discussion of the two exchange systems first takes up the adjustable peg and then turns to flexible rates. It explains how each system operates and examines the arguments for and against each. A characteristic of most literature on this topic is that the arguments for one system consist primarily of arguments against the other [Kindleberger, 17, pp. 403–4]. This discussion also displays that characteristic. For instance, much of the argument for pegged rates appears in the section "The Case Against Flexible Rates." In many instances, an argument and a rebuttal appear together. As a result, neither major section of the chapter discusses just one exchange system. Any disadvantage of this intermixture of the arguments seems to be overcome by the advantage of giving the reader the pro and con arguments together rather than having them widely separated.

To avoid much repetition in the footnotes or in the text, three assumptions are followed throughout the chapter. First, price elasticities are assumed to be high so that the sum of the elasticities of demand for imports is greater than one. Second, exports and imports refer to the values rather than to the physical quantities, unless specified otherwise. Finally, the marginal propensity to import is assumed to be greater than zero but less than one. These assumptions may not appear explicitly in the discussions, although, to repeat, they apply throughout unless stated otherwise.

☐ THE EXCHANGE SYSTEM OF THE ADJUSTABLE PEG

Background

The financial experts who drew up the articles for the International Monetary Fund sought to avoid the disadvantages of the old gold standard which required countries to subjugate domestic policy objectives to the maintenance of equilibrium in their balance of payments. In the 1930's this system promoted the spread of depression from one country to another and led to competitive devaluations in efforts to revive domestic economies. The experts also wanted to devise a system that would avoid the chaotic fluctuations of exchange rates, such as occurred during the 1920's and 1930's when various countries had freely fluctuating rates. They sought, in short, to obtain the advantages of both systems (the rigid gold standard and freely fluctuating rates) without incurring the disadvantages of either.

The resulting agreement was necessarily a compromise between the two systems. It called for individual countries to stabilize their domestic economies at full employment and to seek adjustment of their foreign balances through infrequent changes in otherwise rigid exchange rates. Individual countries established the parity of their currencies with gold (or the dollar) and maintained their values within one per cent of parity. An international body (the IMF) would, after careful consideration, permit a country to adjust its exchange rate when faced with a "fundamental disequilibrium." [2] The purpose of the discussion by the international body was to make certain that countries would change their exchange rates only when justified and not simply to match another's devaluation. Thus, on the one hand, the mixed system, like a system of free rates, permitted adjustment through changes in exchange rates rather than in domestic prices and incomes. As a result, countries could employ domestic policies to achieve high and stable employment. On the other hand, the system sought to obtain the advantages of fixed exchange rates by keeping the rates rigid between the infrequent adjustments.

How the System Works

To show how the system works, assume that a country's imports rise to create a deficit in the balance of payments. The country will draw upon its reserves, borrow abroad, borrow from the IMF, or perhaps do all three to finance the deficit. The increase of imports contracts income through the operation of the foreign trade multiplier. The decline in income causes imports to fall, thus partially offsetting the initial import surplus. If the initial deficit causes the country to lose gold and if the monetary authorities permit the gold outflow to reduce the money supply, interest rates will rise and cause a further contraction in investment and income. This, in turn, will further reduce imports and the payments deficit. Prices generally will not be flexible in the downward direction, so there probably will not be a sufficient price decline to eliminate the deficit. If prices were more flexible downward, countries could, of course, more easily re-establish payments equilibrium. The usual situation is that the decline in imports (and perhaps increase in exports) resulting from income and price changes will not be great enough to restore the balance of payments to equilibrium.

The currency of the deficit country will tend to depreciate, so the monetary authorities will intervene in the exchange market to buy their currency with reserves to keep the depreciation within the 1 per cent allowed by the IMF agreement. If the deficit turns out to be temporary, because of cyclical or random factors or because other offsetting disturbances re-establish equilibrium, no deliberate adjustment policy is necessary. The country would finance the temporary deficit by borrowing or using reserves. If, however, the deficit persists, the country will eventually have to adopt policy measures aimed at restoring equilibrium. The appropriate policies to restore payments equilibrium are deflationary monetary and fiscal measures for the deficit country and inflationary measures for the surplus countries. If the situation should be one of fundamental disequilibrium, the deficit country may devalue its currency or the surplus countries may revalue their currencies upward.

Under the conditions of the nineteenth century, fixed exchange rates seemed to work well.[3] Countries permitted the balance of payments to dictate domestic economic policy and this provided the necessary coordination of monetary policy, i.e., expansion in surplus countries and contraction in deficit countries [Halm, 13, p. 258]. The primary goal of central banks (and other banks too) was to protect their reserves to maintain convertibility at fixed rates. Bank authorities in all countries raised interest rates when reserves fell and lowered them when reserves rose. Such policies were appropriate to restore the balance of payments to equilibrium. Because of this automatic monetary coordination, investors were confident that exchange rates would remain fixed and would move funds from one country to another in response to differences in interest rates. Another common explanation for the success of the gold standard is that prices were more flexible in the nineteenth century. Recent analysis and research suggests, however, that price changes were less important than short-term capital movements in the equilibrating process [Sohmen, 32, pp. 63–64; and Bloomfield, 3].

Conditions today are, however, less favorable than in the nineteenth century for the smooth operation of a system of fixed exchange rates. As explained previously, the IMF represented an attempt to overcome some of the problems encountered in today's world by genuinely fixed exchange rates. But the pegging of exchange rates under the IMF agreement has not been entirely successful, as the discussion in the next section will point out.

Shortcomings of the System

Possible policy conflicts / The authorities in individual countries may not permit gold flows and changes in the trade balance to affect prices and incomes in ways that tend to restore international equilibrium. They normally determine their policies with primary regard to the domestic objective of high and stable employment. If the deficit country is trying to reduce unemployment and the surplus country is fighting inflation, the usual policies to achieve the domestic goals will worsen the international disequilibrium. If the deficit country is fighting inflation and the surplus country has unemployed resources, then the policies that are appropriate for achieving the domestic objectives are also appropriate for correcting the payments imbalance.

With pegged exchange rates, the basic correctives for a deficit country are a decrease of domestic prices and incomes, or a devaluation of the currency, or both.[4] But deflationary policies may cause little downward movement of prices in modern economies because of the downward inflexibility of prices, especially wages. Therefore, attempts to reduce prices will probably cause a reduction in output, employment, and real income but not have much impact on prices. If the reduction of real income goes far enough, it will sufficiently curtail the demand for imports to eliminate the deficit. But the cost is apt to be high in unemployment and foregone income, so high as to make deflation politically unacceptable unless the deficit country is simultaneously fighting inflation. Modern political parties are generally unwilling to sacrifice the domestic goal of high and stable unemployment to the achievement of foreign balance.

The basic correctives for the surplus countries are a rise of domestic prices and incomes, or an upward revaluation of the currency, or both. The authorities may, however, try to prevent any inflation, perhaps because of disastrous experiences with inflation at some previous time or because they want to avoid the shifting of resources required by the unequal response of prices to expansionary policies. Thus, when the deficit country has unemployment and the surplus country has inflation, an adjustment of exchange rates may be the only method of restoring payments equilibrium (except for abandoning convertibility and adopting direct controls) while also allowing the countries to pursue their domestic objectives.

If, however, the deficit country has sufficient policy instruments at its disposal, it should be able to eliminate both unemployment and the payments deficit. Similarly, the surplus country should be able to contain inflation and eliminate its surplus. Mundell [24] has constructed a model in which a country with unemployment and a payments deficit can eliminate both by adopting a tight monetary policy and a loose fiscal policy, i.e., by raising interest rates and increasing the budget deficit.[5] High interest rates attract foreign capital, thus tending to eliminate the payments deficit, while the increased budget deficit stimulates output and employment. By contrast, the surplus country adopts an easy monetary policy and a tight fiscal policy to achieve both its domestic and foreign objectives. A good deal of support has developed for these policy proposals in the present world payments situation. But whether governments can and will promptly adopt such policies in the degree necessary to achieve the twin objectives remains uncertain.

The IMF agreement implicitly assumes that changes in exchange rates will occur only at infrequent intervals — if at all. If countries frequently altered their pegged rates, the system would lose much of the advantage it might have over one with flexible rates. If there is a conflict between the appropriate policies for achieving domestic objectives and payments equilibrium and if the attainment of domestic objectives receives priority, the system of pegged rates provides no variable for effecting international adjustment in the interval between adjustments of exchange rates, unless the countries have and will use adequate policy tools as described in the preceding paragraph. Countries have to meet deficits by using reserves or borrowing. The length of time that they can continue in a disequilibrium will depend upon the size of the deficit, the amount of reserves they possess, and their ability to borrow reserves. In the long run the exchange rate may have to change to restore equilibrium but in the short run and in the medium run the system *per se* may provide no means of adjusting.[6]

Difficulties in managing the rate / Because the system of pegged rates permits occasional changes in exchange rates, some persons call it a system of *managed flexibility*. There are, however, several difficult problems in managing the value of a currency. One problem is that of deciding when to change the value of a currency. When a deficit first appears in the balance of payments, the monetary authorities will probably not be able to determine whether it will be temporary or persistent. Because the authorities are generally reluctant to devalue, they postpone any such action as long as possible. Changes in the pegged rates thus tend to occur infrequently and only after a major and prolonged period of disequilibrium ending in a payments crisis.

Even assuming no reluctance to adjust exchange rates, the problem of establishing acceptable criteria for devaluation is a difficult one [Scammell, 31, pp. 101–103]. Countries are apt to disagree over the need to devalue or over the necessary extent of devaluation, so that rate changes can easily lead to competitive devaluations. The difficulties of determining a single criterion for devaluation suggest the need for judging each case on its merits, as the IMF in effect does by permitting such a move only in situations of "fundamental equilibrium," a term the IMF has wisely not defined. But the absence of clear-cut criteria for introducing a change in the exchange rate will, unfortunately, delay the decision and may permit the disequilibrium to worsen. To avoid a crisis and the undesirable effects of a sudden, large change in exchange rates, the corrective forces should be brought to bear soon after the disequilibrium appears. Such corrective forces appear promptly under the gold standard because the loss of reserves by the deficit country leads to a tighter monetary policy. They also appear promptly under flexible rates because the rate will change. Under pegged rates, however, the deficit country may have to devalue before equilibrating forces take effect.[7] And by delaying the devaluation, the adjustable peg system introduces a lurch in price relationships when devaluation finally occurs, a shock to the economy which gradual changes in exchange rates would avoid.[8]

Another problem arises after a country has decided to devalue its currency: how much devaluation is necessary to re-establish equilibrium in the balance of payments? For guidance, a country may employ a purchasing power parity formula on a comparative basis but this technique involves difficult problems of estimation so that it does not necessarily yield the equilibrium exchange rate [Haberler, 11, pp. 45–50]. Regardless of the method used in selecting the new exchange rate, there is small chance of choosing precisely the equilibrium rate.[9] In fact, a country has a strong incentive to devalue too much. Because the IMF agreement envisages only infrequent adjustments of the rate, a country will want to make certain of setting the rate low enough to eliminate the deficit and to insure that no additional change is needed for several years. Furthermore, the devaluation must be sufficient to convince speculators that additional changes will not come soon.[10] Moreover, if a deficit country has an unemployment problem, it may devalue more than is necessary to eliminate the payments deficit so as to obtain the stimulation to income and employment provided by an export surplus. All of these considerations suggest that when countries adjust their exchange rates under a system of pegged rates, they will tend to make greater changes than necessary or desirable.

Because countries are expected to maintain fixed exchange rates for considerable periods of time, they must hold substantial reserves of gold or convertible currencies, or be able to borrow them, in order to finance deficits that may exist for fairly long periods. The more infrequent the exchange rate changes and the less integrated the national monetary policies, the greater will be the need for reserves, other things being the same.[11] With the current rate of growth of international trade, reserves will soon become inadequate unless the major trading countries succeed in integrating their national financial policies. Manifestations of increasing cooperation in financial policies exist, however, in the informal cooperation among the leading industrial countries, the committees of the Organization for Economic Cooperation and Development (OECD) and in the meetings of the International Monetary Fund and the Bank for International Settlements.

Possible destabilizing speculation / Critics of pegged rates argue that the system can easily lead to large-scale destabilizing speculation. Because countries can change their exchange rates infrequently and then only if they are experiencing a "fundamental disequilibrium," the change will occur after a prolonged period of difficulties during which pressure on the exchange rate builds up. Some time during this period of disequilibrium, speculators will doubt the ability of the weak currency to continue at the existing exchange rate and they will move funds to strong currencies. That a country has a weak currency and may have to devalue becomes obvious to everyone. There is no question as to the direction of change in the rate if it should come. The worst that can happen to speculators under these circumstances is that the authorities in the country with the weak currency will overcome their difficulties without devaluation, in which case the speculators would at most lose the small margin paid to transfer the funds and perhaps some interest earnings if the interest rate is lower in the country with the strong currency. If the expected adjustment in the exchange rate materializes, speculators profit at the expense of the monetary authorities of the deficit country. Such movement of funds from weak to strong currencies can hardly be called speculation at all because there is no real threat that the weak currency will appreciate.[12] Furthermore, it serves no useful purpose[13] and, indeed, it could force a devaluation which would otherwise not occur, force a more drastic devaluation, or force a country to resort to exchange controls.

This possibility of destabilizing speculation is a threat to the present system. Recent arrangements to assure that a large amount of reserves would be available to countries suffering loss of speculative capital attest to the threat. But such arrangements do not help countries effect the fundamental adjustments required to eliminate a persistent disequilibrium and they may not prevent continued speculation as long as the disequilibrium persists. They can, however, buy time to make adjustments in a more orderly manner without abandonment of free trade and convertibility. And buying time may be all that is required of these arrangements because the exchange rate can be changed over longer periods.

Pegged rates are not permanently fixed, so the system may deter some long-term foreign investment that would have occurred under genuinely fixed rates. Furthermore, the possibility of large discontinuous adjustments in pegged rates may also be a threat to commercial trade between countries, particularly because countries frequently resort to exchange and trade controls in efforts to avoid devaluing their currencies. The pegging of spot exchange rates may tend to reduce the amount of trading on the forward markets, so traders may not be able to obtain forward cover when needed for protection against the risk of exchange-rate changes. Critics of flexible exchange rates cite the uncertainty of future rates as a serious deterrent to trade and capital movements. But the present system is subject to a similar though less telling criticism — because it provides for only temporary, not permanent, rigidity of exchange rates.

Thus, there are a number of defects in the current system of pegged rates. Friedman [9, p. 164] has characterized it as the worst of two worlds: it provides neither the expectation of permanently stable rates that would exist under the old gold standard nor the continuous and sensitive adjustments of a freely fluctuating rate. In his view, the experts at Bretton Woods, by trying to obtain the advantages of both the gold standard and flexible rates, succeeded primarily in obtaining the disadvantages of the two systems. If the system is as bad as Friedman suggests, a legitimate question is how it worked at all. Scammell [31, p. 105] suggested that the system has survived since 1945 not so much because of its merits as because many major countries had extensive exchange and trade controls for much of the period during which the United States liberally supplied dollars to the deficit countries. The real test of the present system will come with future disturbances because many countries have dropped their controls.

Defenders of the IMF system do, of course, rebut these criticisms. They say that it has worked satisfactorily in that it handled effectively numerous payments crises in a period of rapidly expanding trade since 1945. Although admitting the system is not perfect, they also argue that alternative systems, particularly flexible rates, have even more serious defects. But rather than present their case in detail at this point, the following subsection describes the system of flexible rates and the case for it. The case against flexible rates then follows and it contains much of the argument in support of the IMF system.

□ THE SYSTEM OF FLEXIBLE EXCHANGE RATES

How the System Works

The basic idea behind a system of fluctuating exchange rates is that of an equilibrium price: there is some exchange rate that will equate the demand for and supply of the home currency. Under ideal conditions, changes in the exchange rate will restore equilibrium by inducing shifts in exports and imports, or short-term speculative capital movements, or both.[14] Any tendency for a deficit or a surplus to appear in the balance of payments will first affect the exchange rate. On the one hand, an incipient surplus (excess demand for the home currency) will cause the exchange rate to fall.[15] On the other hand, an incipient deficit will cause the exchange rate to rise. Thus, the price (exchange rate) responds to changes in demand and supply and it will, in turn, alter both the movement of goods and services and the movement of capital.

To see how the system works ideally, consider first the effects of exchange rate adjustments on the exports and imports of the country with the depreciating currency. The country with the appreciating currency will, of course, experience the opposite effects. Depreciation will cause the export prices of the country with the incipient deficit to fall in terms of other currencies.[16] The decline in price abroad will cause the quantity of exports to rise. The price of exports will rise in terms of the domestic currency, causing a reduction in domestic consumption and an increase in the amount available for export. The rise in prices will increase profits and enable the export industries to bid resources away from other industries. The amount of foreign currency spent on the exports will rise if there is sufficient elasticity in the foreign demand for the country's exports.

The prices of goods imported by the depreciating country tend to rise in domestic currency but to fall in foreign currency. The increase in the domestic price of imported goods reduces the amount purchased from abroad and increases the amount purchased from domestic producers, assuming the existence of import-competing producers. Again the elasticities of supply and demand for imports will determine whether more or less money is spent on imports. The change in exchange rates causes the depreciating country's products to displace products of the appreciating country in the domestic markets of both and in the markets of third countries to which both export. Provided the elasticities are high, the exports of the depreciating country will rise relative to its imports, thereby correcting an incipient disequilibrium in the balance of payments.[17]

A change in the exchange rate will not immediately cause a large shift in commodity trade in accordance with the altered price relationships. The substitution of the depreciating country's products for those of the appreciating country will take time. The speed of adjustment will depend upon the extent of price changes, upon whether or not excess capacity exists, upon the mobility of resources, and upon the ease with which buyers can shift to new suppliers. Because trade tends to be sluggish in responding to the changed price relationships, the immediate depreciation of the exchange rate will have to be large in order to induce sufficient changes in exports and imports to restore equilibrium in the short run. Over a longer period, this large depreciation will cause the exports of the depreciating country to continue to rise and its imports to fall, thus tending to create a payments surplus. The subsequent tendency to a surplus will cause the currency to appreciate, thus partially reversing the initial depreciation.

There is, however, a force that minimizes this initial excessive depreciation: it is the movement of short-term speculative funds. Speculators know that the initial excessive depreciation will be partially reversed when it has had time to have a greater effect on the country's exports and imports. When speculators believe a particular fall in the price of a currency will be temporary, they will buy that currency. After the currency has depreciated more than speculators believe is necessary for long-run equilibrium, they will move funds from the excessively appreciated currency to the excessively depreciated currency to take advantage of the expected reversal in rates. In doing this, they perform the valuable function of moderating the movement in the exchange rate by financing a temporary deficit until the new exchange rate can gradually bring about the underlying adjustment in trade needed to restore the balance of payments to equilibrium.

Some proponents of flexible exchange rates advocate government intervention in the exchange markets to overcome the dangers of misguided speculation and the potential instability of reserve currencies [Meade, 21, p. 250]. An exchange equalization fund will buy gold or other currencies to prevent or reduce an appreciation of the domestic currency or it will buy the domestic currency with gold or other currencies to prevent or reduce a depreciation. Under this plan, the stabilization fund will enter the market only to reduce short-run fluctuations of the exchange rate that are not justified in the eyes of the authorities but will permit the rate to adjust to changes in long-term or fundamental forces of supply and demand. International cooperation would be necessary to insure that two countries did not try simultaneously to depreciate their currencies — one relative to the other's.

Friedman argues against intervention in the exchange market [9, p. 188]. Although recognizing that there may be times when private speculation will be destabilizing while government speculation will be stabilizing, he believes that in general government officials are not apt to be better judges of what the equilibrium exchange rate should be than speculators. Therefore, private speculators can do as well as the official stabilization fund in promoting the appropriate pace and timing of exchange rate adjustments. In fact, Friedman argues that they might do a better job because government officials are likely to be swayed by political pressures to keep a currency from depreciating when it should.

Advantages Claimed for Flexible Rates

Simplicity / The preceding description of a system of flexible exchange rates provides a background for considering the arguments in favor of flexible rates. The first of the advantages claimed for the system of flexible exchange rates is its simplicity.[18] The price — or exchange rate — moves in a free market to equate supply and demand, thus clearing the market and eliminating the problem of scarcities and surpluses of any one currency. Countries do not have to induce changes in prices and incomes to maintain or re-establish equilibrium in the balance of payments.[19] Certainly the exchange rate is the easiest to alter of the variables affecting the demand for and supply of any particular currency and it responds quickly to market forces.

Continuous adjustment / Because a free exchange rate is sensitive, a system of flexible rates provides for continuous adjustment, thus avoiding the adverse effects of prolonged periods of disequilibrium. A persistent disequilibrium permits inappropriate use of resources to continue — perhaps become exaggerated — and it leads to a sudden shock when a country eventually introduces the necessary corrective measures. When long delayed, the resulting changes will be more drastic and difficult to effect. Gradual changes in exchange rates would eliminate these sudden shocks and drastic adjustments. They would not eliminate the need for adjustments but they would permit the necessary changes to take place more slowly.

More independence in domestic policies / Several proponents of flexible exchange rates have argued that it is the only system that will, in the modern world, permit the continued existence of free trade and convertible currencies [Friedman, 9; and Sohmen, 32 and 33]. Most governments today are committed to maintaining full employment and promoting rapid economic growth and will adopt appropriate policies to achieve these goals. Because of their commitment to domestic objectives, governments may not be willing to adopt deflationary or inflationary policies to maintain or re-establish payments equilibrium at some pegged exchange rate. Therefore, governmental policies may prevent adjustments through price and income changes because the automatic coordination of monetary policy does not exist. The alternative means of adjustment are changes in exchange rates and use of direct controls. The widespread commitment to convertible currencies and greater freedom of trade suggests a desire to avoid direct controls, leaving only variations in exchange rates as an acceptable means of adjustment.

A system of infrequently altered exchange rates (pegged rates) cannot exist for long, according to this argument, without widespread use of exchange controls.[20] Although the pegged rates have existed since World War II, many industrial countries continued to maintain extensive direct controls even after recovering from the effects of the war. Strong pressure by international organizations and by the United States to have the controls removed was unsuccessful until recently. If these countries encounter renewed imbalance, they may reimpose direct controls. If countries want to maintain free trade and convertibility in the modern world, they may have to adjust exchange rates more often than they have in the years since 1945.

Although fluctuating exchange rates give countries a certain independence from balance-of-payments considerations in determining domestic policies, national authorities cannot ignore the impact of domestic policies on the balance of payments. In fact, proponents of flexible rates stress that every effort should be made to keep the rates reasonably stable. They particularly try to counter the common view that flexible rates will be unstable ones. Flexible rates will not work if underlying economic conditions are unstable and produce widely varying exchange rates — but no system will work under such conditions. But there is no a priori reason for supposing that policies to achieve domestic stability (full employment, relatively stable prices, and growth) will cause free exchange rates to be unstable ones.

Advocates of flexible rates believe that changes in the rates will not be large if countries follow appropriate policies and these advocates do not believe that the changes will discourage entry into foreign trade. Traders can reduce the uncertainty about the future rate by hedging in the forward markets. If broad forward markets do not develop spontaneously, monetary authorities can promote them [Sohmen, 32, p. 87]. The existence of a broad forward market will bring more buyers and sellers into the exchange market, thus increasing the elasticity of supply and demand in the combined spot and forward market [Sohmen, 32, Chapter 4; and Einzig, 6, Chapter IX].[21] The forward market will also facilitate speculation, which flexible rate proponents believe will be stabilizing.

A system of fixed exchange rates requires countries to harmonize closely their internal monetary policies. Such harmonization is not forthcoming, however, unless governments allow the payments situation to determine domestic policies or otherwise agree on some method of co-ordinating policies. If there is a conflict, the objectives of high level employment and economic growth generally receive priority over the objective of payments equilibrium. When the two objectives require opposite financial policies, there may be no means of adjusting to a payments disequilibrium except by resort to direct controls or by a substantial change in the exchange rates following a payments crisis.[22]

With flexible exchange rates, countries have more freedom to pursue policies independently of balance-of-payments considerations. If one country inflates while others maintain internal price stability, the primary effect is a depreciation of the inflating country's currency.[23] The depreciation counters the effect of inflation on the balance of payments and largely prevents the transmission of inflation to the stable countries. Inflation may alter the real income of the first country and thereby affect other countries but the effects do not flow through monetary channels for the most part, so that monetary policies can to an extent be independent. But the desire to avoid large fluctuations in free exchange rates will certainly limit the independence of countries in choosing their domestic policies; however, a willingness to permit exchange rates to vary by 5 per cent or perhaps 10 per cent should allow considerable leeway in policy decisions without significantly disturbing international transactions. Furthermore, individual countries need not suffer undesirable effects from inappropriate economic policies abroad or originate such undesirable effects by their own mistaken policies.

If all countries achieve their domestic objectives with appropriate policies, the resulting exchange rates should be reasonably stable. Friedman believes that the harmonization of internal monetary policies is more apt to occur under flexible than under fixed exchange rates [9, p. 200]. The main reason for his view is that flexible rates minimize the transmission of economic effects through monetary channels that otherwise might interfere with the operation of internal policies aimed at achieving full employment and satisfactory growth. Variable exchange rates, however, provide no panacea — they will not work satisfactorily if countries follow widely divergent monetary policies (but neither will pegged rates).

Increases effectiveness of monetary policy / Sohmen argues that perhaps the greatest advantage of flexible rates is to reinforce the effectiveness of monetary policy [32, pp. 83–90]. If a country is fighting inflation, it will normally raise interest rates. The increase in interest rates will tend to reduce spending but, in addition, it will cause an inflow of short-term capital seeking the high interest rate.[24] The inflow of capital will depress the spot rate for the currency which will in turn cause imports to rise and exports to fall. The increased imports will tend to push domestic prices down, or to depress income, or both. The change in the trade balance will therefore reinforce the purely domestic effects of higher interest rates and help to choke off inflationary pressures. With pegged spot rates, the increase in domestic interest rates will not directly induce the import surplus that tends to reduce domestic prices and incomes. The higher interest rate will affect the trade balance only insofar as it reduces domestic prices, or incomes, or both. If, on the contrary, a country wants to increase output, it will lower interest rates. Under flexible exchange rates, the decline in interest rates will cause an outflow of capital, a rise in the spot rate, and a rise in exports relative to imports. The favorable movement in the trade balance will reinforce the expansionary effects of lower interest rates on domestic spending. Flexible exchange rates thus enable the foreign account to operate directly to reinforce the purely domestic effects of monetary policy and to make that policy more effective [See also Mundell, 25 and 26; and Fleming, 8].

Reduces need for reserves / Another advantage of flexible exchange rates is that they eliminate the need for official foreign exchange reserves, provided individual governments do not employ stabilization funds to influence the rate. As Sohmen points out, the shortage of international liquidity is the result of pegging exchange rates and the intervention of the monetary authorities to prevent fluctuations beyond narrow limits [33, pp. 71–72]. With flexible rates speculators would supply the exchange to satisfy private liquidity needs. Individuals, traders, banks, governments, and others would, of course, continue to hold liquid assets, some of which would undoubtedly be gold or foreign exchange. But these holdings would be working reserves, i.e., for purposes other than to maintain a certain value for the currency of any country.

The Case Against Flexible Rates

There are basically two general arguments against flexible exchange rates: (1) the elasticities in international markets are too low for exchange rate variations readily to bring about equilibrating adjustments[25] and (2) flexible rates tend to be unstable, thus introducing such uncertainty as to reduce the volume of international trade and investment below optimum levels. There are several more specific objections that are also discussed at the end of this subsection.

Low elasticities / If the elasticities are too low, the exchange market is unstable so that depreciation of the weak currency will simply worsen the payments imbalance. For depreciation to prevent or eliminate a deficit, it must reduce domestic currency expenditures on imports relative to domestic currency receipts for exports.[26] If this is to occur, it is necessary that the sum of the elasticities of demand for imports at home and abroad be greater than one, assuming infinite supply elasticities and a neutral trade balance initially. Critics of flexible rates have argued that the elasticities are, in fact, too low, so that depreciation of the weak currency would worsen the deficit.

This argument was prevalent in the early years following World War II during the debate over whether countries with weak currencies should devalue. There was much support for the position that elasticities were low and that devaluation would make the weak currencies weaker. Those holding this view were called "elasticity pessimists." Their arguments actually implied that the market for foreign exchange was unstable —that a free exchange rate would be subject to drastic fluctuations in response to small disturbances. Subsequent theoretical analysis has shown that if there is an unstable intersection of the supply and demand schedules in the foreign exchange market, there will be stable intersections on either side of the unstable one [Sohmen, 32, pp. 3–11]. In addition, if the demand and supply for foreign exchange derive solely from trade in goods, instability in the foreign exchange market is possible only if at least one commodity market is unstable, an improbable situation [Morgan, 22, pp. 291–92].

Some countries might have an inelastic demand for imports in the neighborhood of current prices so that devaluation of a pegged currency would not easily eliminate a deficit. Even though a large depreciation might result in a stable intersection of supply and demand curves for foreign exchange, it would probably raise extremely difficult adjustment problems and would be unacceptable to the country involved. A country might be in this position, for instance, if its imports were predominantly food and essential raw materials, the demands for which are inelastic.

Exchange rate changes need to be large and businessmen must feel that the change will last for a long time in order to alter trade quickly in accordance with the new exchange rates. For this reason, the short-run elasticity of demand for the imports and exports of any country will probably be low, particularly for small changes in exchange rates. In such cases, critics of flexible rates would argue that equilibration requires an excessive change in exchange rates.

Although at one time there was widespread sentiment that elasticities were low, the difficulties in recovering from the war period probably caused much of this feeling. With the recovery of the devastated economies and with the improved payments position of most such countries, there has been less talk about low elasticities. On the contrary, both the current opinion that international markets are more highly competitive than before and the recent alterations of pegged exchange rates imply that elasticities are high. Thus, the arguments of the elasticity pessimists no longer appear persuasive. With high elasticities, relatively small changes in exchange rates are effective in bringing about necessary adjustments. If elasticities are low, internal price changes induced by changes in the trade balance will not correct payments disequilibria under pegged rates. Unless the income effects are great enough to restore equilibrium without price changes, an appreciation of the currency is the appropriate remedy if the elasticities are low.

Unstable rates reduce foreign trade and investment / The second argument against flexible rates has several aspects and is more difficult to assess. The central part of it is that flexible rates will introduce a degree of uncertainty harmful to international trade and capital flows. The uncertainty would presumably exist because the flexible rates were unstable or because they might become unstable. The points at issue are the probable extent and causes of rate fluctuations and the effect of the fluctuations on trade, investment, and short-term capital flows.

One aspect of the argument is that exchange rate variations under a system of flexible rates will greatly curtail long-term foreign investment because either borrowers or lenders will refuse to conclude long-term contracts. The lender might protect himself by insisting upon repayment and servicing in his own currency but this would merely shift to the borrower the risk of unanticipated gains or losses entailed by exchange rate changes. A shift from pegged to flexible rates will therefore reduce long-term foreign investment because it will increase the risks.

Proponents of flexible rates have several counter-arguments. In the first place, pegged rates assure borrowers and lenders of only temporary rigidity, not long-run stability of exchange rates. With the possibility of periodic adjustments of rates under this system, conversion risks continue to exist over the long run. For long-term investments the risk may not be much different under one system than under the other [Caves, 4, p. 122; Scammell, 31, pp. 95–96; and Sohmen, 33, pp. 64–65]. Moreover, as Scammell suggests, borrowers and lenders may be more concerned with expected price levels in both of their countries than in expected changes of exchange rates [31, p. 96]. He suggests that the true basis for international investment is the expectation of stable domestic currencies. A third argument is that the risk of exchange controls is greater under a system of pegged rates and that this threat could deter long-term investment as much as variations or potential variations of flexible rates [Meade, 20, p. 17]. Finally, Caves points out that the alternative to changes in exchange rates is domestic adjustment of prices, or incomes, or both as a response to disturbances [4, p. 122]. Such adjustments create what he calls "solvency risk," that is, unexpected increases or decreases in quasi-rents that will affect the profitability of a particular investment and its rank on the list of profitable uses of funds. But Caves admits that investors may attach greater importance to conversion risks than to solvency risks, although there is no *a priori* reason for them to do this.

In a similar vein, critics argue that flexible rates restrict commodity trade because buyers and sellers are reluctant to make commitments when the rates fluctuate. The possibility of rate changes creates a risk of lower profits because of a change in the price traders pay or receive for foreign currency. Although they could theoretically hedge such risks in the forward exchange market, this action involves costs and may not be possible if forward markets are thin. The cost of hedging, assuming it is possible, or the added uncertainty concerning the profitability of foreign transactions will discourage foreign trade and investment and thus keep them below optimum levels.

The advocates of flexible rates object strongly to the assumption that flexible rates will be unstable. If flexible rates are unstable, it is because of major disturbances in domestic economies that require large changes in adjustment variables. If the exchange rates do not change, countries will have to induce substantial price and income changes or resort to trade and exchange controls to cope with payments disequilibria. The existence of unstable economies in some countries will discourage foreign trade and investment under either pegged or flexible exchange rates. If the disturbances are such as to cause only moderate changes in free exchange rates, the disturbance to foreign trade and investment might be smaller than that under a pegged rate where the deficit country is apt to impose controls rather than to devalue. Haberler, for instance, argues that minor fluctuations in exchange rates are less disturbing to international trade than the imposition of controls that may wholly or partially close certain markets [12, p. 26].

Furthermore, participation in any market involves some risk; domestic prices as well as exchange rates may fluctuate and give rise to unexpected gains or losses. If exchange rate changes are just as apt to yield windfall gains as losses, a free rate will not affect the expected profit of a trader from a foreign transaction. If, however, the possibility of exchange rate changes increases the variance of the probability distribution of expected profits, the greater uncertainty will undoubtedly deter some traders from foreign transactions. A broad forward market would, of course, permit hedging to reduce uncertainty. An increase in uncertainty would, nevertheless, tend to reduce international trade.

Speculation will be destabilizing / Opponents of flexible rates argue that speculation will be destabilizing and will therefore contribute to rate fluctuations. They point to Nurkse's *International Currency Experience* for empirical evidence in support of their position [27, pp. 117–122]. According to their argument, speculators will interpret a rise in the exchange rate (depreciation of a currency) as a sign that the rate will rise even more in the future. They will therefore sell the depreciating currency, causing even greater depreciation. Such action will depress the price of the first currency more than is justified by the "real" conditions. Some speculators will finally realize that a currency is excessively depreciated and they will start buying it, causing its price to rise. This will be the signal for all other speculators to do the same so that the price of the currency will soon rise above its long-run equilibrium level. If speculators are motivated as suggested, their actions will cause flexible rates to be unstable.

In rebuttal, advocates of flexible rates say that Nurkse's data do not prove anything because speculators were simply attacking overvalued currencies [Friedman, 9, p. 176]. Their action could just as well be called stabilizing as destabilizing because it tended to shift rates closer to their equilibrium levels. When speculation tends to move an exchange rate closer to the equilibrium rate, it is stabilizing; only when it moves the rate away from the equilibrium level is it destabilizing. Proponents of flexible rates go on to argue that speculation is more apt to be stabilizing under flexible rates than under fixed rates. As explained previously, when a pegged rate is clearly wrong, everyone will expect it to change in one direction only. Under flexible rates, by contrast, speculators will not be unanimous in their expectations concerning the future equilibrium exchange rate. At any given time, some will think that a particular currency will appreciate in the future while others will think that it will depreciate. Whenever uncertainty exists concerning the future rate, there will be some risk in shifting funds from, say, a depreciating currency to an appreciating one. The risk is that the appreciating currency may fall in price because it has over-appreciated. Speculators who believe that the currency has over-appreciated will move funds back to the weak currency. As long as there is some doubt about the future equilibrium exchange rate, speculation will not be a one-way street as it is under pegged rates.

Certain conditions are necessary, however, for speculation to be stabilizing under flexible rates and these conditions will not exist in all situations. Speculators must be well informed; if they are uninformed or misinformed about market conditions and act at the wrong time, they will accentuate fluctuations in rates and could cause a breakdown of the payments system. Furthermore, financial authorities in the deficit country must demonstrate their willingness to adopt appropriate policies to help restore equilibrium. If depreciation results from more rapid inflation in one country than in others and if the financial policies of that country are such as to suggest a continuation of this condition, then speculators and others will naturally move funds out of that country's currency.[27]

Friedman has argued that speculators in search of profits will develop an acute understanding of the exchange market and the basic forces underlying it. Therefore, they will quickly recognize when a currency is excessively depreciated or appreciated and will conduct transactions that tend to push the rate toward the equilibrium level, thus reducing fluctuations around that level. In support, he argues that speculators would probably have lost money on the whole if their actions had been destabilizing [9, p. 175]. If they had increased the rate fluctuations, they would have done so by buying when the price of exchange was high and selling when it was low, thus losing money. That speculators continue to speculate implies that they gain and that speculation is therefore stabilizing rather than destabilizing.

Baumol [2], among others, has challenged the Friedman thesis that profitable speculation is normally stabilizing. He has developed a model in which speculators buy after prices start moving up and sell when they start down. He assumed that the price of foreign currency will follow a cyclical path in the absence of speculation but that speculators, through buying on the upswing and selling on the downswing, speed up price movements, increase the frequency of fluctuations, and under certain circumstances increase the amplitude. With Baumol's assumptions, speculation is profitable but destabilizing, provided the cycle is not too short.

Telser [34] in turn criticized Baumol's model and concluded that profitable speculation will normally be stabilizing, as Friedman suggested. He argued that it is just as reasonable to assume that speculators make maximum purchases just before the price upturn and make maximum sales just before the price downturn as it is to adopt Baumol's assumptions. Speculators would thereby make profits and stabilize the price by reducing the amplitude of fluctuations.

The major point of dispute between Baumol and Telser is the proper definition of speculators and nonspeculators. If the buyers and sellers are both speculators, there is, of course, no net gain or loss for speculators as a body (the gains of some are the losses of others) and both arguments break down. Telser argues for a narrow definition of nonspeculators, whereby their actions depend solely upon current prices. If past prices or price trends influence peoples' actions, Telser calls them speculators. Baumol believes the definition should be less rigid. He says nonspeculators would like to avoid risk by hedging but that they must consider price trends in their decisions because there are no perfect hedges. The basic question, according to Baumol, is the effect of professional speculators on the price of foreign exchange.

The debate on the theory of exchange speculation indicates, however, that profitable speculation can be either stabilizing or destabilizing and the same is true for unprofitable speculation [Kemp, 16, Ch. 18]. But the theoretical arguments do not answer the question of whether speculation will be, or has actually been, destabilizing. This is an empirical question and only empirical research can answer it.

Empirical studies have not, however, provided a satisfactory answer to the question. Tsiang [36] analyzed the 1919–1926 data for three countries and concluded that speculation was not generally destabilizing. Indeed, he thought it was stabilizing more often than not. He also examined Peru's experience with flexible rates from 1950 to 1954 and concluded that speculation did not contribute to instability of the rate [35].

Similarly, Rhomberg found that on the whole speculation tended to stabilize the Canadian exchange rate [28].

By contrast, Eastman [5] and Aliber [1] found little or no evidence to suggest that speculation had a stabilizing influence on flexible rates. Aliber studied the interwar period and he admits that it may have had unique problems that make generalizations open to doubt. He feels, however, that his study demonstrates rather clearly that large fluctuations will occur in exchange rates if the market is completely free. The contrasting conclusions arise because the empirical studies encounter difficult problems of definitions, of the proper measures of stability or instability, and therefore of the correct interpretation of the historical evidence.[28]

In a new approach, Kindleberger suggests that the monetary and fiscal policies of countries are more important than the exchange system in determining the nature of speculation [17, p. 417]. With stable monetary and fiscal policies, short-term capital movements will generally be stabilizing, as the Canadian experience suggests. With inappropriate monetary and fiscal policies, short-term capital movements will be destabilizing. Kindleberger concludes, therefore, that under one set of circumstances, speculation will be destabilizing, but under another set it will be stabilizing.

Possible inflationary effects / Another aspect of the instability argument against flexible exchange rates concerns the possibility of a feedback of depreciation upon the domestic price level of a country to produce inflation and therefore the need for further depreciation [Scammell, 31, pp. 97–98]. Suppose that, for some reason, a country has a tendency toward a payments deficit, causing the exchange rate to rise in a free market. Depreciation of the currency increases the cost of imports, thus increasing the cost-of-living and causing labor to push up wage rates. This situation might exist if a country imports a large share of its food and raw materials so that imported commodities carry great weight in the cost-of-living index. Higher wages lead to higher prices and smaller exports, causing a further depreciation of the currency. Such a spiral of depreciation, cost-inflation, deterioration of trade balance, and further depreciation is a particular threat, according to this argument, if a country has full employment. Speculators will anticipate the cumulative domestic inflation and move funds out of this currency into stronger ones. Such action will further weaken the currency, cause more rapid depreciation and domestic inflation, and thus justify the speculation itself.[29]

Lutz argues, however, that for most of the major trading countries, imports do not loom large in the cost-of-living index — domestic goods and services dominate — so that an increase of wages just sufficient to offset the higher cost of imported goods in the wage bill will never fully nullify the depreciation [19, p. 182]. In addition, there will normally be a lag between depreciation and the resulting rise in the cost-of-living, between the latter and an increase in wages, and between a wage rise and an increase in prices. During the lags, depreciation could benefit the payments situation to the full extent.

Nevertheless, depreciation could set off or contribute to an inflationary spiral such that the equilibrating effect of depreciation would be fully lost by the rise in domestic prices. The deficit would still persist and require another round of depreciation that would lead to more inflation and so forth. This possibility points up the fact that a country with full employment and a payments deficit must somehow reduce its real income (reduce absorption or consumption — see the discussion of absorption versus elasticities in Chapter VII) in order to eliminate the deficit. If no group in the country is willing to give up real income, a depreciation that increases the costs of import goods will simply cause a parallel rise in prices. This rise in prices nullifies any beneficial effect that depreciation might have had on the payments deficit. When a country has full employment, devaluation cannot reduce a deficit unless it can reduce the real income of some groups in the country.

When domestic prices, particularly wages, are inflexible downward, the argument for flexible exchanges implies a type of money illusion [Mundell, 26, p. 227]. Downward inflexibility of prices indicates that a country with a deficit is unwilling to accept the needed reduction in real income through changes in domestic prices. To argue that flexible rates will restore equilibrium is to say that the community will accept reduced real income when it results from increased prices for goods traded internationally. As Mundell suggests, the argument is really that when prices are inflexible downwards, a system of flexible exchange rates provides a more acceptable method of changing real income than changes in employment or in domestic prices.

With respect to the problem of inflation, some critics of flexible rates argue that the system imposes little if any discipline on domestic authorities to prevent excessive inflation. Flexible exchange rates would maintain equilibrium in the balance of payments so that individual countries could, if they wanted to, permit domestic inflation to continue more rapidly than abroad without worrying about the foreign balance. In other words, financial authorities would not worry about a depreciating currency because currencies were supposed to fluctuate under the system. By contrast, the loss of reserves and the common feeling of failure and humiliation at having to devalue a pegged exchange rate impose a strong discipline upon officials to prevent inflation.[30]

In rebuttal, proponents of flexible exchange rates argue that a system of fixed rates actually provides the weaker discipline. The issue is whether the loss of reserves and the possible need to devalue constitute stronger pressure to oppose inflation than the actual or threatened depreciation of a flexible rate. Under the IMF agreement, countries may devalue when faced with a fundamental disequilibrium. They may also resort to exchange controls at least for capital movements. Thus, the supporters of flexible rates argue that the pressure to contain inflation is not so strong today, under IMF pegged rates, as it was under the old gold standard when the accepted code of ethics disapproved of both controls and devaluation. Furthermore, a freely fluctuating rate is a more sensitive and a more obvious indicator of inflation than a loss of reserves. Because it is more immediate and more widely noticed, a rapid depreciation will be more apt than a loss of reserves to spur financial authorities to adopt anti-inflationary measures and to call forth the necessary public support for such action.

Need for internal mobility of resources / Still another condition influences the case for and against flexible exchange rates. Mundell [23] has suggested that if factors of production are not highly mobile *within* individual countries, much of the advantage of flexible rates is lost. The reason is that although the variable rate keeps the foreign account in balance and permits the use of monetary policy for domestic stability, the immobility of factors internally prevents domestic monetary policy from achieving full employment without inflation. For example, an increase in foreign demand for an export from one region of a particular country will cause that country's currency to appreciate but this will decrease the exports of the other regions of the country and will cause them to have recessions. If the monetary authorities increase the national money supply to prevent unemployment in the other regions, the result will be inflation in the region with an increased export demand. If the authorities prevent inflation in this region, the other regions will have unemployment. Only if factors move freely within the country will domestic monetary policy be able to perform its stabilizing function. But this problem will exist also under fixed exchange rates as long as factors are not highly mobile. The main point is that the immobility of factors deprives flexible rates of their big advantage in freeing monetary and other policies for use primarily to maintain internal stability.

Flexible rates have not worked / A final argument against flexible exchange rates is that there is no example of the system having worked satisfactorily for an extended period. Opponents of flexible rates say that they were a dismal failure between World War I and World War II and that the Canadians' apparently successful experience with them after 1950 finally ended in ignominy. As the preceding discussion has mentioned from time to time, past experiences with flexible rates are open to various interpretations. Proponents of flexible rates say that the system itself was not to blame for failures — that the cause of failure was unwise financial policies or some other unfavorable condition. The Canadian experience was interesting in that short-term capital movements appeared to be stabilizing but, quite unexpectedly, the long-term capital movements proved to be destabilizing. Long-term investors continued to buy Canadian dollars when they sold for a premium. The import surplus resulting from the long-term capital inflow was deflationary. Canada sought to eliminate the import surplus to increase domestic employment and the policies employed in this effort finally led to speculation against the Canadian dollar and the eventual adoption of a pegged rate in 1961. Defenders of flexible rates say that the problem was simply that the Canadian government adopted the wrong domestic policies. But the Canadian case demonstrates that flexible rates are no panacea — they still require governments to follow intelligent domestic policies.

☐ THE TWO SYSTEMS IN DIFFERENT KINDS OF DISEQUILIBRIA

The desirability of one exchange eystem or the other will depend upon such conditions as the nature of the disturbances to the balance of payments, the number of effective policy tools available to individual governments, and the structure of individual economies. Such an approach suggests that no one system is best for all situations. But it is worthwhile to summarize the arguments to point out those situations favoring flexible rates and those favoring pegged rates.

Price Level Out of Line

First, suppose a country under a system of fixed exchange rates has a deficit because its price level is too high (but not rising) relative to price levels abroad. The best remedy for this situation is a devaluation of the currency by an appropriate amount; a shift to flexible exchange rates would also provide the appropriate depreciation. Had the exchange rate been flexible initially, the deficit would not have arisen, because the exchange rate would have settled at the level necessary to place the domestic and foreign price levels in the correct relationship. Pegged, as well as flexible, rates would work satisfactorily provided the authorities could determine the appropriate amount of depreciation, i.e., the new equilibrium rate.

Changes in Foreign Demand

When the disturbance results from the rise or fall of foreign demand for a given country's exports, flexible exchange rates appear to offer the better means of adjusting. If there is an increase in the foreign demand, the initial impact falls entirely on the export industries under a system of fixed exchange rates. The impact spreads to other parts of the economy as the expansion of exports causes an increase in national income and perhaps some increase in prices. By contrast, a system of flexible rates restores equilibrium immediately — there is no waiting for the gradual increase of income following an expansion of exports. The appreciation of the currency provides an immediate incentive for the appropriate output adjustments throughout the economy so that initial impact is not on the export industries alone.

If there were a fall in incomes and employment abroad, the country would have a deficit under fixed exchange rates while its currency would depreciate under flexible rates. Under fixed rates, the foreign countries would have surpluses in their balance of payments and these surpluses would be a stimulant to income and would tend to offset the deflationary forces. Thus, the first country could assist the foreign countries in their efforts to increase income by permitting the deficit to continue (using its reserves) and by maintaining full employment. If the foreign governments do not try to re-establish full employment but are content to permit continuation of an underemployment equilibrium, the first country will eventually exhaust its reserves and have to act to eliminate its deficit by depreciating, by deflating, or by using direct controls.

With flexible rates, the foreign countries would not have the benefit of a trade surplus to stimulate domestic incomes. Flexible rates would thus make more difficult their task of increasing income and employment. But the flexible rates protect or insulate the first country against income fluctuations abroad, although they do not eliminate the need to reallocate resources when the exchange rate changes. They will generally block the transmission of business cycles through changes in trade balances, although capital flows induced by exchange rate changes may transmit some cyclical effects. The conclusions from this analysis are that flexible rates are (1) advantageous to a country that successfully maintains full employment because rate changes protect it from depressions (and inflations) abroad and (2) disadvantageous to countries that cannot maintain full employment because flexible rates do not permit a trade surplus that would tend to offset domestic deflationary forces.

Changes in Domestic Demand

The case for flexible exchange rates for any one country is weaker when disturbances to the balance of payments typically originate within the country rather than abroad. In this situation, the foreign balance does not contribute to the achievement of domestic objectives if the exchange rate is flexible. Suppose the country is undergoing a recession. With fixed exchange rates, imports decline because of the decline of income, giving the country a trade surplus (or a smaller deficit). If the country's prices fall relative to prices abroad, exports will increase and imports will fall even more, assuming demand elasticities are high. The favorable movement in the trade balance will stimulate the economy and will help counteract the decline of income. It will thus lighten the burden of stabilization measures adopted by the government.

Similarly, if the country is having inflationary problems, a pegged exchange rate will assist in alleviating the problem because the trade balance will tend to become unfavorable. A deficit in the trade balance will be deflationary and thereby relieve some of the inflationary pressure. The fixed exchange rates help smooth domestic business fluctuations by providing an income stimulant during the downswing of the cycle and an income depressant during the upswing. The fixed rates simply cause the income multiplier to be smaller and thus reduce income fluctuations.

Under a flexible rate system, the country undergoing a downswing in business activity will not receive the stimulant of a trade surplus because the currency will appreciate as the demand for imports declines, thus maintaining equilibrium in the foreign account. During a boom, the currency will depreciate to prevent a deficit in the foreign balance, thus preventing a leakage of income that will lessen inflationary pressures.[31] A system of flexible rates does not, therefore, produce counter-cyclical effects through the foreign balance, as does a system of fixed rates. But from a broader point of view, flexible rates may still be preferable because they prevent the transmission of the business cycle from one country to others. Although a country that cannot control its domestic cycles with reasonable success may be better off with fixed exchange rates, it gains an advantage at the expense of other countries who will suffer from the instability transmitted from the first country through changes in its trade balance. If one country is better off, its gain is at the expense of other countries.

If the source of disequilibrium in the balance of payments is excessive domestic demand, flexible exchange rates will not work well. If nothing is done to stop the demand-pull inflation, every one will expect the currency to continue to depreciate and will move funds to stronger currencies, causing the depreciation to be even more rapid. An exchange crisis of this sort will almost inevitably lead to abandonment of convertibility and resort to exchange controls. But this argument applies equally to a system of fixed exchange rates. No system can operate satisfactorily with continuous, excessive inflation in any one country. With fixed rates, the inflating country would incur larger and larger deficits with attendant loss of reserves. Speculation against the currency in anticipation of devaluation could break down the system and force implementation of controls. The only solution to this problem is to bring about a reduction in spending to eliminate the excessive inflation.

The Need for Adequate Policy Instruments

In line with the above arguments, Caves has suggested that if a country does not have adequate policy instruments for controlling internal inflation, it will have to depreciate its currency, either continuously under flexible rates or periodically under the adjustable peg [4, p. 126].

His main point was that the appropriate exchange system for an individual country would depend upon whether it had sufficient policy instruments to achieve both foreign balance and domestic objectives. With policy tools to cause the appropriate changes in relative rates of inflation, the system of fixed rates will work satisfactorily. Those who support this view believe that small changes in relative rates of inflation would be sufficient adjustment for the ordinary disturbances and that countries can, with international cooperation, bring about these small changes without having to sacrifice domestic objectives. Whether this is possible is an empirical question, the answer to which is not known. But the conditions necessary to this kind of adjustment are complicated and delicate [Caves, 4, p. 126].

☐ POSSIBLE EXPLANATIONS OF THE WIDE SUPPORT FOR FIXED RATES

The arguments for and against each of the two exchange systems are rather evenly balanced — there are good arguments for and against each system. Despite the evenness of the debate, business men, government officials, bankers, and economists have overwhelmingly supported fixed exchange rates. Most of these persons are otherwise advocates of a competitive market economy, so their general support of government price fixing in the foreign exchange market may seem somewhat surprising. Proponents of a free market economy commonly support government intervention to control price and other characteristics of a product or service when imperfections in the market are such that competition does not work well. These conditions occur in the public utilities and perhaps in other similar industries or activities. But the foreign exchange market meets none of the conditions commonly accepted as justification for government intervention.

Actually, the foreign exchange market for major currencies comes closer than virtually any other market to meeting the conditions of perfect competition [Sohmen, 33, p. 35]. There are many buyers and sellers because money represents general purchasing power and has many uses. If governments do not intervene in the market, one participant acting independently is rarely big enough to influence the price appreciably.[32] Modern communications facilities permit rapid and easy spread of market information and arrangement of transactions, even though market participants may be widely separated geographically. Consequently, foreign exchange markets tend to become broad, active, and nearly perfect when government authorities permit them to function freely; in fact, strict government control of exchange markets frequently cannot suppress some of these attributes of free exchange markets, as Friedman points out [9, pp. 162–63]. In a free market, the price of foreign exchange should respond to changes in the forces of supply and demand so as to clear the market. Like any commodity price, flexible exchange rates are rationing devices that keep demand from exceeding supply at any given time.

Why do so many people demand government price setting in a market that so closely approaches perfection? The literature on foreign exchange markets provides possible explanations. Sohmen attributes much of the popular support for fixed exchange rates to the feeling by the layman that foreign exchange markets are highly complicated and perhaps mysterious [33, pp. 34–35]. This feeling results from the fact that money is exchanged for money, that no visible commodity is involved in the majority of transactions, and that the operations consist primarily of bookkeeping entries in a number of banks. Sohmen believes that if people generally realized that exchange rates perform the same role as other prices and that exchange markets are potentially more nearly perfect than almost any other markets, they would be more likely to support a free market in foreign exchange. But Sohmen's explanation, however valid it might be in describing the attitude of laymen, does not satisfactorily explain the opposition to flexible rates by businessmen, government officials, bankers, and economists who are well acquainted with the operations of exchange markets.

Halm suggests an explanation that is perhaps more valid in describing their attitudes. His idea is that the prevailing attitude toward foreign exchange and exchange rates closely resembles the prevailing attitude toward domestic money [13, pp. 255–56]. Foreign currencies and exchange rates fulfill the same role in transactions with foreigners as domestic money does in transactions with fellow countrymen — that role being to serve as a means of payment and a unit of account. The common view is that domestic money is in some sense stable in price, as reflected in the saying that "a dollar is a dollar." Because this view is so strong, people do not question the use of domestic money as a unit of account, as a means of payment, and as the most liquid of assets — despite gradual inflation which slowly erodes the value of the currency. The fixing of an exchange rate, according to Halm, is merely carrying over this desire for price stability of money to a foreign currency — the fixed exchange rate makes for absolutely stable prices of money for both currencies. If the price levels of the two countries do not move together, a fixed exchange rate between the currencies means that their relative purchasing powers will change. But people overlook this fact in their desire "to create an international unit of account and a means of payment closely matching the qualities of domestic money" [13, p. 256].

But Halm's explanation is only slightly more satisfactory than Sohmen's. Other explanations are still more plausible for the many economically sophisticated persons who oppose flexible exchange rates. Some undoubtedly feel that fixed exchange rates (the gold standard) worked well "in the good old days, i.e., the 19th century and up to 1913, and they feel that there must be some way of re-establishing this smoothly operating system. The major trading countries have had long experience with fixed rates and only limited experience with flexible rates — generally under seriously disturbed economic conditions, so naturally many people support the familiar and oppose the unfamiliar. Caves, for instance, suggests that government officials regard flexible exchange rates as leading into the dark unknown (4, p. 129). Some persons agree with the logic of the arguments for flexible rates but believe that flexible exchange rates will lead to additional uncertainties and thus reduce businessmen's willingness to engage in international trade. Furthermore, even supporters of flexible rates believe that fixed rates are generally preferable for an area closely integrated economically, particularly if it has integrated monetary and fiscal policies.

Finally, some persons do not accept all the logical arguments for free exchange rates. Viner, for instance, believes that the analogy between the exchange market and commodity markets is invalid [37, p. 291; also see Baumol, 2, p. 270]. He argues that exchange markets have characteristics — decidedly different from commodity markets — that make them especially inviting to speculators. No commodity can approach foreign exchange in homogeneity, standardization, and durability. Storage costs are zero, and the financial carrying charge will vary from zero to the excess of the return the funds would earn in the best alternative use over what they actually earn in exchange speculation. Moreover, the real cost of foreign exchange to the issuer is virtually zero if it is a fiat currency. Therefore, there is no objective cost limitation to its output and no floor to its price in terms of other currencies or other commodities. In addition, there is no price ceiling or floor based on its direct utility as a consumers' good or as an input in production. Therefore, according to Viner, the theory of commodity markets, particularly with respect to speculation, is not applicable to exchange markets because exchange has no cost or demand limitations comparable to those for commodities.

CONCLUDING REMARKS

The logic of the case for flexible exchange rates is compelling — countries should be able to maintain equilibrium in their foreign balances with convertible currencies and free trade without continual crises. The liquidity problem would no longer exist as it now does with a system of pegged rates. The earlier criticism that elasticities were too low to permit easy adjustment through changes in exchange rates appears unjustified. The most serious doubt about the workability of flexible rates derives, of course, from the possibility that the rates will fluctuate excessively. If speculation causes greater variations in rates than are justified by the underlying economic conditions, the result will be to reduce international trade and investment below desirable levels.

The protagonists in the argument over fixed and flexible rates have not been able to agree on the effects of speculation at either the theoretical or the empirical level. At the theoretical level, the disagreement relates to the appropriate assumption with respect to how speculators will act in given circumstances. The resolution of the dispute must obviously come from empirical findings. But the empirical studies have not so far resolved the issue because of disagreement over the correct measures to show whether speculation was stabilizing or destabilizing, over the correct definitions to employ, and over interpretation of data.

A reasonable conclusion is that flexible rates will not lead to large rate fluctuations, provided monetary and fiscal policies are appropriate. But either exchange system should work satisfactorily with appropriate economic policies. The question then becomes which system will work better if countries adopt inappropriate policies or if international disequilibria result from structural changes. The question is not easy to answer; consequently, the argument over the merits of fixed and flexible exchange rates is certain to continue.

FOOTNOTES

1. Rueff [30] and Heilperin [14] argue for a return to the old gold standard but they have few supporters among economists.

2. More exactly, the IMF shall not object to a change in a country's par value provided (1) the country consults with the Fund, (2) the change is to correct a "fundamental disequilibrium," and (3) the change does not exceed ten per cent of the initial par value. For larger changes, the Fund may or may not concur, depending upon whether it believes the change is necessary to correct a fundamental disequilibrium. Concurrence consists of a majority vote with the votes weighted according to quotas.

3. Perhaps the system only seemed to function well. Little information is available to show to what extent income and employment fluctuated because of payments disequilibria. Rapid growth of the world economy made the adjustments less difficult. Furthermore, propitious gold discoveries led to a rapid growth of reserves and that, in turn, enabled countries to finance deficits for relatively long periods. Finally, capital movements were generally stabilizing and therefore helped smooth the adjustments.

4. A common view in recent discussions with respect to the United States payments problem is that financial policies to increase employment and accelerate growth might help the balance of payments in the long run. The argument is that a faster growth rate would lead to greater productivity increases, thus improving the competitive position of U.S. producers in world markets. Also, faster growth would tend to attract capital that is now being invested abroad. Although the initial effect of greater income and faster growth will be to increase imports relative to exports, the long-run effect, according to this argument, will

be to improve the balance of payments. The validity of this argument is uncertain. The analysis of this chapter holds to the traditional view that a rise of income will increase the payments deficit.

5. See the preceding chapter on "the Adjustment Process" for a more detailed description of Mundell's model.

6. Although the system itself may provide no means of adjusting, a country could adopt other policies designed to increase exports and perhaps reduce imports by making domestic producers more efficient or more export minded. Other policies might discourage capital outflows and encourage inflows. The United States has adopted a number of such policies in recent years. (See 38, pp. 35–7 for a list of these policies.)

7. If the deficit country is fighting inflation, its interest rate would presumably be relatively high and would cause a short-term capital inflow that would help finance the deficit. If, however, the deficit country has unemployment and adopts an easy money policy, relatively low interest rates might cause short-term capital to flow out, thus worsening the deficit. These considerations suggest that pegged rates are satisfactory for the first disequilibrium but not the second. (See the later section concerning different kinds of disequilibria.)

8. Gradual changes in the exchange rate will not, of course, avoid reallocation of resources. Any change in the relationship between the prices of internationally-traded goods and nontraded goods, which exchange-rate changes cause, will shift resources.

9. If the country has not exhausted its reserves, it need not precisely hit the equilibrium exchange rate. If it at least comes close, it could probably attain equilibrium by slight changes in other policies and by allowing resources to shift until achieving equilibrium.

10. The appreciation of the mark and the guilder in March 1961 illustrates this problem in the opposite situation. Both currencies were appreciated by 5 per cent, resulting in large-scale movements of speculative funds into both countries. Speculators believed erroneously that further appreciations would soon follow.

11. See the chapter on international liquidity for a detailed discussion of this problem.

12. If the country solves its payments problem without devaluing, the speculators could lose the spread between the gold points in addition to the other costs mentioned.

13. One could argue that this flow of short-term funds serves a useful purpose in forcing an increase of interest rates in the country with the weak currency. But an increase of interest rates might not be desirable if the country had unemployment. Also, only a tremendous increase in interest rates would stem the outflow of funds if investors suspect that the currency may be devalued.

14. The description of the system assumes that conditions are ideal for it to maintain equilibrium. Critics of the system may construe this section to be a presentation of the case for flexible rates. The following section summarizes the arguments for the system in most cases by comparing its operation with the system of pegged rates.

15. The exchange rate is expressed as units of domestic currency per unit of foreign currency. Therefore, a rise in the exchange rate constitutes depreciation of the currency and a fall constitutes appreciation.

16. This discussion of the effects of changes in exchange rates excludes the extremes in supply and demand elasticities for exports and imports, i.e., the elasticities are assumed to be neither zero nor infinity.

17. The operation of a system of flexible rates as described here rests upon the assumption that the exchange market is stable. Some critics of flexible rates argue that the exchange market will be unstable either because of destabilizing speculation or because of inelastic demand and supply curves in the absence of speculation. These arguments are considered later.

18. The system is simple only if it works. Critics of the system argue that it has not worked well and therefore is not simple.

19. Changes in exchange rates would, however, require some shifting of resources into or out of export and import-competing industries.

20. Just how long it can continue without changes in exchange rates or resort to controls depends upon the amount of reserves possessed by deficit countries as suggested previously.

21. Kindleberger [17, pp. 410–12] disagrees with this view. He argues that traders can hedge without forward markets by borrowing in one country and lending in another. A trader can take a long position in one currency by borrowing another currency, converting it to the first currency, and then lending the first currency. The trader has a long position in the first currency and a short position in the second. If such a trader substitutes a forward transaction for the borrowing of one currency and the lending of another, the elasticity in the forward market is merely transferred from the spot market. Kindleberger believes any gain of elasticity in the forward market will be at the expense of the spot market so that the combined markets experience no change in elasticity. He also points out that interest arbitrage is necessary for the interest rate differential to determine the spread between the spot and forward rates. But to achieve sufficient interest arbitrage will, he believes, require institutional changes in many countries that will come about very slowly.

22. As previously mentioned, a country should have as many independent policy instruments as it has policy objectives to insure attainment of all goals. Countries might be able to use monetary policy for attaining payments equilibrium and other policies for attaining domestic objectives, provided there are enough other appropriate policies.

23. The depreciation changes the relationship between prices of internationally traded goods and domestic goods in all countries and therefore it causes a reallocation of resources.

24. If the currency of the country with a high interest rate is weak, short-term capital would not flow in unless forward cover were available. A necessary condition for an inflow of such funds is the existence of sufficient speculation to make a large market in forward exchange so that interest arbitrageurs can obtain forward cover.

25. If elasticities are low, devaluation of a pegged rate would not easily restore equilibrium. The argument applies to depreciation of either flexible or pegged rates.

26. This ignores the possibility of inducing an inflow of long-term capital by the depreciation.

27. Friedman would not call such a movement destabilizing speculation,

however, because the equilibrium exchange rate will clearly have to rise under the circumstances, and the movement of funds abroad will simply speed up the rise.

28. In the case of France from 1919 to 1926, Tsiang [36] attributed the difficulties of the franc to the excessive supply of money in the country. Given the excessive money supply, he concluded that speculation was not destabilizing. Critics of flexible rates argue that speculation was destabilizing even though the cause was an unwise monetary policy. This illustrates a problem of interpretation that arises in such empirical studies.

29. The argument that depreciation will lead to inflation applies to devaluation of a pegged rate as well as to depreciation of a flexible rate.

30. The attitude of a country towards devaluation depends largely upon its tradition. Many countries, particularly industrial countries, will try to prevent or avoid devaluation; others, particularly underdeveloped countries, will not care greatly about changes in exchange rates.

31. If speculators believe that the exchange rate changes are cyclical and thus will later be reversed, they will move funds so as to moderate but not prevent a change in rates.

32. Large corporations with extensive foreign operations have large sums of cash in various financial centers. These companies could undoubtedly affect exchange rates by large purchases or sales of a particular currency. But most buyers and sellers of exchange are too small to affect rates significantly.

BIBLIOGRAPHY

[1] R. Z. Aliber, "Speculation in the Foreign Exchanges: The European Experience, 1919–1926," *Yale Economic Essays* (Spring 1962).

[2] W. J. Baumol, "Speculation, Profitability, and Stability," *REStat* (August 1957).

[3] A. I. Bloomfield, *Short-Term Capital Movements Under the Pre-1914 Gold Standard*, Princeton University, International Finance Section, Princeton Studies in International Finance, No. 11 (1963).

[4] R. E. Caves, "Flexible Exchange Rates," *AER* (May 1963).

[5] H. C. Eastman, "Aspects of Speculation in the Canadian Market for Foreign Exchanges," *CJEPS* (August 1958).

[6] P. Einzig, *A Dynamic Theory of Forward Exchange* (1961).

[7] Federal Reserve System, "A System of Fluctuating Exchange Rates: Pro and Con," *State of the Economy and Policies for Full Employment,* Hearings, Joint Economic Committee, U.S. Congress, 87th Congress, 2d Session (August 7–10, 13–17, 20, 21, and 22, 1962).

[8] J. M. Fleming, "Domestic Financial Policies under Fixed and under Floating Exchange Rates," *SP* (November 1962).

[9] M. Friedman, "The Case for Flexible Exchange Rates," *Essays in Positive Economics* (1953).

[10] F. D. Graham, *The Cause and Cure of 'Dollar Shortage,'* Princeton University, International Finance Section, Essays in International Finance, No. 10 (January 1949).

[11] G. Haberler, *A Survey of International Trade Theory*, Revised Edition, Princeton University, International Finance Section, Special Papers in International Economics, No. 1 (July 1961).

[12] _____, *Currency Convertibility*, No. 541 in the series "National Economic Problems," American Enterprise Association, Washington (1954).

[13] G. N. Halm, "Fixed or Flexible Exchange Rates," in *Factors Affecting the United States Balance of Payments*, Compilation of Studies prepared for the Subcommittee on International Exchange and Payments of the Joint Economic Committee, U.S. Congress, 87th Congress, 2d Session (1962).

[14] M. A. Heilperin, "Monetary Reform in an Atlantic Setting," *International Payments Imbalance and Need for Strengthening International Payments Arrangements*, Hearings before the Subcommittee on International Exchange and Payments, Joint Economic Committee, U.S. Congress, 87th Congress, 1st Session (1961).

[15] H. G. Johnson, "Equilibrium under Fixed Exchanges," *AER* (May 1963).

[16] M. C. Kemp, *The Pure Theory of International Trade* (1964).

[17] C. P. Kindleberger, "Flexible Exchange Rates," in *Monetary Management*, prepared for the Commission on Money and Credit (1963).

[18] F. Lutz, *The Problem of International Liquidity and the Multiple-Currency Standard*, Princeton University, International Finance Section, Essays in International Finance, No. 41 (March 1963).

[19] _____, "The Case for Flexible Exchange Rates," *Banca Nazionale del Lavoro Quarterly Review* (December 1954).

[20] J. E. Meade, "The Case for Variable Exchange Rates," *Three Banks Review* (September 1955).

[21] _____, "The Future of International Payments," in *Factors Affecting the United States Balance of Payments*, Compilation of Studies prepared for the Subcommittee on International Exchange and Payments, Joint Economic Committee, U.S. Congress, 87th Congress, 2d Session (1962).

[22] E. V. Morgan, "The Theory of Flexible Exchange Rates," *AER* (June 1955).

[23] R. A. Mundell, "A Theory of Optimum Currency Areas," *AER* (September 1961).

[24] _____, "The Appropriate Use of Monetary and Fiscal Policy for Internal and External Stability," *SP* (March 1962).

[25] _____, "Flexible Exchange Rate and Employment Policy," *CJEPS* (November 1961).

[26] _____, "The Monetary Dynamics of International Adjustment under Fixed and Flexible Exchange Rates," *QJE* (May 1960).

[27] R. Nurkse, *International Currency Experience: Lessons of the Inter-War Period* (1944).

[28] R. Rhomberg, "Canada's Foreign Exchange Market: A Quarterly Model," *SP* (April 1960).

[29] L. Robbins, *The Economist in the Twentieth Century* (1954).

[30] J. Rueff, "The West Is Risking a Credit Collapse," *Fortune* (July 1961).

[31] W. M. Scammell, *International Monetary Policy*, 2d Edition (1961).

[32] E. Sohmen, *Flexible Exchange Rates, Theory and Controversy* (1961).

[33] _____, *International Monetary Problems and the Foreign Exchanges*, Princeton University, International Finance Section, Special Papers in International Economics, No. 4 (April 1963).

[34] L. G. Telser, "A Theory of Speculation Relating Profitability and Stability," *REStat* (August 1959).

[35] S. C. Tsiang, "An Experiment with a Flexible Exchange Rate System: The Case of Peru, 1950–54," *SP* (February 1957).

[36] _____, "Fluctuating Exchange Rates in Countries with Relatively Stable Economies, Some European Experiences after World War I," *SP* (October 1959).

[37] J. Viner, "Some International Aspects of Economic Stabilization," L. D. White, Editor, *The State of the Social Sciences* (1956).

[38] U.S. Congress, Joint Economic Committee, *The United States Balance of Payments — Perspectives and Policies*, Materials prepared for the use of the Joint Economic Committee, 88th Congress, 1st Session (1963).

CHAPTER 7 / Elasticities and Absorption
in Devaluation Analysis

PREFATORY STATEMENT

When a country faces the prospect of protracted international payments deficits and when international reserves are deficient, the presumptive remedy, all things considered, is probably devaluation. Nevertheless,
presumption alone is a hazardous foundation for policy decisions. Given
the constraints of the international monetary and trading networks, in
the case of devaluation it is necessary to determine not only whether devaluation will in fact reduce the deficit but also the distinct questions of
how much devaluation is required in order to erase a deficit of given size
and of how large a deficit can devaluation of a given amount eliminate
must be deliberated. Only plausible and reliable answers to these issues
will permit the conscientious use of devaluation if, indeed, such a course
commends itself.

To formulate reasonably accurate replies to these questions is at
present no mean undertaking. It would have been an impossible task
twenty years ago. Aside from the still-difficult problems stemming from
the need to quantify a number of complex behavioral relationships, the
mechanism through which a change in the exchange rate affects the
balance on trade account was, until recently, comprehended incompletely
and possibly defectively. And even today the mechanism for establishing
the probable impact of devaluation on capital account transactions remains conjectural.

But if concern is with the probable change in the trade account
balance due to devaluation, serviceable analytical guidelines are now at
hand. Devaluation induces foreign and domestic responses in the demand
for and supply of imports and exports because relative prices are altered.
These responses may effect increases in domestic income and output and
in domestic expenditures on goods and services produced at home and
abroad. Provided that these expenditure changes do not absorb the entire increment to output, the trade balance will improve as a consequence
of devaluation. The influence of devaluation on absorption in turn de-

284

pends upon the increments to hoarding and to net outlays on foreign goods and services induced by the income adjustment. An enlightened monetary policy can be used to buttress these trade-balance effects of devaluation.

These various relationships are nevertheless all conditioned by the environment in which devaluation is implemented. A delineation of the guide lines does not supplant an analysis of the particular conditions of devaluation; it merely provides the analysis with a focus.

Devaluation is a tempting policy for countries faced with the need to eliminate balance of payments deficits. The IMF system permits — even recommends — devaluation if a country is suffering from "fundamental disequilibrium" in its international transactions. This is not to suggest that devaluation is always desirable. The possibility of destabilizing speculative capital movements must be considered. Long-term capital flows are also to some degree influenced by exchange rate adjustments. But the most strategic consideration is the impact of changes of the exchange rate on the balance of trade itself. For most countries, in terms of sheer size, the trade balance accounts preponderantly for the total international payments position; its central place in a discussion of the balance of payments consequences of devaluation is therefore firmly established.

In addition to the potential magnitude of the trade balance, there is another justification for focusing on the balance of trade: it has been long established as a theoretical proposition that increasing the domestic price of the foreign currency, i.e., devaluation, may in fact result in a deterioration of a trade account deficit rather than in an improvement. This possibility must be weighed before devaluation is undertaken. Consequently, the mechanism through which devaluation alters the balance of trade must be explored. Only when the devaluation mechanism has been determined and carefully studied can the objective conditions for effective devaluation be firmly established.[1]

For years economists have been tracing the contours of this mechanism and, until recently, the map appeared to be virtually complete. But soon after World War II, possibly because of the widespread acceptance of Keynesian macroeconomics and the rejection of both fixed and freely fluctuating exchange rate systems in their pure forms, the then accepted model of devaluation, which was thought of in terms of simple price elasticities of supply and demand, was found to be oversimplified, possibly inadequate. The likelihood that devaluation might result in changes in income levels had been largely ignored. This realization led to revision of the traditional model in an effort to enhance its realism. In the analysis of devaluation the effects of income changes were superimposed upon relative price or elasticity effects.

While this further development of the traditional mechanism was in progress, an entirely new formulation of the effects of devaluation, stemming wholly from simple Keynesian theoretical concepts, was proposed and soon further elaborated. The new variant of the devaluation model — the absorption approach — gained its champions, while the revised traditional variant retained many of its own adherents. Inevitably a vigorous and fruitful debate ensued, a debate which has resolved itself for the moment into tentative adoption of a synthesized approach to the analysis of devaluation. After a short and eventful courtship, the elasticities and absorption variants of devaluation analysis have, as it were, been wedded. The marriage of the two devaluation models, and their maturation and courtship, is the focus of this chapter.

☐ AN OVERVIEW

Analysis of the effects of devaluation upon the trade balance was undertaken traditionally in terms of a strict partial equilibrium, elasticities[2] approach in which relative commodity prices were all-important. To determine the probable effectiveness of devaluation, it was necessary first to know the price elasticities of the demand for and supply of goods entering into foreign trade. If devaluation were to have a favorable impact upon the balance of trade, the sum of the elasticities of demand for imports in the devaluing country and for its exports in the foreign market would have to be in excess of some ascertainable critical value. This critical value was given by the so-called conditions of stability in the foreign exchange market.[3] When supply elasticities were assumed to be infinite, so that any amount of the exported or imported goods would be forthcoming at a given price, the exchange market stability condition was that the sum of the two import demand elasticities must be greater than one.[4] As long as this stability condition was met, the efficacy of devaluation as a remedy to a trade deficit was positively related to the sum of the demand elasticities.

In contrast, if the supplies of imports and exports were completely inelastic, with the result that the relevant pre- and post-devaluation prices of traded goods were identical in terms of the producing country's currency, devaluation would always result in an improvement in the trade balance, even though the commodity demand curves might be extremely inelastic. In this instance a given percentage devaluation would result in an equal percentage improvement, relative to the value of exports, in the balance.[5] Intermediate, determinate results were of course possible —

wherein the various elasticities took on any reasonable value. These general results were capable of straight-forward derivation from rather complicated mathematical formulas, such as those in Metzler [50], Allen [4], Kindleberger [35, p. 658], Vanek [75, p. 71], and Kemp [33, Chap. 16] and others. The main point, however, was that even before more realistic complications were superimposed upon the traditional elasticities approach to the analysis of devaluation, a good deal of difficult-to-derive empirical information — the demand and supply elasticities of traded goods — had to be estimated before devaluation could be rationally considered.

This was not, of course, a shortcoming of the theoretical model. Nevertheless, the traditional elasticities devaluation model was deficient on theoretical grounds in several respects. In the initial stages of the discussion of the devaluation model, it was usually considered sufficient to assert that the supply elasticities of a country's exports and imports, together with the demand elasticities, when both sets of elasticities were taken in their *partial equilibrium* senses, determined the exchange stability conditions. That is, the elasticities, and hence the responses of importers and exporters to changes in relative prices, were defined as if both incomes and prices of other commodities (domestic goods) were held constant. This was a logically valid approach to an examination of the balance of trade effects of devaluation; it was also unnecessarily unrealistic. Devaluation itself is a cause of income change, contrary to the *ceteris paribus* assumption of partial equilibrium analysis. Unless the monetary-fiscal authorities take steps to hold income levels constant, it is indefensible to explore the effects of devaluation as though they were. Moreover, prices of other commodities are not in fact likely to remain unchanged after a devaluation; income and substitution effects induced by the import and export price adjustments will usually alter the *ceteris paribus* supply and demand conditions of domestic goods. These shortcomings were soon recognized, by Meade [48], Balogh and Streeten [5; 6], Polak [57], Machlup [44], and Laursen [38], for example, and the early partial equilibrium approach was then amended by including in the analysis the impact of devaluation-induced changes in income and in all prices.

One form this elaboration took, exemplified by Sohmen's approach [63; 64; 65; 66], was to redefine the relevant commodity supply and demand curves in "total" terms. That is, the price elasticities which it was necessary to know in order to assess the effectiveness of devaluation were to be computed as if all adjustments caused by devaluation had been permitted to have their ultimate influence on the price-quantity relationship for the internationally traded goods. While this line of development was an acceptable theoretical "out," it did not solve the empirical problem created by the maze of significant interdependence among the essential elements of an open economy. Indeed, it presupposed that the problem had been previously met and solved. Insofar as the stability condition formulas were designed to illuminate the practical issue of whether to devalue, a reasonably accurate specification of their variables was required. Interpreting the elasticities in the formulas in a "total" sense — as if all the relevant markets (excepting the foreign exchange market) were in general equilibrium — did not lessen the statistical difficulty of estimating these variables.

A more fruitful refinement of the traditional elasticities approach to devaluation analysis was soon presented: continue to define the price elasticities in partial equilibrium terms but make adjustments in the stability conditions themselves so as to allow for significant direct income effects and for the possible interadjustments of all prices, the latter adjustments inducing indirect income effects as well as other salient changes. This approach — called the revised traditional variant above — was first recommended by Tinbergen [73] and Brown [13] and employed empirically by Stuvel [72] and Polak [56], as well as by others to be discussed later. The reformulation of the traditional elasticities approach, incorporating as it did either income elasticities or marginal or average propensities to import and save, gave rise to even more complex stability condition formulas, such as those in Harberger [24], Laursen and Metzler [39], Bell [9, Appendix], and Alexander [1]. Nevertheless, a major advantage of this approach, in comparison with both the *ceteris paribus* and "total" elasticities formulations, was that in explicitly recognizing that devaluation has significant effects beyond merely altering the exchange rate, and hence relative export and import prices, attention is directed to the roles of income effects in the devaluation mechanism.

This was an important development. It was now shown that the conditions for effective devaluation were more stringent than had been previously supposed. With income effects, including those induced by terms-of-trade movements, incorporated in the devaluation model, the beneficial consequences of relative price movements for the payments balance tended to be counteracted. Thus, Harberger [25, p. 51] noted that when supply elasticities were infinite, the critical value of the sum of the price elasticities of demand was no longer one but something greater than one, the excess being dependent on the strength of the income effects.

In retrospect this was a disquieting deduction. The relevance of income effects in devaluation analysis could not be denied, of course, so that devaluation seemed to be a less attractive balance of payments policy than had been imagined. It was bad enough that the sum of the demand elasticities had to exceed unity for effective devaluation; now it had to exceed unity by a substantial margin. Both conclusions were difficult to accept in view of the statistical estimates, from interwar data, that the relevant demand curves were typically inelastic — so inelastic in fact that the sum of the two relevant demand elasticities would frequently fall short of unity. On almost any interpretation, these data would seem to question the advisability of devaluation as a corrective to a trade deficit.

As it turned out, however, devaluation as a cure for a payments deficit was never repudiated. For one thing, most analysts recognized that devaluation of the British pound in September 1949 had alleviated Britain's balance of payments crisis. Moreover, a number of economists, including Machlup [43], Orcutt [53], Letiche [42], and Harberger [25, pp. 507–08], argued that the statistical estimates of the demand elasticities were not only unreliable for forecasting the outcome of devaluation; they were in fact biased downward and, hence, tended to err on the low side.

In part, these judgments were based upon sophisticated statistical theory; but equally it was asserted that the estimators had measured short-run demand elasticities rather than the long-run elasticities that were meaningful in devaluation analysis. Kahn [32, pp. 97–98], following Ellis' lead [17, p. 361], made this point as well as any. It is true, Kahn noted, that short-run elasticity measurements are pertinent to a study of the stability conditions, *per se,* but for an examination of the impact of devaluation, the quantities demanded must be permitted to adjust relatively fully to post-devaluation conditions. After the adjustment the import and export demand elasticities are apt to be appreciably higher. Devaluation is therefore likely to be a useful weapon against a payments deficit even though the measured (short-run) elasticities are low.

This line of reasoning seemed plausible and was widely accepted. However, it overlooked a potentially critical feature of import and export demand curves. No one demands imports and exports for their own sakes. Rather the demand is for, say, products of the type imported. The quantity of imports demanded is the difference, at each of the several hypothetical prices, between the quantity demanded of the type of goods imported and the quantity of these products supplied domestically. That is, the geometric addition (horizontally) of the import demand curve and the domestic supply curve of this type of commodity gives the domestic demand curve of the type of goods imported, as seen in Haberler [22] and Ellsworth [18]. Thus, while the domestic demand elasticity for the type of products imported will increase over the longer period, it does not follow directly that the import demand elasticity will increase also, for the supply relationship for this type of good may change as well. Kreinen, for example [37, p. 311, fn. 3], suggested that the supply curve of the type of goods imported may shift inward with devaluation as a consequence of resource reallocation. There is also evidence to the contrary: in Gillespie's simulation study of various trade balance policies [28, pp. 99, 108], a substantial expansion of capacity in import-substitute goods, particularly capital and intermediate goods, was generated.

Moreover, care must be used in interpreting the time aspect of the supply curve as well as of the demand curves. If the relevant supply curve is construed in its short-run sense, this expansion of capacity would result in an outward shift of the supply schedule and, hence, in an inward shift of and a higher elasticity for the import demand schedule. In contrast, if, as seems more reasonable, the relevant supply curve for deriving the long-run import demand function is also a long-run one, capacity expansion would result simply in a movement along the given, relatively elastic supply function and the import demand curve is unaffected. In the long run, supply curve shifts are induced by technological change or changes in factor prices. Whether devaluation itself causes such technological and factor price changes is of course an interesting and perhaps moot point. If devaluation tends to be inflationary, however, there is at least a presumptive case that prices of inputs, both of factors and of raw materials, will increase as a result of devaluation. The long-run supply curve will then shift upward, the import demand schedule outward, and its elasticity will most likely be lower.[6] The contention that the relevant (to devaluation analysis) import demand function becomes more elastic in the long run must be carefully weighed.

Obviously, the revised traditional variant of the devaluation mechanism complicated analysis at the same time that the analysis became more realistic. The increased realism, moreover, made it much harder to supply the devaluation model with the necessary empirical content required in meaningful policy choices. The revised model itself was difficult to specify in theoretical terms and the problems of estimating the parameters of the model — of sorting out price and income effects — were aggravated. Perhaps another formulation of the devaluation mechanism would reduce these obstacles to manageable proportions.

Alexander [2] thought he had hit upon such a model — his absorption approach — by the straight-forward extension to an open economy of the definitional notions and equilibrium condition of Keynesian macroeconomics for a closed system.[7] Keynesians had asserted a definitional identity, in realized magnitudes, between the value of aggregate output[8] and the value of aggregate expenditure. Yet it was not necessarily true that the more significant production intentions of individual producers added up to the same value as the sum of the spending intentions of individual buyers. When they did not, the familiar adjustments in income and output were set in motion which, in turn, caused further adjustments in expenditure and production intentions. The equality of aggregated production and expenditure intentions was the condition of equilibrium for the economic system. So much was true for a closed economy. Yet no allowance was made for the fact that it is not necessary for all of domestic production to be sold domestically nor for all of domestic expenditure to be solely on domestically produced goods and services.

In an open economy the definitional identity and the equilibrium condition must be recast.

In an open Keynesian system, the trade balance is the difference between total domestic production, including exports, and the total of goods and services purchased domestically, including of course expenditures on imported items; a deficit exists if total domestic expenditures exceed total domestic output.[9] These total domestic expenditures, using Alexander's term, are called absorption. That is, assuming no government expenditures, as will be the case throughout this chapter, imports and a substantial fraction of domestic output are absorbed in the form of consumption and investment by the domestic economy, the remainder being goods and services exported. The key to the effectiveness of devaluation as a balance of payments policy is the direction and extent to which an alteration of the exchange rate induces changes in domestic output relative to changes in absorption. If, and only if, devaluation increases production relative to absorption, a country's trade balance will be improved. The essence of Alexander's analysis is to explain how devaluation will be likely to affect output under specified conditions and, more exhaustively, how devaluation will affect absorption, both because absorption is subject to income-induced phenomena and because devaluation can cause absorption to change independently of the level of income.

A trade account deficit, therefore, must be the result of decisions everywhere in the economy and not just, as might be incorrectly surmised from the elasticities approach, of decisions in the foreign trade sector alone. As Johnson emphasized in a highly instructive article [30], this perspective is very helpful in conceiving a strategy for a balance of payments policy. The strategy must have the consequence of increasing domestic output or reducing domestic absorption relatively. But this statement in itself is not necessarily enlightening. In fact, one normally thinks of domestic output and domestic expenditure as being directly and closely interrelated. If, say, expenditure declines, so too will production. It is critical, however, that the fall in output may follow that in expenditure after an appreciable lag. This lag can be exploited by policies designed to cause the initial reduction to fall on expenditure on domestic output — an impact decrease in expenditure as Johnson called it. Output, of course, will decline eventually and there will be multiplier effects to consider; but it can be shown that as long as the multiplier is not infinite, the multiplier repercussions will fail to overpower the impact effect of the policy [30, pp. 161–62, fn. 12]. An initial reduction in expenditure will then improve the trade balance, notwithstanding the fact that production too will contract.

Alternatively, an impact increase in production could be the aim of balance of payments policy. Multiplier effects would come into play here as well. However, they would not wipe out completely the balance of trade alteration caused by the impact expansion of output unless the relevant marginal propensity to spend exceeded unity.

The distinction in absorption analysis between domestic and foreign production and expenditure can also be utilized to develop another trade balance strategy. Measures, such as devaluation, may be used to switch domestic and foreign spending away from foreign output onto domestically produced goods.[10] The switch will result in an expansion of domestic output relative to domestic expenditure as production of exports and import-substitute products increases with no change in total domestic spending but merely an alteration in the composition of this spending. Thus, a logical development of the absorption analysis leads to a strategic choice between, or combination of, policies to promote impact changes in production and expenditure or expenditure-switching measures — a choice hinging on the degree of unemployment and of resource mobility and on the direction of price level movements.

Supplying guide lines for a strategy to improve the trade balance is only part of the problem of deciding upon policy. As noted by Machlup [44, pp. 275–76], quantitative values must also be assigned. In the case of the absorption approach, this amounts to the empirical estimation of a marginal propensity to spend on the sum of consumption and investment because devaluation will induce changes in output which in turn will cause changes in absorption. Alternatively, a marginal propensity not-to-absorb, i.e., to hoard,[11] can be estimated. Moreover, devaluation will presumably influence directly (without working through output and income) the amount of absorption engendered by a given level of productive activity. The magnitude of this direct effect upon absorption must also be estimated. To put the issue in other terms, think of the existence of a functional relationship between current output and current absorption. The empirical task is to derive the slope of this function and also find out the extent to which this function shifts as a consequence of devaluation.

Seen in this light, the absorption approach loses some of its attractions as a policy tool. The marginal propensity to spend (absorb) is equal to the sum of the marginal propensities to consume and to invest. It has been difficult enough to estimate an acceptable marginal propensity to consume; adding to this the need to derive a marginal propensity to invest greatly compounds the difficulty. Neither consumption nor, particularly, investment outlays can be considered simple functions of output. In addition, it is also necessary to estimate the extent to which devaluation will directly affect the level of absorption from a given level of production — i.e., the extent to which devaluation shifts the output-absorption relationship must be known. Finally, there is the question of the impact of a change in the exchange rate on output itself. Does devaluation lead to an expansion or contraction of output and by how much?

The reasons why these quantitative estimates are needed should be apparent. Estimates of the price elasticities are required in the traditional approach to devaluation analysis in order to ascertain whether the trade balance will be improved. So too it is necessary to quantify the change in output, the marginal propensity to absorb (spend), and the direct effect on absorption in order to determine the trade balance result of devaluation using the absorption approach. To put it in a way discussed below, the numerical values of the estimates determine whether or not the "stability condition" derived from absorption analysis is met.

Merely to state this is not, of course, to derive a quantitative estimate. Machlup, at least, thinks this is likely to be as difficult as deriving reliable price elasticities. Intuitively, he feels that propensities to absorb are less reliable than price elasticities because of the greater changeability of the former [44, p. 276]. And Machlup adds presciently (see also Johnson [30], and Tsiang [74]), ". . . from the point of view of malleability through public policy, one probably should regard the price elasticities as the tougher factors to deal with, and the spending propensities more subject to the influence of (monetary and fiscal) policy — which means that in the last analysis not given propensities but chosen policies will determine the outcome " [44, p. 276].

Alexander's original rendition of the absorption approach was further criticized by Machlup [44, p. 277] for repressing elasticity phenomena that were implicit in the model. For example, one of the revealing uses of absorption analysis is to discover the trade balance effects of devaluation in the alternative situations of unemployment and full employment of resources. The distinctive features of these situations were, in Alexander's presentation, spelled out in differing commodity supply and demand conditions and, ultimately, in terms of their elasticities. The magnitude of the direct effect of devaluation upon the level of absorption from a given income likewise depended upon elasticity assumptions. Alexander was undoubtedly aware of these intrusions of aspects of the elasticities approach into his argument but he chose, probably in order to differentiate distinctly his model from that of the pure elasticities approach, to play down elasticity effects.

In his original exposition of the absorption approach, Alexander also chose to assume that the rest of the world was a passive adjuster to devaluation and balance of trade conditions in the devaluing country and, thus, again overlooked elasticity phenomena. It is identically true that the change in one country's trade balance must be reflected in a change in the trade balance of the rest of the world in the opposite direction. Therefore, the absorption argument — that the way to improve the trade balance is through an increase in domestic hoarding — implies a decrease of equal value in hoarding abroad. How is this decrease in foreign hoarding to be imposed since, presumably, the propensity to hoard abroad should, as in the devaluing country, also be taken as given?

The ultimate effect of these criticisms was a reinterpretation of devaluation analysis so as to include elasticity effects within the rubric of the absorption approach. This was the kind of synthesis Machlup seemed to be driving at and Allen [3] provided its first rudimentary expression. Alexander himself [1] formalized it in a comprehensive model. Alexander's new model of the effects of devaluation on the trade balance used what might be called a two-stage analysis. In the first stage, the initial impact of devaluation on the trade balance depended upon the conventional, constant money income supply and demand elasticities. Since the size of this initial impact depended in part on foreign demand and supply elasticities, as well as on purely domestic elasticities, a passive adjustment abroad was no longer implicitly assumed. If the relevant elasticities were such that devaluation improved the trade balance, income in the devaluing country was increased and that of the non-devaluing country fell. The income changes in turn set in motion a variety of income effects whose outcome, as established via the absorption approach, was a tendency to reverse the initial improvement in the trade balance of the devaluing nation. The adjustment of the initial balance of trade impact by these so-called reversal factors was the second stage — the absorption stage — of Alexander's new analysis.

The varieties of income effects were comprehended in two parameters in each of the countries, a marginal propensity to hoard (not to absorb) and, since the initial income change could alter the local demand for both imports and export substitutes, a resulting marginal propensity for the trade balance to change. As Alexander put it [1, p. 31]: "How much of the initial [elasticities] effect [of devaluation on the trade balance] 'sticks' depends on the relative strength in each of the two countries of the impact of additional money income on money hoarding on the one hand, and on imports and exports on the other." The effects of these propensities in both countries were embraced by a sequential multiplier analysis so that conditions in the non-devaluing country actively contributed to the determination of the devaluing country's ultimate trade balance.

That the absorption approach remains an essential part of this synthesis is most apparent from Alexander's statement of conclusions. The vital role of hoarding is here emphasized, as it was in the earlier simple account of the absorption analysis. If either country's marginal propensity to hoard is zero, the value of the corresponding trade balance marginal propensity and the outcome of the initial elasticities computation are immaterial; devaluation will not result in an improvement in the trade balance. The stability condition continues to be that there must be some hoarding out of the increment to income. In contrast, if both trade balance marginal propensities are zero and the marginal propensities to hoard are positive, the ultimate trade balance effect of devaluation is determined completely by the supply and demand elasticities calculation. Generally, the larger are the hoarding propensities relative to the trade balance propensities the lower will be the improvement in the trade balance from devaluation, given the values of the various elasticities. The ratios of the marginal propensity to hoard to the trade balance propensity in each country determine the strength of the reversal factors. Under various conditions, the first-stage trade balance improvement may be completely reversed or reversal may be nonexistent.[12]

Clearly, the ratios of the marginal propensities are very important to the final outcome of devaluation. It is not surprising, then, that much of the discussion of the absorption formulation has been devoted to an evaluation of the likely magnitudes of the individual components of these ratios. The *a priori* reasoning has generally hinged on the familiar distinction between increases in money income with, on the one hand, a constant price level and with, on the other hand, constant real output and hence price level increases. This discussion will be summarized below so that its elements need not be presented again. The generalization reached, however tentatively, is that devaluation when resources are substantially unemployed is more apt to improve the trade balance than when resources are fully employed. With unemployment the trade balance marginal propensity is likely to be smaller and the marginal propensity to hoard larger than under full employment conditions; the tendency for the initial trade balance improvement caused by devaluation to be nullified is weaker when the economy is depressed.

It is equally essential to point out that the elasticity approach, which the original presentation of the absorption model strongly suggested should be scrapped, is once again an integral part of devaluation analysis. The first-stage improvement in the trade balance, which is reversed by the absorption factors mentioned above, is due to the operation of changes in the exchange rate upon the supply and demand curves. Moreover, as Tsiang has noted [74, pp. 927–28, 934–35], the assumption of constant costs, as in the absorption approach, limits realistic discussion of devaluation. Once income-induced changes in relative prices are superimposed upon the devaluation model synthesized by Alexander, the reversal factors themselves are partially dependent upon the relevant elasticities. In a world with widespread increasing cost conditions, changes in income will have comparatively systematic effects upon relative prices. Tsiang has proposed a devaluation model which incorporates this refinement.

In addition, Tsiang has emphasized the rather "special" character of the devaluation models by exposing some of the relatively neglected implicit assumptions concerning management of monetary conditions. Whether the money supply is completely inelastic, so that the interest rate adjusts freely as devaluation alters economic conditions, or whether it is completely elastic, so that the interest rate is constant, is of material importance. With an implicit assumption that the money supply is completely flexible with respect to the interest rate or, alternatively, that the demand for money is perfectly elastic with respect to the interest rate (the Keynesian liquidity trap), there need be no concern with the effects of non-existent interest rate changes. The consequences of this special assumption on the mechanism of devaluation had previously been glimpsed by others, including Harberger [24], and Johnson [30]. Tsiang, however, showed conclusively [74, pp. 924–34] that this assumption predisposes a devaluation model toward exchange instability: with the interest rate constant, devaluation is more likely to result in a deterioration of the trade balance than when the interest rate is variable. When the interest rate adjusts during the adaptation of the economy to a revision of the exchange rate, interest-induced phenomena will enter the model. Tsiang's conclusion was that interest rate flexibility will yield a higher marginal propensity to hoard. Indeed, even though the marginal propensity to hoard may be negative when interest-induced effects are omitted, inclusion of these effects will lead ultimately to a positive marginal propensity to hoard provided that the velocity of circulation of money has some practical, finite limit. With a variable interest rate and a money velocity ceiling, devaluation will improve the trade balance irrespective of the purely income-induced marginal propensity to hoard.[13] Even though full employment exists, as both Tsiang [74, pp. 931–32] and Alexander [2, pp. 275–78] suggested, the balance of trade can be improved by devaluation if the proper monetary policy is followed.

The discerning reader will have noticed that this development of a devaluation model, synthesizing as it does the elasticities and absorption approaches, has led to a more complicated and refined analytical structure. The reactions of both countries in the model jointly determine the trade balance effects of devaluation in one of them. The reactions are in turn dependent upon four import demand and export supply elasticities, behind which lie eight purely domestic supply and demand elasticities. A further influence on the reactions of the two countries stems from the absorption effects embodied in the ratios of the trade balance marginal propensities to the marginal propensities to hoard. These latter influences in their turn are conditioned by the state of employment, price level development, and the type of monetary policy being pursued. Under plausible conditions the impact in the devaluation model of any one of these aspects of the analytical structure can completely negate the balance of trade effects of the others combined; alternatively, the individual elements can operate within the model so as to strengthen the trade balance effects attributable to each; or more likely some intermediate combination of offsets and reinforcements are appropriate. The complexity of a decision to devalue is apparent. These various influences must be sorted and numerical estimates of their strengths must be attempted. Another level of complication is added by virtue of the need to consider the "other country" of most theoretical devaluation models as being the rest of the world. Only after consideration of these factors can the policy maker determine by what percentage the exchange must be devalued to achieve a given improvement in the trade balance or, for that matter, whether devaluation is an appropriate policy.

☐ ELEMENTS OF THE ELASTICITIES–ABSORPTION SYNTHESIS

The foregoing summary statement of the synthesis of the elasticities and absorption approaches into a sophisticated devaluation model suggests a filling in of detail by discussing first the role that constant-income price elasticities of demand and supply for exports and imports play in the model. This role is given by the familiar presentation of the balance of trade effects of devaluation in a pure elasticities framework. It would be repetitious to elaborate this role completely; neither can it be wholly neglected. For a full comprehension of the synthesized devaluation model, and for an appreciation of its limitations, the elasticity conditions under which devaluation will improve the trade balance — this time denominated in terms of the domestic currency — must be established. The effects of devaluation in the elasticities framework upon the level of real income in the devaluing country must also be determined. Moreover, a distinction between real and monetary changes in income is required. An assumption of the absorption stage of the synthesis is that the initial impact of devaluation gives both an improvement in the trade balance and an initial expansion in real income. The increase in income then generates the types of absorption effects sketched above. There may be situations, however, in which devaluation does not result in a higher level of real income. The likelihood of this condition must be explored. What happens to the terms of trade is a key issue. The absorption analysis presumes that devaluation in the elasticities framework leads to a deterioration of the terms of trade in the devaluing country. Deterioration in its turn tends to change in certain ways the value of the trade balance and hoarding marginal propensities. But the assumption of terms of trade deterioration after devaluation may be a special assumption that is not universally borne out. [See Chapter 3.] This possibility must be considered. Thus, in order to form an opinion of the role of elasticities in the synthesized devaluation model, we must know how the trade balance is affected initially, what the terms of trade are apt to do subsequent to devaluation, and whether the elasticity conditions lead to an improvement in the level of real income. Not that the probable numerical values of the various elasticities are brought into the picture; rather, focus is on the elasticity conditions from which devaluation results in an improvement in the trade balance, an increase in real income, and a turning of the terms of trade against the devaluing country.

Second, a detailed explanation of the role of absorption effects in the synthesized devaluation model is given. Absorption effects account for the reversal factors which dampen the original trade balance impact of devaluation during the elasticities stage of the analysis. This dampening feature is approached in more than one way in the literature. Here the alternatives are presented in rather short compass. A firm grasp of the simple absorption approach itself is, however, requisite to a discussion of the reversal features of the synthesized model. The essentials of the pure absorption approach may therefore be considered a prelude. To lay bare these essentials the discussion will employ the conventional assumptions that devaluation in the elasticities framework does improve (money and probably real) income and causes a deterioration of the terms of trade, even though the preceding section will have shown that this is not always so. It is not necessary here to prejudge the trade balance outcome of the pure elasticities approach, for in a discussion of the simple absorption analysis the elasticities of supply and demand barely enter. Indeed, one of the consequences of the exposition of the simple absorption model is to establish when devaluation causes trade balance deterioration and when it causes trade balance improvement, while the price elasticities are all but ignored.

It should be apparent that a substantial part of the ultimate balance of trade effects of devaluation turns upon the actual values of the absorption variables — the hoarding (or absorption) and trade balance marginal propensities. A discussion of relative quantitative magnitudes of these variables must occupy a visible place in a treatment of devaluation analysis. No one has yet attempted empirical estimates of these within the context of an absorption model, so no numerical estimates can be given. Comments must be limited, rather, to deductions about the relative sizes of the propensities. Since the development of devaluation analysis until now has pivoted on the central question of exchange market stability, the deductive generalizations about the marginal propensity to hoard have been whether it is positive, negative, or zero — or, to take its converse, whether the marginal propensity to absorb is greater than, less than, or equal to unity. While much less thought has been given to the marginal propensity for the trade balance to deteriorate from income-induced phenomena, its value too has been discussed primarily in an exchange market stability context. But all too frequently, the less useful generalization that this or that condition causes these marginal propensities to be larger or smaller is as far as the story can be carried. The derivation of these generalizations is nevertheless important. It is in the specification of the effects of various conditions, such as the level of employment, changes in the income distribution, monetary conditions, and the like, upon the absorption variables that much of the most provocative theoretical work has been done. This work cannot be slighted.

The Role of Elasticities

In an elasticities framework the initial impact of devaluation tends to alter relative prices of imports, exports, and purely domestic goods. Assume for the moment that all commodities are produced under conditions of constant cost, i.e., perfectly elastic supplies. The effect of, say, a ten per cent increase in the domestic price of the foreign currency is to raise ultimately by ten per cent the domestic price of imports while leaving the domestic prices of exports and domestic goods unchanged. In the foreign country, where the relevant price of commodities is the one denominated in that country's currency, devaluation causes the price of imports (exports of the devaluing country) to be lowered by ten per cent. A change in the assumption regarding supply conditions can, of course, offset this. If all supply curves of goods are completely inelastic, devaluation produces no change at all in the domestic price of the imports of the devaluing country and its export price rises by the full percentage of the devaluation; the price (in the foreign currency) of imports abroad is not changed. Domestic prices are unaffected. More generally, for supply conditions in between perfect elasticity and inelasticity, the domestic price of imports in the devaluing country ultimately rises by less than ten per cent and the foreign price of the devaluing country's exports is ultimately reduced by less than ten per cent. This, the more general case, is worth exploring further in order to determine the possible "normal" effects of relative price changes — of elasticities — upon the trade balance and the terms of trade.

Let us refer to Figure 7-1 with given (solid lines) supply and demand curves for imports and exports of the devaluing country. Here the prices are designated in the domestic currency of the devaluing country. The price axes in Figure 7-1 could with equal facility be in terms of the foreign currency. However, the synthesized devaluation model is standardized in terms of the currency of the devaluing country, so it is convenient to derive the effects of relative price changes in terms of the domestic currency.

299

Assume initially that the prices of imports and exports in the devaluing country are, respectively, P_{m_1} and P_{x_1} and that at these prices an amount Q_{m_1} is imported and Q_{x_1} is exported. Assume further, for simplification, that trade is initially balanced so that $P_{m_1}Q_{m_1} = P_{x_1}Q_{x_1}$.[14] The initial (net barter) terms of trade are P_{x_1}/P_{m_1}. Now assume that the country devalues its currency by ten per cent, by decreeing that the domestic price of the foreign currency is now ten per cent higher than previously. The effect of devaluation is shown by the dashed supply and demand curves in Figure 7-1. Since in the diagram the prices are denominated in the currency of the devaluing country, for any given quantity of imports supplied, the foreign producers are able to realize a ten per cent higher price in terms of the devalued currency; the supply curve of imports shifts upward by ten per cent. For any given quantity of exports demanded, foreign consumers must pay ten per cent more in terms of the devalued currency; the curve of foreign demand for exports of the devaluing country shifts upward by ten per cent. It is to be cautioned that these shifts are due solely to a change in the exchange rate and not to any alteration in the underlying real conditions of supply and demand.

What happens to the trade balance after the market adjusts to the devaluation? Clearly the domestic price of exports increases to P_{x_2}. Since this represents less than a ten per cent price increase at the pre-devaluation quantity (Q_{x_1}), the price of exports in the foreign currency will have fallen and, consequently, the quantity of exports will have risen to Q_{x_2}. Unambiguously, $P_{x_2}Q_{x_2} > P_{x_1}Q_{x_1}$; the value of exports in the domestic currency rises. This always happens as long as the demand for exports has some elasticity.

But the trade balance is the difference between the value of exports and the value of imports. What happens to the post-devaluation value of imports? As long as the supply of imports has some elasticity, the price of imports increases. As long as the demand for imports is not perfectly inelastic, the quantity of imports purchased falls. Ordinarily $P_{m_2} > P_{m_1}$ and $Q_{m_2} < Q_{m_1}$. Has the value of imports therefore fallen? Is $P_{m_2}Q_{m_2} < P_{m_1}Q_{m_1}$ so that the trade balance definitely improves? This may or may not be the case. As the import market of Figure 7-1 is drawn, import demand is highly inelastic[15] and $P_{m_2}Q_{m_2} > P_{m_1}Q_{m_1}$. The value of imports has risen as a consequence of devaluation. Thus, it is possible that the trade balance may have deteriorated. If pre-devaluation balance is assumed, this is so if $P_{x_2}Q_{x_2} - P_{m_2}Q_{m_2} < 0$. The smaller is $P_{x_2}Q_{x_2}$ and the larger is $P_{m_2}Q_{m_2}$ the more likely is devaluation to give rise to trade balance deterioration. Conversely, the larger is $P_{x_2}Q_{x_2}$ and the smaller is $P_{m_2}Q_{m_2}$ the more likely is devaluation to bring about an improvement in the balance of trade. A visual adjustment of the components of Figure 7-1 will show when this latter set of conditions is more probable.

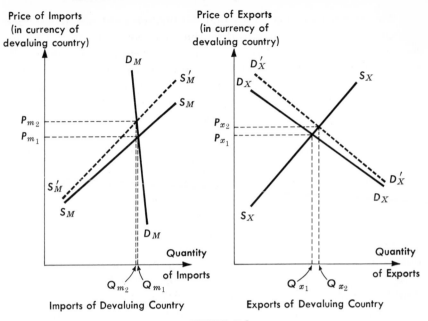

■ FIGURE 7-1

For any given positively sloped supply curves for imports and exports, trade balance improvement is more likely the higher the elasticities of demand for imports and exports. This condition insures that $P_{x_2}Q_{x_2}$ is large and that $P_{m_2}Q_{m_2} - P_{m_1}Q_{m_1}$ tends to be negative. Indeed, if the demand for exports is completely inelastic, a demand for imports in excess of unity permits devaluation to improve the trade balance for then, although $P_{x_2}Q_{x_2} = P_{x_1}Q_{x_1}$, $P_{m_2}Q_{m_2} < P_{m_1}Q_{m_1}$. At the other extreme, when the demand for imports is perfectly inelastic, $P_{m_2}Q_{m_2} > P_{m_1}Q_{m_1}$. Specifically, the post-devaluation value of imports is precisely ten per cent larger than their pre-devaluation value because $P_{m_2} = 1.1P_{m_1}$ while $Q_{m_2} = Q_{m_1}$. If now the elasticity of demand for exports is greater than unity, $P_{x_2}Q_{x_2} > P_{x_1}Q_{x_1}$ by more than ten per cent. Devaluation must have increased the value of exports relative to the increase in import value and the trade balance improves from an initially balanced position.

It can be inferred from this discussion that the necessary condition for trade balance improvement is that the sum of the elasticities of demand for exports and for imports exceeds unity, all elasticities being defined as non-negative. This statement is based on the supposition that both supply curves are fairly elastic. As the supply curves decrease in elasticity, the demand elasticity condition for devaluation to improve the trade balance becomes less stringent. The sum of the demand elasticities may be substantially less than one where the supplies are highly inelastic and devaluation still brings about trade balance improvement.

The above discussion shows that devaluation need not always raise the value of exports relative to the value of imports and, thus, that the conventional assumption of trade balance improvement is not universally valid. Can a second conventional assumption of devaluation models, viz., that devaluation causes a deterioration in the (net barter) terms of trade be verified? In terms of Figure 7-1, the conditions under which devaluation makes $P_{x_2}/P_{m_2} < P_{x_1}/P_{m_1}$ must be shown. Since, in Figure 7-1, P_{m_2} rises relative to P_{x_2}, a case of terms of trade deterioration is depicted. Where the trade balance reacts unfavorably to devaluation this must always be the case, as Haberler has proved [21, p. 154]. Regardless of these possibilities, however, it is convenient to accept the conventional assumptions of the synthesized devaluation model. It is useful to show the terms of trade outcome under elasticities giving rise to improvement in the trade balance. Haberler [21] provides a simple demonstration.

Figure 7-2 is drawn so that both demand curves are elastic. Devaluation, shifting the curves as depicted, improves the trade balance — $P_{x_2}Q_{x_2} > P_{x_1}Q_{x_1}$, and $P_{m_2}Q_{m_2} < P_{m_1}Q_{m_1}$. But, to take an extreme instance, the supply of exports is perfectly elastic while the import supply curve is positively sloped. Devaluation then results in no change in the price of exports; the price of imports rises; $P_{x_2}/P_{m_2} < P_{x_1}/P_{m_1}$; and the terms of trade decline. The same would be true if the supply of imports were perfectly elastic as long as the supply of exports were not completely inelastic. P_{m_2} would rise by ten per cent over P_{m_1}; P_{x_2} would rise by less than ten per cent over P_{x_1}; the terms of trade would deteriorate. The

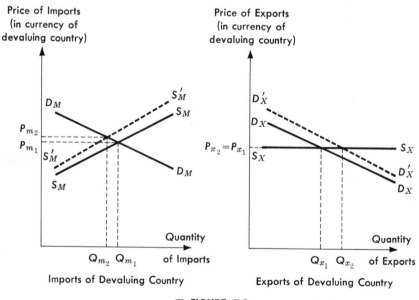

Imports of Devaluing Country · Exports of Devaluing Country

■ FIGURE 7-2

conventional devaluation assumption of terms of trade deterioration seems to have some substance.

Now look at Figure 7-3. Here are drawn positively sloped supply curves, a relatively elastic export demand function, and, importantly, a perfectly elastic demand for imports. In this situation, devaluation shifts the import supply and export demand curves as before. The price of exports rises; the price of imports remains unchanged; $P_{x_2}/P_{m_2} > P_{x_1}/P_{m_1}$; the terms of trade improve! Yet it is clear that the trade balance has also improved, for $P_{x_2}Q_{x_2} > P_{x_1}Q_{x_1}$ and $P_{m_2}Q_{m_2} < P_{m_1}Q_{m_1}$. The terms of trade would rise also if the export demand elasticity were infinite and the import demand elasticity greater than zero.

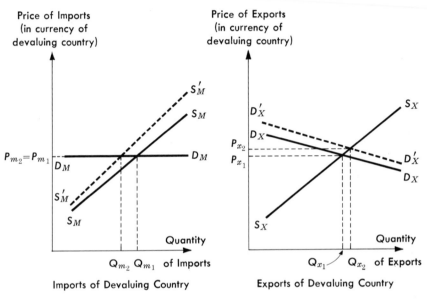

■ FIGURE 7-3

Thus, it is not certain that devaluation, even when it improves the trade balance, causes the terms of trade to turn against the devaluing country. Whether this is the case evidently depends upon the relative sizes of the two demand elasticities and the two supply elasticities. Meade [48, pp. 235–47], for one, proves that the sufficient condition for deterioration in the terms of trade is that the product of multiplying together the supply elasticities is greater than the product of the demand elasticities. This condition is, of course, not entirely unrelated to the stability condition in the elasticities framework. But as long as the stability condition is more than fulfilled, so that devaluation is an effective remedy to a deficit on trade account, *a priori* the terms of trade may rise or they may fall or they may even remain unaltered.

Which result is more likely depends upon actual supply and demand elasticities for international goods. The usual presumption is that supply elasticities are apt to be larger than demand elasticities. This is not based on a belief that demand elasticities are absolutely low, since devaluation is usually assumed to be able to remove a trade deficit. Rather, it is thought that a given economy tends to "specialize in production and exports and generalize in consumption and imports." The demand elasticity for a country's exports is presumed to be relatively low and the elasticity of supply of its imports relatively high. If in turn some unemployment is assumed, the country's supply of exports would also be highly elastic. Terms of trade deterioration is, then, the likely outcome of devaluation.

However, one should not conclude, as Smith seems to [62, pp. 822–23], that in a world of fully employed economies, where supply curves are supposed to be highly inelastic, the terms of trade improve with devaluation. The error of this position is that it ignores the fact that devaluation "at home" must mean appreciation of the exchange rate abroad. If a full employment policy is being pursued in both countries, the supply of exports by the devaluing country may be on the low side but the supply elasticity of imports to the devaluing country is apt to be high. Kleiner, who is responsible for this point, concludes [36, p. 944]:

> It is unlikely, therefore that the supply elasticities will be so low as to move the terms of trade in favor of the depreciating country, given relatively low demand elasticities. Under full-employment conditions it is the supply elasticity of the depreciating country's imports that is likely to be high; under conditions of unemployment of resources, it is the supply elasticity of the depreciating country's exports that is likely to be high.

Still the demand elasticities must be considered in conjunction with the supply elasticities. While the resulting change in the terms of trade should not really be prejudged for any given devaluation, it is assumed, in what follows, that deterioration takes place.

An improvement in the trade balance is tantamount to an expansion in money income and real output in the devaluing country. In Keynesian terms, $Y = C + I + (X - M)$, where Y is income, C is consumption, X is exports, M is imports and, hence, $(X - M)$ is the trade balance. Since an improvement in the trade balance is assumed, X must expand relative to M and, when induced effects are added, multiplier theory asserts that money income rises by a larger amount. Alternatively, if the economy is less than fully employed, so that resources being drawn into expanding production centers need not be shifted from employment elsewhere, expansion of the quantum of exports and contraction of the quantum of imports, with a probable growth in import-substitution production, results in a greater domestic output. As Machlup emphasizes [44; 45], domestic output is also likely to expand under full employment conditions. If prior to devaluation the domestic currency was overvalued, as may be reasonably assumed, with the result that resources were not being allocated optimally, devaluation causes a reallocation of the fully employed resources into more efficient lines of activity and, consequently, real output expands.[16] This implies that productive factors are relatively mobile and that frictional unemployment is not noticeably increased. Thus, if devaluation causes trade balance improvement, it also generates expansion of money income and real output.

It cannot be inferred from this that real income, upon which it is assumed the several absorption variables are based,[17] increases as well. Normally, real output and real income can be considered as being identical but this is not the case in an open economy, as Machlup [45, pp. 440–42] and Jones [31] note. Just as devaluation affects the foreign prices of exports and imports it also affects the wealth positions of people holding assets abroad or owing debts payable to foreigners. If the underlying contractual obligations are denominated in the foreign currency, the position of debtors in the devaluing country is worsened and that of creditors improved. In contrast, where the obligations are denominated in the devalued currency, debtors in the devaluing country are better off while creditors are worse off as a consequence of devaluation. Moreover, the stream of earnings on these wealth obligations are similarly influenced by changes in the exchange rate. Therefore, even though the output, export, and import quanta are unchanged by devaluation, real income is not likely to remain constant.

The direction of the change in real income is determined by whether the devaluing country is a net creditor or debtor and whether, on balance, the contractual obligations and their associated income streams are denominated in the foreign or domestic currency. Moreover, changes in prices of exports or imports affect asset positions, even though real output and the physical volume of exports and imports remain constant. If, for example, export prices rise and import prices remain fixed, the resulting borrowing or asset decumulation by foreigners would result in an expansion of real income relative to the given real output. Changes in real income and real output are apt to differ in an open economy because of devaluation-induced changes in wealth positions and in the income streams arising from international assets.

The effects of changes in the terms of trade upon the relationship between real output, money income, and real income are also significant. Think of real income as the amount of goods and services that may be purchased with a given real output or money income. If real output and money income were unaffected by devaluation, a deterioration in the terms of trade would, according to the usual view, result in a lower real income. Real output and money income would have to be deflated by a higher price level figure as the price of imports rose relatively. Again, Machlup points out the superficiality of this conclusion [45, pp. 421–24]. If the net barter terms of trade are being used, it is necessary to determine the proximate cause of the deterioration. The net barter terms of trade are the export price index divided by the import price index, both indices being computed in terms of the same currency. A decline in the barter terms of trade because of a relative increase in import prices would be the cause of a relative reduction in real income. But suppose that the terms of trade decline because of a reduction in prices received for exports. If this is all that happens, i.e., if money income and real output are constant, real income should remain unchanged. Neither less nor more goods and services can be purchased than before. It is important, as Brems [12, p. 49] emphasizes, to distinguish whether the barter terms of trade fall because imports are more expensive or exports command a lower price due to devaluation.

Moreover, to use the net barter terms of trade in the comparison implies that devaluation has not resulted in a change in productivity. The likelihood of resource reallocation because of devaluation suggests this is not the case. When productivity changes, the single factoral terms of trade[18] are the more relevant concept in computing the consequences of devaluation for real income. Since devaluation usually increases productivity and, by assumption above, causes the net barter terms of trade to fall, it is difficult *a priori* to state whether the theoretically relevant single factoral terms of trade improve or deteriorate. This is the gist of Machlup's claim [45, p. 420] that "even if we knew in what direction and by how much the net terms of trade will change as a result of a devaluation [we cannot] infer by how much and in what direction these changes in the terms of trade will affect real national income."

The complexities of the relationships among changes in real output, money income, and real income are significant in that absorption analysis is normally undertaken by defining functional relationships in terms of real income. As long as output and real and money income move together after devaluation, it may be assumed legitimately that the relationships are stable. When devaluation causes them to move in different ways, however, it is necessary to decide whether real output or money income influences the absorption variables independently of real income. Should this be the case, the functional relationships defined in real income terms shift with devaluation. The parameters of the functions can no longer be taken as given and the ways in which these parameters are likely to change with divergent or opposite movements in real output, money income, and real income must be probed. This entails a discussion of terms of trade effects, distributional effects, substitution and income effects, the possibility of money illusion, and other phenomena as they affect the functional relationship between absorption and real income. Only by pursuing this is it possible to determine how devaluation ultimately causes changes in the trade balance of a country and the direction in which the trade balance is most apt to change. Before this can be done, the absorption approach itself must be developed in some detail.

The Role of Absorption

The fundamental identity from national income accounting in an open economy is $Y = C + I + (X - M)$. The essence of the simple absorption approach to devaluation analysis is to rearrange this identity so as to spotlight the trade balance and then treat the equation as though it were derived from behavioral phenomena. Thus, after rearrangement:

$$(X - M) = Y - (C + I). \tag{7-1}$$

For purposes of simplifying, terms can be combined giving

$$B = Y - A, \tag{7-2}$$

where B is the trade balance, $(X - M)$, Y is income (output), and A is absorption, $(C + I)$, all for the current period. To the extent that Y exceeds A, hoarding (H) will have taken place. Consequently, the identity can be expressed as:

$$B = Y - A = H.^{19} \tag{7-3}$$

Since devaluation analysis is concerned with changes in the trade balance, it is convenient to express this identity as

$$\Delta B = \Delta Y - \Delta A = \Delta H, \tag{7-4}$$

where Δ refers, as usual, to "changes in." It is from this identity that the absorption approach derives the condition for effective devaluation. For the trade balance to improve — for ΔB to be greater than zero — current income must increase relative to current absorption; hoarding must be greater after devaluation than before. Only if devaluation results in $\Delta Y > \Delta A$ (with due regard given to the signs of the terms), so that ΔH is positive, can the trade balance be improved.

So much for the identity. The absorption approach proceeds by noting that devaluation causes a change in absorption for two kinds of reasons. It is assumed, as a behavioral relationship, that decisions to consume and invest depend upon the level of real income. Any increase in real income results normally in an increase in intentions to absorb; intended consumption and investment are both positively related to the level of real income. Moreover, absorption may be affected by devaluation in ways other than through changes in real income. A desire to accumulate additional cash balances, subsequent to devaluation, is an example of a "direct" absorption effect, the realization of which would cause absorption to fall relative to any given level of income. Thus, there are income-induced effects of devaluation upon absorption and direct (or non-income-induced) effects of devaluation upon absorption. Remembering that devaluation causes changes in the level of income directly, the effects of devaluation upon the trade balance may be written out in terms of the following "absorption equation":

$$\Delta B = \Delta Y - \alpha\Delta Y - \beta A = \Delta H. \tag{7-5}$$

Here α is the marginal propensity to absorb income and βA is the expression for the net result of the various direct effects of devaluation upon absorption.[20] In terms of the previous equation, $\Delta A = \alpha\Delta Y + \beta A$. Equation 7-5 merely breaks down the effect of devaluation upon income and upon absorption through its income-induced and non-income-induced components.

For purposes of stating the stability conditions in the simple absorption framework it is desirable that the income effects be combined into one expression. This can be achieved by rearranging equation 7-5, merging the effects of devaluation upon income directly and upon absorption via income changes. The resulting form of equation 7-5 is

$$\Delta B = (1 - \alpha)\Delta Y - \beta A = \Delta H. \tag{7-6}$$

In this equation the term $(1 - \alpha)$ is an expression for the marginal propensity not-to-absorb income or, better, for the marginal propensity to hoard, as it is called previously.

The last equation allows a derivation of the stability relationship (condition) within the absorption framework. Whether devaluation improves the trade balance depends, obviously, upon the relative values of ΔY, α, and βA. Provided that devaluation increases income, so that ΔY is positive, the balance of trade improves if α is less than unity and βA is negative — or if βA is positive, it is less than $(1 - \alpha)\Delta Y$. The change in the trade balance, ΔB, is then positive. Devaluation brings about a larger improvement in the trade balance the larger is ΔY, the smaller is α, and the smaller is βA. Since absorption consists of both consumption and investment expenditures, an α larger than one is a distinct possibility, as noted before. If α exceeds one, with devaluation still causing an expansion of income, the trade balance can only improve if βA is negative and relatively large, i.e., $|\beta A| > |(1 - \alpha)\Delta Y|$. Moreover, since Y is defined as real income, it is also possible that devaluation causes ΔY to be negative, even though real output and money income expand. Then, if devaluation is to improve the trade balance, α should exceed unity or, again, βA should be negative and relatively large in absolute value. All of these combinations of ΔY, α, and βA, and others, of course, bring about an increase in hoarding as a result of devaluation and, hence, by definition, an improvement in the trade balance. Unlike the derivation of the stability condition in the elasticities framework, it need not be specified that the initial position of the trade account must be one of balance, although it is still important that the devaluation be by a relatively small percentage.[21]

These properties of the absorption approach can be illustrated diagrammatically. To conceptualize equation 7-5 in a functional sense, think of devaluation as causing (1) a movement along a function relating absorption and income and (2) a shift of that function due to direct absorption effects. This is shown by Figure 7-4. In Figure 7-4A it is assumed that βA is negative, so that the function shifts downward as a consequence of devaluation, and that $\alpha < 1$. Since the effects of devaluation upon relative changes in income and absorption are being explored, the axes represent these variables. The function is drawn initially to pass through the origin of the diagram.

It is perhaps simplest to think of the initial trade balance as being zero, although this is not necessary and is not implied by the diagram as drawn. Recall that a property of the 45° line is that along it $\Delta A = \Delta Y$. This property is useful in comparing these two variables in order to derive the change in the trade balance and in hoarding.

In the first instance, assume that devaluation increases income by ΔY_1. Because of income-induced effects, absorption increases by ΔA_1. This is derived from the "absorption function," $\Delta A = \alpha \Delta Y$; $\alpha < 1$. If the process initiated by devaluation stopped here, the trade balance would improve by $\Delta B_1 = \Delta Y_1 - \Delta A_1 = \Delta H_1$. But the process goes further. Since devaluation has direct effects upon the level of absorption out of every income level — direct effects equal to βA — the absorption function shifts downward to $\Delta A' = f(\Delta Y)$.[22] Therefore, the change in absorption as a result of devaluation, the consequent increase in income, and the direct effects is $\Delta A_1'$. The ultimate improvement in the balance of trade is $\Delta Y_1 - \Delta A_1' = \Delta B_1' = \Delta H_1'$.

Alternatively, still referring to Figure 7-4A, if it is assumed that devaluation causes an income reduction equal to ΔY_2, an induced decrease in absorption of ΔA_2 occurs. Then, the direct effect of devaluation brings about a further reduction in absorption, so that the total fall in absorption as a result of devaluation is $\Delta A_2'$. The change in the trade balance, $\Delta Y_2 - \Delta A_2' = \Delta B_2' = \Delta H_2'$, is negative. The reduction in income, ΔY_2, is, according to the diagram, greater than the total reduction in absorption. If there had been no direct effect on absorption, the trade balance would have deteriorated to an even larger extent.

Before looking at Figure 7-4B it might be helpful to give a numerical example using Figure 7-4A. Assume that devaluation causes income to rise by $10, that $\alpha = .6$, and that the direct effects of devaluation cause absorption at every level of income to fall by $3, i.e., $\beta A = -\$3$. According to the above analysis, ΔA_1 is $6, due to income-induced changes, but this is offset in part by the direct effects so that the ultimate increase in absörption, $\Delta A_1'$, is only $3. Therefore, the trade balance improves by $7; of the $10 expansion in income, only $3 goes into absorption. Or, using equation 7-6: $\Delta B_1' = (1 - .6)\$10 - (-\$3) = \$7$. In contrast, if income falls by $10 ($\Delta Y_2 = -\$10$) as a result of devaluation, the trade balance deteriorates by $1. The reduction in income causes a fall in absorption of $6 ($\Delta A_2 = -\$6$) and this is further augmented by the direct effects of devaluation upon absorption of $-$3 ($\Delta A_2' = -\$9$). Income falls absolutely by $10 and relatively to the $9 decline in absorption. The trade balance deteriorates by $1. In terms of equation 7-6: $\Delta B_2' = (1 - .6)(-\$10) - (-\$3) = -\$1$. Given the values of α and βA assumed here, the trade balance deteriorates or improves as devaluation causes income to fall or to rise.

Figure 7-4B differs from Figure 7-4A only because α is assumed to be greater than unity. If, in Figure 7-4B, devaluation gives rise to an expansion of income of ΔY_1, there is an induced increase in absorption of ΔA_1. If there were no further effects of devaluation, the trade balance would have deteriorated because $\Delta Y_1 - \Delta A_1 = \Delta B_1 < 0$. However, the direct effects of devaluation, as drawn here, are relatively large: $|\beta A| > |\Delta Y_1 - \Delta A_1|$. In this event, the balance of trade improves because the direct effects more than compensate for the difference between the increase in income and the detrimental, larger induced increase in absorption: $\Delta Y_1 - \Delta A_1' = \Delta B_1' > 0$. Numerically, assuming $\alpha = 1.2$ and ΔY and βA as before, $\Delta B_1' = (1 - 1.2)\$10 - (-\$3) = \$1$, which is an improvement in the balance of trade. If it is posited, however, that devaluation causes a reduction in income, the large change in absorption relative to the fall in income is beneficial to the trade balance. That is, since $\Delta Y_2 - \Delta A_2 > 0$, the trade balance will have improved if only income-induced effects are taken into account. When the direct effects of devaluation are superimposed there is a further improvement in the trade balance. Again, using the assumptions just above, $\Delta B_2' = (1 - 1.2)(-\$10) - (-\$3) = \$5$. Thus, when α is greater than one, if devaluation expands income, it tends also to cause deterioration in the balance of trade, the direct effects acting as offsets. In contrast, if devaluation results in a reduction of income, the induced effect tends to bring about improvement in the trade balance and the direct effects are reinforcing.

It should be noted that these comments about the impact of the direct effects of devaluation, and similar ones above, depend for their validity upon the direction of the direct effects. It has been assumed that the consequence of direct effects is to reduce the amount of absorption at every level of income. In other words, βA is assumed to be negative. However, the direct effects of devaluation may cause absorption at every level of income to increase. In this case, βA would be positive and, in Figure 7-4, the function $\Delta A' = f(\Delta Y)$ would have to lie above the function $\Delta A = \alpha \Delta Y$, rather than as drawn. If this were the case, the

■ FIGURE 7-4

■ Figure 7-4A

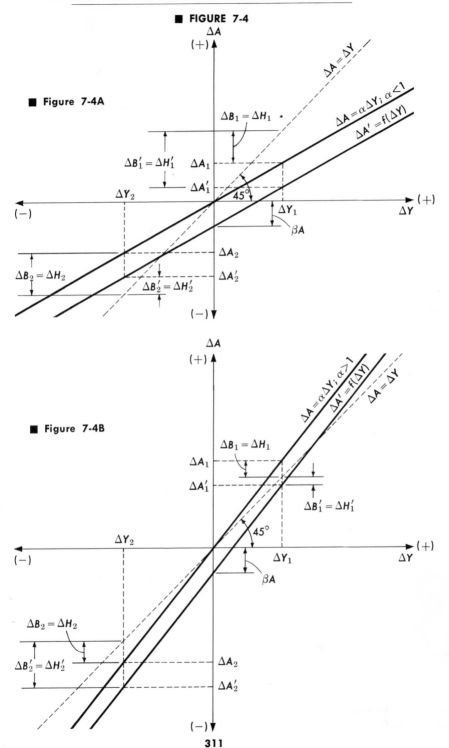

■ Figure 7-4B

impact of the direct effects, *per se*, in either offsetting or reinforcing the income-induced effects upon the trade balance would be the opposite of those stated above. If α exceeds unity and devaluation expands income, direct effects tend to increase further the trade balance deterioration caused by the income-induced effects; when devaluation reduces income, the direct effects offset the tendency of the induced effects to improve the trade balance. Thus, the direction, and of course the magnitude, of the direct effects is an important element of absorption analysis.

The results of devaluation in the absorption framework discussed in the last few paragraphs can be presented perhaps in a more straightforward manner by relating changes in hoarding (ΔH) to changes in income (ΔY). Recalling the identity between ΔB and ΔH, the vertical axis can represent both variables. This is done in Figure 7-5, which simplifies Figure 7-4 by virtue of deriving ΔH and, hence, ΔB directly rather than having to subtract ΔA from ΔY as previously. It should be noted that when $\alpha > 1$, the "hoarding function" will be negatively sloped because $(1 - \alpha)$ is the marginal propensity to hoard. When $\alpha < 1$, the hoarding function is positively sloped. The latter is assumed to be the case in drawing Figure 7-5. Moreover, in plotting ΔH against ΔY, care must be exercised in diagramming the impact of the direct effects of devaluation upon the functional relationship. If it is assumed, as before, that the direct effects are such as to reduce absorption at every level of income ($\beta A < 0$), by definition hoarding at every level of income is increased. If the direct effects of devaluation upon hoarding are denoted by γH, then $-\beta A = \gamma H$. Thus, if direct effects cause the absorption functions of Figure 7-4 to shift downward, they will cause the hoarding functions of Figure 7-5 to shift upward, and vice versa.

To avoid repetition and yet gain familiarity with the hoarding approach to absorption analysis, the notion of the hoarding function can be used to illustrate how the positive and negative direct effects alter the income-induced effects of devaluation. Figure 7-5 is designed to bring this out. Assume, as is drawn, that $\alpha < 1$ and devaluation causes income to increase by ΔY_1. The income-induced change in hoarding and in the trade balance is $\Delta \beta_1 = \Delta H_1$ and, obviously, since $\alpha < 1$, the trade balance improves. Bringing in the direct effects of devaluation, suppose that devaluation causes less to be absorbed at every income level, i.e., $\beta A < 0$. This is the same as saying that γH, the direct effect upon hoarding, is positive; the hoarding function shifts upward to $\Delta H' = f(\Delta Y)$. In consequence the direct effect of devaluation reinforces the induced effects of the income expansion. The change in hoarding for the given increase in income (ΔY_1) is greater, since $\Delta H_1' > \Delta H_1$, and the trade balance is further improved.

But what if the direct effects on absorption are positive and, hence, increase absorption at every income level? In this case, still assuming that

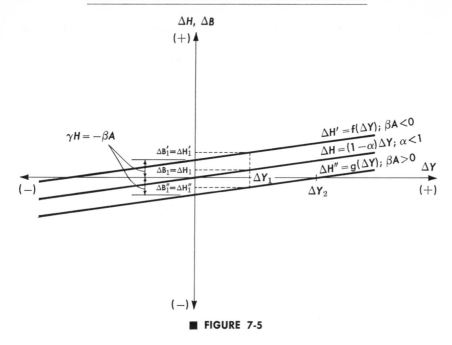

■ FIGURE 7-5

devaluation expands income by ΔY_1, the trade balance deteriorates. The income-induced effects which tend to improve the trade balance are counteracted by the downward shift of the hoarding function to $\Delta H'' = g(\Delta Y)$. While the income effects of devaluation tend to increase hoarding and the trade balance by $\Delta H_1 = \Delta B_1$, the direct effects (on hoarding) change hoarding by $\gamma H = -\beta A$. As the diagram is drawn, for the assumed income increase, ΔY_1, $\beta A > \Delta H_1 = \Delta B_1$ so that $\Delta H_1'' = \Delta B_1'' < 0$. In this case the direct effects of devaluation more than offset the positive income-induced effects and devaluation causes a deterioration in the trade balance.

Several further observations concerning Figure 7-5 are worthwhile, although they could have been made with equal facility by using Figure 7-4. If devaluation had increased income by more than ΔY_2, with the given $\alpha < 1$, the positive direct effects on absorption of $\beta A > 0$ would not have been sufficient to offset the favorable impact of the income-induced effects on the trade balance. The trade balance would have improved, unlike the example above in which devaluation expanded income by less than ΔY_2. Moreover, if the diagram had been drawn with α assumed to be somewhat smaller — so that the three functions would have to be rotated in a counterclockwise direction — a devaluation which increased income by ΔY_1, with the given $\beta A > 0$, might have resulted in an improvement in the trade balance. This would have been so if the new $\Delta H_1 = \Delta B_1$, after the rotation of the functions, would have been larger than βA.

These relationships could be explored further upon the assumption that devaluation causes a reduction in income and upon the assumption that $\alpha > 1$, so that hoarding functions are negatively sloped. This has been done in Figure 7-4 with the absorption functions and is not repeated here. Both Figure 7-4 and Figure 7-5 illustrate, however, the stability relationship (condition) in the absorption framework. In this framework effective devaluation depends upon the relative sizes and signs of ΔY, α, and βA. Moreover, the diagrams serve to emphasize the prior algebraic presentation that for devaluation to improve the trade balance hoarding must increase or, what is the same thing, the change in income brought about by devaluation must be larger, due regard being given to signs, than the total change in absorption. This is the primary policy lesson of absorption analysis.

"Values" of the Absorption Variables

The importance of the magnitudes of the absorption variables, ΔY, α, and βA, in the analysis of devaluation characteristically has given rise to a good deal of discussion of their likely values. This discussion has not been completely satisfactory for purposes of policy decisions. No precise, empirical quantification of the variables has been undertaken; yet quantification is imperative if a high degree of assurance about the trade balance outcome of devaluation is to be achieved. With the given state of knowledge, policy makers must rely on the less complete information on the values of the absorption variables derivable from theoretical considerations. Theoretical discussions have taken the form of speculations about the relative sizes of the variables in differing economic situations and with different assumptions about the motivations of individuals making absorption decisions. These theoretical discussions have been valuable in that they have provided guide lines concerning the likelihood that devaluation will be an effective weapon for improving the balance of trade. Moreover, the discussions provide a more sophisticated understanding of the mechanism of devaluation itself. The kinds of factors underlying absorption decisions are brought to the surface, laying bare the elements of the devaluation mechanism. This facilitates a policy of affecting the results of devaluation by changing or influencing these individual elements of the mechanism.

Income-induced effects of devaluation / It is a reasonable proposition that the state of employment of an economy is a major determinant of the response of income to changes in the exchange rate. It is also reasonable to suppose that the level of employment affects the relationship between changes in income and changes in absorption. That is to say, it is plausible to assume that the marginal propensity to absorb income for income changes associated with output increases might be different from the marginal propensity to absorb income for income changes due to price level increases. This of course is true but one of the clever aspects of Alexander's exposition of the absorption approach is virtually to assume that it cannot be the case. By stating his absorption function in real income terms, he tries to insure that the value of α will not be altered according to the level of employment.

Alexander may not have been entirely successful in this. Real output, which cannot be increased after full employment is reached, is not identical with real income, which may be increased after full employment is reached. When real output and real income move together, α may have one value; it may not retain that value if real income changes while real output is constant. Moreover, as Machlup has emphasized [45; 44, pp. 265–66], real output itself may rise after full employment is reached as resources are reallocated into more efficient activities. The marginal propensity to absorb may be different for output increases achieved by re-employing unutilized resources than for output increases achieved by reallocating resources.

The effects of these complexities on the value of α are perhaps too indistinct to pursue further so that it can be assumed, with Alexander, that the marginal propensity to absorb real income is independent of the level of employment. This, of course, does not insure that the "direct effects" of devaluation upon absorption are independent of the level of employment also. Indeed, in these direct effects, and through them the shift in the absorption function, the differential impact of different states of employment is brought into the analysis. Thus, if the level of employment at which devaluation is implemented has a significant impact upon its effectiveness as a trade balance policy, it is because the state of employment influences ΔY and βA.

If resources are not fully utilized, devaluation results in an expansion of output and income. The normal market response to a devaluation is an increase in the quantity of exports demanded abroad and with idle resources this is met by an expansion of the supply of exports with no curtailment of production in other sectors. This is the cause of an initial expansion in output and income.[23] As Alexander notes [2, p. 267], this increase in output has multiplier effects on the domestic economy and further expansion occurs. The process is limited by the size of the multiplier, of course, but also by the volume of additional exports foreigners are willing to take and by the extent to which output of the devaluing country can be increased without a significant rise in prices. The latter restraint may become critical even before full employment of all resources — or even labor — is reached. Output expansion may proceed more rapidly in particular goods so that specific bottlenecks may arise; as Machlup observes [44, p. 261], specific resources to complement the factors needed for a certain composition of output expansion may not always be available. But until these kinds of limits are reached, it may be assumed that output and income rise together as a consequence of devaluation.

With resources fully employed at the time of devaluation, these kinds of expansionary responses in output and income are ruled out. In Alexander's formulation of the simple absorption approach, devaluation in a fully employed economy can improve the trade balance only if absorption can actually be depressed, it being impossible to rely on an idle-resources effect to increase output further. Since it is unlikely that devaluation would result in a decline in output and income (terms of trade effects aside), the depression of absorption depends solely on the direct effects of devaluation, βA. This leads to the conclusion that, in a state of full employment, devaluation, unaccompanied by deflationary measures, is a poor bet to improve the trade balance.

The conclusion is misleading, however, as Machlup [44, pp. 265–66; 45] points out. Devaluation, because of responses to relative price adjustments that are usually subordinated in the absorption framework, typically improves the allocation of resources in the devaluing country and elsewhere. With increased factor efficiency, even though expansion of factor employment is impossible, output and income expand. While it is recognized that this resource reallocation effect is operative whether or not the economy is at full employment, it is especially relevant at full employment. Devaluation may, then, result in further output and income expansion at full employment and the trade balance is more likely to improve than if changes in resource efficiency are totally neglected. This statement implies, of course, that $\alpha < 1$ with βA not offsetting. Should $\alpha > 1$, the expansion of output and income, if they proceed at the same rate, would tend to cause a deterioration of the trade balance with devaluation.

For one steeped in the traditional elasticities analysis, it is inconceivable that changes in the terms of trade could be ignored entirely. And, of course, Alexander does not do so. He incorporates terms of trade effects into his absorption analysis but, as is discussed below, in a relatively unsatisfactory way. It is generally assumed that devaluation results in a deterioration of the barter terms of trade of the devaluing country. Given that the terms of trade fall, there is an attendant fall in income. If it is further assumed that the reduction in income is not followed by a decline in absorption, according to the absorption equation, the trade balance must deteriorate by the amount that the adverse turn in the terms of trade reduced the income level. This is contrary to the conclusion generally derived as a consequence of the elasticities argument that devaluation improves the (real) trade balance because imports are reduced relative to exports. But, of course, absorption does fall as income declines so that the net result of the terms of trade effect upon the trade balance is given by the reduction in income due to the adverse movement of the terms of trade (call it ΔY^1), less the induced fall in absorption ($\alpha \Delta Y^1$). That is, the change in the trade balance due to the terms of trade effect is $\Delta B^1 = \Delta Y^1 - \alpha \Delta Y^1$. If ΔY^1 is negative, the trade balance tends to deteriorate if $\alpha < 1$; it tends to improve if $\alpha > 1$.

Perhaps, at this point, discussion of these various "income-induced" effects on the trade balance, including some of the noted reservations about them, can be summarized. Use $\widehat{\Delta B}$ and ΔY to represent net (or total) changes in the trade balance (due to income-induced effects) and in income respectively.[24] The change in income, however, may be broken down into subcomponents, ΔY^1 for the terms of trade effect, ΔY^2 for the resource reallocation effect, and ΔY^3 for the idle resources effect. Similarly, α represents a weighted average of α^1, α^2, and α^3, the marginal propensities to absorb income arising from the various effects. This splitting of α reflects a belief, consistent with Spraos' position [67], that the marginal propensity to absorb varies significantly as the change in income is generated via different mechanisms. Using this notation:

$$\widehat{\Delta B} = \Delta Y^1 + \Delta Y^2 + \Delta Y^3 - \alpha^1 \Delta Y^1 - \alpha^2 \Delta Y^2 - \alpha^3 \Delta Y^3 \qquad (7\text{-}7)$$

It has been assumed that the terms of trade deteriorate so that $\Delta Y^1 < 0$. It is also possible that $\Delta Y^1 > 0$. If devaluation takes place during a period of unemployment, $\Delta Y^3 > 0$ and also, presumably, $\Delta Y^2 > 0$. In contrast, if resources are fully employed when the devaluation occurs, $\Delta Y^3 = 0$ while $\Delta Y^2 > 0$. It should be added, although this is not reflected in the notation, that the two ΔY^1's in the right side of the equation need not be equal. Ignoring Machlup's elaboration of the terms of trade effect, as is the case up to now, the first ΔY^1 may well be zero while the second ΔY^1, as noted above, may be either positive or negative.[25] In view of these observations it is apparent that the net income-induced impact of devaluation upon the trade balance depends upon the "composition" of the change in income and the magnitudes of the various α's which hypothetically are determined for the various types of income effects. The net effect of devaluation upon the balance of trade is seen to depend intimately upon the state of employment and, it might be added, upon the mobility of resources and the effectiveness of the market mechanism.

Direct effects on absorption / To these income-induced effects of devaluation must be added a number of direct effects on absorption before the ultimate result of devaluation upon the trade balance can be discerned. It has been noted that if $\alpha > 1$ and $\Delta Y > 0$, the sole hope that devaluation will improve the balance of trade is that the direct effects of devaluation are on balance negative — that $\beta A < 0$. While devaluation then results in a larger income-induced expansion in absorption relative to the increase in income, it is possible that the direct effects may so reduce absorption at every income level that the total increase in absorption falls short of that in income. The trade balance then improves. In contrast, if the direct effects are positive on balance, their impact causes a further deterioration in the balance of trade account. Alternatively, if $\alpha < 1$, and still $\Delta Y > 0$, negative direct effects add to the effectiveness of devaluation while positive direct effects countervail the favorable income-induced effects. For a complete appraisal of devaluation as a policy instrument, the various direct effects must be analyzed and assigned their relative importance. If effective devaluation depends largely upon favorable direct effects, it is important to know how dependable these are and how they might be reinforced.

Devaluation's direct effects on absorption can be isolated from income-induced effects by making assumptions which assure no change in income. Assume, for instance, that resources are fully employed at maximum efficiency, thereby eliminating the idle resources and resource reallocation effects. Further, to eliminate the terms of trade effect upon income, assume that the supply of imports from abroad and the foreign demand for exports are infinitely elastic. Under these assumptions, the terms of trade are constant, regardless of the exchange rate, as the domestic prices of imports and exports increase by the same amount. In these circumstances producers and consumers respond to devaluation by shifting demand from imports to import-substitutes and by expanding exports. Since full employment is postulated, the price level rises in the devaluing country, as does money, but not real, income. The question to be considered is whether the increase in the price level and money income causes a shift in the absorption function and, if so, in what direction the shift occurs.

One way in which absorption is directly affected by an increase in the price level is through a cash balances effect, as suggested by Savosnick [61] and Beckerman [8; 7]. Assume that individuals hold cash balances (in order to make real purchases) in such a way that the volume of intended real purchases determines the desirable holdings of cash. With no change in real income, people would wish to buy the same volume of goods and services. Individuals would, with an increase in prices, attempt to build up their holdings of cash balances. Whether this is possible depends upon the actions of the monetary authorities. If it is assumed, with Alexander, that the money supply is fixed, the desire to increase cash holdings is frustrated. In the process, however, real expenditures on goods and services decline; absorption falls relative to income. Moreover, in trying to increase cash balances, people with liquid securities sell these assets by reducing their prices. Interest rates rise sufficiently to induce the buyers of these securities to cut back consumption and investment expenditures and there is a further reduction in absorption. The frustration of the desire to accumulate cash, as the money supply is constant, results in a downward adjustment of the amount of absorption. To be sure, Hahn [23, pp. 115–16] minimizes the importance of the cash balances effect, believing that the shift in the absorption function would be small in practice and that the effect may be short-lived. There is, however, room for different judgments on this and, moreover, as a theoretical issue the cash balances effect is of some moment.

It might be pointed out that a type of cash balances effect may be operating, given Alexander's assumptions, even though devaluation has not taken place. Assuming an absence of international capital flows, a trade deficit implies a spending of previously inactive cash or an expansion in the money supply. If the monetary authorities prevent monetary expansion, support for a continuing deficit must come from dishoarding. But, as both Machlup [44, p. 273] and Johnson [30, pp. 156–57] emphasize, dishoarding cannot continue indefinitely and ultimately the trade balance must improve. This mechanism cannot, of course, convert the trade balance into a favorable one since there are no inherent forces that generate the required hoarding that would support a surplus.

A second possible direct effect on absorption is attributable to the fact that the increase in the price level may result in a redistribution among the recipients of the given (aggregate) income.[26] Profit takers may gain relative to wage earners if the prices of goods dominant in wage earners' consumption patterns rise relatively. Wage increases may lag behind the increase in prices; or they may precede the price rise with the wage earners increasing their income share. Receivers of relatively fixed incomes suffer, due to the price rise, while factors with flexible incomes benefit. Producers of exports and import substitutes gain appreciably from the devaluation while purchasers of imports and import substitutes are disadvantaged. Rising prices also increase the government's tax take from the given income; the government gains at the taxpayers' expense.

The nature of these devaluation-induced redistributions of income is hard to anticipate and, in order to determine the effects of redistribution on absorption, it is necessary further to know the marginal propensities to absorb of the various income groups. What these marginal propensities are is not altogether clear. Profit receivers, for example, may have lower marginal propensities to consume than wage earners but, for obvious reasons, the profit takers also have higher marginal propensities to invest. The government may or may not have a greater propensity to spend than taxpayers, depending upon the type of fiscal policy it is pursuing. What can be said with certainty is that absorption will be reduced at every level of (aggregate) income if that income is redistributed toward low marginal spenders and away from high marginal spenders. This does not permit a decision as to whether in fact the direct redistribution effect shifts the absorption function downward or upward. It suggests merely that some shift probably takes place and that changes in the income distribution must be considered when analyzing the consequences of devaluation.

Once price level and money income changes are included in the discussion, the possibility of money illusion becomes relevant. In the context of absorption analysis, money illusion may be said to exist if real expenditures are determined with reference to money valued, rather than (or in addition to) real, phenomena. By defining the absorption function with reference to real income, if money income or the price level influences absorption decisions, there is a direct money illusion effect. Again, however, as with the redistribution effect, it is difficult to decide whether absorption is increased or reduced. If the money illusion takes the form primarily of a price-orientation of real spending decisions, the absorption function is shifted downward. A fixation on the rise in prices, even though money income has risen commensurately, causes a downward revision of absorption and the balance of trade tends to be improved. But money illusion could as easily tend to reduce the trade balance. Money illusion may arise from a money income fixation as well as from a price level fixation. Since both the price level and money income, by assumption, rise in the same proportion, a money income-orientation of spending decisions brings about an upward adjustment of absorption relative to real income. The influence on absorption of the expansion in money income relative to real income then tends to cause the balance of trade to deteriorate.

The kind of price expectations held by the community is also likely to affect the level of absorption for a given income. As devaluation generates a price level increase, a reasonable presumption is a continuation of inflation. If this were the case, both consumers and investors would be expected to rush to make the purchases that could not be indefinitely postponed or at least postponed until the price level settled back to its original position. This acceleration of spending might be rather appreciable; current absorption would advance relative to current income. In contrast, if opposite price expectations prevailed — if it were thought that the increase in prices would be temporary — a postponement of current purchases should be anticipated. In normal circumstances the latter assumption about price expectations is less plausible than the former. Therefore price expectations probably have a tendency to make devaluation a less effective weapon against trade balance deficits.

The rise in the price level, specifically the increase in the domestic price of imports, has a further impact on the level of absorption. It may be assumed that investment decisions depend upon the costs of capital equipment as well as upon the interest rate. Insofar as some investment entails the use of imported items, the volume of investment will fall.

Similarly, consumer purchases of imported goods should decline if demand is sensitive to prices. Where government expenditures are disregarded, a reduction in both consumption and investment outlays must, of course, increase hoarding so that the trade balance improves. But if either consumption or investment expenditures (but not both) fall, there may simply be a change in the composition of total absorption with no reduction in that total. It is essential if the trade balance is to be improved by this price-induced effect that the altered spending decisions result in an actual reduction in absorption, as is likely in practice to be the case.[27]

The enumeration of the various direct effects of devaluation on absorption, while fleshing out the devaluation mechanism, possibly does little to clarify the issue of whether devaluation improves the trade balance. Alexander [2] is of the opinion that these direct effects result in a reduction in the level of absorption for any given income. Machlup [44] does not seem inclined to take exception to Alexander. Neither states this position strongly; and the reluctance seems justified. Whether these effects balance out to a reduction or an increase in absorption is highly debatable without knowledge of the particular situation. The size of the various direct effects, as well as the direction of some of them, is indeterminate without information additional to the fact that devaluation has taken place. This being so and it also being the case that a reduction in income is unpalatable, it appears all the more important to try to insure that the marginal propensity to absorb is significantly less than one.

Relative price effects / The direct effects of devaluation adumbrated above do not constitute an exhaustive listing. The discussion proceeded from assumptions that excluded changes in the terms of trade. The initial effect of the devaluation was a rise in the price level because domestic prices of imports and of exports rose in the same proportion. With the exception of the last-mentioned direct effect, wherein imports and absorption were commensurately reduced because of a concern of spenders for relative prices, it was not necessary to stipulate how devaluation affected the prices of domestic goods. In general, the direct effects already mentioned were a consequence of an increase in the price level alone. But, typically, relative prices are also altered by devaluation. Indeed, in the pure elasticities approach, relative price adjustments are the sole force of the devaluation. The ratio of prices of domestic goods to prices of traded goods is changed by devaluation, with domestic goods' prices normally rising by less than the assumed increase in the prices of goods traded internationally.[28] This kind of price adjustment triggers the resource reallocation effect previously discussed. But aside from this important phenomenon, consideration of the effects of changes in relative prices in the absorption framework has been negligible.

This is a significant omission. Hemming and Corden [26, p. 509], Salter [60] and Pearce [55] demonstrate the importance to the effectiveness of devaluation of the fact that, under conditions where commodities are substitutes, it result in a lowering of the prices of purely domestic goods relative to those of internationally traded goods. The neglect of relative price effects is, similarly, a major source of Machlup's remonstrances against the simple absorption approach. Gehrels [20] and Brems [12] extend the absorption analysis by explicitly incorporating relative price effects into their models. Not that Alexander has ignored comparative prices entirely. His terms of trade effect, by altering real income, does cause income-induced changes in absorption. But the working out of this effect hardly stresses conventional adjustments to relative price movements. In any event, there are other significant ways in which changes in relative prices affect absorption and these comprise an important part of the devaluation mechanism. Indeed, as Machlup takes pains to argue [44, pp. 266–68; 45], they may very substantially alter the level of absorption independently of income movements.

Perhaps the best way to account for these relative price effects is to note a theoretical consideration that until now has been largely neglected. Assuming that the economy is fully employed, absorption analysis shows that the trade balance can be improved only if total expenditure is lowered relative to income. It is necessary to consider, however, just where the reduction in absorption takes place. On the one hand, if it falls on spending on domestically produced consumption and investment goods, the lower effective demand may reduce employment and income rather than improve the trade balance. This depends upon the size of the marginal propensity to absorb and upon direct absorption effects. But it depends on more. The mobility of resources and the efficacy of the price mechanism are also relevant. If resources are less than perfectly mobile or if price incentives are weak, the required transfer of resources from domestic production to export goods or to import substitutes is not apt to be forthcoming. Either full employment cannot be maintained (in which case the trade balance may improve) or absorption cannot be reduced and the trade balance cannot become more favorable. On the other hand, if the reduction in absorption falls on imports and exportables, the need to reallocate resources does not exist. Relative price movements may be the motivation for this latter kind of fall in absorption.

This argument, relying as it does on various price elasticities, can be valid only if spenders at home and abroad, as well as producers, are motivated by relative price considerations. The increase in import prices due to devaluation must induce shifts in domestic spenders' outlays in favor of domestically produced goods. The increased prices of exports must cause a shift of resources away from purely domestic commodities into exportable goods. For these shifts to be profitable, foreigners must be willing to purchase more exports. Adjustments of this sort to relative price movements presumably reduce absorption even though money income, because of the operation of price incentives, has been allowed to expand. One way in which absorption might be reduced is through the cash balances effect described above: the reconstitution of spenders' outlays and shift of resources reduce the aggregate supply of domestic goods relative to the aggregate demand for them; the general price level rises as domestic goods' prices increase; the real value of cash holdings declines; individuals, in an effort to recover their real cash positions, reduce absorption relative to income. In short, the devaluation causes relative price adjustments; if price elasticities differ from zero, a different composition of expenditures and allocation of resources ensues; domestic prices increase; and, because of the chain of events generated by relative price shifts, absorption falls compared to income and the trade balance thereby improves.[29]

Machlup notes that this relative price effect may be reinforced by one of a presumably different kind. The relative price change causes not only adjustments in the composition of expenditures but also induces a review of the decisions to spend or not to spend. In consequence, there may be shifts between consumption and asset positions or between investment and liquidity. Recall that an excess of absorption over income, or a trade deficit, implies a reduction in the net asset position of the economy. It is possible that, even apart from the relative price-induced cash balances effect, a change in the ratio of prices of traded and non-traded goods "may affect the willingness of 'absorbers' to run up their debts or run down their liquid asset holdings" [44, p. 267].

While Machlup believes this review of the spending-nonspending decision results in a decline in absorption there are, nevertheless, conflicting views on this point. Harberger [24], Laursen and Metzler [39], and Johnson [30, p. 163] argue that absorption may well be increased because of relative price movements. The reduction in real income due to the relative rise in import prices would lead to a proportionately greater reduction in saving. This could be diagrammed in terms of Figure 7-4 as an upward shift of the absorption function which was derived on the basis of absorption adjustments due solely to income effects. Thus, if the absorption function moves upward, because of relative price effects, at the same time that income and absorption adjust along the function because of the fall in income, the final level of absorption may be higher or lower than, or equal to, the pre-devaluation absorption level. Which of these outcomes is probable depends on the marginal propensity to absorb and the strength of this relative price effect.[30]

In another context, Day [15] suggests that to some extent, in the eyes of consumers, imports may be substitutes for not absorbing, although

Spraos [67] questions the importance of this. Imports of consumer durables, for example, provide a flow of satisfaction similar to that derivable from the interest return on assets acquired through saving. If the "price" of the flow of services from durable goods imports rises relatively, the demand for interest earning assets would rise — supporting Machlup's position, the level of absorption would fall. This ignores, however, the fact observed by Pearce [54] that interest from asset holdings is used to purchase imports and that, therefore, the real value of the interest earnings falls with a rise in import prices. Whether this leads spenders to try to accumulate more assets, in order to maintain their real spending power, or to reduce their asset holdings, because they are no longer as "valuable," is debatable. If the former attitude prevailed, there should be a reduction in absorption; if the latter were dominant, there should be a rise in absorption.

By neglecting these relative price-induced substitutions in expenditure patterns and resource uses, Machlup notes, Alexander's first exposition of the devaluation mechanism failed to give a correct picture of the process by which the trade balance could be improved [44, p. 268]. Alexander assumed that the sole impact on absorption of changes in the terms of trade was through resulting changes in (real) income; the terms of trade effect was an income-induced phenomenon. By overlooking relative price movements and, therefore, possible substitutions in spending patterns, it was fairly easy to assume that the reduction in income due to a worsening of the terms of trade resulted in a matching deterioration of the trade balance. If income fell without a simultaneous reduction in absorption, the trade balance would deteriorate. This assumption led Alexander to conclude that an adverse movement in the terms of trade would result in an unfavorable change in the trade balance, rather than in an improvement — as had been supported by the elasticities approach. His reasoning was straightforward: if devaluation worsened the terms of trade to an extent that income fell by, say ΔY, the trade balance would also simultaneously fall by ΔY because absorption for the moment remained unchanged. As the reduction in income later induced a reduction in absorption equal to $\alpha \Delta Y$, the trade balance would, it is true, tend to improve. But this improvement would not be substantial enough to offset the initial reduction of ΔY in the trade balance unless $\alpha > 1$. That is, the ultimate change in the trade balance in Alexander's use of the terms of trade effect was $\Delta Y - \alpha \Delta Y$ and since ΔY was negative due to worsened terms of trade, the entire expression would be positive only when $\alpha > 1$.

Machlup argues against the validity of this assumption, noting that the relative price effects described above would alter absorption independently of income [44, p. 268]. Relative price adjustments, he observes, would cause income effect*s and* substitution effects and Alexander had discounted the latter. But when these effects are both given their due, devaluation reduces income (through Alexander's "limited" terms of trade effect) and absorption (through a substitution effect) simultaneously. Since absorption changes are not all income-induced, it is then necessary to weigh the relative strengths of these two forces before evaluating the trade balance outcome of a "complete" terms of trade effect due to devaluation. It is not true that $\Delta Y - \alpha \Delta Y$ would provide a measure of this effect. Rather, to this expression must be added another term to account for the downward shift of absorption relative to income because of substitutions. If these substitution effects are large relative to Alexander's "limited" terms of trade effect, the change in the terms of trade and relative prices generated by the devaluation might well cause an initial improvement in the balance of trade.

Therefore, Alexander's pessimism about the effectiveness of devaluation may not be warranted. His limited terms of trade effect, provided the terms of trade worsened due to devaluation, always tended to counteract the idle resources effect. In Machlup's view, the idle resources, resource reallocation, and "complete" terms of trade effects could all reinforce each other in tending to improve the balance of trade, provided of course that the marginal propensity to absorb was less than unity. Where $\alpha > 1$, the terms of trade effect could, if relative price movements and substitutions were sizeable, bring about improvement in the trade balance also. Even when the economy is operating at full capacity, so that the idle resources effect is negligible, devaluation alone might be counted on to improve the trade balance. Other measures — disabsorption policies, as Alexander calls them [2, p. 275] — need not be pursued in order to discourage absorption relative to income. Shifts in expenditure patterns and increases in income because of more efficient resource utilization, both of which are results of devaluation best analyzed in an elasticities framework, are fully capable of bringing about the reduction in the level of absorption relative to income that is required if the trade balance is to improve.

Combining the Elasticities and Absorption Approaches

It is apparent from this review of the "simple" absorption approach to devaluation analysis that the absorption model is only seemingly simple. In emphasizing the significance of income and absorption, the approach focuses on only two variables, unlike the elasticities approach where four variables — and even more in Harberger's [24] and Laursen and Metzler's [39] early elaboration of the traditional elasticities approach to include a consideration of income effects — are salient to the analysis. But the simplicity of the absorption approach is to a large degree artificial. It is necessary to comprehend the relationship between absorption and income as the exchange rate is varied and this relationship is by no means a simple one — even if only linear possibilities are considered. Alexander's exposition is straightforward largely because it plays down the impact of relative price changes on current absorption out of current income and thereby distorts the analysis of devaluation. It is primarily Machlup who questioned this downgrading of the trade balance consequences of relative price movements in the simple absorption approach. His efforts to have elasticities reinstated in the devaluation mechanism were to bear fruit.

Machlup issued yet another challenge to the simple absorption approach as developed by Alexander. Recall that most of the analysis of the absorption model was in "real" terms. In explaining the effects of devaluation upon the trade balance, Alexander discussed a real absorption function, real income, and derived a real trade balance, asserting merely that the basic relationship would hold in money terms as well. Machlup, however, wondered what a "real" trade balance is. While it is reasonable to treat exports and imports as "real quantities," what is the meaning of the difference between the two "treated as a real (physical) quantity?" [44, p. 269]. Moreover, to search for an improvement in the real trade balance ignores the possibility, seen above, that a more favorable real trade balance may be accompanied by a deterioration in the money value of this trade balance. Since this is the case, it is not precisely accurate to leave the implication, as Alexander did, that the analysis, as well as the basic relationship, holds in both real and money terms without requiring significant emendations. "The supposed equivalence between relationships in money and in real terms," Machlup correctly observes, "is sometimes troublesome, occasionally even meaningless" [44, p. 269].

These criticisms of the simple absorption approach to devaluation led Alexander to recast his view of the devaluation mechanism, putting it in money terms and giving elasticities a vital place in the model, while retaining the basic conceptions of the absorption analysis. The synthesis visualized a devaluation model in which the change in the trade balance depended on the net result of superimposed relative price effects and income-absorption effects. The contribution of the former was to bring about initial changes in the money value of the trade balance and in money income; income-absorption effects contributed to the trade balance outcome of devaluation by tending normally to reduce the initial impact of relative price movements. Tsiang has succinctly summarized Alexander's "compromise" on the issues of the elasticities and absorption debate in the following way [74, p. 912]: "Alexander now proposes . . . that the result obtained by the traditional elasticities approach may be treated as the 'initial' (or primary) effect of a devaluation to which a sort of 'multiplier' (normally less than unity), computed from the [marginal] propensities to hoard, to import, etc., is to be applied to yield the final effect of the devaluation." This was, according to Tsiang, a "rather disappointing anticlimax" to the controversy and left him feeling "somewhat let down." For, after all, as he noted, had not others, notably in the models of Meade [49], Harberger [24], Laursen and Metzler [39], and Stuvel [72], already analyzed the effects of devaluation in which output, income, and relative price movement were all strategic? "If," Tsiang asked, "the controversy between the relative-prices and aggregate-spending approaches merely leads to a synthesis which had already been worked out before the controversy, what then has been gained by the debate?" [74, p. 913].

This is a fair rhetorical question. Tsiang answers it only in part. In his opinion, the major contribution of the debate is its emphasis on the vital role of the supply of money and credit in the devaluation mechanism. The significance of monetary conditions (or assumptions) had all but been lost in the simple elasticities approach, in the revised traditional variant of the simple elasticities approach, and in Alexander's simple absorption formulation. The absorption approach and Machlup's comments on it, however, pointed subsequent analytical efforts in the direction of "rediscovering money" by underlining that a trade deficit, with current absorption in excess of current income, could only be sustained by credit creation or dishoarding.

Tsiang's point is well taken and the following section explores the trade balance implications of various monetary assumptions. Nevertheless, the fruits of the absorption-elasticities debate extend beyond this issue. The models of Meade, Harberger, and Stuvel were developed and argued in rigorous mathematical terms: assumptions were made, formulas derived, and conclusions arrived at largely without concern for the etiology of the economic processes involved.[31] With the complicated nature of the problem of plumbing the devaluation mechanism, it is, perhaps, forgivable to settle for an account of *what* will happen to the trade balance *per se* if devaluation is undertaken under certain assumptions. But settling for this should not be satisfying: for satisfaction, no less than an account of *why* the trade balance changes with devaluation under certain assumed conditions is needed. That is, it is important to be able to follow, step by step, not the mathematical derivations of certain conclusions but, rather, the relatively convoluted reality of the economic responses that ensue from devaluation — responses that may or may not achieve improvement in the trade balance. This latter kind of understanding is required in order to increase the range of policy choices.[32] Although a full comprehension of these economic processes is not yet possible, the elasticities-absorption debate, and not so much the development of the revised traditional elasticities variant, is largely responsible for an appreciable increment to understanding them. Alexander and, no less, Machlup, are responsible for this; and in this sense Alexander's synthesis, far from being disappointing, goes beyond the economic analysis derivable in the revised traditional elasticities models.

The synthesis of the elasticities and absorption approaches achieves this deepened understanding of the economic processes produced by devaluation by maintaining a formal dichotomy between the two methods of analysis. Alexander, as it were, first lets devaluation play upon the price elasticities in the devaluing country and in the non-devaluing country. The impact of this, given the elasticities in both countries, is to cause an initial change in money income, in relative prices, and in the money value of the trade balance in the two countries. The relationship between the various elasticities, on the one hand, and the trade balance, income, and relative prices, on the other, has already been examined in discussing "The Role of Elasticities" above. It is not necessary to go into this further.

Nevertheless, in order to facilitate exposition of the synthesis, assume that the elasticities are such that in the devaluing country the terms of trade deteriorate, the ratio of prices of domestic goods to traded goods falls, money income rises, and the money trade balance (measured in the currency of the devaluing country) improves. The converse of these phenomena, of course, occurs in the other country. Again, assume that the marginal propensity to hoard, λ, is not negative.[33] Moreover, in this synthesis it is necessary to adopt a parameter which symbolizes the effects of money income adjustments on exports and imports — a marginal propensity for the trade balance to deteriorate because of money income changes. Call this parameter μ and assume that $0 < \mu < 1$. For further simplification assume also that initially the balance of trade is zero. These assumptions define, of course, a special case as an example. In contrast, Alexander's presentation of the synthesis is completely general in the sense that these restrictive assumptions are not implied by his analysis. His framework is equally useful in analyzing devaluation that brings about an initial deterioration of the trade balance, a rise in the terms of trade, etc., where $\lambda \gtreqless 0$ and where a trade imbalance exists at the time of devaluation.

If it is assumed, then, that devaluation, operating within the pure elasticities framework, causes the devaluing country's trade balance to improve initially by ΔB, there is also an initial expansion of money income by ΔY. The converse is assumed to happen abroad. These income adjustments in the devaluing country and abroad, and their reverberation through the familiar multiplier process, have a further impact on the trade balance which cannot be discounted. Normally these income-induced forces are expected to operate against the initial effects of devaluation. If real output, and therefore real income, can increase in the devaluing country, it is probable that the demand for imports and for those domestic goods using factors eligible for the export sector would rise; the assumed ΔB tends to be reduced by these phenomena. Similarly, if employment is full, the rise in the prices of domestic goods following devaluation tends to reduce devaluation-caused price differences; again, typically, since aggregates of goods (such as "traded" and "non-traded") are usually substitutes, the initial trade balance increase tends to be offset. Corresponding processes, in reverse, are taking place abroad as well.

Thus, under either full employment or unemployment conditions, reversal tends to occur, depending on the values of the marginal propensities to hoard and of the trade balance to deteriorate. Under the assumptions about the sizes of λ and μ and on the further assumption that initially $\Delta B = \Delta Y = \Delta A$,[34] these income-induced adjustments tend to reverse the postulated improvement in the trade balance attributable to the play of devaluation in the elasticities framework. Analysis of this reversal constitutes the second element of the formal dichotomy mentioned above. Reversal is due to the role of absorption in the devaluation process — in this synthesis Alexander embraces absorption analysis in his discussion of "reversal factors" [35] — and this approach has already been described in some detail.

As applied to the synthesis, however, the simple absorption approach must be transliterated because it is superimposed directly upon the elasticities approach and it explicitly incorporates substitutions among the types of commodities. The most effective way to do this is to assume, with Alexander, that the entire initial improvement in the trade balance results in an equal increase in absorption of domestic goods: if the trade balance improvement is due in part to an expansion of exports and in part to a contraction of imports, the increase in the former represents a rise in expenditures on domestic output and the reduction in imports results in a switch of an equivalent amount of expenditures to domestic goods. This expanded outlay on domestic goods is, of course, allocated by its recipients among further expenditures on domestic output, on imports or on goods that otherwise would have been exported had they not been purchased domestically (so-called export substitutes), or, finally, on an increase in hoarding, in accordance to ν, μ, and λ, respectively.

Of this allocation, the additional hoarding and expenditures causing the trade balance to deteriorate are leakages from the income stream; the expenditures on domestic goods constitute income in the succeeding "income period." This is the "first round" of the multiplier process. Income continues to increase in subsequent rounds, inducing all the while further domestic absorption, further deterioration of the trade balance, and further hoarding, until the sum of the leakages is made equal to the value of the initial injection. The total expansion in income as a result of the "first reaction" of the devaluing country is, then, given by $\widetilde{\Delta Y} = \Delta B \frac{1}{\lambda + \mu}$. The leakage into hoarding from this first reaction multiplier process is $\lambda \widetilde{\Delta Y}$ or, alternatively $\widetilde{\Delta H} = \Delta B \frac{\lambda}{\lambda + \mu}$. The leakage caused by the "first reaction" income-induced deterioration of the trade balance is, similarly, $\mu \widetilde{\Delta Y}$ or $\widetilde{\Delta T} = \Delta B \frac{\mu}{\lambda + \mu}$. Thus, as a consequence of the devaluing country's first reaction to devaluation, the trade balance is reduced to:

$$\widetilde{\Delta B} = \Delta B - \widetilde{\Delta T} = \Delta B \left[1 - \frac{\mu}{\lambda + \mu} \right] = \Delta B \frac{\lambda}{\lambda + \mu} = \widetilde{\Delta H}. \qquad (7\text{-}8)$$

But this is only the first reaction in the devaluing country. It should not be forgotten that a corresponding first reaction occurs abroad and that consequently ΔB in the devaluing country would be reduced even further. The reason for this is clear. The equivalent of ΔB abroad is a deterioration in its trade balance of an equal amount and, therefore, a reduction in income and expenditure there. These income and expenditure changes, by a process the reverse of that just described, induce hoarding and trade balance adjustments abroad. These adjustments, having the consequence of a partial reversal of the trade balance deficit abroad, tend to reduce the trade balance surplus of the devaluing country to something less than $\widetilde{\Delta B}$.

These first reaction responses in the two countries, then, tend to eliminate some of the initial improvement in the balance of trade in the devaluing country. They also elicit "second reaction" adjustments in the devaluing country and abroad. These, in turn, induce "third reaction" responses in both areas, and so on. Following the familiar income reverberations of the foreign trade multiplier, the effect upon the trade balance of the devaluing country of secondary and subsequent reaction is always to tend to improve its trade balance, with diminishing force for later reactions; the impact of the secondary and subsequent responses abroad is always to tend to reduce the trade balance surplus of the devaluing country, again with diminishing force. Normally, since the secondary reaction in the devaluing country improves its trade balance relative to what the balance would have been following first reactions in the devaluing country and abroad, the ultimate effect upon the trade balance of the devaluing country, call it ΔB^*, is something less than $\widetilde{\Delta B}$ as well.

The final effect of devaluation upon the balance of trade of the devaluing country (measured in its own currency) is given by the expression

$$\Delta B_1^* = \left[\frac{\left(\dfrac{\lambda_1}{\lambda_1 + \mu_2}\right)\left(\dfrac{\lambda_2}{\lambda_2 + \mu_2}\right)}{1 - \left(\dfrac{\lambda_1}{\lambda_1 + \mu_1}\right)\left(\dfrac{\lambda_2}{\lambda_2 + \mu_2}\right)} \right] \Delta B_1 \qquad (7\text{-}9)$$

where the subscript 1 refers to the devaluing country and the subscript 2 to abroad.[36] It will be remembered that the ΔB_1 is attributable to the impact of devaluation in the simple elasticities framework. It is assumed that the elasticities are such that devaluation brings an initial improvement in the trade balance, i.e., $\Delta B_1 > 0$. This is then multiplied by the bracketed expression derived from the absorption analysis, giving the final trade balance outcome of devaluation. This outcome is determinate given the percentage amount of the devaluation, the pre-devaluation money values of exports and imports, the four relevant price elasticities of supply and demand, and the marginal propensities to hoard and for the trade balance to deteriorate.

As Tsiang points out, however, there is a further required adjustment in the trade balance of the devaluing country [74, pp. 912–13]. This is not reflected in equation 7-9 nor is it encompassed by Alexander's more general formulation of this equation [1, pp. 36–37]. Typically, the sequence of income-induced reactions in the devaluing country and abroad initiate changes in relative price levels. The formula above allows for income-induced effects only, and not price effects, once the process gets beyond the elasticities stage. But at every stage of the multiplier analysis relative prices should have a bearing on expenditure decisions. This was seen in the discussion of the simple absorption approach. It is not enough to account for relative price effects, as Alexander does, in only the stimulus to the first reaction adjustment.[37] In Alexander's synthesis, the effects of relative price movements would be reflected in variations of v, λ, and μ for the secondary and subsequent reactions and, eventually, in the trade balance of the devaluing country. It is only possible to speculate on the nature of these variations and, in any event, the expression giving ΔB_1^* could no longer be as compressed as in equation 7-9.

Alternatively, relative price effects could be incorporated in the synthesis of elasticities and absorption approaches by defining import functions in terms of expenditures, rather than income, and by including a term which denotes the pure substitution (or expenditure compensated) elasticity of import demand with respect to the price ratio between domestic goods and imports. This is the method adopted by Meade [49] and

Tsiang [74]. Except under relatively restrictive assumptions, this alternative seems to provide no simpler basis for predicting the outcome of devaluation than would an extension of Alexander's synthesis. A truly realistic model would have to encompass relative price effects, as well as income effects, but if the price effects are insubstantial compared to the income effects, it would not seem cavalier to neglect relative price adjustments in order to gain analytical simplicity.

Even when price effects are eliminated from the absorption analysis sequence, the resulting expression for the effect of devaluation on the trade balance — equation 7-9 — is not a very manageable formulation. More than casual inspection is needed to determine the likely effects of devaluation, even given the assumption that the price elasticities, export and import values, and percentage devaluation provide an initial improvement in the trade balance of ΔB_1. Fortunately, the expression brackets in equation 7-9 can be greatly simplified so that intuition is more helpful, at least for the special case of pre-devaluation trade balance and a shifting of the total initial change in the trade balance onto domestic absorption. As Alexander points out, the value of the bracketed expression depends only on the ratios of the λ's and μ's in the devaluing country and abroad [1, p. 30]. Equation 7-9 is reducible to:

$$\Delta B_1^* = \frac{\Delta B_1}{1 + (\mu_1/\lambda_1) + (\mu_2/\lambda_2)}. \qquad (7\text{-}10)$$

From this final formulation of the synthesis of the elasticities and absorption approaches, it is apparent that the main lesson of the simple absorption approach has lost none of its force. There it was learned that devaluation improves the trade balance if it causes an increase in hoarding, i.e., if current absorption falls relative to current income. If devaluation generates no increase in hoarding, the trade balance does not improve. In the present formulation, given by equation 7-10, the equivalent of "no increase in hoarding" is a marginal propensity to hoard in the devaluing country of zero. In the limiting case, where λ_1 approaches zero, the denominator of the expression becomes infinite (as long as $\mu_1 \neq 0$) and ΔB_1^* approaches zero regardless of the size of ΔB_1. Thus, irrespective of how favorable to effective devaluation the price elasticities may be, this may be totally negated if the marginal propensity to hoard (either in the devaluing country or abroad) is zero. In contrast, if the λ's are large relative to the μ's in both countries, the denominator of the expression approaches unity and ΔB_1^* tends to be comparatively great, approximating ΔB_1. In this event, the entire trade balance consequence of devaluation in the simple elasticities formulation tends to "stick." The larger is λ relative to μ the greater is the ultimate change in the trade balance; the larger is μ compared to λ the smaller is the ultimate effect of devaluation on the balance of trade. Typically, the relative sizes of the marginal propensity to hoard and the marginal propensity for the trade balance to deteriorate determine the ultimate change in the trade balance, ΔB_1^*, for any given set of determinants of the initial change in the trade balance, ΔB_1. What, then, are the likely relative magnitudes of these marginal propensities?

Alexander proposes an *a priori* response to this question. He first notes the probable value of the ratio of μ to λ when it is supposed that the economy has extensive unemployment of resources. In this case, devaluation causes output to rise by ΔB_1 because of the assumption that the entire improvement in the initial trade balance results also in an equivalent increment to expenditures on domestic goods. In the unemployment case, output and real income rise together. Alternatively, it can be assumed that resources are fully employed at the time of devaluation. As used here, although of course the resource reallocation effect should be allowed for, this is tantamount to fixing output at the pre-devaluation level. Devaluation in this circumstance provides an initial improvement in the balance of trade, ΔB_1, but the consequence for the domestic economy is a pure price rise with no expansion of production in the devaluing county. Finally, Alexander summarizes the general case in which devaluation results in some increment to output and some increase in prices. Here the initial expansion of money income attributable to the devaluation is composed in part of an increase in real income and, since it is assumed that money income rises relative to real income, the excess of the increment to money income over the expansion in real income is due solely to a price rise.

Where output can be expanded without initiating price increases, λ_1 corresponds to the real marginal propensity to hoard, i.e., $\lambda_1 = (1 - \alpha_1)$. This is assumed to be positive and, in view of the discussion in the preceding section, it is most likely not large. In particular, the fact that its converse, the marginal propensity to absorb, includes expenditures on consumption *and* investment should not be forgotten. μ_1, which formally is the marginal propensity for the trade balance to deteriorate, is equal to the real marginal propensity to import when production is expansible. With unemployment, the increase in real income is not apt to pull goods or factors away from exports. Unemployed resources are drawn into use, expanding production of export substitutes as well as of other types of commodities. Thus, any deterioration in the trade balance is due entirely to the reaction of import demand to the expansion of output.

Where full employment exists at the time of devaluation, this, of course. is no longer true. Output is fixed and real income is constant as the prices of domestic goods and money income rise in the same proportion. In this event some of the money income-induced expansion in demand will spill over into the export substitute sector. Commodities which otherwise would be exported are drawn into domestic consumption and investment and factors of production transfer out of the export sector. The trade balance deteriorates because of a money income-induced expansion in imports and reduction in exports. With full employment, μ_1 is greater than with substantial unemployment of resources.

Equation 7-10 states, however, that the effect of devaluation depends on the ratio of μ_1 to λ_1. What influence does full employment have on the size of λ_1? Alexander suggests [1, pp. 32–33] that λ_1 is smaller if resources are fully employed rather than unemployed. With output fixed, λ_1 approximates the *average* propensity to hoard which is assumed to be zero by virtue of the assumption that the trade account is initially in balance. If real hoarding is a function of real income only, the proportional expansion of money income and prices raises money hoarding but not real hoarding. Since pre-devaluation hoarding is already zero, it remains zero after money income increases due to the price rise. But an increase in real income would cause an increase in hoarding equal to the change in real income multiplied by $(1 - \alpha_1)$. Since real income does not increase because of fixed output, λ_1 approximates zero. Of course, the change in prices initiates a cash balances effect which raises λ_1 above zero; but the cash balances effect is also operative in the unemployment case. λ_1 is therefore likely to be lower, even close to zero, when the economy is fully utilizing its resources.

Until now the ratio of μ_2 to λ_2 — the money income-induced response abroad — has been disregarded. In the synthesis it plays a role as significant as the ratio in the devaluing country. Here the relative effects of devaluation under diverse situations in the devaluing country are being discussed. Unless there is a deliberate effort to maintain full employment conditions abroad, it is not necessary to inquire about the difference in μ_2/λ_2 under full employment and unemployment conditions there. The initial impact abroad of a devaluation improving the trade balance of the devaluing country is a trade balance deficit and, correspondingly, a reduction in money income. To be sure, this fall in income breaks itself down into an output reduction component and a price decrease component. But with a positive effect of devaluation in the elasticities framework in the devaluing country, there seems to be no reasonable ground for supposing that this breakdown is different whether employment is full or unfull in the devaluing country at the time of the alteration of the exchange rate.[38] Therefore, the ratio μ_2/λ_2 can be assumed to be identical in the two employment cases. It may still be necessary to ascertain whether $\lambda_2 = 0$, for, if this is the case, there can be no ultimate improvement in the trade balance of the devaluing country. Again, however, this would seem to be invariant with employment conditions in the devaluing country. Only if the focus is on the practical question of the effect of devaluation in conditions existing at a given time must thought be given to μ_2/λ_2. Then equation 7-10 indicates that the money income-induced responses abroad deserve equal attention with those of the devaluing country.

As suggested above, Alexander's more general treatment of these phenomena is to assume that some proportion of the money income increase in the devaluing country is due to a price rise, the remaining proportion being attributable to an increase in real output. μ_1 and λ_1 are then hybrids, derived by taking weighted averages of the marginal propensities to hoard and for the trade balance to deteriorate for each of the pure money income expansion components. The weighting is done in accordance with the importance of the respective components. Thus, denote the proportion of the increase in money income in the devaluing country due to a real income expansion by ω_{1y} and that proportion due to a price rise by ω_{1p}. Then $\omega_{1y} + \omega_{1p} = 1$. Also, let λ_{1y} and μ_{1y} be the marginal propensity to hoard and for the trade balance to deteriorate as real income changes and, similarly, λ_{1p} and μ_{1p} are these marginal propensities for price level increases. Then the hybrid marginal propensities, i.e., those relevant to the expansion in money income due to a combination of real income and price increases, are given by:

$$\lambda_1 = \omega_{1y}\lambda_{1y} + \omega_{1p}\lambda_{1p} \quad \text{and} \quad \mu_1 = \omega_{1y}\mu_{1y} + \omega_{1p}\mu_{1p} \qquad (7\text{-}11)$$

Analogous reasoning could be applied to the non-devaluing country to derive a hybrid λ_2 and μ_2. These two sets of marginal propensities could then be inserted in equation 7-10 to provide an assessment of the effects of devaluation when money income changes in the two countries are composed of real income and price change components.

This is a purely formal procedure, allowing for a "hybrid" money income expansion in a mechanistic way. It does not reflect, as it should, the likelihood that the values of the λ_y's, λ_p's, μ_y's and μ_p's depend in some complicated way upon the relative magnitudes of the ω_y's and ω_p's. Recognition of this subtlety, however, is a frill that does not detract from the basic validity of the approach.

The prospects for improvement in the balance of trade of a country undertaking devaluation may now be summarized. The trade balance outcome, ΔB_1^*, depends, in the first place, upon the price elasticities of the country's import demand and foreigners' demand for the country's exports and the price elasticities of the supply of those imports and exports. Assuming initial trade account balance in the devaluing country, the value of either its imports or its exports and the percentage amount of the devaluation are also pertinent. These factors may give a ΔB_1 which is either positive or negative and also, of course, determine the absolute size of the initial change in the trade balance. This accounts only for the influences of the elasticities upon the trade balance and, since these effects cause changes in income, the influence of income-induced phenomena on the devaluation process must be considered.

These phenomena, in Alexander's synthesis, are encompassed in the ratios of the marginal propensities to hoard and for the trade balance to deteriorate in the two countries. Generally, the income-induced factors are responsible for forces which countervail the initial trade balance change of ΔB_1. On the one hand, these forces are completely offsetting if the devaluation is incapable of evoking any further hoarding in either country, assuming that the μ's are not zero. On the other hand, if both of the μ's are zero (and the λ's are different from zero), equation 8-10 shows that the offset is non-existent and the entire ΔB_1 is reflected in ΔB_1^*.

In the more typical instance, where both sets of the income-induced parameters are positive, it is important to establish their relative sizes. For convenience, assume that the ratio μ_2/λ_2 is constant, irrespective of conditions in the devaluing country. Given this, the synthesis supports the conclusion of the simple absorption analysis that devaluation is not likely to be substantially successful in improving the balance of trade when it is implemented in a fully employed economy: μ_1 is relatively large compared to λ_1, unless the latter is significantly influenced by the cash balances effect. And even so, there is a commensurate cash balances effect in the unemployment case, so that devaluation as a trade balance policy has more to commend it during periods of large-scale unemployment than during periods of full employment. Indeed, in the latter instance, μ_1/λ_1 may be so great that the improvement in the balance of trade from devaluation is negligible.[39] Other measures must then be employed if a sizeable improvement in the trade balance is required.

The Impact of Monetary Conditions

Both the simple elasticities and absorption approaches and, indeed, their synthesis as summarized above have been exceedingly casual about the monetary conditions implicit in the analysis. Generally, with the exception of the cash balances effect, it has been tacitly assumed that the money supply adjusted automatically to economic conditions, with the interest rate remaining constant. Absorption decisions were predominantly based upon changes in income and price levels. Since the interest rate was fixed by the implicit assumption of a completely elastic money supply, it could not affect absorption decisions in any meaningful way. That the rate of investment is somewhat sensitive to changes in the interest rate has no relevance in a constant interest rate devaluation model. Moreover, the possibility that saving is positively related to the interest rate, and hence that consumption is inversely related, has no bearing on the outcome of devaluation. If these hypotheses about investment and saving are valid, absorption should in fact be responsive to interest rate movements. Thus, the exclusion of interest rate adjustments from the devaluation model may lead to oversight of a potentially significant factor in the devaluation process.

Machlup [44] and Johnson [30] both cautioned that an important tacit feature of the absorption analysis is its image in the monetary sphere. Johnson noted the relatively short time limit on a trade deficit not supported by the creation of credit by the monetary authorities. Machlup had already stressed the same point [44, p. 273]: "Without continuing dishoarding or bank credit expansion, the negative trade balance could not continue. Every day of excess imports would bring a further reduction in the money supply . . . and, inevitably, a decline in absorption. A persistent import surplus, in the absence of autonomous capital imports, presupposes a policy of enabling the banking system to expand credit; it disappears when that policy is discontinued." But these two experts did little more than raise their eyebrows at the omission of other permissible assumptions about the efforts of the monetary authorities. In particular, they did not ask the important question of whether a monetary policy might be specifically designed to counteract those elements of the devaluation mechanism which tend to impede or undermine devaluation's effectiveness.

It was Tsiang [74] who, in an adaptation of the devaluation model developed by Meade [49], elucidated the impact of different monetary conditions on the devaluation mechanism. Even though Tsiang's model is possibly too simple, his analysis is mathematically intricate — indeed, his derivations are not presented — and his observations are based largely on the formal mathematical properties of his system. The inferences drawn from his model are, nevertheless, important in that they indicate the need to revise the more pessimistic conclusions of the elasticities-absorption analysis with its permissive monetary policy. The policy program consistent with Tsiang's model is also disarmingly simple compared to what is likely to be required in practice. Tsiang's analysis occurs basically within a two commodity framework. When the model is extended to four commodities, as Mrs. Flanders shows in a provocative article [19, pp. 404–11], it may be no mean feat to alleviate a balance of payments deficit by devaluation and, at the same time, keep the price level reasonably stable. Be that as it may, Tsiang's model is worth exploring further, even in a vastly oversimplified form; it incorporates an additional institutional feature into the analysis of the devaluation mechanism.

Tsiang's major alterations in the structure of the devaluation model based upon superimposing the elasticities and absorption approaches are two in number. First, in terms of the above treatment of the absorption approach, Tsiang assumes that absorption is a function not only of the level of money income but that it is also related to the interest rate.[40]

It has already been suggested that there is reason for supposing an inverse relationship between absorption and the interest rate. As the rate of interest rises, investment would fall and, possibly, consumption also — other things being equal, of course. Since the trade balance reflects the difference between the levels of income and absorption and since absorption is negatively related to the rate of interest, the trade balance itself should display a positive relationship with the rate of interest [74, pp. 916–19, 922].

Second, Tsiang brings a money sector specifically into the devaluation process. The demand for money in his model is directly related to the level of money income and inversely related to the rate of interest [74, p. 922]. It may be convenient to think of this money demand function as being a composite of a transactions demand function and a speculative demand function. These functions are familiar from Keynesian economics: the transactions demand relationship between money demand and income is positively sloped since it is assumed that an increase in income also increases the amount of money needed to meet payments arising from income-generating transactions; the speculative demand function, relating the demand for money for speculative purposes to the interest rate, is negatively sloped.[41]

Since it has heretofore been assumed that the money supply adjusted automatically to meet the economy's needs, a money demand function would have added nothing to the discussion of devaluation. But in making the contrary assumption, as Tsiang does, that the monetary authorities hold the supply of money constant, the money demand function becomes strategic. For if the money supply is fixed, any attempt to shift money balances between satisfying transaction demands and satisfying speculative demands is likely to induce changes in the level of income and in the interest rate. If, for example, the initial impact of a devaluation improves the trade balance and, hence, raises money income, a greater amount of money is then demanded for transactions purposes. With the supply of money held constant by the monetary authorities, fewer funds are available to meet the speculative demand for money and the interest rate tends to rise. If the hypothesis of an inverse relationship between absorption and the interest rate is accepted, an increase in the interest rate causes an interest-induced reduction in absorption and, presumably, an improvement in the trade balance.

Tsiang is even more deeply impressed with the positive role that the monetary authorities can play in the devaluation process. Not only does this interest-induced phenomenon tend to improve the trade balance; it is typically of enough significance to override destabilizing elements in the foreign exchange market. Indeed, Tsiang contends that interest-induced changes in absorption normally cause an improvement in the trade balance, even though devaluation occurs in a fully employed economy and even if the marginal propensity to hoard out of increases in money income is negative. Discussion of the simple absorption model concluded that full employment was not conducive to effective devaluation and that a marginal propensity to absorb in excess of unity, i.e., $\alpha > 1$, hence, $\lambda < 0$, results in devaluation causing a deterioration in the trade balance unless "direct effects" are countervailing. But this conclusion was based on the implicit assumption of a perfectly elastic money supply. Tsiang is assuming that the money supply is completely inelastic. With this sort of monetary policy, interest-induced hoarding is eventually capable of outweighing income-induced dishoarding, unless of course the speculative demand for money becomes infinitely elastic. Dishoarding cannot continue for long and if the interest elasticity of money demand remains finite and absorption is negatively related to the interest rate, a policy of holding the money supply constant eventuates in devaluation always improving the balance of trade [74, pp. 930–32].

CONCLUDING REMARKS

Devaluation analysis, intricate as this summary has shown it to be, has still somewhat further to go before it can be an absolute guide to policy makers. The analysis has yet to take into account a number of phenomena that complicate a real-life decision on whether or not to devalue. It has not considered the impact on the effectiveness of devaluation of meeting increased demands for traded goods out of previously accumulated inventories. Analysis has generally been conducted within a framework which precludes economic growth. Absorption has been related to the level of income but little consideration has been given to the possibility that absorption may also be related to rates of change in income, i.e., possible acceleration effects have been omitted from the analytical picture. The effects of competitive devaluation remain to be evaluated. There are other, perhaps significant, omissions but even without these additional complexities it would be taxing to weigh the pros and cons of devaluation in any particular situation.

Unless income can be increased, absorption must be reduced. That much is apparent. Whether devaluation can reduce absorption relative to income is the issue. The effectiveness of devaluation, it was noted, is intimately related to the type of monetary policy being pursued. Particularly when the devaluing economy is already operating at full capacity, a restrictive monetary policy is helpful. When the economy is underemployed, devaluation is doubly effective, improving the balance on trade account and expanding income and employment — although the devaluing country must be prepared to withstand the charge that it is "exporting its unemployment."

All this takes for granted fairly reliable estimates of the values of the relevant elasticities and marginal propensities and the availability of information about the importance of the direct effects. It also implies definite knowledge about the response of productive factors and output to the operation of the price mechanism. Yet information on elasticities and marginal propensities is far from reliable; knowledge of the internal response is incomplete. Given the understandable hesitancy of policy makers to eschew decisions which have far-reaching and uncertain results, without further analytical and empirical research (even in the limited sphere of trade balance measures), devaluation will receive less attention than it merits.

FOOTNOTES

1. Machlup asserts [44, p. 255] that in contemplating devaluation three questions of fact are significant. Will devaluation result in an improvement in the balance of payments? How much devaluation is required in order to eliminate a deficit of a given size? What is the magnitude of a deficit that can be eliminated by devaluation of a given amount? The answer to each of these questions depends equally on *a priori* reasoning and empirical determinations. The theoretical issues, *per se*, are probably best revealed by an examination of the first of these questions. Thus, throughout this chapter the devaluation mechanism must be primarily construed as encompassing those forces generated by devaluation which permit economists to determine whether the trade balance is likely to be improved. In focusing on this issue, deductions relevant to answers to the second and third questions can be inferred.

2. Unless otherwise stated, the term "elasticities," without a modifier, will mean price elasticities.

3. These conditions, especially when derived in a partial equilibrium context, are frequently called Marshall-Lerner conditions. The appellation does injustice to a host of other substantial contributions to the subject of exchange stability. In addition to Marshall [47, App. J] and Lerner [40, Chap. 28], see also Bickerdike [10], Yntema [77], Mrs. Robinson [59], Brown [14], Machlup [46], Meade [48], and Haberler [21; 22].

This "stability condition" approach to specifying the effectiveness of devaluation is not entirely appropriate on two counts. First, as Kemp warns [34, p. 314]: "The problem of determining the impact of a once-over devaluation on the balance of payments has often been identified with *the question of dynamic exchange stability*. In fact the questions are quite dissimilar. Moreover, a model which can answer one question cannot answer the other. The question of exchange stability calls for a model in which the rate of exchange appears as a *variable*, the value of which is to be determined by the system itself. [To determine the consequences of devaluation] however, call[s] for a model in which the rate of exchange appears as a *parameter*. We wish to know the implications of a once-and-for-all policy adjustment of the exchange rate." Second, the stability condition approach implies a balance in the exchange market, whereas devaluation would be contemplated only when an imbalance exists. Vanek [75, pp. 71, 72–76] rightly points out that the correspondence between the stability conditions and the specification of devaluation effectiveness is lost when imbalance is assumed. That the stability conditions themselves were modified by the pre-existence of a trade imbalance was noted much earlier in Hirschman [27].

It is appropriate to note at this point an interesting demonstration by Smith [62, pp. 815–16] that the size of the initial imbalance may be relevant to consideration of the effectiveness of devaluation. He shows that when the demand of the devaluing country for imports is inelastic, a large deficit may be improved by an increase in the domestic price of the foreign currency whereas a small deficit may be caused to deteriorate further.

4. Technically, since demand elasticities are normally negative, the statement should read, "must be less than minus one" in the algebraic sense. In the text, however, algebraic signs of the elasticities are ignored, reflecting conventional usage.

Moreover, the statement assumes that the trade account is in balance and that the percentage devaluation is relatively small. When it is assumed that the devaluation starts from a position of imbalance, the critical value for stability is altered. Additionally, it is necessary to specify whether the analysis is to be in terms of the foreign currency or in terms of the domestic currency. The imbalance is here taken to be measured in foreign currency terms. Devaluation will then improve a trade deficit, even though the sum of the demand elasticities is slightly less than one. See Hirschman [27] and Harberger [24, pp. 48–49]. A short derivation is found in Kindleberger [35, pp. 656–58]. A somewhat different approach, using exchange elasticities at the outset, is in Vanek [75, pp. 70–72].

5. The discussion in the text is based upon elasticities of supply and demand for exports and imports. Thus, it starts at an intermediate point unless complete specialization is assumed. Ellsworth [18] goes behind the export and import demand and supply curves by discussing their derivation from eight curves of purely domestic origin. This method eliminates the need to assume, unrealistically, that production is completely specialized.

6. With respect to relevant price elasticities, see the interesting remarks of Polak and Chang [58, pp. 51–54] and Mrs. Flanders [19, pp. 398–400].

7. It would be unfair to overlook the important, largely neglected contribution of Stolper [68; 69; 70; 71]. In many ways, his work presages the absorption approach. He demonstrates that a balanced change in trade turnover has varying effects upon income and employment depending upon the nature of the shift in the domestic average propensity to spend on consumption and investment.

8. For the present, assume that income and production or output are synonymous terms. This is in fact not true and important issues hinge upon distinguishing between them. To simplify exposition, these distinctions will for the moment be disregarded.

9. In an ingenious interpretation of the absorption approach, Johnson [30, pp. 158–59; also 29] classifies deficits according to whether they arise from stock or flow decisions and whether either of these types of decisions shows up in deficits on current or capital account. Stock decisions are those leading to an altered composition of a country's assets by substitutions between financial securities or goods and domestic money. Flow decisions are reflected in relative changes in current expenditures and current receipts. A balance of payments deficit is therefore a manifestation of dishoarding, or credit creation, or both. A deficit because of a stock decision is temporary, being self-correcting as the new asset composition is achieved, and will be of some, although not great, concern in this chapter. See also Machlup [44, pp. 272–73]. Following custom, a capital

account deficit, arising from a stock decision to convert domestic money into securities or from a flow decision to lend more than is currently saved, will not be admitted to the discussion. The discussion will therefore center on current flow decision deficits — those arising from decisions to absorb a greater amount of goods than is being currently produced domestically. This is consistent with the deficit concept usually implied by both "absorptionists" and proponents of the elasticities viewpoint. Some explanations of facets of the absorption analysis rest, however, on a stock decision concept of a current account deficit.

10. Black [11, p. 272] discusses the role of elasticities in facilitating or impeding this shift. This is also an important ingredient of Machlup's analyses [44; 45].

11. Alexander [2, p. 267] defines (real) hoarding as the difference between (real) production or income and (real) expenditure (absorption) on goods and services. This definition seems to conflict with the more conventional one, developed in monetary theory, of an increase in holdings of money balances. But Alexander simplifies, as does Black [11], by assuming the absence of international capital movements. With this assumption, the conflict is eliminated. Absorption can only exceed income if dishoarding — the spending of previously inactive cash holdings — takes place. If income exceeds absorption, idle cash balances will increase; hoarding, in both of the above senses of the word, will have occurred.

12. The conclusions of this paragraph are based on several simplifying assumptions. First, none of the marginal propensities can be negative. Second, the supply and demand elasticities must be such that devaluation results in an initial improvement in the trade balance. It is also helpful to assume that the entire initial change in the foreign trade balance of the devaluing country is reflected in an increase in domestic expenditures on domestic goods. Not until this totally domestic increase in expenditure causes induced income effects are there assumed to be leakages into hoarding. The consequences of relaxing this last assumption, as well as the assumption that devaluation starts from a position of initial trade balance, are elaborated in Alexander [1, pp. 34–37].

13. It should be apparent from this paragraph that Tsiang conceives of a composite marginal propensity to hoard made up of a change in hoarding due to a change in income and a change in hoarding due to changes in the interest rate. The latter component is usually positive and may be large. The former component may be negative. It is, however, the overall composite marginal propensity to hoard which is relevant to the outcome of devaluation. This is more likely to be positive when interest-induced phenomena are included in the argument.

14. This is not a necessary assumption for the demonstration. It is made for pedagogical reasons. Note that it is not required that $P_{m_1} = P_{x_1}$, and therefore that $Q_{m_1} = Q_{x_1}$, since trade is balanced. The condition of balance is merely that $P_{m_1}Q_{m_1} = P_{x_1}Q_{x_1}$ but for simplicity of demonstration it is assumed also that $P_{m_1} = P_{x_1}$. The diagrams are drawn to reflect this.

15. For this discussion when a demand or supply curve is said to be elastic (or inelastic) it must be assumed that the elasticity (or inelasticity) persists, even though the curve may have shifted or the relevant price-quantity "position" may have changed. One could, alternatively, assume that the percentage of devaluation is infinitely small. There would then be inappreciable shifts of or movements along the curves.

16. Díaz Alejandro [16] shows that, under certain assumptions, the trade balance may improve and output fall as a result of devaluation. The major assumptions — that the supply of domestically produced goods is completely elastic; that the supply schedule for internationally traded goods is "kinked," being perfectly elastic for price reductions and perfectly inelastic for price increases; and that devaluation redistributes income against wage earners — seem, as he suggests, to be most applicable to underdeveloped countries.

17. Machlup feels that careful distinctions should be made in absorption analysis in specifying the relevant functional relationships. He queries which among real domestic production, or real income, or real absorption is the crucial determinant of consumption, of income-induced investment, and of imports [45, pp. 443–45].

18. The single factoral terms of trade are a measure of the volume of imports that can be obtained for a given amount of factor input. An improvement in productivity improves the single factoral terms of trade, even though the net barter terms of trade remain constant. Thus, let the single factoral terms of trade be represented by $(P_{m_1}/P_{x_1})\phi_1$, where P_m and P_x are defined as before and ϕ is an index of productivity of the export sector. The numerical subscripts refer to time periods. For the single factoral terms of trade to improve $(P_{m_2}/P_{x_2})\phi_2 > (P_{m_1}/P_{x_1})\phi_1$. This may occur because $\phi_2 > \phi_1$ with $P_{m_2}/P_{x_2} = P_{m_1}/P_{x_1}$, or because $P_{m_2}/P_{x_2} > P_{m_1}/P_{x_1}$ with $\phi_2 = \phi_1$. It may also occur, even though $P_{m_2}/P_{x_2} < P_{m_1}/P_{x_1}$, i.e., net barter terms of trade deterioration, provided that $\phi_2 > \phi_1$ by a sufficiently large amount.

19. Recall that hoarding (H) is defined as $Y - A$ and, hence, equals B.

The discussion of this and the next section is in real terms. This suffices to illustrate the absorption approach and, as Alexander suggests [2, p. 266], the basic relationship of equation 7-2 holds in money terms as well. Machlup [44, pp. 269–70] has reservations about the equivalence of the absorption analysis in real and in money terms. He would argue for a discussion couched in money terms but he does not attempt to spell out an analytical framework in money terms.

A slightly different development of this equation, in which domestic production is broken down into output of "exportables" for home consumption and for export and output of purely domestic goods, can be found in Hemming and Corden [26, pp. 483–84, fn. 3]. The derivation leads to identical results, however.

20. In other words, βA shows how devaluation causes a change in absorption on the assumption that real income is fixed at its predevaluation level. This is an adaptation of the notation developed by Machlup [44]. It differs from Alexander's original notation [2] where equation 7-5 would have been expressed, with some obvious translations, as $\Delta B = \Delta Y - \alpha Y - \delta$, where δ may be considered as equivalent to βA.

The difference in notation has not raised any comment but it may be useful to point out that, strictly interpreted, equation 7-5 implies that the magnitude of the direct effects of devaluation upon absorption depends upon the level of absorption prior to devaluation. Devaluation's direct effects are encompassed in β and this changes the level of absorption, A, by the proportion given by β. Presumably, the greater A the greater is the change in absorption due to the direct effects of devaluation. This is not implied by Alexander's notation, where δ, the change in absorption due to the direct effects of devaluation, may or may not be independent of the level of absorption prior to devaluation. This difference, while inconsequential to the validity of the analysis, should be borne in mind when the direct effects of devaluation on absorption are discussed below. Is their magnitude dependent, or independent, of the prior level of absorption?

There is another ambiguity, in equation 7-5, arising from the use of ΔY to represent changes in both output and real income. For the trade balance to improve, output must rise relative to absorption. Interpreting ΔY in equation 7-5 in light of this, the first ΔY (just to the right of the equality sign) must denote changes in real income since it is assumed that absorption is a function of real income. But, as noted above, it is inaccurate to equate output and real income in every instance and the consequent inaccuracy is explored further below. Nevertheless, the tendency to ignore this distinction is understandable, simplifying the exposition as it does. Generally it is assumed in the exposition given here that changes in output and in real income are usually equal. The convenience of this is even more apparent in the alternative statement of the absorption equation in equation 7-6. Moreover, a moment's reflection on the problems of diagramming the absorption analysis, as is done below in Figures 7-4 and 7-5, if a distinction between output and real income is made, reinforces the convenience of this simplification.

21. This is important conceptually if the functional relationships are nonlinear, as they might well be. Moreover, as Alexander realizes [2, p. 274], the direct effects of devaluation on the level of absorption might vary significantly for small and large devaluations. As he puts it, some of the direct effects may be non-proportional in terms of the size of the devaluation.

22. The functional relationship between $\Delta A'$ and ΔY is here left unspecified. Consistent with Alexander's overall viewpoint, the diagram is drawn on the presumption that α is the same before and after devaluation — that α is unrelated to the magnitude of ΔY. It also presumes, as drawn, that βA is independent of ΔY. Neither of these presumptions may be true. Machlup [44; 45] is leery of the first; Alexander himself [2, p. 274] questions the second. In consequence of these two possibilities, the diagram merely states that $\Delta A'$ is some function (f) of ΔY. As it is drawn, however, the function is clearly specified as $\Delta A' = \alpha \Delta Y + \beta A$. The diagram has been drawn in this manner in order to simplify the exposition and to eliminate further complications from the diagram. See also the discussion of equation 7-7 below.

23. Note that none of the initial expansion can be due to an increase of import-substitute production. It has not yet been stipulated that the domestic price of imports rises due to devaluation and that, consequently, import substitution occurs. Indeed, there have so far been no domestic terms of trade changes admitted to the analysis of this section. Only the foreign price of exports has fallen because of devaluation; domestic export prices are as yet unaffected. In Alexander's analysis, and Machlup's extension of it, these price and substitution phenomena are encompassed by a "terms of trade" effect.

24. It is not necessary to "cap" ΔY, as it is ΔB, because the direct effects of devaluation do not affect income whereas they do affect the trade balance. Since the direct effects are excluded from the discussion here a distinction between ΔB and $\widehat{\Delta B}$ is necessary. There is no need for this with ΔY.

25. Moreover, the first three ΔY's in equation 7-7 stand for output changes while the second three refer to real income changes. As noted previously, in an open economy these need not be identical.

26. Michaely [51] provides an elaborate analysis of the impact of various income redistribution assumptions on the effectiveness of devaluation. The effects of devaluation upon the trade balance and income depend upon whether some productive factors suffer a reduction in their income shares and whether the money supply expands as rapidly as the price level increases.

Kahn [32, pp. 100–01] discusses the shift of income to exporters. He expresses a concern that income redistribution may be undesirable and that, therefore, unless the trade balance is substantially improved or income is substantially increased, devaluation may not be worth the costs. See also Smith [62, p. 813].

27. The brief interchange between Stopler [68; 69] and White [76] on the substitutability of import expenditures, outlays on domestically produced goods, and saving explores the devaluation consequences of the alternative possibilities of import reduction and an offsetting expansion of home-good expenditures or an offsetting increase in saving.

28. Letiche [41, pp. 130–51] shows that the validity of this conclusion depends upon the nature of money expenditure movements in the devaluing country and abroad. The simplest assumption to give a reduction in this price ratio is that expenditures in both places are constant.

29. Michaely [52] justifies the operation of this mechanism by proving that, on the one hand, if prices of traded goods rise relative to prices of domestic goods, absorption must fall; whereas, on the other hand, if absorption does not fall the relative price of traded goods cannot increase.

30. Jones [31, pp. 75–76] adds complexity to this situation by distinguishing between short-run and long-run effects of relative price changes upon the level of consumption and, hence, absorption. He defines his relationships in money terms but assumes that the basic "decision-relevant" relationship is in real terms. Shifts in (money) consumption outlays as (real) income changes depend, as he notes, on the (real) income elasticity of (money) consumption expenditures, which varies cyclically. Therefore, the relative price effects on absorption would depend upon the stage of the business cycle in which devaluation occurred.

31. This comment applies with much less force to Laursen and Metler [39] than to Meade [49], Harberger [24], and Stuvel [72]. It does not apply to Meade [48]. However, Laursen and Metzler analyze an issue quite different from the trade balance effects of devaluation. Their primary concern is with the impact of changes in the exchange rate on relative income levels. A high degree of economic sophistication is needed to reorient their analysis to explain the process by which the trade balance adjusts.

32. To overstate the case somewhat, a knowledge of *what* will happen to the trade balance with devaluation permits policy makers to decide whether to devalue. A knowledge of *why* the trade balance changes permits policy makers to decide how to change structural conditions in the economy so that devaluation will always improve the trade balance, and, further, gives some indication of the probable consequences of these structural changes for performance with respect to other economic goals.

33. It should be noted that this is not identical with the assumption that α, the real marginal propensity to absorb, is unity or less. λ is the marginal propensity to hoard increments of money income. Hence, only when money and real income change together is $\lambda = (1 - \alpha)$. This distinction is useful in the discussion below of the size of λ under full employment conditions.

34. The assumption that the initial impact of devaluation is $\Delta B = \Delta Y = \Delta A$ ignores the possibility, which Machlup stresses and Alexander appreciates, that the relative price movements caused by devaluation may force a direct adjustment in money absorption relative to money income. Thus, generally $\Delta B \neq \Delta Y \neq \Delta A$. Alexander explores the consequences of this inequality in [1, pp. 36–37] and provides there formulas which allow for its effects.

35. Both Allen [3] and Jones [31] consider the same kind of reversal factors. Indeed, Allen's discussion of his "final-balance ratio" and his use of the concept anticipates in crude form the basic approach of Alexander's synthesis. Allen notes that changes in exports and imports due to devaluation are counteracted to some extent by the impacts of foreign and domestic marginal propensities to save and to import. He did not work out the details of this effect to nearly the degree that Alexander did.

Jones' "dampening coefficient," which performs the same functions as Alexander's "reversal factors," compares the balance of trade outcome of devaluation when output in all countries is variable with the outcome when output is fixed.

36. The complete derivation of an expression equivalent to equation 7-9, along with a listing of the "necessary conditions," is in Alexander [1, Appendix]. The expression can also be obtained, with less mathematical elegance, by following the argument in the text of the article [1, pp. 26–30].

37. Alexander recognizes [1, pp. 36–37] the possibility that "money income induced price changes, or distributional or taxation effects, or whatever," as well as changes in real income, affect the relationships between changes in money income and hoarding and the trade balance. He allows for this, however, only by altering the assumption that the entire initial improvement in the trade balance, ΔB, results in an equal initial increase in money income and absorption.

38. If, contrary to the present assumption, it had been assumed that the devaluation in the pure elasticities framework had caused a trade deficit in the devaluing country, i.e., $\Delta B_1 < 0$, the effects of employment levels on μ_2/λ_2 would become relevant, for then money income abroad would be expanding.

39. Gehrels [20, p. 77] concludes, in his extension of the simple absorption approach, that the marginal propensity to hoard would have to be extremely close to zero in order that the balance show "no significant improvement." This finding does not seem inconsistent with Alexander's subsequent restatement of the position as expressed in this sentence. μ_1 is normally small and, hence, for the trade balance improvement to be negligible, λ_1 must be very small.

40. In Tsiang's approach (and Meade's too) the demand for imports is made a function of absorption rather than money income. This is an important distinction, providing a more stable import function than an import-income function would give. In Tsiang's model the relationship between absorption and income is influenced by the interest rate and the terms of trade. If imports were then related to income (but determined by absorption), the import-income relationship would be altered with changes in the interest rate and in the terms of trade. To consider how these changes affect the import-income relationship it is appropriate that imports be related functionally to absorption [74, pp. 920–21].

41. It is assumed that the speculative demand for money never becomes perfectly elastic with respect to the interest rate. That is, the possibility of a "liquidity trap" is assumed away. If the economy were in a liquidity trap, there would be no way to alter the interest rate. Since the effects of changes in the

interest rate upon the balance of trade are being pursued here, it is convenient to set the liquidity trap aside. Tsiang, however, includes this in his analysis. See, for example, his discussion of "Keynesian neutral monetary policy."

BIBLIOGRAPHY

[1] S. S. Alexander, "Effects of a Devaluation: A Simplified Synthesis of Elasticities and Absorption Approaches," *AER* (March 1959).

[2] _____, "Effects of a Devaluation on a Trade Balance," *SP* (April 1952).

[3] W. R. Allen, "A Note on Money Income Effects of Devaluation," *Kyk*, Fasc. 3 (1956).

[4] _____, "Stable and Unstable Equilibria in the Foreign Exchanges," *Kyk*, Fasc. 4 (1954).

[5] T. Balogh and P. P. Streeten, "Exchange Rates and National Income," *BOUIS* (April 1951).

[6] _____, "The Inappropriateness of Simple 'Elasticity' Concepts in the Analysis of International Trade," *BOUIS* (March 1951).

[7] W. Beckerman, "National Income, Exchange Rates and the Balance of Trade: A Note," *Econa* (August 1951).

[8] _____, "Price Changes and the Stability of the Balance of Trade," *Econa* (November 1952).

[9] P. W. Bell, "Model of Elasticity and Income Conditions for 'Perfect' Automatic Adjustment to Shifts in a Country's Export and Import Prices," Appendix to Bell, *The Sterling Area in the Postwar World: Internal Mechanism and Cohesion, 1946–1952* (1956).

[10] C. F. Bickerdike, "The Instability of Foreign Exchange," *EJ* (March 1920).

[11] J. Black, "A Savings and Investment Approach to Devaluation," *EJ* (June 1959).

[12] H. Brems, "Devaluation, A Marriage of the Elasticity and the Absorption Approaches," *EJ* (March 1957).

[13] A. J. Brown, "Trade Balances and Exchange Stability," *OEP* (April 1942).

[14] _____, "The Fundamental Elasticities in International Trade," in T. Wilson and P. W. S. Andrews (eds.), *Oxford Studies in the Price Mechanism* (1951).

[15] A. C. L. Day, "Relative Prices, Expenditures and the Trade Balance: A Note," *Econa* (February 1954).

[16] C. F. Díaz Alejandro, "A Note on the Impact of Devaluation and the Redistributive Effect," *JPE* (December 1963).

[17] H. S. Ellis, "The Dollar Shortage in Theory and Fact," *CJEPS* (August 1948).

[18] P. T. Ellsworth, "Exchange Rates and Exchange Stability," with a "Mathematical Supplement" by M. Bronfenbrenner, *REStat* (February 1950).

[19] M. J. Flanders, "The Balance-of-Payments Adjustment Mechanism: Some Problems in Model-Building," *Kyk*, Fasc. 3 (1963).

[20] F. Gehrels, "Multipliers and Elasticities in Foreign-Trade Adjustments," *JPE* (February 1957).

[21] G. Haberler, "Currency Depreciation and the Terms of Trade," in E. Lagler and J. Messner (eds.), *Wirtschaftliche Entwicklung und Soziale Ordnung* (1952).

[22] _____, "The Market for Foreign Exchange and the Stability of the Balance of Payments," *Kyk*, Fasc. 3 (1949).

[23] F. H. Hahn, "The Balance of Payments in a Monetary Economy," *REStud* (February 1959).

[24] A. C. Harberger, "Currency Depreciation, Income, and the Balance of Trade," *JPE* (February 1950).

[25] _____, "Some Evidence on the International Price Mechanism," *JPE* (December 1957).

[26] M. F. W. Hemming and W. M. Corden, "Import Restriction as an Instrument of Balance-of-Payments Policy," *EJ* (September 1958).

[27] A. O. Hirschman, "Devaluation and the Trade Balance: A Note" *REStat* (February 1949).

[28] E. P. Holland with R. W. Gillespie, *Experiments on A Simulated Underdeveloped Economy: Development Plans and Balance-of-Payments Policies* (1963), Part II, "The Balance of Payments of a Growing Economy," by R. W. Gillespie.

[29] H. G. Johnson, "The Balance of Payments," in Johnson, *Money, Trade and Economic Growth* (1962). Reprinted from *Pakistan Economic Journal* (June 1958).

[30] _____, "Towards a General Theory of the Balance of Payments," in Johnson, *International Trade and Economic Growth* (1958).

[31] R. W. Jones, "Depreciation and the Dampening Effect of Income Changes," *REStat* (February 1960).

[32] R. F. Kahn, "The Dollar Shortage and Devaluation," *Econia Internaz* (February 1950).

[33] M. C. Kemp, *The Pure Theory of International Trade* (1964).

[34] _____, "The Rate of Exchange, the Terms of Trade and the Balance of Payments in Fully Employed Economies," *International Economic Review* (September 1962).

[35] C. P. Kindleberger, *International Economics,* 3rd ed. (1963).

[36] G. Kleiner, "Exchange Rate Adjustments and Living Standards: Comment," *AER* (December 1955).

[37] M. Kreinen, "Effect of Tariff Changes on the Prices and Volume of Imports," *AER* (June 1961).

[38] S. Laursen, "The Market for Foreign Exchange," *Econia Internaz* (November 1955).

[39] _____ and L. A. Metzler, "Flexible Exchange Rates and the Theory of Employment," *REStat* (November 1950).

[40] A. P. Lerner, *The Economics of Control* (1944).

[41] J. M. Letiche, *Balance of Payments and Economic Growth* (1959).

[42] _____, "A Note on the Statistical Results of Studies on Demand Elasticities, Income Elasticities, and Foreign Trade Multipliers," *Nordisk Tidsskrift for Teknisk Økonomi* (1953).

[43] F. Machlup, "Elasticity Pessimism in International Trade," *Econia Internaz* (February 1950).

[44] _____, "Relative Prices and Aggregate Spending in the Analysis of Devaluation," *AER* (June 1955).

[45] _____, "The Terms-of-Trade Effects of Devaluation upon Real Income and the Balance of Trade," *Kyk,* Fasc. 4 (1956).

[46] _____, "The Theory of Foreign Exchanges," *Econa* (November 1939, February 1940). Reprinted in American Economic Association, *Readings in the Theory of International Trade* (1949).

[47] A. Marshall, *Money Credit and Commerce,* 1st ed. (1923).

[48] J. E. Meade, *The Balance of Payments* (1951).

[49] _____, *The Balance of Payments: Mathematical Supplement* (1951).

[50] L. A. Metzler, "The Theory of International Trade," in H. S. Ellis (ed.), *Survey of Contemporary Economics,* I (1948).

[51] M. Michaely, "Devaluation, Cost Inflation, and Supply of Exports," *Econia Internaz* (February 1956).

[52] _____, "Relative-Prices and Income-Absorption Approaches to Devaluation: A Partial Reconciliation," *AER* (March 1960).

[53] G. H. Orcutt, "Measurement of Price Elasticities in International Trade," *REStat* (May 1950).

[54] I. F. Pearce, "A Note on Mr. Spraos' Paper," *Econa* (May 1955).

[55] _____, "The Problem of the Balance of Payments," *International Economic Review* (January 1961).

[56] J. J. Polak, *An International Economic System* (1953).

[57] _____, "International Trade Theory — Discussion," *AER* (May 1952).

[58] _____ and T. C. Chang, "Effect of Exchange Depreciation on a Country's Export Price Level," *SP* (February 1950).

[59] J. Robinson, "The Foreign Exchanges," in American Economic Association, *Readings in the Theory of International Trade* (1950). Reprinted from Robinson, *Essays in the Theory of Employment,* 2d ed. (1947).

[60] W. E. G. Salter, "Internal and External Balance: The Role of Price and Expenditure Effects," *Ec Rec* (August 1959).

[61] K. M. Savosnick, "National Income, Exchange Rates and the Balance of Trade," *Econa* (May 1950).

[62] W. L. Smith, "Effects of Exchange Rate Adjustments on the Standard of Living," *AER* (December 1954).

[63] E. Sohmen, "Demand Elasticities and the Foreign Exchange Market," *JPE* (October 1957).

[64] _____, "The Effect of Devaluation on the Price Level," *QJE* (May 1958).

[65] _____, "The Effect of Devaluation on the Price Level: Reply," *QJE* (November 1958).

[66] _____, *Flexible Exchange Rates: Theory and Controversy* (1961).

[67] J. Spraos, "Consumers' Behaviour and the Conditions for Exchange Stability," *Econa* (May 1955).

[68] W. F. Stolper, "The Multiplier, Flexible Exchanges, and International Equilibrium," *QJE* (November 1950).

[69] _____, "The Multiplier, Flexible Exchanges, and International Equilibrium: Reply," *QJE* (February 1953).

[70] _____, "A Note on Multiplier, Flexible Exchanges and the Dollar Shortage," *Econia Internaz* (August 1950).

[71] _____, "The Volume of Foreign Trade and the Level of Income," *QJE* (February 1947).

[72] G. Stuvel, *The Exchange Stability Problem* (1950).

[73] J. Tinbergen, "Unstable and Indifferent Equilibria in Economic Systems," *Revue de l'Institut International de Statistique* (1941).

[74] S. C. Tsiang, "The Role of Money in Trade-Balance Stability: Synthesis of the Elasticity and Absorption Approaches," *AER* (December 1961).

[75] J. Vanek, *International Trade: Theory and Economic Policy* (1962).

[76] W. H. White, "The Multiplier, Flexible Exchanges, and International Equilibrium: Comment," *QJE* (February 1953).

[77] T. O. Yntema, *A Mathematical Reformulation of the General Theory of International Trade* (1932).

CHAPTER 8

Persistent Disequilibrium: Dollar Shortage and Dollar Glut

PREFATORY STATEMENT

A country's international transactions on trade account are rarely in balance. For one thing, net flows of intended international capital transactions must be offset. But assuming these net intended capital movements to be zero, the values of exports and imports are seldom equal. Trade imbalance of this sort may be due to transitory and random phenomena, or to conditions whose effects on the balance of trade cancel out over the course of a business cycle, or to factors giving rise to long-term payments deficits or surpluses. Conventionally, only trade imbalances attributable to the last set of influences are encompassed by the term persistent disequilibrium. In "normal" times, these long-term imbalances are the source of greatest concern about balance of payments problems. If they persist long enough, they can be the cause of substantial reductions in a country's standard of living; their long endurance can also cause severe disruption of the operation of the international economy.

It is not without reason, then, that the potential sources of persistent balance of payments disequilibrium have been carefully studied. This interest was accentuated in the first years of the postwar era by a shortage of dollars, wherein foreigners found it difficult to acquire the means of meeting their payments obligations to the United States. Interest was further heightened when the dollar shortage turned, too abruptly it would seem, into an apparent dollar glut. The fear of recent years that foreign holdings of dollar balances are in excess of the amount deemed desirable and that the United States faces potential embarrassment in meeting its foreign obligations are manifestations of this. One of today's vital economic issues is whether the sustained international payments imbalance of the United States is an endemic feature of the world economy and, if so, whether the imbalance tends to be self-reversing within a reasonable period of time.

This issue cannot be judged, of course, without some analytical explanation of persistent payments disequilibrium. In fact, there is no

351

dearth of hypotheses about postwar international payments behavior. Naturally, not all are equally supportable or reliable. Which among the several better hypotheses best fits the facts of the period — which offers the best explanation upon which to base policy decisions — remains a moot question.

Immediately after World War II and well on into the decade of the fifties, economists throughout the world were troubled by the disparity between American receipts and expenditures on international account. Foreigners were wanting to spend more dollars on international transactions than Americans, at going exchange rates, were willing to supply on the basis of normal economic motivations. There is little doubt that this situation had existed for some time. Some scholars believe it began during the mid-nineteenth century. Other — and perhaps more authoritative — sources suggest that it began just after World War I. Like World War II, the events of 1914–18 gave rise to a nearly insatiable demand for dollars for reconstruction and rehabilitation. But the general deficiency of dollars did not disappear in the Twenties and Thirties. Rather the dollar deficit of these decades was accommodated by the extensive private capital outflows from the United States during the 1920's and by persistent depression in the United States and a vast redistribution of international reserves during the depression decade. The term "dollar shortage" was coined to encompass and dramatize the persistence of these phenomena.

In view of the evidence of the years through 1949, it is not surprising that dollar shortage was expected to be a reasonable projection for the future. Keynes' dissenting position that there were strong, natural equilibrating forces — so that "the chances of the dollar becoming dangerously scarce in the course of the next five to ten years [were] not very high" [44, p. 185] — was, in view of the eminence of the man, most notable for its inability to gain adherents. What is surprising is that the belief in dollar shortage should have continued into the late 1950's. Except for the moderate balance of payments surplus of 1957 (an aberration attributable to the Suez crisis in the fall of 1956), the U.S. balance of payments has been in deficit since 1949.[1] As a consequence of these continuing deficits, the dollar is no longer in short supply; rather it is readily available to most of the developed nations, although not, apparently, to the underdeveloped ones. Moreover, since 1958 the dollar has been merely one among many freely convertible currencies whereas in the early postwar years it was virtually alone in being generally convertible.

One would think that these changes would be reflected in attitudes toward dollar shortage. Yet, in a series of lectures given in April 1957,

Crowther, the Managing Director of *The Economist,* revealed that he had become "more convinced" that the worldwide deficiency of dollars was "permanent and organic" [18, p. 34]. Even as late as mid-1960, when most experts were alerted to the precarious international position of the dollar, MacDougall, author of the most comprehensive empirical study of the dollar problem [60], remained skeptical. He found no persuasive reasons in the payments data for the 1950's indicating anything more lasting than a brief respite from the dollar shortage. "The view that my previous judgment should," he summarized, "be reversed — that, far from the trend in the U.S. balance of payments being favourable, it is more likely to be adverse — is not, therefore, one to which I should subscribe" [61, p. 63].

It is not necessary to search far for an explanation of what might appear to be a substantial recognition lag. In the first place, with the dollar being demanded for use as international reserves, some deficit in the U.S. balance of payments is entirely consistent with external equilibrium [see Chap. 9 below]. Second, if a temporary shortage of real resources abroad undergirded the postwar payments problem, then a U.S. surplus followed by a deficit when foreign resource positions are recovered is, as Bernstein suggests [10, p. 101], a realistic policy goal. Third, U.S. foreign commitments in a period of "cold war," especially when one's allies cannot be expected to carry a significant share of the burden, seem to have entailed a rather substantial payments deficit.[2] These are reasons for not accepting at first blush the U.S. payments deficits since 1949 as evidence of the demise of the dollar shortage and for not proposing its replacement by a "dollar glut."

Nevertheless, after so many years of U.S. balance of payments surpluses, deficits for more than a decade could not help but arouse suspicions of a surfeit of dollars. Quite naturally, Americans became apprehensive about the long-run prospects of the U.S. payments position — an apprehension directly responsible for two quickly mounted appraisals of the situation, one by the Joint Economic Committee [80] and a second by Salant *et al* [74]. Some of this concern was a direct outgrowth of fears of the impact on the U.S. economy of integration in Western Europe — fears which gained currency because of the noticeable deterioration of the net U.S. international reserve position in the first year of European Economic Community operations. But more to the point, the concern was also due to the behavior of U.S. exports and imports relative to GNP: compared to the early postwar years, during the Fifties the ratio of exports to GNP fell at the same time that there was an increase in the import-GNP ratio. This pattern pointed to a lack of "competitiveness" of U.S. productive activity, relative to that abroad, as a source of the payments difficulty. The U.S. balance on trade account, therefore, became the subject of careful scrutiny.

Emphasis on the trade position might seem somewhat misplaced. A very substantial expansion in dollar payments abroad has occurred on capital and government accounts in the latter half of the 1950's. Williamson [85, esp. pp. 526–29] reasons that the causes of the payments deficit are to be found in the net private capital account. The capital account responds to profit opportunities so that when United States growth is sluggish, as it has been since 1955, there is an expanding net export of capital. Conversely, if the United States is growing rapidly, capital exports fall off. Furthermore, the longer the periods of stagnation or exhilaration the greater is the change in the net capital account. A similar position is that of Bernstein. His provocative thesis [79a, esp. p. 968; 27a, pp. 77–78] attributes the U.S. deficit primarily to a relatively large increase in capital and government outlays overseas.

Nevertheless, focus on the trade position in today's world is justified. It reflects the attitude that the existing international balance on trade account is not so sacrosanct that all other components of the balance of payments must adjust to it. Rather, it is as defensible — perhaps more so — to posit that the U.S. trade position itself must adjust or be adapted to whatever foreign commitments, especially of a political nature, Americans decide to incur. According to this approach, the degree of competitiveness of American productive effort, i.e., the trade account position, is to be judged relative to U.S. foreign commitments and not vice versa.

Much of the intensive empirical research on U.S. international competitiveness has focused almost exclusively on the relative position of American export goods. This focus is found, for example, in the studies of Miss Romanis [73], the Department of Commerce [82], Balassa [80a], the Department of Agriculture [81], Fleming and Tsiang [21], and the British National Institute of Economic and Social Research [68]. Why this is the case may not be obvious since the observable import-GNP ratio has until recently risen much more, proportionately, than the observable export-GNP ratio has fallen.[3] The stress on export competitiveness rests on the belief that the trade figures are, in part, deceptive indicators of changes in the trade position. Specifically, the reduction in the export-GNP ratio understates the true loss of export competitiveness, although the movement of the import-GNP ratio is a fairly accurate representation of U.S. import-substitute competitiveness. Among the reasons for this assertion are, as Harris suggests [27d, pp. 6–7], the widespread relaxation abroad of discriminatory practices against U.S. goods and services, particularly since 1955, and the fillip to exports given by P.L. 480 in which U.S. agricultural exports are subsidized and "local currency" is accepted in payment.

Yet, empirical research on competitiveness, either export or import-substitute, skirts the heart of the dollar problem unless it comes to grips with the assignment of possible causes of the change in international competitive positions. At a level of causality suggested by Cooper [27b, p. 139], alterations of competitive position may be accommodating or autonomous. Only the latter give rise to a change in the international payments balance. For example, if the foreign expenditures of the U.S. government were to be drastically curtailed because of an easing of "cold war" tensions, a relative increase in domestic demand and prices should induce, with a time lag, an accommodating deterioration of the U.S. trade position so that external balance is retained. In contrast, if there is a reduction in the trade position due, say, to a change in tastes for foreign products — that is, an autonomous change in the trade account balance in the sense that change is not induced by the domestic adjustment process — the decline in the trade position is not necessarily accompanied by an equivalent offsetting change elsewhere in the payments balance. In this event, the external balance deteriorates. At the more fundamental level, then, the assignment of causes to "the" dollar problem consists of specifying and analyzing the possible reasons for autonomous changes in the competitive position of the U.S.

Before turning to this task, it is advisable to reiterate several points about the issues of competitiveness and the ascription of causation to balance of payments problems. It must be remembered, as Balassa points out [80a, pp. 29–30], that the doctrine of comparative advantage places limitations on the meaning of changes in international competitive positions. The concept is, in a real sense, meaningful only under a regime of fixed exchange rates. When exchange rates are flexible, although frictions are a relevant consideration, autonomous changes in international conditions result in adjustments in the commodity composition and geographical pattern of trade, rather than in the competitive position. Changes in competitiveness, in the conventional sense of generally enhanced or diminished ability to sell at home and abroad, are the product of autonomous international phenomena when relative prices are not adjusted automatically by movements in the exchange rate. Moreover, while a country's competitive position may be altered for all commodities, the operation of the law of comparative costs requires that, at any point in time, the change in international competitiveness relates only to a limited number of specific types of commodities. As a static phenomenon, heightened or reduced international competitiveness cannot logically be attributed to all commodities produced. In a dynamic situation, however, this conclusion does not hold. When the bases of comparative advantage are undergoing quick transformations and the internal adjustment processes are impeded by imperfections and frictions, competitive positions may well be deteriorating or, alternatively, improving in every line of economic activity.

The relationship between the adjustment mechanism and the size and progression of international disturbances determines the extent and nature of the payments imbalance. A perfectly efficient adjustment process, no matter what the upsetting condition, eliminates the possibility of payments imbalance. However, following Harris's lead [28, p. 170], if the adjustment mechanism is relatively halting or incomplete,[4] given the nature of the disturbance, a payments imbalance can be lasting and serious. Alternatively, given the existing, imperfect adjustment mechanism, the size and timing aspects of the international disturbance will set the tone of the imbalance.

In focusing on the dollar problem, the international disturbances themselves are conventionally subjected to analysis; discussions of the adjustment mechanism are typically considered independently, with almost no attempt to integrate the two issues. The resulting analysis of the dollar problem is artificial but also pedagogically convenient. This artifice will be followed here as well. But it must always be borne in mind that any treatment of the dollar problem which ignores the adjustment process is, itself, based upon an implicit conception of the degree of efficiency of the adjustment mechanism. Different opinions of the efficiency of the adjustment process, as well as of the relative importance assigned to different possible disturbances, are sources of experts' disagreements about the dollar problem. There is no way to resolve this, however, short of an unattainable quantification of the efficiency of the adjustment process, together with an accurate, detailed evaluation of the relative significance of unsettling disturbances.

A further elementary point needs clarification. It is asserted above that analysis of the *trade* position is warranted from a review of existing balance of payments data. To a large extent this too is done as a matter of convenience. Although there are significant exceptions — Kenen [43], Williamson [85], Bell [80b], and Salant *et al* [74] are examples — the vast bulk of the studies of the dollar problem has been concerned with commodity exports and imports. Non-trade account items have been shortchanged. The most rudimentary knowledge of balance of payments analysis warns against singling out any particular component of the payments statement. Many of the items in the balance are very intimately interrelated. Should one of the components change, alterations in other components will be induced. It is questionable procedure, then, to examine balance of payments statements, *per se,* for "causes" of possible disequilibria, although this is not to deny that the examination may suggest avenues of approach. Rather, to explore the basis of the dollar problem the analyst must go behind the payments accounts. He must, within the context of a given adjustment mechanism, seek out "real" explanations of changes in comparative cost conditions, of relative profitability of foreign and domestic investment, and of attitudes and commitments of a politico-international nature.

356

Extended polemics on the meaning of dollar problem lead very quickly to diminishing returns. Depending upon the definition of the concept, some scholars have denied the existence of the dollar problem, as, for example, Harrod [30, pp. 42–43] (but note also his [31, chap. IV]) and Bloomfield [12]. However, a much larger number believe that the dollar problem exists — an attitude which must be adopted if the problem is to be discussed at all. Still, among those who accept the reality of the dollar problem, there is reasonable divergence of opinion as to its conceptual basis. The most tenable concept seems to be one which equates the dollar problem with a relatively persistent disequilibrium in the balance of payments of the U.S. The payments disequilibrium is usually designated as a payments surplus or deficit, even though that shorthand is not precisely accurate. A payments disequilibrium in which intended expenditures exceed intended receipts (when converted at the appropriate exchange rates) may nevertheless be realized as a balance of payments surplus.

The tendency to equate the dollar problem with a payments disequilibrium is fortunate.[5] While any single definition of dollar shortage or glut would not command majority acceptance, there is widespread agreement on the general dimensions of payments disequilibrium. This agreement follows the usage of disequilibrium developed by Nurkse [69] and later elaborated by Meade [65, Chap. I]. Meade's definition follows [65, p. 15]:

. . . an 'actual' balance-of-payments deficit [may be defined] as the actual amount of accommodating finance used in any period of time . . . and a 'potential' balance-of-payments deficit as the amount of accommodating finance which it would have been necessary to provide in any period in order to avoid any depreciation in the exchange rate without the employment of exchange controls, import restrictions, or other government measures especially devised to restrict the demand for foreign currencies. It is, of course, this 'potential' deficit (or the corresponding 'potential' surplus) which is the proper measure of . . . disequilibrium.

In order to constitute a dollar problem, this disequilibrium should be a general phenomenon vis-a-vis the vast majority of the other trading nations, as indeed it has been. While the existence of a multilateral trading network serves to dilute exchange pressures, manufacturing and primary producing countries alike must experience a dollar pinch if a dollar shortage is to be diagnosed. As Balogh notes, a more complicated situation exists when the U.S. payments disequilibrium is not generalized to most countries [5, pp. 250–51]. If primary producing areas generally are capable of exporting to the U.S. and earning dollars at the same time that manufacturing nations are not, a competition between the U.S. and "other" manufacturing countries might well develop in the primary producer markets. The primary producing countries would then feel no ill effects from the "quasi-dollar shortage." [6] Quite the contrary; they would be able to select and effectively bargain among the various suppliers of manufactured goods, to the particular disadvantage of the "other" manufacturing nations if, as is assumed here, the U.S. has a competitive superiority in manufactured items. The quasi-dollar shortage of the other manufacturing countries would be aggravated by the ability of primary producers to exercise freedom of import choice but the primary producers can only gain.

The matter of the degree of persistence required of a payments disequilibrium before it can properly be called a dollar problem is not precisely definable; or if definable the definition must be largely arbitrary. On pragmatic grounds, the amount of international reserves dictates the duration of a disequilibrium that can be sustained without the need to undertake conscious adjustment measures. With fixed exchange rates any country without international reserves would almost certainly have a continuous "dollar problem." But a dollar problem, in the sense developed in the literature, is not established by the mere fact that a country is forced into overt adjustments. Rather it seems preferable to define a dollar problem on the assumption that international reserves are adequate [see Chap. 9]. Then a dollar problem surely implies a payments disequilibrium of longer duration than the business cycle. Beyond that, however, it is not possible to designate an agreed-upon time period. Dollar problem, then, means persistent balance of payments disequilibrium, where persistence is interpreted to mean extending beyond the length of a business cycle and ideally over several cycles.

Persistence does not mean that the disequilibrium, as manifested in the balance of payments accounts, must be continuous, although it should be one-directional on the whole. That is, a disequilibrium that vacillates between payments deficits and surpluses must be found either to be associated with one of the two apparent manifestations of dollar problems — excessive dollar demands or excessive dollar supplies — or to be simply an equilibrium situation. It would be the latter if the payments deficits and surpluses normally tended to cancel out over the cycle, assuming, of course, that demand and supply curves in the exchange markets have not been artificially altered. Suspicion of the non-existence of a dollar problem would also be justified if, over a series of cycles, there were payments deficits in the "on" cycles and surpluses in the "off" cycles, with a long-run cancelling. A dollar problem is presumed to exist if the deficits and surpluses did not average out over the cycle. The fact that what is being studied is the "marginal part of a marginal part" [7] and that sporadic and exceptional circumstances affecting the payments balance arise from time to time warns the analyst not to expect uniformity — deficit or surplus but not both — in the realized payments magnitudes. It is uniformity in the underlying causes of persistent disequilibrium that must be sought.

That the causes of payments imbalances must be inherent in the economic organism is a further requirement for existence of the dollar problem. Hard and fast rules of what is and what is not intrinsic to the economic system are not necessary. The analyst must exercise his judgment. On the one hand, wars, reconstructions, and natural catastrophes are possible causes of disequilibrium that are probably inadmissible on the ground that they are not inherent in the economic system. Depressions, on the other hand, are admissible. Inflations are less clear-cut. It is difficult to make a case that inflation can be self-generating without passivity on the part of the government. Is it therefore advisable to exclude inflation as a possible source of the dollar problem because the government may be considered a political instrument which does not inhere in the economic system? An affirmative answer would be an unnecessarily strict interpretation of the scope of the economy. In any event, the consensus is that inflation must be included among the possible causes.

☐ CAUSES OF PERSISTENT PAYMENTS DISEQUILIBRIUM

The sufficient condition for a dollar problem is, then, a payments disequilibrium of a long-term nature — the cause of which inheres in the operation of the world economic system. The disequilibrium manifests itself in a U.S. payments deficit or surplus. Permanence of the disequilibrium is not essential; persistence is. But this implies merely two types of dollar problem, definable in terms of the net payments balance. When, as here, the dollar problem is classified according to causation, rather than according to its accounting manifestations, the number of types is greater.

Short-term Causes and Skeptical Approaches

The incorporation of the time dimension and of the inherence quality means that disequilibria caused by forces of a short-term or transitory character or of an extrinsic nature can be excluded from analysis of the dollar problem. These kinds of forces fall into three categories, all of which have appeared in the literature with notable frequency and authority. Insofar as the U.S. payments imbalance rests on these types of forces, it would not be, according to the definition above, a dollar problem. Rather these explanations of the disequilibrium represent a discrediting of the dollar problem concept itself. In view of their persistence, however, these short-term explanations merit some attention.

Perhaps the most noted proponent of a short-term rationale of the U.S. payments imbalance is Lary. He invokes special disturbances which, coinciding in a relatively short time-span, have forced the U.S. payments position into substantial deficit [52; 53, pp. 23ff]. He cites the non-parallelism of business cycles at home and abroad, the upsurge of U.S. demand for foreign automobiles, the Suez crisis and its aftermath, the 1959 steel strike in the U.S., and shifts in U.S. cotton pricing policies. These events are relatively recent and would be responsible for the "dollar glut" of the last few years. Perhaps it is not so unusual to attribute a deficit of a few years standing to exceptional circumstances. The dollar shortage, in contrast, lasted for several decades. Yet, even here, according to Lary [53, pp. 6–7], the persistence of imbalance ". . . did not repose . . . on some unyielding structural disequilibrium. . . . It derived rather from the extraordinary concatenation of misfortunes that befell the world over this period." [8]

A similar argument weighing against the dollar glut hypothesis, although there is no proposed analog for the dollar surplus, is that the behavior of certain commodity markets has been the chief culprit.[9] Steel, engineering products, automobiles, aircraft, cotton, and others are often noted. Much of the empirical work cited above points to this conclusion. Evidence of this sort can be misleading, however. Any of the major long-run causes of the dollar problem could well reveal themselves in disruptions in particular commodity markets, especially in an imperfect economic situation with relatively immobile factors of production. As Balassa [80a, pp. 41, 49–50] and Lary [52, pp. 422–23] suggest, if a "localized" cost-push explanation of inflation is plausible in the steel industry, for example, relative inflation could underlie many of the special commodity situations. Special commodity problems are even more apt to arise if the dollar problem is caused by technological change considerations or demand effects of the demonstration variety. It is not to be expected that technological improvements will occur largely simultaneously in a whole host of goods or that changes in tastes will affect a relatively large number of commodities, except insofar as these changes are a consequence of new accessibility rather than of altered production costs and tastes themselves. All this is, of course, accepted. Nevertheless, possibly because of an understandable reluctance to face squarely the possibility of a dollar glut — but possibly because it is correct — special commodity conditions continue to be used to explain the current U.S. payments position.

The concept of accessibility — of the availability of commodities and of markets — is the basis for the third of the short-term causes of U.S. payments disequilibrium.[10] It has been employed to explain both the durable U.S. payments surplus and, lately, its payments deficit. Again the implication is that neither imbalance is a dollar problem. In explaining both the surplus and deficit, accessibility has taken on a hybrid aspect. If, on the one hand, accessibility of foreign commodities accounts for the recent U.S. deficit, then the imbalance will not be persistent. The idea, as suggested by MacDougall [61, pp. 41–42] and Lary [53, p. 53], is that Western Europe and Japan have only recently begun to exploit the vast opportunities of the U.S. market. For several decades these opportunities were open to them in terms of product costs and design but were foreclosed to them by wars, capacity shortages, depressions, steep trade restriction measures, poor sales organizations, and the like. Progressively, and especially since 1955, these barriers to foreign exports to the U.S. have been reduced with a resulting U.S. payments deficit. Once this relative foreign supply shortage is eliminated, the U.S. payments deficit will presumably disappear (via something like an acceleration effect) and perhaps a surplus will reassert itself.

On the other hand, if the sources of inaccessibility to the U.S. of foreign goods just mentioned were at the bottom of the U.S. payments surplus, inaccessibility, as an independent cause, lacks the quality of inherence. To be sure, some of its elements are intrinsic, as indicated above. But some are not. The relative importance of these various elements of accessibility cannot be quantified and whether capacity shortages (in the sense above) and trade restrictions inhere in the operation of the economy—and not in the political system — is a moot question. Moreover, once the supply deficiencies are substantially eliminated, they will no longer be an important element of the payments disequilibrium, although relative price considerations may well supplant shortages in the analysis. Thus, as applied to either type of imbalance, the accessibility argument disallows the existence of a dollar problem unless the bases of accessibility are relative prices and incomes. Then, of course, accessibility is subsumed under one of the long-term explanations compatible with the dollar problem.

Cyclical Causes and Asymmetries

Cyclical fluctuations in income and prices are certainly an inherent characteristic of Western economies. Their pervasiveness and generality and the Keynesian emphasis on the foreign trade multiplier in the adjustment process have led a number of scholars to seek the cause of the dollar problem in cyclical ups and downs. Unlike the short-term forces depicted above, cyclical factors can indeed be the source of a truly persistent dollar problem if the economies' reactions to the cyclical mechanism are in some sense asymmetrical.[11]

Hoffmeyer [36, p. 64] shows that even in those dynamic income adjustment models that assume that at least one economy is unstable in isolation,[12] a persistent payments disequilibrium will not arise from symmetrical responses to the business cycle. A symmetrical cyclical response will generate payments surpluses and deficits; the process is all too familiar. But unless the argument partakes of the features of relative secular exhilaration or stagnation, a cyclically symmetrical response will wipe out, during the expansion phase of the cycle, the payments imbalance it has created during the contraction phase. As an explanation of the dollar problem, asymmetries must be discovered in the adjustments of economies to cyclical disturbances.

One of the first to stress the possibility of asymmetrical reactions to income fluctuations was Kindleberger [46, Chap. 5]. He ventured that a dollar shortage would occur if the U.S. were to overcompensate for payments deficits and undercompensate for surpluses — and conversely in the rest of the world.[13] This was possible, he surmised, if the U.S. were more depression-prone than the rest of the world; that is, if the U.S. tended relatively to enter contractions earlier, if U.S. contractions progressed more rapidly, and if they were more protracted than in other countries. The suggestion of these particular compensation asymmetries was, as Kindleberger recognized, at variance with traditional income analysis, wherein it was asserted that most countries tended to undercompensate for surpluses. However, Kindleberger felt that domestic investment effects were an important consideration which the traditional multiplier analysis usually ignored. If the U.S. tended to be relatively depressed and have underutilized capacity, so that domestic investment was unlikely to respond to an export surplus, the surplus would be undercompensated. But under the same stagnant conditions, if a payments deficit developed because of an autonomous reduction in exports, investment in the export industries might be reduced sufficiently to over-balance the drop in saving induced by the income change. In this event, the U.S. could overcompensate for the payments deficit, tending to generate an over-all payments surplus over the business cycle.

This over-all U.S. surplus is only possible, in what is essentially a two-country model, if the rest of the world has the opposite compensation asymmetry. And probably it does. Other countries, especially the developing nations, may tend toward excessive aggregate demand and an increase in their exports might induce further domestic investment. Income would over-expand relative to the needs of payments balance; a deficit could result. If exports were to decline, however, the buoyant conditions might cause domestic investment to be well-maintained so that income would not fall sufficiently to induce the required reduction in imports. None of this was established inductively but at the *a priori* level a plausible case can be made for a cyclically generated, persistent dollar shortage.[14]

Taking another approach, MacDougall observes [59, pp. 198–99] that the U.S. response to price fluctuations may also represent an asymmetrical pattern giving rise to a dollar shortage, although it does not seem reasonable that a reversal of the reactions of the U.S. and the rest of the world would suffice to explain a dollar glut. (Nor does MacDougall suggest that it would.) In this proposal MacDougall utilizes the kinked demand curve, so familiar in the theory of oligopoly, but with a new twist. The U.S. long-run price elasticity of demand for imports, Mac-Dougall believes, is relatively higher for price increases than for price reductions,[15] while presumably this is not the case abroad. If this is granted, an increase in the prices of U.S. imports will result in a substantial reduction in the volume of imports and the development of alternative domestic supplies. The establishment of import-substitute industries will, by increasing domestic output of import-type goods, shift inward (to the left) the U.S. demand curve for imports. Thus, even though import prices subsequently fall to their previous level, producers abroad will not be able to recover their original share of the U.S. market. Since the foreign demand for imports is not kinked, this kind of response will not be found abroad. The consequence would be a tendency, over the cycle of price fluctuations, for the U.S. to run a payments surplus.

Moreover, by altering relative mechanisms of adjustment, a kinked U.S. demand curve for imports may cause further dollar shortage. On the one hand, in a world of existing dollar shortage, a relative downward adjustment of foreign prices would bring about an expansion of U.S. expenditures on imports of relatively modest proportions. On the other hand, during a dollar surfeit, foreign price increases would elicit a substantial reduction in U.S. import expenditures. Given, then, the kinked import demand curve and the comparative strengths of the reactions to upward and downward price movements, purely random fluctuations in the factors affecting world trade would establish a tendency toward dollar shortage.

If relative differences in price flexibility in the U.S. and abroad are considered, there is yet another candidate for a cyclical cause of the dollar problem. In this instance, the evidence seems to support the likelihood of a dollar glut rather than a shortage. Cooper has suggested [27b, p. 162] that the existence of excess industrial capacity is less likely to result in price cuts in the U.S. than in the rest of the world. Assuming, therefore, equi-elastic import demand schedules and assuming that cyclical activity creates initially the same degree of underutilization of plant — or a greater underutilization abroad — a deficit would tend to develop in the U.S. balance of payments during worldwide contractions. Since presumably foreign producers respond to excessive pressures on plant capacity by raising prices to the same extent as their American counterparts, there is no offsetting tendency for the U.S. to run payments surpluses during cyclical expansions. Furthermore, raw materials prices are, generally speaking, relatively more flexible and represent a comparatively larger component of product costs abroad which, as prices fall, further reduces the prices of foreign goods relative to American ones. The combined effect is a relative downward, but not upward, stickiness of U.S. prices, and a likelihood of a U.S. payments deficit over the business cycle as a whole.

Long-term Causes and Relative Competitiveness

Neither the short-term phenomena nor asymmetrical cyclical reactions have held center-stage in scholarly discourses on the causes of the dollar problem. The controversy over causation has concerned itself primarily with the forces of a secular nature which determine shifts in relative competitive trade positions and, through them, the character of the dollar problem. As Fleming and Tsiang observe [21, p. 219], this is not to imply that all long-term factors which affect the balance of payments must work through competitive positions when, as is usually the case, competitiveness is defined in terms of export supply conditions in exporting countries. One of the more popular explanations of the dollar problem — that based on the demonstration effect — does not affect competitiveness at all. In general, though, explanations of the dollar problem which highlight long-persisting phenomena have had relative competitiveness as their direct focus.

The complexity of these long-term causes varies considerably. In at least one case — the explanation which ascribes the dollar problem to relative rates of productivity change — the discussion has taken on a definite labyrinthine quality. In other cases, the supporting argument is less tortuous. Fortunately, the number of classes of long-term cause is not great; but the variations within some of these classes are significant and a high tribute to scholarly imagination. Rarely is one of these long-term explanations found in a straightforward and unadulterated form. Amalgams are the rule, even though this is sometimes painstakingly suppressed. Moreover, any number of the protagonists can, with modest effort, be found to have changed ground radically; not only because what seemed to be a dollar shortage has now seemingly become a dollar glut and the abrupt and largely unpredicted shift must somehow be explained but also because new evidence continues to come to light.

These are facts of life that must be accommodated. They complicate the task lying ahead. While it is possible, without much unfairness, to assign the various contributors to the discussion to their "camps," it must be acknowledged that no one champion of any long-term explanation could properly be called a purist. Certainly none would deny the relevance of the short-term and cyclical factors. But more than that; even within the categories of long-term explanations, no purist will be found. Rather, positions are matters of emphasis, of degree, and, frequently, of pragmatism. In what follows, these issues will not be stressed but it is essential that they be kept in mind. Insofar as possible the various categories of long-term cause will be expounded in essentially a pure form, with detail and nuance as seems warranted by the pedagogical value of the theoretical arguments.

Currency valuations and productive capacity / When the accessibility of goods that could be traded was discussed above, under the heading of short-term factors, it was not at that time associated with the possibility of under- or overvaluation of the dollar vis-a-vis other currencies. Recognizing that the U.S. payments deficit first appeared in 1950 — in the year following the widespread devaluations of approximately 30 per cent relative to the dollar — it seems reasonable to attribute the change from long-standing dollar surplus to "persistent" deficit to the currency revaluations. Yet apart from the substantial deficit in 1950 (related to exceptional Korean War conditions), it was necessary to explain why the 1949 devaluations took until the latter half of the 1950's to have a sizeable impact on the U.S. payments balance. The inaccessibility argument was called upon to explain this sluggish adjustment. Thus a hypothesis combining elements of relative currency valuations and of productive capacity conditions was proposed, notably by Hinshaw [35] but also by Furth [23, p. 433], Triffin [27e, p. 232] and Schlesinger [75, p. 288], to account for the switch-over from dollar shortage to dollar glut.

While Cooper does not support this hypothesis,[16] he provided, in his doctoral dissertation [16, pp. 166–68], a careful elaboration and critical assessment of its theoretical merits and implications. Foreign currencies (at least those of industrial countries) were overvalued, it is maintained, relative to their equilibrium prices in the immediate postwar period. This overvaluation was to a substantial degree responsible for the U.S. payments surpluses. When it finally became apparent that devaluation was a necessary condition to eliminate foreign payments deficits, the consequent changes in exchange rates were made excessively large in order to insure confidence in the devaluing currencies and to reduce speculation.[17] As it turned out, the price elasticities of demand for imports were greater than had been anticipated and supply elasticities for exports were lower. The devaluations therefore created an excess demand gap for European and Japanese industrial products which could not be eliminated until productive capacity expanded. Capacity expansion was a slow process despite government measures to reinforce normal market incentives, since prices abroad were not allowed to rise sufficiently relative to prices in the U.S.[18] Thus, although the devaluations made foreign industrial products potentially price competitive with U.S. products — probably excessively so — the shortage of productive facilities in overseas industrial areas permitted the U.S. for a time to overbalance a price competitive disadvantage by a superior advantage on non-price competitive grounds. In due course growth of capacity abroad erased the U.S. non-price competitive margin; the relative price competitive positions achieved by the devaluations, heretofore latent, asserted themselves; and consumers in the U.S. and elsewhere transferred their purchases away from U.S. suppliers.

The validity of this hypothesis as a theoretical explanation of the dollar glut rests upon a breakdown or short-circuiting of the price mechanism. When the demand gap opened up because of the devaluations, why did not relative prices adjust to clear the market? Why did not the devaluations begin immediately to have an impact? The premise is, of course, that the demand gap endured because relative prices did not adjust even with the lapse of adequate time. Since these markets are highly oligopolistic and controlled, the short supply abroad was rationed through a non-price method. Cooper [16, pp. 169–73] suggests, if prices had adjusted as called for by the competitive pricing model, these European producers, having relatively low costs after the devaluations, would have received substantial economic rents. Since negotiated wages are highly sensitive to profit levels, the European producers chose to ignore the possibility of immediate, large profits — which would have been bargained away too quickly. They took refuge in their capacity shortages rather than raise prices to the competitive level and hence did not satisfy a significant portion of the potential demand. Choice of this option was warranted also on the ground that internal demand pressures in Europe were, during the first half of the 1950's and earlier, particularly insistent and if producers had succumbed completely to these, any international price advantage they had gained would have rapidly evaporated.[19] Presumably European productive capacity, in some absolute sense, was recovered around 1953 but when it was juxtaposed to internal and external demand conditions, the more meaningful concept of capacity, it was found to be relatively deficient until after the 1956 Suez crisis.

While this analysis was proposed as a separate category explaining the dollar problem, Cooper maintains that it was fundamentally a variety of the inflation-deflation thesis. Presumably Triffin would also defend this position, although probably for different reasons. Cooper's supporting logic [16, pp. 174–75] rests on an examination of the potential and actual effects of capacity growth on relative price levels. The rapid expansion of production facilities abroad helped restrain price increases there, a process facilitated by high elasticities of supply of other factor inputs as well. There is no doubt but that foreign industrial productive capacity was catching up with a demand that could have been growing more rapidly. Exports of industrial products of foreign countries did, after all, increase. Hence, especially after 1953, the progressive reduction of supply shortages abroad made foreign prices lower relative to those in the U.S. than they otherwise would have been. The shift in relative price levels in favor of other industrial countries reduced, possibly eliminated, the necessary competitive advantage of American industrial products and the

U.S. payments balance went into deficit. As MacDougall observes: "The important thing is whether there are sufficient items whose costs are lower at home, and sufficiently lower, to give a balanced trade, or rather, in the case of the United States, a trade surplus sufficient to cover heavy non-trade expenditure" [61, p. 14]. The extraordinary expansion of overseas industrial capacity in an inflationary context in the U.S. and abroad, in Cooper's view, mitigated foreign price increases there; no commensurate effects were felt in the U.S. Certainly, excessive devaluation contributed to this condition but, in the absence of capacity growth and an economic structure which facilitated non-price rationing, the once-for-all competitive advantage gained from the devaluations would have been quickly wiped out by foreign inflationary pressures. The currency valuation and productive capacity thesis, then, could really appear as an elaboration of the inflation-deflation argument.

Size and self-sufficiency / An obvious fact stands out in the figures on world and U.S. international trade: the U.S. is a gargantuan economy which participates relatively little, compared to its own national output, in international trade. Yet, of the world's aggregate of international trade, the share contributed by the U.S. is exceptionally large. That this large relative and absolute size and the self-sufficiency of the U.S. economy may have an important bearing upon the world payments disequilibrium has not escaped attention. The U.S. economy, because of size and autarky, felt less of the strains of an open economy and was less likely to adapt to these strains than any other participant in the world trading system. This placed a considerable bias in the world economy favoring persistent surplus in the U.S. payments. Notably, this line of argument was not concerned with a cause of disequilibrium, *per se,* but rather with degrees of proneness to economic adjustment in the event of payments disequilibrium. Nor can this argument, without becoming grossly unrealistic, be turned around to explain a dollar glut.

The large absolute and relative size of the U.S. meant that it did not have to respond to the inflow or outflow of international reserves to as great an extent as the foreign countries had to respond to reserve flows.[20] With this relative immunity from payments pressures and the fact that surpluses are rarely if ever as embarrassing as deficits, there was a tendency toward deflation abroad. But with deflation just as intolerable abroad as in the U.S. and with the U.S. and the various international organizations discouraging use of trade and payments controls, it was natural that the foreign deflationary tendencies should have been effectively countered. In consequence, a world shortage of dollars arose.

The subtlety of this argument should be noted. Foreign countries were not relatively inflation prone; they were, rather, relatively adjustment prone to deficits — compared with the U.S. Because of its size, the U.S. could bear, if no other factors were pertinent, greater reserve losses

— greater payments deficits — than foreign countries. But at least one other factor was pertinent. Deflation, as a means of adjustment, was no more permissible abroad than in the U.S., the result being a tendency to payments deficits abroad.[21] This argument was differentiated from the inflation-deflation hypothesis by its emphasis on market size and by the fact that the inflation or deflation proneness in the U.S. and abroad was assumed to be equal. Like the preceding argument, however, this analysis of the effects of size and autarky could easily be treated as a subset of the inflation-deflation thesis.

A somewhat different case that size matters is attributable to MacDougall [60, pp. 346–48]. Again the presumption was that there is no real basis for a persistent payments disequilibrium; rather the adjustment process is one-sided and weighted in favor of a U.S. payments surplus. If payments surpluses, and hence deficits, are entirely random (in terms of time sequences and location) among the various countries, only a surplus of the U.S. is likely to be substantial enough to cause worldwide difficulties. Because GNP in the U.S. is so large, it could absorb with no appreciable inflationary effects a payments surplus of several billion dollars. If any other country were to generate a surplus of this magnitude, that surplus would represent such a large proportion of that country's GNP that inflation could not be avoided without extreme effort. Since a payments surplus is a form of saving, another way of stating this position, according to Kindleberger [47, p. 389], is that foreign countries, unless acting in concert (which is ruled out by the randomness assumption), would have to save an impossibly large share of their GNP, over and above their domestic investment outlays, if they were to be able to discomfort the whole world. The share would not, however, be impossibly large for the U.S. to save; rather in the case of the U.S. it need not even be exceptional.

The effect of the assumption of randomness takes on special significance in this argument. It implies a high improbability of appreciable U.S. deficits. It rules out any systematic reason for a group of foreign countries, whose aggregated impact may well be substantial, to run a payments surplus. If payments disequilibria are random, however, there is by assumption no necessary tendency for the U.S. to incur a persistent payments surplus. This can only occur, given the assumption, where the countries' adjustment processes are skewed.

This form of the size argument resolves itself into one of relative adjustment proneness. More to the point, however, the assumption of random imbalances undermines the underlying approach of students of the dollar problem. Their quest is precisely for forces giving rise to systematic, non-random payments disequilibria. If these forces can be found, differential adjustment processes become merely refinements. Moreover, the forces causing systematic disequilibria offer prospects of credible explanations of both dollar glut and shortage, whereas size and skewed response patterns can reasonably explain one or the other, not both.

Disparate and biased productivity changes / Differences in productivity provide the basis for international trade. But, according to the doctrine of comparative advantage, these differences are of a special sort. That international differences in over-all average levels of productivity exist is obvious — but not particularly relevant in the pure theory of international trade. If productivity differences are the same for all products, discrepancies in levels of productivity between nations can, and under the usual classical assumptions would, be completely offset by international differences in money income and by exchange rate adjustment so that international trade would not take place. Transportation costs aside, if only productivity levels differed, commodity prices, when converted at the equilibrium exchange rate, would be identical for all countries. The special sense in which productivity differences make international trade economically advantageous is that productivity differences between countries must vary from one industry to another. The internal "productivity structures" must differ between countries. This is the situation which Ricardian comparative cost analysis presupposed and which the Heckscher-Ohlin model attempts to explain.[22]

So much is elementary. Nevertheless, assuming that productivity structures vary internationally so that there is a basis for trade, a number of scholars have asserted that differences in levels of productivity are the cause of the dollar problem. None of these arguments is in strictly static terms. For then, complete absence of an international adjustment mechanism would have to be assumed. If there is an operative adjustment mechanism, given international productivity differences cannot underlie the dollar problem unless the adjustment forces are very sluggish and weak. Indeed, just after World War II, Graham contended that the dollar shortage is to be explained by a breakdown which resulted from the fact that the world's "pecuniary institutions [were] all but perfectly designed to prevent" international equilibrium [24, p. 1].

At that time, however, no one had emphasized international differences in productivity change as an explanation of the dollar problem, although in a series of studies [8; 7; 3; 4] Balogh had earlier offered disparate productivity changes as a possibility and was soon to formulate an emphatic but vague statement. Williams [83; 84] and Haberler [25, pp. 438–39], too, were to pinpoint relative productivity changes in their analyses of the dollar shortage. Even when changing productivity is stressed, however, a perfectly effective adjustment mechanism would prevent the appearance of persistent payments imbalance. But given the imperfect international adjustment processes, a dollar problem is a distinct likelihood in a dynamic setting, a point stressed by both Robertson [72, pp. 53–62] and Bernstein [10, p. 103]. Those who espouse disparate rates of productivity change as a cause of the dollar problem are assuming implicitly that technical change disrupts worldwide competitive advantage patterns systematically and too rapidly for the imperfect adjustment mechanism. Johnson [40c, esp. pp. 105–10], however, explicitly incorporates aspects of the adjustment process into his analysis.

The seminal work on the consequences of different rates of productivity change is the renowned lecture of Hicks on the long-run dollar problem [34]. The primary focus of his analysis was the consequences of reductions in the real costs of production[23] for the various terms of trade and for real income and much of the subsequent discourse his ideas generated has had this emphasis. This perspective derives largely from Hicks' assumption that international adjustments in relative prices and incomes would maintain payments equilibrium. His primary interest was in comparing the welfare and terms of trade conditions of the pre-productivity change and post-productivity change equilibria. Hicks' analysis, and that of ensuing elaborations, was essentially comparative statics. Only by expert between-the-lines reading could the dynamic properties of his model be discerned. This framework tended to gloss over some of the interesting payments problems, the offspring of a sluggish adjustment mechanism in a world economy continuously subjected to disparate rates of technological progress.

To illustrate the balance of payments effects of technological change, imagine two countries in initial trade balance each producing an import-substitute and a commodity for export.[24] Assume that a uniform (over the export good and the import-substitute) increase in productivity takes place in country A, productivity in country B remaining unchanged. On the further assumption that money income in B is constant while it rises in A proportionately to the increase in productivity, commodity prices in both countries will remain unchanged.[25] The potential price effects of the assumed productivity change in A are cancelled by the assumptions about income. The income increase in A, however, is most likely to result in an expansion of A's expenditures on imports (B's exports) and an increased domestic demand for A's export goods. With a uniform productivity increase, country A tends to develop a deficit in its trade balance. Only if A's income rises by less than its productivity increase, initiating price effects in the export and import-substitute sectors favoring A's trade balance and countering the income effect,[26] can A's payments remain in equilibrium. Thus with a uniform productivity increase in A, the net barter terms of trade will move in favor of B; the price of A's exports falls relative to the (fixed) price of its imports. Conversely, the factoral terms of trade move in A's favor; the value of A's productive factors rises relative to that of B's factors. But here the argument creates an internal inconsistency: an improvement in A's factoral terms of trade, if productivity and income in B are constant, requires a substantial, rapid increase in A's income.

What is the likelihood that A's income will rise sufficiently and that B's income will in fact remain unchanged? The adjustment mechanism helps supply the answer. Hicks thought that A's income is not likely to expand rapidly enough to permit B's income to be constant. He assumed, therefore, that B will be forced to deflate. This is necessary for balance of payments equilibrium. If A's income does not rise sufficiently, the income effect favoring B's trade balance may be smaller than the price effects favoring A's balance. The deflation in B sets in motion compensatory income and price effects, tending to improve B's trade position. Evidently, the balance of payments outcome of a uniform productivity change in A depends upon whether A lets its income increase rapidly enough and upon the income and price elasticities of demand.

If A's income adjustment is inadequate and B is willing to deflate, B's trade balance is the better off (relative to what it would be if income adjustments are ruled out) — since its income elasticity of demand for A's exports is high and its price elasticity is low, preferably inelastic. B's balance is also improved more if A's income elasticity of demand for B's exports is high and its price elasticity for B's exports is low, again preferably inelastic.[27] If B does not deflate, however, A's income elasticity of demand for B's exports must be even higher and its price elasticity lower still. Thus, while there is an improvement in B's real income as a consequence of uniform productivity change in A, the trade balance effects are anything but obvious. The initial impact of a uniform innovation is to give A a trade surplus. The less prone A is to an upward income adjustment and the less likely B is to deflate the greater is the presumption that B's trade balance will tend to remain unfavorable. If A stands for the United States and B for the rest of the world, a dollar shortage may or may not develop from a rapid, uniform increase in American productivity. The demand elasticities, as noted above, are an essential consideration. Under the simplifying assumptions of this analysis — constant costs, price and income elastic demands, and fixed exchange rates — a dollar shortage is likely.

So much for uniform, disparate rates of productivity change. The major contribution came as Hicks explored the consequences of biased productivity change. Again following his treatment, imagine that a productivity improvement occurs in making A's export good but with no change in productivity in making A's import-substitute or in the production of either of B's goods; that is, assume an export-biased technological change in A. If money income remains constant in both countries, the price of A's export good will fall relative to the prices of all other goods which do not change. The quantity of A's exports to B must increase.

What happens to the value of A's exports depends, of course, on B's price elasticity of demand for imports. Hicks supposed that A's export value will remain unchanged, implying unitary demand elasticity, and that trade will continue to be balanced. Under the usual assumption of relatively elastic import demand, A's export-biased innovation would open up a trade surplus for it if, as is assumed, income in each country is stable. But the barter terms of trade turn in favor of B.

Should A's income increase rather than remain fixed, the export-price effect favoring A's balance will be weaker, assuming B's price elasticity of demand for imports is greater than one. Moreover, an income effect would be brought into play, tending to improve B's trade balance. The barter terms of trade are less favorable to B than when A's income is stable and the factoral terms of trade turn in A's favor. Should B deflate, a further improvement in B's trade balance would result. Both the new price and income effects would tend to expand the value of B's exports and decrease its imports.

Again, it can be seen that the balance of payments result of an export-biased productivity change in A is determined by the relevant income and price elasticities and by the efficacy of the adjustment process. The case of export-biased productivity change is similar to that of uniform technical change. With uniform, disparate productivity change, A's income had to expand less than proportionately to the decrease in its real production costs in order to prevent its trade balance from becoming adverse. With export-biased improvement in A, any expansion in A's income, B's income being constant, tends to open up a trade deficit by increasing A's imports (an income effect) and decreasing, relative to a fixed income, its exports (a price effect).

So far it has been implicitly assumed that the income expansion in A is restricted to the export sector.[28] This is unlikely. Since factor prices will rise with a general income increase in A, the price of A's import-substitute will increase along with the price of the export good. A's imports will therefore grow because of income and price effects, along with the shrinkage of its exports. This import-substitute price effect has no exact analog in the case of uniform productivity improvement. There, as A's income increased, it resulted in a movement of the price of A's import-substitute back towards the pre-innovation price. In effect, the income movement in A tended to eliminate a favorable (for A's trade balance) import-substitute price effect created by the uniform productivity change. An export-biased technological change, in contrast, resulted in no such favorable initial import-substitute price effect. Nevertheless, general income expansion in A does bring an import-substitute price effect into operation which engenders an expansion in A's imports. With uniform productivity change, A's income increase tends to eliminate the drop in imports — as a consequence of the cost reduction in A's import-substitute.

With export-biased technological improvement, there is no initial drop in imports to eliminate. Thus, given the adjustment mechanism and the demand elasticities, there is a presumption that export-biased innovation in A is more favorable to B's trade balance than is uniform, disparate technological progress.

Hicks claimed that the innovating country was most favorably affected, and the non-innovating country unfavorably affected, by a productivity change that reduced the production cost of the import-substitute. In the United States, he asserted, productivity was forging ahead more rapidly than elsewhere during the twentieth century and, since a dollar shortage had arisen, the rapid productivity change must have been heavily import-biased.[29] Contrastingly, during the nineteenth century innovation was predominantly export-biased — not only in the U.S. but in the United Kingdom — so that neither a dollar nor a pound shortage materialized.[30]

The mechanism by which import-biased, disparate technological progress influences the trade balance follows a pattern similar to the patterns above. Assume that productivity in the import-substitute sector of A increases, productivity in A's export sector and in B remaining constant. If income in each country remains fixed, the price of A's import-substitute falls relatively and, assuming price elastic demand, A's expenditures on imports (B's exports) should fall. If trade is to remain balanced, A's income must rise. In the unlikely event that the increase in income is limited to the import-substitute sector, a rise in factor prices in this sector will prevent the price of the import-substitute from falling as far and a sectoral income effect favorable to B will be activated. The extent of the increase in A's income that is required to return to trade balance, given the import-biased innovation, varies inversely with the price and income elasticities of demand for A's imports. Moreover, with income change restricted to the import-substitute sector, there is no change in either the barter or the factoral terms of trade.

It is more probable, however, that A's income will increase in both its import-substitute and export sectors. The resulting impact on the balance of payments, once again, is complex. The import-biased innovation with income in A held constant tended to open up a surplus in A's trade balance as A's consumers shifted away from imports into the import-substitute. Relative price movements initiated this adjustment. As before, expansion of A's income tends to reverse this import-substitute price effect, diminishing A's surplus. In addition, as income and factor prices rise in the export sector, the price of the export good rises relatively, since productivity there remained constant. Therefore, assuming B's demand for A's export good is price elastic, the value of A's exports drops. These effects, tending to eliminate A's trade surplus, are reinforced by the income effect in A. The barter terms of trade turn against B, since the price of its export good is constant, whereas the price of A's export good rises, due to the increase in factor prices.

Thus, the export good price effect under import-biased innovation serves the same purpose as the import-substitute price effect under export-biased innovation. They both, as do income effects, tend to reduce the initial trade balance impact of the innovation. But in the case of an import-biased productivity change, the initial trade balance surplus of A is the result of an import reduction. The expansion of income in A not only reduces its trade surplus from the import side but from the export side as well. Again it appears that import-biased innovation in A is more favorable to B's trade balance than is uniform productivity change, although finally it may still be unfavorable depending upon elasticity conditions.

To summarize, the probable balance of payments effects of disparate productivity change cannot be predicted without careful estimates of the prospective path of income change and rate and bias of technological progress. Knowledge of income and price elasticities of demand is also vital. To use differential rates of productivity change to explain the dollar shortage implies that this information is available. It is to be noted, and this is Johnson's contribution [40c; 38], that with alternative assumptions about the elasticities and growth rates, the disparate technical progress argument can support either dollar famine or dollar surfeit.

It must now be asked whether the hypothesis of disparate rates of productivity change is consistent with a relatively rapid and complete reversal of the dollar problem from a persistent U.S. surplus to a seemingly protracted deficit. A priori, abrupt, substantial changes in income and price elasticities are not likely nor is a rapid switch between unbiased, export-biased, and import-biased progress probable. But, in a careful exposition, Johnson shows [40c, pp. 102–05] that when money income changes in one or both countries a complex relationship among the elasticities and technical progress determines the specific trade balance outcome and that marginal changes in these parameters, if the parameters approximate certain critical values, may be sufficient to tip the balance from dollar shortage to glut. The disparate productivity change hypothesis has the advantage of being able, without stretching credibility, to explain the two dollar problems interchangeably. The situation is just more complex than Hicks' analysis would lead us to believe.

The model just set forth was extended in several ways. The simplifying assumption of constant, rather than rising, productivity in the second country (B) was attacked as being unrealistic and resulting in an unnecessarily gloomy outlook. Because of this assumption, logic led Hicks to conclude that B must deflate in order to keep its trade in balance. The impracticability of a deflationary policy suggests that a persistent payments problem would arise. If, however, productivity is increasing in B, though not as rapidly as in A, the income adjustment is not as distasteful as under the stationary productivity assumption. Indeed, if innovation in B is appreciable (relative to the sluggish income rise in A), B need not deflate absolutely but only relatively to A in order to maintain balanced trade. Thus, as Balogh [5, pp. 247, 275], MacDougall [57, pp. 191–92], and Machlup [62, pp. 262–64], among others, suggest, when technological improvements in both countries are admitted to the analysis, a dollar problem caused by productivity changes is not as likely.

Further extension in the direction of more countries, by Balogh [5; 6] Basu [9] and especially Bernstein [10] and Laursen [54], and in the direction of more commodities, by Bernstein [10] and Johnson [38, p. 6], also occurred. When the model is made more realistic, however, the disparate productivity hypothesis loses much of its impact as an explanation of a general dollar shortage.[31] If, for example, productivity in A is export-biased, there being no technological progress in the import-substitute and purely domestic good sectors, and B's productivity growth is in the import-substitute and domestic good without improvement in the export sector, there may be a deterioration in B's competitive position in C, a third country, where B's exports compete with those of A. But the consequences of this disparate productivity change in B's and A's home markets are more problematical. In B's home market A's exporters are competing with B's domestic good and its import-substitute. In A's markets B's exports compete with the domestic good and import-substitute sectors in A. The effects on the balances of payments, as distinct from the competitive positions, of the three countries depends on the configuration of the sectoral productivity changes, sectoral wage developments, and income and price effects.

Alternatively, it can be assumed that innovation in A's purely domestic sector occurs, all other productivities remaining constant. Here the eventual outcome depends, in part, upon whether the demand for the domestic good is price elastic or inelastic. This in turn determines whether productive factors are drawn from or released to the import-substitute and export sectors. The change in output in these sectors will be a function of the factor intensity in the domestic sector. Therefore, productivity change in the domestic good may increase or decrease, say, the quantity of imports due to factor substitution effects. Working out the result for the value of imports is further complicated by the need to include income and price effects as well.

Thus, when the disparate productivity model is made more general by incorporating additional countries and commodities, the generality of the conclusion is reduced. Bernstein sums up the whole argument by distinguishing between specific and general effects [10, p. 109]:

The effects of a rapid increase in United States productivity are too complex and too diverse to explain the payments problems of so many different countries. The effects of an increase in American productivity must be analyzed in specific terms and in general terms. The increase in productivity in each specific industry must be considered in relation to its effect on export competitors, import suppliers, and on the terms of trade. The specific effects may be adverse for some countries, beneficial for others. The aggregate of the specific effects on the balance of payments of all other countries with the United States may be favorable under certain conditions and at certain times, adverse under other conditions and at other times. No firm conclusion as to the aggregate impact of *specific* effects can be drawn even from historical experience.

There can be no doubt, however, as to the *general* effects of an increase in United States productivity. An increase in productivity . . . is merely the counterpart of an increase in real incomes. An increase in incomes means an increase in demand for imports, as well as for home goods. Unless the specific effects of an increase in United States productivity are clearly adverse to the payments position of other countries, the general effects are certain to be such as to lead to a strengthening of the dollar payments position of the rest of the world. Indeed, the greater the increase in United States productivity, the wider the field over which the increase in productivity has taken place, and the more sustained the increase in productivity, the more likely it is that the general effects will be favorable to the payments position of the rest of the world as a group.

Varying technological gap / The argument that disparate, biased growth in productivity is responsible for the dollar problem depends substantially on relative cost and price conditions. It is for this reason that demand elasticities and relative income adjustments occupy a central place in the analysis. Aside from specifying that technological change takes place and pinpointing the sectors in which it occurs, little attention is paid to the nature of technological progress itself. An alternative hypothesis about the dollar problem, offered by Hoffmeyer [36, Chaps. 5–8], is based upon different *types* of productivity change. Innovation is again emphasized but, as Cooper notes [27b, p. 151], relative price differences are largely ignored or even extraneous in that normal responses to price differences may be overshadowed by non-price considerations. This hypothesis attributes the dollar gap to asymmetrical reactions to kinds of and specializations in productivity change found in the real world.

The U.S., it is asserted, has from past and continuing efforts developed a comparative advantage, vis-a-vis the rest of the world, in research intensive or research oriented products and a comparative disadvantage in "traditional" goods. The basis for this assertion is an examination of trade data which show for the U.S. a much larger expansion of research oriented exports than of "traditional" exports and, conversely, a much larger growth of "traditional" imports than of research intensive imports over the period from 1890 to the mid-1950's.[32] Progress, in the sense of reductions in producing costs, takes place continuously and throughout the world in both types of goods; differentials in the rate of progress and biased change need not be hypothesized. Progress may also take the form of developing new products and this, it is noted, is more likely when the commodities are research oriented.

Taking a clue from oligopolistic reaction patterns, national responses to innovation in these two types of commodities are assumed to be different. On the one hand, technological changes in the production of traditional goods are propagated abroad almost as quickly as they filter through the innovating economy. On the other hand, there is an extensive lag in the international propagation of innovations in research oriented goods and in dissemination of new products.

The U.S., it is implied, finds its technological gap widening as it becomes relatively better in producing research intensive goods and also relatively more proficient (although still relatively inferior) in making traditional commodities. The comparative cost position becomes increasingly favorable to the U.S. because of a differential adaptability to the forms of progress. It is not that capacities to transform differ so significantly among nations but that nations are forced to transform for different reasons; and so long as there is a general inability to transform as rapidly as the changes in comparative cost conditions require, a persistent payments imbalance will exist. A static theory of comparative advantage, wherein a protracted disequilibrium is shown to be impossible, is invalidated by the dynamic elements of this hypothesis.

An interesting facet of this explanation of dollar shortage is that the U.S. need not be price competitive in order to support a long-term export surplus. Cooper indicates how this is possible [16, p. 107]. International price differences could be such that the U.S. would sustain a long-run static equilibrium payments deficit. Yet in a dynamic setting, if the U.S. were to innovate and were to penetrate foreign markets with new products with sufficiently greater rapidity than the innovations themselves were propagated abroad, it could maintain continuous balance in its external payments. It need only be added that if the pace of progress were slightly more rapid, a dollar shortage could result, although certainly there is some relative price relationship which would prevent it. In short, relative price movements can obviate the balance of payments advantages derived from research oriented technological change; but they may not be of sufficient order of magnitude to do so.

The degree of payments disequilibrium, then, is a function of the size of the technological gap and the sluggishness of adjustment of relative price structures. For a given lack of responsiveness of prices, any widening or narrowing of the technological gap — any lengthening or shortening of the lag in transmitting abroad new technologies and products or any change in relative rates of progress internationally — will be reflected in the balance of payments. For there to be a switch from a payments surplus to a deficit, the technological gap itself need not be reversed; it need only be narrowed sufficiently. Moreover, the narrowing may be a "one-shot" affair or it may be continuous. In the latter instance, the deterioration in the payments position will be progressive. Thus, to explain the transition from dollar shortage to dollar glut, it is enough to find the cause of the reduction in the technological gap favoring the U.S.

That the technological gap has narrowed, especially since 1955, seems *a priori* plausible. Cooper mentions [17, p. 136], as tending in this direction, the relatively higher rates of investment abroad, the more rapid international transmission of technological change, and the expanded opportunities in Western Europe for scale economies in production and research. The fact that the poor export performance of the U.S. in the last few years has been restricted to a relatively few categories of goods is similarly indicative of a compression of the technological gap. Vanek [27f, pp. 170–71] relied upon the same explanation when he argued that the structure of economic growth is a relevant consideration. Growth has been more rapid in Europe than in the U.S. and "owing both to catching up abroad with American techniques and to a gradual tendency toward the equalization of factor endowments . . . the comparative advantage of the United States, and consequently the European propensity to import from the United States, has diminished." American exports have therefore declined relatively whereas U.S. imports have continued their rapid growth due to altered American demand conditions and to rigidities in the operation of the U.S. price mechanism.

This latter point can, of course, be considered as a manifestation of the demonstration effect, as also, but less clearly, can Vanek's hypothesis about the recent structure of comparative growth. While Vanek's argument is depicted in terms of shifting production possibilities curves, its upshot is that foreigners' demand for dollars has, as a consequence of the narrowing of America's technological lead, fallen relative to the U.S. supply of dollars. This, combined with the relatively sluggish response mechanism, is the cause of the present dollar surfeit.

Basis of economic growth / The preceding two sections discuss the trade balance consequences of productivity change by stressing the rates and locus of technological improvements. In this emphasis they become dynamic analyses and it is principally because of this dynamism that the conclusions derived from the static comparative doctrine were found wanting in content. While these analyses were careful to explore the income generating aspects of technological change, the other side of the coin — that technological change increases the capacity to produce as well — was largely ignored. Nevertheless, "capacity effects" are important in expounding a dynamic balance of payments model. Perhaps they can best be analyzed by taking economic growth, generally, as a point of departure and then noting that growth can occur because of technological progress or, alternatively, because of net capital accumulation. Does growth via net investment potentially have different capacity effects and hence a different impact on the trade balance than growth via innovation? [33]

The payments effects of growth generated by technological progress have been discussed above. In contrast, the balance of payments consequences of growth through capital formation have received little attention. Johnson's article [40b], which is path breaking in some respects, is not precisely to the point. It emphasizes the equilibrium rate of growth which is required by given values of, *inter alia,* the marginal propensity to import, the rate of expansion of exports, and the capital-output ratio if an open economy is to fully utilize its productive capacity when investment is expanding. In other words, Johnson's complicated analysis was in the strictest tradition of the Harrod-Domar discussion.

Yet it is possible, following Johnson's lead [40b, p. 124], to derive the conditions under which a country will be tending to develop a trade account surplus or deficit. If, to simplify, the rate of growth of demand for exports (determined by foreign conditions) is lower than the country's equilibrium growth rate[34] the country will be tending to open up an import surplus as well as encountering greater difficulties in fully utilizing its productive facilities. Conversely, when the equilibrium growth rate is lower than the growth rate of exports the country will tend toward a payments surplus. It is apparent that growth through capital accumulation expands trade by raising incomes; capital formation, by changing relative factor proportions, also alters comparative advantage positions. As in the discussion of the impact of technical change on the payments position, the net effects are contingent on income elasticities and the rate of income adjustment.

Few economists have taken a stand on the ultimate payments effects of the two types of growth. Kindleberger, in his brief examination of the problem [48, pp. 23–26; 49, pp. 191–94], concluded that, on balance, when economic growth is due to investment in new plant and equipment, the country's balance of payments probably turns unfavorable. Much depends on whether the investment is concentrated in the domestic goods sector or in the export and import-substitute sectors. Much depends also on whether the stimulus to investment is domestic or external in origin and whether the capacity expansion precedes or is called forth by an increase in demand. When the capital formation is primarily in the domestic goods sector, when the demand stimulus comes from within the home economy, and when the expansion of capacity antedates the increase of demand, the payments balance is most likely to be adversely affected. Even when investment expands export capacity and, to a lesser extent, the capacity to produce imports, if it precedes demand growth, the trade balance will initially be more unfavorable. Possibly, even in the longer run, the expansion in income via a multiplier process, and hence the induced increase in imports, will be even more substantial. Presumably, the growth of exports and contraction of imports made possible by the additions to productive facilities will be outweighed by the income effect on imports. When capacity expansion occurs in response to a demand shift, however, there is an *a priori* indeterminate offset to these conclusions.

If a country's economic growth is generated by technological change, particularly if the change is in the foreign trade sectors, the payments balance is likely to move toward a surplus. The role of the source of demand stimulus is important here as well. Kindleberger implies that if the stimulus is from abroad, technical progress will be primarily in the trade sectors. Typically, progress in these sectors will expand exports and reduce imports, in both quantum and value terms. Even where the technological change takes place in domestic goods production, the general reduction in unit costs will tend directly to expand exports and to contract imports. Indirectly the cost reduction in the domestic goods sector will tend to release resources to the foreign trade sectors so that exports and import-substitutes can expand. To be sure, income effects will cause a countervailing expansion of imports; but these will normally be overpowered by capacity effects. The increase in capacity because of innovation will, through extending the line of products available for export, through increasing the price competitiveness of existing exports in foreign markets, and through the development of new and effective facilities to produce import substitutes, augment exports and hold back the growth of imports.

Kindleberger puts great stock in the basis of growth hypothesis of payments disequilibrium. He concludes that the different bases of growth are fundamentally responsible "for the recent disparate balance-of-payments behavior of Britain and the United States, on the one hand, and Germany, France, Italy, and Japan, on the other" [49, p. 194]. In the former group of countries, investment-based growth has predominated of late and international payments are in deficit; in the latter countries, growth is primarily due to technological change with a recent tendency toward payments surplus. In addition, growth in the latter group is initiated to a large extent by capacity expansion rather than by demand expansion. The lag between the creation of exports and the induced expansion of imports tends to reinforce the payments surplus growing out of technological progress.

Relative price level movements / In analyzing the balance of payments effects of disparate, biased productivity changes, the outcome depended as much on assumptions concerning price adjustments (through assumed income movements) as on the locus and rate of technological progress. Less obviously perhaps the same was true of the explanation of the dollar problem in terms of a changing technological gap. In neither instance did price movements take an active role; nevertheless, price phenomena entered the argument at nearly every stage. It is not surprising, therefore, that divergent movements of national price levels have been suggested — Haberler [26; 27c] being the foremost supporter of this view — as the cause of persistent payments imbalances.

Much of the discussion, exemplified by Cheng [15], Cooper [27b, pp. 151–55], Lary [53, pp. 56–58], and MacDougall [61, pp. 13–25; 60, Chap. IV], has focused on such factual matters as the international relative price trends. Others, Cooper [16, pp. 129–34] being a case in point, examine what available price indices are most meaningful for international comparison. All price indices suffer from the common disadvantages that their component series and weights are not commensurate country-to-country. For intertemporal comparisons, effects on prices of changes in commodity composition of exports and imports cannot be adequately allowed for. Particularly in a dynamic world, where relative price adjustments and innovation lead to rapid changes in the commodity composition of trade, it is difficult to judge the degree to which a relative price movement shown by the available statistical series can be said to represent a similar trend in the theoretically relevant price level. For theoretical comparisons the ideal is to have price indices net of the effects of changes in the relative weights of their component commodities.

Moreover, it must be remembered that the comparison should be in terms of the prices of goods that can be traded internationally. Two frequently used series, the GNP deflator and the consumer price index (CPI), include a host of items connected with the service and housing sectors which do not enter trade. The CPI suffers from the further defect that a number of commodity categories of importance in world trade — crude materials, semifinished manufacturers, and finished producer goods — are excluded from the direct index computations and therefore affect the CPI only indirectly. In contrast, the wholesale price index (WPI), which specifically includes these items, reflects domestically generated inflation or deflationary pressures rather poorly. The prices of a great many of its component commodities are determined in international markets so that the WPI's in the various advanced countries are likely to move in the same direction, although not to the same extent. The close agreement between the WPI and the index of export "prices" for the U.S. may attest to this. A similar condition in foreign countries, where the international trade sector is much larger relative to the purely domestic sector than in the United States, almost surely does.

Vanek [27f. p. 178], however, suggests that where the trade sector is relatively inconsequential, domestic conditions, rather than conditions abroad, will have an overwhelming impact upon export prices. This latter consideration suggests using an export price index for international comparisons. These should reflect price pressures rather faithfully. Unfortunately, the "price" indices of traded goods are in reality unit value indices,[35] making virtually impossible their use for theoretical purposes. Moreover, no price series can take account of the various non-price rationing devices that have been so significant in much of the postwar period.

There is no easy solution to the problem of theoretically pertinent measurement of price level movements. One analyst will opt for one type of price index for international comparisons; another analyst, with equal justification, will opt for another. The compromise position — to look to several indices for empirical corroboration of the relative price level hypothesis — normally will not work. As likely as not, the relative movements of the various price series will be contradictory. The relevant price index concept must be chosen *a priori* in order to test the hypothesis; but no available index is likely to reproduce this concept. As always, the empiricist must make a difficult, debatable choice between degrees of imperfection.

Theoretical examination of the relative price level hypothesis has been rather superficial. The literature on the various causes of domestic inflation has barely been considered in analyses of the international consequences of divergent price trends. With few exceptions the level of theoretical contribution is that, regardless of the basis of relative international price movements, changes in relative price levels are largely, if not solely, responsible for the protracted payments difficulties of the postwar period.

It is not stated this baldly, of course. For example, Haberler concludes [27c, p. 65]: "The plain fact is that in view of this rising competition by increasingly efficient and financially increasingly disciplined rivals, the United States had more inflation during the last five years than was compatible with an equilibrium in its balance of payments . . . whatever may be the *comparative* magnitude of inflation. . . ." This statement places relative price movements in a dynamic setting, to be sure, and has the dubious merit of being irrefutable if an operative price adjustment mechanism is presumed to exist. But, as Cooper observes [16, p. 127], the statement amounts to a tautology. It is of little real help in delimiting the causes of the dollar problem and greatly oversimplifies the choice among alternative remedial policies.

Be that as it may, a relative price movement hypothesis has at least one attraction. Built-in international asymmetries in the long-term price response to changes in effective demand and to institutional pressures certainly exist and have been called upon on numerous occasions as a basis for the hypothesis. On the one hand, an assertion found rather frequently — in Schlesinger [75, pp. 289–90], Johnson [41, p. 227], and Vanek

[27f, p. 178] — is that the U.S., being less subject to the pressures of a balance of payments deficit or being relatively free from international competition, is likely to find its prices creeping upward comparatively. Moreover, American businessmen are thought to be reluctant to reduce prices in slack periods. The proportionately lower raw materials content of U.S. manufactured goods, combined with relatively stable raw materials prices in the U.S., results also in downward price stickiness, a phenomenon noted by Cooper [27b, pp. 162–63] and MacDougall [60, p. 19]. On the other hand, Balogh [8] argues that by being a relatively high saving economy, the U.S. is likely to be prone to depression and presumably deflation. Additionally, Furth [23, p. 433] takes note of the fact that the U.S. economy, relative at least to that of Western Europe, has been comparatively free of general capacity shortages and excess demand pressures. The built-in asymmetries support either dollar shortage or dollar glut and during the appropriate time-span. Indeed, the matching is so felicitous as to suggest that the factors enumerated may be rationalizations rather than explanations.

One way to meet this objection is to begin the analysis by examining each of the probable causes of inflation (rather than the causes of payments problems) and tracing out the resulting balance of payments implications. This is the approach used by Cooper [16, Chap. IV]. If, to take up his argument, a country is undergoing a relative excess demand inflation, it will tend toward a payments deficit as an income effect expands imports and absorbs goods otherwise available for export, even though relative prices remain unaltered. A price effect will reinforce this response under conventional elasticity assumptions. It must be recognized, however, that if import competition is particularly strong in some production sectors, these sectors will not experience a price effect. There would be no inflationary price rise in these sectors, even though the trade balance would deteriorate. But in sectors not subject to intense import competition prices would increase, as would the general price level.

If the inflation is assumed to result from cost-push phenomena, a different and more complicated mechanism is involved. The price effect will be as above.[36] The income effect will be of a special sort. In analysis of cost-push inflation money income is normally assumed to remain constant. The effect of successful cost-push pressures is not only an increase in the price level but also a redistribution of the given money income. The resulting money income redistribution effect on the balance of payments, therefore, depends on the relevant marginal propensities of the various income receiving groups. Little can be said about the net outcome *a priori;* imports may increase or they may decrease, exportable goods may be absorbed domestically or released for the export market.

The income effect during cost-push inflation is, of course, not limited to a money redistribution effect; a real income effect also occurs. As the price level increases, money income being fixed, real income must fall and with its fall comes a reduction in the demand for goods and services. Where this drop in demand hits hardest depends, ultimately, on the sectoral focus of the price effect. On the one hand, if foreign competition holds down price increases in the export and import sectors, so that most of the cost-push vents itself on domestic goods prices, the demand reduction from the real income effect will be heavily concentrated on domestic goods. Nevertheless, some reduction in demand will fall on imports, import substitutes, and exportable goods. There will in all probability be a small real income effect tending to improve the trade balance of the inflating country. Coincidentally, the price effect will also be altered. If only domestic goods prices rise, international relative prices will not change. The price effect will therefore influence the trade position indirectly. Demand will be deflected from the domestic sector to the trade sector. If there are supply shortages, this could result in a reduction in exports and expansion in imports. The indirect response to a price change localized to the domestic sector tends to counteract the effect of the real income reduction on the payments balance. On the other hand, if cost-push raises prices generally, the price effect will clearly work against an improvement in the payments position. The indirect price effect just mentioned will not come into play. The real income effect will fall equally on domestic, import substitute, and exportable goods but less heavily on imports. The trade balance will presumably deteriorate.

Plainly, the balance of payments consequences of cost-push inflation are quite complex. To the usual need to consider price and real income elasticities must be added concern for the sectoral location of price changes and income elasticities (or marginal propensities) of various groups of income recipients. Moreover, the degree to which non-price rationing will in fact replace the price mechanism must be estimated. But this assumes that cost-push pressures raise prices despite a constant level of effective demand. If an expansion in aggregate demand "validates" the cost-push, so that further unemployment does not arise and money income effects must be weighed, the payments impact of cost-push inflation will, as Cooper notes [16, p. 122], be virtually indistinguishable from the consequences of excess demand inflation.

The difficulty with the excess demand inflation analysis of the dollar problem is that it does not jibe with the observable evidence of the last few years. In order to explain a dollar surfeit, excess demand inflation would have to result in a relative rise in a general price index, such as the consumer price index, in the U.S. Yet the consumer price index in the U.S. has not risen relative to those in Western Europe during a period when the U.S. balance of payments has deteriorated. In contrast, the U.S. export unit value index has inched up compared to similar indices abroad. These movements are hard to justify by a demand inflation hypothesis. Nor, barring extreme circumstances, does a cost-push thesis find support in the facts. If U.S. export prices have been rising relatively and its general price level falling relatively, by what means are cost-push price increases restricted to the export sector? Why have they not spilled over into the domestic goods sector where, of all places, the price-holding pressures of foreign competition are minimized?

Cooper's resolution of this dilemma is clever [16, pp. 155ff.]. He invokes the demand-shift hypothesis of inflation.[37] This hypothesis is based on an assumption that changes in sectoral demand, total demand being neither excessive nor deficient, elicit an irreversible price response in the several sectors. In sectors subjected to intense demand pressures prices will rise; in sectors where demand, by assumption, is slack prices do not drop. The movement of the general price level, while rising, will not be as rapid as may occur in some of the sectoral price indices. In the U.S. domestic demand pressures seem to have been particularly heavy in a number of industries producing commodities for export — for instance, the steel industry whose output is exported directly and indirectly in the form of fabricated commodities has been singled out. Exports of these commodities fall off and since the prices of other export goods do not decline, even though demand for these commodities slackens, no compensating increase in the exports of these other goods can occur. Exports drop; the export price index climbs upward; the general price index increases but by a somewhat smaller amount. Meanwhile, in Europe the prices of exports need not have risen any more rapidly than the general price index. In fact, they probably rose by less as the upward price movement was particularly rapid in goods which typically do not enter the export trade. The consequence of this configuration of demand shifts was, then, a relative deterioration of the U.S. payments position — so that the dollar tended to glut its market — even though the trend of the U.S. general price index would have indicated otherwise.

There is, undoubtedly, more to the explanation of events of the last few years than this hypothesis. Yet the extension of the demand-shift inflation argument is a sufficient explanation. Even so it is difficult to see how it can be turned upside down to explain the dollar shortage of prior years. Nothing suggests that in prior years U.S. domestic demand for export goods was less intense or that demand for import substitutes was more intense. Moreover, it could be argued that capacity shortages abroad augmented the demand on U.S. export goods, although, of course, contrary to present conditions, demand for these same goods from European facilities was equally heavy. It cannot reasonably be presumed that the irreversibility in the price response to demand shifts previously worked the other way, so that prices were inflexible upward. Nor are there reasons to suspect appropriate demand-shift response conditions abroad. Thus, while the demand-shift formulation suffices to explain the advent of dollar surfeit it does not come to grips with dollar shortage. Some other explanation must be called upon for this purpose.

Demonstration effects / Yet another theory of the dollar problem attributes protracted payments disequilibria to persistent attempts of groups of people (nations) to emulate the standards of living and production techniques of others. At one time it was fashionable to believe that this phenomenon was partly responsible for dollar shortage. It was suggested by Nurkse [70, pp. 91–92] and MacDougall [59, pp. 189–91; 60, pp. 60–64], among others, that the high standard of living attained by the U.S. served as a magnet or target for the current standards of consumption of less well-endowed nations. The aspirations of these nations to imitate Americans resulted also in their undertaking heavy investment programs in the hope that the higher consumption levels would soon be sustained by higher productivity. Unwittingly, the U.S. was serving as a "demonstration model" for the consumption patterns and the production techniques of the rest of the world. However, the rest of the world, while aspiring to American living standards, did not yet have American productive capabilities. While their imports of consumer and producer goods from the U.S. rose in response to emulation pressures, their output was neither high enough nor growing rapidly enough to sustain the growing deficits on trade account without at the same time an increase in the inflationary pressures.[38] The rest of the world was, perpetually it seemed, tending to live beyond its means of support.

The validity of this thesis was dependent on two conditions: that discrepancies in levels of living did exist and that the higher level was being communicated to people living on a lower plane. There can be no denial of the first condition. Since the time of the Industrial Revolution at least, the "Western" standard of living has been substantially higher than that of "non-Western" areas. Moreover, beginning after World War I, it was generally accepted that the level of economic comfort and well-being in the U.S. was appreciably higher than that of the European countries. The spreading abroad of knowledge of this standard had also, certainly during and after World War II, taken place on the required scale.

Thus, the demonstration effect seemed to be a plausible hypothesis of dollar shortage. Nevertheless, even before concern shifted to fear of a dollar glut, the thesis was questioned at several points. First, why was the desire to emulate restricted solely to consumer behavior? Was it not feasible that producers abroad, especially in the underdeveloped areas where market incentives may be deficient, would imitate Americans by exerting greater effort and devoting more thought to organizational and technical skills? Were there not, in short, both consumption and production effects as a consequence of the "American demonstration?" If this was so, as MacDougall believed [60, p. 63], the demonstration effect need not cause either inflationary pressures or persistent payments deficits.

More superficially, MacDougall [60, pp. 62–63] observed from empirical data that neither those countries with the largest deficiencies in their levels of living relative to that of the United States nor those with the closest American contacts tended necessarily to have the largest deficit, contrary to the inference from the demonstration hypothesis. This ostensible failure of the demonstration effect can be explained, however, by virtue of the fact that an excessively large gap between living standards serves as no stimulus at all. If income level differences are great, the possibility of emulation is utopian rather than real. Not only, as suggested by Nurkse [71, p. 67], are the means of communication apt to be absent where the living standard is extremely meager but also the means of effectuating a desire to emulate (even where the difference in living levels is understood) is for all intents and purposes non-existent. When a country is at the margin of subsistence, imitation of an American consumption pattern or production techniques is virtually impossible. It takes some income in excess of the subsistence level in order to have anything to "dissipate" on an American living standard. Prodigality, where emulation can be called that, is a luxury of the relatively well-off. By this line of reasoning then, the higher the level of income above subsistence the more likely is a deficit in the balance of payments due to the demonstration effect. A balancing factor is, of course, that disparities in living levels must be of some significant size but not so large as to make imitation a hopeless task.

If these strictures impair the demonstration effect hypothesis of the dollar shortage, they do not unseat it. As long as dollar shortage was the focus of attention, this version of the demonstration effect seemed reasonable. Furthermore, except upon such inconsequential grounds as those cited above, the thesis could not be invalidated empirically. No one has devised a method by which to "test" the demonstration effect hypothesis. Yet the switch in the character of the dollar problem from a U.S. payments surplus to a sustained deficit should have signaled a need for second thoughts. In fact, it did. As a consequence the demonstration effect was not junked; rather the effect itself was reversed. Now, the U.S. was trying to emulate foreigners.[39]

The reverse demonstration effect is not without its persuasive supporters. Kindleberger has argued that the perspectives of American consumers *and* businessmen have extended to encompass the entire world. "The widening of the American consumer and business horizon to a world view is expanding direct foreign investment on the one hand, and changing the relationship between national income and imports on the other" [79c, p. 956]. In the process of transmitting their own living standard abroad, American consumers have learned of exciting, new foreign goods. Consumer parochialism of the past has broken down.[40] Moreover, the kinds of foreign goods that have whetted American appetites have become so attractive that American capital, direct and indirect, is being invested in foreign productive facilities. And these conditions, it is specifically noted, are not merely because of relative price movements or recovery of productive capacity in Western Europe and Japan but also because of a structural change in demand — a pure change in tastes — on the part of Americans.

Vanek too [27f] underscored the reverse demonstration effect, stating it in a context of income growth in the U.S. Thus, with respect to Vanek's analysis, it is difficult to determine whether American preferences for foreign commodities have shifted favorably, *per se*, or whether American income has risen and, for Americans, foreign products have a high income elasticity of demand [27f, pp. 170, 179]. Both elements are undoubtedly present and from an empirical point of view the distinction may be uninteresting. From a theoretical viewpoint, however, there is an ambiguity. If the income adjustment is the true source of the change in American consumption patterns because foreign goods have a higher income elasticity than domestic goods, then, as Cooper notes [27b, p. 148], it is unwise to call the change in demand a structural change. There has been no change in tastes if tastes are considered to be determined not only relative to given price ratios but also to given income levels. If the altered demand pattern is due to income change, in what sense is it possible to distinguish between a reverse demonstration hypothesis of dollar glut and a theory based upon relative income and relative price adjustments? Thus, unless care is exercised in expressing the cause of the altered consumption pattern, the demonstration effect can shade into relative price level phenomena.

An interesting facet of the reverse demonstration effect is that, apparently, nations with low living standards no longer try to imitate a high living standard country. Indeed, it would seem quite the reverse. A careful look at the hypothesis reveals that this sort of "reversal" is not true in a significant sense. Perhaps Americans are conditioned to think in terms of "the" standard of living but even in the United States this is an oversimplification. Living standards are complex. They may be thought of in some average sense; in which case, even though average levels of living may be substantially different, some perhaps significant components of the lower standards may yet be higher than the average of the higher standard. Alternatively, within any country there may be strata of living standards. In either case, what Americans with their high average level of living seem to be trying to emulate is the higher strata or higher components of the lower average foreign living standard. That this can result in a payments deficit for the U.S. is not doubted. With the highest per capita income in the world, Americans can implement their changed tastes on a truly mammoth scale. Indeed, as Vanek pointed out [27f, p. 170], the low ratio of imports to GNP in the U.S. means that a relatively small shift in expenditures from domestic to foreign goods would result in a sizable balance of payments shift.

□ A THEORY OF PAYMENTS DISEQUILIBRIUM

In setting forth in more or less detail the various long-term explanations of the dollar's persistent disequilibrium since World War II — of first its shortage and then its glut — the reversibility of the argument, in the sense that it can plausibly encompass an explanation of both types of disequilibrium, has perhaps been insufficiently stressed. The idea of reversibility of course need not be central to hypotheses designed to explain observable facts, for it is not necessary that observable facts be accounted for by only one sequence of logic. Dollar shortage may be due to one cause or one group of causes and glut to others. Yet it would seem reasonable that those explanations of persistent disequilibrium that are capable of demonstrating the reversal of the dollar problem within a single analytical framework are preferable on theoretical grounds.

On this criterion, the long-term causes of disequilibrium come off relatively poorly. It is to be expected that the "currency valuation and productive capacity" hypothesis would receive a high score because it was offered expressly to explain the switch in the dollar payments position. The category of explanations embracing adjustments in relative price levels should also score well *a priori*. That the group has been viewed with some skepticism is due more to the morass of conflicting empirical evidence than to its inability to explain both glut and shortage in terms of relative movements in price levels. It is fair to say, however, that the other arguments discussed above were not proposed with this sort of reversibility specifically in mind. How do they fare according to this criterion?

The demonstration effect, and its reverse, naturally explain the dollar problem switch but, it is to be noted, not within a single analytical framework. To be sure, emulation is at the heart of both types of demonstration. Nevertheless, if the demonstration effect and its reverse are classified as one argument, it must be shown within the body of the hypothesis how the direction of demonstration itself becomes reversed. This is precisely what the proponents of this argument have been most vague about. In the discussion above of the demonstration effect it was suggested that the patterns of living cannot be too disparate and that one must consider that these patterns may be stratified. These suggestions, however, have nowhere been incorporated within the demonstra-

389

tion effect hypothesis in order to explain its reversal. The demonstration effect, then, cannot be considered to meet satisfactorily the criterion adopted above, although it does not fail absolutely.

It was also shown that the matter of whether economic growth is based on technological change or on capital accumulation with existing techniques will also affect systematically a country's payments balance. To explain the switch in the U.S. payments position, this hypothesis must show that the early postwar growth of the U.S. arose predominantly from the former cause and that growth in the rest of the world was primarily due to the latter; that this geographical pattern of the bases of growth was reversed sometime during the 1950's; and, moreover, that this reversal was inherent in the growth process in an open economic system. Factual evidence supporting this differential basis of growth between the U.S. and elsewhere — and a reversal of this basis — is not apparent. Intuitively, one may feel that this is the case but intuition is never good support for a theoretical hypothesis. In addition, the argument has not shown why the bases of growth should reverse themselves. Why, that is, should the U.S. base its growth upon, say, technological innovation for a period of years and then, either because other countries' growth has been based on capital accumulation or because its own growth has been due to technological change for a long enough period, start building its growth upon investment in existing techniques? And why should the opposite occur abroad? No mechanism has been developed, or even suggested, which justifies this transition. The "basis of growth" hypothesis of disequilibrium fails, then, on the same ground as the demonstration effect — and probably with a poorer mark.

Similarly, the "size and self-sufficiency" hypotheses fail to meet the test of being capable of explaining the switch in the payments position of the U.S. It can hardly be argued that the relative size or self-sufficiency of the U.S. has altered in the postwar period. Even now, the E.E.C. cannot be reasonably treated as a monolithic economic entity; surely it was not one from its inception, as it would have had to have been to explain even the U.S. payments deficit since 1958. For the same reason, it cannot be considered that there has been a substantial increase in the absolute size of any trading country. Western Europe is not yet a "country" in a meaningful sense.

This leaves but two hypotheses which more or less meet the standard of reversibility: disparate and biased productivity change and a widening and narrowing of the technological gap between the U.S. and the rest of the world. As noted above, Johnson has demonstrated that the first of these hypotheses can explain the switch. Provided that price and income elasticities are of a certain magnitude, that income changes at a certain rate, and that technological developments take a certain form, the U.S. payments balance can go from surplus to deficit with small, incremental changes in these magnitudes, rates, and forms. But little is known of the size and character of these various parameters. They may, or they may not, approximate the required, critical values. It would not be particularly wise, in the absence of tangible evidence, to assume that they do. And only *if* they do, can it be said that the disparate and biased productivity hypothesis is a plausible explanation of the U.S. payments performance in the postwar period.

Nor does the varying technological gap argument come away unblemished. It is reasonable to expect that the technological gap that exists between countries will widen and narrow over time, of course. And, it should be recalled, this is all that is necessary to explain shifts in the payments balance from deficit to surplus to deficit; reversal of the gap is not required at all. What must be shown is that the technological gap widens and narrows somewhat systematically and for rather protracted periods of time. This is precisely what a Schumpeterian explanation of the process of innovation would achieve. Innovation leads to a swarming process by imitators, the resulting increase in output eventually saturates the market, profits decline, and innovation ceases. But the economy reacts to this so that periodically the stage is set again for the innovator and the whole sequence is repeated. The duration of the sequence depends upon the "stature" of the innovation.

With a Schumpeterian-type innovation underpinning the varying technological gap argument is superficially reasonable. When innovation occurs in one country, the width of the technological gap will change. Depending upon where innovation occurs the gap may widen or narrow. During a process of innovation and imitation in the U.S. it is likely that the gap will widen, tending to cause a U.S. payments surplus. But this assumes that technological progress abroad is constant. It cannot, however, be assumed that innovators do not exist abroad. Given that there will be innovation overseas, so that technological progress there will accelerate and decelerate, the phasing of the innovation and swarming in the various countries becomes a critical feature of the varying technological gap hypothesis. Only a particular phasing will permit the hypothesis to explain the disequilibrium shift. There is nothing in the hypothesis that insures the proper kind of phasing. Thus, depending upon the timing of innovation in the various countries, the technological gap argument may or may not be able to explain the reversal of the dollar problem on a consistent basis.

The discussion of this section suggests that a truly useful hypothesis of the dollar problem is yet to be proposed. Of those discussed, and they are thought to be exhaustive, most are reasonable explanations of the dollar's persistent glut or shortage. Since they are more or less compatible with the empirical evidence of the postwar period, some are more plausible than others. Some are capable of explaining both shortage and glut but only on a haphazard basis. None is capable of explaining fully and plausibly the circumstances in which a shortage might turn into a glut and vice versa. In the present state of empirical knowledge, none gives a reliable mechanism for predicting when any given persistent disequilibrium may reverse itself. There is, in short, no generally acceptable theory of balance of payments disequilibrium.

FOOTNOTES

1. See the table in Lary [53, pp. 163–67]. It should be noted that the size of the balance in the international accounts depends upon the method used to derive the balance. The Department of Commerce concept of balance, which attempts to highlight the liquidity condition of the U.S., is generally accepted and is the basis for the assertion in the text. Lary, in an interesting discussion [53, pp. 137–61; 52, pp. 418–20], proposes an alternative formulation based on sensitivity of the balancing items to monetary policy. See also the article by Johnson [39].

2. This assessment is only seemingly inconsistent with the position sponsored by Bernstein [11, pp. 67–76; 79a]. In particular, opinions can differ concerning the extent of U.S. foreign commitment required by the "cold war," the share of these commitments that should be borne by the allies of the U.S., and the time at which these allies are in a position to reasonably assume the burdens of their share.

3. It should be noted that relatively (compared to imports) favorable export performance is not incompatible with pessimism about a country's competitiveness. Lary [53, pp. 84–85] ingeniously couches a supporting argument in terms of differences between short-run and long-run import demand elasticities, market imperfections, and terms of trade effects.

4. The prospects for overcomplete adjustment have also received attention in the literature. See Kindleberger [50] and Bloomfield [12].

5. Hicks [34] interprets dollar shortage in a real sense as well. He asserts that a country, in order to avoid a payments deficit (e.g., dollar shortage), may have to accept a worsening of its barter terms of trade. This permits him to conclude that an import-biased innovation in, say, the United States would make the rest of the world unambiguously worse off. Johnson suggests, in addition to a "normal" monetary trade balance concept, a "real" concept in which the trade balance is measured as the ratio of a country's import or export surplus to its imports. The dollar problem would then be represented by the "proportion of the imports of the rest of the world from the United States not paid for by exports to the United States" [40c, p. 98]. In practice, Johnson adopts the ratio of the value of exports to the value of imports of a country as a measure of its real balance. See also Machlup [63] for an instructive discussion of payments imbalance.

6. The term "quasi-dollar problem" refers to the situation where some specialized group of nations has developed an immunity; that is, where the problem is not general. A dollar shortage would be "quasi" for the, say, manufacturing nations in the sense that they could earn dollars by incurring sufficient losses in the primary producing areas but only as long as the primary producers themselves have continued access to dollars.

7. MacDougall states that the payments "balance is a marginal part of total trade and trade is in turn a marginal part of the national income" [61, p. 64].

8. Ellis [20] expresses a similar view. Other researchers, however, find these same phenomena to be indicative of a dollar shortage. Hoffmeyer, for one [36, p. 23], asserts that the ". . . signs of disequilibrium have been so numerous that it seems worthwhile to investigate whether there is a common explanation."

9. There is support as well, in Miss Romanis [73] and the Department of Commerce study [82], for a "geographical" explanation of dollar glut. Markets in which the U.S. share of imports is relatively high (e.g., Canada and Latin America) were relatively stagnant in the latter half of the 1950's. This relative stagnation is in turn reflected in a slower growth of U.S. exports as a whole.

10. See, especially, Kravis' provocative but little noticed article [51]. Also note Lary [52, p. 423], Cooper [27b, p. 148], and Frank [22, p. 314].

11. The issue of the balance of payments effects of synchronization, or lack thereof, of U.S. and foreign business cycles is not discussed here. MacDougall [60, Chap. II], Mintz [66; 67] and Chang [14] give specific attention to this.

12. By unstable in isolation is meant that the slope of the aggregate demand function, i.e., the sum of intended expenditures, at the relevant income level is greater than one. This is usually expressed, although with oversimplification, as $MPC + MPM > 1$, where MPC and MPM are the marginal propensities to consume home produced goods and to import. These instability models are summarized in Hoffmeyer [36, pp. 60–64]. Note also the comments of Mac-Dougall [61, p. 29] and Harris [80c, p. 18].

13. Over- and undercompensation, in this context, refer to the ability of an autonomous change in exports to call forth a greater or smaller change in imports in the same direction via income effects.

14. It is of interest that in his subsequent writings on the dollar problem Kindleberger has not revived this asymmetrical cycle argument, even though a case for dollar glut can be made by positing a tendency for relatively excessive demand in the U.S. compared to the rest of the world. The reason is perhaps obvious. It would be difficult to defend this assumption over the recent past, with the U.S. suffering substantial unemployment and Western Europe being reasonably fully employed. Thus, Kindleberger (see below) now supports a noncyclical explanation of the dollar problem.

15. MacDougall's analysis of this point implies that though the U.S. import demand curve is kinked it is still elastic throughout the relevant price range.

16. Note, however, Cooper [27b, pp. 154–55] where the exceptional export performance of Japan and Germany (relative to performance in other industrialized countries) is adduced as "perhaps lending some credence to the 'excessive devaluation *cum* growth in capacity' argument."

17. It is perhaps necessary to recall that some of this "over-devaluation" was justifiable in light of the deteriorated international capital positions of many of the devaluing countries.

18. Indeed, in its purest form the theoretical argument would assume that prices in the United States did not rise after the 1949 devaluations. This prevents admixture, in any simple fashion, of the devaluation-capacity hypothesis and the inflation-deflation hypothesis considered below. This is clearly what Cooper means by his assertion that according to the devaluation-capacity hy-

pothesis the U.S. did not price itself out of world markets following the 1949 devaluations [16, p. 166].

It should be noted that "pricing out of the market" is an ambiguous term. At least four distinct meanings are suggested by MacDougall [61, pp. 13–14].

19. Triffin [78, Chap. 2, especially pp. 84–85] believes that in fact producers were not able to resist the internal demand pressures and therefore that the relative price competitiveness gained by the devaluations could not become effective until European inflation was brought under control. European inflation was contained, he felt, in the early 1950's.

20. This statement of relative structural patterns is now, in light of the extensive deterioration of the U.S. international reserve position, questionable. In the mid-1950's it was undoubtedly correct.

21. This argument, together with the assumption of substantial scale economies in productive activity which the U.S., by virtue of its size, can more fully exploit to the benefit of its competitive position, seems to be the logic underlying Balogh's assertion that size, *per se*, is important to the dollar shortage [6, p. 151; 5, pp. 264–65].

22. The argument assumes that taste patterns among nations are identical. If tastes differ significantly trade will be profitable even though the "productivity structures" in the several countries are identical.

23. It is clear from Hicks' context and the context of most of the discussion that "productivity change" is limited to a decrease in the real cost of a given output aggregated over sectors or over the whole economy. As Johnson observes [38], a more precise term for this is "technical change." Productivity changes can occur because of occupational shifts and accumulation of capital embodying the extant technology. [See also Harris, 29, p. 442.] Johnson uses the terms precisely and would like to see the distinction explored, as he does to some extent in [40a] and [37]. Johnson also pursues the effects of whether the technological innovation is intensive-factor using or saving [38]. Again these extensions of the Hicksian framework have been analyzed largely for their impact on the terms of trade. In this chapter, productivity change, technological improvement, and innovation are used interchangeably, however.

24. What follows is an elaboration of Hicks' model. Hicks is rightly criticized by Johnson [40c; 38], Balogh [5], and Kindleberger [45] for underplaying demand conditions in his analysis. Moreover, in order to highlight the balance of payments features of this model it has been extended in a direction elucidated by Johnson [40c]. Johnson underscores the significance of various uniform rates of productivity increase and income and price elasticities in a two commodity-two country format in order to analyze trade balance consequences. Hicks' model is a four commodity-two country one incorporating biased as well as uniform productivity change. The following discussion weaves aspects of the adjustment mechanism into the analysis, emphasizes balance of payments phenomena, and simplifies the picture compared to Johnson's statement by restricting the assumptions about income and price elasticities. It has therefore been necessary to take some liberties with the expositions of Hicks and Johnson. Hicks' argument is faithfully summarized by Machlup [62] and Letiche [55, pp. 179–84]. Bruton [13] uses the Johnson framework to examine the relative impact of technological progress in developed and underdeveloped countries.

25. Hereafter income without the antecedent will mean money income. Real income will be so specified. Income effects are mentioned by many scholars,

among them Laursen [54], Balogh [5], MacDougall [59; 60, Appendixes VI.B and VI.C], Basu [9], and Bernstein [10]. Kemp [42] and Asimakopulos [2] give rigorous demonstrations that the strict Hicksian conclusion that import-biased innovation is detrimental to the non-innovating country is challengeable with certain income effects. Johnson [38] suggests that simple income effects must be augmented by income redistribution considerations in the event that the various commodities require different factor intensities in production and that the factors have different marginal propensities to consume the various commodities. Laursen [54, p. 185] and Letiche [55, p. 183] point out that even with constant money income, real income effects are unavoidable and would work in the same direction as the absent money income effects.

26. The analysis assumes constant production costs for all goods and a fixed exchange rate system. It is also assumed that each country's price elasticity of demand for imports is greater than one for both price increases and decreases. In addition, no good is inferior in consumption, i.e., income elasticities of demand for imports are positive.

27. Concerning the "low, preferably inelastic" price elasticities, it is implied that the income adjustments in the two countries are such as to reduce the price of A's exports relative to B's import-substitute and to raise the prices of B's exports relative to A's import-substitute. Under the assumed conditions, of course, all prices will fall in absolute terms. Price elasticities should be as high as possible, to favor B's balance, if the income changes result in the opposite relative price movements.

28. Laursen [54, p. 184] brings up a similar point. He notes that the balance of trade results of innovation depend partly upon whether wages move with average over-all productivity or with productivity in the export-good sector. See also Bernstein [10, pp. 103–5].

29. The factual validity of several important assumptions of Hicks has been examined, specifically whether U.S. productivity has risen more rapidly than elsewhere (usually the United Kingdom) and whether it has recently been import biased. See Balogh [5, pp. 248–49], Laursen [54, pp. 185–86], MacDougall [57; 58; 60, Chaps. IV and V], and Letiche [55, pp. 186–98].

Note also that Hicks has clarified his interpretation of import-biased productivity change [33]. The usage in the text follows that generally accepted from the inaugural lecture of Hicks and does not reflect the subtleties of his clarification.

30. An alternative hypothesis concerning the absence of dollar shortage during the nineteenth century is that of Matthews [64, p. 400]. Even though during that century U.S. technological progress was in the vanguard, productivity growth and expansion of income in the U.S. caused a reduced dependence on foreign loans and on foreign goods alike, with the two phenomena being offsetting.

31. In particular, as concerns the effects of disparate progress in the U.S., it is important to draw distinctions between predominantly industrial countries and predominantly agricultural countries, as in Despres [79b, p. 1024] and Basu [9].

32. Cooper points out that this pattern can also be explained by relative international income changes and differing income elasticities of demand [16, pp. 113–15].

33. The two types of growth model are frequently called, after the names

of those economists who developed them, Abramovitz-Solow type growth (through technological progress) and Harrod-Domar type growth (through investment). These models of growth are formulated in Abramovitz [1], Solow [77], Harrod [32], and Domar [19].

It should be cautioned that whether or not innovation can occur without investment — even without *net* investment — is a moot and interesting point. Exploring the issue does not offer the prospects of great rewards in this context. Therefore, it will be assumed that there is in fact a sharp dichotomy between the capital accumulation and technological change types of growth.

34. As Johnson [40b, pp. 121–22] notes, the Harrod-Domar equilibrium rate of growth in investment, productive capacity, and income in an open economy is inversely related to the level of productive capacity and the average propensities to save and to import.

35. That is, they are computed by dividing the index of value by the index of quantum. These latter two series are independently compiled; the unit value series is derivative.

36. The role of foreign competition in this instance is ambiguous. Will factors of production insist on raising returns in the face of foreign competition when the by-product is apt to be unemployment? Or will the cost-push pressures be restricted to sectors free of competition from abroad?

37. Demand-shift inflation was first proffered by C. L. Schultze [76] as an explanation of the rapid rise in prices in the U.S. during 1955–57, when the evidence seemed incompatible with either cost-push or excess demand inflation.

38. To the extent that inflationary pressures enter the analysis, the demonstration effect hypothesis takes on elements of the argument that the dollar problem arises from relative price level movements. If the pressures are permitted to affect prices, exports will decline and imports will rise; if the pressures are frustrated and price increases averted, imports will still increase and export goods will be absorbed by the domestic market. The important point, however, is that the inflationary pressures themselves are a response to partly fulfilled attempts to emulate.

39. An alternative, little noted, extremely tentative hypothesis explaining the switch is suggested by Kindleberger [49, pp. 58–59], based upon a finding of Linder [56, Chap. 3]. Kindleberger notes that countries typically export the kinds of goods embodied into the standard of living of their population masses. This, he reasons, might partly explain why Britain lost its export market for low-grade cotton textiles. The British level of living exceeded the point where these goods were important elements in domestic demand. Similarly, he reasons, because of the upgrading of the American automobile as U.S. incomes rose, its quality now surpasses that required by countries which formerly imported American cars. It is fair to note in passing that this argument would seem to have its greatest plausibility for explaining a declining export market of countries in which domestic demand, not foreign, dominates the total market. Thus, it is perhaps more relevant for the U.S. than for the U.K.

40. Alternatively, Cooper [27b, p. 151] implies that the American consumer's myopia is as strong as ever but that relative prices of American and foreign goods have shifted sufficiently to offset the consumer's inertia. American consumers, in consequence, are buying more abroad, even though their tastes are unchanged.

BIBLIOGRAPHY

[1] M. Abramovitz, "Resource and Output Trends in the United States Since 1870," *AER* (May 1956).

[2] A. Asimakopulos, "A Note on Productivity Changes and the Terms of Trade," *OEP* (June 1957).

[3] T. Balogh, "The Concept of a Dollar Shortage," *Man Sch* (May 1949).

[4] _____, *The Dollar Crisis: Causes and Cure* (1949).

[5] _____, "The Dollar Crisis Revisited," *OEP* (September 1954).

[6] _____, "The Dollar Shortage Once More: A Reply," *Scottish Journal of Political Economy* (June 1955).

[7] _____, "The United States and International Economic Equilibrium," in S. E. Harris (ed.), *Foreign Economic Policy for the United States* (1948).

[8] _____, "The United States and the World Economy," *BOUIS* (October 1946).

[9] P. K. Basu, "Theoretical Dollar Shortage," *Indian Economic Journal* (April 1955).

[10] E. M. Bernstein, "American Productivity and the Dollar Payments Problem," *REStat* (May 1955).

[11] _____, *International Effects of U.S. Economic Policy*, Study Paper No. 16 in U.S. Congress, Joint Economic Committee, Study of Employment, Growth, and Price Levels (86th Cong., 2d Sess., 1960).

[12] A. I. Bloomfield, "Induced Investment, Overcomplete International Adjustment, and Chronic Dollar Shortage," *AER* (September 1949).

[13] H. J. Bruton, "Productivity, the Trade Balance and the Terms of Trade," *Econia Internaz* (August 1955).

[14] T. C. Chang, *Cyclical Movements in the Balance of Payments* (1951).

[15] H. S. Cheng, "Relative Movements in the Prices of Exports of Manufactures: United States Versus Other Industrial Countries, 1953–59," *SP* (March 1962).

[16] R. N. Cooper, "American Competition in World Markets, 1953–1960." Unpublished Ph.D. dissertation, Harvard University (October 1961).

[17] _____, "International Aspects," in American Assembly, Columbia University, *Automation and Technological Change* (1962).

[18] G. Crowther, *Balances and Imbalances of Payments* (1957).

[19] E. V. Domar, "Capital Expansion, Rate of Growth, and Employment," *Emet* (April 1946).

[20] H. S. Ellis, "The Dollar Shortage in Theory and Fact," *CJEPS* (August 1948).

[21] J. M. Fleming and S. C. Tsiang, "Changes in Competitive Strength and Export Shares of Major Industrial Countries," *SP* (August 1956).

[22] H. J. Frank, "The United States Balance of Payments Problem: Causes and Cures," *Econia Internaz* (May 1960).

[23] J. H. Furth, "Unbalanced International Accounts: Diagnosis and Therapy," *AER* (May 1961).

[24] F. D. Graham, *The Causes and Cure of the "Dollar Shortage,"* Princeton University, International Finance Section, Essays in International Finance No. 10 (January 1949).

[25] G. Haberler, "Dollar Shortage?" in S. E. Harris (ed.), *Foreign Policy for the United States* (1948).

[26] _____, *Growth and Balance in World Trade,* the Galen L. Stone Inaugural Lecture, Harvard University (1958).

[27] S. E. Harris (ed.), *The Dollar in Crisis* (1961).
a. E. M. Bernstein, "The New Administration and the Dollar-Payments Problem."
b. R. N. Cooper, "The Competitive Position of the United States."
c. G. Haberler, "Domestic Economic Policies and the United States Balance of Payments."
d. S. E. Harris, "Introduction."
e. R. Triffin, "The International Monetary Position of the United States."
f. J. Vanek, "Long-Run Factors in the United States Payments Disequilibrium."

[28] _____, "Dollar Scarcity: Some Remarks Inspired by Lord Keynes' Last Article," *EJ* (June 1947).

[29] _____, *International and Interregional Economics* (1957).

[30] R. F. Harrod, *Are These Hardships Necessary?* (1947).

[31] _____, *The Dollar* (1954).

[32] _____, *Toward a Dynamic Economics* (1948).

[33] J. R. Hicks, "A Further Note on 'Import Bias,' " in Hicks *Essays in World Economics* (1959).

[34] _____, "An Inaugural Lecture," *OEP* (June 1953).

[35] R. Hinshaw, "Implications of the Shift in the U.S. Balance of Payments," *AER* (May 1959).

[36] E. Hoffmeyer, *Dollar Shortage and the Structure of U.S. Foreign Trade* (1958).

[37] H. G. Johnson, "Economic Expansion and the Balance of Payments," *BOUIS* (February 1955).

[38] _____, "Effects of Changes in Comparative Costs as Influenced by Technical Change," *Malayan Economic Review* (October 1961). Reprinted in R. Harrod (ed.), *International Trade Theory in a Developing World* (1963).

[39] _____, "The International Competitive Position of the United States and the Balance of Payments Prospect for 1968," *REStat* (February 1964).

[40] _____, *International Trade and Economic Growth* (1958).
a. "Economic Expansion and International Trade." Reprinted from *Man Sch* (May 1955).
b. "Equilibrium Growth in an International Economy." Reprinted from *CJEPS* (November 1953).
c. "Increasing Productivity, Income-Price Trends and the Trade Balance." Reprinted from *EJ* (September 1954).

[41] _____, "Statement" in U.S. Congress, Joint Economic Committee, Subcommittee on International Exchange and Payments, *International Pay-*

ments Imbalances and Need for Strengthening International Financial Arrangements: Hearings, May 16, June 19–21, 1961 (87th Cong., 1st Sess., 1961).

[42] M. C. Kemp, "Technological Change, the Terms of Trade and Welfare," *EJ* (September 1955).

[43] P. B. Kenen, "Short-Term Capital Movements and the U.S. Balance of Payments," in U.S. Congress, Joint Economic Committee, *The United States Balance of Payments: Hearings,* July 8 and 9, 1963 (88th Cong., 1st Sess., 1963).

[44] J. M. Keynes, "The Balance of Payments of the United States," *EJ* (June 1946).

[45] C. P. Kindleberger, "Anciens et Nouveaux Produits en Commerce International," *Économie Appliquée* (July–September 1954).

[46] _____, *The Dollar Shortage* (1950).

[47] _____, "The Dollar Shortage Re-Revisited," *AER* (June 1958).

[48] _____, "Foreign Trade and Growth: Lessons from British Experience Since 1913," *Lloyds Bank Review* (July 1962).

[49] _____, *Foreign Trade and the National Economy* (1962).

[50] _____, "The Foreign-Trade Multiplier, the Propensity to Import and Balance-of-Payments Equilibrium" *AER* (March 1949) and his "Rejoinder," *AER* (September 1949).

[51] I. B. Kravis, " 'Availability' and Other Influences on the Commodity Composition of Trade," *JPE* (April 1956).

[52] H. B. Lary, "Disturbances and Adjustments in Recent U.S. Balance-of-Payments Experience," *AER* (May 1961).

[53] _____, *Problems of the United States as World Trader and Banker* (1963).

[54] S. Laursen, "Productivity, Wages, and the Balance of Payments," *REStat* (May 1955).

[55] J. M. Letiche, *Balance of Payments and Economic Growth* (1959).

[56] S. B. Linder, *An Essay on Trade and Transformation* (1961).

[57] G. D. A. MacDougall, "British and American Exports: A Study Suggested by the Theory of Comparative Costs, Part I," *EJ* (December 1951).

[58] _____, "Does Productivity Rise Faster in the United States?" *REStat* (May 1956).

[59] _____, "A Lecture on the Dollar Problem," *Econa* (August 1954).

[60] _____, *The World Dollar Problem* (1957).

[61] _____, *The World Dollar Problem: A Reappraisal,* Princeton University, International Finance Section, Essays in International Finance No. 35 (November 1960).

[62] F. Machlup, "Dollar Shortage and Disparities in the Growth of Productivity," *Scottish Journal of Political Economy* (October 1954).

[63] _____, "Three Concepts of the Balance of Payments and the So-called Dollar Shortage," *EJ* (March 1950).

[64] R. C. O. Matthews, "Review of J. E. Meade, *The Theory of International*

Economic Policy, Volume I: The Balance of Payments," *EHR,* Vol. IV, No. 3 (1952).

[65] J. E. Meade, *The Balance of Payments* (1951).

[66] I. Mintz, *American Exports During Business Cycles, 1879–1958,* National Bureau of Economic Research Occasional Paper No. 76 (1961).

[67] _____, *Trade Balances during Business Cycles: U.S. and Britain since 1880,* National Bureau of Economic Research Occasional Paper No. 67 (1959).

[68] National Institute of Economic and Social Research Staff, "World Trade in Manufactures," *National Institute Economic Review* (July 1960).

[69] R. Nurkse, *Conditions of International Monetary Equilibrium,* Princeton University, International Finance Section, Essays in International Finance No. 4 (Spring 1945). Reprinted in American Economic Association, *Readings in the Theory of International Trade* (1949).

[70] _____, "A New Look at the Dollar Problem and the United States Balance of Payments," in Nurkse, *Equilibrium and Growth in the World Economy* (1961). Reprinted from *Econia Internaz* (February 1954).

[71] _____, *Problems of Capital Formation in Underdeveloped Countries* (1953).

[72] D. H. Robertson, *Britain in the World Economy* (1954).

[73] A. Romanis, "Relative Growth of Exports of Manufactures of the United States and Other Industrial Countries," *SP* (May 1961).

[74] W. S. Salant *et al., The United States Balance of Payments in 1968,* "The Brookings Report" (1963).

[75] E. R. Schlesinger, "Discussion of 'International Trade and Payments in an Era of Coexistence,' " *AER* (May 1959).

[76] C. L. Schultze, *Recent Inflation in the United States:* Study Paper No. 1 in U.S. Congress, Joint Economic Committee, *Study of Employment, Growth and Price Levels* (1959).

[77] R. M. Solow, "Technical Change and the Aggregate Production Function," *REStat* (August 1957).

[78] R. Triffin, *Europe and the Money Muddle* (1957).

[79] U.S. Congress, Joint Economic Committee, *Employment, Growth, and Price Levels, Hearings, Part 5: International Influences on the American Economy* (1959).
a. E. M. Bernstein
b. E. Despres
c. C. P. Kindleberger

[80] U.S. Congress, Joint Economic Committee, *Factors Affecting the United States Balance of Payments* (87th Cong., 2d Sess., 1962).
a. B. Balassa, "Recent Developments in the Competitiveness of American Industry and Prospects for the Future."
b. P. W. Bell, "Private Capital Movements and the U.S. Balance-of-Payments Position."
c. S. E. Harris, "The U.S. Balance of Payments, the Problem and Its Solution."

[81] U.S. Department of Agriculture, *Competitive Position of United States Farm Products Abroad, 1958* (January 1958).

[82] U.S. Department of Commerce, "Analysis of Changes in United States Shares of Export Markets for Manufactures, 1954–1958" by Carl Blackwell (mimeographed, n.d.).

[83] J. H. Williams, *Economic Stability in the Modern World* (1952). Republished as *Trade Not Aid: A Program for World Stability* (1954).

[84] _____, "International Trade Theory and Policy — Some Current Issues," *AER* (May 1951).

[85] J. G. Williamson, "Dollar Scarcity and Surplus in Historical Perspective," *AER* (May 1963).

CHAPTER 9 / The Adequacy of International Reserves

PREFATORY STATEMENT

Autonomous international payments conventionally arise because individuals and governments purchase goods and services produced abroad, invest in foreign countries, and speculate and conduct arbitrage activities in foreign currencies. When a country's autonomous international receipts fall short of its autonomous international payments, some means of settling its resulting indebtedness to the rest of the world is required. Ultimately, settlement takes the form of intercountry transfers of international reserves. Without international reserve holdings, no country could sustain deficits in its balance of payments; indeed, the size and duration of a payments deficit that a country can endure without remedial actions is very directly related to the volume and liquidity of its international reserves. Since the mechanism that tends to equilibrate a country's autonomous international expenditures and receipts is sluggish in meeting the strains put upon it by participation in the world economy, the volume and liquidity of international reserves are strategic facets of the viability of the international economic system.

With relatively fixed exchange rates inadequate international reserves predispose countries, and hence the world economy, toward slower growth rates, deflationary economic policies, and restrictions on movements of goods and productive factors. Inadequate reserves increase the world's proneness to crises in foreign exchange markets. Insufficient reserves can also disrupt normal patterns of international trade and payments and lead to a reduction in the level of foreign trade and investment. Contrastingly, with excessive international reserves, prices in the world economy tend to rise secularly and productive factors tend to be malallocated. The goal is to find the "golden mean" between these untenable positions so that the volume and liquidity of international reserves is just adequate.

It is decidedly easier to specify a goal than to attain it, however. A consensus on the goal itself may be lacking. The present structure of

402

the international monetary system may frustrate attempts to achieve the goal within the system's framework. An alteration of the system, however, besides disturbing vested interests, generates its own set of uncertainties. There is, then, no ready solution to the range of problems resulting from an insufficiency or surfeit of international reserves. Yet, the initial step toward the ultimate remedy to these problems, whatever it may be, is to set forth concretely the conditions which adequate international reserves must fulfill.

International reserves[1] enable countries to incur temporary balance of payments deficits while holding their exchange rates steady. This vital function, which reserves have always performed, has only recently received emphasis. In particular, it has come to the fore as nations have desired to take a more active part in the determination of relative economic well-being. International reserves in effect free countries to undertake policies whose implementation, in the absence of adequate reserves, would involve very costly economic sacrifices. Countries rather have released themselves from the conventional "rules" of the gold standard.

Under the classical explanation of the operation of the gold standard, countries were expected to adjust to balance of payments difficulties by changes in the domestic price level, production costs, and, in all likelihood, employment. Changes in the level of gold reserves were to trigger and transmit the adjustment process and relative interest rates played an important role in this explanation. That the gold standard ever functioned along these lines may be, as Triffin suggests [57, pp. 2–20], a popular myth. Nevertheless, there is no doubt that the present commitment of governments to the goals of reasonable price level stability and full employment makes this supposed mechanism of adjustment under the fixed exchange rates of the international gold standard unpalatable and inoperative. Still, it is the intent of the present international monetary system that countries maintain highly stable or occasionally adjusted rates of exchange in the face of inevitable payments deficits and surpluses.

An obvious and critical question arises, therefore: if nations troubled by payments imbalances do not allow income and price level correctives, if exchange rate adjustments are ruled out except in extraordinary circumstances, and if imposition of direct controls is frowned upon, how, then, do such nations adapt to balance of payments difficulties? The answer, somewhat oversimplified, is that in most instances countries do not consciously adjust by actively attempting to eliminate the imbalances. Rather, deficits are sustained and there is a loss of international reserves.

External economic events are no longer permitted to force a compromise of domestic stability. This strategy is appropriate, however, only when the excess of international payments over receipts is short-lived or when international reserves are adequate.[2] Under these conditions, as Nurkse [48, pp. 11–14; 49, pp. 212–19] described concisely, holdings of international reserves serve effectively as a buffer and temporarily insulate the domestic economy from outside forces.

It would be a happy fortuity if all payments imbalances were short-lived. Even excluding those imbalances arising during the course of economic development of underdeveloped countries — imbalances incidentally that should be met by long-term capital flows rather than by resort to international reserve balances — many payments disequilibria will be prolonged and more fundamental. In order to eliminate these imbalances, exchange rate adjustments, deflation, trade and exchange restrictions, or structural changes are needed. Nevertheless, in actual practice the character of the disequilibrium is usually not immediately evident, nor is the nature of the required adjustment policy always obvious. Indeed, some of these adjustments are so attractive — they produce results quickly — that they are tempting even when inappropriate. Thus, on the one hand it is important to stress, as do the Joint Economic Committee [62, pp. 10–11] and the "Group of 32" [22, pp. 48, 50], that the existence of ample international reserves insures that these remedial steps need not be undertaken prematurely or without reasonable prospect that they are appropriate. On the other hand, it must not be forgotten that if a country is too liberally supplied with reserve balances necessary adjustment to fundamental disequilibrium may be inordinately postponed, making eventual adjustment more difficult. This too is acknowledged by the "Group of 32"; indeed, the fears of many experts that reserves are, or may soon be, excessive are based on this argument. Patently, reserves in any amount are not an unmitigated blessing.

International reserves must also accommodate the speculative capital movements and interest arbitrage which occur under a system of freely convertible currencies. The world economy becomes especially prone to crippling international capital movements when there is shaken confidence in the ability of reserve centers to convert their currencies into gold at a given price. It may seem, at first blush, that such short-term capital flows will not be large but it is important to point out that the limits of short-term capital movements of this variety are not set by the amount of a country's currency held by foreigners. Normally the liquid asset holdings of a country's own citizens are freely transferable abroad.[3] Thus, the potential drain from speculation and arbitrage is truly enormous.

It is evident, then, that an adequate supply of liquid international reserves is essential to the continued viability of the current international monetary system.[4] Assuming that payments imbalances continue, quasi-fixed exchange rates and the independent governmental pursuit of internal economic stability are incompatible in the absence of adequate international reserves. Where both of these goals are sought, reserves in sufficient volume and liquidity are essential to the continued growth of international trade and capital movements. They are also vital if the world's resources are to be optimally allocated. The question of the adequacy of international reserves does indeed justify the attention economists have given it.

☐ THE GOLD EXCHANGE STANDARD

The importance of an adequate volume of international reserves has long been recognized. It was an urgent issue after World War I; experts then, as now, anticipated an increasing need for international reserves, while gold production had been falling. Faced with this problem, the monetary authorities recommended that holdings of foreign exchange balances as well as gold be used as international reserves.[5] In response, holdings of exchange, primarily of pounds sterling, dollars, and short-term sterling and dollar assets, supplemented gold as international reserves. Thus, as a practical matter, exchange reserve holdings became concentrated in London and New York. This system enabled reserves to increase relative to gold and during 1927 and 1928 approximately 40 per cent of the international reserve holdings of European central banks was in the form of foreign exchange.

By the end of the 1920's, however, the gold exchange standard was prostrate. Its collapse was attributable to a lack of liquidity of international reserves: Nurkse [49, p. 46] asserted that coordination among central banks was poor; the IMF staff noted that a high proportion of the foreign exchange reserves were not in fact "owned" but had been borrowed at short term [30, pp. 17, 27–28]. In the terminology of later sections, the problem was more a matter of the illiquidity of reserves than of insufficient volume. Significantly, and somewhat ironically, no contemporary analyst ascribed the downfall of the international monetary system of the Twenties to a long-run inability to supply reserves in sufficient volume. In contrast, many of today's critics of the system condemn it because of its incapability of providing over the long pull the necessary reserve volume: the Joint Economic Committee, for example, reported that "the special weakness of the gold-exchange standard is that it does not provide adequate reserves" and from the context it can be inferred that the committee meant the volume of international reserves in the long-run [62, p. 7].

Because of its success in economizing gold supplies, the gold exchange standard' of the Twenties cannot be deemed a failure. Indeed, when fears of a shortage of reserves reappeared following World War II, the international monetary network, after a frustrating period of extensive exchange control and inconvertibility, gravitated toward a gold exchange standard. Consequently, over time foreign exchange holdings have become an impressively large segment of the total of international reserves. In the decade of the 1950's more than half of the increase in world reserves was due to the use of short-term dollar balances, with Western gold production contributing less than a third of the expansion in reserves. Moreover, toward the end of the decade a substantial proportion of the increment to global reserves came from gold sales by the U.S.S.R. to the West, a phenomenon which gave rise to auguries that the viability of the gold exchange standard was closely tied to the vicissitudes of the Cold War.

Nevertheless, the international monetary system that has evolved differs from its prototype of the 1920's in several important respects. Friedman [18] and the IMF staff [30, pp. 27–28] argue that today's system is in some ways less stable. For example, while the system still has two reserve centers, dollars now bulk much larger than pounds in official exchange holdings. One consequence of this change in the composition of reserves, noted by the Joint Economic Committee [62, p. 6], is an increase in the relative volatility of the exchange component of reserves: the allegiance of sterling holders to the London reserve center traditionally has been much stronger than that of dollar holders to New York. In the 1920's the U.K. was providing exchange reserves, in effect, by virtue of its sizable trade account deficit; in the 1950's, by contrast, the U.S. was running trade account surpluses but was contributing to world international reserves through its larger deficits on private long-term capital and government accounts. This also tends to augment the instability inherent in the gold exchange standard; a capital-cum-government account deficit in the reserve center country is a less dependable, although in the short-run perhaps a more stable, source of reserves than is an import surplus. Finally, because of the greater reluctance to permit adjustment to occur through deflation and unemployment there is probably less assurance today relative to the Twenties that current exchange rates will be maintained. This increases the probability of speculative exchange movements from one currency to another.[6]

In contrast, some elements in the current situation tend to counter these destabilizing developments. Unlike the 1920's, the majority of the present exchange reserves today is "owned" rather than borrowed, as the IMF staff stresses [30, pp. 7, 94]. This adds to the liquidity of total international reserves and to the stability of reserves as long as the viability of the international monetary system itself is not seriously challenged. In part, changes in composition of the exchange component of reserves and in the over-all liquidity of exchange holdings are the result of the large sterling balances carried over from Britain's efforts to finance its wartime and immediate postwar needs. They are also the result, until relatively recently, of a conscious effort on the part of U.S. government to permit foreign authorities to accumulate larger dollar reserve holdings.

The activities of the IMF and the European Economic Community have improved the operation of today's international monetary system. Central bankers, too, have firmly grasped the lessons of the interwar period; in the event of a run on a major currency, central bankers have several times in the last few years demonstrated an aptitude for rescuing the currency with suitably tailored assistance arrangements. The first and most publicized of these arrangements occurred in March 1961 when the British pound was subjected to adverse pressures following the German and Dutch revaluations. At that time Western European central bankers negotiated the so-called Basel agreement to discourage destabilizing speculation and ameliorate the effects of "hot" money movements.[7] International financial negotiations, since the 1961 breakthrough, have produced a number of innovations (described clearly by Aliber [2]) which at the very least have provided short-run defenses at several points where the monetary network has been under attack. Moreover, recent reports of the so-called "Group of Ten" [21] and of the IMF [31, Chaps. 3 and 4] and the articles by Altman [3] and Fleming [16] indicate that further innovations are in the offing.

Finally, in the postwar period purely domestic business cycles have not caused such serious strains as in the past. Moreover, the cycles that have occurred do not appear to have been transmitted to other countries to the extent that they formerly were. Because of these many structural differences, then, several sources of instability in the gold exchange standard of the Twenties are no longer significant.

Nevertheless, a gold exchange standard with more than one reserve center inherently tends to be unstable. This is so for two reasons. First, the existence of two (or a few) reserve centers, such as New York and London, makes it possible for third parties to take advantage of international interest rate differentials in their investing-borrowing decisions[8] or to speculate on exchange rate movements by converting one reserve currency into the other without an appreciable deterioration of their reserve positions.[9] Such transfers usually begin when a reserve currency displays some weakness and they intensify the pressures causing the weakness. Capital outflows from the reserve center may indeed precipitate devaluation or exchange control, both of which would seriously damage the reserve currency status of the center.

There is, of course, a corresponding net gain by the reserve center whose currency is being purchased by speculators or arbitrageurs. Its gold holdings and its exchange liabilities will increase to the same degree. Initially this will tend to improve its liquidity position and enhance its strength as a reserve center. Thus, despite the disadvantages of having two or a few more reserve centers, such a system may provide a greater growth of international reserves than the more stable single-center system. It will do so as long as an identical expansion of gold holdings and exchange liabilities in one center — and decreases in gold and liabilities in the other — are not treated symmetrically, the effects of the gold loss in the one center and the effects of the exchange liability increase in the other both being somewhat discounted. Whether the world as a whole is better off as a consequence — whether the increase in the system's instability through increasing the possibility of profitable short-term capital movements counterbalances the growth potential of reserves — remains at present a debatable issue.

The inherent instability of the gold exchange standard is apt to be increased because such a system is prone to a limited multiplication of reserve centers. Currently there is evidence that other currencies are assuming the role of an international reserve currency, alongside the dollar and the pound. For a country to become a reserve center it must have a strong currency and it must be a substantial international creditor. In practice this means that the nascent reserve center must, for a time, run a balance of payments surplus. In so doing, it usually accumulates substantial amounts of reserve currencies and ultimately converts some of these into gold. Since gold in "mature" reserve centers provides the backing for a pyramided system of international reserves throughout the world economy, a gold loss by mature centers may precipitate a multiple contraction of international reserves throughout the world, provided that it is the gross, rather than net, international reserve position which is the basis for calculating the effective international "reserve ratio." Eventually, of course, the currency of the nascent reserve center will become widely held as exchange reserves. There is, nevertheless, a considerable period during which the liquidity, if not the volume, of international reserves is reduced.

To this consideration must be added the possibility, first mentioned by Tew [61h, p. 289], that new reserve currency countries might well, because of the lesson of the experiences of the U.S. and the U.K., maintain something like 100 per cent reserves against their short-term liabilities and not permit their payments balance to deteriorate sufficiently to become the source of significant increments in total reserves held by other countries. Nevertheless, the consensus seems to be that the end result of proliferation of reserve centers is to enlarge the possibilities for growth of reserves. Again there is a risk in that a multiplication of reserve centers increases the probability of destabilizing speculation but this is at least partly offset because of the greater prospects for mutual support among the reserve centers and because it offers additional currencies as alternatives to holding gold.

While these destabilizing features of the gold exchange standard are debilitating, the standard's most serious drawback is the way in which it provides for over-all increases in international reserves. When current gold production is insufficient to supply the needed growth in global international reserves, the deficiency can only be filled by the acquisition of balances of reserve currencies. This means that the reserve centers must be prepared to run payments deficits to facilitate reserve currency accumulation by other countries. The effect of such deficits is to reduce the liquidity of the reserve centers by causing a deterioration in their net reserve positions. Ultimately, there may be a loss of confidence in one of the reserve currencies with a growing likelihood of destabilizing capital flight. Naturally, this basic dilemma of the gold exchange standard has caught the experts' attention as is manifest in the report of the "Group of 32" [22, esp. pp. 32, 34–36]. Kaldor's apt statement of this issue is worth repeating: "The basic shortcoming of a '[reserve] currency' system lies precisely in the fact that it only provides international liquidity when the [reserve] currencies are 'weak,' whereas the whole system presupposes that the currencies which serve as the reserves for others should be exceptionally 'strong' " [33, p. 277]. Triffin, the pre-eminent expositor of the inconsistencies of the current international monetary system, dramatizes the dilemma by categorically asserting that the present international monetary system's "long term survival is admittedly impossible" [55, p. 48; also Triffin, 56 and Angell, 1, pp. 696–97].

It should be clear that the current international monetary system requires sustained confidence in the ability of the reserve centers to convert their currencies into gold and other currencies at fixed prices. Confidence in a reserve currency is conditioned by a complex set of factors, most of which are noted in the Committee for Economic Development's study of international liquidity [12, p. 24]. Because the psychological climate is so vital, appraisal of these factors is indeed difficult. It is generally dangerous to infer from a given balance of payments deficit and a given volume of exchange indebtedness to foreigners that some particular level of gold reserves is safe. It can be said, however, that if the liquidity of a reserve center should fall because of some combination of a larger payments deficit, gold losses, or increased foreign holdings of the currency, the margin of safety provided by a given amount of gold reserves is reduced. In recent years, where the reserve currencies are, in Yeager's stressed term, "precariously pegged to gold on a fractional-reserve basis" [65, p. 302], it is likely that the touchstone to expectations of confidence is gold movements alone. Loss of gold, even though on a relatively minor scale and unaccompanied by other alarming signs, may be enough to shake confidence in a reserve currency and threaten the effectiveness of a center country. The gross reserve positions of reserve centers, as well as their net positions, have an important bearing on confidence. Thus, even though foreign exchange holdings can replace gold as international reserves in non-reserve currency areas, the role of gold is still central to the viability of the international monetary system.

□ A STATEMENT OF THE ISSUES

This survey of the difficulties inherent in a multi-center gold exchange standard suggests that there are three major issues in the general problem of the adequacy of international reserves.[10] While the issues clearly are not separate, they are separable. It will contribute to the effectiveness of the subsequent discussion if they are presented individually.

First, a long-run issue arises over whether the international monetary system will permit the amount of international reserves to grow so as to accommodate the expected secular increases in international trade and long-term capital flows. This issue will be called the long-run *expansibility* of the international monetary system. Doubts that the system might fail to provide sufficient reserve expansion, and hence that it might choke off the growth of foreign trade and investment, are widespread and have provoked several explicit recommendations for improving the long-term effectiveness of the system. It is clear that the expansibility problem involves primarily the adequacy of future supplies of (non-Communist) world reserves. The liquidity of these reserves, insofar as that can be divorced from their volume, is of some, although not of great, concern. Necessarily the particular asset composition of the reserve holdings and the geographical distribution of reserves must be considered: since the growth of reserves under a gold exchange standard regime depends importantly upon the strength of and confidence in the reserve currencies, stockpiles of gold in the center countries are strategic. Difficult problems are also posed by a perennial shortage of international reserves in the underdeveloped areas.

The second issue is of a short-term nature and should be clearly distinguished from long-run expansibility. Reserves perform a useful function by allowing countries to ride out short-term balance of payments difficulties, speculative storms, and uncovered arbitrage movements without instituting drastic defensive measures. To fulfill this purpose, the international monetary system must provide short-run reserve *flexibility*, that is, ability of reserves to expand and contract in response to short-run payments disequilibria and violent speculative and arbitrage flows. This is fundamentally a matter of reserve liquidity, although rapid and reversible changes in the level of reserves are not without significance. It should be noted, as Triffin has suggested [25c, p. 227], that insolvency, defined as a condition where liabilities owed abroad are larger than domestic ownership of foreign assets, is not an issue.

The problem of flexibility is almost solely concerned with the circumstances of reserve centers. Reserve currencies, in particular, must be always above suspicion. Until the world economy has become acclimated to the situation where reserve centers meet liquidity crises by, say, borrowing or swap arrangements, it is hazardous to try to cope with speculative flights by these instruments. If there has been no precedent established, further doubts about a reserve center's status may be raised. Non-reserve center countries, however, can borrow reserves in virtually any amounts up to the extent of their credit capacities without compromising the viability of the international monetary system. Thus, in the instance of reserve flexibility, it is not so much the world's reserves but the liquidity of reserve currencies that must be preserved.

Whether or not the current volume and liquidity of international reserves are *adequate* to support the current level of world payments — the third issue — is of great immediacy. On it hinges the decision of whether or not emergency treatment of the system is mandatory. The problem, in the final analysis, is one of assessing qualitative arguments because objective, measurable criteria of reserve adequacy do not exist. Experts have wrestled with this problem for some time and have managed only to reach an *ex post* consensus that reserves were insufficient in the late Twenties, but there is little agreement as to cause.

At the moment, however, the adequacy of the present reserve level does not seem seriously questioned. A few scholars — Busschau [10] and Harrod [25b; 26] for example — judge that the present level of reserves is crippling the world economy. Most economists range throughout the spectrum to the position of virtual certainty that reserves are presently sufficient to meet most current needs — a position taken by Altman [5; 25a] and the IMF [30] — and to the position at the polar extreme, exemplified by Holtrop [27, p. 42], of present international reserve redundancy. These disparate views suggest that there is little accepted doctrine to discuss here. Nevertheless, the issue of present adequacy is so vital that the difficulties in appraising the adequacy of reserves at a given time must be considered.

The discussion is bound to be inconclusive. In part, the assessment of reserve adequacy entails a difficult judgment of whether or not the world's economic resources are reasonably optimally allocated at the present time. The problem is further enormously complicated by the fact that the relatively specific questions of appropriate level, liquidity, geographical distribution of reserves, and asset composition of reserves are admixed with the more general and deep-seated questions of the effectiveness of the existing international adjustment process and the political "hot potato" of acceptable domestic macroeconomic goals and monetary and fiscal policies. Feasible mechanisms of adjustment to payments imbalances and the potential types of balance of payments disequilibria to which economies must adapt are also especially relevant to the "determination" of reserve adequacy, as Lary [42, pp. 99–117], Williamson [64, pp. 427–28], Fleming [15], and, more recently, the "Group of 32" [22] have underlined.

There is, for countries in payments deficit, an inverse relationship between the efficacy of the adjustment mechanism and the need for reserves. The quicker and more thorough the adjustment process the fewer international reserves are required. Conversely, the larger the volume of international reserves the less likely is the adjustment process to work effectively. The adjustment mechanism is both automatic and contrived by policy measures and, to the extent that the automatic aspects of adjustment have undesirable effects upon, say, employment or the price level, they may be offset or even reversed by policy instruments. This course of action is facilitated by the existence of a large volume of international reserves.

In the surplus payments countries, however, the relationship between the adjustment mechanism and the amount of international reserves is apt to be the reverse. The larger the volume of reserves the more likely will it be that the automatic adjustment mechanism will be allowed to work — and even be reinforced by conscious policy measures. Mundell notes that "the speed of adjustment may itself be influenced by the availability of reserves. A country with no reserves or borrowing power has to adjust immediately, while a country with limitless reserves does not have to adjust at all. This means that an increase in liquidity, which eventually increases the reserves of surplus countries, shifts the burden of adjustment from deficit to surplus countries" [63d, p. 544]. The statement, of course, assumes that surplus countries do not have to adjust to their payments imbalances while adjustments in the deficit countries will always be painful and, hence, avoided if possible. Since this is indeed the case, Mundell's is a synoptic statement of the relationship between payments adjustment and international reserves. Characteristically, Mundell asserts that the international liquidity problem is a "gold herring": the adjustment mechanism, and not the means of providing international reserves, has failed [63d, pp. 544–49].

There is a similar relationship between the adjustment mechanism, the volume of reserves, and the need for reserve flexibility. Flexibility is needed primarily to meet exchange crises. As reserve currency countries fail to adjust to payments deficits, the amount of international reserves expands and the probability of exchange crises rises. If the deficit is adjusted rapidly, reserves do not grow and crises are less likely. If a reserve center wishes to increase confidence in the exchange value of its currency it may run a payments surplus and international reserves are reduced. Slow adjustment by reserve currency countries to either deficits or surpluses, therefore, affects the volume of international reserves and the need for flexibility in opposite directions. The efficiency of the adjustment mechanism is evidently relevant to the required degree of flexibility as well as volume of international reserves.

These two relationships suggest that the distinction between flexibility of reserves and adequacy of reserve volume is not entirely artificial. If the volume of reserves is permanently expanded because of the possibility of exchange crises in the reserve centers, the adjustment of the world economy to payments imbalances will tend to be inflationary overall. Deficit countries are not so apt to find adjustment imperative and surplus countries will be more likely to respond to the inevitable pressures to expand and inflate. To avoid this, the possibility of exchange crises should be met by enhancing the flexibility of reserves rather than by increasing their volume. Moreover, the need for an appropriate long-run expansion of global reserves is also highlighted. If the rate of required expansion is misjudged on the high side, the world economy is biased in an inflationary direction; if the rate of growth of global reserves errs on the low side, a deflationary bias is imparted to the world economy. Inappropriate growth of reserves biases the adjustment process just as the adjustment process affects the need for reserves.

These examples of the involvement of an assessment of the adequacy of international reserves with the issue of the effectiveness of the adjustment mechanism serve as a reminder that the issue of balance of payments adjustment cannot be wholly ignored. It will come up again and again. Yet, the following sections will not be deeply concerned with the adjustment process; nor, for that matter, will they discuss the causes of disequilibrium. These topics are treated fully in Chapters 5 and 8. Rather, the adjustment mechanism and causes of disequilibrium will come into the discussion to a relatively minor extent and usually by indirection and implication, as is the case in virtually all recent work on the problem of international reserves.

Adequacy

The initial statement of the issue of reserve adequacy begged the question of the geographical unit to which the problem is most relevant. Is it the world's international reserves or is it the availability of a nation's international reserves relative to the need for them that should be the criterion of reserve adequacy? Of course, the notion of adequacy will be imprecise, even under the best of circumstances. But, where feasible, ambiguity should be limited. A brief discussion of the concept of adequacy as it applies at the global or aggregate level accomplishes this.

Scammell [51, pp. 80–81] suggests that the adequacy of global international reserves is a useful, and presumably determinable, concept. The volume of these reserves, it is said, determines the extent of permissible disequilibria that can be successfully borne by a quasi-fixed exchange rate standard in a free, multilateral trading system where the participating nations are singly devoted to seeking high levels of domestic employment and rapid growth. The validity of this assertion is undeniable. Yet, as the IMF staff points out [30, pp. 42–43], the necessary conditions for the statement to hold are fundamentally nationally determined conditions. That is, the important individual countries must not resort to flexible exchange rates; each must not compromise its pursuit of full employment and growth; each must accept multilateralism and free, unfettered trade. Therefore, adequacy of the world's aggregate reserves is not, in the abstract, an operationally meaningful concept. Global reserve adequacy is, at bottom, definable only within a framework of given national policies. And, of course, inadequacy of national (as distinct from global) international reserves is a major constraint upon the policy freedom of the participating countries. Reserve deficiency might compel a country to install trade restrictions or unpeg its exchange rate, in which case a determination of global adequacy becomes impossible.

This view of the meaningfulness of global adequacy was adopted by the Joint Economic Committee in its assessment of international liquidity and payments. "So long as there is any deficiency of reserves in any country," it reported, "there is an overall deficiency, in any meaningful sense" [62, p. 5]. The irrelevance of determining whether global reserves, *per se*, are sufficient or insufficient was recognized. Appropriately, it was concluded that global reserves are almost certainly deficient because "it would be a remarkable coincidence if each country's reserves were adequate" [62, p. 5]. The Joint Economic Committee saved itself from a logical embarrassment, however, by finding that an explicit determination of reserve inadequacy for a particular country is feasible. Thus, there is agreement that the problem of global inadequacy reduces itself to a determination of the reserve adequacy of individual countries.

A clarification must be made at this juncture, however. It may seem, as is suggested by the context of the Joint Economic Committee statement and from general *a priori* notions, that the position taken just above should refer to any *major* country (reserve or non-reserve currency area) rather than to any country at all. On a loose interpretation of the function of reserves, the restriction to major countries would be necessary. The plain fact is that developing countries will typically be short of international reserves in the sense that reserves can be used interchangeably to finance long-term development programs as well as short-term payments deficits. But the analysis here has restricted reserves to the functions of tiding countries over periods of speculative or arbitrage flights, of short-term payments imbalances, and of correction of fundamental payments disequilibria (the last defined so as to exclude balance of payments problems arising from development efforts). When reserves are used only for these purposes, the delimitation of a determination of reserve deficiency to major countries only need not be made.

The conditions that determine a country's need for international reserves are familiar to anyone contemplating the causes of short-run movements in the balance of payments. These are aptly catalogued by Familton [14, pp. 216–17] and the IMF staff [29, pp. 188–89], among others. Cyclical variations in the value of current account items, including exports and service transactions as well as imports; the likelihood and size of equilibrating and disequilibrating short-term capital flows; amplitudes, durations, and synchronization of domestic and foreign business cycles are examples of these causes. Nurkse [49, p. 91] suggested, additionally, that long-term capital movements create a need for reserves in that these capital flows are cyclically unstable so that a borrowing country, in order to smooth out its importing capacity, must set reserves aside. Intercountry differences in conditions such as these go far toward explaining the theoretical existence of some optimum geographical pattern of reserve holdings. Presumably, this optimum pattern will not be one which provides countries with equal reserves per dollar of foreign trade or per dollar of per capita income. Nevertheless, differences in these conditions do not completely explain optimum geographical distribution. The inclination and the ability of a country to hold reserves enter the calculation too, as Nurkse [48, pp. 14–17] also underscored.

The fact that inclination and ability to hold international balances influence the determination of reserve adequacy suggests that there is more to assaying the need for reserves than an evaluation of the causes of short-term payments imbalances. The degree of a country's dependence on imports, the amount of accumulated inventories of internationally traded goods, the country's general level of economic well-being, and similar conditions are factors affecting the ability of a country to tolerate or adjust to a deficit. The inclination to hold reserve balances is determined by less objectively established factors, such as the national financial psychology and the intensity of desires to avoid balance of payments emergencies. Clearly, these factors also vary among countries, especially as between non-reserve and reserve areas. But the factors underlying the inclination to accumulate reserves, while salient, are very subjective. There is little hope of formally including them in an estimate of the need for reserves, although Kenen [38] has provided a framework by which the reserve demands of central banks might be measured.[11]

The roles of a balance of payments model and policy goal / One way to allow for these subjective factors is to admit that reserve adequacy pertains not to a given volume of reserves but to a certain range for the volume of international reserves. A range of reserve adequacy recommends itself for a theoretical reason as well. Both Scitovsky [52, pp. 101–09] and Gemmill [19, pp. 53–54] stress that the degree of adequacy of reserves is determinable only within the framework of a given balance of payments model. Model, in this context, refers not only to the pertinent (for purposes of the adequacy determination) causes of balance of payments disequilibrium but also to a specification of related domestic policy feasibilities and commitments. Balogh affirms this: the need for international liquidity is basically "determined by the policy framework (in particular the range of 'admissible' means of readjustment) and the ends of policy, especially how much unemployment and slowing down of growth countries will tolerate" [7, p. 362, italics omitted]. This, too, is the significance of the IMF staff's assertion that "countries are able," when reserves are adequate, "to make . . . adjustments when they wish without seriously disturbing the system and without initiating a series of deflationary or countervailing actions" [30, p. 43; see also Bernstein 8, p. 79; and Fleming 17, p. 440]. It is also the basis of IMF staff's vigorous contention, typified by Altman's rebuttal [5, p. 164] to Triffin, that a determination of adequacy cannot be made according to any rigidly mechanistic format.

Indeed, the relevance of a "balance of payments model" to an evaluation of the adequacy of international reserves is unanimously agreed upon. Yet, there is nothing approaching unanimity in the evaluation of reserve adequacy itself. How is this possible? The figures on reserves and data on the balances of payments are available for all to study. Further, it must be assumed that the experts are competent and impartial. Much of the disagreement about reserve adequacy stems, in fact, from different implicit assumptions about the currently relevant "balance of payments model." Rather than discuss these different assumptions specifically, attention will be directed to the kinds of considerations that are entailed in formulating a relevant balance of payments model. The difficulties these involve for a determination of reserve adequacy should be evident.

First of all, the model must incorporate some blueprint of the underlying international financial and trading network. Thus far, it has been assumed that the adjustment mechanism is constrained by an adjustable peg exchange rate system, i.e. quasi-fixed rates, in a context of widespread convertibility and transferability. This assumption is generally supported. Yet, as can be imagined, the specific requirements of quasi-fixed exchanges and the practical context for convertibility and transferability are subject to diverse interpretation. Even the institutional framework, about whose features there is common agreement, is a stumbling block to a generally acceptable determination of reserve adequacy. For example, Balogh [7, pp. 361–63] notes that the degree to which multilateralism is *actually* practiced must be assessed.

Sources of even greater difficulties are international differences in admissible policy alternatives and feasible policy objectives. The IMF staff [29, pp. 187–88] enumerates four illustrative combinations. The combinations start from a standard of reserve adequacy which entails the maintenance of currency convertibility in the face of a modest reduction in demand for exports by resorting to exchange and trade restrictions and to a moderate deflationary policy. And they range to a standard implying maintenance of convertibility during a severe decline of export earnings without the need to institute trade and exchange controls and without being forced to invoke deflationary measures. Thus, among other factors, what is involved in the acceptance of any one standard of adequacy is the degree of national dedication to full employment, economic growth, and a world of free trade and payments. Clearly, the standard which involves ability to weather a serious loss of exchange earnings without recourse to deflation or restrictions is more exacting and requires far larger reserves than other feasible policy mixes in order to attain reserve adequacy.

It might be reasonably assumed that all countries would aim for a level of reserves consistent with this standard. After all, it would permit them to adopt most conceivable domestic policy goals with reasonable expectations of successfully achieving them. This, however, is not the case. On the one hand, the accumulation of reserves, even though eminently desirable, entails lost opportunities. It absorbs savings that might otherwise have gone into investment or growth enhancing projects or into greater satisfaction of immediate human wants. The opportunity cost of reserve accumulation, therefore, provides an upper limit to the desirable level of international reserves — a conclusion accepted by the IMF staff [29, pp. 193–94]. The possibility of redundancy is, indeed, the reason Scitovsky asserts that an adequate volume of international reserves "would create an incentive for the surplus countries to share and thus lighten the burden of adjustment of the deficit countries" [12] [61f, p. 175]. On the other hand, failure to accumulate adequate reserves also involves a cost. If reserves are deficient, a country may have to give up convertibility, its employment target, unfettered trade, and so forth — all of which cause serious economic disadvantage. There is also, then, an objective lower limit to the desirable level of reserves.

This kind of rationale for the existence of limits to the desirable level of reserves suggests that it may be possible to derive a single figure for an optimum level of reserves. Two scholars, Fleming and Balogh, have independently developed a theoretically determinable optimum reserve level for a given country, although the bases for their analyses are different and presumably the optimum derived by each would be at different reserve levels. Fleming [17, p. 442] proposes that since reserve increments are subject to diminishing, and eventually negative, marginal usefulness an optimal level exists. Marginal usefulness of increments to reserves diminishes because growing credit ease will ultimately generate inflation. Moreover, increases in reserves will permit liberalization of trade and payments and, after the more onerous restrictions are lifted, further liberalization gives a marginally less effective resource reallocation. Further liberalization is also less likely. Thus, basic to Fleming's position is the hypothesis that the economic gain from incremental reserves becomes progressively smaller and finally negative. Not all are convinced of the evil of gradual inflation and this is reflected in Fleming's analysis where the "costs" of reserve accumulation are given a subsidiary role. Yet inflation can be ignored and it is still possible to find disutility in reserve accumulation. Fleming states that the ultimate disutility of adding to reserves arises if countries become blinded to payments situations requiring structural adjustments.

In contrast, Balogh [7, pp. 363–64] emphasizes the costs of excessive reserve accumulation in his discussion of the optimum level of reserves. While Fleming seems most concerned with relatively short-run consequences of holding reserves, Balogh takes the longer view. Indeed, Balogh assumes in his formulation that economic growth is the essential aim of policy. In view of this key assumption of a growth preoccupation, Balogh's analysis, unlike Fleming's, seems primarily applicable to the liquidity problems of underdeveloped areas.

Balogh's hypothesis is that the sacrifice involved in adding reserves may be that a country's growth rate is reduced. Reserve accumulation, in effect, means that real net investment, the necessary condition for economic growth, has been foregone. Consistent with this hypothesis, there is just one way in which reserve accumulation can be justified: only if the availability of reserves permits an increase in the rate of growth and investment over time by avoiding the adverse effects of balance of payments disturbances and trade restrictions — the adverse effects being weighed, of course, in terms of their consequences for the growth rate. Thus, the optimum level of reserves is one which permits an open economy to obtain a maximum rate of growth from a given resource base and with a given rate of saving.

A difficulty with the Balogh framework is that it is not truly representative of the policy objectives of economically advanced societies. Where the average level of living already greatly exceeds subsistence, it is unlikely that any single economic goal, let alone growth, will be dominant. Hence, Balogh's analysis is not generally applicable. Nevertheless, it accurately reflects the position of the underdeveloped (and reconstructing) areas. In this instance, however, if an optimum reserve level does in practice exist, the level would seem exceptionally low by the standards of advanced countries. This, it appears, is the significance of the frequent observation, illustrated by the IMF staff [29, pp. 193–94], that if a country's international payments are not brought into balance over the business cycle, but rather suffer a persistent, long-term imbalance, as would be the case for an urgently developing country, no amount of reserves will be sufficient. It is also the reason that most observers, of whom Nurkse [48, pp. 1–5] and Kindleberger [61e, pp. 284–85] are typical, insist that the concept of reserve adequacy is relevant only in the context of a balanced or strong payments position over the length of the business cycle.

In view of Balogh's point, this observation is somewhat amiss. It oversimplifies for countries suffering from "other-than-developmental" long-term disequilibria, as well as for developing countries. In the former a positive optimum level of international reserves exists since, even though too many reserves will be likely to delay and worsen the eventual readjustment, some reserves are needed in order to avoid mis-diagnosis and incorrect prescriptions. Still, it has an element of truth in a system where the use of reserves for riding out short-term imbalances cannot be separated from their use for palliating fundamental (developmental) disequilibria. Countries' holdings of international reserves will be highly unequal — some would say maldistributed. Nevertheless, a disparate geographical reserve distribution is the normal condition. With the insistence of development and the substitutability of reserve accumulation and investment, any change in the geographical distribution of reserves would be unsustainable. The "maldistribution" would eventually reassert itself. This is not to say that geographical maldistribution of reserves is impossible. If individual country optima do exist, as both Fleming and Balogh would insist, maldistribution is distinctly possible. But, clearly, disproportionate reserve holdings by particular countries are not *prima facie* evidence of maldistribution.

If Balogh's analysis is most pertinent for growth-oriented economies, Fleming's is most relevant to multi-goal economically advanced countries. For developed economies, unlike underdeveloped economies where no conventional reserve level has been observed, experts have noted what seems to be a "normal" ratio between the value of international reserves and the value of imports. The IMF staff, for example, finds that industrial countries have usually held the reserve-import ratio in the range of thirty or forty to fifty per cent [30, p. 48], a view independently supported by Triffin [58, pp. 45–46]. Thus there is a rough empirical verification of Fleming's hypothesis. If this historically achieved reserve ratio means that countries do hold expectations of normal reserve levels, the possibility of increasing the incentive to undertake payments adjustments in surplus countries, as well as in deficit countries, during payments imbalances becomes an attractive aim of international reserve policy.

In like manner, when the objective of economic growth dominates an advanced country's policy, the fear that too much international liquidity will be conducive to inflationary pressures may be well founded. If international reserves can increase without limit, the traditional disciplinary nature of reserve losses is ineffective. In a world where purely domestic conditions seem capable of generating their own inflationary pressures it may not be desirable to deprive reserve losses of their normally attendant adjustment effects.[13]

Beyond these purely monetary and balance of payments considerations in specifying a target for international reserve adequacy a further criterion stems from the well-established conditions for optimizing consumer satisfaction in an open economy. Reserves should be large enough so that purchasers of goods and services, and investors as well, need not feel constrained, by virtue of a payments deficit or a reserve loss, to divert some of their expenditures from foreign to domestic markets. As a practical matter, this implies that widespread currency convertibility must be maintained and that trade and payments restrictions for balance of payments reasons should be minimized. The point is perhaps too obvious but about the only clear-cut expression of it to be found in the literature is that of Salant [50].

The relevance of this "optimizing" condition suggests that reserves can be inadequate but not excessive. Unlike the balance of payments considerations, no boundary conditions for reserve adequacy are established by this criterion. Moreover, it seems likely that the minimal international reserve level required in order to yield optimal purchaser satisfaction will be comprehended by the range for reserve adequacy that exists, as has already been suggested, on monetary and balance of payments grounds.

The determination of reserve adequacy is thus clearly a task requiring subtlety of analytical judgment. Formulating a realistic balance of payments model is at the heart of the matter. Such things as the speed and strength of the equilibrating adjustment mechanism, the permissible variables in the adjustment process, the general international institutional framework, and the benefits and costs of reserve accumulation must be considered. The distinctive problems of reserve currency countries, essentially the ones posed by speculation, add another layer of complexity, tending to increase the ambiguities of evaluating the degree of reserve adequacy. They force an assessment of the trend of the reserve position, as well as of the "level" of that position, and impose the need for a "cushion" of international reserves over and above the more objectively determined reserve requirements. An evaluation of the adequacy of the current level of international reserves is not simple. The relevant analytical variables are legion; the battle lines can be drawn only indistinctly. Little wonder that opinions about reserve adequacy are widely divergent.

Flexibility

The foregoing discussion suggests that a country's need for international reserves is determined by the likely instability and duration of payments disequilibria. The adoption of this approach involves an implicit assumption about the flexibility of reserves and renders impossible a definitive evaluation of the adequacy of a given amount of reserves without some assumption pertaining to reserve flexibility.[14] The reason for this is straightforward. The level of reserves and their flexibility are to some extent substitutable characteristics in their contribution to a country's reserve adequacy. Indeed, the combination of the level of reserves and their flexibility are generally embraced by the term international liquidity. Under any given adjustment mechanism and payments disequilibrium, a smaller amount of reserves will be judged an adequate level where the international financial system provides reserve flexibility; under an inflexible reserve regime a larger volume of reserves is typically necessary before reserves can be judged adequate.

Flexibility and reserve volume are not perfect substitutes, however. Only if the amount of reserves of a country is very substantially redundant can reserve flexibility be disregarded. Correspondingly, only under conditions of absolutely perfect flexibility and of immediate impact of reserve movements is the amount of reserves largely immaterial. In normal circumstances, where reserves of most countries are at best marginally excessive and where power of the countries to increase or decrease their reserves is not infinite, cannot be immediately implemented, and is not quickly effective, both some volume of reserves and some flexibility in reserves are clearly desirable.

What factors in the present international situation make reserve flexibility mandatory? Two conditions are necessary and sufficient. First, for the world as a whole and for most countries individually, international reserves are certainly far from substantially redundant.[15] There is no significant cushion of excess international reserves to serve in place of reserve flexibility. Still, the absence of surplus reserves is not a sufficient condition. Even with a bare minimum adequacy of reserves, flexibility would be unnecessary were international payments to remain stable. The second condition, which along with a minimum operational reserve level constitutes sufficient conditions for flexibility, that is, a positive need for flexibility, is that the amount of international payments not covered by current, normal receipts is subject to short-term fluctuation. This is perhaps so obvious as to be trite. Nevertheless, an enumeration of the factors responsible for the short-term volatility of the need for reserve balances will reveal that reserve flexibility is currently absolutely vital to the continued viability of the international monetary system. The amount of flexibility which somehow must be provided is truly quite large.

Twenty years ago Nurkse asserted that the total demand for reserves was partly determined by the degree to which business cycles in separate countries were synchronized with each other [49, p. 14]. Synchronization of cyclical movements, he suggested, would require a smaller volume of reserves — in accordance with the distinction being made between level and flexibility of reserves, would require less flexibility — in order to fulfill the buffer function. If, for example, all economies are expanding and contracting simultaneously and at approximately the same rate, international payments and receipts in individual countries would be moving in the same direction. It is true, of course, that payments surpluses or deficits could emerge, requiring greater reserve financing. But the imbalance would not grow as rapidly as when payments and receipts had opposite movements — as would be likely to occur with cycles completely out of phase.[16] Non-synchronization would produce an international payments-receipts gap of intermediate magnitude.

Interestingly, Nurkse believed that there had been a reduction in synchronization during the 1920's. This is even more evident now. As often as not postwar business cycles in Western Europe have been independent of U.S. cyclical activity. Synchronization has been barely noticeable. A structural short-circuit in the mechanism by which cycles formerly were transmitted internationally may explain this. Most countries are unswervingly dedicated to a policy of full employment and this commitment tends to heighten the desirability of reserve flexibility, both of global and of individual countries' reserves. At the same time a full employment policy also undoubtedly increases the level of reserves needed to meet the criterion of adequacy.

Moreover, it is significant that the amplitude and duration of the cyclical swings in the balance of payments caused by domestic business cycles have been altered in the postwar period. Both in the U.S. and abroad the amplitude and duration of cyclical expansions have been stretched out, and those of cyclical contractions have been damped, compared to historical experience. A result of these changes, in the context of lack of synchronization, would appear to be an increase in the rate at which individual countries would need to expand reserves in order to retain, through time, a given degree of reserve adequacy.

Recall, also, that international reserves function not only as a buffer; they also ease the equilibrating adjustments that are necessitated by structural payments imbalances. Anything requiring that more reserves be devoted to this latter function, such as an intensified incidence of structural disequilibria, would also require greater reserve flexibility. This follows from the inability to forecast where and when structural disequilibria will strike.[17] In view of this uncertainty, the alternatives of any country wishing to hedge against structural imbalances are either a continuously larger volume of reserves (in excess of the amount required in the absence of structural disequilibria) or more flexibility. There are, of course, real costs involved in accumulating and continuously holding more reserves than are absolutely essential. An inflationary bias in the adjustment process has already been mentioned. Whether greater flexibility entails commensurate costs is debatable, in view of the fact that flexibility means that any given country can obtain and hold a larger volume of reserves when they are sorely needed and can release them when the emergency has passed. Flexibility of reserves is an alternative to reserve stockpiling and seems preferable where it can be satisfactorily established. While the possibility of acceleration of structural imbalance cannot be explored here, there is good reason to believe, with the Joint Economic Committee, that ". . . in recent years, payments imbalances . . . have had their origin in dynamic factors which have created structural disequilibria" that are "relatively persistent" [62, p. 3]. Reserve flexibility would seem to be useful on this count too, especially where the types of domestic changes required to adjust to the structural disequilibrium could be undertaken with some facility if only there were time to perceive accurately the kinds of changes needed.

The tenuous position of reserve currencies / The most urgent need for reserve flexibility stems from enhanced possibilities for speculative flight under the current international monetary system, especially speculation against the currencies of reserve centers. The international liabilities of reserve centers are particularly liquid and potentially volatile. At the same time, in a gold exchange standard system, with growing reserve requirements and a shortfall of gold production, the net reserve positions of the reserve centers themselves must deteriorate through time. The exchanges of the reserve centers become increasingly susceptible to capital flight. Few experts doubt, for example, that the high volatility of short-term sterling balances, together with a relatively low net reserve position, was largely responsible for the speculative pressures on the pound which, in March of 1961, resulted in the Basel agreement. Similarly, speculation against the dollar led in 1960 to the rather large flow of gold into Switzerland, despite relatively low interest rates there.[18] The evidence has convinced a large number of experts, including Kenen [36, p. 16], Coombs [61a, p. 97], Johnson [61c, p. 173], and Kindleberger [61e, p. 284], that under a multi-center gold standard "hot" money flows are a potentially very serious peril.

But speculation against reserve currencies is not the only cause of financial pressures on reserve centers. The strains caused by speculation against non-reserve currencies also fall, by and large, on the reserve currencies. The reserves that non-reserve currency areas hold in reserve centers are essentially insurance against imperfectly predictable contingencies. One of these contingencies is speculative pressure on the exchange rate. To meet this pressure, a country may call upon its reserves; it may draw down its exchange balances in the reserve centers, in effect transmitting some of the pressure to reserve currency areas. It cannot be assumed that simultaneously with the withdrawal of these short-term exchange funds will occur a building up of the reserve balances of other countries. Hence the short-term withdrawal may be in the form of gold losses by reserve centers and not simply a geographical redistribution of the pre-existing amount of dollar and sterling holdings. The result of pressure upon the exchange of a non-reserve currency may well be a significant deterioration of the reserve position of the reserve currency centers, with the added possibility of speculation against their currencies.

It should also be noted that exchange crises are frequently precipitated by exporters and importers who, by their actions, take on speculative positions in the exchange market, a phenomenon played up by Katz [34] and Hansen [24]. When doubts arise in traders' minds about the stability of a quasi-fixed rate of exchange, payments to the country for its exports will be deferred and payments by the country for its imports will be hastened. The working balances of foreign exchange become the instrument of speculation. This so-called leads and lags problem cannot be disregarded. It is possible, of course, that the potential size of leads and lags may not be large enough to cause an exchange crisis. Postponement and acceleration of payments for goods and services can only be for comparatively short periods and international reserves may be sufficient to meet these short-term capital swings. Nevertheless, leads and lags activity is capable of triggering movements of purely speculative funds; as Katz describes [35], they have done so with annoying frequency, particularly in the U.K. But whether or not payments leads and lags are against reserve centers or against non-reserve countries, the ultimate consequence is that the financial resources of reserve centers must be drawn upon in order to shore up deteriorating exchange positions.

Thus, potentially sizeable short-term capital flows can exert heavy pressures upon the exchanges of reserve currency centers. This need not be the case, of course. Where the reserve positions of these countries are impregnable, the existence of a substantial volume of short-term exchange holdings is clearly beneficial. Private flows of short-term funds will be of a stabilizing character. The more smoothly and automatically the short-term exchange market functions the less is the need for international reserves. With stabilizing capital movements one country's loss of reserves and other countries' gains would, through a money market propagation mechanism, tend to buoy up interest rates in the former and depress them in the latter. These flows will also be reflected in minor adjustments in exchange rates, although within a fixed rate structure.[19] The counter-movements of respective interest and exchange rates will tend to induce a reversal of private short-term capital flows; because of speculative transactions short-term capital flows are stabilizing.

In the converse situation, however, when the reserve position of reserve centers is somewhat doubtful, insufficient reserve flexibility and exchange rate speculation via short-term capital movements may become reinforcing and compounding. Flows of funds which under more favorable circumstances would be the result of covered arbitrage operations may be left in uncovered positions. Payments leads and lags on trade transactions may become more pronounced and one-directional. Those with liquid funds, both domestic and foreign holders, will almost certainly catch a "speculative fever." Thus reserve flexibility and short-term capital movements can be complementary. Nurkse appreciated long ago [49, pp. 15–16] that, when flexibility is already satisfactory, private capital flows in response to minor exchange rate adjustments and interest rate changes will most likely make it more so; when flexibility is inadequate private destabilizing speculation compounds the inflexibility.

The possibility of arbitrage operations, initially independent of any speculative activity, is of some further concern to reserve currency centers. Imagine a situation in which the reserve position of a country, while not currently under suspicion, might be shaken by a substantial withdrawal of short-term funds for interest arbitrage purposes. The potential outflow of such funds is, of course, very large for reserve countries. But there is doubt as to the size of the feasible withdrawal when the short-term flow is pure arbitrage. It can be argued, for example, that the ability of other economies to absorb the short-term capital flows is substantially limited by the size of their money markets, to the effect that significant interest rate adjustments would quickly be induced by a relatively small capital inflow. The interest rate differential which first motivated arbitrageurs would not be sustainable; arbitrage activity would cease after a short period and without too great a loss of reserves by the reserve center. Moreover, the differential between the spot exchange rate and the forward rate is also likely to be adjusted by arbitrage flows so as, ultimately, to remove the advantage based upon interest rate differences. It might be concluded, therefore, that reserve currencies are not seriously disadvantaged by the possibility of short-term capital movements in search of greater interest return.

Now the mechanism of arbitrage, if operating in isolation, is capable of reversing short-term capital flows. It does not follow, however, that arbitrage can be ignored. Disruption in the exchange market may be severe before arbitrage reversal takes place. Arbitrage transactions can be safely disregarded by a reserve currency center only if it is assured that the swings in arbitrage are manageable — only if the automatic reversal of short-term flows occurs before the flows become inordinately large. It would be hard to find such assurance in current conditions.

The anticipation of moderate arbitrage swings depends upon several alternative implicit assumptions which are not realistic. To be valid, the argument may imply, on the one hand, that the international financial network has only one center. Arbitrage must therefore be between the reserve currency area and the non-reserve currency countries where money markets are not apt to be tremendously absorptive. Interest rates would then quickly reflect the short-term capital flows with inappreciable loss to the reserve center. This is patently unrealistic. On the other hand, for a multi-centered system the argument is relevant only for a center whose money market is large, indeed massive, compared with those of other reserve centers. A great size disparity in reserve centers is implied by the argument. Size disparity of money markets is essential in a multi-centered system because it is probable that arbitrage will take place among the reserve centers, this being the surest means of maintaining reserve liquidity while gaining additional interest return. With the current bi-polar reserve situation in which the U.S. money market appreciably exceeds in size that of the U.K., monetary authorities in the U.S. might be heartened by the above logic. Contrastingly, British authorities are not likely to be set at ease.

Both of the above assumptions — of a single center or a multi-centered system with great size disparity — require an additional institutional feature if arbitrage is not to be a possible cause of speculative difficulties. The additional requirement is that the world's money markets must be largely independent or isolated. The reason for this is that the absorptive capacity of countries receiving the arbitrage flows must be relatively limited. This is entirely possible when only one or a few countries are the recipients. But since the size of the money market in any single country, even if it serves as a reserve center, is not likely to be large relative to the aggregated money markets of all other countries, the absorptive capacities of all countries combined is quite substantial. In this case, the potential loss of reserves in the center country due to arbitrage can be ignored only if the arbitrage is limited to one (comparatively small) country and if there is no further spill over from that country into third countries.

The existence of a multi-centered exchange network cannot be denied. It is also difficult to imagine that the world's money markets are fragmented to a significant degree. Therefore, the magnitude of short-term arbitrage flows can be substantial. This being so, a reserve center must be continually aware of the possibility that arbitrage is capable of raising doubts about the impregnability of its reserve position. The

426

arbitrage nature of flows of funds can always be misconstrued. Under realistic conditions speculative capital flows can be set in motion by arbitrage and under the circumstances these speculative movements will be destabilizing. Speculative flows are not likely to be reversed by any feasible alteration of interest rates or adjustments of spot-forward exchange rate gaps, even though, once "hot" money flights occur, the recipients' absorptive capacity, in the sense used above, may be regarded as relatively small. But absorptive capacity is largely irrelevant in the case of speculative capital flights. Therefore, arbitrage possibilities, even though in and of themselves they are inherently stabilizing, cannot be ignored by reserve centers. Before the reversal of short-term capital flows takes place, the size of the arbitrage outflow may be more than enough to trigger destabilizing speculative movements.[20]

It is apparent, then, that private short-term capital flows are potentially able to provide the kind of flexibility that is needed by a viable international monetary system. They may even be able to provide the amount of flexibility required. To do so, short-term capital movements must be stabilizing which is to say that an effective international credit mechanism must exist. Unfortunately, the international monetary network seems now capable of engendering destabilizing capital flows at all-too-frequent intervals. The flow of private capital is no longer a reliable element in the reserve picture; the private international credit system apparently loses a great deal of its stabilizing effectiveness at the precise time that it is most urgently needed.

This turn of events was not unanticipated. Governmental authorities have built a system in which official arrangements are used to insure reserve flexibility. Until now, these have given adequate service but perhaps only barely. It has been necessary, for example, to resort to *ad hoc,* makeshift rescue arrangements. The IMF's fund of gold and currencies has been enlarged by a substantial increase in the quotas of its member countries. Additionally, the IMF has negotiated permanent, virtually automatic, lines of credit in the world's financial centers. The U.S. Treasury has set up a series of exchange "swap" arrangements with other developed exchange market countries and has issued securities denominated in foreign currencies — the so-called "Roosa bonds." [21] These are all devices by which it is hoped that the efficiency, that is, the ability to support a substantial and volatile level of international payments, of a given amount of international reserves can be augmented. Moreover, there is some responsible feeling, as described by Kindleberger [40, pp. 383–89; 63b, pp. 383–90], that these measures have at the very least reduced the financial strains that might otherwise have fallen on the international monetary system. There is almost no doubt, however, that all efforts to give reserves greater flexibility ultimately will prove unsuccessful unless reserves are capable of a reasonable rate of expansion in the longer run. Thus it is necessary to evaluate the reserve expansion capabilities of the current international monetary system.

Expansibility

Experts unanimously agree that the secular trend of demand for international reserves will be upward. The reasons for this agreement are easy to find. As the world economy grows so will the value of international transactions, both on trade and long-term capital account. Additionally, as underdeveloped nations try to expand, relative to the rates of growth in the advanced economies, reserve positions of the less developed countries will be perennially unsatisfactory. The incessant demands of the underdeveloped nations for the means of international payment — for international reserves if these countries would only retain gold and foreign exchange earnings — will carry more weight as they gain in political power and influence. Impetus for reserve expansion will come from the developed areas as well. If wage-cost inflation tends to occur relatively independently of aggregate demand, the primacy of the full employment goal implies a larger volume of reserves. Finally, it is possible that the prices of internationally traded raw materials will increase secularly, further reinforcing the demand for international reserves.

These factors suggest that the demand for reserves will increase appreciably over time. Can it also be inferred that the optimal level of international reserves should grow at a matching rate? In large part, it seems, it can. Fleming, with some qualification, believes that "a change in the demand for reserves will involve a similar change in the need for (i.e., the optimal level of) reserves" [17, p. 444]. In a fixed exchange rate system there is a close, but not necessarily proportional, relationship between international reserves and the purchasing power of domestic currencies. As the price level rises, assuming of course that an excess supply of reserves is not responsible, additional reserves are required to support the expanded value of foreign transactions.[22]

Nevertheless, as the preceding paragraph implies, the demand for reserves is not the sole determinant of the optimal reserve level which may vary quite apart from changes in demand. The desirability of reserve balances in the event of structural payments disequilibria has already been noted. In effect, reserves grubstake government authorities while they decide what remedial steps are necessary. But because of this, reserves can impede progress toward ultimate readjustment if there are plausible grounds for delaying. Hence, while demand for reserves is clearly generated by structural imbalances, it is not evident that the optimum level of reserves is commensurately increased thereby.

This factor seems, incidentally, to be the basis of a good deal of the criticism which is directed at the IMF and a valid reason for increasing the flexibility of reserves without at the same time undertaking a real reserve expansion. The IMF, quite reasonably, seems attracted to the concept of an optimal reserve level and to its maintenance as the volume of international reserves found in practice. Perhaps, in view of political realities, it is justifiable that the IMF should view this volume as the long-run optimum level of reserves. When this long-run optimum diverges from the level of reserves that is demanded, it is to be expected that the IMF will come under increasingly severe pressure.

An even more obvious cause of discrepancy between the demand for reserves and their optimum level has been noted in the perpetual reserve deficiency of the developing nations. It is no doubt true that the drive for economic development requires a higher optimum level of reserves than would otherwise be warranted. But it is equally true that the underdeveloped countries' appetite for international exchange is virtually insatiable. Until some mechanism, internal to the development process, is constructed whereby this appetite can be controlled, it is unlikely that there will be a balance between the aggregate needs and demands for international reserves.[23] But these exceptions mean merely that the demand for reserves will run ahead of the need for them. No one denies that the need for reserves — their optimum level — will also expand secularly.

It should not be inferred from these statements, however, that international reserves and the volume of international payments are somehow related in a relatively strict quantity theory sense. As international payments grow, the optimal level of reserves need not rise proportionately. For one thing, it should be remembered that the liquidity and volume of international reserves are to a degree substitutes and, hence, increasing or decreasing liquidity will alter over time the optimal ratio of reserve volume to payments. Moreover, since an optimal level of reserves can only be defined in the context of a given balance of payments model and given policy constraints, any alteration in these underlying conditions will likewise affect the optimal ratio of international reserves to international payments. The brief conclusion of the "Group of 32" is worth quoting: "There are thus no solid theoretical or empirical grounds for believing that the ideal is a growth rate of international reserves invariantly related to the normal rate of growth of world output or world trade and payments" [22, p. 33]. But if there is no constant of proportionality between the volume of reserves and the level of international payments, it is nevertheless true that the anticipated future growth of trade, if it is to be realized, will compel a rather substantial expansion of global reserves.

Here, then, is the major problem of expansibility — the dilemma of the gold exchange standard. Given that the optimum level of international reserves will rise through time, can the present monetary framework continue to bring forth an increase in reserves as rapidly as the mounting needs call for? This is the elemental question. More is entailed, however, than just securing a rapid increase in reserves. Implicit in the question is the requirement that as the need for reserves expands, the supply of reserves should grow at an appropriate rate. Given sufficient flexibility, an equality between the optimum level of reserves and the volume of reserves must be maintained over time. This latter aspect of expansibility tends to be stressed by those individuals of an anti-inflation inclination. Of late, however, concern about the adverse effects of a failure of reserves to keep up with the need for them has been predominant. A long-run deficiency of reserves is likely to result in trade and exchange controls and poorer resource allocation; in an unpegging of exchange rates; or in unnecessary deflation and a slowing down of the rate of economic growth throughout the world.

Inconvertibility, or the possible freeing of exchange rates, is not an issue here. As long as the current institutional framework is in effect, these alternatives are inadmissible. The possibility that a secular deficiency in reserves will retard growth and in general be responsible for a systemic deflationary bias must, however, be considered. A number of critics, among them Balogh [7], Harrod [25b], and Triffin [58], level this charge at the current gold exchange standard and at the IMF's management of it. Contrastingly, the IMF staff [29; 30] and at least two of its influential members, Altman [5] and Fleming [17], writing privately, imply that to accede to the demands of these critics would be to subject the world to inflationary pressures. Before any assessment of the various proposals to alter the existing monetary framework is even feasible, the relative merits of these antagonistic positions must be summarized.

If the dilemma of the gold exchange standard is a true dilemma, there exists the possibility of a global shortage of reserves. Now as long as world reserves are not excessive, no single country is apt to be saturated with international reserves. As already noted, developing countries are chronically short of reserves. Additionally, for the advanced economies there seems historically to have been some empirically established, individual optimum reserve level in the neighborhood of forty per cent of the value of annual imports. This implies that if ever global reserves were in oversupply a somewhat commensurate world expansion and increase in the value of imports tended to eliminate the surplus. Where the world's real output is relatively fixed, as it would presumably be if the major industrial countries were approaching full employment of their resources,[24] the tendency to erase the reserve surplus would most likely operate via a mechanism of general price increase, a point suggested by Fleming [17, pp. 442–43]. Pumping reserves into the world economy in excess of a clear-cut need for them would generate inflation. But it should be stressed that this is not a consequence of the international monetary system nor of the excessive reserves; rather it results from the actions of individual nations. As both Nurkse [49, pp. 25–26] and Yeager [65, pp. 294–95] note, global reserves in excess of the world's need are merely a permissive factor. National prodigality is to be condemned. Thus, while the IMF's fears of inherent inflation are not without basis, emphasis on the possibility of excessive reserves might seem misplaced.

Whether or not the above argument is valid rests upon the realism of the assumption of full employment in the advanced economies. If there is less than full employment and if the supplies of the products of these countries are relatively elastic, expansion of output may not be accompanied by a general price rise. Under these conditions, it is desirable to induce growth. Assuming there are "normal" reserve levels, a rapid expansion of reserves may provide the needed fillip through interim price increases. Then as output responds to these price incentives, the price level may return to approximately its original level. Presumably, expansion of world output is desirable as long as it is accompanied by relatively stable prices.

It is unlikely, however, that the growth of world output will occur without a rising price level. For one thing the increase in aggregate demand inspired by the expansion of international reserves cannot be directed solely to the under-employed advanced nations. Some of the enlarged demand will spill over into the underdeveloped areas whose principal commodities are produced under relatively inelastic supply conditions. This spill over of demand will eventuate in an increase in the world's price level. Additionally, if cost push-price pull or demand-shift types of inflation are meaningful experiences in the advanced economies, there is reason to question whether growth is compatible with stable prices, even without a spill over of aggregate demand into the underdeveloped areas. Thus, those who abhor inflation on a world scale have more to fear than national prodigality; national drives for higher growth rates underlie the inflationary potential of excess international reserves. In a sense, this too is prodigal behavior, for the analysis is based on the assumption that nations are driven to grow at rates in excess of those which are supportable by domestic saving.

Nevertheless, it may still be doubted that the evils of potential inflation outweigh the likelihood and disadvantages of world-wide deflation and slower growth rates. There is good reason to believe that world reserves are likely secularly to fall short of needs, rather than to be excessive. In Balogh's view [7, p. 361], when there is a reserve deficiency, if nations seek to achieve a normal relationship between reserves and imports, deflationary pressures will predominate and excess economic capacity will be likely to arise. Indeed, Harrod, consistent with his view that reserves are currently deficient, has noted abnormally high (i.e., deflationary) interest rates in non-dollar countries [25b, p. 47]. If the reserve centers should run short of reserves, they would of necessity reduce their payments deficits, cutting down on their output of exchange reserves. This, too, Balogh suggests [7, pp. 359–60], would force restraint in other countries with a distinct possibility that the process could become cumulative. In fact, in any situation where global reserves are inadequate, the oligopolistic relationship among nations will put a premium on national behavior that will gain reserves. As Balogh puts it, with a general reserve deficiency "Safety first would counsel deflation" [7, p. 363].

The historical behavior of the international reserve ratio may not, of course, be a valid reason for predicting a similar normative ratio between reserves and trade in the future. The evolution of many international monetary institutions can be explained in terms of husbanding international reserves. Yet, even if a normal reserve ratio cannot be identified, guidelines to an appropriate rate of reserve expansion are available. Reserves ideally should grow along a path which lies between inflation-permitting excesses and deflation-inducing shortages. But in a system where the expansion of international reserves is left largely to chance, this ideal is beyond attainment. Almost certainly the system will err on one side or the other. On theoretical grounds there is merit in both the anti-inflationist and anti-deflationist cases. But in reality the probability of error in the rate of growth of reserves is asymmetrical. With a few important exceptions no one believes that international reserves, for any long period, will exceed legitimate needs for them. Rather the belief is widespread that the current international monetary system cannot continue to produce the amount of international reserves required by an expanding world economy.

The basis of this belief is, of course, not groundless. Global reserves can only be expanded through an increase in the monetary gold stock — by sales of gold by the U.S.S.R. as in the late 1950's, or by private dishoarding of gold, or by new gold production — or through an increase in foreign holdings of reserve center currencies. Few would care to see the viability of the free world's monetary standard dependent upon decisions of the Soviet Union. But unless there is substantial gold dishoarding, or the West's gold output increases, or the exchange component of reserve holdings rises commensurately with the expanding need for reserves, this is a real possibility.

Unfortunately, it appears unlikely that production of new gold will grow apace with reserve needs. While gold output will expand somewhat (see Altman [4] and Coombs [61a, pp. 93–100]), there is almost no expectation that the foreseeable expansion will suffice. It must be remembered, furthermore, that not all new gold will find its way into official monetary coffers. Indeed, in some years the loss of new gold to non-monetary uses has represented a serious drain and probably a substantial fraction of this drain was into gold hoards.[25] The major hurdle to increasing gold output is rising production costs in the face of a fixed gold price, gold mining being a profit-motivated operation in which the long-standing subsidy is no longer as generous as it once was. It seems unlikely, short of acceptance of the recommendations of Harrod [25b; 26] or Busschau [10] to increase substantially the price of gold, that production will rise in the future. The exploitation of existing, sub-marginal deposits will not become suddenly profitable. Certainly, the viability of the world economy should not be gambled on the possibility that rich, easily recoverable ore deposits will again be discovered.

Therefore, it would seem that the hopes of the international monetary system rest upon the possibility of an ever-increasing use of foreign exchange as international reserves. How realistic are these hopes? Assuming the continuation of a bi-polar gold exchange standard, the increase in official exchange reserve holdings is limited by the cumulative payments deficits of the U.S. and the U.K. The cumulative deficit gives the maximum possible growth in the exchange component of reserves. But actual expansion is certain to fall far short of this maximum — to the extent that dollar and sterling exchange flows into private rather than into official balances and to the degree that the gold reserves of the U.S. and the U.K. are absorbed by third countries. The only dependable incentives for holding exchange balances are convenience and interest return but these can be offset by possible losses due to devaluation. Thus, the greater is the confidence in the reserve center currencies the more likely it is that increases in reserve currency availability will be absorbed in private holdings. In this event, the payments deficits of the U.S. and the U.K. will at least in part be wasted as concerns the expansion of international reserves. In contrast, when the reserve currency seems shaky, rational behavior of private individuals would involve drawing down reserve center currencies in favor of other currencies whose gold parity seems secure or in favor of gold. So if the reserve currency is under pressure, more of the payments deficit is available for official holdings. But these are precisely the conditions under which monetary authorities of non-reserve centers would question the wisdom of accumulating the currencies of reserve centers. Indeed, in recent years it appears that they have converted exchange reserves into gold on an appreciable scale, as Kenen's empirical findings [38; 61d, pp. 179–96] suggest.

In consequence, the Joint Economic Committee concludes that ". . . if there is no lack of confidence, official holdings of reserve currencies would be bound to rise by less than the payments deficits of the [reserve] currency countries; while if there is not full confidence, the results might be the same, though for different reasons" [62, p. 5]. The "Group of 32" agrees with this point, asserting [22, p. 37] that ". . . the rate at which a reserve-currency country runs a deficit cannot simultaneously perform two functions: that of increasing liquidity at an appropriate rate and that of maintaining confidence in the convertibility of its currency into gold."

Obviously, it is preferable to maintain confidence in the reserve currency. It is better that the payments deficits of the reserve centers be inefficient generators of international reserves than that they not generate reserves at all. But to maintain confidence in reserve currencies is a taxing problem when there is a continuous need to expand world reserves without adequate gold production. Under these conditions, a secular payments deficit by the reserve centers can only result in a deterioration of their net reserve positions. Ultimately, doubt about the stability or convertibility of their exchange is bound to arise.[26] Indeed, in the extreme, reserve center deficits could be responsible for the disintegration of the gold exchange standard.[27] But the apparent "solution" — elimination of the deficits — is no solution. It is true, of course, that just as third countries may not want to hold dollars or sterling as the net reserves of the reserve centers dwindle, so the reserve centers will be reluctant to continue running payments deficits. The point is, however, that under the posited conditions reserve center deficits are essential if global reserves are to expand. Is there no relief from within the current international monetary system for this dilemma?

Possibly there is really no problem at all. There will over the years be some increase in the world's supply of monetary gold. Additionally, until quite recently, a payments deficit in the reserve centers seemed to be called for in order to satisfy the desires of third countries to hold additional exchange balances. Bernstein [8, pp. 80–82] estimates, for example, that there was a tendency to accumulate official holdings of dollars at the rate of one billion dollars per year, although this "propensity" cannot be expected to last indefinitely. Indeed, an alternative finding, not necessarily inconsistent with Bernstein's, but not necessarily consistent either, is that of Høst-Madsen wherein countries other than the United States have, as a group, generally taken about 60 per cent of their increases in international reserves in the form of new acquisitions of gold from either U.S. coffers or new production [28, p. 251]. But as long as either of these tendencies persists and as long as U.S. payments deficits do not exceed a certain amount, there is no cause for alarm. Nevertheless, that the growth in international reserves due to gold production and such limited deficits will be sufficient to satisfy the expanding need for reserves cannot be assured. In fact, the evidence seems to point inevitably to a growing shortage of reserves. Undoubtedly, there is a serious problem here.

One possible solution is a geographical redistribution of the current stock of monetary gold. Some countries, Switzerland, for example, are notorious sponges for gold. Yet their currencies do not serve as exchange reserves. A relocation of gold holdings from non-reserve centers that hold their reserves substantially in gold to the reserve centers would permit the existing gold supply to support a much higher level of global reserves. This policy has serious limitations, however. It would serve merely as a stopgap. Redistribution of gold would be unlikely to permit the supply of reserves to expand apace with reserve needs for more than a relatively short period of time. But more than that, relocation of gold is politically unfeasible. Furthermore, it seems unlikely that the level of gold reserves which individual countries will think desirable, and therefore will seek to obtain, is compatible with the optimum distribution of global gold stocks from the viewpoint of the continued viability of the gold exchange standard.

A somewhat analogous possibility is the proliferation of reserve centers as proposed by Lutz [45; 46]. If the gold stock cannot be redistributed, then the existing stock can be made to support more reserves by the simple expedient of worldwide acceptance of holdings of a greater number of currencies as the exchange component of international reserves. But, as Williamson points out [64], multiplication of reserve centers serves to increase total reserves available only if the new centers can behave asymmetrically with respect to assets and liabilities. That is, a new reserve center must be able to view an equal increase in international assets and liabilities as though the assets enhanced its reserve position to a greater degree than the liabilities caused the reserve position to deteriorate. This, Williamson notes, can happen under four circumstances: (1) if part of the new-center exchange holdings of the non-reserve center countries serve as balances to meet payments on international commodity transactions; (2) if non-reserve center countries have no equally attractive alternative currency in which to hold their reserve balances; (3) if existing reserve centers need have no greater fear of loss of reserves under an extended reserve-center system than under a two-center system; and (4) if reserve centers can rely upon the willingness of their creditors to subordinate self-interest and thereby avoid actions that would embarrass the reserve centers. In Williamson's view, the first condition would not be likely to apply to new reserve centers, although it does apply to the U.S. and the U.K. The validity of the second and third reasons for treating increases in assets and liabilities as non-offsetting would, however, be reduced by further multiplication of reserve centers. Williamson concludes that proliferation of reserve centers, far from expanding the volume of international reserves, might rather lower it unless safe asymmetrical treatment of new assets and liabilities can be institutionally guaranteed by circumstances comprehended by point (4) above. And these circumstances, it is important to note, depend for their effectiveness on sovereign nations acting in ways that are generally contrary to their own best interests in the short-run and possibly in the long-run.

Thus, a multiple currency gold exchange standard may not come to grips with the problem of reserve expansibility. Moreover, as already noted, the limited multiplication of reserve centers creates an environment which enhances the possibility of perverse flexibility. And, finally, Kaldor's arguments that a multiple reserve currency system may tend to have a relatively deflationary bias because it is heavily dependent on mutual confidence, and hence on some degree of coordination of monetary and fiscal policies among the reserve currency countries, and that it makes changes in the exchange rate in the face of fundamental payments disequilibrium more difficult [33, p. 283] seem weighty.

There is still a possibility that increasing the mobility or flexibility of international reserves might, by permitting a given volume of reserves to fill the need for reserves more effectively, tide the world economy over the gap between the expanding reserve optimum and reserve supplies. The implicit basis for this statement contains a great deal of truth. As noted before, flexibility and reserve volume are to a degree substitutable so that increasing one reduces the need for the other. But there are persuasive reasons for insisting upon an increase in reserve flexibility, in its own right, and there are some reservations, given the political and economic environment, about the capability of doing so. The burden for reserve flexibility to carry out its own urgent role is perhaps already too great. It would seem unwise, therefore, to place upon flexibility the additional load of filling the gap, which will probably widen secularly, between the need for international reserves and their supply.

CONCLUDING REMARKS

It must be concluded, in agreement with a majority of specialists in international monetary affairs, that there is no practicable way, short of a relatively comprehensive renovation of international monetary institutions, to provide a volume of reserves over the long pull that will be consistent with the expanding optimum reserve level. This defect of the current gold exchange standard, alone, is enough to cause grave concern and to have resulted in numerous proposals for overhauling present institutional arrangements.[28]

It is more difficult, as has been seen, to come to grips with the issue of the present adequacy of the volume of reserves. Adequacy cannot be evaluated without making assumptions about the kind of adjustment mechanism that is most desirable, about whether resources are optimally allocated, ultimately about the generally accepted goals of economic activity, and about the types of payments disequilibrium that the world is facing. The assumptions adopted in each of these areas will hinge importantly on value judgments and consequently it should not be expected that a definitive or even a widely-accepted assessment of the extent of current international reserve adequacy or inadequacy will ever be available.

The flexibility of international reserves, the need for which arises primarily because of the possibility of exchange crises and uncertainties and errors of diagnosis and policy prescription, can be increased without major changes in the international monetary system. But even with greater flexibility, the world economy would probably tend to have an endemic shortage of reserves. The fact is that a chronic reserve shortage is incompatible with national full employment, unrestricted trade and payments, and stability of exchange rates. If these economic goals are to remain paramount, new ways to increase the expansibility of the international monetary system must be found.

FOOTNOTES

1. The meaning of international reserves, and of their liquidity, will become apparent as the discussion proceeds. There are, nevertheless, difficult conceptual problems in defining these terms. These are not discussed in the text because they are largely peripheral to the subject matter. They are presented, however, in Arndt [6], Brown [9], Gemmill [19], Goodman [20], Lederer [43, part IV], and Clement [11].

2. Holtrop [27] provides a useful summary of the types of adjustment which are available in the event that disequilibrium is protracted. His examples are taken largely from the experiences of the Netherlands. Tobin [63e] and the so-called "Group of 32" [22, pp. 43–53] also give enlightening discussions of the possible methods of adjusting to payments disequilibrium.

3. Sohmen, for example, states: "It is practically impossible for the American and British authorities to throw the shadow of a doubt on their determination to preserve the established par values for their currencies . . ." because liquid domestic holdings will be quickly transferred [53, p. 21].

4. The structure of the world's monetary system will not be described here. Good, brief discussions are to be found in Day [61b], Bloomfield [63a], and Lutz [63c].

5. The role of gold in the contemporary international monetary system is the specific focus of the pamphlet by Kriz [41].

6. The IMF study [30, p. 75] points out that with sufficiently flexible credit policies being pursued by trading countries the substantial amounts of private short-term exchange holdings might be used in an equilibrating fashion. This is true, of course, only as long as the exchange component of international reserves remains sound.

7. The mechanism by which the agreement was to accomplish this is straightforward: countries receiving pounds through speculative movements were to hold them in larger than normal amounts rather than convert the newly acquired pounds into gold. This was tantamount to lending to the U.K., at

short term, currencies needed to meet any private speculative withdrawals. The mechanics are set forth by Coombs [60a; 61a, pp. 100ff.] and *The Economist* [13, pp. 645–48].

8. Kenen [39] gives evidence of the importance of the interest rate in generating short-term capital movements.

9. The account of Stein [54, Parts II and III] is a lucid description of these types of activities, as well as interest arbitrage operations, in the foreign exchange market. See also the description of Trued [59].

10. Lieftinck [44, p. 6] adopts the same tripartite breakdown of the problem of ascertaining the adequacy of reserves. He refers to these as the issues of: (1) present adequacy; (2) the long-term problem of whether reserves will grow adequately in the future; and (3) the short-term problem of maintaining confidence in the reserve currencies. In the terminology of this chapter these are, respectively, the issues of adequacy, expansibility, and flexibility. The same taxonomic scheme is suggested by Johnson [32, pp. 1–4].

11. Note that Williamson [64] does include this feature of reserve need in his discussion of adequacy. While he gives some relevant qualitative guides, he does not attempt to quantify.

12. Scitovsky would support an increase in global reserves in order to insure that if some countries were to lose reserves, thus becoming deficient, other countries would gain, thereby becoming over-supplied with reserves. If world reserves were inadequate, the gaining countries would not necessarily feel surfeited of reserves and, hence, would not be induced to take steps to eliminate their payments surpluses [61f., pp. 175–76, 237–38]. A presumed deficiency of global reserves also explains Balogh's fears [7, pp. 361–66] that the current international financial system is biased toward deflation and a relatively slow rate of economic growth. Tobin's statement [63e, pp. 554–55] is consistent with both of these views.

13. Kindleberger [40, p. 382] is apprehensive about this possibility. The traditional discipline of reserve losses — deflation — may now be channeled in less desirable directions than formerly. For example, Harris [25, p. 32] points out that where prices and wages are rigid in a downward direction, the "corrective" effects of a reserve loss may hit employment and output; they will not result in price level adjustments. Under these circumstances it may be desirable to render ineffective a loss of reserves. See also Sohmen [53, pp. 8–13].

14. This is one of the reasons why the issues of adequacy and flexibility (and expansibility) are not distinctly demarcated problems.

15. If this were not so, it would be difficult to understand why there is such a furor about international liquidity. There may have been a time in the not too distant past when U.S. reserves were plainly so large that a selfish concern for their flexibility would have been fatuous. This is no longer the case, despite Holtrop's inclination ". . . that there is too much liquidity around" [27, p. 42].

16. This statement is vastly oversimplified but nevertheless seems to hold generally. The oversimplification results from the fact that the composition of imports and exports, the configuration of domestic adjustments during the cyclical movement, and the price and income elasticities of demand should be considered in making statements about the difference through time between international payments and receipts.

17. By structural disequilibria is meant payments problems created by such

events as changes in the pattern of international demand, intercountry shifts in technology, and the like. Historically, the unpredictability of these events has been striking.

18. Perhaps more indicative that this was a speculative movement of funds is the fact that they went to Switzerland, in spite of a Swiss interest charge on foreign balances.

19. The arguments here and in succeeding paragraphs assume no "sterilization" of the short-term capital flows. Several years ago this assumption would have bordered on unrealism for the U.S., when interest rate movements because of international financial flows would not have been permitted to subvert the achievement of purely domestic goals. This is no longer the case, however. In the U.K. and some other European countries, moreover, the interest rate corrective is undoubtedly allowed considerable play. The operation of this corrective in the U.K. is thoroughly examined by Kenen [36].

20. Ideas such as these may be responsible for the real concern of some experts, for example Bernstein [8, pp. 80–82], that the current net reserve position of the U.S. ties the hands of its monetary and fiscal authorities as concerns measures to combat recessions and growth slow-downs. Worry over the possibly adverse effects of arbitrage was partly responsible for the U.S. policy, initiated early in 1961, of trying to "twist" the structure of interest rates — raising short-term rates (to hold short-term dollar balances in this country) and maintaining low long-term rates (to provide incentive for expansion of domestic investment).

21. These activities are described in various recent issues of the *Monthly Review* of the Federal Reserve Bank of New York and by Coombs [60a].

22. Fleming recognizes that the immediate and short-run requirements for an optimum reserve level may differ from the optimum long-run level. See [17, p. 444]. When evaluating the expansibility of reserves the long-run optimum seems to be the relevant period. In this regard see also Nurkse [49, p. 13] and Yeager [65, pp. 293–94].

23. The article by Balogh [7] is a vigorous discussion, mostly taking an opposing view, of these ideas.

24. The assumption here is that until full employment is reached the supplies of goods from the industrial economies are relatively elastic; beyond full employment these supplies become inelastic. For raw materials, which are the major exports of the underdeveloped areas, supplies seem inelastic regardless of the level of employment.

25. Figures compiled by the staff of the Federal Reserve Bank of New York, reported by Coombs [61a, p. 99], show that in each year of 1956–1960 the drainage of newly produced gold into non-monetary uses exceeded fifty per cent of the free world output. During this period annual free world production averaged $1,070 million. U.S.S.R. sales contributed, on the average, another $207 million per annum. It is significant that in 1960, a year of substantial reserve loss by the U.S., Western gold production was estimated to be $1,175 million, Soviet sales $210 million, and of this $1,385 million of new gold available to the West $1,045 million found its way into non-monetary uses.

26. It is assumed that doubt about exchange rate stability is inversely related to the net reserve position. Some authorities believe that the net position is largely irrelevant. This latter position is perhaps best expressed by Halm [60b].

27. Kenen [37] has formally specified the conditions under which the system

439

is likely to disintegrate. His argument is applied to a single reserve center system and contains various reserve components and "the" interest rate as parameters of action.

28. These proposals are legion and a description, let alone analysis, of them is out of the question. Many of the citations given above outline and evaluate these proposals. It is not necessary to range so widely in order to gain knowledge of the various recommended revisions. Grubel [23] presents most of the major suggestions in comparatively short compass. Machlup [47] provides a more analytical treatment of a number of the proposals. The renovations are also summarized by Fleming [17], Stamp [61g], Tew [61h], and the Joint Economic Committee [62].

BIBLIOGRAPHY

[1] J. W. Angell, "The Reorganization of the International Monetary System: An Alternative Proposal," *EJ* (December 1961).

[2] R. Z. Aliber, *The Management of the Dollar in International Finance,* Princeton University, International Finance Section, Studies in International Finance No. 13 (1964).

[3] O. L. Altman, "The Management of International Liquidity," *SP* (July 1964).

[4] _____, "A Note on Gold Production and Additions to International Gold Reserves," *SP* (April 1958).

[5] _____, "Professor Triffin on International Liquidity and the Role of the Fund," *SP* (May 1961).

[6] H. W. Arndt, "The Concept of Liquidity in International Monetary Theory," *REStud*, No. 1 (1947–48).

[7] T. Balogh, "International Reserves and Liquidity," *EJ* (June 1960).

[8] E. M. Bernstein, *International Effects of U.S. Economic Policy*, Study No. 16 in U.S. Congress, Joint Economic Committee, *Study of Employment, Growth and Price Levels* (January 25, 1960).

[9] W. M. Brown, "Concept and Measurement of Foreign Exchange Reserves," *EJ* (September 1955).

[10] W. J. Busschau, *Gold and International Liquidity* (1961).

[11] M. O. Clement, "A Functional Approach to the Concept of International Reserves," *Kyk*, Fasc. 3 (1963).

[12] Committee for Economic Development, *The International Position of the Dollar* (May 1961).

[13] *The Economist* (London), "Exchanges after the Storm" (August 12, 1961).

[14] R. J. Familton, "Balance of Payments Equilibrium and Monetary Policy," *Ec Rec* (November 1954).

[15] J. M. Fleming, "Developments in the International Payments System," *SP* (November 1963).

[16] _____, "The Fund and International Liquidity," *SP* (July 1964).

[17] _____, "International Liquidity: Ends and Means," *SP* (December 1961).

[18] I. S. Friedman, "The International Monetary System: Part I, Mechanism and Operation," *SP* (July 1963).

[19] R. F. Gemmill, "Notes on the Measurement of International Liquidity," *JFin* (March 1960).

[20] B. Goodman, "The Price of Gold and International Liquidity," *JFin* (March 1956).

[21] "Group of Ten," *Ministerial Statement of the Group of Ten and Annex Prepared by Deputies* (mimeographed, August 10, 1964).

[22] "Group of 32," *International Monetary Arrangements: The Problem of Choice: Report on the Deliberations of an International Study Group of 32 Economists*, Princeton University, International Finance Section (1964).

[23] H. G. Grubel (ed.), *World Monetary Reform, Plans and Issues* (1963).

[24] B. Hansen, *Foreign Trade Credits and Exchange Reserves* (1961).

[25] S. E. Harris (ed.), *The Dollar in Crisis* (1961).
  a. O. L. Altman, "Professor Triffin, International Liquidity, and the International Monetary Fund."
  b. R. Harrod, "The Dollar Problem and the Gold Question."
  c. R. Triffin, "The International Monetary Position of the United States."

[26] R. Harrod, "A Plan for Increasing Liquidity: A Critique," *Econa* (May 1961).

[27] M. W. Holtrop, *Monetary Policy in an Open Economy: Its Objectives, Instruments, Limitations, and Dilemmas*, Princeton University, International Finance Section, Essays in International Finance No. 43 (September 1963).

[28] P. Høst-Madsen, "Gold Outflows from the United States, 1958–63," *SP* (July 1964).

[29] International Monetary Fund Staff, "The Adequacy of Reserves," *SP* (October 1953).

[30] ————, *International Reserves and Liquidity* (August 1958).

[31] ————, *1964 Annual Report* (1964).

[32] H. G. Johnson, "International Liquidity — Problems and Plans," *Malayan Economic Review* (April 1962).

[33] N. Kaldor, "The Problem of International Liquidity," *BOUIS* (August 1964).

[34] S. I. Katz, "Leads and Lags in Sterling Payments," *REStat* (February 1953).

[35] ————, *Sterling Speculation and European Convertibility: 1955–1958*, Princeton University, International Finance Section, Essays in International Finance No. 37 (October 1961).

[36] P. B. Kenen, *British Monetary Policy and the Balance of Payments, 1951–1957* (1960).

[37] ————, "International Liquidity and the Balance of Payments of a Reserve-Currency Country," *QJE* (November 1960).

[38] ————, *Reserve-Asset Preferences of Central Banks and Stability of the Gold-Exchange Standard*, Princeton University, International Finance Section, Studies in International Finance No. 10 (1963).

[39] ————, "Short-Term Capital Movements and the U.S. Balance of Pay-

ments" in U.S. Congress, Joint Economic Committee, *The United States Balance of Payments: Hearings, Part 1, Current Problems and Policies*, July 8 and 9, 1963 (88th Cong., 1st Sess., 1963).

[40] C. P. Kindleberger, "The Prospects for International Liquidity and the Future Evolution of the International Payments System," in R. Harrod and D. Hague (eds.), *International Trade Theory in a Developing World* (1963).

[41] M. A. Kriz, *Gold in World Monetary Affairs Today*, Princeton University, International Finance Section, Essays in International Finance No. 34 (June 1959).

[42] H. B. Lary, *Problems of the United States as World Trader and Banker* (1963).

[43] W. Lederer, *The Balance on Foreign Transactions: Problems of Definition and Measurement*, Princeton University, International Finance Section, Special Papers in International Finance No. 5 (September 1963).

[44] P. Lieftinck, *Recent Trends in International Monetary Problems*, Princeton University, International Finance Section, Essays in International Finance No. 39 (September 1962).

[45] F. A. Lutz, *The Problem of International Equilibrium* (1962).

[46] _____, *The Problem of International Liquidity and the Multiple-Currency Standard*, Princeton University, International Finance Section, Essays in International Finance No. 41 (March 1963).

[47] F. Machlup, *Plans for Reform of the International Monetary System*, Princeton University, International Finance Section, Special Papers in International Economics No. 3, rev. ed. (March 1964).

[48] R. Nurkse, *Conditions of International Monetary Equilibrium*, Princeton University, International Finance Section, Essays in International Finance No. 4 (Spring 1945). Reprinted in American Economic Association, *Readings in the Theory of International Trade* (1949).

[49] _____, *International Currency Experience: Lessons of the Inter-War Period* (League of Nations) (1944).

[50] W. S. Salant, "Does the International Monetary System Need Reform?" in J. C. Murphy (ed.), *Money in the International Order* (1964).

[51] W. M. Scammell, *International Monetary Policy*, 2d ed. (1961).

[52] T. Scitovsky, *Economic Theory and Western European Integration* (1958).

[53] E. Sohmen, *International Monetary Problems and the Foreign Exchanges*, Princeton University, International Finance Section, Special Papers in International Economics No. 4 (April 1963).

[54] J. L. Stein, *The Nature and Efficiency of the Foreign Exchange Market*, Princeton University, International Finance Section, Essays in International Finance No. 40 (October 1962).

[55] R. Triffin, "Altman on Triffin: A Rebuttal," *Banca Nazionale del Lavoro Quarterly Review* (March 1961).

[56] _____, "The Dollar and International Liquidity Problem Reconsidered," *Kyk*, Fasc. 3 (1958).

[57] _____, *The Evolution of the International Monetary System: Historical Reappraisal and Future Perspectives*, Princeton University, International Finance Section, Studies in International Finance No. 12 (1964).

[58] _____, *Gold and the Dollar Crisis*, rev. ed. (1961).

[59] M. N. Trued, "Interest Arbitrage, Exchange Rates, and Dollar Reserves," *JPE* (October 1957).

[60] U.S. Congress, Joint Economic Committee, *Factors Affecting the United States Balance of Payments: Compilation of Studies* (87th Cong., 2d Sess., 1962).
a. C. A. Coombs, "Treasury and Federal Reserve Foreign Exchange Operations."
b. G. N. Halm, "Special Problems of a Key Currency in Balance-of-Payments Deficit."

[61] U.S. Congress, Joint Economic Committee, Subcommittee on International Exchange and Payments, *International Payments Imbalances and Need for Strengthening International Financial Arrangements: Hearings*, May 16, June 19–21, 1961 (87th Cong., 1st Sess., 1961).
a. C. A. Coombs
b. A. C. L. Day
c. H. G. Johnson
d. P. B. Kenen
e. C. P. Kindleberger
f. T. Scitovsky
g. A. M. Stamp
h. B. Tew

[62] _____, *International Payments Imbalances and Need for Strengthening International Financial Arrangements: Report* (87th Cong., 1st Sess., 1961).

[63] U.S. Congress, Joint Economic Committee, *The United States Balance of Payments: Hearings, Part 3, The International Monetary System: Functioning and Possible Reform*, November 12–15, 1963 (88th Cong., 1st Sess., 1963).
a. A. I. Bloomfield
b. C. P. Kindleberger
c. F. A. Lutz
d. R. A. Mundell
e. J. Tobin

[64] J. Williamson, "Liquidity and the Multiple Key-Currency Proposal," *AER* (June 1963).

[65] L. B. Yeager, "The Triffin Plan: Diagnosis, Remedy, and Alternatives," *Kyk*, Fasc. 3 (1961).

SUBJECT INDEX